HATE SPEECH IN JAPAN

This book explains the past and present status of hate speech regulations in Japan. The United States and European countries have adopted different approaches to resolve their respective hate speech problems. Both of them, however, continue to confront the dilemma that freedom of speech and anti-racism are fundamental values of human rights. Some scholars criticize the US approach as too protective of freedom of speech, while other scholars criticize the European approach as impermissibly violating that freedom. Compared to these countries, Japan is unique in that it does not criminalize hate speech and hate crime other than in the recently enacted Kawasaki City Ordinance criminalizing some kinds of hate speech. Japan basically relies on a comprehensive set of non-regulative tools to suppress extreme hate speech. This volume analyses Japanese hate speech laws and suggests a unique distinctive model to strike a balance between both core values of democracy.

SHINJI HIGAKI is Associate Professor of Law at Fukuoka University, Japan. He has been a visiting scholar at the U.S.–Asia Law Institute of New York University School of Law and the Peter A. Allard School of Law of the University of British Columbia. He earned his Ph.D. in Law from Doshisha University in 2015. He specializes in constitutional law, particularly freedom of speech. He is the author of numerous works on free speech issues, including *Heito Supīchi Kisei no Kenpōgakuteki Kōsatsu* [A constitutional analysis on hate speech regulation] (Horitsubunkasha, 2017).

YUJI NASU is Professor of Law at Seinan Gakuin University, Japan, where he teaches constitutional and comparative law. His research interests are primarily in freedom of expression, with a particular focus on hate speech and definitional balancing. He has written numerous articles on free speech, which have been published in Japanese periodicals such as *Hōgaku Seminā* [Legal seminar] or *Amerika Hō* [American law]. He recently published *Heito Supīchihō no Hikaku Kenkyū* [A comparative study of hate speech laws] (Shinzansha, 2019), analysing the laws of the United States, the United Kingdom, Canada, and Japan.

HATE SPEECH IN JAPAN

HATE SPEECH IN JAPAN

The Possibility of a Non-Regulatory Approach

Edited by

SHINJI HIGAKI

Fukuoka University

YUJI NASU

Seinan Gakuin University

CAMBRIDGE
UNIVERSITY PRESS

University Printing House, Cambridge CB2 8BS, United Kingdom

One Liberty Plaza, 20th Floor, New York, NY 10006, USA

477 Williamstown Road, Port Melbourne, VIC 3207, Australia

314-321, 3rd Floor, Plot 3, Splendor Forum, Jasola District Centre, New Delhi - 110025, India

103 Penang Road, #05-06/07, Visioncrest Commercial, Singapore 238467

Cambridge University Press is part of the University of Cambridge.

It furthers the University's mission by disseminating knowledge in the pursuit of education, learning and research at the highest international levels of excellence.

www.cambridge.org
Information on this title: www.cambridge.org/9781009256520
DOI: 10.1017/9781108669559

First published 2021
First paperback edition 2022

A catalogue record for this publication is available from the British Library

Library of Congress Cataloging in Publication data
Names: Higaki, Shinji, author. | Nasu, Yūji, author.
Title: Hate speech in Japan : the possibility of a non-regulatory approach / edited by Shinji Higaki, Fukuoka University; Yuji Nasu, Seinan Gakuin University.
Description: Cambridge, United Kingdom ; New York, NY : Cambridge University Press, 2021. | Includes index.
Identifiers: LCCN 2020041200 | ISBN 9781108483995 (hardback)
Subjects: LCSH: Hate speech – Law and legislation – Japan. | Discrimination – Law and legislation – Japan. | Race discrimination – Law and legislation – Japan. | Freedom of speech – Japan. | Constitutional law – Japan.
Classification: LCC KNX4147 .H54 2021 | DDC 342.5208/53–dc23
LC record available at https://lccn.loc.gov/2020041200

ISBN 978-1-108-48399-5 Hardback
ISBN 978-1-009-25652-0 Paperback

CONTENTS

TABLES

FIGURES

CONTRIBUTORS

AYAKO HATANO is a doctoral researcher at the University of Tokyo, Japan, with a research interest in the internalization of international law. She was a visiting scholar at the U.S.–Asia Law Institute of New York University School of Law. Her recent work includes 'Can Strategic Human Rights Litigation Complement Social Movements? A Case Study of the Movement against Racism and Hate Speech in Japan', in Myungkoo Kang (ed.), *Hate Speech in Asia and Europe: Beyond Hate and Fear* (Routledge, 2020).

SHINJI HIGAKI is Associate Professor of Law at Fukuoka University, Japan. He specializes in constitutional law, particularly in freedom of speech. He is the author of numerous works on hate speech, hate crime, critical race theory, and free speech issues in the Roberts Court of the Supreme Court of the United States, including *Heito Supīch Kisei no Kenpōgakuteki Kōsatsu* [A constitutional analysis of hate speech regulation] (Horitsu Bunkasha, 2017).

NAOTO HIGUCHI is Professor of Sociology at Waseda University, Japan. His recent works include *Japan's Ultra-Right* (Trans Pacific Press, 2016) and 'The Radical Right in Japan', in Jens Rydgren (ed.), *The Oxford Handbook of the Radical Right* (Oxford University Press, 2018) as well as 'The "Pro-Establishment" Radical Right', in David Chiavacci, Simona Grano, and Julia Obinger (eds.), *Civil Society and the State in Democratic East Asia: Between Entanglement and Contention in Post High Growth* (Amsterdam University Press, 2020).

KENSUKE KAJIWARA is Associate Professor of Constitutional Law at Kyushu University, Japan. He has written many articles on free speech issues. Those relevant to the subject matter of this volume include 'Heito Supīchi Gainen no Gaien to Naihō ni Kansuru Ichikōsatsu' ['The intention and extension of the concept of hate speech'] (2015) 27

Hikaku Kenpōgaku Kenkyū [Japanese journal of comparative constitutional law] 127.

MASAYOSHI KANEKO is Professor of Law at Hosei University, Japan. He specializes in constitutional law and human rights policy, particularly in national and local administrative human rights systems such as national human rights institutions. He has authored numerous articles and other contributions, including 'Kyūsai no Gainen' ['Concept of remedy'], in Kiyoshi Hamakawa, Kaoru Inaba, and Kosuke Nishida (eds.), *Gyōsei no Kōzōhenyō to Kenrihogoshisutemu* [Change of administrative structure and system to remedy rights] (Nihon Hyoronsha, 2019).

ATSUSHI KONDO is Professor of Constitutional Law at Meijo University, Japan, and Director of the Japan Association for Migration Policy Studies. He has been a visiting fellow at Stockholm University, the University of Oxford, and Harvard Law School. He has authored and edited several books, including *Citizenship in a Global World* (Palgrave Macmillan, 2001), *New Concept of Citizenship* (CEIFO Stockholm University, 2003), *Migration and Globalization* (Akashi Shoten, 2008), and *Migration Policies in Asia* (Sage, 2020).

RYANGOK KU is a third-generation Korean Japanese attorney: a human rights lawyer based in Osaka. She specializes in providing legal services to foreigners and foreign companies, including business, immigration, labour, and family law. From 2009 to 2014, she served as a lead counsel on a prominent case relating to hate speech against a Korean school in Japan (*Kyoto Korean Elementary School* case). She got her LL.M. in international human rights law in 2019 from the University of Essex, UK.

SHIGENORI MATSUI is Professor at the Peter A. Allard School of Law, the University of British Columbia, Canada. He holds an LL.B., LL.M., and LL.D. from Kyoto University and a J.S.D. from Stanford University. He is a well-known expert in the fields of constitutional law, mass media law, and internet law, and is the author of many books and articles, including *The Constitution of Japan: A Contextual Analysis* (Hart, 2011).

TORU MORI is Professor of Law at Kyoto University, Japan. He was formerly a scholarship researcher at the Alexander von Humboldt Foundation (2006–07) at Frankfurt University. He is the author of numerous works on the normative theory of democracy, freedom of speech, and constitutional litigation, including 'Justice Frankfurter as the Pioneer of the Strict Scrutiny Test' (2012) 7 *National Taiwan University L. Rev.* 91 and 'Die Rolle von Verfassungsrecht', (2016) *Jahrbuch des öffentlichen Rechts*, N.F. 64, S.795–813.

HIDEKI NAKAMURA is Professor of Constitutional Law at the University of Kitakyushu, Japan. He has written numerous articles and book chapters on public law, specifically on local ordinances and on media law. He has recently published two influential articles on local government hate speech regulations in *Hōgaku Seminā* [Legal seminar]. He was a member of the panel that examined the Tottori Prefectural Ordinance on Human Rights Protection, which attempted to regulate hate speech.

IL-SONG NAKAMURA is a freelance journalist. His work focuses on Korean residents in Japan, migrant workers, and the death penalty. His reportage on the *Kyoto Korean Elementary School* case, *Rupo: Kyoto Chōsen Gakkō Shūgeki Jiken* [Reportage: the *Kyoto Korean School* case] (Iwanami Shoten, 2014), is one of the most influential works on hate speech in Japan. He is also the author of *Rupo: Shisō to Shiteno Chōsen Seki* [Reportage: Korean nationality as an idea] (Iwanami Shoten, 2017).

YUJI NASU is Professor of Law at Seinan Gakuin University, Japan, where he mainly teaches constitutional law. He is an expert on hate speech law. He has published *Heito Supīchihō no Hikaku Kenkyū* [A comparative study of hate speech laws] (Shinzansha, 2019), analysing the laws of the United States, the United Kingdom, Canada, and Japan.

KEIGO OBAYASHI is Professor of Law at Chiba University Law School, Japan. He teaches constitutional law and public law, and is one of the most prolific law authors in Japan. His works include *Amerika Kenpō to Shikkō Tokken: Kenryoku Bunritsu Genri no Dōtai* [Executive privileges in the US Constitution: the dynamics of the separation of powers principle] (Seibundo, 2008) and *Kenpō to Risuku* [The Constitution and risks] (Kobundo, 2015). His research interests are constitutional order, judicial review, and freedom of speech.

KAZUSHI OGURA is Professor of Law at Otaru University of Commerce, Japan. He is a scholar of and teaches constitutional law, in addition to information law. He is widely known as a pioneering scholar in the field of internet law. His main works include *Intānetto, Kōdo, Hyōgen Naiyō Kisei* [Internet, code, and content-based regulation] (Shogakusha, 2017) and *Saibāsupēsu to Hyōgen no Jiyū* [Cyberspace and freedom of expression] (Shogakusha, 2007).

OSAMU SAKURABA is Associate Professor of Criminal Law at Yamaguchi University, Japan. He is known to be an expert on hate speech, having written numerous articles and book chapters on the theme. He is the author of *Doitsu ni Okeru Minshūsendōzai to Kako no Kokufuku* [The prohibition of incitement to hatred and the struggle to overcome the past in Germany] (Fukumura Shuppan, 2012) and the co-author of *Heito Supīchi no Hōteki Kenkyū* [A legal study of hate speech] (Horitsu Bunkasha, 2014).

FUMIAKI TAKA is a lecturer at Kanagawa University, Japan. He is a social psychologist who obtained a Ph.D. in psychology from the University of Tokyo and who has studied racism against Zainichi Koreans (Korean residents in Japan). His book, *Reishizumu o Kaibōsuru: Zainichi Korian eno Henken to Intānetto* [The anatomy of racism: prejudice against Zainichi Koreans in the age of the Internet] (Keiso Shobo, 2015), which investigated this issue empirically, was ground-breaking in Japanese psychology and other relevant fields.

SHIKI TOMIMASU is an attorney who acted as a lead counsel in the *Kyoto Korean Elementary School* case. He has outlined his legal analysis of that experience in practice, combined with his experience of the *Tokushima* case, in articles such as 'Heito Supīch Jian ni Okeru Fuhōkōihō Tempo Baishō Hōri no Ninau Yakuwari no Saihyōka' ['A re-evaluation of the role played by compensatory principle of torts law on hate speech cases'] (2018) 61 *Kanazawa Hōgaku* [Kanazawa law review] 199.

SHINJI UOZUMI is Associate Professor at Kansai Gaidai University, Japan. He served as an organizer of the Media Law/Ethics Research Division at the Japan Society for Studies in Journalism and Mass Communication, and facilitated a workshop about the Osaka City Ordinance against Hate Speech. His recent publication is 'Split Decision in the 51st Year of the U.S. Public Access TV: *Manhattan*

Community Access Corp. v. Halleck, 139 S. Ct. 1921 (2019)' (2020) 23 *Jinken o Kangaeru* [Thinking about human rights] 1.

KATSUO YAKURA is a member of the Upper House of Japan. He was elected from Saitama District in 2013 and is currently serving his second term. He belongs to Komeito, one of the ruling coalition parties in Japan. He is one of the leading drafters of the Hate Speech Elimination Act and co-authored its commentary, *Heito Supīchi Kaishōhō: Seiritsu no Keii to Kihontekina Kangaekata* [The Hate Speech Elimination Act: its history and basic idea] (Daiichi Hoki, 2016).

TAKANORI YAMAMOTO is Associate Professor of Social and Human Studies at Shizuoka University, Japan. He is co-editor of *Ima Buraku Mondai o Kataru* [Talking about the Buraku problem] (Seikatsu Shoin, 2019) and *Jūmin Undō to Gyōsei Kenryoku no Esunogurafī: Sabetsu to Jūmin Syutai o meguru Kyoto ron* [An ethnography of residents' movements and administrative power: Kyoto studies on social discrimination and the subject of residents] (Koyo Shobo, 2020).

ACKNOWLEDGEMENTS

This project was conceived around spring 2017, when one of the editors, Shinji Higaki, was a visiting scholar at the U.S.–Asia Law Institute of the New York University (NYU) School of Law. Professor Jerome A. Cohen of the School recommended that Higaki translate his book *Heito Supīch Kisei no Kenpōgakuteki Kōsatsu* [A constitutional analysis of hate speech regulation] (Horitsu Bunkasha, 2017), which had been published in Japan a few months earlier. Higaki, however, preferred to publish an entirely *new* book in English that would focus on Japanese hate speech law. Although many works had been published on this theme in Japan, especially after an upsurge in hate demonstrations in the late 2000s, no such book had been published in English and it is anticipated that this volume will be the first. It was Professor Frank Upham of NYU School of Law who introduced Higaki to Joe Ng of Cambridge University Press, while the School's Professor Jeremy Waldron kindly oversaw the book proposal and provided valuable advice. We sincerely appreciate the encouragement that these professors gave us to publish this book.

After consulting with Joe, we submitted our book proposal and sample chapters for peer review. Three anonymous referees provided detailed and thought-provoking critique, contributing to the clarification and refinement of our project. We are deeply grateful to them. The staff of Cambridge University Press tolerantly took charge of this endeavour from the outset; this book would not have materialized without Joe's assistance in particular at the early stages. We truly appreciate his understanding of the significance of our project. During the editing process, Gemma Smith was particularly helpful, doing a masterly job of arranging the entire composition of and proposing a fine cover design for this book, and we are much obliged to Joe and Gemma for their brilliant work. We are also grateful to Vanessa Plaister and Subathra Manogaran for refining this book at the later stages of editing.

We invited reputable scholars, attorneys, a journalist, and a statesman notable for their work on hate speech in Japan to contribute chapters to this volume; we are indebted to their collaboration. We are also beholden to scholars, journalists, editors, and attorneys who did not participate directly in this project, but who provided continuous support for our research activities. Their innovative ideas became valuable contributions to various parts of this book.

* The publication of this book was supported by the Suntory Foundation's Overseas Publication Grant Program.

ABBREVIATIONS

AEDB	Act for Eliminating Discrimination against Buraku
ARP	Anti-Racism Project
BBS	bulletin board service
BCYP	Broadcast Committee for Youth Programming (BPO)
BPO	Broadcasting Ethics and Programme Improvement Organization
BRC	Broadcast and Human Rights/Other Related Rights Committee (BPO)
CERD	Committee on the Elimination of Racial Discrimination (UN)
CIBE	Committee for the Investigation of Broadcasting Ethics (BPO)
CPPCG	Convention on the Prevention and Punishment of the Crime of Genocide (UN)
CRC	Convention on the Rights of the Child (UN)
DPJ	Democratic Party of Japan
ERD Net	Network for the Elimination of Racial Discrimination Japan
FCC	Federal Communications Commission (US)
G7	Group of Seven
GHQ	General Headquarters
HRB	Human Rights Bureau
HRC	Human Rights Commission
HSEA	Hate Speech Elimination Act
ICCPR	International Covenant on Civil and Political Rights (UN)
ICERD	International Convention on the Elimination of All Forms of Racial Discrimination (UN)
IMADR	International Movement against Discrimination and Racism
IT	information technology
JBA	Japan Commercial Broadcasters Association
JRU	Japan Confederation of Railway Workers' Union
KKK	Ku Klux Klan
Komei PT	Project Team to Deal with Hate Speech Problems of Komei Party
LDP	Liberal Democratic Party
LGBTQ+	lesbian, gay, bisexual, transgender, queer/questioning and others
LRA	less restrictive alternative
MBS	Mainichi Broadcasting System
MEXT	Ministry of Education, Culture, Sports, Science and Technology

MIC	Ministry of Internal Affairs and Communications
MIPEX	Migrant Integration Policy Index
MOJ	Ministry of Justice
MPT	Ministry of Post and Telecommunications
MXTV	Tokyo Metropolitan TV
NGO	non-governmental organization
NHK	Japan Broadcasting Corporation
NHRIs	national human rights institutions
Norikoe Net	*Heito Supīchi to Reishizumu o Norikoeru Kokusai Nettowāku* ('International Network to Overcome Hate Speech and Racism')
PTSD	post-traumatic stress disorder
RWA	right-wing authoritarianism
SCAP	Supreme Commander for the Allied Powers
SDO	social dominance orientation
SEM	structural equation modelling
SNS	social network services
TBA	Tokyo Bar Association
TBS	Tokyo Broadcasting System
UDHR	Universal Declaration on Human Rights
UN	United Nations
UNESCO	United Nations Educational, Scientific and Cultural Organization
UPR	Universal Periodic Review
URL	uniform resource locator
Zaitokukai	*Zainichi Tokken o Yurusanai Shimin no Kai* ('Association of Citizens against the Special Privileges of Korean Residents in Japan')

Introduction

YUJI NASU AND SHINJI HIGAKI

Countries around the world are commonly troubled with the problem of hate speech, but their responses vary. Constitutional law scholars often use two models for analysis: the US model, which hesitates to regulate hate speech not directed at particular persons, and the European model, which favours regulation, including of hate speech not directed at particular persons.[1] Most governments regulate hate speech broadly, meaning that the European model has so far held sway,[2] but this simple classification has been under reconsideration recently.[3] On the one hand, the United States strictly regulates hate speech targeting particular individuals and it does so by means of hate crime or harassment laws. It is also said to adopt a rigid distinction between private and public spheres, tolerating a wide variety of private regulation in broadcasting, universities, workplaces, and so on. On the other hand, some European nations are unwilling to execute regulatory laws, thus watering down their effect. Still, the contrast between the US and European models is useful for researchers. As the 2017 rally in Charlottesville, VA, exemplifies, it remains significant that the United States does not regulate hate speech in public places.[4]

[1] See, e.g., Eric Barendt, *Freedom of Speech*, 2nd ed. (Oxford University Press, 2005), 183–84; Michel Rosenfeld, 'Hate Speech in Constitutional Jurisprudence: A Comparative Analysis', in Michael Herz and Peter Molnar (eds.), *The Content and Context of Hate Speech: Rethinking Regulation and Responses* (Cambridge University Press, 2012), 242.

[2] See, e.g., Frederick Schauer, 'The Exceptional First Amendment', in Michael Ignatieff (ed.), *American Exceptionalism and Human Rights* (Princeton University Press, 2009), 33–34.

[3] See generally 'Interview with Robert Post', in Herz & Molnar, note 1, at 11; Arthur Jacobson and Bernhard Schlink, 'Hate Speech and Self-Restraint', in Herz & Molnar, note 1, at 217.

[4] For a legal analysis of the Charlottesville affair, see Frederick Schauer, 'When Speech Meets Hate', *Virginia*, Winter 2017, at 40, available at https://uvamagazine.org/articles/when_speech_meets_hate [accessed 28 August 2019].

Japan has never had civil or criminal laws regulating hate speech that is not targeted at particular persons. In this sense, the country appears to adopt the US model. It can also be noted that Japan is much more negative towards the regulation of hate speech than the United States, in that not only does it have no hate crime and harassment laws, but also there are generally no special rules for hate speech within private institutions. The Japanese model is unique in the world and civil libertarians may applaud it as respecting freedom of speech. However, Japan has not deliberately privileged free speech over minority interests as a consequence of battles against government suppression; rather, the country might be criticized as simply apathetic about minority interests. In this regard, Japan differs from the United States, where the people, including minorities, have consciously opted for free speech in a long-term struggle against government censorship.

In Japan, however, this landscape began to change in the late 2000s,[5] when large numbers of extremists began to call vehemently for the exclusion of Koreans and Korean-Japanese from the Korean neighbourhoods of major cities and elsewhere across the country. This compelled the national and local governments to review a traditional Japanese model that is largely indifferent to minority interests. Since then, while Japan has not yet punished hate speech in national law, it has developed a wide variety of innovative measures to counter it.

At the national level, the Japanese Diet enacted the Hate Speech Elimination Act (HSEA) in May 2016. This law does not criminally regulate hate speech; rather, it declares that 'unfair discriminatory speech and behaviour will not be tolerated'. However, it is not a wholly symbolic law. Those who proposed the Act explained that *every* statute should be interpreted in the light of this law, and that public officials and administrative organs should refer to it when enforcing any law or regulation. One of its principal proposers and a contributor to this volume, Katsuo Yakura, emphasized the US-style principle of content neutrality during deliberations of this law. However, US scholars may have some doubts about this perception of the content neutrality principle and argue that this directing of interpretation violates the principle itself.

[5] See Shigenori Matsui, 'The Challenge to Multiculturalism: Hate Speech Ban in Japan' (2006) 49 *U.B.C. L. Rev.* 427, at 427–28; Shin Hae Bong, 'Legal Responses to Racial Hate Speech in Japan' (2018) *Droits Fondamentaux*, at 3–4, available at www.crdh.fr/wp-content/uploads/legal_responses_to_racial_hate_speech_in_japan.pdf [accessed 13 September 2020].

Japanese courts have been particularly noteworthy in inventing creative measures.[6] As the chapters in this volume highlight, some courts have awarded significant damages for harms caused by hate speech, referring to relevant articles of the International Convention on the Elimination of All Forms of Racial Discrimination (ICERD), the HSEA, and the Japanese Constitution. Yokohama District Court's Kawasaki Branch issued an injunction for a hate demonstration in an area with a large minority population on 2 June 2016, although this rally did not target a particular person. In this ruling, the court invented the right to live in one's own home in peace and with honour as a subcategory of the personality right. A few years later, the Osaka High Court recognized that a website had caused original and unique harms by selecting and editing hate speech from 2channel (the biggest bulletin board system in Japan, called 5channel at time of writing), although the website's editors added no further hateful comments. More recently, various courts have issued injunctions for the online publication and sale of a book listing Buraku.[7] *Buraku* is a term that originates in Japan's pre-modern caste system, referring to the areas in which *Burakumin* ('Buraku people') live, and publishing a list of Buraku may lead directly to discriminatory conduct. The Tokyo High Court held that this publication would infringe upon the interest to live without unjust discrimination as a subcategory of personality rights.

Since the enacting of the HSEA, the administrative branch of government has also been active in campaigning against hate speech. The Ministry of Justice has dispatched advertising vans to some neighbourhoods that have been experiencing problems with hate speech.[8] These vans display anti-hate messages on big screens mounted on their sides. The Ministry of Justice also confirmed that hate speech will not be tolerated even in the course of election campaigns – a point to be laboured in light of the recent rise of the far-right *Nippon Daiichitō* ('Japan First Party').[9] Moreover, in enforcing the HSEA, the police have clearly shifted their stance to guard counter-demonstrators rather than those voicing hate at demonstrations.

[6] See Shin, note 5, at 4.

[7] For details, see www.stop-burakuchousa.com [accessed 17 September 2020].

[8] The Ministry of Justice website introduces various anti-hate campaigns: see www.moj.go.jp/ENGLISH/m_jinken04_00001.html [accessed 17 September 2020].

[9] See 'Three Years after Enactment of Japan's Hate Speech Law, Politicians Call for Increased Efforts to Eradicate Discrimination', *The Japan Times*, 31 May 2019, available at www.japantimes.co.jp/news/2019/05/31/national/three-years-enactment-hate-speech-law-politicians-call-increased-efforts-eradicate-discrimination/ [accessed 17 September 2020].

As Chapter 9 details, local governments have been the sites of experimentation of policies against hate speech. Kawasaki City in Kanagawa Prefecture and several other municipalities have enacted guidelines to judge whether it is constitutional to deny extremists the right to use public facilities. Osaka City in Osaka Prefecture enacted a hate speech ordinance in January 2016. It does not criminally regulate hate speech, but rather permits the mayor to take measures against hate speech, such as by publishing the name of or other information about those voicing hate. Kobe City in Hyogo Prefecture enacted its anti-discrimination ordinance in June 2019, which merely declares in its preamble that the city will tackle the promotion and incitement of discrimination. This ordinance, like the HSEA, does not contain any provisions for punishing hate speech. In the same month, Kawasaki announced that it would create an ordinance that included the criminal regulation of hate speech – the first of its kind in Japan.

In December 2019, Kawasaki enacted its anti-discrimination ordinance, which included various measures against hate speech. The most notable is that it *criminally* regulates some kinds of hate speech for the first time in Japan.[10] This could be recognized as foreshadowing a departure from the unique position of Japanese hate speech law. However, Kawasaki's new ordinance contains distinctive provisions to protect free speech, in the event that it disconnects from the existing framework of hate speech law.

When a violation of ordinance is found, the mayor issues to the offender a *recommendation* not to repeat the same or similar speech. If the offender were to defy this recommendation, the mayor would then issue an *order* requiring the speaker not to repeat the same or similar speech. Should this order then be violated, the offender would be criminally punished, and relevant facts – including the speaker's name and address – would be made public. In short, someone found to be voicing hate speech would be punished *only after repeating the same or similar speech three times.* It is also notable that this ordinance obliges the mayor to consult the expert committee it established, and that the offender is provided opportunities to give their opinions and to submit evidence. Moreover, the ordinance targets only hate speech in *physical* public spaces (streets, parks or forums). It also limits regulated hate speech to three extreme types:

[10] See Kazuo Ichimura, 'Kawasaki Plans Japan's 1st Ordinance Punishing Hate Speech', *The Mainichi*, 25 June 2019, available at https://mainichi.jp/english/articles/20190625/p2a/00m/0na/015000c [accessed 17 September 2020].

- speech that incites the exclusion of minorities;
- speech that incites infliction of some harm to life, body, freedom, reputation, and property of minorities; and
- highly insulting speech against minorities that typically suggests they are something other than human.

Finally, this ordinance does not allow the city to punish any offender by means of an administrative procedure; instead, it requires normal criminal procedure to be used against them.

Impatient endeavours for combating hate speech can be seen in the private sphere as well. Numerous counter-demonstrators organized after the late 2000s[11] and they have grown substantially in power, even pushing back some extremists. Bookstores, publishers, and writers launched campaigns against so-called hate books that mainly feature anti-Korean and anti-Chinese discourse.[12] Hateful comments on Twitter, Yahoo!, and other web services are regarded as serious problems by anti-hate activists, and IT companies have started to examine measures.[13] Additionally, hate speech is regarded as a cause for penalty in the workplace and at least one corporation is reported to have disciplined an employee because of hate speech.[14]

Japan has developed a highly unique model by means of these efforts at both national and local levels of government, as well as in the private sphere. It is non-regulatory in nature and similar to the US model in that respect. However, the Japanese model is not the same as the US model, in that Japan has no hate crime and civil rights laws, nor does it prefer clear-cut distinctions between individually directed hate speech and public hate speech, as does the United States. As has been evident in injunctions against hate demonstrations targeting the minority-populated area in

[11] On detailed explanation of counter-movements, see, e.g., Hajime Kanbara, *Heito Supīchi ni Kōsuru Hitobito* [People resisting hate speech] (Shin Nihon Shuppansha, 2014).

[12] See, e.g., Heito Supīchi to Haigai Syugi ni Katan Shinai Shuppan Kankeisha no Kai [Publishers and related actors who do not participate in hate speech and exclusion] (ed.), *No Heito! Shuppan no Seizōsha Sekinin o Kangaeru* [No hate! Thinking about the product liability of publication] (Korokara, 2014).

[13] See Alisa Yamasaki, 'Twitter Japan Confronts Hate Speech with Mixed Results', *The Japan Times*, 28 October 2017, available at www.japantimes.co.jp/news/2017/10/28/national/media-national/twitter-japan-confronts-hate-speech-mixed-results/ [accessed 17 September 2020].

[14] See 'Tokyo Pension Office Head Replaced over Hate Speech Tweets, Some Targeting South Koreans', *The Japan Times*, 26 March 2019, available at www.japantimes.co.jp/news/2019/03/26/national/japan-pension-branch-head-replaced-hate-speech-tweets/ [accessed 17 September 2020].

Kawasaki and the publication of a book revealing Buraku, the Japanese model resorts to restrictions even in certain grey areas. Japan does not clearly define private and public spheres. In other words, the HSEA has a role to play in interpreting private laws and consequently affects hate speech in the private sphere.

Certainly, the Japanese model is far from perfect. Some commentators fiercely advocate criminal regulation against certain extreme kinds of hate speech, because the HSEA has been powerless to repress obstinate racists. Conversely, civil libertarians criticize the HSEA for skewing the marketplace of ideas by inviting government bias in by the back door, thus violating the principle of content neutrality. There are various possibilities for improvement in the future:

- Japan might look at the European model and adopt criminal regulations;
- it might purify the non-regulatory model by making the HSEA a literal principle law that is not used as an interpretation standard; or
- it might strengthen the current Japanese model by resolving existing problems and supplementing the current system with other legal and non-legal measures.

In any event, the contributors to this book firmly believe that it would be useful to introduce the Japanese model to the rest of the world, which similarly struggles with the problem of hate speech. This volume is written by notable experts in hate speech in Japan, including not only legal scholars, but also practicing lawyers who have participated in hate speech cases, academics in social psychology and sociology, and a member of the Diet, who is one of the leading drafters of the HSEA. Various aspects of the Japanese hate speech law are thus analysed and, by means of this project, the contributors aim to illuminate the *whole picture* of the Japanese model, clarifying both its possibilities and limitations.

The volume develops as follows.

Part I outlines the current legal status of free speech protection and hate speech laws in Japan. Chapter 1 provides an overview of the debates over hate speech regulation in Japan. Atsushi Kondo criticizes Japan for the absence of a law regulating hate speech, even though it ratified the International Covenant on Civil and Political Rights (ICCPR) and acceded to the ICERD. He asserts that Japan must interpret its Constitution in accordance with international human rights treaties that impose obligations to enact hate speech laws on signatory nations. From this perspective, he analyses the hate speech laws of other countries and argues that Japan ought to adopt regulations including criminal regulation, administrative measures, and regulation of ethnic harassment in the workplace. However, Japanese constitutional law scholars have been reluctant to enact such laws because most privilege freedom of speech in the hierarchy of constitutional values. Kondo criticizes these scholars and provides a theoretical basis for regulation.

In Chapter 2, Shigenori Matsui provides an outline of the free speech doctrine in Japan and how Japanese scholars have come to accept the doctrine of the US First Amendment. He examines the jurisprudence of the Supreme Court of Japan on freedom of expression and demonstrates that the Court has accepted broad restrictions on that right. He then criticizes the Court for being highly deferential to the political branch, and suggests that it has been reluctant to inquire into whether the restriction is really necessary and narrowly drawn as a means for realizing legislative ends. He also points out that constitutional academics in Japan have criticized the Court's doctrine and attempted to incorporate US First Amendment jurisprudence into Japan. Many Japanese scholars tend to oppose hate speech regulation, in accordance with the prevalent negative attitude to it in the United States. Matsui concludes that if hate speech regulations were to be introduced to Japan, it would be difficult to satisfy the requirements imposed by free speech jurisprudence espoused by academics.

In Chapter 3, Ayako Hatano explores international treaties that require signatory nations to eradicate racist speech. In particular, she analyses how the Japanese government has implemented international treaties in the field of hate speech. She particularly focuses on the ICERD and its implications for Japan. She explores whether the HSEA actually responds to the recommendations from the UN human rights treaty bodies. Her conclusion is that, despite some shortcomings, the HSEA has been gradually made effective by means of various actors embedding international human rights laws and norms into Japan, including the judiciary, the legislature, administrative bodies, and civil society.

Part II describes the history of hate speech in Japan, most of which used to be aimed at Burakumin – modern-day descendants of Japan's feudal outcast group. In Chapter 4, Takanori Yamamoto chronicles past attempts to regulate hate speech against Burakumin. He explains the problems that Burakumin face, based on their history, referring to their characteristics and transition. He also mentions some relevant key cases. Despite recommendations of the UN Committee on the Elimination of Racial Discrimination (CERD), Japan has not enacted sufficient laws to eliminate discrimination against the Burakumin. According to the Japanese government, Buraku people are not classified as either a race or an ethnic group nor are they a special group distinguished by 'descent' under Article 1(1) ICERD. It can therefore be said that the ICERD does not apply to them – but the Diet enacted the Act for Eliminating Discrimination against Buraku in 2016, although the Act does not include hate speech provisions. Yamamoto concludes this chapter by suggesting some possible solutions to hate speech against the Burakumin.

In Chapter 5, Ryangok Ku, a third-generation Korean resident of Japan, describes the history of anti-Korean hate speech in Japan. She points out how the *Kyoto Korean Elementary School* case triggered a national debate about establishing a new law against hate speech and hate crime, and ultimately led to the enactment of the HSEA. To examine the impact of this Act, she analyses the case and its background. She argues that Japanese racism against Korean people has deep historical roots and has been continuously found in governmental policies, legislative decisions, and courts' rulings. She finds that, because it has some fatal defects, the HSEA cannot play any role in deterring such racism. She concludes that a comprehensive anti-discrimination law is needed to combat racism in Japan.

In Chapter 6, Masayoshi Kaneko provides an outline of the Human Rights Vindication Bill, which was submitted to the Diet in 2002 and was to have been the first national legislation on hate speech, and he analyses why it failed. First, he gives an overview of the history of human rights policies in Japan, in particular the Human Rights Volunteer system and the Buraku Liberation Policy (also known as the Dōwa Policy), and he criticizes these for lack of comprehensiveness and flexibility. He goes on to describe the legislative history of the Human Rights Vindication Bill and explains its substance. The Bill included various legal measures, such as injunctions against discriminatory speech and behaviour, but it was criticized by many politicians, scholars, lawyers, and the mass media, and it was abandoned the year after its submission. Similar attempts have been made by national and local governments since then, but to no avail, and Kaneko examines the causes and the effects of those failures. He argues that the Human Rights Vindication Bill would not solve current hate speech problems, but suggests that the Bill's remedial procedures could transform the discriminatory atmosphere latent in Japanese society. For this reason, he regrets that the Human Rights Vindication Bill came to naught.

Part III explores Japan's existing laws relating to hate speech. While Japan neither criminally nor civilly regulates hate speech directed to the public, some legal provisions such as defamation, threat, or insult have been considered applicable to some types of hate speech. Chapters 7–9 outline the frameworks of those provisions, including criminal and civil laws, as well as local ordinances.

In Chapter 7, Osamu Sakuraba clarifies the current legal situation surrounding the criminal regulation of hate speech. He gives an overview of the Japanese Penal Code, focusing on the provisions regarding defamation and insult. He points out that the Code punishes only defamation or insult that targets specific individuals or organizations and explains that is why the majority of hate speech cannot be prosecuted. He also states that although most Japanese academics have been sceptical about criminal regulation, some have recently begun to argue for the enactment of criminal provisions. Sakuraba himself thinks that while criminal law is not powerless, it is capable of only partially addressing the problem of hate speech.

Kensuke Kajiwara discusses the question of the extent to which tort law can provide relief for victims of hate speech in Chapter 8. As in the case of criminal law, with regard to the typical types of hate speech that defame and degrade a group as a whole, it is difficult – if not totally impossible to impose tort liability on the speaker. Kajiwara introduces the Japanese tort law system and addresses what sorts of tort liability might be imposed on hate speakers. On the one hand, he argues that the remedy of monetary compensation by tort law may not be what victims seek; on the other, he points out that there are some advantages to civil lawsuits, in that victims can take the initiative in pursuing legal assessment and judgment.

In Chapter 9, Hideki Nakamura examines how local governments in Japan have addressed the problem of hate speech. He first explains the framework of the system of local autonomy in Japan; he then examines some ordinances on hate speech. After tracking the history of various local governments' hate speech measures, he describes and analyses the Osaka City ordinance dealing with hate speech enacted in 2016. Nakamura provides detailed explanation on this ordinance's novel approach, including the disclosure of names of or other information on those voicing hate speech. He concludes by pointing towards the future challenges to and prospects for local governments in the area of hate speech.

As mentioned earlier, the Japanese Diet enacted the HSEA in 2016: the first statute to prevent hate speech in the country. In Chapter 10, Katsuo

Yakura – a member of the House of Councillors and a principal proposer of the HSEA – explains the background and legislative history of the Act. He reveals that the rapid increase of xenophobic groups in Japan since the early 2000s, made particularly evident in the *Kyoto Korean Elementary School* case, prompted the national government to address the problem of hate speech. After the initial Bill proposed by the opposition parties failed, the ruling coalition of the Liberal Democratic Party and the Komeito (to which Yakura belongs) submitted the Hate Speech Elimination Bill to the Diet. Following vigorous discussion, this Bill was enacted as the HSEA. Yakura provides a first-hand account of this legislative process and emphasizes its significance in Japanese society.

In Chapter 11, one of the editors of this volume, Shinji Higaki, presents an outline of the HSEA and analyses some of its issues. He analyses the Act from a number of viewpoints, indicating that it is unique because while it clearly declares hate speech to be impermissible, it does not impose any penalties. He emphasizes that the HSEA calls on national and local governments to implement educational activities to eliminate unfair discriminatory speech and behaviour, as well as to spread awareness among the general public about the issue. Such government activities can be interpreted as a type of government speech, which can be used to discourage and deter hate speech while avoiding constitutional problems. In this way, he concludes, despite some theoretical problems, the Japanese hate speech law may present a modest model that can strike an appropriate balance between freedom of speech and anti-racism.

Part IV elaborates on judicial rulings on hate speech. In Chapter 12, Il Song Nakamura details the history of the most significant hate speech case in Japan, the *Kyoto Korean Elementary School* case, in which some well-known xenophobic groups had held protests in front of the school. He describes the history of Korean schools in Japan and analyses the reasons why xenophobic groups attacked them. Nakamura reports on the actual picture of the harms done in the Kyoto case, as explored through interviews. In response to these harms, the only counter-measure available to the Kyoto Korean Elementary School was legal action – but it took the school a long time to decide to fight back in court. Nakamura describes the difficulties of the legal battle – and he reveals the many problems that linger even though the school ultimately won the case.

In Chapter 13, Shiki Tomimasu, who represented the school in the *Kyoto Korean Elementary School* case, analyses it from a legal perspective. On the one hand, Kyoto District Court ordered the defendant to pay damages, which amounted to approximately US$120,000 – an exceptionally large sum for a Japanese civil lawsuit. On the other, this decision revealed the limitations of existing laws, which clearly state that one cannot seek remedy for hate speech that is not directed at a specific target. This case triggered a nationwide debate about whether and how the Japanese government should regulate hate speech, ultimately leading to stronger public demand to enact hate speech laws.

In Chapter 14, Toru Mori analyses another important case, in which a xenophobic group announced in 2016 that it would march in the district of Sakuramoto in Kawasaki City, Kanagawa Prefecture, where many ethnic Koreans live. A social welfare corporation, whose president and the majority of whose staff are Korean-Japanese or Korean permanent residents, filed for an injunction against the demonstration. Yokohama District Court's Kawasaki Branch accepted the claim, which became the first case in which a court cited the HSEA. Mori criticizes the court's use of the HSEA, which does not include legal prohibitions against hate speech. He also emphasizes specific facts of the case, such as that the demonstration was planned in an area in which many residents of Korean descent live. He cautions that this court decision should not be regarded as general permission for the restraint in advance of hate demonstrations.

Part V outlines some of the debates relating to hate speech from multidisciplinary perspectives and considers possibilities for further regulation. In Chapter 15, Keigo Obayashi examines hate speech law from the perspective of comparative law. Although the Japanese legal system has been strongly influenced by that of the United States since World War II, Japan has also adopted British, German, and French legal doctrines since the Meiji Era (1868–1912). Accordingly, Japanese law is a sort of an amalgam of Anglo-American and Continental laws. As Obayashi points out and Matsui pointed out in Chapter 2, however, the Supreme Court of Japan has failed to use judicial review properly. Japanese constitutional law scholars have therefore tried to change this situation by applying the study of comparative law. Obayashi explains the differences between American and German doctrines, and how Japanese academics have supported the former. He points out that, despite their preference, the Supreme Court has tended to go in a different direction. He analyses hate speech issues in the light of this general tendency of judicial scrutiny in Japan.

Chapters 16 and 17 approach hate speech from the perspective of sociology and sociological psychology, and the authors analyse why and how hate speech has existed and spread in Japan. In Chapter 16, Naoto

Higuchi claims that, because legal measures against hate speech cannot solve the root cause of the problem, different approaches are also needed. He focuses on the targets of hate speech, which embody the historical and structural conditions of the rise of nativism, and points out that Koreans have accounted for the overwhelming majority of victims of recent hate speech and hate crimes. He analyses why Koreans are so targeted by hate groups and describes the characteristics of hate speech in Japan.

In Chapter 17, Fumiaki Taka focuses on hate speech in Japan from the perspective of social psychology and adjacent fields. He explains that an intergroup phenomenon such as hate speech can be understood by means of three concepts: stereotypes, prejudice, and discrimination. After explaining these three, Taka examines racism in Japan. He focuses on hateful content on the Internet, specifically social networking services (SNS). Although his research illuminates that only small numbers of SNS users post hateful comments, he believes that their comments negatively affect the entire marketplace of ideas. He is generally pessimistic about the current state of online racism in Japan.

Part VI explores a number of ongoing issues. An enormous amount of hate speech exists on the Internet and Kazushi Ogura introduces some instances in Chapter 18. He finds that there are some differences between hate speech on the Internet and that in other media. Describing the characteristics of hate speech on the Internet and how laws have dealt with it, he claims that although hate speech is unpleasant, the fact that discriminatory expressions often take on a political character should not be overlooked. He therefore suggests alternative solutions for hate speech online, such as voluntary initiatives (self-regulation) by service providers.

Chapter 19 deals with issues relating to public facilities. In Japan, as in other countries, groups must seek permission from national and local governments to hold assemblies in facilities under their jurisdictions. Article 21 of the Constitution of Japan protects freedom of assembly, while article 244(2) of the Local Autonomy Act provides that local government shall not reject citizens' applications to use public facilities without 'due reason'. The other editor of this volume, Yuji Nasu, explains the Japanese legal framework regarding national and local public facilities. Recently, several local governments have issued guidelines for considering citizens' applications to use public facilities and they have relied on these to deny applications from xenophobic groups. Nasu introduces these guidelines, and examines their pros and cons as argued by academics, going on to suggest a way in which it might be possible to accommodate both perspectives. He further justifies a limited mechanism for denying permission to xenophobes applying for permission to assemble.

Chapter 20 covers hate speech in the mass media, particularly on television. Japanese law imposes special regulations only on broadcasting media. As Shinji Uozumi explains in this chapter, broadcasting stations are regulated and must not air extreme speech. In addition, they are subject to codes of ethics and they have also established systems of self-regulation. Using the *News Joshi* case as an example, in which some defamatory language condemning protesters in Okinawa was aired, he outlines these systems and considers how to apply them.

This book aims to compare the various measures taken by Japan with those taken by other countries, and the authors examine the nature and character of the current non-regulatory approach against hate speech in Japan. Although their conclusions vary, all of the contributors are certain that the Japanese model has the potential to stimulate discussion among international academics on the law of hate speech.

PART I

Outline

1

Hate Speech Regulation and Anti-discrimination in Japan

ATSUSHI KONDO*

I. International Human Rights Treaties and Their Ratification in Japan

Japan attempted to include a racial equality clause in the Covenant of the League of Nations in 1919, but ultimately it failed because of opposition from the United Kingdom, the United States, and others.[1] Since World War II, human rights protection has been developed under international treaties. The International Convention on the Elimination of All Forms of Racial Discrimination (ICERD) was adopted on 21 December 1965 by the General Assembly of the United Nations, provoked by the struggle against anti-Semitism, apartheid, and colonialism. The General Assembly subsequently adopted the International Covenant on Civil and Political Rights (ICCPR) on 16 December 1966. The government of Japan ratified the ICCPR in 1979; it finally acceded to the ICERD in 1995 as the 146th State Party. Its accession was delayed because the constitutionality of enacting a law punishing hate speech had been the subject of intense debate.

Article 20(2) ICCPR provides that '[a]ny advocacy of national, racial or religious hatred that constitutes incitement to discrimination, hostility or violence shall be prohibited by law'. The term 'shall be prohibited by law' does not stipulate criminal punishment. Discussions on the drafting of this Article were quite controversial. In view of experiences with powerfully manipulative modern propaganda, on the one hand, positive commentators stressed that this law could be enforced only through criminal prohibition. On the other, negative commentary held that the limitation clause in Article 19(3) was enough to prevent racial hatred and that

* This chapter was supported by JSPS KAKENHI Grant No. 19K01290.

[1] Paul Gordon Lauren, 'Human Rights in History Diplomacy and Racial Equality at the Paris Peace Conference' (1978) 2 *Diplomatic History* 262.

provisions extending beyond this would endanger freedom of expression; thus the formulation did not necessarily require a criminal punishment or authorize censorship.[2] However, the UN Human Rights Committee (HRC) requested the enactment of a law in which 'propaganda and advocacy . . . are contrary to public policy and providing for an appropriate sanction in case of violation'.[3] There are various ways of imposing civil and administrative sanctions. Civil sanctions may be considered, including pecuniary and non-pecuniary damages, along with the rights of correction and to reply.[4] Administrative sanctions should also be considered, including an order to delete the hate expression, removal of the right to benefits granted by public bodies, the suspension of licences, disciplinary action,[5] and an order to dissolve the group.

On the one hand, Article 4(a) ICERD requests that the State Parties 'declare an offence punishable by law' all dissemination of ideas based on racial superiority or hatred and incitement to racial discrimination. On the other hand, Article 4(b) ICERD demands that entities 'declare illegal and prohibit organizations' and other propaganda activities that promote and incite racial discrimination. In ratifying the ICERD, the Japanese government maintained the following reservation: 'Japan fulfils the obligations under those provisions to the extent that fulfilment of the obligations is compatible with the guarantee of rights to freedom of assembly, association and expression and other rights under the Constitution of Japan.'[6] The reason for this reservation is that, under the Japanese Constitution, 'excessively broad restrictions on freedom of expression are interpreted not to be permitted under the Constitution' (article 21), and 'the criminal laws

[2] Manfred Nowak, *UN Covenant on Civil and Political Rights: CCPR Commentary*, 2nd rev. ed. (Engel, 2005), 40–71. The adoption of Article 20 means that, in human rights conflicts, the prohibition of discrimination set forth in Articles 2(1) and 26, as well as, indirectly, the right to life in Article 6, were given certain priority over the rights of political liberty.

[3] HRC, *General Comment No. 11* (27 July 1983), para. 2.

[4] UN Human Rights Council, *Annual Report of the United Nations High Commissioner for Human Rights: Addendum – Report of the United Nations High Commissioner for Human Rights on the Expert Workshops on the Prohibition of Incitement to National, Racial or Religious Hatred* (11 January 2013), para. 34.

[5] Denial of the Holocaust led the HRC to state that 'the removal of the author from a teaching position can be considered a restriction necessary to protect the right and freedom of Jewish children to have a school system free from bias, prejudice and intolerance': *Ross* v. *Canada*, UN Doc. CCPR/C/70/D/736/1997, 26 October 2000, para. 11.6.

[6] The US Senate qualified its consent to the ratification of the ICERD with the reservation of obligation under Article 4 and the declaration of the non-self-executing status of the ICERD provisions. The UK and France declared their release from the obligation to enact anti-discrimination legislation, which was incompatible with the freedoms of opinion and expression and peaceful assembly and association.

provisions shall be as concrete and clear as possible' (article 31).[7] The UN Committee on the Elimination of Racial Discrimination (CERD) believes the prohibition of racial hate speech to be compatible with freedom of expression and recommends that the government penalize racial discrimination, as well as ensure access to effective protections from and remedies for any act of racial discrimination.[8]

II. The Possibility of Regulating Hate Speech under the Constitution of Japan

Under the influence of US constitutional theory, a negative attitude towards regulating hate speech has dominated in Japanese constitutional theory. First, the 'marketplace of ideas' posits that ideas compete in the free market and that truth eventually wins out over falsehood; therefore, the best way of combating hate speech is 'counter-speech' or education. Second, in view of the evaluation of 'clear and present danger', the regulation should be limited to cases in which an entity incites 'imminent lawless action', since content-based restriction on speech is vulnerable to abuses of governmental power. Third, under the 'void for overbreadth' doctrine, hate speech regulation is unconstitutional if it is written so broadly that the fear of legal sanction has a 'chilling effect' on public discussion. Fourth, hate speech should be guaranteed as a form of freedom of expression because hate speech is sometimes related to political issues, and it is not easy to distinguish between political opinion and hate speech.[9] Fifth, a government should not judge the value of speech, because to restrict hate speech as a low-value expression is to overlook the constitutive 'justification ground' upon which that freedom of speech is guaranteed regardless of social utility.[10]

[7] *Japan's First and Second Periodical Report on the ICERD* (June 1999), para. 50.

[8] Article 2(2) ICPPR states that, '[w]here not already provided for by existing legislative or other measures, each State Party to the present Covenant undertakes to take the necessary steps, in accordance with its constitutional processes and with the provisions of the present Covenant, to adopt such laws or other measures as may be necessary to give effect to the rights recognized in the present Covenant'. A similar formulation is provided for under Article 4 ICERD.

[9] Junko Kotani, 'Genron Kisei Shōkyokuron no Igi to Kadai' ['Significance and challenges of negative view on regulation of speech'], in Sangyun Kim (ed.), *Heito Supīchi no Hōteki Kenkyū* [Legal study of hate speech] (Horitsu Bunkasha, 2014), 96–100.

[10] Megumi Saito, 'Hyōgen no Jiyū no Genkyō: Heito Supīchi o Sozai to shite' ['Current situation of freedom of expression: hate speech as a material'] (2015) 13 *Quarterly Jurist* 62.

On the one hand, unlike a political speech, it is possible to punish speech that is terribly insulting of particular ethnic groups.[11] One example is 'conditional constitutionality theory', which is a middle ground between positivist and negativist approaches, and which allows punishment for hate speech if it is clearly limited to instances in which an insult is made as its own end or violent acts are instigated that pose imminent danger to specific ethnic groups.[12]

On the other hand, in recent years, hate speech with the goal of harassment by insulting a certain ethnic group has become a serious problem in Japan; therefore, positive opinions towards regulating hate speech have increased, in accordance with the recommendation of UN human rights institutions. In this context, first, the 'marketplace of ideas' theory is not convincing given the historical fact that the Nazis exercised their freedom of expression, frequently used hate speech, took power, and then destroyed any opposition parties. The 'counter-speech' argument is not supported given that hate speech discourages minorities from voicing their opinions publicly and hence silences them.[13] Second, the restriction of speech is possible if there is an objective risk to the peaceful coexistence of people in society.[14] Hate speech regulation is allowed according to the jurisprudence of the Supreme Court of Japan, as illustrated by *Shibuya Riot*,[15] in which case the prohibition of inciting lawless action was held to be constitutional.[16] It is somewhat odd that the Japanese government has been so reluctant to impose a ban specifically on hate speech.[17] Third, regarding a lack of clarity in the scope of hate speech, we can utilize a legislative technique to determine the judicial operation of the interpretation as clearly as possible whereby the court will find that the law is constitutional only if it is read in accordance with the guidelines in the judgment. Fourth, even in the case of political

[11] Masato Ichikawa, 'Hyōgen no Jiyū to Heito Supīchi' ['Freedom of expression and hate speech'] (2015) 360 *Ritsumeikan Hōgaku* [Ritsumeikan law review] 130.

[12] Yuji Nasu, 'Waga Kuni ni okeru Heito Supīchi no Hōkisei no Kanōsei' ['Possibility of hate speech regulation in Japan'] (2013) 707 *Hōgaku Seminā* [Legal seminar] 27.

[13] Yasuko Morooka, *Heito Supīchi to wa Nani ka* [What is hate speech?] (Iwanami Shoten, 2013), 157–61.

[14] Toru Mori, 'Heito Supīchi no Hōteki Kisei ni tsuite: Amerika Doitsu no Hikakuhōteki Kōsatsu' ['On the regulation of hate speech: comparative legal study in the US and Germany'] (2014) 176 *Hōgaku Ronsō* [Kyoto law review] 235.

[15] Supreme Court, 2nd Petty Bench, 28 September 1990, 44 Keishū 6, 463.

[16] Masahiro Sogabe, 'Heito Supīchi to Hyōgen no Jiyū' ['Hate speech and freedom of expression'] (2015) 14 *Quarterly Jurist* 153.

[17] Shigenori Matsui, 'Challenge to Multiculturalism: Hate Speech Ban in Japan', (2016) 49 *U.B.C. L. Rev.* 427, at 435.

speech, we must bear in mind that political speech to incite hatred towards certain religions and ethnic groups, such as the persecution of the Jews in Nazi Germany and that of the Tutsis in Rwanda, brought about genocide.[18] Fifth, even if public speech is important, it cannot be protected absolutely; we must consider the balance of 'other democratic values', such as human dignity and equality.[19]

From my viewpoint of the constitutional interpretation, adjusted for the provisions of international human rights treaties, article 13 of the Constitution, in conjunction with article 21, protects the freedom to live without infringement on human dignity by means of statements comprising ethnic, racial, and religious hatred, and it permits criminal punishment for hate speech. The regulation of freedom of expression is justified in cases in which hate speech against ethnic groups is an expression that harms human dignity by insult or defamation, incitement with imminent lawless action, and true threats of an act of unlawful violence.[20] Article 13 of the Constitution provides that 'all of the people shall be respected as individuals. Their right to life, liberty, and the pursuit of happiness shall, to the extent that it does not interfere with the public welfare, be the supreme consideration in legislation and in other governmental affairs.' In my interpretation, the term 'public welfare' is the key word for the proportionality principle, and 'the supreme consideration' provides that the restrictive measure in question must be appropriate and necessary to achieve its objectives. According to the dominant theory, the sentence 'all of the people shall be respected as individuals' in article 13 of the Constitution protects human dignity.[21] Thus expression that infringes on human dignity interferes with the public welfare and can be restricted as an abuse of freedom of expression. Article 21 of the Constitution stipulates that '[f]reedom of assembly and association as well as speech, press and all other forms of expression are guaranteed', and there is no limitation clause. However, the situation in Japan is different from that in the United States, because the US

[18] Morooka, note 13, at 61–62.

[19] Shinji Higaki, 'Heito Supīchi Kiseiron to Hyōgen no Jiyū no Genriron' ['Constitutional considerations about hate speech regulation: contemporary problems with freedom of speech'] (2013) 64 *Dōshisha Hōgaku* [Doshisha law review] 3045.

[20] Atsushi Kondo, *Jinkenhō* [Human rights law] (Nihon Hyoronsha, 2016), 222.

[21] Nobuyoshi Ashibe, *Kenpō* [Constitutional law] (Iwanami Shoten, 2015), 82; Toshiyoshi Miyazawa, *Kenpō II* [Constitutional law II], rev. new ed. (Yuhikaku, 1974), 13–14. Recently, some researchers have stressed the distinction between human dignity and individual dignity. Individual dignity covers not only universal human dignity, but also individual autonomy and diversity.

Constitution does not have a human dignity clause; rather, the US government reserved Article 20 ICCPR, and the US Senate declared most international human rights treaties to be non-self-executing. Japan's Constitution does have a human dignity clause; the Japanese government ratified Article 20 ICCPR without reservation, and article 98(2) of the Constitution of Japan provides that '[t]he treaties concluded by Japan and established laws of nations shall be faithfully observed'.

Article 19(2) ICCPR provides for 'freedom of expression', and Article 19(3) limits the necessary restriction for 'respect of the rights or reputations of others', as well as for 'the protection of national security or of public order (ordre public), or of public health or morals'. To determine whether a restriction for such purposes is necessary, the HRC performs a strict review of the proportionality principle.[22] In Article 19(3), the term 'others' includes members of ethnic groups, and the term 'rights or reputations' includes human dignity. The damage caused by hate speech should not be regarded as a problem only of honour but as one related to human dignity.[23] We need protections against group-directed attacks that proclaim all or most of the members of a given group to be, by virtue of their ethnic, racial, or religious characteristics, unworthy of being treated as members of society in good standing.[24] Hate speech violates the most basic right of all: the right to recognition as a human being.[25] Thus domestic and international human rights principles call for the legal system to evaluate whether hate speech violates human dignity in view of the proportionality principle under article 13 of the Constitution and Article 19 ICCPR.

It is also important to establish laws and ordinances for necessary administrative measures such as censure of the perpetrators of discriminatory practices and suspension of authorizations. Moreover, efforts to ban ethnic harassment are necessary in many workplaces and universities, in the same way as rules aiming to prevent sexual harassment have spread throughout Japan. It should be noted that many local governments have enacted an ordinance for the promotion of gender equality, but only three have enacted the ordinance for the promotion of intercultural co-living. Setagaya Ward enacted an ordinance for the promotion of gender equality and intercultural co-living (*Tabunka Kyōsei*) in

[22] Sarah Joseph and Melissa Castan, *The International Covenant on Civil and Political Rights*, 3rd ed. (Oxford University Press, 2013), paras 18.30–31.

[23] Sogabe, note 16, at 155.

[24] Jeremy Waldron, *The Harm in Hate Speech* (Harvard University Press, 2012), 106.

[25] Steven J. Heyman, *Free Speech and Human Dignity* (Yale University Press, 2008), 183.

2018. This ordinance prohibits discrimination based on citizenship and ethnicity, although there is no penalty provision. Many local governments have established active plans for the promotion of intercultural co-living, including the elimination of hate speech.

Let us examine the case law on hate speech in Japan. In the criminal case *Kyoto Korean Elementary School*,[26] the Supreme Court rejected an appeal and affirmed the decisions of the High Court and Kyoto District Court, which had ruled that the street protest against ethnic Koreans constituted 'illegal actions beyond the limits of legitimate political expression'. The Court sentenced participants to between one and two years in prison, with a probation of four years, under articles 231 (insults), 234 (forcible obstruction of business), and 261 (damage to property) of the Penal Code. In the absence of a law to punish hate speech against ethnic groups, such as insults, existing punishments were applied to the case of a corporation (the school). Previously, the Japanese government had reported that 'racist motivation adequately proves as a malignancy of motivation in the criminal trial procedure of Japan and recognizes it as being considered on sentencing in the court'.[27] However, in the absence of a hate crime statute that enhances penalties for crimes based on racial hatred, the legal basis on which crime motivated by racism would be heavily punished is not clear.

The Kyoto Korean School brought civil suits against the protesters, to which Kyoto District Court responded by admitting damage in tort under article 709 of the Civil Code and granting an injunction; the Osaka High Court upheld Kyoto District Court's ruling, which ordered the group 'to pay about 12 million yen ($100,000) in compensation to the school'. The Supreme Court dismissed the defendant's appeal and confirmed this compensation.[28] It is noteworthy that Kyoto District Court ruled that, in cases in which a tort such as defamation involved racial discrimination or was motivated by racial discrimination, the ICERD directly affected the application and interpretation of the Civil Code, and it ordered that intangible damages be awarded when specific harms arose from it. However, it did not apply the ICERD itself; the court merely cited

[26] Kyoto District Court, 21 April 2011, LEX/DB 25471643; Osaka High Court, 28 October 2011, LEX/DB 25480227; Supreme Court, 1st Petty Bench, 23 February 2012, LEX/DB 25480570. See Chapter 13.

[27] *ICERD Seventh, Eighth and Ninth Reports of the Japanese Government* (January 2012), para. 93.

[28] Kyoto District Court, 7 October 2013, 2208 Hanji 74; Osaka High Court, 8 July 2014, 2232 Hanji 34; Supreme Court, 3rd Petty Bench, 9 December 2014, LEX/DB 25505638.

the Convention as a factor that weighted the accreditation of damage. It should be also highlighted that the Osaka High Court recognized the defendants' protest as 'an abuse of freedom of expression, contrary to "public welfare" under Article 13 of the Constitution'.

In recent years, hate speech incidents involving racist and discriminatory propaganda against Koreans have occurred at street rallies in Kawasaki City, Kanagawa Prefecture. The city mayor issued a provisional disposition order seeking an injunction to prevent the execution of a racist rally in a Korean community in Kawasaki. In *Kawasaki Hate Demonstration Prohibition*,[29] Yokohama District Court ruled that hate-fuelled rallies are illegal actions that violate personal rights derived from article 13 of the Constitution and that 'if there is significant illegality in the action, it falls outside the scope of freedom of expression and assembly guaranteed under the Constitution' (article 21).

As an aside, the Supreme Court has consistently ruled that 'vulgar and insulting expression for disabled persons' violates the provisions of article 150–2 of the Public Offices Election Act, which bans the degrading of other persons during election broadcasts, such as intentionally damaging other persons' honour.[30] I therefore believe that a similar prohibition of degrading speech on the part of a racist party candidate is constitutional under the case law.

III. Hate Speech Regulations in Several States

In Germany, article 130(1) of the Criminal Code, as revised in 1960, prohibits the speech that incites hatred against segments of the population, calls for violent or arbitrary measures against them, or assaults the human dignity of others by insulting, maliciously maligning or defaming them. The key notion of this article is the concept of *Menschenwürde* ('human dignity'), enshrined in article 1(1) of the German Constitution.

In the United Kingdom, section 18(1) of the Public Order Act 1986 prohibits incitement to racial hatred. According to section 17, 'racial hatred' means 'hatred against a group of persons defined by reference to colour, race, nationality (including citizenship) or ethnic or national origins'. In addition, stricter requirements such as intention were imposed and limited to threatening cases, religious hatred was added

29 Yokohama District Court, Kawasaki Branch, 2 June 2016, 2296 Hanji 14. See Chapter 14.

30 Supreme Court, 3rd Petty Bench, 17 April 1990, 44 Minshū 3, 547 (Election Broadcast Delete Case).

in 2006, and hatred on the basis of sexual orientation was added in 2008.[31]

In Sweden, Chapter 16, section 8 of the Penal Code, revised in 1988, prohibits the threatening of ethnic groups. In 2002, the Act expanded the offence to include threats on the basis of 'sexual orientation'.[32] The European Court of Human Rights ruled that the Swedish Supreme Court, which imposed fines on applicants for distributing, in a secondary school, leaflets containing offensive statements about gay and lesbian people, did not breach the European Convention on Human Rights because its interference was proportional to the aim of 'the protection of the reputation and rights of others' and 'necessary in a democratic society'.[33]

In France, the revised Law on the Freedom of the Press of 1972 prohibits anyone from publicly inciting another entity to discriminate against, or to hate or harm, a person or group for 'belonging or not belonging to an ethnicity, a nation, a race, or a religion'. In 2004, the Law was revised to include 'a sex, a sexual orientation, or a gender identity, or for having a handicap' (article 24). The Gayssot Act of 1990 establishes a punishment of five years' imprisonment and a €45,000 fine for the public expression of ideas that challenge the occurrence of the Holocaust. When Robert Faurisson denied the Holocaust in a journal, the restriction served as a gesture in support of the Jewish community's right to live freely without fear of an atmosphere of anti-Semitism, and the HRC concluded that the restriction on the author's freedom of expression was permissible under Article 19(3)(a) ICCPR.[34]

In Canada,[35] the Criminal Code of 1970 prohibits the public incitement or wilful promotion of hatred against any identifiable group under

[31] In this Act, 'religious hatred' means hatred against a group of persons defined by reference to religious belief or lack of religious belief (section 29A); 'hatred on the grounds of sexual orientation' means hatred against a group of persons defined by reference to sexual orientation, regardless of what that orientation may be (section 29AB).

[32] Since 1948, there have been regulations related to agitation against a national or ethnic group, which were then expanded to include race and colour as the result of the influence of the ICERD.

[33] *Vejdeland and Others* v. *Sweden* [2012] ECHR 242.

[34] *Robert Faurisson* v. *France*, Communication No. 550/1993, UN Doc. CCPR/C/58/D/550/1993 (1996), para. 9.6.

[35] Section 13(1) of the Canadian Human Rights Act, enacted in 1977, prohibited the telephonic communication of matter that is likely to expose persons identifiable based on race and religion to hatred or contempt. Taylor and the party of white supremacists were repeatedly communicating messages by telephone that were likely to expose Jewish people to hatred and contempt, and hence they were issued a cease-and-desist order, sentenced to one year's imprisonment and fined for their violation of section 13(1). In

section 319. Under this Code, 'identifiable group' means any section of the public distinguished by colour, race, religion, national or ethnic origin, age, sex, sexual orientation, gender identity or expression, or mental or physical disability (section 318(4)). A high school teacher was charged under section 319(2) of the Criminal Code with wilfully promoting hatred against an identifiable group by communicating anti-Semitic statements to his students. The Supreme Court of Canada found that section 319 violated freedom of expression under section 2(b) of the Canadian Charter of Rights and Freedoms; however, the violation was justified under section 1 of the Charter because the law had a rational connection to its objective to prohibit hateful expression and minimized impairment of freedom of expression without including in the criminalized expression statements made 'in private conversation'. Furthermore, the effects of section 319(2) of the Code are not of such a deleterious nature as to outweigh any advantage gleaned from the limitation of section 2(b) of the Charter.[36]

Conversely, the US Supreme Court is hesitant to confirm hate speech regulation. For example, the Court deemed unconstitutional a city ordinance prohibiting certain symbolic conduct, including the burning of crosses, because it imposed special prohibitions on those speakers who express views on the disfavoured subjects of 'race, color, creed, religion or gender'. A strict scrutiny test was applied in this perspective on discrimination.[37] However, the Supreme Court found the statute to be constitutional regarding the language limiting the burning of crosses to the extent that the intent of the burning constituted a 'true threat' of an act of unlawful violence towards a particular individual or group of individuals.[38] Additionally, based on the concept of 'clear and present danger', the Supreme Court ruled to permit a state to forbid or proscribe advocacy aiming to incite or produce imminent lawless action or likely to incite or produce such action.[39] Moreover, 'genocide' is defined in 18 U.S. Code Chapter 50A; inciting genocide can result in up to five years' imprisonment and a fine of up to US$1 million

Canada (Human Rights Commission) v. *Taylor* [1990] 3 SCR 892, the Supreme Court of Canada ruled in favour of the constitutionality of section 13(1) because there was clearly a rational connection between the restriction on communicating hate messages and the objective of promoting equality for racial and religious minorities. However, section 13 was repealed by a federal statute that was passed in 2013 and came into force in 2014, because it was an overly broad prohibition of discrimination.

36 *R* v. *Keegstra* [1990] 3 SCR 697.

37 *RAV* v. *St. Paul*, 505 U.S. 377 (1992).

38 *Virginia* v. *Black*, 538 U.S. 343 (2003).

39 *Brandenburg* v. *Ohio*, 395 U.S. 444 (1969).

under 18 U.S. Code §1091(c). Furthermore, some US states have retained regulations criminalizing the defamation of groups of people.[40]

There are many countries with regulations that include criminal sanctions for hate speech. States differ widely on the maximum prison sentence that should be imposed for incitement to hate; the punishments range from three months to fifteen years. A maximum penalty of two or three years' imprisonment appears to be most common.[41] European Union member States ensured that certain serious manifestations of racism and xenophobia were punishable by effective, proportionate, and dissuasive criminal penalties under Council Framework Decision 2008/913/JHA of 28 November 2008, which focused on combating certain forms and expressions of racism and xenophobia by means of criminal law.[42]

The United States is notable in its hesitation to regulate hate speech based on the marketplace of ideas theory, chilling effect doctrine, and viewpoint discrimination doctrine.[43] Meanwhile, EU member States and

[40] Alex Brown, *Hate Speech Law: A Philosophical Examination* (Routledge, 2015), 20, 42. Chapter 272, section 98c of the Massachusetts General Law stipulates that '(w)hoever publishes any false written or printed material with intent to maliciously promote hatred of any group of persons in the commonwealth because of race, color or religion shall be guilty of libel and shall be punished by a fine of not more than one thousand dollars or by imprisonment for not more than one year, or both'. Section 609.765 of the Minnesota Statute provides:

> Subdivision 1. Definition. Defamatory matter is anything which exposes a person or a group, class or association to hatred, contempt, ridicule, degradation or disgrace in society, or injury to business or occupation.
> Subdivision 2. Acts constituting. Whoever with knowledge of its false and defamatory character orally, in writing or by any other means, communicates any false and defamatory matter to a third person without the consent of the person defamed is guilty of criminal defamation and may be sentenced to imprisonment for not more than one year or to payment of a fine of not more than $3,000, or both.

[41] Jeroen Temperman, *Religious Hatred and International Law: The Prohibition of Incitement to Violence or Discrimination* (Cambridge University Press, 2015), 343–44.

[42] Regarding its implementation, see European Commission, *Report from the Commission to the European Parliament and the Council on the Implementation of Council Framework Decision 2008/913/JHA on Combating Certain Forms and Expressions of Racism and Xenophobia by Means of Criminal Law*, COM/2014/027 final (2014).

[43] Hungary was exceptional in Europe, the Hungarian Constitutional Court imposing an 'incitement to violence' standard by stating that actual incitement to hatred produce a 'clear and present danger' of violence, like the US Supreme Court: Michael Rosenfeld, 'Hate Speech in Constitutional Jurisprudence: A Comparative Analysis', in Michael Herz and Peter Molnar (eds.), *The Content and Context of Hate Speech* (Cambridge University Press, 2012), 271–72. However, the first provision of article 269 of the Hungarian

Canada permit minimum necessary regulations that make a rational connection between criminal punishment and the purpose of preventing the incitement of hatred towards ethnic groups. Comparisons between positive US and negative European approaches towards the regulation of hate speech are often explained by the concept of 'liberty over equality' in US law and that of 'equality over liberty' in European law.[44] Another explanation is that US exceptionalism was strongly influenced and reinforced by the civil rights movement; this is more likely the case than another idea that has been proposed, which holds that Americans have a more robust attachment to liberty, while Europeans are more imbued with the values of personal honour and dignity.[45] The difference was also likely caused by the differing political culture, foundational legal texts, and jurisprudential norms.[46] If we focus on article 13 of the Constitution of Japan, the human dignity clause, the constitutional text of Japan is more similar to that of Germany than to that set out in the US Constitution.

IV. Challenges to Japanese Hate Speech Regulations

According to the Ministry of Justice's Human Rights Bureau, 1,152 demonstrations characterized by hate speech occurred in Japan between April 2012 and September 2015.[47] There is a legislative basis in Japan to regulate hate speech.

In May 2016, the Diet, the Japanese national legislature, passed the Act on the Promotion of Efforts to Eliminate Unfair Discriminatory Speech

Criminal Code was ruled constitutional because the incitement of hatred against national groups, etc. can stir up intense emotions in most people, and it results in a disturbance of the social order and peace: Peter Molnar, 'Towards Improved Law and Policy on "Hate Speech": The "Clear and Present Danger" Test in Hungary', in Ivan Hare and James Weinstein (eds.), *Extreme Speech and Democracy* (Oxford University Press, 2009), 249; András Koltay, 'The Appearance of the Clear and Present Danger Doctrine in Hungarian Hate Speech Laws and the Jurisprudence of the European Court of Human Rights' (31 August 2018), 7–11, available at https://ssrn.com/abstract=2457903 [accessed 6 September 2020].

44 Eric Heinze, *Hate Speech and Democratic Citizenship* (Oxford University Press, 2016), No. 3413.

45 Erik Bleich, *The Freedom to Be Racist? How the United States and Europe Struggle to Preserve Freedom and Combat* (Oxford University Press, 2014), 136–37.

46 Erik Bleich, 'Freedom of Expression versus Racist Hate Speech: Explaining Differences between High Court Regulations in the USA and Europe', in Marcel Maussen and Ralph Grillo (eds.), *Regulation of Speech in Multicultural Societies* (Routledge, 2015), 124.

47 See www.moj.go.jp/content/001206812.pdf [accessed 5 September 2018].

and Behaviour against Persons Originating from Outside Japan (known as the Hate Speech Elimination Act or HSEA). In this Act, 'persons originating from outside Japan' means persons originating exclusively from a country or region other than Japan or their descendants, who are lawfully residing in Japan. This Act applies only to 'lawfully residing' persons with an immigrant background. Thus it is narrower than that of Article 20 ICCPR and Articles 1 and 4 ICERD. If we are to include the Ainu (Japan's indigenous people) and Okinawans (who are indigenous people or a national minority), as well as all other ethnic, racial, and religious minorities, we must expand the scope of the Act. Indeed, the ICERD appropriately highlights 'that legislative guarantees against racial discrimination apply to non-citizens regardless of their immigration status, and that the implementation of legislation does not have a discriminative effect on non-citizens'.[48] Accordingly, limiting the Act's application to 'lawfully residing' persons is contrary to the spirit of the ICERD. The House of Councillors Committee on Judicial Affairs and the House of Representatives Committee on Judicial Affairs have adopted supplementary resolutions to address this fact in view of the Act's purpose, as well as the spirit of the Japanese Constitution and the ICERD;[49] therefore, the Act can now be expected to address broader hatred against ethnic and racial groups regardless of their legal status under immigration law. The government of Japan is responsible at a national level for improving the system of consultation, enhancing education, and raising awareness, and municipal measures merely impose an obligation to make an effort; there is a problem with the anti-discrimination law, because it lacks substance.

In January 2016, Osaka City was the first local government to enact a hate speech ordinance. The Osaka City Ordinance for Dealing with Hate Speech is an important milestone in the hate speech debate in Japan because it is the first written law that legally defines the phenomenon.[50] In this ordinance, 'hate speech' is said to be an act of expression:

48 CERD, *General Comment No. 30* (5 August 2004), para. 7.

49 Ministry of Justice, 'Promotion Activities Focusing on Hate Speech', available at www.moj.go.jp/ENGLISH/m_jinken04_00001.html [accessed 5 September 2018]. In the supplementary resolution, both local and national governments shall endeavour to keep track of the actual situation related to unfair discriminatory treatment through the Internet and shall take measures that are necessary for their elimination.

50 Koji Higashikawa, 'Japan's Hate Speech Laws: Translations of the Osaka City Ordinance and the National Act to Curb Hate Speech in Japan' (2017) 19 *Asian Pac. L. Pol'y J.* 4.

- the 'purpose' of which is to exclude from society any person or group of persons who has or have specific characteristics pertaining to race or ethnic origins, to limit their rights or freedoms, or to incite hatred, a sense of discrimination, or violence against those specific persons;
- the 'content' of which is to insult or substantially defame the specific persons, to make them (or a substantial number of them, if directed to a group) feel threatened; and
- which is carried out in a 'way' and in a place where many anonymous individuals are aware of the content of the act.

Under the ordinance, the mayor is mandated to hear the opinion of the review board, to take necessary measures to prevent the dissemination of hate speech, and to publish the name of the actor.

Kawasaki City subsequently introduced guidelines for refusing the use of municipal facilities for gatherings in which hate speech activities are expected. In 2018, Tokyo Prefecture, as host to the 2020 Olympic Games in 2021, enacted an Ordinance for Realization of the Olympic Charter Goal of Respect for Human Rights to give effect to the International Olympic Committee's anti-discrimination policy. This regulates the use of public spaces to prevent groups from promoting hate speech targeting minorities on the basis of their ethnicity or sexual orientation. Like the Osaka City ordinance, the Tokyo regulation provides for publication of the name of the actor responsible for the hate speech.

V. Conclusion: The Need to Enact an Anti-discrimination Act

Generally, democratic states all have a dedicated anti-discrimination law[51] and independent equality bodies. According to the Migrant Integration Policy Index (MIPEX),[52] Japan, Switzerland, and Turkey are notable exceptions. Table 1.1 ranks states in terms of their anti-discrimination efforts as at 2014; Japan ranked 37th among 38 states. Only Iceland fared worse, having joined the list for the first time that year and being negatively evaluated for its lack of a specific anti-discrimination Act, scoring 0 for the regulation of hate speech. Article 233(a) of the Icelandic General Penal Code does, however, provide that

[51] European Network of Legal Experts in Gender Equality and Non-discrimination, *A Comparative Analysis of Non-discrimination Law in Europe 2017* (European Union, 2017), 132–42.

[52] Atsushi Kondo and Keizo Yamawaki, 'MIPEX and Japan: Findings and Reflections' (2014) 4 *OMNES: The Journal of Multicultural Society* 59–80.

Table 1.1 *Anti-discrimination*

Ranking	State	Score	Ranking	State	Score	Ranking	State	Score
1	Canada	92	**14**	Netherlands	73	**27**	Denmark	50
2	United States	90	**15**	Slovakia	72	**27**	Cyprus	50
3	Bulgaria	89	**16**	Slovenia	67	**29**	Luxembourg	49
4	Portugal	88	**17**	Ireland	66	**29**	Spain	49
5	United Kingdom	85	**18**	Italy	61	**31**	Czech Republic	48
5	Sweden	85	**18**	Croatia	61	**32**	Lithuania	43
7	Hungary	83	**20**	Greece	60	**33**	Latvia	34
8	New Zealand	79	**21**	Norway	59	**34**	Estonia	32
9	Belgium	78	**22**	Germany	58	**35**	Switzerland	31
9	Romania	78	**23**	Austria	57	**36**	Turkey	26
11	Finland	77	**24**	Poland	52	**37**	Japan	22
11	France	77	**24**	South Korea	52	**38**	Iceland	5
13	Australia	74	**26**	Malta	51			

Source: www.mipex.eu/anti-discrimination [accessed 6 September 2020].

'(a)nyone who does by means of ridicule, calumniation, insult, threat or otherwise assault a person or group of persons on account of their nationality, colour, race, religion or sexual inclination shall be subject to fines or imprisonment for up to two years'.

The United Kingdom, the Netherlands, the United States, South Korea, Sweden, Finland, and other countries all have laws in place that prohibit direct and/or indirect discrimination, and/or harassment, and/or incitement to discriminate on the grounds of race and ethnicity, religion or belief, and nationality or national origin. For example, section 9(1) of the Equality Act 2010 in the United Kingdom and section 1(1) of the Dutch Equal Treatment Act prohibit discrimination on the grounds of 'nationality', while Title VII, 42 U.S.C. §2000e-2 and article 2(4) of the National Human Rights Commission of Korea Act stipulate 'national origin'. It should also be noted that section 5(3) of the Swedish Discrimination Act uses the term 'ethnicity' rather than 'race', defining it as 'national or ethnic origin, skin colour or other similar circumstance'. Section 8(1) of the Finnish Non-discrimination Act also stipulates 'origin' rather than 'race'.

Japan has no special anti-discrimination Act, but article 3 of its Employment Security Act prohibits discrimination on the grounds of 'race, nationality and creed', and article 3 of the Labour Standards Act and article 27 of the Act for Worker Dispatching stipulates 'nationality and creed', while Article 5–2-4 of the Labour Union Act states 'race and religion'. Although there are judgments that have allowed for compensation in discrimination cases among civil parties, it is desirable that Japan enact anti-discrimination law for administrative regulation as well. In doing so, it might consider whether to do as Sweden and Finland have done by following the advice of the United Nations Educational, Scientific and Cultural Organization (UNESCO), which recommends dropping the term 'race' on the ground that all human beings belong to the same species, homo sapiens, and using instead the terms 'ethnicity' or 'ethnic origin'.

Table 1.2 sets out the scope of states' regulation of hate speech, spanning:

(a) public incitement to violence, hatred, or discrimination based on race or ethnicity, religion or belief, or nationality;
(b) racially or religiously motivated public insults, threats or defamation;
(c) instigating, aiding, abetting or attempting to commit such offences; and
(d) racial profiling.

The United States, Canada, the United Kingdom, France, Germany, and others regulate all four, but the United States prohibits only hate crimes.

Table 1.2 *Scope of national anti-discrimination law*

The law prohibits: (a) public incitement to violence, hatred or discrimination on basis of race or ethnicity, religion or belief, or nationality; (b) racially or religiously motivated public insults, threats or defamation; (c) instigating, aiding, abetting or attempting to commit such offences; and (d) racial profiling	
All of (a)–(d)	Australia, Canada, France, Germany, Hungary, Netherlands, Slovenia, Sweden, United Kingdom, United States
(a)–(c) only	Austria, Belgium, Bulgaria, Croatia, Czech Republic, Denmark, Finland, Greece, Italy, Lithuania, Luxembourg, Malta, New Zealand, Norway, Poland, Portugal, Romania, Slovakia, Spain, Switzerland, Turkey
Two of these or fewer	Cyprus, Estonia, Iceland, Ireland, Japan, Latvia, South Korea

Source: www.mipex.eu/download-pdf#/add-selection [accessed 6 September 2020].

Germany prohibits three of the activities listed, excluding only racial profiling. However, the Supreme Administrative Court of Rheinland Pfalz has nonetheless prohibited police officers from checking the documents of passers-by based on their skin colour because it breaches the ban on racial discrimination under article 3(3) of German Basic Law (Germany's constitution).[53] In Japan, such checks are not illegal. In fact, the Supreme Court of Japan upheld the religious profiling of Muslim residents as 'necessary and inevitable' to guard against the threat of international terrorism – although it granted compensation of ¥90,200,000 ($880,000) on the basis that a leak of that profiling data had violated the residents' privacy.[54]

This chapter has examined human rights treaties on hate speech and constitutional responses, discussed the regulatory situation of several countries, and considered the need for Japan to enact a comprehensive anti-discrimination law, as well as to conduct a review of issues related to the legal development of the issue. We must pay attention to the fact that

[53] OVG Rheinland-Pfalz – Az.: 7 A 10532/12.OVG (29 October 2012).

[54] Supreme Court, 3rd Petty Bench, 31 May 2016 (unpublished).

Japan makes constitutional provision for human dignity, and that article 13, in conjunction with article 21, of the Constitution guarantees freedom from infringements on human dignity by means of hate speech. Japan has no legal provisions prohibiting discrimination in terms of access to housing. It is expected to enact a comprehensive anti-discrimination Act as soon as possible as a basis for an administrative action to prevent discrimination – an Act that must define the scope of discrimination and regulation, and consider implementation mechanisms such as support for litigation and shifts in the burden of proof. Furthermore, Japan must also consider establishing a dedicated equality body and what measures it can take towards positive action. As the original bill of the Osaka City Ordinance outlined, there are ways in which an administration can help to resolve discrimination, including by supporting litigation. According to the UN Special Rapporteur on the right to freedom of opinion and expression, adopting a broadly applicable anti-discrimination law is a critical first step towards tackling hate speech.[55]

[55] David Kaye, *Preliminary Observations by the United Nations Special Rapporteur on the Right to Freedom of Opinion and Expression* (12–19 April 2016).

2

Freedom of Expression in Japan

The Constitutional Framework of Protection

SHIGENORI MATSUI

I. Introduction

The Constitution of Japan,[1] enacted in 1946 and in effect since 1947, stipulates that '[f]reedom of assembly and association as well as speech, press and all other forms of expression are guaranteed'.[2] It also provides that '[n]o censorship shall be maintained'.[3] Under this protection, the Supreme Court of Japan, exercising the power of judicial review,[4] has developed jurisprudence on freedom of expression.

This chapter will examine this jurisprudence, focusing on the various restrictions on the content of that expression, as well as restrictions on public demonstration and public assembly.[5] Principally, it will examine to what extent freedom of expression is restricted for the purposes of public safety and individual dignity, and to what extent it may be restricted. It will illustrate that the Supreme Court's jurisprudence on freedom of expression is highly deferential to the government and is not underpinned by any serious analysis, resulting exclusively in decisions that sustain restrictions on freedom of expression. In other words, when the Diet, the national legislature, passes a statute restricting freedom of expression, it is highly likely that the Supreme Court will sustain its constitutionality.

Constitutional academics have criticized this toothless jurisprudence. They have argued for the introduction of jurisprudence from the United

[1] Constitution of Japan (promulgated in 1946).

[2] *Ibid.*, art. 21(1).

[3] *Ibid.*, art. 21(2).

[4] *Ibid.*, art. 81 ('The Supreme Court is the court of last resort with power to determine the constitutionality of any law, order, regulation or official act').

[5] For a general overview of the Constitution of Japan and especially of the constitutional protection of freedom of expression in Japan, see Shigenori Matsui, *The Constitution of Japan: A Contextual Analysis* (Hart, 2011).

States and have developed an alternative jurisprudence on the freedom of expression. These prominent academics adopt the position that freedom of expression deserves to be protected much more vigorously by the courts, making legislative restrictions on freedom of expression more difficult to impose. Right now, there is no criminal ban on hate speech in Japan.[6] This chapter will show that a ban on hate speech, if introduced, would most likely be sustained by the Supreme Court, but that it would be more difficult to justify under the alternative jurisprudence developed by these constitutional academics.[7]

II. A Framework of Analysis by the Supreme Court

A. *The Scope of Protection*

Under article 21(1) of the Constitution, the 'freedom of assembly, freedom of association and freedom of speech, press and all other forms of expression' are protected. Traditionally, this provision has been interpreted as protecting freedom of expression generally. Indeed, the Supreme Court does not make any clear distinction among speech, the press, and 'all other forms of expression'. Since all forms of expression are taken to be constitutionally protected, there has been no need to clearly distinguish the three.

The Supreme Court has not clearly defined the meaning of 'expression'. However, it has granted protection to some forms of contested expression, such as obscenity[8] and commercial expression.[9] It has also extended protection to television broadcasting[10] and expression in the cyberspace,[11] even though neither form of expression was anticipated at the time the Constitution of Japan was enacted.

Although the Constitution merely refers to 'expression' and suggests that all expressive conduct comes under its protection, the Supreme Court has held that the right to receive information is also protected.[12]

[6] It must be noted, however, that some kinds of hate speech are subject to criminal punishment under different provisions. See notes 69 and 101.

[7] For a more detailed analysis of the constitutionality of a hate speech ban in Japan, see Shigenori Matsui, 'The Challenge to Multiculturalism: Hate Speech Ban in Japan' (2016) 49 *U.B.C. L. Rev.* 427; Craig Martin, 'Striking the Right Balance: Hate Speech Laws in Japan, the United States and Canada' (2018) 45 *Hast. Con. L.Q.* 455; Junko Kotani, 'Proceed with Caution: Hate Speech Regulation in Japan' (2018) 45 *Hast. Con. L.Q.* 603.

[8] Supreme Court, Grand Bench, 13 March 1957, 11 Keishū 997.

[9] Supreme Court, Grand Bench, 15 February 1961, 15 Keishū 347.

[10] Supreme Court, 1st Petty Bench, 12 June 2008, 62 Minshū 1656.

[11] Supreme Court, 1st Petty Bench, 15 March 2010, 64 Keishū 1.

[12] Supreme Court, Grand Bench, 22 June 1983, 37 Minshū 793.

The Supreme Court has also noted that the right to gather information must also be respected,[13] although it did not go so far as to say that the right to gather information is protected constitutionally.[14] The Supreme Court denied, however, that the protection applies to a right of access to government information, thus rejecting any constitutional challenges against the government's refusal to disclose government information.[15]

B. *A Restriction: Blanket Acceptance*

Despite the constitutional guarantee of freedom of expression, the protection is not absolute and may be restricted under certain circumstances. Although there is no explicit limitation within article 21 itself, other articles – especially articles 12[16] and 13[17] – imply that any fundamental human rights protected under the Constitution can be restricted for the sake of 'public welfare'. The Supreme Court confirmed this in the case *Lady Chatterley's Lover.*[18]

The case also manifestly showed that the Supreme Court would adopt a highly deferential stance towards restrictions on freedom of expression imposed by the legislature. At issue was the constitutionality of article 175 of the Criminal Code, which prohibited the publication, distribution, and public display of obscene materials.[19] In this case, the publisher and translator of D.H. Lawrence's book *Lady Chatterley's Lover* into Japanese were prosecuted for publication of obscene materials in violation of article 175. The defendant translator argued that imposing criminal punishment for such publication violated his freedom of expression, as protected under article 21 of the Constitution.

The Supreme Court held that one aim of the provision was to protect sexual morality and that the protection of sexual morality was a matter of public welfare. It reasoned that all human beings share a sense of shame

[13] Supreme Court, Grand Bench, 26 November 1969, 23 Keishū 1490.

[14] *Ibid.*

[15] Supreme Court, 3rd Petty Bench, 16 February 1990, 254 Saishū Keiji 113.

[16] Constitution of Japan, note 1, art. 12 ('The freedoms and rights guaranteed to the people by this Constitution shall be maintained by the constant endeavour of the people, who shall refrain from any abuse of these freedoms and rights and shall always be responsible for utilizing them for the public welfare').

[17] *Ibid.*, art. 13 ('All of the people shall be respected as individuals. Their right to life, liberty, and the pursuit of happiness shall, to the extent that it does not interfere with the public welfare, be the supreme consideration in legislation and in other governmental affairs').

[18] See note 8.

[19] Keihō [Criminal code], art. 175.

and that this sense of shame will manifest when someone engages in sex in public. The Supreme Court was convinced that the principle that sex should not be performed in public supported a prohibition on the publication of obscene materials. It thus readily upheld the constitutionality of a ban on the publication of obscene materials for the purpose of protecting sexual morality. Accepting that *Lady Chatterley's Lover* was obscene, the Supreme Court upheld the conviction.

This holding exemplified the typical early constitutional jurisprudence of the Supreme Court: an eager willingness to accept a legislative purpose or goal as legitimate and important, and a reluctance to inquire into whether the means chosen was actually necessary or justified. The Supreme Court adopted a similar highly deferential attitude in all freedom of expression cases in its early days.[20] Despite strong criticisms from constitutional academics,[21] the Supreme Court has followed these earlier decisions in subsequent decades and has upheld all challenged restrictions on freedom of expression.

C. *Reasonable and Necessary Restrictions*

At other times, the Supreme Court has indicated that a reasonable and necessary restriction on freedom of expression could be permissible, and it has demonstrated its willingness to make that inquiry rather than base its reasoning solely upon legislative declaration. The conclusion that a restriction was reasonable and necessary has come easily each time, however, without any substantial inquiry. For example, in *Door-to-Door Canvassing I*,[22] the Supreme Court readily sustained the constitutionality of a total ban on door-to-door canvassing during election periods as reasonable even without delineating the government's goals or questioning whether a complete and total ban was really necessary. It simply noted that door-to-door canvassing was banned because it was accompanied by various harms. It conceded that freedom of expression could, to some extent, be limited by the ban, yet it held that the protection of freedom of expression was not absolute and was subject to reasonable restrictions on time, place, and manners for the public welfare. It concluded that the restriction on freedom of expression resulting from the

[20] Supreme Court, Grand Bench, 18 May 1949, 3 Keishū 839 (holding that advocacy of a violation of the mandatory food supply and distribution system infringed the public welfare and was beyond the scope of the protection of freedom of expression).

[21] See note 33.

[22] Supreme Court, Grand Bench, 27 September 1950, 4 Keishū 1799.

ban on door-to-door canvassing to secure election fairness could not be unconstitutional.

Other decisions concluding that restrictions on freedom of expression are reasonable and necessary have been similar.[23] These decisions might therefore be viewed as continuing the earlier pattern of blanket acceptance of government restrictions.

D. *Balancing Interests*

In other cases, the Supreme Court has adopted an explicit, but ad hoc, balancing of interests as a standard. For instance, in *Sarufutsu*,[24] the constitutionality of a total ban on political activities by public officials under the National Public Workers Act[25] was challenged. The Supreme Court reasoned that since public workers are servants of the public, and there is a need to maintain political neutrality within the public administration and to secure public trust in that political neutrality, a reasonable restriction on the political freedom of public workers is justified.

To determine whether the ban was justified, the Court was required to balance consideration of: (a) the purpose of the ban; (b) the relationship between the banned conduct and the purpose of the ban; and (c) the balance between the interest obtained and the cost of what would be lost.[26] The Supreme Court held that the purposes were legitimate and that the ban was rationally connected to them. It specifically held that a rational connection could be found even though *all* political activities were banned regardless of the type of job, the rank, whether or not the activity took place during work hours, whether the activity took place in the workplace, or whether the ban was limited to activities that would cause direct and specific harm. Viewing the ban only as precluding political activity and preventing no other methods of expression, the Supreme Court then held that any incidental or indirect cost to freedom

[23] Supreme Court, Grand Bench, 20 July 1960, 14 Keishū 1243 (sustaining the comprehensive permit requirement for public demonstration as necessary and minimal to maintain law and order); Supreme Court, Grand Bench, 18 December 1968, 22 Keishū 1549 (sustaining the ban on postering on facilities in public places such as utility poles as necessary and reasonable); Supreme Court, Grand Bench, 17 June 1970, 24 Keishū 280 (sustaining the ban on postering on the private property of others as necessary and reasonable); Supreme Court, 3rd Petty Bench, 3 March 1987, 41 Keishū 15 (sustaining the ban on attaching placards to public trees as necessary and reasonable).

[24] Supreme Court, Grand Bench, 6 November 1974, 28 Keishū 393.

[25] National Public Workers Act, arts 102 and 110(1), item 19.

[26] See note 24.

of expression was easily outweighed by the more important general public interest of maintaining political neutrality and securing public trust.

In *Hakata Station Television Film Production*,[27] the Supreme Court used the same ad hoc interest-balancing standard. The question at issue was whether a judge-issued production order for video clips shot and aired of a demonstration and confrontation between demonstrators and police was justified. The order was issued in a case determining whether criminal charges should be laid for abuse of power or brutality by police officers. The Supreme Court noted that freedom to gather information for the purpose of news reporting should be respected but could be restricted under the aim of achieving criminal justice. It then held that determining the permissibility of such a restriction should be decided by:

> . . . considering the nature, manner and seriousness of the crime under review as well as the value of the film as evidence, ultimately the necessity of accomplishing the fair administration of criminal justice on the other hand, and balancing it against the degree of interference into the freedom to gather news by mass media via the production order as well as the impact on freedom of the press and other relevant factors.[28]

Applying this standard, the Supreme Court held that since it was very hard to identify the assailant, the films were vital as evidence, and the films had already aired, saying that the only disadvantage to the mass media would be the possibility of a negative impact on future news gathering. The Supreme Court concluded that this degree of disadvantage must be accepted to achieve criminal justice.

The adoption of the interest-balancing approach was an improvement on the earlier constitutional jurisprudence, which had simply upheld the constitutionality of restrictions on freedom of expression without making any further inquiries. Nevertheless, the Supreme Court has used this ad hoc interest-balancing approach in few other cases[29] and nowhere has it led to the striking down of any legislated restriction. It has clung to its highly deferential approach in other cases and, ultimately, the Supreme Court has never once struck down any legislative restriction on freedom of expression.

[27] See note 13.

[28] *Ibid.*

[29] Supreme Court, 3rd Petty Bench, 16 March 1993, 47 Minshū 3483 (sustaining censorship of school textbooks); Supreme Court, 3rd Petty Bench, 18 September 2007, 61 Keishū 601 (sustaining the local anti-gang ordinance that authorized a mayor to issue a stop order to motorcycle gangs and similar groups gathering, with criminal punishment for breach).

E. *Indirect and Incidental Restrictions*

Sometimes, the Supreme Court has held that a particular restriction was merely indirect and incidental, and it has easily upheld it on that basis.

For instance, in *Sarufutsu*,[30] the Supreme Court viewed the ban only as precluding political activity and not as preventing other methods of expression. It held that any incidental and indirect cost to freedom of expression was easily outweighed by the more important goal of the general public interest in maintaining political neutrality and securing public trust. Similarly, in *Door-to-Door Canvassing II*,[31] the Supreme Court – in confirming the constitutionality of the total ban on door-to-door canvassing during election periods, under the Public Office Election Act[32] – held that the restriction on freedom of expression was merely incidental and indirect, and that any cost to freedom of expression was easily outweighed by a much more important interest in preventing the various harms arising from door-to-door canvassing and securing election fairness.

III. Academic Criticisms

A. *The Critical Drawbacks of the Jurisprudence of the Supreme Court on Freedom of Expression*

Constitutional academics have criticized the jurisprudence on freedom of expression established by the Supreme Court. They have criticized the Supreme Court for too easily allowing restrictions on freedom of expression by invoking the concept of 'public welfare'.[33] They have argued that the Supreme Court should instead rely upon much more specific criteria to determine whether restrictions are justified. Under such a revised approach, merely invoking the public welfare as talismanic justification would be insufficient.[34]

This criticism is, in reality, a criticism of the Supreme Court's blind acceptance of the legitimacy and the necessity of restrictions in furthering important government goals or purposes. In other words, constitutional academics criticize the Supreme Court's reluctance to inquire what precise goal or purpose the government is attempting to protect, whether

30 See note 24.

31 Supreme Court, 2nd Petty Bench, 15 June 1981, 35 Keishū 205.

32 Public Office Election Act, art. 138.

33 Toshiyuki Miyazawa, *Kenpō II* [Constitution II], new ed. (Yuhikaku, 1971), 232, 369.

34 Koji Sato, *Nihonkoku Kenpōron* [Japanese Constitution] (Seibundo, 2011), 133.

such a goal or purpose is legitimate, and whether it is sufficiently important, substantial, or compelling to justify the restriction on freedom of expression. There is simply no serious concern with the goals or purposes of the restrictions.

Constitutional academics also question the Supreme Court's reluctance to inquire into whether a particular restriction on freedom of expression is truly necessary and is narrowly drawn as a means of accomplishing its intended purpose. The Supreme Court has generally sustained comprehensive bans as reasonable and necessary even in cases in which there might be less-restrictive means or in which the ban is overly broad. In other words, academics generally have insisted that the Supreme Court should employ much more careful scrutiny of the means.

On this basis, academics have generally insisted that the jurisprudence of the Supreme Court on freedom of expression was no different from the pre-war jurisprudence on the same. Before the enactment of the Constitution of Japan, the Meiji Constitution protected freedom of expression, but that protection was graciously granted by the sovereign emperor to his subjects and was specifically confined within the statute.[35] As a result, when the Imperial Diet passed a statute restricting freedom of expression, there was no way of challenging the permissibility of the restriction. Moreover, it was generally believed that the courts did not have a power of judicial review.[36] The judicial courts had no means of examining the constitutionality of restrictions on freedom of expression imposed by statute. As a result, freedom of expression was subject to very broad and intrusive restrictions both before and during the war.[37]

Based on this history of serious infringement of freedom of expression, and on the sober reflection that such infringement led to the rise of extreme militarism and ultimately Japan's invasion of Asian countries, the drafters of the Constitution of Japan decided to protect freedom of expression as a fundamental human right. It is no longer a right granted graciously by the emperor; rather, it is one of the inherent rights of all individuals, binding upon the Diet as well. Furthermore, the drafters

[35] Constitution of the Empire of Japan, 1889 (Meiji Constitution), art. 29 ('Japanese subjects shall, within the limits of law, enjoy the liberty of speech, writing, publication, public meetings and associations').

[36] There was no provision for judicial review in the Constitution of the Empire of Japan. National Diet Library, *Nihonkoku Kenpō no Tanjō* [Birth of the Constitution of Japan], available at www.ndl.go.jp/constitution/ronten/05ronten.html [accessed 31 January 2020].

[37] Newspaper Act (repealed in 1949); Publication Act (repealed in 1949); Public Safety Preservation Act (repealed in 1945).

decided to explicitly grant the power of judicial review to the courts. Thus the Constitution of Japan apparently anticipates that the Diet should not be free to arbitrarily restrict freedom of expression and that the judiciary should function as an ultimate guardian of freedom of expression. Constitutional academics have condemned the stance of the Supreme Court as a total abdication of that judicial duty, which seriously undermines the very foundation of the constitutional protection of freedom of expression and the explicit grant of the power of judicial review to courts.[38]

B. A Theory of Constitutional Double Standards

Constitutional academics have therefore attempted to reinvigorate the constitutional protection of freedom of expression and urge the courts to play a much more active role in safeguarding it. To this end, they have looked to the jurisprudence developed by the Supreme Court of the United States and have argued for establishing a freedom of expression jurisprudence similar to that approach.

The key to establishing such alternative jurisprudence would be a recognition that the courts should play different roles in freedom of expression cases and economic freedom cases.[39] This is supported by two arguments: freedom of expression is vital to representative democracy; and there is a limit on the judicial capacity to evaluate the regulation of economic freedoms based on social policy.[40] As a result, leading academics argue that restrictions on freedom of expression should be subjected to much more vigorous scrutiny, applying a standard of review more demanding than mere rationality, which requires that legislation needs to be a rational means with which to accomplish some legitimate rational goal.[41] This can be described as a theory of constitutional double standards.[42]

These leading academics note, however, that there is a difference between content-based restrictions and content-neutral restrictions. They have therefore followed the US Supreme Court to introduce that

[38] Miyazawa, note 33, at 226–27.

[39] Sato, note 34, at 249, 254; Nobuyoshi Ashibe (supplemented by Kazuyuki Takahashi), *Kenpō* [Constitution], 7th ed. (Iwanami Shoten, 2015), 105, 202–03.

[40] Ashibe, note 39, at 194.

[41] *Ibid.*

[42] The term 'double standards' has a negative connotation in many states, but in Japan, following the same usage in the United States, this term is widely used in a positive sense.

dichotomy in Japan.[43] When the government attempts to introduce content-based restrictions on freedom of expression, such as a ban on the advocacy of illegal action, there is a much more serious risk of the government simply prohibiting speech that it itself opposes. Thus these academics insist that much more demanding criteria should be applied to sustain the constitutionality of a content-based restriction. An example of this is the 'clear and present danger' test.[44] This test, initially espoused by Justice Oliver Wendell Holmes, Jr. and accepted by the US Supreme Court, demands that restrictions on freedom of expression be justified by a clear and present danger of serious harm.[45] The test requires not only the presence of very serious harm to justify a restriction but also the existence of an immediate danger that such harm could be caused by the expression. In addition, some academics argue for an application of strict scrutiny that demands the existence of compelling government interests to justify a content-based restriction – that is, a government interest far more overriding than the rational, or even important, interest.[46] Further, the means needs to be narrowly drawn: it must be the least restrictive method available and not overly broad. They would thus support a presumption that a content-based restriction is unconstitutional and impose a very heavy burden of proof on the government to justify restriction on freedom of expression.[47]

Content-neutral restrictions on freedom of expression may be granted somewhat less stringent protection because the danger of allowing the suppression of government-opposed expression is less significant. But it should be protected more vigorously than economic freedoms by applying a standard of review slightly more demanding than the rationality standard, because such restrictions still result in curtailing the freedom of expression. Leading academics have generally insisted that content-neutral restrictions should be justified by important or substantial

43 Ashibe, note 39, at 195.

44 *Ibid.*, at 208. Masami Ito, *Genron/shuppan no Jiyū* [Freedom of speech and of the press] (Iwanami Shoten, 1959).

45 *Thornhill* v. *Alabama*, 310 U.S. 88 (1940); Hans A. Linde, 'Clear and Present Danger Reexamined: Dissonance in the *Brandenburg* Concerto' (1970) 22 *Stan. L. Rev.* 1163; Martin H. Redish, 'Advocacy of Unlawful Conduct and the First Amendment: In Defense of Clear and Present Danger' (1982) 70 *Cal. L. Rev.* 1159; David R. Dow and R. Scott Shieldes, 'Rethinking the Clear and Present Danger Test' (1998) 73 *Ind. L.J.* 1217.

46 Ashibe, note 39, at 195; Shigenori Matsui, *Nihonkoku Kenpō* [Constitution of Japan], 3rd ed. (Yuhikaku, 2007), 448; Shigenori Matsui, *Masu Mediahō Nyūmon* [Introduction to mass media law], 5th ed. (Nihon Hyoronsha, 2013), 48–50 (hereinafter Matsui, MMN).

47 Sato, note 34, at 254; Ashibe, note 39, at 195.

government goals or purposes, and should be supported by a substantial relationship between those goals and the means.[48] For such restrictions, although a presumption of unconstitutionality is not attached, neither is a presumption of constitutionality granted. The government owns the burden of proof to justify the restriction.[49] If the restriction is, in reality, triggered by the content, then it should be regarded as a content-based restriction and not as a content-neutral restriction.[50]

Naturally, this freedom of expression jurisprudence in theory is much more demanding compared with the freedom of expression jurisprudence of the Supreme Court in practice. It would render unconstitutional many restrictions that the Supreme Court has sustained. A ban on hate speech, if introduced, would likely be sustained by the Supreme Court as it stands, but if it were to be evaluated in light of this alternative academic freedom of expression jurisprudence, it would face much more difficulty.

IV. Restrictions Based on the Content of Expression

A. *Advocacy or Solicitation of Violence*

The discrepancy between the freedom of expression jurisprudence adopted by the Supreme Court and that proposed by academics is most clear in respect of a ban on advocacy of illegal conduct. There is no consensus on the definition of hate speech, but it is clear that it includes advocacy or solicitation of violence towards a group of people marked by some criteria, such as race, ethnic origin, or religion.[51] It is useful to compare how the ban on advocacy or solicitation of illegal conduct would be handled under the freedom of expression jurisprudence adopted by the Supreme Court or that proposed by constitutional academics.

The ban on advocacy of illegal conduct, such as revolution or violent overthrow of the government, is the most typical content-based restriction of political freedom. The Supreme Court held in *Emergency Food Supply Order*[52] that such advocacy risked bringing about social harm and therefore that the Diet could ban it. During the extreme food shortage after the Pacific War, the government maintained the mandatory food

48 Ashibe, note 39, at 197; Matsui, MMN, note 46, at 50.
49 Ashibe, note 39, at 210.
50 *Ibid.*, at 198.
51 Matsui, note 7.
52 See note 20.

distribution system under the Food Supply Control Act[53] and mandated that farmers sell their crops to the government at a designated price. It then prohibited any solicitation of violation of this obligation under the Emergency Food Supply Order.[54] The defendant, a farmer who was frustrated by the government's policy, stood before other farmers at a farmers' meeting and argued that they should resolve not to sell their crops to the government. The defendant was prosecuted for advocating a violation of a statutory obligation. The Supreme Court upheld the resulting conviction without regard to what the farmer had actually said or whether the speech actually risked bringing about a violation. In this case, it was evident that if the Diet believes that a certain type of advocacy is dangerous, then it can be banned; the Supreme Court will not inquire into whether the ban is justified.

This judgment clearly indicated denial of the significance of constitutional protection for freedom of expression – and the Supreme Court affirmed its position in *Riot against the Return of Okinawa*.[55] The defendant in this case was the leader of a radical student group critical of the return of Okinawa to Japan without the removal of US military bases. He gave a speech to protesters, urging them to attack and eliminate the riot police. The group, consisting of roughly 400 radical students, attacked the police station in the National Railroad (now JR) Shibuya Station, set fires, and killed one police officer and injured several others. The defendant was prosecuted for solicitation to commit arson for the purpose of accomplishing a political agenda, in violation of the Subversive Conduct Prevention Act.[56] The Supreme Court upheld the resulting conviction, holding that the solicitation banned was capable of provoking damage to public safety and not deserving of protection as freedom of expression, and hence that the Diet could rightfully ban such expression.

Academics criticize the Supreme Court for providing virtually no protection to freedom of expression in these cases. Some academics have argued for the use of the clear and present danger test, once adopted by the US Supreme Court as a standard with which to judge the constitutionality of bans on the advocacy of illegal actions, requiring that there must be a clear and present danger of the expression causing serious

[53] Food Management Act (repealed in 1994).

[54] Emergency Food Supply Order, Imperial Prescript No. 86 of 1946, art. 10 (repealed in 1994).

[55] Supreme Court, 2nd Petty Bench, 28 September 1990, 44 Keishū 463.

[56] Subversive Conducts Prevention Act, art. 39 (prohibiting advocacy or solicitation of arson with the purpose of advancing, supporting or opposing political causes or policies).

harm before it can be prohibited.[57] Other leading academics have insisted on the application of the *Brandenburg* test,[58] justifying a ban only when it is targeting direct incitement of unlawful conduct and where there is a real likelihood that unlawful conduct will manifest. *Emergency Food Supply Order* would not be sustained under either test because the restriction was not so narrowly targeting advocacy as to prohibit only the unprotected conduct.

There is no case in which the ban on advocacy of illegal conduct has been applied to advocacy of violence against a particular person or group of persons. Incitement to commit homicide or assisting a homicide could be subject to punishment,[59] and, theoretically, groups that advocate or solicit arson with a political agenda could be punishable under the Subversive Conduct Prevention Act.[60] Moreover, a group that advocates or solicits illegal violent conduct such as homicide for political causes could be targeted under the same Act.[61] If the clear and present danger test or the *Brandenburg* test were applied, then criminal punishment would not be possible unless there were an apparent substantial likelihood of harm and the criminal ban could not be sustained unless the ban were narrowly limited to target only conduct immediately likely to cause serious harm. This approach would make it very difficult to ban the advocacy of violence against a particular person or a group of persons.

B. *Insult and Offensive Speech*

Another form of hate speech is insult of a particular group of people characterized by certain criteria such as race, ethnic origin, or religion.

Insult or offensive speech could be banned for the protection of public safety. In the United States, although the US Supreme Court once held that offensive speech did not deserve constitutional protection,[62] the law now limits permissible punishment only to 'fighting words' that have an immediate risk of triggering public disturbance.[63] If a similar approach

57 Ashibe, note 39, at 208; Sato, note 34, at 62–63, 263.

58 *Brandenburg* v. *Ohio*, 395 U.S. 444 (1969); Sato, note 34, at 263. See Staughton Lynd, 'Comment, *Brandenburg* v. *Ohio*: A Speech Test for All Seasons?' (1975) 43 *U. Chi. L. Rev.* 151; Thomas Healy, '*Brandenburg* in a Time of Terror' (2009) 84 *Notre Dame L. Rev.* 655.

59 Criminal Code, note 19, arts 61 and 62.

60 Subversive Conduct Prevention Act, note 56, art. 39.

61 *Ibid.*, art. 4(2). The Public Safety Review Board can issue an order to end a demonstration or publication of such a group, or an order to disband it: *Ibid.*, art. 7.

62 *Chaplinsky* v. *New Hampshire*, 315 U.S. 568 (1942).

63 *Cohen* v. *California*, 403 U.S. 15 (1971).

were also adopted in Japan, a prohibition on insult or offensive speech directed at a person or group of people could not be justified unless there were an immediate danger that the speech could cause public disturbance, making such a prohibition very difficult to sustain.

There is a criminal ban on insult in the Criminal Code.[64] But, historically, this provision has largely been interpreted as a means of protecting the social reputation of a person, intended to protect the same interest as criminal defamation and covering statements other than statements of fact[65] rather than protecting public safety. As a result, it was used only to punish extremely derogatory and outrageous speech towards a person, and thus prosecution and conviction under it is rare. Moreover, there has been no judicial consideration of the constitutionality of the criminal insult provision, although it is likely that both the Supreme Court and constitutional academics would be willing to sustain its constitutionality to protect the dignity of a targeted person. Such insult could also be a tort and raise civil liability. Courts in Japan are more willing to order damages be awarded for insult if the words used are hateful or spiteful.[66] However, giving courts the power to impose punishment or to award remedy for insult, could allow judges to deny protection to the apparently vulgar or distasteful words likely to be used by any dissenting minority in society.[67] Critics therefore argue that the government should not be allowed to ban offensive speech unless the speech poses a clear and present danger of serious social disturbance or is directly directed to a particular individual.[68]

The criminal insults provision has also been interpreted only as protecting individuals and not a group of individuals; hence insults targeting a particular group cannot be criminal insults. Since a tort action for insult cannot be filed unless it is targeting a particular person, insults targeting a group cannot justify the award of damages in Japan. As a result, it is wholly unclear whether the legislature could impose punishment for insult of a group or allow damages to be awarded where insult harms a group.[69]

The ban on hate speech as insult of a targeted group, if it is to be introduced, needs to be justified by something other than the individual

64 Criminal Code, note 19, art. 231.

65 Supreme Court, 1st Petty Bench, 1 November 1983, 37:9 Keishū 1341.

66 Supreme Court, 3rd Petty Bench, 24 September 2002, 207 Shūmin 243; Tokyo District Court, 27 November 1985, 1174 Hanji 34.

67 Matsui, MMN, note 46, at 84–85.

68 *Ibid.*

69 If the hate speech is targeting a particular person, then it may be an insult and could be subject to criminal punishment.

interest in reputation. The Supreme Court might be willing to accept such justification, but, in light of the much more demanding requirements recommended by constitutional academics, it will be a serious challenge for it to do so.

It is true that some of the commentators argue that there is no room for any speech that violates human dignity. It is likely that many people agree with this argument. But when we move to define 'human dignity' and what speech could be banned as violating human dignity, then the agreement begins to disappear. Human dignity is too abstract and vague concept to ground a decision on whether or not a particular speech should be excluded.

C. *Defamation or Vilification*

Hate speech also usually includes defamation or vilification of a particular group characterized by some criteria, such as race, ethnic origin, or religion.

Defamation gives rise to both criminal liability and civil liability in Japan (and there is no distinction between libel and slander). Article 230 of the Criminal Code prohibits the publication of defamatory statements that point out facts in public.[70] This provision was inserted into the Criminal Code under the Meiji Constitution. It prohibited the publication of defamatory statements regardless of whether or not they were true. When the Japanese Constitution was enacted, the question was raised whether article 230 could be squared with the constitutional guarantee of freedom of expression. The Diet amended the Criminal Code and added article 230–2,[71] thereby giving immunity to those who publish defamatory statements when they relate to matters of public interest, when they are published with the sole purpose of advancing the public interest, and when it can also be proven that the statement is true.

The Supreme Court held that criminal liability for defamation was constitutional because a defamatory statement is an abuse of freedom of expression and is beyond constitutional protection.[72] It initially construed article 230–2 literally and held that there would be no room for immunity if a defendant were to fail to prove that the statement was true.[73] Yet, in *Evening Wakayama News*,[74] the Supreme Court expanded

[70] Criminal Code, note 19, art. 230.
[71] *Ibid.*, arts 230–32.
[72] Supreme Court, 1st Petty Bench, 10 April 1958, 12:5 Keishū 830.
[73] Supreme Court, 1st Petty Bench, 7 May 1959, 13:5 Keishū 641.
[74] Supreme Court, Grand Bench, 25 June 1969, 23:7 Keishū 975.

its interpretations of article 230–2, construing it as also giving immunity where there are reasonable grounds to *believe* that the statement at issue is true, even if the defendant cannot *prove* it. The Supreme Court held that this judicially created immunity was necessary to balance freedom of expression and protection of the reputation of individuals.

Defamation also gives rise to tort liability under article 709 of the Civil Code.[75] The Supreme Court has afforded the same protection in civil suits against defamatory statements[76] and it has upheld the constitutionality of awarding civil damages against those who publish defamatory statements.[77]

This is in sharp contrast with the position of the US Supreme Court, which, in *New York Times* v. *Sullivan*,[78] barred the award of civil damages for defamatory speech directed towards public officials unless the defendant had 'actual malice'. Although the actual malice standard is not applicable to private plaintiffs, they still need to prove that the defendant was at least negligent and, by implication, that the statement was false.[79] Moreover, the US Supreme Court acknowledged that the same protection should be granted in criminal defamation cases.[80] In the United States, however, while criminal defamation used to be justified by reason of public safety, it is now widely believed that criminal punishment for defamatory speech is very difficult to justify in light of the development of jurisprudence on incitement to illegal conduct and offensive speech.

Compared with the United States, where the truth of a defamatory statement is generally an absolute defence, it is only truth about a matter of public interest uttered for the sole purpose of advancing the public interest that is protected in Japan. Moreover, while in the United States the plaintiff (or prosecutor) must prove that a defamatory statement is false (and that the defendant had actual malice, in the case of defamation against a public figure), in Japan it is always the defendant who must prove that a statement concerns a matter of public interest, that it is expressed with the sole purpose of advancing the public interest, and that the statement is true – or at least that there are reasonable grounds to believe it is true. Furthermore, while in the United States damages could not be ordered unless the defendant had actual malice in defaming

[75] Civil Code, art. 709.
[76] Supreme Court, 1st Petty Bench, 23 June 1966, 20:5 Minshū 1118.
[77] Supreme Court, Grand Bench, 4 July 1956, 10:7 Minshū 785.
[78] *New York Times* v. *Sullivan*, 376 U.S. 254 (1964).
[79] *Gertz* v. *Robert Welch, Inc.*, 418 U.S. 323 (1974).
[80] *Garrison* v. *Louisiana*, 376 U.S. 64 (1964).

a public person, in Japan damages can be ordered unless the defendant can prove that there was a reasonable ground to believe that the statement was true. As a result, although the amount of damages awarded is generally limited because punitive damages are not awarded in Japan, the protection of defamatory speech is considerably limited.[81] Leading academics seem to support the Supreme Court in sustaining the constitutionality of both criminal and civil defamation law on condition that the requirements imposed by the Supreme Court are satisfied. However, there is strong criticism of the lack of protection for defamatory statements and strong endorsement of the idea that Japan ought to adopt the US Supreme Court's 'actual malice' standard.[82]

Nevertheless, in Japan, criminal defamation law and civil defamation law preclude only defamation against a particular person or a group of persons that may be easily identified. There is therefore no criminal or civil liability when someone utters hate speech by way of defamation or vilification of a particular group broadly. Unless the group is small and it is easy to identify individually those who are targeted, then no criminal punishment would be imposed nor would civil damage liability be found. In other words, there is no such thing as group defamation or group vilification in Japan.[83]

If hate speech is banned as group defamation or group vilification, then, such a ban needs to be justified by some interest other than the personal reputation of the persons targeted. The Supreme Court might be willing to sustain it – but, in light of the alternative academic freedom of expression jurisprudence, which attempts to balance the interest in reputation with freedom of expression and to limit the reach of defamation law, it might be much more difficult to justify it.

D. *Promotion of Hate*

Some countries, such as Canada, ban the wilful promotion of hate towards a particular group.[84] In addition to the need to protect the feelings of the

[81] Moreover, judicial injunctions are available in defamation cases: Supreme Court, Grand Bench, 11 June 1986, 40 Minshū 872.

[82] Matsui, MMN, note 46.

[83] Ministry of Justice, *Jinken Kyūsai Seido no Arikata ni Kansuru Chūkan Torimatome* [Intermediate summary of the discussion on human rights complaint system], available at www.moj.go.jp/JINKEN/public_jinken04_settlemen04.html [accessed 31 January 2020] (suggesting government condemnation as one remedy).

[84] Canada's Criminal Code, s. 319(2).

people belonging to the targeted group, it might be argued that there is a need to prevent division in society or to maintain a social harmony.[85]

Since there is no similar ban in Japan at the present time, it is very difficult to say whether such a ban would be accepted. In light of the possibility of prohibiting group insult or group defamation (group vilification), however, it may be seriously questioned whether the harmed feelings of the people belonging to a targeted group justify criminal punishment. Moreover, it may also be seriously questioned whether the need to prevent division in society or to maintain social harmony could justify criminal punishment. The Supreme Court might be willing to accept these justifications, but it would be much harder to satisfy the more stringent requirements imposed by constitutional academics.

The same could be said of the need to demonstrate a social commitment that hate speech should never be acceptable in a liberal democratic society to justify a hate speech ban. The government is surely permitted to ban hate crimes or illegal discrimination; it is a totally different matter whether the government can ban speech to show its commitment to the idea that a particular type of speech is never acceptable.

V. Restricting Public Demonstration and Public Gathering

A. *The Rights of Public Gathering and Public Demonstration*

Often, hate speech is used during public gatherings or demonstrations. Those who are opposed to hate speech will naturally want to restrict those public demonstrations or gatherings at which it is used. It is consequently imperative to examine whether the rights of public demonstration and public gathering could or should be restricted on the basis of hate speech used by a leader or by the participants.

The Constitution of Japan explicitly protects 'freedom of assembly' and there is no doubt that public gatherings receive constitutional protection. Public demonstrations similarly attract constitutional protection as a form of moving assembly or as an 'other' form of expression. The Supreme Court has confirmed that public demonstration is constitutionally protected.[86]

The Supreme Court has, however, accepted that the right of public gathering and the right of public demonstration are subject to reasonable restriction for the public welfare.[87] Whether a restriction on public

[85] *R* v. *Keegstra* [1990] 3 SCR 697.

[86] Supreme Court, Grand Bench, 24 November 1954, 8 Keishū 1866.

[87] *Ibid.*

demonstration or public gathering is permissible therefore depends upon whether it is reasonable to protect the public welfare.

B. *Public Assembly*

Members of the public have an apparent right to public assembly. In general, members of the public may assemble in public parks and other public places. However, the use of public parks for public gathering is partially restricted by the National Park Act and other legislation.[88] Although the government does not have a constitutional duty to build civic centres and other facilities or to make them available as public forums, members of the public have a right to use those facilities for expression as long as the facilities remain open. The Local Autonomy Act thus obliges local governments not to refuse the public use of 'public facilities' without legitimate reasons[89] and prohibits discrimination.[90] Applications to use these public facilities may consequently be denied only in exceptional cases.

With respect to public gatherings in public parks, the Supreme Court has granted very broad discretion to the government to manage the use of such spaces. For instance, in *May-Day Parade*,[91] an application for a permit to use the exterior garden of the Imperial Palace for a May Day rally was denied because of the risk of possible damage to the park. The applicants filed a suit seeking judicial revocation of this denial. The Supreme Court rejected the constitutional attack because the case became moot when the planned date for the rally had passed. Yet the Supreme Court added its opinion on the merits, rejecting the constitutional argument and holding that the denial was a result of the reasonable exercise of the administration's discretion to manage public parks. It may be questioned, however, whether there was indeed an apparent danger that the rally could seriously damage the park.

With respect to the regulation of gatherings at public facilities, applications to use a facility have sometimes been refused on the basis of a concern that the gathering could be harmful to public safety. In *Izumisano City Civic Centre*,[92] the denial of an application to use the centre for a gathering of a group opposing the construction of Kansai

[88] Natural Park Act; Metropolitan Park Act.
[89] Local Autonomy Act, art. 244(2).
[90] *Ibid.*, art. 244(3).
[91] Supreme Court, Grand Bench, 23 December 1953, 7 Minshū 1561.
[92] Supreme Court, 3rd Petty Bench, 7 March 1995, 49 Minshū 687.

International Airport was challenged. The manager believed that the applicants were a radical group and had engaged in a series of bombings, and hence the manager decided to refuse the group the use of the centre on the basis of possible danger to the public order. The Supreme Court interpreted the provision in the Local Autonomy Act to allow refusal only when there was a clear and imminent danger that public safety would be jeopardized. Applying this standard, it nonetheless concluded that the refusal was justified.

Sometimes, applications for the use of public facilities may be rejected because of concern over potential disturbances expected to be caused by opposing groups. In *Ageo City Welfare Centre*,[93] an application to use the centre for funeral services of union leaders was refused because of the fear that opposing radical groups could gather and cause a disturbance. The Supreme Court held, however, that such a disturbance must be specifically predicted based on objective facts and that the centre could not refuse such use because of a fear of disruption by opposing groups unless the potential disruption could not be adequately handled by the police. The Supreme Court invalidated the refusal in this case, holding that there were no circumstances to justify it.

Academics have insisted that a right of public assembly is a vital right for average citizens who do not have access to mass media, and that it should not be prevented unless there is a clear and present danger that the assembly causes serious public disturbance.[94] They generally oppose the denial of permits on the grounds that gatherings could damage the parks, since the public clearly have a right to their use for public gatherings and the probability that those gatherings could cause serious damage to the park is often questionable.[95] Academics have also insisted that public assembly should not be banned unless there is a clear and present danger of serious public disturbance and that potential activities of opposing groups should not be invoked as a justification to shut down assemblies.[96]

On the basis of the requirements imposed by the Supreme Court and by academics, it should be hard to refuse applications for public gathering by hate groups either in public parks or public facilities. This is because there would most likely be no clear and present danger that serious harm to public safety would result, because the likelihood of the gatherings causing serious damages is highly uncertain, and because potential

93 Supreme Court, 2nd Petty Bench, 15 March 1996, 50 Minshū 549.
94 Ashibe, note 39, at 215.
95 Yoichi Higuchi *et al.*, *Kenpō II* [Constitution II] (Seirin Shoin, 1997), 28–29.
96 Sato, note 34, at 287.

disturbances by opposing groups should not be accepted as a justification for refusal. The Supreme Court might be willing to accept other restriction on public gathering if the purpose or manner is so offensive as to justify it – but it would be hard to satisfy the requirements proposed by constitutional academics in this case, because such a refusal would be a content-based restriction.

C. *Public Demonstration*

With respect to demonstrations on public streets, local public safety ordinances regularly demand prior notification or permits for such demonstrations and will deny permits if there is a risk that public safety could be endangered. They also may impose various conditions even when a permit is issued.

The Supreme Court held in *Niigata Prefecture Public Safety Ordinance*[97] that, although the comprehensive prior permit requirement for public demonstration was not acceptable, the permit requirement for demonstration in a particular place or of a particular manner under reasonably clear standards or the system of prior notification could be upheld. It concluded that a permit could be denied or demonstrations could be prohibited when there was a clear and present danger to the public safety. Yet the Supreme Court essentially reversed this holding and sustained the prior comprehensive permit system in *Tokyo Public Safety Ordinance*.[98] The Supreme Court's current position is that public demonstrations are capable of turning into riots and that local governments can prohibit demonstrations if there is a possibility that public safety might be jeopardized. The Supreme Court affirmed this holding in *Tokushima City Public Safety Ordinance*[99] and held that a condition attached to a permit not to disturb traffic was not vague enough to invalidate it.

Academics have insisted that a right of public demonstration is also a vital right for average citizens who do not have access to mass media, and that a public demonstration should not be denied unless there is a clear and present danger of causing serious public disturbance.[100]

In light of the Supreme Court's decisions, public demonstrations can be subject to a permit system and applications may be refused if there is

97 Supreme Court, Grand Bench, 24 November 1954, note 86.

98 See note 23.

99 Supreme Court, Grand Bench, 10 September 1975, 29 Keishū 489.

100 Sato, note 34, at 290; Ashibe, note 39, at 217 (to preserve public safety, an advance notification requirement should be sufficient).

a danger that a demonstration could disturb public safety. It would be difficult, however, to deny an application by hate groups to hold a public demonstration because of danger to public safety.[101] As it stands, there can be no legal restriction on public demonstration other than in the interests of public safety.[102] As in the case of public gatherings, the Supreme Court might be willing to accept other restrictions on public demonstration when the purpose or manner of demonstration is so offensive – but it will be hard to satisfy the requirements proposed by the constitutional academics, because such a restriction is content-based.

VI. Conclusion

This chapter has shown that the Supreme Court has accepted broad restrictions on freedom of expression in Japan. By accepting at face value the arguments of the government that restrictions are necessary for public welfare, easily accepting the ends or goals invoked by the government to justify restrictions and the means as reasonable and necessary without inquiry, or using the interest-balancing standard, the Supreme Court has been eager to sustain the constitutionality of such restrictions. There is thus no judgment of the Supreme Court that has struck down a statutory restriction on freedom of expression in Japan.

Academics have insisted, however, that the stance of the Supreme Court is a total abdication of its judicial duty to safeguard freedom of expression. They propose to reinvigorate judicial review, especially with respect to restrictions on freedom of expression. Leading academics focus on the freedom of expression jurisprudence established by the US Supreme Court, which comprises a more protective framework for freedom of expression than that found in Japan. They therefore cast doubt on

[101] In some cases, a hate demonstration could constitute a forcible obstruction of business if it were to target a particular organization and prevent normal business by force: Criminal Code, note 19, art. 234. Although there is no precedent on the punishment for a hate demonstration as a forcible obstruction of business, the Supreme Court would be likely to uphold it, while most academics would probably uphold it if there were a clear and present danger of obstructing the normal operation of the organization by force.

[102] Road Traffic Act, art. 77(1), requires a permit for any use of a public road that might have serious effect on traffic and obliges the police chief, in art. 77(2), to grant a permit if there is no such danger or there would be no such danger if attached conditions were complied with, which conditions art. 77(3) authorizes the police chief to attach. This regulation is, however, designed to secure traffic safety and is wholly unrelated to the content of the activity or message conveyed.

the constitutionality of many current restrictions on freedom of expression and would prefer to make it more difficult to introduce new restrictions.

It is against this background that Japan must consider introducing a ban on hate speech. As this chapter has shown, if such a ban is introduced, regardless of its definition and requirements, the Supreme Court will be willing to sustain its constitutionality – but it will be hard to satisfy the requirements proposed within an alternative freedom of expression jurisprudence, as espoused by Japan's leading constitutional academics.

3

Hate Speech and International Law

The Internalization of International Human Rights in Japan

AYAKO HATANO*

I. Introduction

The recent rise of xenophobia and hate speech in Japan has caused serious concern at both national and international levels.[1] Since the

* This chapter is based on the author's previous work, including Ayako Hatano, 'Kokusai Jinken no Naimenka – Nihon ni okeru Han Reishizumu Undō to Heito Supīchi Kaishōhō o Jirei ni shite' ['Internalization of international human rights: the anti-racism movement and the Hate Speech Elimination Act in Japan'], in Toru Oga *et al.* (eds.), *Kyōsei Shakai no Saikōchiku III* [Reconstructing a coexistent society III] (Horitsu Bunkasha, 2020), 195–220. The author is immensely thankful to the editors of the book, and all those who made helpful comments and revisions, and especially those who kindly shared insightful experiences and thoughts in interviews. The author also expresses deepest appreciation to the Davis Projects for Peace by the Davis United World College Scholars Program, the Asia Leadership Fellow Program by the Japan Foundation and the International House of Japan, the Grants-in-Aid for Scientific Research (A) of the Japan Society for the Promotion of Science, 2016–21: Network Governance for Access to Justice in East Asia, and all organizations and individuals who generously supported this research. All opinions and errors remain strictly the author's own.

1 There is no established legal definition of hate speech, and its defining characteristics are controversial and disputed. See, e.g., Sangyun Kim, 'Heito Supīchi no Teigi' ['The definition of hate speech'] (2015) 48 *Ryūkoku Hōgaku* [Ryukoku law review] 19; Yasuko Morooka, *Heito Supīchi to wa Nani ka* [What is hate speech?] (Iwanami Shoten, 2013), at 38–50, 61–71. For the purposes of this chapter, informed by relevant international human rights instrument, hate speech is understood as a manifestation of hatred that constitutes incitement to discrimination, hostility, or violence towards a group of people or a single person, on the basis of various elements of identity, such as race, ethnicity, language, religion, national origin, colour, descent, age, disability and gender. See the International Convention on the Elimination of All Forms of Racial Discrimination (ICERD) (adopted 21 December 1965, entered into force 4 January 1969) 660 UNTS 195 (Arts 1, 2 and 4), the International Covenant on Civil and Political Rights (ICCPR) (adopted

2000s, hateful demonstrations that incite discrimination and violence targeting minorities – particularly ethnic Korean residents in Japan known as Zainichi Koreans – have been conducted publicly throughout the country.[2] While there has long been prejudice and discrimination against Zainichi Koreans in Japanese society, several political and social incidents in the 2000s between Japan and the Korean peninsula fuelled nationalism among the Japanese.[3] The trend was reinforced by the rise of

16 December 1966, entered into force 23 March 1976) 999 UNTS 171 (Art. 20(2)), and UN Committee on the Elimination of Racial Discrimination, *General Recommendation No. 35: Combating Racist Hate Speech*, UN Doc. CERD/C/GC/35 (26 September 2013). In this chapter, the term 'racial discrimination' shall broadly include discrimination on the basis of race, colour, descent, and national or ethnic origin, as defined by ICERD (Art. 1). This chapter focuses on discriminatory expression and behaviour aimed at individuals or specific groups on the basis of ethnic or national origin.

[2] *Zainichi* Koreans literally means 'Koreans staying or being in Japan' and is used to refer to settled permanent residents with ethnic Korean roots – especially to those who came or were brought to Japan during Japan's colonial rule of the Korean peninsula and to their descendants. Some of these individuals have acquired Japanese nationality, while others remain foreign residents with special residential status in Japan. This chapter uses 'Zainichi Koreans' in broad terms to include both those who have either *Chōsen-seki* (a domicile assigned to ethnic Koreans in Japan when the Japanese government revoked their Japanese citizenship after World War II) or South Korean citizenship, and Japanese citizens of Korean descent who acquired Japanese nationality by naturalization or by birth. See Soo im Lee, *Diversity of Zainichi Koreans and Their Ties to Japan and Korea* (Afrasian Research Centre, Ryukoku University, 2012), at 4–11 (describing the historical background of Zainichi Koreans). For a discussion of Zainichi Koreans in international law, see, e.g., Yasuaki Onuma, 'Interplay between Human Rights Activities and Legal Standards of Human Rights: A Case Study on the Korean Minority in Japan' (1992) 25 *Cornell Int'l L.J.* 515; Yasuaki Onuma, *Zainichi Kankokujin no Kokuseki to Jinken* [The nationality and human rights of Zainichi Koreans in Japan] (Yuhikaku, 2004). For a history of Zainichi Koreans' civil rights movements, see Kiyoteru Tsutsui, *Rights Make Might: Global Human Rights and Minority Social Movements in Japan* (Oxford University Press, 2018), at 82–149.

[3] These incidents may include North Korean abductions of Japanese citizens, which North Korea recognized officially in 2002, nationalistic attitudes among South Korean supporters booing the Japanese team in the 2002 FIFA World Cup co-hosted by South Korea and Japan, and recurring issues over historical perceptions, followed by a boom in anti-Korean publications after 2005. This trend has been reinforced by North Korea's missile tests and the territorial dispute between Japan and South Korea since around 2012. See Morooka, note 1, at 4–5; Rumi Sakamoto and Matthew Allen, 'Hating "The Korean Wave" Comic Books: A Sign of New Nationalism in Japan?' (2007) 5 *Asia-Pacific J. Japan Focus* 1. To connect the historical context with recent xenophobic movements against Zainichi Koreans in Japan, see generally Naoto Higuchi, *Nihongata Haigaishugi: Zaitokukai, Gaikokujin Sanseiken, Higashi Ajia Chiseigaku* [The radical right movement in contemporary Japan: East Asian geopolitics and the rise of xenophobic violence] (Nagoya University Press, 2014). See also Chapter 16.

the Internet, which made it possible to swiftly spread discriminatory discourse and information of unknown authenticity nationwide.[4] In 2007, an ultranationalist group calling itself *Zainichi Tokken wo Yurusanai Shimin no Kai* ('the Association of Citizens against the Special Privileges of Zainichi Koreans') (*Zaitokukai* for short) was established and began actively demonstrating its radically xenophobic and exclusionary claims.[5] Data from the Japanese Ministry of Justice shows that, between April 2012 and September 2015, there were at least 1,152 hate-based demonstrations.[6] In 2013, these demonstrations became more extreme, participants shouting slogans such as 'You Koreans are cockroaches!' and advocating for the extermination of 'all Koreans, good or bad', while waving Japanese national flags and swastikas.[7] Videos of these hate rallies were uploaded online, spreading on social media and other online communication tools, where anonymous discriminatory postings have become rampant. This rise in hateful demonstrations and online vitriol in Japan has drawn not only domestic but also international criticism, particularly from the human rights treaty bodies of the United Nations. In mid-2014, the UN Human Rights Committee (HRC) and UN Committee on the Elimination of Racial Discrimination (CERD) strongly recommended that the Japanese government take steps to curb hate speech.[8]

[4] Tomomi Yamaguchi, 'Xenophobia in Action: Ultranationalism, Hate Speech, and the Internet in Japan' (2013) 117 *Radical History Review* 98, at 100–01 (pointing out the notable surge of online xenophobic discourse since 2000). See generally Koichi Yasuda, *Netto to Aikoku* [The Internet and patriotism] (Kodansha, 2012) (describing how right-wing groups use Internet media extensively and strategically to communicate ideas and organize, and how racist and xenophobic movements have spread by means of Internet media). See also John Boyd, 'Hate Speech in Japan: To Ban or Not to Ban?', *Al Jazeera*, 19 March 2015, available at www.aljazeera.com/indepth/features/2015/03/hate-speech-japan-ban-ban-150310102402970.html [accessed 27 April 2019]. See also Chapters 17 and 18 for analysis of hate speech on the Internet.

[5] See in general Yasuda, note 4; Koichi Yasuda, *Heito Supīchi: 'Aikokushatachi' no Zōo to Bōryoku* [Hate speech: the hate and violence of 'patriots'] (Bungeishunju, 2015).

[6] Centre for Human Rights Education and Training, Ministry of Justice, *Heito Supīchi ni Kansuru Jittai Chōsa Hōkokusho* [Report of the survey about actual conditions of hate speech] (2016), at 62, available at www.moj.go.jp/content/001201158.pdf [accessed 26 May 2019]. This number is likely to be a very conservative estimate as it only counts publicly observed demonstrations. See Craig Martin, 'Striking the Right Balance: Hate Speech Laws in Japan, the United States, and Canada' (2018) 45 *Hastings Const. L.Q.* 461.

[7] Centre for Human Rights, note 6, at 33. See also Julian Ryall, 'Japan Conservatives: "Hate Speech Goes Too Far" ', *Deutsche Welle*, 7 September 2013, available at www.dw.com/en/japan-conservatives-hate-speech-goes-too-far/a-16938717 [accessed 27 April 2019]; Morooka, note 1, at 2.

[8] Human Rights Committee, *Concluding Observation on the Sixth Periodic Reports of Japan*, UN Doc. CCPR/C/JPN/CO/6 (20 August 2014); Committee on the Elimination of

On 24 May 2016, the Japanese National Diet passed its first law against hate speech, the Act on the Promotion of Efforts to Eliminate Unfair Discriminatory Speech and Behaviour against Persons Originating from Outside Japan (known as the Hate Speech Elimination Act, or HSEA), and the Act came into force on 3 June 2016.[9] According to the Ministry of Justice, this law was developed 'in response' to the recommendations set out in '[the] Concluding Observations on the Sixth Periodic Report of Japan by the UN Human Rights Committee in July 2014 and [the] Concluding Observations on the Combined Seventh to Ninth Periodic Reports of Japan by the UN Committee on the Elimination of Racial Discrimination in August of the same year'.[10] A resolution that the House of Councillors of Japan adopted on 26 May 2016 also confirms that the Act is a response to the requests from the HRC and the CERD.[11] However, the burning question before us is: does the HSEA effectively respond to the recommendations from the UN human rights treaty bodies, as is claimed? Specifically, does it in fact 'internalize' international human rights norms at the domestic level?

This chapter defines 'internalization' as the domestic penetration of international law and norms – that is, the process by which states accept international standards domestically.[12] In doing so, states embed international law and norms into the domestic domain by means such as legal incorporation, legislative materialization, or enforcement, through which they become accepted as appropriate standard behaviours in a compliant

Racial Discrimination, *Concluding Observations on the Combined Seventh to Ninth Periodic Reports of Japan*, UN Doc. CERD/C/JPN/CO/7-9 (26 September 2014).

[9] The term 'unfair discriminatory speech and behaviour against persons originating from outside Japan' in the Act, despite its problematic scope (addressed later in this chapter), is considered to be equivalent to what is known as 'hate speech' in principle, as indicated on the website of Japan's Ministry of Justice. See Ministry of Justice, 'Promotion Activities Focusing on Hate Speech', available at www.moj.go.jp/ENGLISH/m_jinken04_00001.html [accessed 5 May 2019]. See Chapter 11.

[10] *Ibid.*

[11] Committee on Judicial Affairs of the House of Councillors, *Heito Supīchi no Kaishō ni Kansuru Ketsugi* [Resolution of the elimination of the hate speech] (26 May 2016), available at www.sangiin.go.jp/japanese/gianjoho/ketsugi/190/i065_052601.pdf [accessed 16 May 2019].

[12] See Martha Finnemore and Kathryn Sikkink, 'International Norm Dynamics and Political Change' (1998) 52 *International Organization* 887, at 904–05; Sarah Cleveland, 'Norm Internalization and U.S. Economic Sanctions' (2001) 26 *Yale J. Int'l L.* 6; Harold Hongju Koh, 'Why Do Nations Obey International Law?' (1997) 106 *Yale L.J.* 2599, at 2602; Dana Zartner, 'Internalization of International Law', *Oxford Research Encyclopedias International Studies* (2019), available at https://oxfordre.com/internationalstudies/view/10.1093/acrefore/9780190846626.001.0001/acrefore-9780190846626-e-225 [accessed 16 May 2020].

society.[13] While states are technically bound by the international treaties that they have ratified and by international customary law, if such standards are to be effective as appropriate codes of conduct, they must be internalized at the national level.[14] This is particularly important in the context of international human rights treaties because the treaty bodies, while overseeing states' compliance with the treaties, do not have sufficient authority or resources to ensure effective implementation at the domestic level.

Previous literature has described the stages and mechanisms through which international norms can lead to change in domestic practice and political behaviour as a process of 'socialization'.[15] International political scientists Finnemore and Sikkink divide the dynamic socialization process into three stages, referring to the 'lifecycle of a norm': 'norm emergence', 'norm cascade', and 'norm internalization'.[16] According to international law scholar Harold Hongju Koh, the internalization of international law is effected by the repeated interaction of diverse actors both nationally and internationally, with global norms applied domestically by means of interpretation and translation, giving them domestic value.[17] Goodman and Jinks also emphasize the importance of 'acculturation' in the process of internalizing international law – that is, of the general process by which actors adopt the beliefs and behavioural patterns of a surrounding culture as an important mechanism influencing state practice.[18]

[13] See James G. March and Johan P. Olsen, 'The Institutional Dynamics of International Political Orders' (1998) 52 *International Organization* 943.

[14] Amichai Cohen, 'Bureaucratic Internalization: Domestic Governmental Agencies and the Legitimization of International Law' (2005) 36 *Georget. J. Int'l L.* 1079, at 1081. See generally Louis Henkin, *How Nations Behave* (Columbia University Press, 1979); Finnemore & Sikkink, note 12; Koh, note 12, at 2659; Harold Hongju Koh, 'Bringing International Law Home' (1998) 35 *Houston L. Rev.* 623, at 681.

[15] Thomas Risse and Kathryn Sikkink, 'The Socialization of International Human Rights Norms into Domestic Practices: Introduction', in Thomas Risse *et al.* (eds.), *The Power of Human Rights: International Norms and Domestic Change* (Cambridge University Press, 1999), 1–38.

[16] Finnemore & Sikkink, note 12, at 895–905.

[17] Koh, note 12, at 2646; Koh, note 14, at 623, 680 (calling transnational the legal process with which public and private actors interact to internalize the rules of transnational law); Harold Hongju Koh, 'How Is International Human Rights Law Enforced?' (1999) 74 *Ind. L.J.* 1397, at 1406 (claiming that international human rights law is enforced not only by nation states but also by people with a commitment to human rights by means of a transnational legal process of interaction, interpretation, and internalization). See also, e.g., Harold Hongju Koh, 'Transnational Legal Process' (1996) 75 *Neb. L. Rev.* 181.

[18] Ryan Goodman and Derek Jinks, 'How to Influence States: Socialization and International Human Rights Law' (2004) 54 *Duke L.J.* 621, at 626 (analysing the

A question that can be raised here again is whether the internalization of international human rights law and the 'socialization' of the state has been evident in Japan's development of its Hate Speech Elimination Act, purported to be a response to the recommendations of UN human rights treaty bodies. This chapter examines the enactment of the anti-hate speech law in Japan in the context of the impact of transnational legal processes on national obedience to international human rights law and norms. By analysing the legal and political process and its interaction with civil society, as mobilized in an anti-racism social movement, this chapter reveals the complicated mechanisms of internalization at different levels. There are diverse domestic actors with influence on the internalization of international law beyond the legal text itself and its interpretation. Examining their interaction in the legislative process leading to the Hate Speech Elimination Act may reveal whether or not internationally established human rights norms have indeed been domestically transposed and embedded in the national social context.

The importance of this examination is underlined by the fact that not only is internalization realized when there is legitimacy and support at the local level, but also the factors that promote or impede internalization of international law, including the ways in which it is legitimized and supported, are diverse and complex among nations because internalization among them will take different forms and require differing processes.[19] Because of this complexity, inductive and empirical studies of individual cases of the internalization of international law have not been sufficiently covered in the literature. This chapter offers a case study on the internalization of international law in Japan to contribute to filling this gap. Notably, this study examines how a society can move from textual internalization of international norms to 'internalization on the ground' – that is, genuine social acceptance of human rights norms, and the appropriation and local adoption of globally generated ideas and strategies, which anthropologist Sally Engel Merry and sociologist Peggy Levitt call the 'vernacularization' of international human rights

mechanisms that influence the behaviour of states when implementing international human rights law, with a particular focus on acculturation as a process through which human rights cultures are built). See also Ryan Goodman and Derek Jinks, *Socializing States: Promoting Human Rights through International Law* (Oxford University Press, 2013), at 4.

[19] Steven Ratner, 'Does International Law Matter in Preventing Ethnic Conflict?' (2000) 32 *N.Y.U.J. Int'l L. & Pol.* 591, at 680.

law.[20] This study, based on a socio-legal analysis of the role of national and transnational actors in the development of anti-hate speech regulation in Japan, provides a solid example of how international human rights work in practice and aims to inspire discussion on how to implement international human rights law effectively to protect minorities from exclusion in a global context.

Section II of this chapter, after reviewing the international and domestic legal frameworks concerning hate speech and racial discrimination, examines the text of the Hate Speech Elimination Act and its effects. Section III subsequently provides analysis of the internalization of international law in courts of law, administrative authorities, legislative bodies, and civil society in Japan, both during the process of development and in application of the Hate Speech Elimination Act. Section IV concludes that the dynamic process of internalizing international law and norms in society may remedy a weak legal framework and its effective implementation on the ground.

II. The Legal Framework of Hate Speech and Racial Discrimination in International and Domestic Law

A. The International Legal Framework

International law has developed standards against hate speech on the basis that it undermines the fundamental rights of others to equality or to freedom from discrimination, as well as based on a history of racial discrimination that has led to massive violations of human rights.[21] Promoting substantive equality among human beings, including freedom from discrimination, is a foundational idea in human rights. Even though hate speech is not explicitly defined or enshrined in international law, there are provisions that identify expressions considered hate speech. Article 1 of the Universal Declaration on Human Rights (UDHR), adopted by the UN General Assembly in 1948, states that '[a]ll human

[20] Peggy Levitt and Sally Merry, 'Vernacularization on the Ground: Local Uses of Global Women's Rights in Peru, China, India and the United States' (2009) 9 *Global Networks* 441, at 446 (calling the process of appropriation and local adoption of globally generated ideas and strategies 'vernacularization'). See also Sally Engle Merry and Peggy Levitt, 'The Vernacularisation of Women's Human Rights', in Stephen Hopgood, Jack Snyder, and Leslie Vinjamuri (eds.), *Human Rights Futures* (Cambridge University Press, 2017), 213–36.

[21] See also Chapter 1 for more on the international human rights framework regarding hate speech.

beings are born free and equal in dignity and rights'.[22] Article 2 UDHR reiterates equal enjoyment of the rights and freedoms proclaimed, 'without distinction of any kind', and Article 7 provides for equal protection against any discrimination in violation of the Declaration and against any incitement to such discrimination. The first international treaty to deal directly with the issue of hate speech was the International Convention on the Elimination of All Forms of Racial Discrimination (ICERD), adopted by the UN General Assembly in 1965.[23] The ICERD requires States parties to prohibit racial discrimination in all of its forms and to bring an end to racial discrimination by persons, groups of persons or institutions, and to ensure that all public authorities and public institutions, national and local, shall act in conformity with this obligation, including equal treatment and protection before the law and justice (Arts 2(1)(d), 5 and 6 ICERD). The ICERD demands that States parties must make 'an offense punishable by law' the dissemination of ideas based on racial superiority or hatred, the creation or participation in organizations that promote racial discrimination, and the provision of any assistance, financial or otherwise, to racist activities (Art. 4(a)(b) ICERD).[24] The International Covenant on Civil and Political Rights (ICCPR), adopted by the UN General Assembly in 1966, places an obligation on States parties to prohibit hate speech in rather different terms than those of the ICERD.[25] While Article 19(2) ICCPR guarantees the right to freedom of expression, Article 19(3) also outlines possible restrictions on this right, including those required 'for respect of the rights or reputations of others'. Article 20(2) ICCPR subsequently provides that '[a]ny advocacy of national, racial or religious hatred that constitutes incitement to discrimination, hostility or violence shall be prohibited by law'.[26] In 2013, the CERD issued its General Recommendation No. 35 on

[22] UNGA Res. 217 A (III), UN Doc. A/RES/3/217 A (10 December 1948).

[23] UNGA Res. 2106 A (XX), UN Doc. A/RES/20/2106 (21 December 1965).

[24] The CERD has also highlighted the involvement of private actors in hateful discrimination and asked the State party to implement legislative measures rendering private actors liable. See, e.g., Jóna Pálmadóttir and Iuliana Kalenikova, *Hate Speech: An Overview and Recommendations for Combating It* (Icelandic Human Rights Centre, 2018), 1–27.

[25] UNGA Res. 2200 A (XXI), UN Doc. A/RES/2200A(XXI) (16 December 1966).

[26] The HRC requests the States parties to prohibit incitement, as described in Art. 20 ICCPR, by law with sanction: Human Rights Committee, General Comment No. 11 (27 July 1983), para. 2, suggests that imposition of civil and administrative penalties could fulfil the requirement under the ICCPR. See William A. Shabas, *U.N. International Covenant on Civil and Political Rights: Nowak's CCPR. Commentary*, 3rd rev. ed. (Engel, 2019), 587.

combating racist hate speech in a reaction to widespread racist hate speech around the world.[27] It outlines diverse measures to combat racist hate speech effectively while protecting the legitimate right to freedom of expression, providing a detailed interpretation of Article 4 ICERD, as well as Articles 5 and 7.[28]

B. *The Domestic Legal Framework*

Despite these international rules against hate speech, the Japanese government had long refrained from taking legal measures to curb hate speech until its recent effort in the form of the Hate Speech Elimination Act. Japan ratified the ICCPR in 1979 and acceded to the ICERD in 1995. However, it entered reservations on Article 4(a) and (b) ICERD, which calls for the criminalization of racial hate speech, the Japanese government claiming that the provision could conflict with the strong protection of freedom of speech under article 21 of the Japanese Constitution, as well as the principle of legality of crime and punishment under article 31 of the Constitution.[29] Japan further claimed that racial discrimination in Japan was not at so serious a level that legal action was necessary.[30]

Against this background, the Japanese government has not enacted comprehensive legislation prohibiting discrimination nor a specific law

[27] Committee on the Elimination of Racial Discrimination, *General Recommendation No. 35: Combating Racist Hate Speech*, UN Doc. CERD/C/GC/35 (26 September 2013).

[28] *Ibid.* See also the Rabat Plan of Action on the prohibition of advocacy of national, racial or religious hatred that constitutes incitement to discrimination, hostility or violence (Conclusions and recommendations emanating from the four regional expert workshops organized by the Office of the High Commissioner for Human Rights in 2011, and adopted by experts at the meeting in Rabat, Morocco, on 5 October 2012), A/HRC/22/17/Add.4 (11 January 2013).

[29] *First and Second Combined Periodic Report by the Government of Japan under Article 9 of the ICERD*, UN Doc. CERD/C/350/Add.2 (26 September 2000), para. 73. See also Chapters 1, 2 and 15.

[30] Despite the CERD's recommendation in 2010 that urged Japan to adopt 'specific legislation to outlaw direct and indirect racial discrimination', a report by the Japanese government submitted to the CERD in 2013 reiterated that '[t]he Government of Japan does not believe that, in present-day Japan, racist thoughts are disseminated and racial discrimination is incited, to the extent that . . . legislation to impose punishment against dissemination of racist thoughts and other acts should be considered even at the risk of unduly stifling legitimate speech': Committee on the Elimination of Racial Discrimination, *Concluding Observations on the Combined Seventh to Ninth Periodic Reports of Japan*, UN Doc. CERD/C/JPN/CO/3–6 (6 April 2010) paras 9 and 13–14; *Seventh, Eighth, and Ninth Combined Periodic Report by the Government of Japan under Article 9 of the ICERD*, UN Doc. CERD/C/JPN/7–9 (10 July 2013), para. 84.

to ban hate speech. The government, in principle, asserts that the current legal framework and its efforts to raise awareness are enough to deal with the issue[31] – even though, under domestic law as it stands, regulating hateful speech directed at an unspecified group of people is not straightforward. Under the Penal Code, discriminatory words and actions that provoke violence against a specific person or group based on prejudice can be subject to actions of intimidation (article 222 of the Penal Code), insult (article 231 of the Penal Code), and defamation (article 230 of the Penal Code), as well as the crime of defamation of trust (article 233 of the Penal Code). Those provisions, however, can be applied only where victims are specifically identified as individuals or institutions, and these categories do not apply to identifiable groups in general, such as those categorized by race, nationality, and ethnicity.[32] There are only a limited number of situations in which action for obstruction of business by force (article 234 of the Penal Code) can be applied.[33] Also, civil law regulation (in tort under article 709 of the Civil Code and defamation under article 723 of the Civil Code) has been found to be less effective in countering hate speech directed at unspecified groups.[34] As a result, hate speech targeting minorities in general, regardless of how derogatory and insulting, is not prohibited and falls into a legal limbo in Japan. In other words, Japan has long tolerated what Goodman and Jinks call 'decoupling' – that is, a 'disconnect between local circumstances and universally applicable global models'.[35] While the Japanese government made formal commitments to global values when it ratified the UN human rights treaties, it failed to change its concrete practices at the national level in regard to hate speech.

[31] See *First and Second Combined Periodic Report*, note 29, para. 75. See also Chapter 6.

[32] Daishin'in, 24 March 1926, 5 Daihan Keishū 117 (describing that the object of these crimes is to protect the 'honor of people', in which people includes 'natural person[s]', 'corporation[s] (legal person[s])', and 'organization[s] without corporate status', but does not include general groups). See also Takahiro Akedo, 'Heito Supīchi Taisakuhō 'Yotōan' ni tsuite Kangaeru – 'Tekihō Kyojū' Yōken wa Naze Okashii no ka' ['Thinking about the anti-hate speech law proposal by the ruling parties: why the "legal resident" condition is inappropriate'], *Synodos*, 25 April 2016, available at http://synodos.jp/politics/16944 [accessed 28 April 2019].

[33] For instance, the crime of forcible obstruction of business is not directly applicable to mere speech, which does not constitute a hindrance to business activities. See Chapter 7 for issues related to the Penal Code.

[34] Masato Ichikawa, 'Hyōgen no Jiyū to Heito Supīchi' ['Freedom of expression and hate speech'] (2015) 360 *Ritsumeikan Hōgaku* [Ritsumeikan law review] 122.

[35] Ryan Goodman and Derek Jinks, 'Toward an Institutional Theory of Sovereignty' (2003) 55 *Stan. L. Rev.* 1749, at 1760–61.

In light of this inadequate domestic legal framework, the HRC and the CERD, in 2014 expressed strong concerns about a worrying rise in hate speech in Japan and called for comprehensive measures, including criminal punishment for hate speech. The HRC, in its Concluding Observations on the Sixth Periodic Report of Japan adopted in July 2014, recommended that Japan adopt comprehensive legislation prohibiting discrimination on all grounds.[36] It further asked the Japanese government to 'prohibit all propaganda advocating racial superiority or hatred that incited discrimination, hostility or violence, and to prohibit demonstrations that are intended to disseminate such propaganda, as well as to take all necessary steps to prevent a racist attack to ensure that the alleged perpetrators are thoroughly investigated, prosecuted and, if convicted, punished with appropriate sanctions', as well as to spare resources for 'awareness-raising campaigns against racism and increase its efforts to ensure that judges, prosecutors and police officials are trained to detect hate and racially motivated crimes'.[37] It also recommends that Japan should 'take all necessary steps to prevent racist attacks and to ensure that the alleged perpetrators are thoroughly investigated, prosecuted and, if convicted, punished with appropriate sanctions'.[38]

Subsequently, in August 2014, the CERD adopted its Concluding Observations on the Combined Seventh to Ninth Periodic Reports of Japan, in which it commented extensively on hate speech.[39] The CERD expressed its concerns at the spread of hate speech, including 'incitement to imminent violence by right-wing movements or groups that organize racist demonstrations and rallies against foreigners and minorities, in particular against Koreans', and at the fact that 'such acts are not always properly investigated and prosecuted' in Japan.[40] The CERD specifically recommended that the Japanese government should:

(a) Firmly address manifestations of hate and racism, as well as incitement to racist violence and hatred during rallies;
(b) Take appropriate steps to combat hate speech in the media, including the Internet;

[36] Human Rights Committee, *Concluding Observation on the Sixth Periodic Report of Japan*, UN Doc. CCPR/C/JPN/CO/6 (20 August 2014), para. 11.
[37] *Ibid.*, para. 12.
[38] *Ibid.*
[39] Committee on the Elimination of Racial Discrimination, note 8. It should be noted that the CERD has repeatedly recommended that the Japanese government take measures on hate speech in its previous Concluding Observations in 2001, 2003, and 2010.
[40] *Ibid.*, para. 11.

(c) Investigate and, where appropriate, prosecute private individuals, as well as organizations, responsible for such acts;
(d) Pursue appropriate sanctions against public officials and politicians who disseminate hate speech and incitement to hatred;
(e) Address the root causes of racist hate speech and strengthen measures of teaching, education, culture and information, with a view to combating prejudices which lead to racial discrimination and to promoting understanding, tolerance and friendship among nations and among racial or ethnic groups.[41]

It also recommended the enactment of a comprehensive law to prohibit racial discrimination.[42]

C. *The Hate Speech Elimination Act and Its Effects*

The Hate Speech Elimination Act is said to be a response to these recommendations.[43] We might consequently ask whether the Hate Speech Elimination Act does indeed reflect the required international human rights law and norms – particularly those highlighted in the recommendations of those human rights treaty bodies that monitor the implementation of the international human rights law with which Japan has pledged to comply. The answer, we can summarily conclude, is that it does not: the substance of the Hate Speech Elimination Act does not fully comply with the obligations set out under international human rights law for the following reasons.[44]

First, the law neither criminalizes hate speech nor holds it to be illegal, which makes it a so-called law on basic principle. The Act, after declaring in its preamble that unfair discriminatory speech and behaviour is neither permissible nor shall be tolerated, stipulates in article 3 the basic principles for efforts towards the elimination of hate speech in regards to the general public, and sets out in article 4 the responsibility of the national and local governments to make such efforts to eliminate such speech and behaviour. According to the commonly accepted theory

41 *Ibid.*
42 *Ibid.*, para. 8.
43 See text accompanied by notes 10 and 11. The Hate Speech Elimination Act is also mentioned as an achievement in response to the recommendation of the CERD in the *Tenth and Eleventh Combined Periodic Report by the Government of Japan under Article 9 of the ICERD*, UN Doc. CERD/C/JPN/10–11 (25 September 2017), paras 105–07. See also Chapter 10 for the legislative process leading to the Hate Speech Elimination Act.
44 Martin, note 6, at 466–81; Tamitomo Saito, 'Heito Supīchi Taisaku o Meguru Kokunaihō no Dōkō to Kokusaihō' ['The situation of domestic and international laws over the measures against hate speech'] (2016) 19 *Quarterly Jurist* 91, 91–94.

that the preamble is not legally binding, the law does not have the legal effect of directly outlawing or prohibiting hate speech, nor does it create a concrete right to counter hate speech.[45] In other words, the law lacks the critical provision of punishment of or penalties for those who perpetrate hate speech, contrary to the recommendations of the international human rights treaty bodies calling for its prohibition.[46] Ultimately, the Japanese government neither withdraws its reservation of Article 4(a) and (b) ICERD nor imposes criminal, civil or administrative penalties specifically on hate speech.

Second, the scope of the Act is extremely narrow in defining hate speech. Under article 2, 'unfair discriminatory speech and behaviour' covers only hateful speech targeting persons originating exclusively from a country or region other than Japan, or their descendants and lawfully residing in Japan. This means that the law is designed to protect legal residents of overseas origin and their descendants, but that other ethnic minorities or persons who do not reside legally in Japan and other Japanese minority groups are not eligible for protection under the Hate Speech Elimination Act.[47] This is far from the 'comprehensive' anti-discrimination law recommended by the treaty bodies.

The Act stipulates the national and local governments' responsibilities to set up consultation systems to prevent and resolve disputes regarding hate speech (article 5), to implement educational activities (article 6), and

[45] Junko Kotani, 'Proceed with Caution: Hate Speech Regulation in Japan' (2018) 45 *Hastings Const. L.Q.* 610. When Japan reserved Art. 4(a) and (b) ICERD, it declared: 'In applying the provisions of paragraphs (a) and (b) of article 4 [ICERD,] Japan fulfils the obligations under those provisions to the extent that fulfilment of the obligations is compatible with the guarantee of the rights to freedom of assembly, association and expression and other rights under the Constitution of Japan, noting the phrase "with due regard to the principles embodied in the Universal Declaration of Human Rights and the rights expressly set forth in article 5 of this Convention".' See International Convention of the Elimination of All Forms of Racial Discrimination, *Declarations and Reservations: Japan*, UNGA Res. 2106 (XX), UN Doc. A/RES/2106(XX) (21 December 1965), para. 49. There is ongoing argument over whether criminalization of hate speech would be acceptable under the Constitution. While the Committee recommends that Japan withdraw its reservation of the paragraphs.

[46] See Chapter 1.

[47] For example, those who are deemed to originate from Japan, including Buraku people (a group long discriminated against in Japan on the basis of a pre-modern caste system), people from Okinawa, Ainu people, persons with disabilities, LGBTQ+ people, and those who are not legally resident are not subject to the direct protection of the Hate Speech Elimination Act. It should be noted that supplementary resolutions to the law suggest a broader interpretation of its art. 2, as discussed later. See Chapter 4 for more on Buraku discrimination and hate speech.

to enhance awareness-raising activities for the general public (article 7), aiming to eliminate hate speech. While these provisions may correspond to some parts of the recommendations of the international human rights treaty bodies, it makes no reference to international human rights law and standards, while its preamble positions the principle of unfair discriminatory speech and behaviour 'in light of Japan's position in the international community'. It provides for the promotion of educational measures and raising of awareness to counter hate speech, but it makes no provision that sufficient resources must be allocated to these activities. Moreover, there is no regulation of online hate speech or specific provisions centred on hate speech by public officials. It is for these reasons that its critics have decried the Act as so 'toothless' and 'narrow' as to be ineffective.[48]

This textual analysis demonstrates that the Hate Speech Elimination Act is far from comprehensive in reflecting the critical elements of the recommendations by the human rights treaty bodies and the principles stipulated in international human rights law. It might be described, as it is by Goodman and Jinks, as 'incomplete internalization of international law', whereby a state publicly conforms to global norms without privately accepting them, implementing only 'shallow, formal reforms' that exert little influence on actual state practice.[49]

However, has the enactment of the Hate Speech Elimination Act really been nothing more than a shallow and symbolic reform? In addressing this question, it would be important to examine the supplementary resolutions attached to the law, as well as its actual effects on various actors on the ground. Although the Hate Speech Elimination Act itself includes no mention of any international human rights treaty in its text, two supplementary resolutions to the Act adopted by the Committees on Judicial Affairs both of the House of Councillors and the House of Representatives do make clear references to such. The supplementary resolution of the Committee on Judicial Affairs of the House of Councillors that:

> [I]nterpretation of article 2 of this Act that certain form of discriminatory speech and behaviour may be allowed as long as it is not the 'unfair discriminatory speech and behaviour against persons originating from

[48] Tomohiro Osaki, 'Diet Debates Hate-Speech Bill that Activists Call Narrow and Toothless', *The Japan Times*, 19 April 2016, available at www.japantimes.co.jp/news/2016/04/19/national/politics-diplomacy/diet-debates-hate-speech-bill-activists-call-narrow-toothless/ [accessed 28 April 2019].

[49] Ryan Goodman and Derek Jinks, 'Incomplete Internalization and Compliance with Human Rights Law' (2008) 19 *Eur. J. Int'l L.* 725, at 748.

> outside Japan' is not correct and any form of discriminatory speech and behaviour shall be appropriately dealt with in view of the intent of this Act, and the spirit of the Japanese Constitution and *the International Convention on the Elimination of All Forms of Racial Discrimination.*[50]

The supplementary resolution of the House of Representatives also emphasizes that:

> [I]n view of the intent of this Act, and the spirit of the Japanese Constitution and the *International Convention on the Elimination of All Forms of Racial Discrimination*, and with the basic awareness that it is not correct to believe that certain forms of discriminatory speech and behaviour may be allowed as long as it is not the 'unfair discriminatory speech and behaviour against persons originating from outside Japan' provided for in article 2, all discriminatory speech and behaviour shall be dealt with appropriately.[51]

Both resolutions further note that 'the national government and local governments shall endeavour to keep track of the actual situation of unfair discriminatory treatment, and shall conduct a review so as to take the necessary measures for their elimination', referring to measures to tackle hate speech on the Internet.[52] These supplementary resolutions are not legally binding, yet the government is expected to respect them in its implementation of the law.

In regard to the actual effects of the Hate Speech Elimination Act, despite criticism of its weakness absent provisions for punishment, enactment of the law is reported to have led to a swift response to hate speech in relevant ministries, local governments, and the judiciary of the country. Although there is no specific penalty set out in the law, it has been confirmed that the Act can be the basis for administrative or legal decisions such as refusing permission for the use of roads and public spaces for demonstrations.[53] For example, on 30 May 2016, less than

[50] House of Councillors Committee on Judicial Affairs, *Supplementary Resolution for the Act on the Promotion of Efforts to Eliminate Unfair Discriminatory Speech and Behavior against Persons Originating from Outside Japan*, available at www.moj.go.jp/content/001199551.pdf [accessed 24 June 2018] (emphasis added).

[51] House of Representatives Committee on Judicial Affairs, *Supplementary Resolution for the Act on the Promotion of Efforts to Eliminate Unfair Discriminatory Speech and Behavior against Persons Originating from Outside Japan*, available at www.moj.go.jp/content/001199555.pdf [accessed 24 June 2018] (emphasis added).

[52] House of Councillors Committee on Judicial Affairs, note 50; House of Representatives Committee on Judicial Affairs, note 51.

[53] Yuichiro Uozumi *et al.*, *Heito Supīchi Kaishōhō – Seiritsu no Keii to Kihonteki na Kangaekata* [The Hate Speech Elimination Act: the process of the development of the Act and its basic principles] (Daiichi Hoki, 2016), at 162.

a week after the enactment of the Hate Speech Elimination Act, Kawasaki City – inhabited by many people who have foreign heritage, including Zainichi Koreans, and who have been targeted by various hate groups – denied a group that repeatedly conducted rallies centred on hateful remarks targeting those inhabitants permission to hold demonstrations on 5 June at two parks in the city on grounds of their 'unfair discriminatory speech and behaviour'.[54] The decision took into account the provisions of the new Hate Speech Elimination Act, which urges central and local governments to implement measures curbing hate speech as racist actions.[55] On 2 June 2016, the Kawasaki Branch of Yokohama District Court issued its first-ever provisional injunction preventing an anti-Korean activist from holding rallies, again referring to the Hate Speech Elimination Act. The ground-breaking judgment provided that the hateful demonstrations and hate speech were not protected by freedom of assembly and expression, and that they violated personal rights.[56] As Japanese law professor Akira Maeda comments, 'the legislation spells out for the first time what kind of language constitutes hate speech. This was critical in the court's determination that the man's activities constitute a tort, which is prohibited by law.'[57] Yasuko Morooka, an attorney-at-law and an advocate against hate speech, also remarks that '[t]he hate speech legislation, which calls discriminatory language "not permissible" regardless of whether it targets a specific audience, has made it easier for the court to determine

[54] 'Heito Dantai no Kōen Shiyō Fukyoka Shobun o Happyō, Kawasaki-shi' ['Kawasaki City announces denial of permission for hate group's park use'], *Asahi Shimbun*, 31 May 2016, available at http://digital.asahi.com/articles/ASJ503QY5J50ULOB01B.html [accessed 28 April 2019].

[55] *Ibid.*

[56] Yokohama District Court, Kawasaki Branch, 2 June 2016, 2296 Hanji 14; see also Tomohiro Osaki, 'Japanese Court Issues First-Ever Injunction against Hate-Speech Rally', *The Japan Times*, 3 June 2016, available at www.japantimes.co.jp/news/2016/06/03/national/crime-legal/japanese-court-issues-first-ever-injunction-hate-speech-rally/ [accessed 28 April 2019] (reporting on a decision by Yokohama District Court); Akihiro Kawanishi, 'Nihon ni Okeru Heito Supīchi Kisei: Heito Supīchi Kaishōhō o Megutte' ['Hate speech regulations in Japan: a focus on the Hate Speech Elimination Act'] (2018) 807 *The Reference* 51, at 68–69. For analysis of the decision as a positive outcome of the Hate Speech Elimination Act, see, e.g., Kensuke Ueda, 'Heito Demo Kinshi Karishobun Meirei Jiken' ['A case of preliminary injunction against hate demonstrations'] (2016) 433 *Hōgaku Kyōshitsu* [Law classroom] 153; Sangyun Kim, 'Keihō Kaisei, Heito Supīchi Kaishōhō Kaisei no Kanousei' ['The possibilities of amending the Penal Code and the Hate Speech Elimination Act'] (2018) 757 *Hōgaku Seminā* [Legal seminar] 18.

[57] Osaki, note 56.

that what residents in that area have faced amounts to a tort'.[58] Furthermore, the Hate Speech Elimination Act has influenced the practices of the police: on 3 June 2016, the National Police Agency issued a directive to prefectural police throughout the country, calling for them to respond strictly to hate speech and discriminatory behaviour in light of the principles set out in the Hate Speech Elimination Act.[59] In fact, on 5 June 2016, anti-hate speech and anti-racism protests by hundreds of citizens and persuasion by the police resulted in suspension of the demonstration by a group targeting Zainichi Koreans immediately after its departure.[60] Moreover, on 20 December 2016, Osaka District Court issued a provisional injunction prohibiting a hate demonstration in the Korean town in Osaka.[61] Taking all of these incidents into consideration, the Hate Speech Elimination Act seems to have a certain significance and effect in guiding interpretation and action among courts and government agencies.

[58] *Ibid.* However, Morooka, note 1, also points out the limitation of the law and seeks a comprehensive anti-discrimination law with penalties for those responsible.

[59] 'Heito Demo ni Genkaku Taisho, Kizon no Hō Katsuyō – Tsūtatsu' ['Firmly addressing hateful demonstrations by taking advantage of the existing law: an announcement'], *Mainichi Shimbun*, 3 June 2016, available at https://mainichi.jp/articles/20160603/k00/00e/040/255000c [accessed 28 April 2019]; Director General of the Security Bureau and Commissioner of the General Secretariat of the National Police Agency, *Honpōgai Shusshinsha ni taisuru Futō na Sabetsuteki Gendō no Kaishō ni Muketa Torikumi no Suishin ni Kansuru Hōritsu no Sekō ni tsuite (Tsūtasu)* [In re enforcement of the Act on the Promotion of Efforts to Eliminate Unfair Discriminatory Speech and Behavior against Persons Originating from Outside Japan], Circular, 3 June 2016, available at www.npa.go.jp/pdc/notification/keibi/biki/keibikikaku20160603.pdf [accessed 23 May 2020]. The directive also calls for cooperation among ministries to raise awareness of hate speech, as well as to enhance knowledge of the law and hate speech among police personnel. See also Kawanishi, note 56, at 69.

[60] 'Heito Demo Shuppatsu Chokugo ni Chūshi – Kōgi no Sūhyakunin ga Kakomu Kawasaki' ['Hate speech demonstration interrupted immediately after beginning: Kawasaki surrounded by several hundred people protesting'], *Mainichi Shimbun*, 5 June 2016, available at https://mainichi.jp/articles/20160606/k00/00m/040/013000c [accessed 28 April 2019].

[61] The court did not clarify the ground of decision, but the Korea NGO Centre, which made an application to the court for a provisional injunction, presented as legal ground for its petition the ICERD, the Hate Speech Elimination Act, and the Osaka ordinance against hate speech. See Asia-Pacific Human Rights Information Centre, 'Osaka Chisai Heito Demo no Karishobun Kettei' ['Osaka District Court's decision on hate demonstration provisional injunction'], *HuRights Osaka*, undated, available at www.hurights.or.jp/archives/newsinbrief-ja/section3/2016/12/1220.html [accessed 24 June 2018]; 'Heito Supīchi San Seireishi ga Jōrei Seitei o Kentō Yokushi Mokuteki ni' ['To curb hate speech, three municipalities considering ordinance enactment'], *Mainichi Shimbun*, 31 May 2017, available at https://mainichi.jp/articles/20170601/k00/00m/040/133000c [accessed 28 April 2019].

Furthermore, the Ministry of Justice clearly states that the recommendations of the UN human rights treaty bodies were the impetus for its own activities focusing on hate speech and for its implementation of nationwide anti-hate-speech campaigns.[62] While disseminating information about enforcement of the law, including publishing the recommendations from the HRC and the CERD as the background to its activities tackling hate speech and translating the Act into foreign languages on its website, the Ministry of Justice distributed 60,000 posters throughout the country and conducted awareness-raising activities, especially in those areas that could anticipate hate demonstrations. Not only did the Ministry establish a team within its Human Rights Bureau specifically to deal with issues of hate speech, but also a Hate Speech Special Subcommittee was established within the Liaison Council of Ministries and Agencies for Human Rights Education and Awareness, aiming to promote cooperation among relevant ministries, government agencies, local governments, and civil society in the light of the Act.[63]

Meanwhile, the vague definition of 'hate speech' in the Hate Speech Elimination Act has led to demands for a more distinct definition and guidelines for local governments, to support front-line staff in deciding whether or not certain speech and behaviour should be considered hate speech and hence whether or not to permit the use of public facilities for demonstration or assembly. Responding to these demands, the Ministry of Justice provided local governments with criteria to guide such decisions, including typical examples of hate speech as reference material when implementing the Hate Speech Elimination Act.[64] In June 2017, the Ministry of Justice further announced the results of its first survey of

[62] Interview with a government official at the Human Rights Bureau, Ministry of Justice in Tokyo (29 July 2016). See also www.moj.go.jp/JINKEN/jinken04_00108.html [accessed 17 May 2020].

[63] *Ibid.*

[64] *Ibid.* A special team has been set up within the Ministry of Justice to respond to hate speech, actively promoting cooperation with government agencies and local public bodies, as well as cooperation with civil society: 'Japanese Government Gives Examples of What Qualifies as "Hate Speech" in Anti-Discrimination Law', *Sora News 24*, 7 February 2017, available at https://soranews24.com/2017/02/07/japanese-government-gives-examples-of-what-qualifies-as-hate-speech-in-anti-discrimination-law/ [accessed 28 April 2019]; 'Hōmushō, Heito Supīchi no Gutairei o Hyōji' ['Ministry of Justice gives examples of hate speech'], *Nikkei Shinbun*, 4 February 2017, available at www.nikkei.com/article/DGXLASDG04H53_U7A200C1CR8000/ [accessed 28 April 2019]; 'Hōmushō 'Korega Heito Supīchi' Tenkeirei o Hyōji' ['Ministry of Justice: "this is hate speech" showing typical examples'], *Mainichi Shinbun*, 6 February 2017, available at https://mainichi.jp/articles/20170206/k00/00e/040/213000c [accessed 26 May 2019].

foreigners living in Japan and their experiences of discrimination.[65] The Ministry of Education, Culture, Sports, Science and Technology also issued a notice to prefectural boards of education and deans of public and private universities, requesting them to respond appropriately to enforce the Hate Speech Elimination Act with reference to the supplementary resolutions,[66] to promote human rights education, and to help to raise awareness.[67]

Furthermore – and somewhat ironically – the vague definition of hate speech and the weak enforcement measures stipulated in the Hate Speech Elimination Act have prompted some municipal governments to develop their own anti-hate-speech guidelines and ordinances.[68] In April and July 2017, Kannonji City in Kagawa Prefecture amended some of its ordinances concerning the use of public parks and car parking areas to prohibit racially discriminative behaviour.[69] In October 2016, a few months after the enactment of the Hate Speech Elimination Act and during his election campaign, the mayor of Kawasaki City promised to draw up an ordinance to eradicate discrimination, saying that '[h]ate speech goes against the policy of the city, which aspires to guarantee respect for human rights and create an inclusive society'.[70] Subsequently, in November 2017, Kawasaki City set out

[65] Centre for Human Rights, note 6.

[66] Ministry of Education, Culture, Sports, Science and Technology, *Honpōgai Shusshinsha ni taisuru Futō na Sabetsuteki Gendō no Kaishō ni Muketa Torikumi no Suishin ni Kansuru Hōritsu no Sekō ni Tsuite (Tsūchi)* [Notification on enforcement of the Act on the Promotion of Efforts to Eliminate Unfair Discriminatory Speech and Behaviour against Persons Originating from Outside Japan], 20 June 2016, available at www.pref.osaka.lg.jp/attach/6686/00223248/01_kuni_tuuti_honnpou_.pdf [accessed 17 May 2020].

[67] Kawanishi, note 56, at 69; Ministry of Justice and Ministry of Education, Culture, Sports, Science and Technology (ed.), *Jinken Kyōiku Keihatsu Hakusho Heisei 27 Nen Ban* [White Paper on human rights education and awareness-raising, 2017 edition], available at www.moj.go.jp/content/001253816.pdf [accessed 17 May 2020].

[68] Osaka City established its anti-hate ordinance even before the enactment of the Hate Speech Elimination Act. See Eric Johnston, 'Osaka Enforces Japan's First Ordinance against Hate Speech, Threatens to Name Names', *The Japan Times*, 1 July 2016, available at https://www.japantimes.co.jp/news/2016/07/01/national/crime-legal/osaka-enforces-japans-first-ordinance-hate-speech-threatens-name-names/ [accessed 20 October 2020]; see also Chapters 1 and 9 for hate speech regulations enacted by local governments.

[69] 'Kagawa-ken Kannonji-shi de Heito Taisaku Jōrei ga Senshinteki na Riyū' ['The reason why the enactment of the anti-hate ordinance in Kannonji City of Kagawa Prefecture is progressive'], *47NEWS*, 12 September 2019, available at www.47news.jp/3987426.html [accessed 5 May 2020]. For the restriction of the use of public facilities, see Chapter 19.

[70] 'Kawasaki Draws up Japan's First Local Guidelines to Prevent Hate Speech', *The Japan Times*, 11 November 2017, available at www.japantimes.co.jp/news/2017/11/11/national/social-issues/kawasaki-draws-japans-first-local-guidelines-prevent-hate-speech/#.Wy4BU6czaUl [accessed 28 April 2019].

administrative guidelines on the use of 'public facilities' based on the Hate Speech Elimination Act.[71] Similar guidelines were developed in Kyoto Prefecture in March 2018 and Kyoto City in June 2018.[72] They were followed by the anti-discrimination ordinances developed in Setagaya Ward in Tokyo in March 2018 and Kunitachi City in the same metropolis in December 2018.[73] In October 2018, the Tokyo Metropolitan Government adopted an ordinance to curb hate speech – the first such ordinance in Japan at the prefectural level.[74] Kobe City also passed a city ordinance against hate speech in June 2019, with a unanimous vote in the city council.[75] In December 2019, Kawasaki City went even further to enact Japan's very first ordinance imposing criminal penalties on hate speech.[76] It is

[71] *Ibid.*

[72] *Kyoto-fu Ōyake no Shisetsu nado ni okeru Heito Supīchi Bōshi no tame no Shiyō Tetsuzuki ni Kansuru Gaidorain* [Kyoto Prefecture Guideline on procedure on use of public facilities for the prevention of hate speech], March 2018, available at www.pref.kyoto.jp/jinken/documents/kyotogl.pdf [accessed 26 May 2019]; *Heito Supīchi Kaishōhō o Fumaeta Kyoto-shi no Ōyake no Shisetsu nado no Shiyō Tetsuzuki ni Kansuru Gaidorain* [Kyoto City Guideline on procedure on use of public facilities based on the Hate Speech Elimination Act], available at www.city.kyoto.lg.jp/bunshi/cmsfiles/contents/0000239/239867/guideline.pdf [accessed 29 June 2019].

[73] See 'Setagaya-ku ga Sabetsu Kinshi Jōrei LGBTI to Gaikokujin ni Tokka' ['Setagaya Ward's anti-discrimination ordinance focused on LGBTI people and foreigners'], *Nikkei Shinbun*, 2 March 2018, available at www.nikkei.com/article/DGXMZO27620600S8A300C1CC1000/ [accessed 28 April 2019]; 'Kunitachi-shi, Arayuru Sabetsu wo Kinshi Heito nado no Jōrei Seitei he' ['Kunitachi City to pass ordinance to prohibit hate and all forms of discrimination'], *Nikkei Shinbun*, 3 December 2018, available at www.nikkei.com/article/DGKKZO38869780T11C18A2CC0000/ [accessed 2 February 2020].

[74] It also aims to curb discrimination against LGBTQ+ people, in line with the fundamental Olympic principles in light of Tokyo's hosting of the 2020 Olympics in 2021: Magdalena Osumi, 'Tokyo Adopts Ordinance Banning Discrimination against LGBT Community' *The Japan Times*, 5 October 2018, available at www.japantimes.co.jp/news/2018/10/05/national/tokyo-adopts-ordinance-banning-discrimination-lgbt-community/#.XOU7rcj7TIU [accessed 26 May 2019]; Yuichi Inoue, 'Tokyo's Vague Anti-Hate Speech Ordinance Raises Legal Concerns', *Asahi Shimbun*, 4 October 2018, available at www.asahi.com/ajw/articles/AJ201810040040.html [accessed 26 May 2019].

[75] 'Kobe shi Heito Yokushi Jōrei, Raishun Seko, Shigikai de Zenkai Itchi' ['Kobe City ordinance to curb hate passed with unanimous vote in the City Council, to be enforced next spring'], *Mainichi Shimbun*, 5 June 2019, available at https://mainichi.jp/articles/20190605/ddf/007/010/011000c [accessed 2 February 2020].

[76] *Kawaski shi Sabetsu no nai Jinken Sonchō no Machizukuri Jōrei* [Kawasaki City ordinance on establishing a city with no discrimination and respecting human rights], available at www.city.kawasaki.jp/250/page/0000113041.html [accessed 2 February 2020]; Shigehiro Saito, 'Kawasaki Eyes Criminal Action for Those Who Stir Hate Speech', *Asahi Shimbun*, 25 June 2019, available at www.asahi.com/ajw/articles/AJ201906250041.html [accessed 26 June 2019]; 'Kawasaki Enacts Japan's First Bill Punishing Hate Speech', *The Japan Times*, 12 December 2020, available at www.japantimes.co.jp/news/2019/12/12/national/

noteworthy that international human rights norms against racial discrimination and hate speech have been observed rather directly incorporated into the ordinances of local municipalities.[77]

In light of all of this, it is true that Japan's first law to curb hate speech can be said to be too weak because it too narrowly defines potential victims and does not legally ban hate speech.[78] Further, it is hard to say that the substance is sufficient, from the perspective of international human rights standards, because the law stipulates only a basic principle and partners this with the general responsibilities of the relevant parties, lacking comprehensive and detailed provisions. However, in fact, it has had a certain significance and effects, influencing various related administrative and judicial measures, and it has had symbolic effect in declaring hate speech intolerable in society. The law also seems to have functioned as a guideline granting local and judicial bodies the authority to control the dissemination of hateful speech in some cases, as well as in helping to raise awareness among the public that hate speech is not acceptable.[79]

The Hate Speech Elimination Act can also be deemed to have had effect in that there have been fewer rallies and less racist invective since its enactment.[80] Indeed, according to the National Police Agency, the number of xenophobic rallies nearly halved in the 11 months after the Diet enacted the Hate Speech Elimination Act.[81] Subsequent data reveals that the number of hate demonstrations by ultra-nationalistic groups has continued to decline since July 2016, which may indicate that the Act

crime-legal/kawasaki-first-japan-bill-punishing-hate-speech/#.XjelPWj0lPY [accessed 2 February 2020]. As is noted later in the chapter, civil society and human rights advocates played an important part in the development of this anti-hate ordinance in Kawasaki.

77 See also Komae-Shi, 'Jinken Sonchō Kihon Jōrei' ['The ordinance to protect basic human rights'], adopted on 26 March 2020, with reference to hate speech, See also 'Jinshu nado Sabetsu Kinshi no Jourei Seiritsu Tokyo Komae Sekuhara mo' ['The ordinance adopted to ban the discrimination based on race, sex and other grounds at Komae City, Tokyo'], available at https://news.yahoo.co.jp/articles/fd9915c1ad26183c4235d7e838f803d960471d40 [accessed 12 September 2020].

78 Saito, note 44, at 93–94.

79 Martin, note 6, at 455.

80 'A Year after Enactment of Hate Speech Law, Xenophobic Rallies Down by Nearly Half', *The Japan Times*, 27 May 2017, available at www.japantimes.co.jp/news/2017/05/22/national/social-issues/year-enactment-hate-speech-law-xenophobic-rallies-nearly-half/#.WhSvI4anFph [accessed 28 April 2019].

81 *Ibid.* From 3 June 2016 through to the end of April 2017, police nationwide tallied 35 demonstrations involving hate speech versus 61 in the same period a year earlier. A National Police Agency officer attributes the change to the law's entry into force and increased social interest in the matter.

has had an impact at least on mass demonstrations on the street and the extreme speech that accompanies them.[82]

So why has the Hate Speech Elimination Act made these effects possible without strong enforcement measures, which is deemed a legislative deficiency in light of the recommendations of treaty bodies? To analyse this phenomenon, we may need to look at the process whereby the law developed more broadly in terms of the internalization of international human rights law. In the next sections, this chapter will examine the internalization of international law in the judiciary, politics, and society, which may be the foundation of the apparently effective implementation of the Hate Speech Elimination Act.

III. Internalizing International Law and Norms on Racial Discrimination and Hate Speech in Japan

A. *Internalizing International Human Rights Law among the Judiciary*

As the background to the court's and the administrative organs' willingness to take steps to tackle hate speech, judicial rulings in a particular sequence of cases have also had a significant impact on the social movement against hate speech and the development of the Hate Speech Elimination Act.[83] In these cases, a school for children with ethnic Korean roots in Japan, the Kyoto Chōsen First Elementary School (known as the Kyoto Korean Elementary School), was attacked by ultranationalistic groups who shouted racist and xenophobic slogans nearby, damaged school property, and posted video footage of the demonstrations repeatedly throughout 2009 and 2010.[84] On 7 October 2013, in the resulting civil lawsuit,[85] Kyoto District Court took the unprecedented step of ordering those groups to stop their hateful protests and pay the

[82] National Police Agency, *Chian no Kaiko to Tenbō* [Overview and outlook of security] (2015–19).

[83] See Ayako Hatano, 'The Internalization of International Human Rights Law: The Case of Hate Speech in Japan' (2018) 50 *N.Y.U. J. Int'l L. & Pol.* 637.

[84] *Ibid.* See also Morooka, note 1, at 18–20; Il-song Nakamura, *Rupo Kyoto Chōsen Gakkō Shūgeki Jiken: 'Heito Kuraimu' ni Kōshite* [Reportage on the Kyoto Korean School attack case: fighting against 'hate crime'] (Iwanami Shoten, 2014), 1–20, 111–31. See also Chapters 5, 8, 12 and 13 for more details on the case.

[85] Both civil and criminal cases have been brought to the court in relation to the Kyoto Korean School incident.

school a high amount of compensation.[86] The Osaka High Court upheld the ruling on 8 July 2014[87] and the Supreme Court affirmed it on 9 December 2014.[88] This case has been seen as an opening volley, triggering legal discussion of hate speech in Japan.[89]

The decision of Kyoto District Court – the court of first instance in this case – has attracted both domestic and international attention, not only because of the serious nature of the case, but also because of its unique reference to international human rights law.[90] A Japanese international law professor Koji Teraya notes, even though Kyoto District Court drew on the immaterial damage caused by the demonstrations to find liability for damages in tort under article 709 of the Civil Code and, in this sense, the judgment fell within the existing legal framework, the ruling remains significant for several reasons as an interpretation of domestic law in light of international law.[91]

First, Kyoto District Court made it clear that the national courts have a 'direct obligation' to interpret domestic laws to conform with the ICERD, referring to Articles 2(1) and 6 of the Convention.[92] Japanese international law scholar Tamitomo Saito considers that this landmark decision demonstrates a positive attitude among the judiciary towards acknowledging its own role in realizing international human rights law in the form of judicial redress for victims.[93]

Second, the court interpreted the Civil Code without referring to the Constitution, relying solely on the ICERD, which it considered to be a direct influence on the interpretation and application of domestic Civil Code. Teraya considers the ruling to show that a human rights treaty that

86 Nakamura, note 84, at 214–18; Kyoto District Court, 7 October 2013, 2208 Hanji 74. The court approved the plaintiff's claim, holding that the defendants were no longer allowed to stage protests near the school and ordering them to pay the unprecedented amount of ¥12.26 million (approximately US$110,000) in compensation.

87 Osaka High Court, 8 July 2014, 2232 Hanji 34.

88 Supreme Court, 3rd Petty Bench, 9 December 2014.

89 Kim, note 56, at 18.

90 It should be noted that this incident was also assessed as a hate crime and that the demonstrators were convicted in a criminal case: Koji Teraya, 'Heito Supīchi Jiken' ['Hate speech case'] (2014) 1466 *Jurist* 292; Saito, note 44; Martin, note 6; Hatano, note 83.

91 Teraya, note 90, at 293. To apply international law in Japanese national courts, the domestic effect and domestic applicability (direct applicability or self-execution) are important. Article 98(2) of the Constitution provides that 'treaties concluded by Japan and established laws of nations shall be faithfully observed'. Consequently, these treaties in principle enter the domestic legal system without the need for special legislative procedures.

92 Teraya, note 90, at 137.

93 Saito, note 44, at 94.

sets out its content with precision can be more useful than the Constitution in pointing the way towards concrete application and interpretation.[94]

Third, in determining the unlawfulness of the perpetrators' activities, the court referred to the definition of 'racial discrimination' in Article 1(1) ICERD and found that the conduct in question constituted such. That finding led it to conclude that the same acts were both unlawful as tort under the Civil Code and amounted to illegal racial discrimination under the ICERD.[95]

Fourth, the court ruled that, when a tort is racially discriminatory or racially motivated, the intangible damage the court determines would be 'aggravated based on the direct influence of the ICERD on the interpretation of the Civil Code'.[96] The court explained that 'the amount of compensation should be enough to ensure effective protection and remedy against the racial discrimination' under Article 6 ICERD, which is specifically addressed to national courts.[97] Never before had a Japanese court based calculation of compensation due on a violation of the ICERD – but it is a finding that follows from CERD General Recommendation No. 26 (although it is not cited per se in the reasons for the decision):

> [T]he right to seek just and adequate reparation or satisfaction for any damage suffered as a result of such discrimination, which is embodied in article 6 of the Convention, is not necessarily secured solely by the punishment of the perpetrator of the discrimination; at the same time, the courts and other competent authorities should consider awarding financial compensation for damage, material or mental, suffered by a victim, whenever appropriate.[98]

Namely, the court decided to award high intangible damages on the grounds that the tort in question constitutes racial discrimination, which is illegal under the ICERD.[99] Teraya notes that this decision is

94 Teraya, note 90, at 292.

95 Saito, note 44, at 94.

96 *Ibid.*, at 157–58.

97 *Ibid.*, at 138–41. See Art. 6 ICERD: 'States Parties shall assure to everyone within their jurisdiction effective protection and remedies, through the competent national tribunals and other State institutions, against any acts of racial discrimination which violate his human rights and fundamental freedoms contrary to this Convention, as well as the right to seek from such tribunals just and adequate reparation or satisfaction for any damage suffered as a result of such discrimination.'

98 Committee on the Elimination of Racial Discrimination, *Report of the Comm. on the Elimination of Racial Discrimination: Fifty-Sixth Session (6–24 March 2000), Fifty-Seventh Session (31 July–25 August 2000), annex V(B)*, UN Doc. A/55/18 (17 October 2000).

99 Teraya, note 90, at 293; Saito, note 44, at 94.

significant because it articulates the principle under human rights treaty that intangible damage can give rise to monetary remedy.[100]

Fifth, in interpreting the Civil Code, the court referred not only to treaty provisions, but also to the concluding observations in the review of government reports before the CERD.[101] The judgment can be deemed to respond in part to the recommendation of the CERD that 'relevant constitutional, civil and criminal law provisions [should be] effectively implemented, including through additional steps to address hateful and racist manifestations by, inter alia, stepping up efforts to investigate them and punish those involved'.[102]

The Osaka High Court ruling handed down on 8 July 2014, after the Kyoto District Court ruling, did not apply the ICERD as directly as Kyoto District Court did. Most of those positive references of the trial court to the ICERD noted thus far disappeared from the appellate decision.[103] However, the High Court affirmed the decision of Kyoto District Court, supporting the unusually high amount of compensation and recognizing the hateful demonstrations as 'racial discrimination' under Article 1(1) ICERD. The court reinforced the purpose of the ICERD as being to eliminate racial discrimination, underlined the viciousness of the acts concerned, and held that this should be certainly taken into account in considering the magnitude of intangible damages such as mental distress caused by unreasonable torts.[104] It further noted that the ideals of the ICERD should be realized even among private persons when interpreting the Constitution and related legislation.[105] Given that judges had upheld the rather classical view of international law as a set of principles regulating state relations, but not private ones, in the 1980s and 1990s, the outcome in *Kyoto Korean Elementary School* may also reflect a change of attitude towards international law among the judiciary.[106] The ultra-nationalist groups claimed that their demonstrations should be protected by freedom of expression, believing it to be in the public interest to criticize 'the (unfair) privileges of Zainichi

100 Teraya, note 90, at 293.

101 *Ibid.*, at 293; Saito, note 44, at 94.

102 Committee on the Elimination of Racial Discrimination, *Concluding Observations on the Combined Third to Sixth Periodic Reports of Japan*, UN Doc. CERD/C/JPN/CO/3–6 (6 April 2010), at 131.

103 Osaka High Court, note 87.

104 *Ibid.*, at 38.

105 *Ibid.*

106 Timothy Webster, 'International Human Rights Law in Japan: The View at Thirty' (2010) 23 *Colum. J. Asian L.* 242, at 245.

Koreans' and media bias.[107] The Osaka High Court rejected these arguments and held that protestors intended to stir up discriminatory attitudes among the public: a goal that was neither for the public benefit nor within the scope of protection under freedom of speech.[108] On 9 December 2014, five Supreme Court judges affirmed the earlier rulings, unanimously dismissing the appeal.[109]

In light of the fact that Japanese courts had historically been relatively unresponsive to international legal claims in domestic litigation and had either denied the direct effect of international human rights law or ignored such claims altogether, these rulings are ground-breaking – in particular, the ruling of Kyoto District Court, which directly refers to an international human rights treaty, rather than to provisions of the Constitution, in interpreting article 709 of the Civil Code.[110] Human rights advocates have often criticized the Japanese courts for not seriously considering in their judgments the international human rights treaties that Japan has ratified. Yuji Iwasawa, a Japanese international law scholar and incumbent judge at the International Court of Justice, also points out that Japanese courts have long dismissed arguments based on international human rights law or the recommendations of international organizations.[111] While the courts have made some decisions with reference to the international treaties, they remain 'generally reluctant to adjudicate on the basis of international human rights law';[112] instead, Japanese courts 'often restrict their interpretation to the Japanese Constitution, ignoring arguments based on international human rights law'.[113] It might be said that this is because of unfamiliarity with this new branch of law and because of

[107] Osaka High Court, note 87, at 39.

[108] *Ibid.*, at 40.

[109] Supreme Court, note 88; John Boyd, 'Hate Speech in Japan: To Ban or Not to Ban?', *Al Jazeera*, 19 March 2015, available at www.aljazeera.com/indepth/features/2015/03/hate-speech-japan-ban-ban-150310102402970.html [accessed 28 April 2019].

[110] Although the plaintiff's arguments in the complaint refer to art. 13 of the Constitution (the right to life, liberty, and the pursuit of happiness), and art. 26 of the Constitution (the right to an equal education), the court does not mention them in the rulings. See Osaka High Court, note 87.

[111] Yuji Iwasawa, *International Law, Human Rights, and Japanese Law: The Impact of International Law on Japanese Law* (Oxford University Press, 1998), 288–306; Dana Zartner, *Courts, Codes, and Custom: Legal Tradition and State Policy toward International Human Rights and Environmental Law* (Oxford University Press, 2014), 241–44.

[112] Iwasawa, note 111, at 294.

[113] *Ibid.*, at 294. See Takashi Ebashi, 'Kenri Hoshō Kihan to shite no Kenpō to Kokusai Jinken Kiyaku' ['The Constitution and the international covenants on human rights as norms to guarantee rights'] (1994) 1037 *Jurist* 109.

a belief within the Japanese courts that the standards of protection required under international human rights treaties are already realized in the protection provided for under the Japanese Constitution.[114] However, American legal scholar Timothy Webster observes a shift in Japan's incorporation of international human rights law since the late 1970s, when Japan ratified several international human rights treaties.[115] He notes that the Japanese court has gradually warmed to claims brought under international law, and has applied the ICCPR and the ICERD in domestic litigation to hold acts of racial discrimination illegal even though no domestic law specifically proscribes such conduct.[116] Says Webster:

> Judges claimed that they were using international law merely as an interpretive standard by which to define legal norms ... But this interpretive method, or indirect effect, turns out to be the major conduit through which the normative power of international human rights conventions is channelled ... [J]udges [in Japanese courts] hesitated to apply international legal provisions against private persons in the 1980s and 1990s, but this seems to have changed with a recent series of racial discrimination lawsuits.[117]

For example, throughout the legal challenges of the 1980s and 1990s, the court ruled the repeated fingerprinting of resident aliens constitutional in light of article 14 of the Constitution without substantially referring to international law, even though it was alleged to be contrary to the ICCPR and other international human rights treaties.[118] However, in the late 1990s and 2000s, international human rights law played an increasingly prominent role in a series of racial discrimination lawsuits. In 1997, in relation to a dispute over the property rights of the ethnic Ainu minority, the native inhabitants of northern Japan, Sapporo District Court recognized Ainu people as 'indigenous' and ruled that an administrative approval that permitted the forcible seizure of their land did not comply with Japan's obligations under the ICCPR.[119] Moreover, in regard to the

[114] Iwasawa, note 111, at 288; Teraya, note 90, at 292.

[115] Webster, note 106, at 245.

[116] *Ibid.*, at 243.

[117] *Ibid.*, at 267.

[118] Iwasawa, note 111, at 150–54.

[119] Sapporo District Court, 27 March 1997, 1598 Hanji 33 (*Nibutani Dam*). See Art. 27 ICCPR, which safeguards an ethnic minority's rights to enjoy their own culture alongside other members of their group. Iwasawa explains that this may be an example of indirect application of the treaty: Yuji Iwasawa, 'Nibutani Damu Hanketsu no Kokusaihōjō no Igi' ['The significance of the Nibutani Dam decision for international law'] (1999) 9 *Kokusai Jinken* [Human rights international] 56, at 59.

application of the ICERD, in a ground-breaking ruling in 1999, Shizuoka District Court applied the ICERD to private relations and as judgment criteria to acknowledge the tort.[120] Sapporo District Court followed that ruling in 2002, also acknowledging that the act of private person can comprise racial discrimination as defined under that ICERD, and it used international law as 'interpretative standards' to create the tort of racial discrimination.[121] Webster argues that these lawsuits have helped to blur the public–private divide that traditionally insulated people from international law and that the application of the ICERD to the private sphere marks a critical passage in Japan's ongoing integration of international law norms into its domestic law.[122] He also points out that this development is in part because Japan introduced no new legislation to implement the ICERD after its accession to the treaty in 1995.[123] In the absence of domestic legislation, judges can step in to fill a legislative void, and they may apply international law in bold and often unprecedented ways.[124] In essence, without legislative guidance on a point, individual judges must decide whether the narratives they hear and the evidence supporting those narratives constitute illegal acts of racial discrimination.

In *Kyoto Korean Elementary School*, aligning with this trend among the judiciary, the court found a more direct and concrete standard for the interpretation of domestic law in international human rights law than in the Constitution.[125] Even though the ruling did not use the term 'hate speech', the court still found that the conduct amounted to racial discrimination under the ICERD.[126] The court may have adopted the definition of racial discrimination under the ICERD because it deems the human rights treaty more practical, prescribing racial discrimination

120 Shizuoka District Court, Hamamatsu Branch, 12 October 1999, 1045 Hanta 216, 217 (*Hamamatsu Hoseki-sho*). For the detail of the case, see Timothy Webster, '*Bortz* v. *Suzuki* (Translation and Commentary)' (2007) 16 *Pacific Rim P. & Pol. J.* 631.

121 Sapporo District Court, 11 November 2002, 1150 Hanta 185 (*Otaru Gaikokujin Nyūyoku Kyohi*). In this case, a plaintiff sued both a bathhouse that refused non-Asian-looking foreigners entry to the public bath for racial discrimination and the Otaru municipal government for not taking adequate measures to prohibit racial discrimination.

122 Webster, note 106, at 265.

123 *Ibid.*, at 267.

124 *Ibid.*

125 Kyoto District Court, note 86.

126 Teraya, note 90. Notably, the reason why the court does not use the specific definition under Art. 4 ICERD, but uses the general definition under Art. 1 may be a result of the Japanese reservation of Art. 4 of the Convention.

more precisely and in more detail than the Japanese Constitution and other domestic laws.[127] As in previous cases, in this case judges used international law that provides basic standards and clearer language for rights relating to racial discrimination as a yardstick by which to evaluate conduct.[128]

In summary, the rulings in *Kyoto Korean Elementary School* took Japan farther along a path reflecting a gradual change in the attitude of the Japanese judiciary towards international law. While these cases may not have drastically changed the existing framework of jurisprudence, *Kyoto Korean Elementary School* is a solid example of a shift in the Japanese courts towards internalizing international human rights law and it points towards further development likely in the future. This case embedded international law relating to hate speech and racial discrimination in Japan's judicial system as part of the long process of development of the Hate Speech Elimination Act. The case offers a model of how international human rights norms may be internalized among the judiciary, particularly when there are no effective or concrete domestic laws with which to address the issue.[129]

Furthermore, not only the impact on court jurisprudence but also the *social* impact of the case should be noted in terms of the impact of the case on internalizing international human rights norms.[130] Kyoto District Court's ruling was covered in the national newspapers and broadcast on television nationwide, drawing public attention to the problem of hate speech.[131] The conclusions of the decisions in the case that hate demonstrations constituted 'racial discrimination' under the terms of international human rights law, which uphold universal human rights norms, contributed to growing the anti-hate-speech movement nationwide, engaging not only the ethnic Korean residents targeted, but

[127] Teraya, note 90.

[128] Webster, note 106, at 245.

[129] More research is necessary to fully understand the changing attitudes of judges in Japan, who have shown a greater fidelity to international human rights obligations than they did a generation ago.

[130] For the effects of *Kyoto Korean Elementary School* on anti-racism movements in Japan, see also Ayako Hatano, 'Can Strategic Human Rights Litigation Complement Social Movements? A Case Study of the Movement against Racism and Hate Speech in Japan', in Myungkoo Kang *et al.* (eds.), *Hate Speech in Asia and Europe: Beyond Hate and Fear* (Routledge, 2020).

[131] Centre for Human Rights, note 6, at 79–86 (citing more than 30 newspaper and television news articles, including most major news media, which covered the Kyoto District Court decision on the case).

also the general public, including Japanese majorities.[132] Indeed, human rights advocates who fought for the enactment of anti-hate-speech law emphasize that the courts' rulings in this case assisted their movement by making the issue of hate speech highly visible.[133] Moreover, the rulings influenced subsequent cases. For example, in April 2016, in a case in which a group of ultra-nationalistic people including members of *Zaitokukai* had stormed the office of the Tokushima prefectural teachers and staffs union in 2010,[134] the Takamatsu High Court ordered *Zaitokukai* to pay more than ¥4 million in compensation for the mental suffering of teachers and union members: double the amount of compensation the court at first instance had awarded. This ruling, referring to the act of the group as 'racial discrimination' under the ICERD, clearly follows the rulings in *Kyoto Korean Elementary School.*[135] People encouraged by the decision have also pursued their rights in the courts, further raising awareness of issues of racism and hate speech in Japanese society. For example, in August 2014, a Zainichi Korean freelance writer filed lawsuits against *Zaitokukai* and its former chair, and against the webmaster of conservative website *Hoshu Sokuho* ['News flash for the conservative'], seeking compensation for her mental suffering as a result of their publishing on the Internet defaming words and ethnic discriminatory remarks on the basis of her ethnicity. Both lawsuits ended in 2018 with the upper court ruling in her favour, concluding that derogatory speech targeting the writer constituted insult banned under the ICERD.[136] In both cases, the claimants

[132] Kyongho Cho, 'Han Reishizumu Undō to Zainichi Korian' ['The anti-racism movement and Zainichi Koreans'], in Takahiro Akedo *et al.*, '*Gendai Nihon ni Okeru Han Reishizumu Undō' Kyōdō Kenkyū Chūkan Hōkokusho* [Mid-term report of the joint research project 'Anti-Racism Movement in Modern Japan'] (2015), ch. 6, available at https://researchmap.jp/blogs/blog_entries/view/83222/6cf80dadc928454b6ca87f503113049e?frame_id=673887 [accessed 20 September 2020).

[133] Interview with an IMADR project coordinator in Tokyo (27 July 2016).

[134] The intruders were subsequently sued over forcible obstruction of business, unlawful entry, and threatening the union's officers and members.

[135] Takamatsu High Court, 25 April 2016, aff'd Supreme Court, 1 November 2016; interview with Shiki Tomimasu (13 November 2016); Shiki Tomimasu, 'Tokushimaken Kyōso Shūgeki Jiken: Heito 'Kuraimu' Taiō ni Kansuru Kōsatsu Taishō to shite' ['Tokushima prefectural teachers and staff union attack case as an object of analysis of a response to a hate "crime" '] (2018) 757 *Hōgaku Seminā* [Legal seminar] 50.

[136] 'Court Orders Anti-Korean Group to Compensate Woman over Hate Speech', *Mainichi Shinbun*, 28 September 2016, available at http://mainichi.jp/english/articles/20160928/p2a/00m/0na/003000c#csidx69617aa1ac377d89b57d93b680900da [accessed 28 April 2019]; 'Zaitokukai Heito Saiban Ri Shine San Songen Kaifuku no Tatakai' ['Ms. Lee Shinhae, legal battle against Zaitokukai's hate speech for restoring the dignity'], *Mainichi Shinbun*, 9 March 2018, available at https://mainichi.jp/articles/20180310/k00/00m/040/095000c

argued that the malice underpinning racial discrimination should be taken into account in calculating damages – an argument clearly inherited from Kyoto District Court's decision in *Kyoto Korean Elementary School*. In August 2015, another claimant living in Osaka lodged a case against the company for which she worked and its representative, who distributed discriminatory materials to ethnic Koreans in the workplace.[137]

In these ways, the *Kyoto Korean Elementary School* rulings and subsequent hate-related judgments have highlighted universal international human rights as a legal norm to be observed by domestic courts, both inside and outside the court. Anti-racism social movements in Japan have been invigorated and legitimized by those judicial rulings that realize the recommendations of the international human rights treaty bodies, influencing the formation of public opinion against hate speech and racial discrimination, and underpinning the development of the Hate Speech Elimination Act.

B. *Internalizing International Human Rights Law in the Legislative Process*

Since the internalization of international law is ultimately the domestic realization of international norms, it goes without saying that the role of domestic politics in the process is highly important. An analysis of the power relations, structure of the interests of stakeholders, and their bargaining power is essential in any discussion of the domestic implementation of human rights.

Japanese sociologist Naoto Higuchi argues that the development of the Hate Speech Elimination Act is not the result of norm cascade, but better explained as a political process of compromise between the ruling Liberal

[accessed 28 April 2019]. See Osaka District Court, 27 September 2016, Osaka High Court, 19 June 2017, and Supreme Court, 2nd Petty Bench, 29 November 2017, for a case against *Zaitokukai* and its former chair; Osaka High Court, 16 November 2017, Osaka High Court, 28 June 2018, and Supreme Court, 3rd Petty Bench, 11 December 2018, for the lawsuit against a conservative website. See also Hiroko Kotaki, 'Han Heito Supīchi Saiban: Ri Shine san no Futatsu no Saiban wo megutte' ['Anti hate speech: a focus on two lawsuits of Ms. Lee Shinhae'] (2018) 757 *Hōgaku Seminā* [Legal seminar] 43. See also Chapter 17 for a detailed analysis of hate speech on social media.

137 A Zainichi Korean woman sued the company Fuji Jutaku for hate harassment in the workplace: Mieko Takenobu, 'Shokuba no Heito to Nihongata Rōmu Kanri no Ayausa' ['Hate speech in workplaces and the danger of Japanese personnel management'], *Webronza*, 2 August 2016, available at http://webronza.asahi.com/business/articles/2016072800005.html [accessed 26 May 2019]. The case is ongoing as of October 2020.

Democratic Party (LDP) and the opposing Democratic Party of Japan (DPJ).[138] It is true that one of the reasons why the LDP, which had been reluctant to take legislative measures against hate speech, changed its stance and proceeded to enact the law at extraordinary speed is that political concessions were made during its drafting in terms of the bill's narrow scope and the absence of criminal punishment for or prohibition of hate speech. At the initial stages of the legal development process, a bipartisan group of lawmakers led discussion proposing a basic law to eliminate racial discrimination.[139] The Komeito Party, partner in a ruling coalition alongside the LDP, incorporated the ideas of the opposition parties and presented a policy proposal that the LDP deemed acceptable. The bill submitted by the LDP–Komeito government passed in the National Diet in May 2016.[140] This compromise explains why the enacted Hate Speech Elimination Act has not significantly changed the existing political and legal structure, and why its text insufficiently incorporates the recommendations of the international human rights treaty bodies.

However, what should not be overlooked here is the magnitude of the international human rights law and norms considered in a series of processes leading to this legislative work.[141] After the human rights treaty bodies delivered its recommendations in 2014, many local governments across Japan submitted statements of opinion asking the national government to adopt measures tackling hate speech, including legislative

138 Naoto Higuchi, 'Heito ga Ihō ni Naru Toki – Heito Supīchi Kaishōhō Seitei o Meguru Seiji Katei' ['When hate speech becomes illegal: the political process regarding the development of the Hate Speech Elimination Act'] (2018) 62 *Leviathan* 96, at 115.

139 Takahiro Akedo, '2015 Nen Jinshu Sabetsu Teppai Seisaku Suishin Hōan Shingi no Haikei to Katei' ['2015 racial discrimination abolition policy background and process'] (2016) 8 *Imin Seisaku Kenkyu* [Immigration policy research] 180, at 182. In April 2014, the non-partisan Parliamentary League for the Enactment of the Basic Law against Racial Discrimination (*Jinshusabetsu Teppai Kihonhō o Motomeru Giinrenmei*) was formed. The League is represented by Toshio Ogawa, a Democratic Party of Japan (DPJ) legislator and former Minister of Justice during the DPJ administration. The draft bill the League proposed has a broader scope of protection and declared hate speech illegal, while it does not make any provision for punishment: Daiki Shibuichi, 'Countering Japan's Hate Speech Groups', *East Asia Forum*, 12 May 2016, available at www.eastasiaforum.org/2016/05/12/countering-japans-hate-speech-groups/ [accessed 28 April 2019]; Mari Yamaguchi, '"Hate Speech" not Free Speech, Says Japan; Korean School Awarded Compensation for Rally', *Thestar.com*, 7 October 2013, available at www.thestar.com/news/world/2013/10/07/hate_speech_not_free_speech_says_japan_korean_school_awarded_compensation_for_rally.html [accessed 28 April 2019].

140 Higuchi, note 138, at 111.

141 Gaikokujin Jinkenhō Renrakukai, *Q&A Heito Supīchi Kaishōhō* [Q&A Hate Speech Elimination Act] (Gendai Jinbunsha, 2016), 5–10.

amendments making explicit reference to international human rights law and the treaty bodies' recommendations.[142] For example, following in the footsteps of the first statement of opinion delivered by Kunitachi City in Tokyo in September 2014, the statements of opinion delivered by the Hiroshima Prefectural Assembly and the Kagawa Prefectural Assembly included the recommendations of the HRC and the CERD, and cited the rulings in *Kyoto Korean Elementary School*, which recognized racial discrimination based on the CERD.[143] In addition, the statement of Yamagata City of Yamagata Prefecture referred to the recommendation of the CERD, and even asked the government to prohibit and punish hate speech, withdrawing its reservations of Article 4(a) and (b) ICERD.[144] The efforts of those local governments that have formally criticized hate speech and made it harder for hate groups to use public areas are another sign of the momentum behind Japan's anti-hate-speech movement. Here, it is worth observing that local governments were aware of international human rights norms and the recommendations of international human rights treaty bodies regarding measures to address hate speech, which is indicative of the penetration of the norms. It is consequently ironic that the inadequacy and abstract nature of the provisions at national level – the Hate Speech Elimination Act itself – has played a part in promoting development of local regulations and guidelines aiming to remedy the shortfall, and in combination with the civil society and local community movements at which the chapter looks in the next section.

Furthermore, in November 2014 – shortly after the treaty bodies made their recommendations in mid-2014 – the Ministry of Justice initiated a campaign aiming to raise awareness of hate speech, using eye-catching font and the phrase 'HEITO SUPĪCHI YURUSANAI' ['STOP HATE

[142] The number of statements amounted to more than 300 as at end of May 2016: *Ibid.*, at 7.

[143] Hiroshima Prefectural Assembly, 'Heito Supīchi no Konzetsu ni Muketa Hōseibi o Fukumu Taisaku no Kyōka o Motomeru Ikensho' ['Statement of position for strengthening measures including legal development for eradication of hate speech'], 10 March 2015, available at www.pref.hiroshima.lg.jp/site/gikai/hatsugi27-3.html [accessed 1 April 2018]; Kagawa Prefectural Assembly, 'Heito Supīchi Taisaku no Kyōka o Motomeru Ikensho' ['Statement of position for strengthening measures against hate speech'], 15 December 2015, available at www.pref.kagawa.lg.jp/gikai/jyoho/giketsu/2711_hatugi02.pdf [accessed 1 April 2018].

[144] Yamagata Shigikai, 'Jinshu Sabetsu o Sendō Suru Heito Supīchi o Kinshi shi Shobatsu Suru Hōritsu no Seitei o Motomeru Ikensho' ['Statement of position for establishment of a law to ban and punish hate speech that incites racial discrimination'], December 2015, available at www.city.yamagata-yamagata.lg.jp/gikai/kaigikekka/teireikai/201512teireikai/201512teireikaiikensyo.html [accessed 30 August 2018].

SPEECH!']. This was a leap for the conservative Ministry, with its initiative based on no law or policy guidance defining 'hate speech' at the time.[145] In March 2016, the Ministry issued research on hate speech in Japan, citing the concluding observations published by the CERD in August 2014 as the background to the survey.[146] The initiative also demonstrates how seriously the Ministry took the CERD's call for 'measures against the expression of hatred and racism, and the incitement of racist violence and hatred in demonstrations and meetings', the recommendation triggering concrete campaigns and the survey paving the way for anti-hate legislation by revealing the shocking impact of hate speech in Japan.[147]

Higuchi took particular note of the significant role played by Yoshifu Arita, a member of the House of Councillors and the DPJ, in putting anti-hate-speech legislation at the top of the political agenda.[148] Since March 2013, Arita and other concerned legislators from the DPJ and the Social Democratic Party (SDP) had held several meetings at the House of Councillors, inviting lawyers, journalists, and anti-racism activists well versed in the issue to join them. Arita himself went to Geneva and observed the CERD's review of the Japanese government's report in 2014. He actively advocated for implementation of the CERD's recommendations both inside and outside the Diet, which resulted in frequent references to the CERD as the Diet debated hate speech.[149] Higuchi considers himself to be an 'insider activist' – that is, an individual who is both in the government and working closely with civil society to effect a social movement.[150] In collaboration with civil society groups, Arita implanted international human rights norms into the political process. In April 2014, Arita led the way in establishing the non-partisan Parliamentary League for the Enactment of the Basic Law against Racial Discrimination. In May 2015, the Parliamentary League submitted to the House of Councillors a bill that would outlaw racist acts and hate speech. The proposed law was held back in the Diet by opposition from the ruling LDP and the initiative for the legislature was transferred to the

[145] Interview with a government official at the Human Rights Bureau, the Ministry of Justice in Tokyo (29 July 2016).
[146] Centre for Human Rights Education and Training, note 6, at 1–2.
[147] *Ibid.*
[148] Higuchi, note 138, at 104.
[149] Uozumi *et al.*, note 53, at 105–96.
[150] Lee Ann Banaszak, *The Women's Movement Inside and Outside the State* (Cambridge University Press, 2010), 12.

ruling coalition.[151] However, both the Parliamentary League and the Komeito Hate Speech Project Team have been maintained, and they continue their activities while monitoring the implementation and effect of the Hate Speech Elimination Act.

In summary, in the development of the Hate Speech Elimination Act, the internalization of international human rights law and norms has been evident in various political channels, including central and local governments, and international human rights bodies have laid the groundwork for implementation of the Hate Speech Elimination Act and other measures aiming to tackle the issue of hate speech.

C. *Vernacularizing International Human Rights into Japanese Civil Society*

As this chapter has demonstrated, a series of events including a surge of demonstrations by hate groups and legal cases on racial discrimination, as well as the timely review by international treaty bodies and media coverage, have raised awareness of hate speech across Japanese society.[152] It is also true that politics among parties played a significant role in building political momentum for anti-hate legislation, but behind these passionate legislators and public opinion are the tenacious efforts of civil society and non-governmental organizations (NGOs) that have long been performing ardent advocacy before domestic lawmakers, local regulators, and UN human rights treaty bodies.

One of the NGOs leading international advocacy in this field is the NGO Network for the Elimination of Racial Discrimination Japan (ERD Net), a nationwide network of NGOs and individuals working on issues relating to racism and racial discrimination. ERD Net has been involved with the issue of racial discrimination and hate speech since its establishment in 2007, when the UN Special Rapporteur on Contemporary Forms of Racism, Racism, Xenophobia, and Related Intolerance visited Japan, emphasizing the United Nations' solidarity with various minority groups such as Zainichi Korean, Buraku, Ainu, and Okinawan peoples. *Gaikokujin Jinkenhō Renrakukai* ('Association for Protection of Human Rights of Foreigners') is another NGO, formed in 2015 by lawyers,

[151] See Higuchi, note 138, at 108–10.

[152] See Ryan Goodman and Derek Jinks, 'International Law and State Socialization: Conceptual, Empirical, and Normative Challenges' (2005) 54 *Duke L.J.* 983, at 996.

activists, and researchers aiming to work on advocacy for the protection of foreigners and minorities.

These organisations have actively engaged in advocacy for anti-discrimination legislation, both at home and abroad, including by submitting the NGO report to the human rights treaty bodies, and through direct advocacy before the CERD and HRC at the review sessions of government reports.[153] In interview with the author, one NGO staff member from the network said:

> [In the session of the CERD for consideration of the Japanese report] after we showed a video of an actual hate demonstration in Japan, the Committee members were shocked and speechless. That qualitative and quantitative evidence we brought to the international fora moved the Committee to issue a stern recommendation for Japan to rectify the problem of hate speech in the summer of 2014, I believe.[154]

It is observed that those advocacy efforts were reflected in the recommendations on hate speech delivered in 2010 and 2014 by the CERD and in 2014 by the HRC. These civil society groups also advocated at the domestic level, holding study sessions and meetings with civil servants and parliamentarians (including Arita), to secure their commitment to implementing the recommendation of the human rights treaty bodies.

Another active NGO in advocacy against hate and racism is *Heito Supīchi to Reishizumu o Norikoeru Kokusai Nettowāku* ('International Network to Overcome Hate Speech and Racism', or *Norikoe Net*), a civic group in Japan, established in 2013, and specializing in anti-discrimination and anti-racism. Group representatives include the many celebrities and leftist elites, lawyers, journalists, intellectuals, and academics in diverse fields, such as former Prime Minister Tomiichi Murayama. They engage in a wide range of activities, such as disseminating news and information on racism in Japan, organizing and supporting counter-demonstrations, and producing anti-discrimination media programmes.[155] In its mission statement, *Norikoe Net* declares that it takes a universal human rights approach

[153] Interview with a project coordinator of the International Movement against Discrimination and Racism (IMADR) in Tokyo (27 July 2016); Morooka, note 1, at 12–17.

[154] Interview with an IMADR project coordinator in Tokyo (27 July 2016).

[155] Shibuichi argues that *Norikoe Net* seems to be successfully sustaining all of those daunting tasks because of the resources and capability of the leftist elites: Daiki Shibuichi, 'The Struggle against Hate Groups in Japan: The Invisible Civil Society, Leftist Elites and Anti-Racism Groups' (2016) 19 *Soc. Sci. Japan J.* 71, at 78; https://norikoenet.jp/ [accessed 7 March 2019].

against discrimination, noting that hate speech affects various minority groups, with a reference to the UDHR. It is noteworthy that, based on this approach, the network cooperates with a variety of established civic groups and associations, including even a well-known radical right-wing group that has been critical of *Zaitokukai*.[156]

Furthermore, in May 2015, the Japan Federation of Bar Association, the largest nationwide civic organization of lawyers in Japan, issued a statement that asked the government to adopt measures against hate speech based on the principles of the ICERD.[157] Its president's statement – issued in May 2016 when an anti-hate-speech bill was under discussion in Parliament – criticized the bill and called for a more comprehensive ban on discrimination.[158] On 8 June 2018, the Tokyo Bar Association requested that its local authorities enact an ordinance for the elimination of racial discrimination in line with international standards and it proposed a draft model ordinance, with points of concern based on the recommendations of the human rights treaty bodies.[159]

However, a question may be raised about whether movements led by activists or so-called "leftist elites" at home or abroad could reach a point at which the slow systemic change becomes irreversible, triggering dramatic consequences – that is, a tipping point with a critical mass.

In this regard, it is noteworthy that many participants in the counteraction that has been surging since 2009, demonstrating opposition to hate groups at their rallies and solidarity with the minorities targeted, are not conventional human rights activists, but so-called ordinary citizens

156 Shibuichi, note 155, at 79. Kunio Suzuki, a founder of a well-known radical right-wing group, joined *Norikoe Net* as one of its co-representatives.

157 Nihon Bengoshi Rengōkai [Japan Federation of Bar Association], 'Jinshutō o Riyū to Suru Sabetsu no Teppai ni Muketa Sumiyakana Shisaku o Motomeru Ikensho' ['Statement of opinion for swift measures for the abolition of discrimination on the basis of race'], 7 May 2015, available at www.nichibenren.or.jp/activity/document/opinion/year/2015/150507_2.html [accessed 26 May 2019].

158 Nihon Bengoshi Rengōkai [Japan Federation of Bar Association], 'Honpōgai Shusshinsha ni taisuru Futō na Sabetsuteki Gendō no Kaishō ni Muketa Torikumi no Suishin ni Kansuru Hōritsuan no Ichibu Kaisei o Motomeru Kaichō Seimei' ['President's statement calling for partial revision of the Hate Speech Elimination Act'], 10 May 2016, available at www.nichibenren.or.jp/document/statement/year/2016/160510.html [accessed 26 May 2019].

159 Tokyo Bengoshikai [Tokyo Bar Association], 'Chihō Kōkyō Dantai ni Jinshu Sabetsu Teppai Jōrei no Seitei o Motome Jinshu Sabetsu Teppai Moderu Jōreian o Teian Suru kotoni Kansuru Ikensho' ['Statement of opinion asking local governments to establish a racial discrimination abolition ordinance and proposing a racial discrimination abolition model ordinance draft'], 8 June 2018, available at www.toben.or.jp/message/pdf/180608ikensho.pdf [accessed 26 May 2019].

who have never before been involved in human rights or other social movements. For example, one founder of a group calling itself the Anti-Racism Project (ARP), established in November 2013, works at an IT company in Tokyo and had never before participated in nor been strongly interested in social activism at all before engaging in the anti-racism movement in 2013.[160] After he became involved in counter-hate activism, he also joined gatherings of and study groups within human rights NGOs working for international advocacy.[161] Being active in the counter-movement in Tokyo, he became involved in advocacy before lawmakers and ministries, providing opinion and information based on his lived experience.[162] While there are various approaches among these counter-groups, the interesting point is that the ARP's activities are based on universal human rights values and it takes a peaceful approach, focusing on protecting the rights of individuals. 'Our organisation is driven by the concept of universal human rights. Through spreading of the concept, we aim to eliminate hate speech', says the founder.[163]

All of this suggests that the human rights norms that recognize hate speech as an issue affecting the whole of society – an issue for everyone's concern, rather than only the concern of targeted minorities – are to some extent pervasive in Japanese society. A sociological survey observes as a feature of the anti-racism movement since 2013 the spread of the idea that racial discrimination and hate speech are problems that Japanese society as a whole – the majority – should address as its own.[164] In fact, in September 2013, more than 2,000 participants took part in the 'Tokyo Anti-Discrimination March' including not only Zainichi Koreans, but also numerous small groups advocating a variety of issues such as anti-war, anti-nuclear, environmental protection, and protection of other minority rights, as well as individuals including students, retirees, lawyers, office workers, lawmakers, and academics, gathering under the banner of 'anti-discrimination'.[165] They adopted a resolution calling for

160 Skype interview with a member of the Anti-Racism Project (24 November 2016).
161 *Ibid.*
162 *Ibid.*
163 *Ibid.*
164 Akedo *et al.*, note 132, at 2.
165 '2,000 Rally against Hate Speech in Tokyo's Shinjuku', *Japan Today*, 23 September 2016, available at https://japantoday.com/category/national/2000-rally-against-hate-speechin-tokyos-shinjuku [accessed 26 May 2019]; 'Sabetsu Teppai Tokyo Daikōshin no Daiippō Repōto' ['First report of March on Freedom in Tokyo'], *Independent Web Journal*, 22 September 2013, available at http://iwj.co.jp/wj/open/archives/102809 [accessed 26 May 2019'.

the Japanese government to act in good faith with the ICERD – a resolution indicative of the spread of the anti-racism movement into the majority, based on a universal human-rights-centred approach.[166] It is indeed distinctive that this anti-hate and anti-racism social movement involves not only the people targeted and activists, but also so-called ordinary citizens under the banner of 'universal human rights' or 'anti-discrimination'.[167]

In this way, NGOs that have worked in international advocacy, lawmakers, and journalists have not only raised the local issue into the international sphere, but also brought international standards on hate speech and racial discrimination to bear in the local context, cooperating with local civic groups, human rights lawyers, Zainichi Koreans affected by hate demonstrations, and anti-racism counter groups. They have done so by means of seminars, gatherings, and collaborative advocacy, all of which seems to be reaching critical mass – becoming a critical agent of change – in the process of internalizing these international norms.[168]

Furthermore, in the process of lawmaking, a local community within the Sakuramoto area of the City of Kawasaki played an important role in the internalization of international human rights norms.[169] Sakuramoto,

166 *Ibid.* See also 'Anti-Hate Speech March Fills Streets around Shinjuku', *Mainichi Shimbun*, 23 September 2016, available at http://mainichi.jp/english/english/newsselect/news/20130923p2a00m0na010000c.html [accessed 28 April 2019].

167 It is symbolic that the phrase 'hate speech' was selected as one of the top ten Japanese buzzwords in 2013. However, popularization of human rights norms may have overly generalized the issue, and held the movement back from going beyond slogans such as 'anti-racism' and 'live together'. Some scholars also point out that frontline activists in the anti-nuclear movement that arose after the 2011 incident at Fukushima Daiichi have gone on to join the anti-racism social movement. The common ground is that anti-nuclear demonstrations are mostly organized by small groups of concerned individuals with no connection to existing political parties. People can participate in rallies spontaneously and/or casually in response to rallying calls shared on the Internet even though they are not part of any organization – in sharp contrast to the tightly organized social movements of the 1960s. See Shibuichi, note 155, at 77; Eiji Oguma, 'A New Wave against the Rock: New Social Movements in Japan since the Fukushima Nuclear Meltdown', *Asia Pacific Journal*, 1 July 2016, available at http://apjjf.org/2016/13/Oguma.html [accessed 15 May 2020].

168 It is observed that Japanese activism against racism is influenced by global ideas and a transnational social movement, which "have inspired some activists to see their battle as part of a larger one for democracy": Vivian Shaw, 'How Fukushima Gave Rise to a New Anti-Racism Movement', *Al Jazeera*, 12 March 2017, available at www.aljazeera.com/indepth/features/2017/03/fukushima-gave-rise-anti-racism-movement-170310103716807.html [accessed 28 April 2019].

169 See generally Kanagawa Shimbun 'Jidai no Shōtai' Shuzaihan (ed.), *Heito Demo o Tometa Machi – Kawasaki Sakuramoto no Hitobito* [A town where hate demonstrations are ceased:

which is home to many Zainichi Koreans, was targeted by numerous hate demonstrations, and residents faced unbearable intrusions into their daily lives and violations of their dignity.[170] Kan-Ija Choi, a third-generation Zainichi Korean resident of Sakuramoto, has taken a stand against hate in Kawasaki City. Her approach is strongly inclusive in both words and deeds, reflecting universal human rights values such as tolerance and diversity.[171] She seeks collaboration with anyone who shares her values of anti-discrimination, regardless of political standpoint, asking that they all fight 'together' against hate speech and racial discrimination in Kawasaki and beyond – and this approach has resulted in her engaging with many supporters, both online and offline.[172] Choi was invited to speak in support of anti-hate speech legislation at an official hearing of the Committee on Judicial Affairs at the House of Councillors on 22 March 2016.[173] She provided information about the negative effects of hate speech on her local community and advocated for legislation against hate speech based on human rights.[174] This desperate voice of a direct victim moved the lawmakers, including the conservative party, to visit Sakuramoto and hear local people's serious concerns and victims' trauma on 31 March 2016.[175] After the visit, the chair of the Committee on Judicial Affairs of House of Councillors said, 'I understand the hate speech destroyed everyday [lives] of people and we need to work on the extermination of the hate speech.'[176] Even a notably conservative LDP politician agreed: 'I understand *Zainichi* Korean people want to live as they are, not hiding their ethnic roots. This is a common ground for everyone, not only *Zainichi* Koreans, but all Japanese and all people in

people in Sakuramoto, Kawasaki] (Gendai Shicho Shinsha, 2016) (describing how the local community in the Sakuramoto area in Kawasaki City is fighting back against hate groups that targeted the area, which has a long history of Koreans and Japanese people living together). See also Chapter 14.

170 Kanagawa Shimbun 'Jidai no Shōtai' Shuzaihan, note 169, at 18.

171 She emphasizes, 'I would like to cooperate with anyone in the fight against hate, as long as everyone shares the idea that discrimination is not to be tolerated': interview with Kan Ija Choi, staff member, Kawasaki Fureaikan, in Kawasaki City, Kanagawa (21 August 2017).

172 *Ibid.*

173 Kanagawa Shimbun 'Jidai no Shōtai' Shuzaihan, note 169, at 103.

174 *Ibid.*, at 103–12.

175 *Ibid.*, at 112–15. See also Heito Supīchi o Yurusanai Kawasaki Shimin Nettowāku, *Konzetsu! Heito to no Tatakai: Kyōsei no Machi Kawasaki kara* [Fight for extermination of hate speech: from Kawasaki, City of Coexistence] (Ryokufu Shuppan, 2017), 75.

176 Kanagawa Shimbun 'Jidai no Shōtai' Shuzaihan, note 169, at 112; Heito Supīchi o Yurusanai Kawasaki Shimin Nettowāku, note 175, at 74.

general. In our society, it is intolerable to neglect the act to harm the dignity as a human being.'[177] The role played by Kawasaki in the process of enacting the anti-hate-speech law was significant, its activism triggering an official visit that allowed the Committee to hear and recognize the serious damage that hate speech does to the dignity and human rights of residents.[178]

A solid bond between the community and others tackling hate speech and racial discrimination propelled the city of Kawasaki and the judiciary to respond to a call for citizens to rally against hate demonstrations in Kawasaki. On 5 June 2016, a remarkable gathering of some 1,000 protestors staged a sit-in against the scheduled demonstration of a right-wing group in Kawasaki, successfully stopping it and demonstrating the power of the local community and its support.[179] A group, *Heito Supichi wo Yurusanai Kawasaki Netttowaku* ('Kawasaki Network of Citizens against Hate Speech'), was established to facilitate an 'all-Kawasaki' anti-racism movement in collaboration with stakeholders including citizens, journalists, lawyers, and lawmakers. In November 2017, the Network's active engagement was instrumental in translating the principles set out in the Hate Speech Elimination Act into a set of guidelines restricting the use of public facilities should there be risk of hate speech.[180] Furthermore, in December 2019, the Network's effort led Kawasaki to become the first municipality in Japan to pass an ordinance bill imposing penalties for hate speech.[181]

177 Kanagawa Shimbun 'Jidai no Shōtai' Shuzaihan, note 169, at 115–16 (quoting the words of Shoji Nishida, member of the Liberal Democratic Party and a member of the House of Councillors in the Diet after his visit to Sakuramoto).

178 Uozumi *et al.*, note 53, at 105–26.

179 Kanagawa Shimbun 'Jidai no Shōtai' Shuzaihan, note 169, at 180–88; Manabu Ishibashi, 'Kawasaki no Heito Demo to Chiiki no Han Sabetsu no Chikara' ['Hate demonstrations in Kawasaki and the power of local communities against discrimination'], in Hōgaku Seminā Henshubu (ed.), *Bessatsu Hōgaku Seminā Heito Supīchi to wa Nanika; Minzoku Sabetsu Higai no Kyūsai* [Legal seminar annex: what is hate speech? Relief for victims of ethnic discrimination] (Nippon Hyoronsha, 2019), 148–59.

180 Interview with Takayuki Yamada, Member of the Kawasaki Network of Citizens, Kanagawa (21 August 2017); Yasuko Morooka, 'Kawasaki-shi ni yoru Heito Supīchi eno Torikumi ni tsuite: Kōkyō Shisetsu Riyō Gaidorain o Chūshin ni' ['Efforts against hate speech from the example in Kawasaki City: with a focus on public facility use guidelines'] (2018) 757 *Hōgaku Seminā* [Legal seminar] 34, at 34–35.

181 'Kawasaki Enacts Japan's First Bill Punishing Hate Speech', *The Japan Times*, 12 December 2019, available at www.japantimes.co.jp/news/2019/12/12/national/crime-legal/kawasaki-first-japan-bill-punishing-hate-speech/#.XjelPWj0lPY [accessed 2 February 2020]; Ishibashi, note 179, at 156–59.

In this way, the surge of the anti-hate social movement in Japan, based on a long-standing foundation of advocacy efforts among NGOs and civil activists, as well as local activism underlined by multiculturalism nurtured in a long history of people of diverse ethnicity coexisting in harmony, provided solid support throughout the development and enactment process of the HSEA. While the law itself may not fully comply with the recommendations of the international human rights treaty bodies, anti-discrimination campaigns and advocacy mobilized by civil society resulted in important deliverables: the supplementary resolutions of the House of Councillors and House of Representatives, which clearly indicate the compliance with international human rights law.[182] In this regard, the penetration of the concept of international human rights into Japanese society has reinforced implementation of the Act, compensating for its shortcomings and underpinning its application at the municipal level. Japan does not establish anti-discrimination or hate speech law in the form of prohibition required under the international human rights law – but its local communities, in collaboration with local government and civic organizations, have narrowed the space for those who would speak hate in a variety of ways, including restrictions on the use of public facilities and roads by hate groups, and in some cases delivering sanctions against them. This is a twofold example of how a society can 'vernacularize' international human rights norms.[183] On the one hand, international human rights norms mobilized through a social movement may apply in different forms within the constraints of a domestic legal framework and social circumstances. On the other hand, the implementation of international human rights law depends on publicity and on public pressure, at both domestic and international levels, to urge a government towards change. In such a social context, the country's symbolic declaration and confirmation of hate speech as 'intolerable' becomes more substantial and effective, even though it may not be the exact effect that international organizations and agreements might anticipate. We noted earlier that the development of the anti-hate-speech law in Japan is the result of political compromise, but we cannot underestimate the importance of civil society in vernacularizing the human rights discourse, engaging socially and politically not only to shape but also to direct implementation of the HSEA.

[182] Interview with an IMADR project coordinator in Tokyo (27 July 2016).
[183] See Levitt & Merry, note 20, at 458–59.

IV. Conclusion: A Dynamic Process of Internalizing International Law

As globalization and the sovereignty of nation states clash, xenophobia and hate speech are on the rise in countries around the world, Japan among them. Despite the enactment of a law aiming to counter hate speech, critics say that Japan's response is too weak, with an overly narrow definition of potential victims and no ban on hate speech. Textual analysis shows that, despite an official claim that it is a response to the recommendations of international human rights treaty bodies, the Hate Speech Elimination Act does not fully comply with international human rights law nor with the treaty bodies' recommendations.

In this chapter, however, it has become evident that internalization of international human rights law and norms has gradually progressed among the judiciary, legislative, and administrative bodies, as well as civil society, even since before the recommendation of the international human rights bodies in 2014, and that this allows the Hate Speech Elimination Act to have effect. To some extent and somewhat paradoxically, the 'decoupling' of those human rights law that were officially pledged by the state and the reality of racial discrimination that should be addressed on the ground has helped human rights norms to spread among those multiple stakeholders.[184] The courts' jurisprudence demonstrating internalization of international human rights law have had an effect on subsequent cases and on administrative decisions regarding racial discrimination. The declaration by the judiciary that certain speech is deemed racial discrimination has not only legal meaning but also social impact, as does the symbolic condemnation of hate speech as 'intolerable'. In the context of these domestic cases and subsequent hateful rallies highlighted by media, lawmakers have recognized the timely recommendation issued by the human rights treaty bodies, supported by the efforts of 'insider norm entrepreneurs' who tenaciously work with civic activists towards the development of law. Behind the recommendations of the human rights treaty bodies and awareness among those lawmakers lies a long history of activism in civil society, including ardent advocacy at both transnational and national levels. International and domestic attention focused on hate speech has engaged the majority in an anti-racism social movement, supported by the idea of universal human rights to protect and promote the dignity of all regardless of nationality, ethnicity,

[184] Goodman & Jinks, note 49, at 728, 734–37.

and any other characteristics. Furthermore, the anti-racism social movement, connected with local government initiatives, has propelled not only development of anti-hate legislation in Japan, but also its effective implementation after enactment. The process of 'vernacularization' discussed in this chapter suggests that compliance with international norms does not necessarily come in the form of a formal legal text, but arrives in a variety of forms, including judicial rulings interpreting existing laws in alignment with international human rights standards, and civil society movements driving the efforts of municipalities to tackle hate speech and racism. International human rights law and norms strongly informed the process that produced the Hate Speech Elimination Act and continue to inform its implementation, even if the text of the law falls short of those standards. As a result, an inadequate legal framework has been complemented by the detail of its application in trials and administrative practices, as well as its symbolic use in anti-discrimination initiatives by, civil society seeking to secure the normative effects of the law.[185] This argument also recalls Beth Simmons' assertion that leaders sometimes sign human rights treaties not necessarily expecting that they will implement all of the things they promised – and yet they find that, because the legal system has a degree of independence and because civil society actors have room to mobilize, forces are brought to bear that nonetheless push the state towards greater compliance.[186]

If we consider such social acceptance as a process of implementing the international human rights law, the human rights treaty bodies' review of the government reports on the implementation of the human rights treaties has played a certain role in the enactment and implementation of the Hate Speech Elimination Act. In that sense, sustained channels of communication among the international organizations, the government, and civil society are essential in promoting domestic and international dialogue on the protection and promotion of human rights in any specific

[185] Haley analyses Japan's paradoxical phenomenon, i.e. penalties and weak enforcement laws, and systems that strengthen informal social norms and institutions for compliance with the law: John Owen Haley, *Authority without Power: Law and the Japanese Paradox* (Cambridge University Press, 1991); John Owen Haley, *The Spirit of Japanese Law* (University of Georgia Press, 1998). However, this does not lessen the importance of the legislative laws, because in many cases the legal and administrative decision primarily relies on the interpretation and application of domestic law and regulation.

[186] See generally Beth A. Simmons, *Mobilizing for Human Rights: International Law in Domestic Politics* (Cambridge University Press, 2009).

local context and issues on the ground, making international human rights a living norm, beyond the beautiful ritualistic mantra.

Although not directly discussed in detail in this chapter, hate speech is a matter of fundamental values in a multicultural society, such as freedom of expression, equality, and inclusiveness, and there is an ongoing debate about how to regulate it such that we strike a balance and protect those fundamental rights. Connected with this is strong criticism of the 'leniency' of the Hate Speech Elimination Act, which does not confront human rights violations with severe punishment.[187] Critics say it therefore masks human rights violations against minorities and may even structurally encourage such violations, undermining not only equality but also freedom of expression for minorities and society as a whole.[188] Furthermore, even after the enactment of the Hate Speech Elimination Act, there have been calls to improve the operation of the current legal framework, including procedural laws, as well as to enact laws and ordinances with more detailed provisions and penalties, including a blanket prohibition of discrimination.[189]

In this context, this chapter, which discusses the internalization of international human rights law and norms by means of a case study of the anti-racism social movement and development of the Hate Speech Elimination Act in Japan, deals only with a small part of the multifaceted issue around hate speech and its regulation. Many other questions should be addressed such as: what is the most effective and desirable way of regulating hate speech in each country and community, and what practical counter-measures can be sought within the various constraints? For designing and operating effective regulations, and enhancing social awareness, there is an urgent need for discussion and practical collaboration among various stakeholders, including national and local governments, businesses, international and local government, multinational corporations, national enterprises, civil society bodies, academic experts,

[187] Tomofumi Kinoshita, 'Sabetsuteki Hyōgen' ['Discriminatory expression'], in Makoto Oishi and Kenji Ishikawa (eds.), *Kenpo no Soten* [Issues in the Constitution] (Yuhikaku, 2008), 126; Ichikawa, note 34; Takashi Narushima, 'Heito Supīchi Saihō (1)' ['Revisiting hate speech (1)'] (2013) 92 *Dokkyō Hōgaku* [Dokkyō law review] 328; Takashi Narushima, 'Heito Supīchi Saihō (2)' ['Revisiting hate speech (2)'] (2014) 93 *Dokkyō Hōgaku* [Dokkyō law review] 762. For categorization of the arguments, see Yuji Nasu, 'Heito Supīchi Kisei Shōkyokusetsu no Saikentō' ['Revisiting the passive hate speech regulation theory'] (2016) 736 *Hōgaku Seminā* [Legal seminar] 18.

[188] Martin, note 6, at 465–66 and 470.

[189] Morooka, note 1, at 185–88; Morooka, note 180; interview with an IMADR project coordinator in Tokyo (27 July 2016).

community leaders, religious figures, media personalities, and other groups and individuals, based on the principle of respect for human dignity and diversity. It is my hope that this chapter will serve as a stepping stone, helping to deepen our understanding of plural channels to counter hate speech, racism and discrimination with international human rights instruments, by looking into a case of hate speech regulations and internalisation of international law and human rights norms in Japan.

PART II

History

4

Buraku Discrimination and Hate Speech

Complex Situations of Classical and Contemporary Discrimination in Japan

TAKANORI YAMAMOTO*

I. Enactment of the Act for Eliminating Discrimination against Buraku

In December 2016, the *Buraku Sabetsu Kaishō Suishinhō* ('Act for Eliminating Discrimination against Buraku', or AEDB)[1] was enacted and brought into force. Nearly 15 years had passed since a sequence of statutes, starting with the 1969 Law for Special Measures for Dōwa[2]

* This chapter is a revised version of Takanori Yamamoto, 'Buraku Sabetsu Kaishō Suishin Hō to Chiiki Shakai: Buraku Sabetsu no Gendaiteki Keitai to Sono Taiō ni Tsuite' ['Act for Eliminating Discrimination against Buraku and Community: Contemporary Form of Buraku Discrimination and the Measures'], in *Toi Toshite no Buraku Mondai Kenkyū: Kingendai Nihon no Kihi, Haijo, Hōsetsu* [*Buraku* studies as problematic: evasion, inclusion and exclusion of modern Japan] (Kyoto Human Research Institute, 2018).

1 Buraku discrimination refers to discrimination that has been present in Japan since before modern times. The targets of such discrimination have been called *Eta* or *Hinin*, which are highly discriminatory terms and refer to a pre-modern caste system. The terms *Hisabetsu Buraku* ('discriminated area'), *Hisabetsu Burakumin* ('discriminated people'), and the abbreviations *Buraku* and *Burakumin* are favoured at present. Buraku is a word that refers to an area the size of a hamlet (smaller than a village). The characteristics of Buraku with Hinin heritage are that they are (a) not designated administratively as Dōwa districts, (b) designated as another type of district (e.g. a welfare district) in need of and receiving measures, and (c) included in Buraku with Eta heritage or separately designated as Buraku. As such, there are various types of Buraku and they are not uniform.

2 *Dōwa* can be translated as 'assimilation' and it is an administrative term that is commonly used in relation to Buraku discrimination. The word Dōwa was first used in 1941 to mobilize Burakumin in an imperial regime, but it is a negative word and there are those who are critical of the idea of assimilation. These people will tend to favour the language of Buraku and Burakumin. However, as a word that usually means 'village' or 'hamlet', Buraku itself is a word that has nothing to do with discrimination and it may not be understood in that way, especially in East Japan.

Projects, had expired, in March 2002. Since then, a perception that Buraku discrimination is gradually improving and the loss of their statutory basis have led many local governments to reduce or abolish their Dōwa policies: what has been the effect in the 15 years since?

The Japanese government has neglected the recommendations of the United Nations' Committee on the Elimination of Racial Discrimination (CERD). From the government's perspective, according to a report by the *Dōwa Taisaku Shingikai* ('Council for Dōwa Policy'), published on 11 August 1965, Buraku people are not a different race or ethnic group and are, without a doubt, Japanese. By the time of the CERD's report, the Japanese government believed that the 1969 Law had been enough to effect Dōwa measures. In other words, the Japanese government ignored the CERD's inclusion of 'descent' in its definition of discrimination on grounds of race or ethnicity, even as article 1 of the AEDB states that 'Buraku discrimination still exists, and with the progress of informatization, the situation regarding Buraku discrimination is changing'. (By 'informatization', the Act means the Internet and its impact on the sharing of hate speech.)

The structure of this chapter is as follows. In section II, I briefly review legal progress at both national and local levels towards eliminating Buraku discrimination. In section III, I attempt to classify Buraku discrimination based on its characteristics and changes over time. In section IV, I examine specific cases that have involved Buraku discrimination (especially hate speech) in recent years. In the last section, I seek to clarify the legal issues arising.

II. Changing the Law for the Purpose of Eliminating Discrimination against Buraku

A. *Legal Changes and Features*

The Buraku civil rights movement has sought to develop a comprehensive legal system that prohibits Buraku discrimination; the movement continues even today.[3] The 1969 Law was a ten-year time-limited law. It was extended for three years from 1979 and *Dōwa Taisaku Jigyō Tokubetsu Sochihō Kyōka Kaisei Yōkyū Kokumin Undō Chūō Jikkō Iinkai* (the 'National Movement Central Executive Committee for Strengthening and

[3] Takanori Yamamoto, 'Buraku Mondai to Sabetsu Kisei no Kadai ni Kansuru Yobiteki Kōsatsu: Hate Speech o Chūshin ni' ['Preliminary thinking about the Buraku problem and anti-discrimination regulation: the case of hate speech'] (2015) 20 *Sekai Jinken Mondai Kenkyū Center Kiyō* [Bulletin of the Kyoto Human Rights Research Institute] 137.

Revising of the Law for Special Measures for Dōwa Projects') first published its *Zenkoku no Aitsugu Sabetsu Jiken* ('Report on National Discrimination Incidents') in 1981. In 1985, under the Act on Special Measures concerning Community Improvement, the Committee of the National Movement Calling for Enactment of a Basic Act on Buraku Liberation was established. In 1987, the Act on Special Measures for National Finance concerning Specific Community Improvement Projects was enacted. In 1992, and then again in 1997, the 1987 Law was extended for five years, expiring in March 2002 and bringing the statutory effect of the special measures aimed at implementing the Dōwa policy to an end. With that, the Committee's name changed to *Buraku Kaihō Jinken Seisaku Kakuritsu Yōkyū Chūō Jikkō Iinkai* (the 'Central Executive Committee Calling for Establishment of a Buraku Liberation and Human Rights Policy').

The sequence of special measures that came to an end in 2002 were not Acts prohibiting Buraku discrimination; to the last, these Acts were the statutory basis for Dōwa projects. The Buraku rights movement has continued to seek regulation against discrimination and redress from harm. The Dōwa administration was a significant policy device aiming to rectify Buraku discrimination and its projects cost about US$136 billion in total. To its credit, it facilitated improvements in housing and the environment, and it narrowed economic and educational gaps. Yet those who harboured bias against the marginalized Burakumin now harbour jealousy and prejudice is on the rise, motivating hate speech and other discriminatory action on the Internet. In addition, the corruption that can contaminate social movement groups and the problems of 'welfare dependency' that are said to occur in Buraku communities continue today.

Published in May 1996, *Chiiki Kaizen Taisaku Kyōgikai Iken Gushin* ('the Opinion Report of the Council for Community Improvement Measures') noted a need to restructure human rights education and to raise awareness, as well as to establish a system of relief for human rights abuses. In December 1996, the Act for the Promotion of Human Rights Protection Measures was enacted, aiming to clarify the responsibilities of the state and promote measures for the protection of human rights, and *Jinken Yōgo Suishin Shingikai* ('the Council for Promoting Human Rights') was established. The Council's July 1999 report, *Basic Matters on the Comprehensive Promotion of Measures for Education and Enlightenment to Deepen Mutual Understanding of the People on the Principle of Respect for Human Rights*, detailed more on education and December 2000 was the launch of the Act on the Promotion of Human Rights Education and Enlightenment.

The Opinion Report extended the focus of Japan's human rights efforts beyond the issue of Buraku discrimination. Buraku rights activists regarded this as a dangerous trend that diminished the issue of Buraku discrimination – especially in the field of education.

In addition, in May 2001, the Council published *Jinken Kyūsai Seido no Arikata* ('A Vision for a System of Relief for Human Rights Violations') and, in 2002, the Koizumi National Administration submitted its Vindication of Human Rights Bill in the 154th session of the Diet. The Bill was dropped at the Diet's dissolution in October 2003. Subsequently, at the 162th session of the Diet in 2005, the Democratic Party submitted a Bill on Remedy for and Prevention of Damages from Human Rights Violations. The Bill was dropped before it had been discussed. In 2012, the Noda National Administration revised the Vindication of Human Rights Bill and drafted a Bill on Establishment of a Human Rights Committee. Although the Bill was submitted to the Diet, the House of Representatives was again dissolved before the Bill could pass.

Between 2002 and 2016, there was consequently no statutory basis at all for resolving at the national level the problems facing the Buraku people. Meanwhile, Buraku discrimination entered a new phase, fuelled by the appearance of the Internet and the emergence of hate speech. It is into this context that the AEDB was enacted.

Article 1 of the AEDB outlines its purpose as follows: 'Buraku discrimination still exists, and with the progress of informatization, the situation regarding Buraku discrimination is changing.' Article 3 affirms the country's responsibility for eliminating Buraku discrimination and the local government's obligation to make efforts. In terms of concrete measures, the Act mandates improvement of the system of public consultation (art. 4), implementation of education and awareness-raising (art. 5), and a survey of lived experiences of Buraku discrimination (art. 6). A supplementary resolution points out that extremism has historically played a part in limiting the impact of efforts aiming to eliminate Buraku discrimination. And it warns that education, awareness-raising, and investigation should not fuel new forms of discrimination. Yet even this law does not provide for the regulation of discrimination, including hate speech.

B. *The Possibility of Regulation at the Local Level*

It is noteworthy that Osaka Prefecture enacted its Ordinance Regulating the Investigation of Buraku Discrimination in 1985. The Ordinance institutionalized the regulation of conduct such as private investigation that may lead to discrimination in marriage and employment opportunities based on residence in a Dōwa district. In addition to seeking self-regulation among private investigation companies, the governor stipulated that businesses in breach of the regulations would be suspended under administrative procedures. A third chapter headed 'Land Survey, etc.' was added to the Ordinance in March 2011, revised under Governor Tōru Hashimoto, to regulate discrimination in surveys of land by construction and real estate companies.

The reason why this Ordinance was enacted is that, in 1975, a booklet listing Buraku was found to exist. Many companies had bought this list and used it to make discriminatory employment decisions. While the Ordinance does not regulate discriminatory behaviour such as hate speech, it imposed administrative sanctions on any businesses seeking to investigate Buraku and identify Burakumin. Similar Ordinances are enacted in Fukuoka, Kumamoto, Kagawa and Tokushima Prefectures. However, the fact that no case has been prosecuted under any of them demonstrates that these Ordinances have not been effectively implemented despite the fact that Buraku discrimination is evident in each prefecture.

Regarding regulations on Buraku discrimination at local government level, the forerunner, the Anan City Ordinance on the Eliminating Discrimination against Buraku and the Protection of Human Rights, was enacted in June 1993. This trend expanded to the many local governments and by 2004 the number of local governments (city and town) in which such instruments had been enacted stood at 764 (16 prefectures); after fundamental local governments merged during the Heisei era,[4] the number stood at 396 city and town governments (17 prefectures).[5] In large part, these ordinances implement the Basic Act on Buraku Liberation at the local government level and their contents are more about raising awareness than about financial commitment. Regulation and protection remain insufficiently provided for, so these ordinances do not regulate discriminatory speech and behaviour; they are far from effective instruments for tackling discrimination.

[4] In modern Japanese society, basic local governments have been merged some three times, in the Meiji, Shōwa, and Heisei eras.

[5] Kenzo Tomonaga, 'Buraku Sabetsu Teppai/Jinken Jōrei no Seitei no Keika, Genjō, Kongo no Kadai' ['Process, present conditions and issues concerning the abolition of Buraku discrimination and the establishment of human rights ordinance'] (2007) 175 *Buraku Kaihō Kenkyū* [Buraku liberation studies] 5.

Based on this discussion of attempts to regulate against Buraku discrimination at the national and local levels, the next section will consider the relationship between Buraku discrimination and hate speech.

The Acts about Buraku that were in place until 2002 centred on business. Specifically, these focused on improving poor housing and closing the economic and educational gaps. Since 2002, there has been no legislation for human rights enforcement and relief. The regulation of discriminatory behaviour against Burakumin remains absent at the national level and only limited at the local level.

III. The Characteristics of Buraku Discrimination

A. *From Substantive to Relational*

Sociologically, Buraku discrimination should be understood as based on a social construct rather than a material concept.[6] In particular, in terms of the interaction between substantive discrimination and psychological discrimination reported by *Dōwa Taisaku Shingi Kai* ('the Council for Dōwa Policy') in 1965, it is hard to accurately explain the phenomenon of Buraku discrimination, because the substantive situation has gradually improved for Burakumin since that time. Thus a perspective that captures Buraku discrimination as 'relational' is important, not substantive or essentialist. Furthermore, the concept of Burakumin has become nebulous: everyone can be Burakumin and everyone can be the object of Buraku discrimination; its character as social construct has become clear.[7] Ultimately, being Burakumin is based on self-identification ('I am Burakumin'); it is also based on others identifying a person as such ('They are Burakumin'). Only by ignoring these factors can we continue to regard Buraku discrimination as essentialist; however, the nebulous nature of the social construct cannot be avoided even in the naming of Buraku or Burakumin. If these points are to be fully considered, it may not be possible to theorize Buraku discrimination in the conventional way.

[6] Takanori Yamamoto, 'Sabetsu Ron no Sobyō: *Buraku* Sabetsu o Toraeru tameni' ['A sketch of discrimination theory: understanding Buraku discrimination'] (2014) 32 *Nara Jinken Buraku Kaihō Kenkyūjo Kiyō* [Bulletin of the Nara Human Rights and *Buraku* Liberation Institute] 1.

[7] Michihiko Noguchi, *Buraku Mondai no Paradigm Tenkan* [A paradigm shift in the Buraku problem] (Akashi Shoten, 2000). For more on the construction of Burakumin, see Timothy Amos, *Embodying Difference: The Making of Burakumin in Modern Japan* (University of Hawai'i Press, 2011).

The current debate on Buraku discrimination involves the penetration into Japan of the idea of intersectionality. The intersectional approach to discrimination recognizes that the relationship between the discriminated and those discriminating against them is not singular and fixed; it captures the myriad axes of discrimination, which can be layered and combined, and it recognizes discrimination as relational. Certainly, Buraku discrimination occurs between Burakumin and non-Burakumin. At the same time, ethnic discrimination can occur, for example, between Burakumin and Koreans: Koreans can discriminate against Burakumin under the old caste system, while Burakumin, as Japanese, can discriminate against Koreans, as migrants in Japan. The same applies to discrimination on the basis of gender, sexual orientation or disability, as well as Ainu and Okinawan ethnicities. Social theory suggests that discrimination is an expression of paralysed intergroup relations.

B. *Classifying Buraku Discrimination*

What are the components of Buraku discrimination? The idea of 'discrimination as a tripartite relationship' was proposed by Yutaka Sato.[8] Even if Burakumin (marginalized people) or *Hisabetsu Buraku* ('marginalized communities') are not present in an instance, their devaluation as a minority (i.e. discrimination) can be established as the joint act of the person performing the discriminatory act and a third party. This means that not only can discrimination occur regardless of whether there is an intention to discriminate directly against a specific person or area, but also the victims (the minorities) do not bear the excessive burden of proving discrimination by evidencing actual damage.

In situations in which the person being discriminated against is present and the act of discrimination is conscious and explicit, discrimination is self-evident and does not need to be proved. Likewise, if the geographical object is Buraku or if the object is Burakumin, the discrimination is self-evident. This chapter will shortly look at the case in which

[8] Yutaka Sato, *Sabetsu Ron: Henken Hihan Riron* [The theory of discrimination: a critique of prejudice theory], new ed. (Akashi Syoten, 2018). This theory points out that discrimination can be established even in the absence of the person being discriminated against. Discrimination is established only when there is a person who behaves in a discriminatory way and an 'accomplice' (a third party) who agrees with that person. It is therefore effective even when a victim does not receive a discriminatory message and for informing a response to the discrimination that goes beyond the actor's original intention to function as a disincentive to others.

hate speech was delivered in front of the Suiheisha History Museum: an easy-to-understand case in which the requirements necessary to identify the objects of the speech as Burakumin and Buraku were jointly made out. However, can it always be assumed that the target of a discriminatory act is geographical and personal – that is, genuine Burakumin who now live in genuine Buraku? Officially, it is impossible to identify areas of Japan that are Buraku and people who are Burakumin because such identification would likely lead to discrimination and human rights violations. Yet there are those who argue that only with such identification can people be authentically Burakumin.

On the one hand, it is to some extent possible to trace Buraku heritage through historical and administrative materials; on the other, Burakumin identity is supported by a sense of belonging and characteristics that cannot be traced in such materials. Moreover, Buraku discrimination is not always based on a socially constructed definition of Buraku and Burakumin. Discrimination at its most base is rooted in the premise that the person's Burakumin status is biologically essential. In that sense, it can be said that Buraku discrimination exists regardless of whether or not it is targeted at actual Buraku or Burakumin. However, even when it is not substantively directed, negative use of the categories perpetuates their marginalization. There is no limit to its relevance and influence.

I illustrate this point in Figure 4.1: the vertical axis indicates the spectrum between the biological essentialism and social construction of

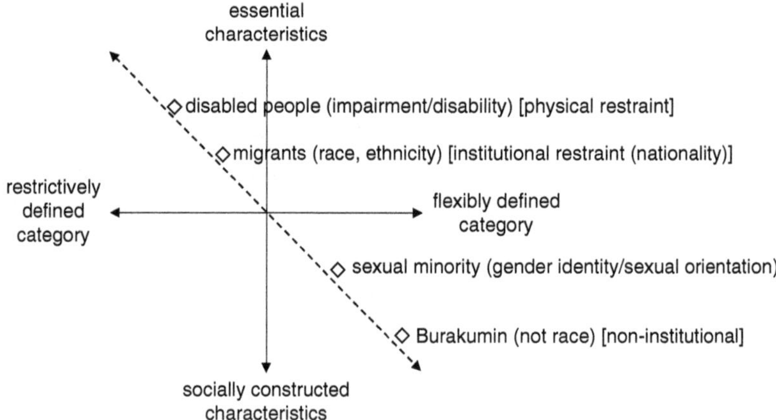

Fig. 4.1 Comparing the characteristics and categorization of minority groups
Source: Yamamoto (2018)

the characteristic, while the horizontal axis indicates the range between restrictive and flexible definitions of category. As flexibly defined and socially constructed, Buraku and Burakumin could be positioned in the lower right-hand quadrant. For comparison, the attributes sexual orientation, migrant status and disability might be positioned as ranging progressively nearer to the top left-hand quadrant. It can be seen that, overall, attributes commonly considered to be biologically essential tend to range towards the more restrictive side of the category spectrum; in contract, more flexibly defined categories tend to be those with socially constructed characteristics.

The AEDB is problematic in that it provides no definition of Buraku discrimination. The supplementary resolution calls attention to the absent definition of Burakumin and Buraku as a deliberate choice, aiming to avoid reviving discrimination. There is in this a deep-rooted idea of *Neta Ko [sabetsu] o Okosuna* ('Do not wake up a sleeping child', whereby the child is discrimination). This nebulous and flexible categorization of Burakumin and Buraku does, however, make it difficult to implement a law that aims to regulate Buraku discrimination.

C. *Changes in Buraku Discrimination*

I would like to examine changes in Buraku discrimination in recent years, focusing in particular on *Zenkoku no Aitsugu Sabetsu Jiken* ('National Discrimination Cases'), published between 1981 and 2018 in *Kaihō Shimbun* (the 'Liberation Newspaper').[9] The first point of note is that the number of discrimination cases recorded is on a downward trend; the second, that persistent discrimination has continued and its form has diversified.

Figure 4.2 is an attempt to categorize the wide range of cases. The vertical axis maps the nature of the discriminatory act, from unconscious bias to explicit discrimination, while the horizontal axis indicates the identity of the actor, from a specific person (individual or corporate) through to indeterminate (anonymous). An important element of discrimination is the motive or purpose at play, indicating whether the discrimination is conducted consciously or unconsciously. The discriminator's identity or anonymity is also important. With the advent of the Internet, anonymized and explicit discrimination has become frequent. In comparison with older cases of explicit discrimination expressed anonymously through methods

[9] The newspaper is published by the Headquarters of the Buraku Liberation League.

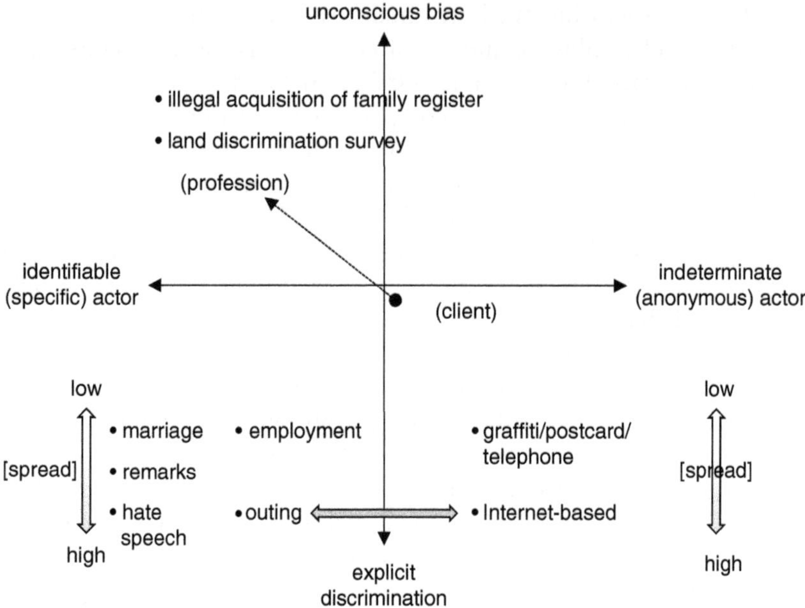

Fig. 4.2 Classification based on form of Buraku discrimination
Source: Yamamoto (2018)

such as graffiti, Internet-based discrimination has greater reach and is more socially influential. These cases land in the lower right-hand quadrant.

Hate speech, meanwhile, lands in the lower left-hand quadrant, being a type of discrimination in which actors are identifiable and the discrimination is explicit. This category has features in common with discriminatory remarks,[10] employment discrimination, and marriage discrimination. However, hate speech is similar to in terms of its reach and impact to Internet-based discrimination. In recent years, it has been increasingly the case that the identity of the actor is clear.

Many cases have historically not been identified as hate speech on the basis of the personal disposition of the actor and whether their discrimination was explicit or unconscious, as well as the reach and influence of the expression and the extent of its incitement of others to discrimination. The phrase 'hate speech' has, however, become more widespread in Japan since the 2010s. While the Japanese translation of the phrase as

[10] These remarks can be defined as unfair discriminatory behaviour not communicated via the Internet or civil movements and not including inciting discrimination.

Futō na Sabetsu teki Gendō ('unfair discriminatory speech and behaviour') is somewhat unnatural, discriminatory speech and behaviour that should properly be called hate speech has existed for a long time. Indeed, while there is a room for misinterpretation even in the Hate Speech Elimination Act of 2016, which defines the object of discrimination as *Honpōgai Shusshinsha* ('migrants'), there is a continuous history of hate speech evident across more than 30 years of National Discrimination Cases.[11] Demonstrating that hate speech is not new as a form of Buraku discrimination, these cases define it as:

(a) targeting a specific individual or group;
(b) with a clear intention to discriminate;
(c) predicting that it would reach a specific audience;
(d) repeating an aggressive discriminatory expression; and
(e) inciting others to discriminate, including by means of the Internet and other electronic media.

It may be said that hate speech is novel in that these elements are combined and take the form of civil movement. In that sense, it is thought to be equivalent to traditional Buraku discrimination, with the addition of the element of incitement and the nature of it as civil movement.

In the next section, we will further examine the relationship between *Buraku* discrimination and hate speech by focusing on three cases of discriminatory incitement since the 2000s

IV. Three Cases

A. *Consecutive Mailing of Discriminatory Postcards*

In the *Consecutive Mailing of Discriminatory Postcards* case, discrimination was evidenced against various minorities, including Buraku (targeting *Buraku Kaihō Dōmei*, the 'Buraku Liberation League'), Koreans in Japan (targeting *Zai Nippon Chōsenjin Kyōkai*, the 'Korean Association in Japan'), disabled people (targeting *Shōgaiji o Futsū Gakkō e Zenkoku Renraku Kai*, the 'National Association of Disabled Children to Normal School'), people recovering from leprosy (targeting *Kikuchi Keifū En*), and migrant workers (targeting *Gaikokujin Rōdōsha o Tsunagu Chiba no*

[11] Some examples are provided in the National Discrimination Cases, *Discriminatory Letters, Doodles, and Telephones at Ikue* (Osaka, 1987 ed.), *Discrimination Incitement: Poster Case in Nagoya* (Aichi, 1992 ed.), *Discrimination Incitement Case by S* (Aichi, 1997 ed.), and *Discrimination Statement Tape Case in Shinyashiki* (Kochi, 1998 ed.).

Kai, the 'Chiba Meeting to Connect Migrant Workers'). The case involves one individual who sent discriminatory postcards of a period of 18 months. The activity would fall within the lower right-hand quadrant in Figure 4.2. Discriminatory postcards cases had occurred in the past, but this case rose to prominence because of the viciousness of the language and persistence of the sender.

The following text was written in the contents of the postcards:

> Even if Eta is dead, it is still Eta.
>
> Reborn as cockroaches, flies, and ticks, they can be disposed of with insecticide. It is good that there is an insecticide that can kill them: it can be used when you are executed.[12]
>
> You are a tick, and Hinin from Tokusyu Buraku.
>
> Eta is a plague, a devil that brings misery to humans. We decided to kill these lower creatures because we could not keep them alive anymore. It is also good to burn off Tokusyu Buraku, and it's fun to kill them, soaking them in poisonous gas and sticking them in coal mines. It is better to kill them with poisonous gas rather than to kill them one by one, when they attack collectively.[13]

The sender portrayed Buraku and Burakumin as less than human, using slurs such as 'Eta', 'Hinin' and 'Tokusyu Buraku'. Malicious threats of execution and killing are repeated. The sender initially remained anonymous, but went on to identify himself repeatedly claiming responsibility before the police and was also identified by a victim who conducted their own investigation.

In court, the defendant alleged that the Edo government had 'purposely created Buraku to divert people's dissatisfaction', as state-sanctioned target that 'we can attack with confidence'.[14] Affirming his allegiance to Japan ('I think that the nation and the system are very important and I should respect them above all'), he went on to claim that Buraku discrimination was not a violation of the law: 'I think that my actions are not a crime. If I do not violate the law, I think that I am free to do anything.'[15]

The prosecution, meanwhile, commented on 'the viciousness of this Buraku discrimination case', such that 'has rarely been seen in recent years', and highlighted that 'this series of crimes has been carried out with

[12] Yoshifumi Uramoto, *Renzoku Tairyō Sabetsu Hagaki Jiken: Higaisya tositeno Hokori o Kaketa Tatakai* [The *Consecutive Mailing of Discriminatory Postcards case*: a fight for victims' dignity] (Kaiho Syuppansha, 2011), 244 (author's translation).

[13] *Ibid.*, at 245 (author's translation).

[14] *Ibid.*, at 134.

[15] *Ibid.*

a clear intention of Buraku discrimination. The victim who is Burakumin was not only threatened daily by the defendant's discriminatory intentions, but [also] has experienced increased prejudice as a consequence. Remedying the damage to his human rights that the victim has suffered will be extremely difficult.'[16]

In July 2005, the court found the defendant culpable and held that he should two years in prison for defamation (under art. 230 of the Penal Code), intimidation (under art. 222 of the Penal Code), and the counterfeiting of private documents (under art. 159 of the Penal Code):

> In this case, the accused sent postcards with threatening statements containing discriminatory expressions to five victims and threatened them. He also sent postcards to the residents of the area in which the three victims live stating that they belonged to a violent group, discrediting their honour. He also used the victim's name to send three sealed letters that slandered others, forging the victim's signature.[17]

At first, because there is no law that regulates the Buraku discrimination itself, both the Legal Bureau and the police had been disinclined to act. When the defendant repeated the offence, the damage expanded and the incident was escalated. The only existing law (the Penal Code) that could be called upon for remedy found defamation and damages in tort. Yet while it might be said that the case involved only the sender and his victims directly, the broader impact was to incite the victims' neighbours to discrimination.

In addition, the necessary aggression that defines this as Buraku discrimination is clear in words such as 'execute' and 'kill'. While it may not have been framed as a group action directly on the street as is commonly considered a quality of hate speech, it is extremely discriminatory. And, as the prosecutor stated, the sender was wholly conscious of the inevitable impact of his action.

B. A Discriminatory Demonstration at the Suiheisha History Museum

Next, let us discuss the case of the discriminatory demonstration in front of the Suiheisha History Museum.[18] The trial, titled only as 'the case for

[16] *Ibid.*, at 155–56 (author's translation).

[17] *Ibid.*, at 242.

[18] Suiheisha is an association for Buraku people that was founded in 1922. The museum is located in Nara Prefecture, where a few original members of Suiheisha gathered to found it.

claiming palimony, no. 686 in 2008 (Wa)', was held from September 2011 to June 2012. The incident occurred in January 2011 in Gose City, Nara Prefecture, as the Suiheisha History Museum prepared to open an exhibition on 'Korea and Japan: One Hundred Years after Colonializing Korea' (December 2010–March 2011).[19] The actor was identifiable and the discrimination explicit, and the incident could be positioned in the lower left-hand quadrant in Figure 4.2, taking the form of a demonstration, the substance of which was shared on the Internet. The plaintiffs sought compensation of ¥10 million (US$91,487); the court awarded damages equivalent to ¥1.5 million ($13,723).

The substance of the demonstration was as follows:

> This Suiheisha History Museum is an Eta, they say that 'comfort women' are sex slaves. Eta, if you have any complaints, you're welcome. Here is the birthplace of Eta, and it seems to be a holy place.
>
> Speaking of Eta and Hinin, long ago, a large number of people would gather and hold impeachment meetings. Come out, Eta! Eta, some people are listening to this! There is only Eta here. I hear that it is a holy place. Eta, come out! You guys, don't some fun things happen in Japan!
>
> Here, if I am doing this, a large number of people would gather, I would be surrounded, and a serious situation would occur. I was listening to it in advance. Thus, I do not expect to be able to demonstrate calmly. I do not think about what to say.
>
> Out of nowhere, come out, Eta! Eta, Hinin, Hinin! The word 'Hinin' is written as 'not human'. Are you really human?

In defence, the demonstrator asserted simply that 'Eta and Hinin are not discriminatory terms. I who used these terms was not engaging in unfair discrimination.'

The court found as follows:

> The defendant gave a speech on the road in front of the plaintiff's Suiheisha History Museum with a handheld microphone using words such as Eta and Hinin. *It is a public fact that these words are discriminatory terms*, taking into consideration the purpose and status of the plaintiff's establishment, and the timing and place of the defendant's behaviour. Thus, it is appropriate to recognise that the defendant's behaviour can be considered defamation of the plaintiff.[20]

[19] The substance of this exhibition included material on the plight of 'comfort women', said to have been forced into sexual slavery by the Japanese army during the colonial era and an issue that continues to be troubling for Japan–Korea relations.

[20] Nara District Court, *The Case for Claiming Palimony, No. 686 in 2008 (Wa)* (2012) (emphasis added).

The plaintiff's counsel praised the judgment, in which the court acknowledged the illegality of discriminatory demonstration and committed to continuing to denounce those who perpetuate unfair discriminatory behaviour.[21] However, counsel asserted that, 'on its surface, the defendant's demonstration did no direct defamation or financial damage to the plaintiff. We must therefore address the specific kind of damage that occurred in the museum forged using the language of discrimination.'[22]

As hate speech, it was possible to pursue remedy under the Civil Code for the act that had been found to have been illegal and the amount of damages made available were relatively high. 'With or without legal restrictions,' counsel added, 'as civil society matures, the existence of diverse citizens is taken for granted and hate speech should have no power; that situation is desirable.'[23]

While this case was dealt with successfully under the existing law (the Civil Code), this judgments in cases of subsequent demonstrations by the same person in the same place were not effective. It is therefore evident that the legal environment needs to be improved.

The Buraku Liberation League of Nara Prefecture Federation says that it 'aim[s] to establish a relief system by clarifying the current legal system, which can currently challenge discriminatory demonstrations only under libel law'.[24] This claim is correct. However, given that there have been effective responses to hate speech in instances in which minority groups have been the target of discrimination, as we saw in the *Postcards* case, there are unresolved issues.

What, then, does this case illustrate? In the first instance, an act of Buraku discrimination was prosecuted under civil law – and that means that that the burden of proof fell on the plaintiff. The other is that the object of damage – the corporation that operates Suiheisha History Museum – was clear. The damage to Burakumin in this area, however, who were the subject of the hate speech, was not raised and discrimination against an unspecified number of Burakumin in other areas remains unchallenged.

21 'Sabetsu Gaisen Saiban de Shōri: Sabetsu de Fuhōkōi to Nara Chisai' ['A win in the Discriminatory Demonstration trial: illegal action by discrimination at Nara District Court'] (2012) 2576 *Kaihō Shimbun* [Liberation newspaper] 1.

22 Msarou Furukawa, 'Suiheisha Hakubutsukan Sabetsu Gaisen Jiken' ['The case of discriminatory demonstration before the Suiheisha History Museum'], in *Naze Ima Hate Speech nanoka: Sabetsu, Bouryoku, Kyouhaku, Hakugai* [Why is it hate speech now? Discrimination, violence, intimidation, persecution] (Sanichi Shobō, 2013), 70.

23 *Ibid.*, at 78.

24 *Ibid.*

C. *Republication of the* National Buraku Survey

Alongside the two cases at which this section has so far looked, that involving republication of the *National Buraku Survey* is a recent example of an action that would fall in the lower left-hand quadrant of Figure 4.2, as Buraku discrimination that – like hate speech – involved an identifiable actor and explicit discrimination.

The case centred on a deal to sell on Amazon a reprint of the *National Buraku Survey* conducted in 1935 by *Chuō Yūwa Jigyō Kyōkai* (the 'Central Integration Business Association'). Although the reprinted version (a booklet) was not sold, the data was posted on the Internet and could be viewed on website named 'Dōwa WIKI'.

In March 2016, the Buraku Liberation League applied to Yokohama District Court for a provisional disposition on an injunction prohibiting publication. The provisional disposition was granted that same month. In April, the Buraku Liberation League applied for another provisional disposition, this time prohibiting posting on the Internet. In the same month, Yokohama District Sagamihara Branch granted the application. In addition, the Buraku Liberation League lodged a suit in Tokyo District Court seeking a ban on publication and posting on the website, and also for damages. In November 2017 and January 2018, the Supreme Court dismissed the defendants' appeals of the ban on publication and the ban on the website, respectively. The original legal suit of this case is pending in Tokyo District Court at the time of writing.

The interesting thing in this case is that the decisions in each of the provisional dispositions recognized the 'right not to be discriminated against' under article 14(1) of the Constitution. It might be hoped that Tokyo District Court will decide such that it treads new legal ground bringing emerging discrimination law into the modern world.[25]

While it might be argued that, in this case, the information being disseminated is rooted in administrative materials and academic research – that is, fact-based material rather than incorrect information or demagogy – that argument is irrelevant to those whom it marginalizes. The point is that the use of such material to inform discrimination is odious.

Even in a society in which only one person has roots in Buraku, zero discrimination or disadvantage would be the ideal. In a society in which

[25] Masayoshi Kaneko, 'Sabetsu sarenai Kenri' no Kenrisei: "Zenkoku Buraku Chōsa" Jiken o megutte' ['Right of "the right not to be discriminated against": the case of the *National Buraku Survey*] (2019) 768 *Hōgaku Seminā* [Legal seminar] 7.

there are many, the spread of information on Burakumin and Buraku without the consent of the parties and stakeholders is seriously problematic. In supplying not only the names of places, but also the names and addresses of individuals belonging to social movement groups and a list of *Rimpokan* ('settlement centres')[26] located in Buraku, the potential of the publication to cause damage is enormous.

Appealing the case, one of the defendant publishers argued that identifying Buraku was the key to effective 'debate on Buraku problems', claiming that the goal of the publication was 'freedom of research'. He alleged that those who experience discrimination are 'very few' and that publishing would have 'merit', including the potential to 'eliminate discrimination'.[27]

In December 2018, the Ministry of Justice's Human Rights Protection Bureau issued a notification on the making and processing of information identifying Dōwa areas on the Internet.[28] The notification covers the actions taken by the defendant in this case and provides, in principle, that the disclosure of information identifying Dōwa districts is illegal. In light of this, it seems likely – at time of writing – that the plaintiffs will win the case before Tokyo District Court. However, this case is similar to that of the *Suiheisha History Museum*. It is an action in which not only does a specific individual act as plaintiff and seek compensation for damage, but also must prove themselves to be true Burakumin.

It is likely that the plaintiffs will seek a verdict that refers to the AEDB – but whether or not that verdict will pave the way towards eliminating discrimination against any number of Burakumin is as yet unknown.

[26] These are regulated under art. 2 of the Act on Social Welfare and are mainly for social work in Buraku. In the 19th century, Toynbee Hall in London and Hull House in Chicago were famous settlement houses, i.e. charitable institutions set up in poor areas such as slums, aiming to bring all members of the community together to improve conditions.

[27] 'Net ga Sarasu *Hisabetsu Buraku*: Giron Saketa Shakai, Fukameta Sabetsu' ['The Hisabetsu Buraku the Internet exposed, the society that avoided discussion, deepened discrimination'], *Asahi Shimbun*, 13 May 2019, available at https://digital.asahi.com /articles/ASM516DSJM51PTIL00Z.html [accessed 20 May 2019].

[28] This notice is interesting because it pre-dates the case of the republication of the *National Buraku Survey*, available at www.moj.go.jp/content/001290357.pdf [accessed 25 September 2020]. It explains:

> It can be evaluated that identifying a specific person as a resident or a native of the Dōwa area infringes privacy, honor, legal interests that ought not to be unfairly discriminated against. The act of pointing out that a particular area is, or was, a Dōwa area, even if it is not an identification against a specific person, is highly likely to be such a violation of human rights. That is, these acts are illegal.

V. Conclusion

The frequency with which hate speech is occurring in Japanese society in the shape of intense demonstrations on the streets is decreasing; at the same time, hate speech on the Internet is on the rise. This clearly shows both the outcome of and challenges faced by those relying on the 2016 Hate Speech Elimination Act (HSEA).

The impact of the AEDB is significant, particularly in relation to the Internet monitoring activities in which some 200 municipalities are now engaging. Such monitoring is not new, however, having been implemented in recent years before the legislation aiming to eliminate discrimination was enacted.

These efforts are conducted independently of one another and are not systematic; there is demand for development of a system that operates at the national level. It is therefore necessary to revise the AEDB and the HSEA, and to pass regulatory laws on human rights violations on the Internet.

Compared with hate speech directed at migrants, public concern about Buraku discrimination is very low, with public backlash a problem, of the sort that is endemic in response to anti-racism. Sadly, this has not changed since the 1970s, shortly after the Law for Special Measures for Dōwa Projects was enacted, because Buraku discrimination is a problem that seems to be simultaneously visible and invisible.

In that sense, improvement of the situation in Japan may depend on Tokyo District Court and the path it treads in the disputed case of republication of the *National Buraku Survey*.

5

The Current Movement of Hate Speech

Focusing on Hate Speech Directed at Korean Residents in Japan

RYANGOK KU

I. The Leading Case on Hate Speech in Japan: *Kyoto Korean Elementary School*

A. *An Outline of the Case and Judgment*

As has already been made clear in this volume, an understanding of the *Kyoto Korean Elementary School* case is essential in any analysis of the background to the Hate Speech Elimination Act (HSEA). The facts of this case are essentially that *Zainichitokken o yurusanai shimin no kai* ('Group of Citizens Who Do Not Tolerate Privileges for Ethnic Korean Residents in Japan', known as *Zaitokukai*) – an anti-Korean, ultra-nationalist organization in Japan – had organized three threatening hate demonstrations in front of the Kyoto Korean Elementary School, on 4 December 2008, 14 January 2009, and 28 March 2010. Zaitokukai distributed videos of the demonstrations on YouTube and the home page of its website.

The school filed a lawsuit against Zaitokukai on 28 June 2010, asking for ¥30 million (US$270,000) in total damages[1] (¥10 million, or $90,000, for each demonstration) and an injunction against any further demonstrations within 200 metres of the school.

On 7 October 2013, Kyoto District Court ordered Zaitokukai to pay ¥12,263,140 (about $114,000) in damages and issued the requested injunction. The Osaka High Court affirmed the District Court's ruling on 8 July 2014. Zaitokukai appealed to the Supreme Court, but its appeal was

[1] Japanese judicial systems do not recognize punitive damages, so 'damages' in the Japanese courts means only compensation and damages for pain and suffering. Judges can use their discretion to calculate the quantum of pain and suffering (Supreme Court, 5 April 1910, 16 Minroku 273).

rejected without a hearing on 9 December 2014 and, at the same time, the Supreme Court affirmed the District Court decision.

The courts' rulings are remarkable in three ways. First, this is the first case in Japan that acknowledges the illegality of a demonstration against the Korean minority motivated by racial discrimination. Second, the courts based their judgments on international human rights law – more specifically, on the United Nations' International Convention on Elimination of All Forms of Racial Discrimination (ICERD) – which is rarely cited as a binding source of law in Japanese courts. Third, the courts recognized and awarded a significant amount of compensation for intangible damage compared to other cases, such as defamation cases, in which intangible damages had been in question.

While coverage of the case was broadcast all over the world[2] and it has been mentioned in the literature, the details of this case and the historical background of the Korean minority in Japan have not been explored to any meaningful extent. Yet the details of this case reveal significant insights into the situation that members of the Korean minority face and how far the HSEA yet has to go in tackling the core of this problem.

B. *Institutional Racism*

(a) First Demonstration

As will be explored in Chapter 12, which looks in more detail at the facts of the case, the school officials had been made aware that Zaitokukai

[2] In the United States, see Martin Fackler, 'Japanese Court Fines Rightist Group over Protests at a School in Kyoto', *The New York Times*, 7 October 2013, available at www.nytimes.com/2013/10/08/world/asia/japanese-court-fines-rightist-group-in-elementary-school-protest.html [accessed 5 March 2019]. In the United Kingdom, see 'Japan Court in Korean Discrimination Ruling', *BBC News*, 7 October 2013, available at www.bbc.com/news/world-asia-24427921 [accessed 1 March 2019]. In France, see Arnaud Vaulerin, 'Le Racisme Anti-coréen Condamné au Japo: un Cas d'École' ['Anti-Korean racism condemned in Japan: a case study'], 27 October 2013, available at www.liberation.fr/planete/2013/10/27/le-racisme-anti-coreen-condamne-au-japon-un-cas-d-ecole_942769 [accessed 1 March 2019]. In China, see 'Rì "zài tè huì" bùfú yīshěn pànjué jiāng shàngsù céng zǔzhī fǎn hán shìwēi' ['Japan's "Zaitokukai" which organized an anti-Korean demonstration dissatisfied with the initial judgment, will appeal'], *China News*, 9 October 2013, available at www.chinanews.com/gj/2013/10-09/5355856.shtml [accessed 1 March 2019]. In the Republic of Korea, see Pil-Seong Kim, 'il hyeomhansiwineun pyohyeon-ui jayu ani wibeob' ['Anti-Korean demonstration in Japan is illegal'], *SBS News*, 7 October 2013, available at http://news.sbs.co.kr/news/endPage.do?news_id=N1002016750&plink=OLDURL [accessed 1 March 2019]. In Kenya, see Agence France Presse, 'Anti-Korean "hate speech" in Japan ruled illegal', available at www.capitalfm.co.ke/news/2013/10/anti-korean-hate-speech-in-japan-ruled-illegal/ [accessed 1 March 2019].

intended to protest by a video notice that the group released. However, at that time, Zaitokukai was an unknown quantity and there was little information on the detail of the planned protest.

On 4 December 2009, around 1pm, when the students were eating lunch in the school building, more than ten men, including members of Zaitokukai, suddenly appeared at the school gate and started demonstrating in a 'threatening' way, yelling through loudspeakers slogans such as 'Open the gate!', 'Yah! Spy school!', 'A Korean school is not a school!', 'Yah! Korean Buraku![[3]] Come out!', 'Kick Korean schools out of Japan!', 'You eat shit: go back to Korea!', 'You are spies' children!', 'Kimchi[[4]] stinks!', 'Illegal immigrants!', and 'Promises are made between human beings, [but] Koreans are not human beings. So promises cannot be made between the Japanese and Koreans!' Soon after the demonstration started, school staff called the police, gathered at the gate, and started recording the protest.

Some 10 minutes after the protest began, police officers arrived at the gate of the school – yet they did not stop the demonstration. School staff and teachers agreed to say nothing in response to the threats. Likewise, when students' parents arrived and sought to respond to the demonstrators, school staff asked them to remain silent.

The demonstration escalated. Members of Zaitokukai began to destroy school property, such as speaker cord. The demonstration was clearly beyond the limits of reasonable speech both in regard to its time, place and nature, and because it was obviously threatening. The demonstration continued for more than one hour and Zaitokukai posted a video of that day's video was to YouTube shortly afterwards.

On their return home, students watched that video, asking their parents questions such as 'Mom, is the word "Korean" a bad word?', 'Why are they angry?', and 'Did we something wrong?' The impact of the threats on the school was severe: the school administration held faculty and parent meetings, putting in place requirements that students be escorted to and from the school every day, and employing security for two hours daily. Because the police were uncooperative, the school staff and parents felt compelled to take these steps themselves despite being the targets of the attack.

[3] *Buraku* refers to one of the minority groups among Japanese nationals. Although *Burakumin* ('Buraku people') are ethnically and linguistically indistinguishable from other Japanese, they have been regarded as a distinct group since the pre-modern caste system and have undoubtedly been discriminated against as a consequence. When the word Buraku is combined with the word 'Korean', it is a slur of the highest order.

[4] *Kimchi* are traditional Korean pickles.

(b) Second Demonstration

On 4 January 2010, Zaitokukai gave notice on its website of plans for a second demonstration.[5] The school held an emergency meeting and decided to host classes outside the school. Arrangements were made, buses were chartered, and the kindergarten students were moved to other Korean kindergartens. The sudden change in the school schedule led some students to ask their teachers: 'Why are we leaving school?', 'Are we running away?', 'Did we do something wrong?', and 'Is this because Zaitokukai is coming again?' Teachers tried to reassure students: 'We're not doing anything wrong', 'We're not running away', and 'We're just trying to be safe.'

Because the second hate demonstration went on for longer than expected, students were forced to wait in a bus for its end, returning to the school well after 5pm. When they came back, 100 police officers were surrounding the school and 10 security vehicles, and students were protected with shields when they got off the bus.

One student described it as 'war time'.

(c) Third Demonstration

We, the school's legal representatives, had organized immediately after the first demonstration. We reported the incident to the police and asked for their help, and we negotiated with Kyoto City Council, asking them to deny permission for Zaitokukai's demonstrations. Neither the police nor city officials were interested in cooperating, demonstrating disinterest in defending the targeted school. Prosecutors refused to accept our criminal complaint and were reluctant to investigate Zaitokukai members. And this disinterest allowed the hate group to carry out a third demonstration.

The overall explanation for these failures can be said to be institutional racism among the police and prosecutors – that is, the collective failure of an organization to provide an appropriate and professional service to people because of those people's ethnic origin. It can be seen in processes, attitudes, and behaviours that amount to discrimination in the form of unconscious bias, ignorance, thoughtlessness, and racist stereotyping (or racial profiling), which disadvantage minority ethnic people.[6]

It was this institutional racism that led to the third demonstration – even though, four days before the demonstration, Kyoto District Court

[5] See Chapter 12.

[6] Colin Webster, 'England and Wales', in John Winterdyk and Georgious Antonopoulos (eds.), *Racist Victimization: International Reflections and Perspectives* (Routledge, 2008), 70.

had finally ordered a preliminary injunction to prohibit demonstrations within 200 meters of the school and Zaitokukai members had been notified of the order. The group ignored the order, appearing at the school on 28 March 2014, shouting, 'Kill Koreans at a health centre!', 'Dogs are better than Koreans!', 'Garbage – to the trash box!', 'Cockroach, Scum, Koreans: go back to Korean peninsula!', 'Beat [Koreans] to death!', and 'Futei Senjin!'[7] A feeling of helplessness seized students, parents, and staff: 'What can we do if the court order could not stop their demonstration?' 'We do not even have human rights.'

Again, Zaitokukai recorded the demonstration and distributed the videos on YouTube and its website. All three harmful demonstrations were shared widely, reaching around the world. Students watched the videos in their own homes and the damage done by the demonstrations was perpetuated by the videos. These demonstrations and these videos have had a huge negative impact on Korean children's ethnic identity.

It was not only students but also the school itself that was affected by the demonstrations. Simply in terms of the time teachers spent responding to Zaitokukai, the demonstrations cost at least 765.5 work hours.[8] After the demonstrations, neighbours were scared that they themselves would be targeted by Zaitokukai and it became difficult for the school to ask for neighbours' help or cooperation.

The Kyoto Korean Elementary School closed in March 2012, at a time when it was taking its case to the civil courts.

Zaitokukai declared its 'victory' online.

(d) The Last Resort: Civil Litigation

As will be examined in more detail in Chapter 12, the police, prosecutors, and other public officials were uncooperative towards the victims of these racially motivated incidents. When we, as the school's counsel, sought a criminal action, prosecutors refused to accept our complaint for more than six months and were evidently reluctant to investigate Zaitokukai members; instead, they asked us to change our claim from defamation to insult, which is a lesser crime under the Japanese Criminal Code. The prosecutor aimed to avoid any burden of proving whether or not Zaitokukai's claims about the school – that Korean students are illegal immigrants, Korean schools are spy schools, and

[7] *Futei Senjin* is a slur meaning 'evil Korean'. The phrase first appeared in public in relation to the Korean massacre in Japan during the Great Kanto Earthquake of 1923, when Korea was under Japanese colonial rule.

[8] See the table, Beppyō Otsu, attached to the court judgment.

so on – were true.[9] It is self-evident that these claims cannot be true, and the effect of the case would have been to drill down into how the police, prosecutors, and public officials ought to react to such kinds of racial discrimination.

Six months on, we gave up and agreed to the lesser charge, and four perpetrators received a suspended sentence of imprisonment in April 2011; their discriminatory motivation was not taken into account in the sentencing. This means that the police officers who came to the school could, in fact, have arrested them immediately, but had chosen not do so.

Only one option remained to us: the 'last resort' of filing civil litigation. There was a high risk that the conservative Japanese courts would overlook the core of this case, as they had in previous cases in which discrimination had been in question. At that time, the words 'hate crime', 'hate speech', or even Zaitokukai were relatively unfamiliar. To make matters worse, the courts in Japan tend not to understand the issues facing the Korean minority and so the courts had historically declared that discrimination was not illegal or had recognized only a small amount of damage. In addition, the Japanese judicial system does not adopt punitive damages.

Even if the school was willing to swallow this, it was likely that the final decision would be a long time coming and that, during the lawsuit, the harms would likely be repeated. The victims had to make a very difficult decision whether to suffer in silence or to fight on, despite these risks.

The school decided to take its case to the civil courts and we filed it in June 2010, six months after the first of the incidents.[10]

B. *The Judgment*

(a) The Kyoto District Court Ruling

After a struggle spanning some four years, on 7 October 2013 Kyoto District Court ordered damages of ¥12,263,140 (about US$114,000) – a remarkably high figure – and granted an injunction prohibiting demonstrations within 200 metres of the school.[11]

9 Insult imposes no burden of proof on the prosecution.

10 For a legal analysis of this case, see Chapter 13.

11 Kyoto District Court, 7 October 2013, 2208 Hanji 74. The whole ruling (only in Japanese) can be found online at www.courts.go.jp/app/hanrei_jp/detail4?id=83675 [accessed 15 September 2020].

The main parts of the opinion can be summarized as follows.

(1) In relation to the court's responsibility under the ICERD:

> Since Japan is a signatory country that has ratified[[12]] the International Convention on the Elimination of All Forms of Racial Discrimination . . . the Court examines in advance how the Convention affects civil litigation in which racial discrimination has occurred between individuals. . . . Article 2(1) of the Convention asks State parties to take appropriate steps to prohibit racial discrimination and bring it to an end, and *Article 6 of the Convention asks State parties to assure effective remedies against racial discrimination through the tribunals*. . . . These tasks will be achieved not only to impose obligation of international law on State parties, but also to *impose obligation directly on the courts* of the State parties. . . . *That's why the Japanese courts have an obligation to interpret domestic laws based on the Convention.*[13]
>
> [D]amages for pain and suffering should be calculated at the discretion of the court taking into account the extent of illegality and severity of damage. *In the event that intangible damage has occurred as a result of racial discriminative action*, the courts should calculate damages to such amount that it will be effective protection against and remedy of any acts of racial discrimination based on Article 2, section 1, and Article 6 of the Convention.[14]

(2) In relation to racial discrimination, the three demonstrations organized by the defendants and the videos that they uploaded were held not only to be defamation and interference with school business, but also:

> . . . activities . . . based on intention to spread their discriminatory message against Korean residents in Japan throughout

[12] The court said 'ratified', but more accurately it should be 'acceded to'.

[13] Kyoto District Court, 7 October 2013, 2208 Hanji 74, emphasis added. This part was rewritten by the Osaka High Court on 8 July 2014, as follows:

> [T]he convention stipulates the international responsibility of each state party and provides for the relationship between public authority and individuals. . . . [T]hat is why, if racially discriminative speech among individuals is to be held unlawful, it is required that *the speech lacks a rational basis and goes beyond permissible limits in view of articles 13 and 14 of the Constitution and the spirits of the ICERD* if it is to be considered a 'violation of the rights or legal interests of another people' under article 709 of the Civil Code.

See Osaka High Court, 8 July 2014, 2232 Hanji 34.

[14] Kyoto District Court, 7 October 2013, 2208 Hanji 74, emphasis added.

Japanese society ... *So these demonstrations are 'exclusion' based on the ethnic origin of Korean residents in Japan and they are intended to obstruct the enjoyment of human rights and fundamental freedoms of Korean residents in Japan in equal position with the Japanese.* They therefore fall under the definition of 'racial discrimination' in Article 1, section 1, of the Convention as a whole.

... That is why these activities are illegal [in tort] not only as violation of article 709 of the Civil Code, but also as consisting of racial discrimination.[15]

(3) In explaining its reasoning with regard to the quantum of damages:

When a court calculates invisible damage, how serious the damage is and the extent to which the violation is illegal should be taken into account. In 1988, the UN Committee on the Elimination of Racial Discrimination, which is established under the Convention, asked the Japanese government whether it considers 'racial motivation' in criminal cases or not. The government replied that, 'In cases of racism, the judges often refer to racial motivation in view of bad faith and such motivation can be reflected in the severity of sentencing.' In response, the Committee asked the government to 'take additional measures against hate-motivated and racist expression', especially recommending that the government should ensure the compliance of its Constitution, Civil Code, Criminal Code, and other laws. This fact means that, when a crime is conducted based on racial discrimination, such motivation can be an element justifying imposition of heavier punishment in the assessment of culpability in criminal cases, so it is approved as a matter of course that the treaty can directly affect the interpretation and application of domestic law. *Similarly, when the tort of defamation is racially motivated or can be defined as racial discrimination, the courts cannot deny that the treaty can directly affect the interpretation and application of civil law and can be a primary factor justifying increased damages for pain and suffering.*[16]

(4) The defendants argued that their activities should be protected as freedom of speech, asserting that their demonstrations were 'reasonable

[15] *Ibid.*, emphasis added.
[16] *Ibid.*

criticism' or 'reasonable statement', which is a defence against illegality and responsibility. In response, the court said:

> [Zaitokukai's] argument is merely *a veil laid on the surface and we can easily see that from the videos.* ... The defendants argue that their demonstrations should be justified as reasonable speech, but *they are straightforwardly contempt, so-called insult, rather than 'criticism' or 'statement' that can be justified as reasonable speech*, so they cannot be justified as any type of 'criticism' or 'statement'.[17]

This ruling is remarkable in ordering payment of so a high a figure of damages for racially motivated hate speech, as well as for rooting its finding in international human rights law (the ICERD), which is rarely mentioned in the Japanese courts.

(b) The Osaka High Court Ruling

Zaitokukai appealed to the Osaka High Court. On 8 July 2014, the Osaka High Court supported the first-instance decision and added a reference on the right of minorities in Japan to ethnic education.

In its opinion, the court noted that the school corporation 'has an *interest in conducting ethnic education*', going on to say: 'Korean schools [in Japan] are ... *evaluated because of their social value as places where ethnic education* in addition to general education are conducted. ... [However, Zaitokukai's activities] destroyed not only the plaintiff's educational environment but also as a social environment performing ethnic education for the Korean minority in Japan.'[18]

In the courts, we argued that Zaitokukai's demonstrations and its distribution of the videos were illegal, based on two main points: that their activities were hate speech and racial discrimination; and that their activities were a violation of the right to ethnic education of the Korean minority in Japan. The latter point was our main claim. Indeed, most of our claim and evidence (more than 80 per cent) centred on the violation of a right to ethnic education. The activities of a hate group can be a serious violation because they intentionally target not only Koreans in general, but specifically Korean children who were in an ethnic Korean elementary school – that is, Korean children aged 4–12 who were only beginning to develop their ethnic identity.

[17] *Ibid.*, emphasis added.

[18] Osaka High Court, 8 July 2014, 2232 Hanji 34, emphasis added.

The Osaka High Court responded to our main claim by recognizing the social value of Korean schools in Japan and by acknowledging that Korean schools in Japan have an 'interest in conducting ethnic education'. It is true that this case has since become well known as a leading case on 'hate speech', but it is equally significant as the first case in which a right to 'ethnic education' was granted special significance for Korean children in Japan. The case, as a benchmark reference for the right to 'ethnic education', contributes to restoring the very ethnic identity and dignity that Zaitokukai sought to destroy.

(c) The Supreme Court Decision

Zaitokukai attempted to take its appeal to the Supreme Court in Japan, but its request was rejected without a hearing, and the Supreme Court of Japan affirmed the remarkable lower-court decisions on 10 December 2014.

The Supreme Court ruling in *Kyoto Korean Elementary School* is remarkable in three ways:

(a) it is the first case to have acknowledged the illegality of discriminatory demonstrations against the Korean minority in Japan and to have mentioned the legal interest of conducting ethnic education;
(b) the decision was based on international human rights law (the ICERD), which is rarely cited as a binding source of law in Japanese courts other than in its ideological (or declarative) capacity; and
(c) the quantum of the intangible damages ordered was the highest yet in comparison with other cases, such as those for defamation, in which damages for pain and suffering had been in question.

Accordingly, this Supreme Court ruling has had a historic impact on the practice of law in Japan. But the school itself was closed because of the racially motivated attacks. A secure, safe, and peaceful community for children who belonged to a Korean minority in Japan was destroyed. Police officers, prosecutors, courts, attorneys, teachers and other adults would or could not stop the hate demonstration, and videos of the three demonstrations were shared all over the world. The impact of these incidents – of this case – has been a denial of ethnic identity and harm to the self-esteem and dignity of Korean children in Japan.

This is harm that is irreparable.

This case triggered national debate about the need to legislate against hate speech and hate crimes; in May 2016, the HSEA was enacted. Yet even as this law condemns unfair discriminatory behaviour, it does not make it illegal. The law has no binding power and makes no mention of penalties for acts such as holding a hate rally in public spaces. Instead, the law was enacted to raise awareness among the general public, to promote understanding and cooperation by means of further human rights education and awareness-raising activities, and to strengthen efforts to eliminate unfair discriminatory speech and behaviour. Is this – can this become – an effective measure to prevent hatred and racism in Japan?

The next part of this chapter will position the roots of racism in Japan in historical context to allow us to analyse the ways in which the law is fundamentally lacking.

II. Racism in Japan

A. *Netto Uyoku*

In Japan, xenophobia targeting ethnic minorities, primarily Koreans, has spread rapidly on the Internet since the 2000s. Anonymous discriminatory remarks against ethnic minorities, especially Koreans, are rampant online. Hostile demonstrations and rallies targeting Korean residents in Japan have been gathering steam. Xenophobic groups have mobilized members on the Internet, repeatedly holding demonstrations and rallies filled with hate speech and intimidation targeting Koreans. These groups are collectively known as *Netto Uyoku* ('Net Far-Right'). Zaitokukai is the largest among them. The *Kyoto Korean Elementary School* litigation between 2010 and 2014 made Zaitokukai the most famous of the Net Far-Right groups. Founded in 2006 by former civil servant Makoto Sakurai, its original 'supporters' (i.e. members) numbered only 500; by 2016, its membership had increased to more than 16,000.[19] Like other xenophobic groups, it has spread its ideas and gathered support by announcing its planned demonstrations and attacks on the Internet, encouraging participation, and then releasing videos of that hate speech and those attacks filmed by group members on various websites.

Zaitokukai, in collaboration with other xenophobic groups, has repeatedly held demonstrations and rallies filled with hate speech targeting and intimidation of Korean communities, including Korean schools and

[19] Kikuko Nagayoshi, 'Nihon no Haigai Ishiki ni Kansuru Kenkyū Dōkō to Kongo no Tenkai Kanōsei' ['Research trends and future possibilities for Japanese exclusionism'] (2017) 66 *Tōhoku Daigaku Bungaku Kenkyūka Kenkyū Nenpō* [Tohoku University graduate course annual report] 89.

Korean towns.[20] Participants describe ethnic Koreans as 'criminals' and 'cockroaches', and call for them to be killed. Their slogans comprise threats such as 'Good or bad, kill all Koreans!', 'Korean, hang yourself! Drink poison! Leap to your death!', 'Turn Shin-Okubo[[21]] into a vacant lot, and build gas chambers here!', and, more simply, 'Kill! Kill! Kill Koreans!' Only when directed towards specific identifiable targets (such as particular individuals, particular schools or particular institutions), these behaviours are crimes such as threat, insult or interference with business[22] under Japan's Criminal Code. When these demonstrations are organized on the streets to demonstrate hate more generally, targeting no specific named target as such, it is argued that these hate demonstrations can be protected as 'freedom of speech', defined under the Japanese Constitution,[23] or as beyond the scope of the law.

In reality, the extreme hate expressed at these demonstrations is such that many Korean residents in Japan feel physically threatened regardless of whether that speech names them or targets them individually. In addition, hate speech has a huge negative psychological impact, especially among Korean students.

B. *The Absence of Hate Crime Law*

Despite widespread hatred and the enormous damage it does to Korean residents, the Japanese government has failed to take effective steps to prevent hate speech and hate crimes. Because there is no specific law governing hate crime, these threatening demonstrations tend to be considered as nothing more than minor offences under the Criminal Code, and so police and prosecutors are reluctant to arrest participants. As the *Kyoto Korean Elementary School* case shows, this kind of institutional racism among public officers empowers the more direct racism of non-state actors,

[20] On 30 March 2016, the Ministry of Justice released a report on hate rallies. According to the report, there were 1,152 demonstrations in 29 prefectures across Japan that reportedly involved associations targeting specific races and ethnicities between April 2012 and September 2015. A total of 237 such demonstrations were held between April and December 2012, 347 in 2013, 378 in 2014, and 190 in the first nine months of 2015. This report is available (in Japanese only) at www.moj.go.jp/content/001201158.pdf [accessed 15 September 2020].

[21] Shin-Okubo is an area in which one of the biggest Korean towns is located.

[22] There are many Korean small businesses in the Korean towns in Shin-Okubo, Tokyo, and in Tsuruhashi, Osaka.

[23] Article 21 of the Japanese Constitution guarantees '[f]reedom of assembly and association, as well as of speech, press and all other forms of expression'.

whose actions become more extreme, and it leads to the misrepresentation of threatening demonstrations (sometimes accompanied by violence) as freedom of speech.

The lack of a law regulating hate crime in Japan is crucial. In my opinion, the most critical problem is that the present Criminal Code completely lacks any provision for hate crimes. Another critical issue is that the courts regularly fail to take account of discriminatory motivation in sentencing. When we consider the HSEA, we must not forget that Japan has no hate crime law and that, as a consequence, these demonstrations of hate can only ever be prosecuted as minor offences – which means that, commonly, they are simply ignored.

C. *Racism in Government: The Root of Racism*

What, then, is the root of this type of racism in Japan? The preamble to the HSEA makes assertions such as 'In recent years in Japan, unfair discriminatory speech and behaviour have been practised' against people with foreign heritage, but is this true? Is this trend *recent*?

The answer is 'No'. In reality, hatred, violence and harassment targeting a Korean minority in Japan has been a matter of grave concern in Japan for over 70 years. Discriminatory and threatening graffiti is nothing new. Yet no attention has been given to racism directed towards the Korean minority; rather, it has been hidden, both deliberately and unconsciously, in many ways. The governmental attitude towards the Korean minority in Japan is characterized by ignorance on their suffering and it is this attitude that has allowed Japan to become a hotbed of racism perpetuated by non-state actors.

(a) The Origin of Racism in Japan

Japanese racism has deep historical roots, tracing back through Japan's historical hatred of Asians and other marginalized racial and ethnic minorities in Japan.

The Western concept of 'race' was introduced into Japan in the late nineteenth century and 'racialized' ideologies were promoted in the project of building a new nation-state.[24] These ideologies included an imagined national unity based on divine cultural roots in the '3,000-year

[24] Hiroshi Fukurai and Alice Yang, 'The History of Japanese Racism, Japanese American Redress, and the Dangers Associated with Government Regulation of Hate Speech' (2018) 45 *Hastings Const. L.Q.* 533.

history' of the imperial family, a myth of racial homogeneity of its national subject, and claims of Japanese racial superiority over other Asian races. Japan's nation-building project and efforts to strengthen the centralized authority of the national government led to imperial projects including the 1868 annexation of Ezo, northern islands including Hokkaido, which had been the homeland of the indigenous Ainu people, and the annexation and dissolution of the Ryukyu Kingdom in Okinawa in 1879. The supposed supremacy of the 'Japanese race' was an ideology also propagated to justify and facilitate Japanese imperial ventures into Asia, leading to the invasion and annexation of Taiwan in 1895, of South Sakhalin in 1905, of Korea in 1910, and of Manchuria in the north-eastern region of China in 1931. Japan's participation in World War I and the defeat of Germany also led to its mandated control of islands in the North Pacific in 1919.[25]

(b) Remembering Genocide

The rhetoric of 'Japanese supremacy' provided justification for Japan's aggressive colonial policies and brutal rule over ethnic Asians both abroad and within Japan itself. In 1923, when Korean uprisings were rumoured in Tokyo metropolitan areas in the aftermath of the Kantō Great Earthquake,[26] more than 6,000 ethnic Koreans were killed by Japanese militias.

It was at during this incident that the key phrase *Futei Senjin*[27] first emerged, meaning 'Evil Korean'. Zaitokukai and other racist organizations frequently use the same phrase today, reminding Korean people of the genocide that followed the Great Earthquake in 1923. The same hatred and incitement to genocide has been seen in the aftermath of recent earthquakes. When Osaka was hit in 2018, rumours spread on social media such as that 'Koreans are conducting theft everywhere in Japan'; hence the impact of that genocide still inspires deep fear among Koreans in Japan nearly 100 years after it happened.

[25] See *Ibid.*, at 534.

[26] On 1 September 1923, an earthquake of 7.9 magnitude struck the Kantō area of Japan, which includes Tokyo. False rumours about *chōsenjin sawagi* (a 'Korean revolt') – e.g. that Korean residents in Japan intended to poison the wells or that Koreans were carrying bombs (when they were, in fact, carrying apples) – spread around Tokyo, which was in a state of disorder because of the earthquake. These rumours led directly to a sudden wave of killings in the disaster area, with more than 6,000 Korean people murdered by vigilante groups, police, and soldiers.

[27] For example, on 3 September 1923 *Tokyo Nichinichi Shimbun* ('Tokyo Daily Newspaper') reported on its front page that 'Futei Senjin set fires everywhere'.

D. *Racism and the Marginalization of a Korean Minority*

In spite of Japan's atrocities, the government has never acknowledged the role of racism, or 'Japanese supremacy', in justifying colonialism; instead, the government stripped the Korean minority of their Japanese nationality after World War II. From a legal perspective, it is this that has continuously impacted on the Korean minority such that they have become the most marginalized group in Japan.

(a) Depriving Those of Korean Heritage of Japanese Nationality

When World War II ended and the Korean peninsula was released from Japanese colonial rule, it was estimated that around 2 million Koreans lived in Japan. As of December 2016, there were approximately 500,000 Korean residents living in Japan on a permanent basis.[28] Among them, around 330,000 Koreans live in Japan as *Tokubetsueijūsha* ('special permanent residents')[29] – that is, residents of Japan with ancestry related to its former colonies, Korea or Taiwan, when they were under Japanese colonial rule.

These special permanent residents or their ancestors used to have Japanese nationality under Japanese colonial rule, but they were stripped of that in 1952 when Japan signed the Treaty of San Francisco (the so-called Peace Treaty). Although the Treaty of San Francisco did not include a specific clause on the citizenship of those Koreans who would continue to reside in Japan, the Japanese government nonetheless used it to deprive Korean and Taiwanese residents of their Japanese citizenship after the treaty became effective. Executed under an official notice from the head of the Civil Affairs Bureau in the Ministry of Justice on 19 April 1952, this was a unilateral procedure that ignored the voices of the residents themselves. Moreover, the measure was applied to a small group – approximately 500,000 – of a population in Japan that, at the time, stood at approximately 85 million. It was a measure that specifically targeted only individuals from Korea and Taiwan on ethnic or racial grounds.

The Supreme Court of Japan continues to uphold this action to this day, despite criticisms highlighting that such unilateral deprivation

[28] For basic background information about Koreans in Japan in English, see Erin Aeran Chung, *Immigration and Citizenship in Japan* (Cambridge University Press, 2010).

[29] In 1991, the Japanese government established a special permanent residency system for individuals born in former Japanese colonies before the Japanese defeat in 1945 (Koreans and Taiwanese) and their descendants.

of nationality violates both the Japanese Constitution and international human rights law.[30]

(b) The Result of Stripping Korean Minorities of Japanese Nationality: Denying Them Participation in Japanese Society

Stripped of Japanese nationality, Korean minorities were excluded from participation in Japanese society. We, the Korean minority, are second, third, and fourth generations born and living in Japan, but we remain subject to deportation and still now experience marginalization and denial of participation in Japanese society:

- we cannot vote or stand for election at either local and national levels;
- we can hold only limited positions in public office and are unable to seek advancement; and
- we cannot become judges or prosecutors.

All of this is simply a consequence of our forebears' loss of Japanese nationality in 1952.

And such exclusionary measures sustained by the Japanese government have only encouraged discrimination based on nationality and ethnicity in the private sector.

(c) Denying Korean Minorities of the Rights to Vote and to Be Elected

Under Japanese law, voting rights in both national and local government elections are limited to those who hold Japanese nationality. Japanese

[30] See Supreme Court, Grand Bench, 5 April 1961, 15 Minshū 657, available at www.courts.go.jp/app/hanrei_en/detail?id=17 [accessed 15 September 2020]. In this case, the Supreme Court justified depriving people of Japanese nationality, saying that:

> The Peace Treaty with Japan in article 2(a) provides that 'Japan, recognizing the independence of Korea, renounces all right, title and claim to Korea, including the islands of Quelpart, Port Hamilton and Dagelet'. To put it simply, it provides that Japan recognises the independence of Korea and renounces sovereign rights to the territory which belongs to Korea. There is no doubt that this provision renounces [Japan's] sovereign rights over the territory (territorial sovereignty) as well as the sovereignty over the people who belong to Korea (personal sovereignty) . . . The recognition of the independence of Korea means that Korea is recognised as an independent state and Korea is recognised to have people who belong to Korea, the territory and the government. Therefore, through the Peace Treaty, Japan is understood to have renounced sovereignty vis-à-vis all people who belong to Korea. This means that, in relation to those who belong to Korea, Japanese nationality would be lost.

nationality law adopts the principle of *jus sanguinis* ('right of blood'), and Japanese nationality is granted to those with at least one Japanese parent. Under this nationality law, descendants of former colonial residents cannot obtain Japanese nationality unless one of their parents marries a Japanese person or they naturalize.

As a result of this law and election laws, some 330,000 Koreans cannot vote in either local or national elections, even though the vast majority of them were born and raised in Japan. Ironically, their forebears could vote during the colonial era, because those ancestors were Japanese nationals at that time – yet a unilateral action stripped the descendants of these Japanese nationals of the ability to participate in Japanese politics at any level.

Moreover, while Japan's nationality law provides for naturalization, the Japanese government controls the naturalization process in Japan and demands assimilation. In Japanese society, there is a strong tendency to regard naturalization not only as the legal acquisition of nationality, but also as ethnic and cultural assimilation into the larger Japanese populace. This and the fact that are no specific provisions in Japan to ease naturalization requirements for former subjects of the sort that exist among other former colonial powers are the reason why multiple generations of special permanent resident Koreans in Japan have hesitated to naturalize.

(d) Denying Korean Minorities the Opportunity to Become Public Officials

Japanese government has taken the position that 'Japanese citizenship is a requirement in order to be a public servant who is involved in the exercise of government authority or the formation of public will', and the Supreme Court has supported this interpretation.[31] As a result, Korean

[31] In one example, when a nurse who was a Korean resident with special permanent resident status was refused permission to take the management selection examination because she was not a Japanese citizen, the Supreme Court ruled that measures that grant management opportunities only to employees who are Japanese citizens are reasonable and valid: Supreme Court decision of 26 January 2005, available at www.courts.go.jp/app/hanrei_en/detail?id=732 [accessed 15 September 2020].

In another example, in 1991, the Minister of Education, Science and Culture issued a notification to local governments that allowed foreign nationals to take the appointment examination to become teachers at public schools, but indicated that they should not be granted the status of 'instructor' that is given to Japanese teachers, but instead titled 'full-time lecturer with no fixed term of employment'. Because only instructors can access management opportunities, it is impossible for foreign nationals to hold management positions in teaching.

residents and other foreign nationals in Japan cannot become public servants who are 'involved in the exercise of government authority or the formation of public will', and in most local governments their appointment or promotion to management positions is restricted.

In addition, a Korean resident or foreign national is completely excluded from positions such as civil and domestic relations counsellor,[32] judicial commissioner,[33] and firefighter, as well as human rights commissioner,[34] welfare commissioner,[35] commissioned child welfare volunteer,[36] and similar public posts.

Excluding all foreign public servants from management positions despite the fact that they have shouldered work responsibilities that in no way differ from those of Japanese persons and possess the same level of abilities is irrational discrimination based on ethnic origin and represents an excessive limitation on the freedom of foreigners to choose their professions. Moreover, most of the Korean minority who had their citizenship unilaterally revoked in 1952 or their descendants were born in Japan, live within a Japanese culture, speak perfect Japanese, and live the same community lives as Japanese persons. Even in some public positions that are open to foreigners,[37] the promotion opportunities available to the Korean minority are largely restricted without legitimate

[32] A civil and domestic relations counsellor is appointed by the Supreme Court from among attorneys recommended by a bar association. A civil and domestic relations counsellor is assigned to mediate and coordinate discussions between parties to reach an agreement in the court.

[33] A judicial commissioner is appointed by a district court from among attorneys recommended by a bar association. A judicial commissioner is assigned to act as an assistant to a court to coordinate discussion between parties in a summary settlement procedure.

[34] Based on the Civil Rights Commissioner Act, human rights commissioners are civilian volunteers who facilitate human rights consultations and engage in activities to raise awareness of human rights. The human rights commissioner system was established to raise awareness of human rights in a broad range of fields and protecting human rights, aiming to prevent human rights violations in local communities. Although human rights commissioners are not paid, as of January 2017, approximately 14,000 had been commissioned by the Minister of Justice and were assigned to municipalities around the country.

[35] Welfare commissioners are commissioned by the Minster of Health, Labour and Welfare, and work to further the interests of residents in local communities by facilitating consultations and providing necessary assistance, and by promoting social welfare.

[36] Commissioned child welfare volunteers provide consultations, support, and other services for child protection, and they respond to concerns over child welfare or during pregnancy, so that children in a community can live in good health and safety.

[37] In 1982, national and public universities abolished the requirement of Japanese nationality for appointment to any position higher than lecturer. In 1986, some local governments abolished the requirement of Japanese nationality as a qualification for appointment as a public health nurse or a midwife.

reason. Yet the government maintains that 'Japanese nationality is required for civil servants who participate in the exercise of public power or in the public decision-making'.[38]

These situations and the denial of participation in Japanese society to the Korean minority continues to position them as the most marginalized group in Japan. Koreans in Japan have been the victims first of colonialism and war, thereafter of governmental discrimination and exclusion, and now of extreme racial harassment and discrimination in the private sector.

Their basic rights have been violated for almost 80 years.

(e) Explicit Racism in Government

Not only is there institutional racism in the government of Japan, but also more explicit racism is readily evident. A similar stance justifying the exclusion of the Korean minority in Japan can be found, for example, in the words of then Counsellor of the Ministry of Justice Tsutomu Ikegami, published in a book titled *Hōteki Chii 200 no Shitsumon* ('200 questions on the legal status [of Korean residents in Japan]') in 1965.[39] Here, we read that foreigners have no right to reside in Japan and can be kicked out of the country arbitrarily. We read that the principles of international law are such that 'it is free to boil and eat or bake and eat foreigners'.

This book is indicative of why the Japanese government has dealt with the rights of people with foreign heritage or nationality, especially the Korean minority in Japan, and the same racist, or 'Japanese supremacist', attitudes can be found in the courts in both the *McLean* case (at which we look next) and in the HSEA itself.

E. Racism in the Courts in Japan

The Supreme Court of Japan has long been empowered to perpetuate racist attitudes in its judicial decisions. In the 1978 *McLean* case[40] – a leading case on the guarantee of constitutional rights for foreign nationals in Japan – we can easily recognize such a stance.

[38] Opinion issued by the Cabinet Legislation Bureau in 1953. The same position can be seen, for example, in Japanese Government, *Periodic Report Submitted to the UN Committee on the Elimination of Racial Discrimination*, CERD/C/350/Add. (2000), at para. 30.2.

[39] Tsutomu Ikegami, *Hōteki Chii 200 no Shitsumon* [200 questions on legal status] (Kyobunsha, 1965).

[40] Supreme Court, Grand Bench, 4 October 1978. The summary of the judgment is available at www.courts.go.jp/app/hanrei_en/detail?id=56 [accessed 15 September 2020].

The plaintiff, Ronald Alan McLean, a citizen of the United States, was refused renewal of his visa by the Immigration Bureau of the Ministry of Justice, partly because he had changed his employment without obtaining Bureau approval as required by law and partly because he had been participating in activities protesting the Vietnam War (i.e. political activities). Mr McLean asked the court to nullify the Ministry of Justice's decision.

The Supreme Court refused, supporting a broad discretionary power for the Ministry of Justice to make such decisions, saying that:

> [T]he Court . . . examines whether the factual basis for the decision was *totally missing or not*, such as in cases in which there was *an error in the material fact* that served as a basis of the decision, or whether it is evident that the decision *significantly lacks appropriateness* in the light of socially accepted views, such as in cases in which the assessment of facts was evidently unreasonable. Only when these points are found to be in the affirmative will the court find a decision to be in excess of the scope of discretionary power or abuse of such power and to be unlawful.[41]

This standard grants the Immigration Bureau of the Ministry of Justice a broad discretion and it remains the courts' precedent.

In addition, the Supreme Court said in this case that the 'constitutional guarantee of fundamental human rights for foreign nationals does not extend as far as to bind the exercise of discretionary power of the state, i.e. does not include a guarantee that acts that are guaranteed as fundamental human rights under the Constitution during the period of stay should not be considered as negative circumstances in renewing the term of that stay'.[42] This Supreme Court ruling has been criticized by lawyers, scholars, non-governmental organizations (NGOs), and others on the basis that the Supreme Court subjected a foreigner's fundamental rights to immigration order. However, this case remains the leading case on the fundamental rights of foreigners in Japan more than 40 years after the ruling – and it is why the plaintiff in refugee or deportation cases is so unlikely to win.

F. Racism in the HSEA Itself

Article 2 of the HSEA provides that, '[i]n this Act, "unfair discriminatory speech and behaviour against persons originating from outside Japan" shall mean unfair discriminatory speech and behaviour aiming to incite

[41] *Ibid.*, emphasis added.
[42] *Ibid.*

the exclusion of persons originating exclusively from a country or region other than Japan or their descendants who are *lawfully residing in Japan*' (emphasis added). In other words, the HSEA protects only 'lawfully residing' foreigners.

It should not need to be said that all human beings are equal and are entitled to the same human rights regardless of their residential status. The principle of non-discrimination or equality has fundamental significance, which is reflected in the article 14 of the Japanese Constitution. Yet the principle of non-discrimination has been rendered subordinate to the domestic law system of immigration control. It is true that the supplementary resolution to the HSEA refers in its 'provisional translation' of article 2 of the Constitution on 'unfair discriminatory speech and behaviour against persons originating from outside Japan', saying that 'any form of discriminatory speech and behaviour shall be appropriately dealt with in line with the intent of this Act',[43] and that 'all discriminatory speech and behaviour shall be dealt with appropriately'.[44] However, the HSEA itself does not include this crucial provision and it risks misleading civil society that once someone's visa has expired, they are no longer protected under a legal system that prioritizes their immigration or visa status over their right to freedom from racial discrimination, as the *McLean* case demonstrated.

G. A Combination of Racism in Both Government and the Private Sector

In summary, racism, or 'Japanese supremacy', has deep historical roots in Japan, and it was used to justify an imperial project that led to colonialism both before and during the war. This racism has been continuously found in governmental policy, legislative policy, and judicial principle or Supreme Court rulings on Korean and other foreigners. This racism, or 'Japanese supremacy', is now combining with extremist groups of the Net Far-Right, which call to mind wartime discrimination against the Korean minority in Japan and the genocide in the aftermath of the Kanto Great Earthquake. The spirit of 'Japanese supremacy' still even now be found in the new HSEA, which implicitly denies human rights and fundamental freedoms to illegal immigrants and other minorities in Japan. As asserted earlier in this chapter,

[43] House of Councillors Committee on Judicial Affairs, Supplementary Resolution for the HSEA (1).

[44] House of Representatives Committee on Judicial Affairs, Supplementary Resolution for the HSEA (1).

it is evident that while the *Kyoto Korean Elementary School* case triggered establishment of a new law focusing on hate speech and hate crimes, the scope of that law falls far from the real needs of the victims.

The next section will analyse the effect of the HSEA in that regard by examining current issues in Japan regarding hate demonstrations.

III. The Reach of Japanese Racism: From the Internet to the Election and the United Nations

The HSEA proclaims that hate speech against foreign nationals should not be allowed, and it requires improvements to the system of public consultation, activities centring on education, and activities to raise awareness.

It is true that enactment of this law is to some extent a first step towards tackling hate speech, but the HSEA is fatally flawed in three main respects:

(a) it does not impose sanction on those who utter hate speech[45] and says only that it must 'not be permissible'[46] – vague terminology compared to those laws that explicitly declare something 'illegal' or 'unlawful' – and hence the effectiveness of the law is unclear;

(b) this law addresses hate speech only against 'foreigners' and so people who belong to other minority groups, such as indigenous Ainu people (in Hokkaido) and Ryukyuans (in Okinawa), or Buraku[47] people, are excluded from its scope; and

(C) as has just been explored, the law protects only 'lawfully residing' foreigners in Japan, such that domestic acts on immigration control take priority over fundamental human rights and universal principles of equality and non-discrimination, which are included in the Constitution of Japan.[48]

These problems reach beyond the HSEA itself into the mechanisms with which Japan can combat discrimination. For instance, Japan has no

[45] To make matters worse, Japan has no statutes on hate crime.

[46] The HSEA says that hate speech is not 'permissible' – a word that leaves some discretion for judges to interpret whether hate speech is 'illegal' or not.

[47] See note 3.

[48] The principle of equality and non-discrimination is reflected in art. 14 of the Japanese Constitution: 'All of the people are equal under the law and there shall be no discrimination in political, economic or social relations because of race, creed, sex, social status or family origin.'

comprehensive anti-discrimination law, Japan has no hate crime law, Japan has no national human rights institution, and Japan has failed to collect data about minorities and has neglected to educate its citizens about minorities in schools. It is against this background that Japan enacted the HSEA.

In that light, how effective can the Act be? After the enactment of the law, racist speech and racist activities remain rampant in Japan. Discriminatory text targeting the Korean minority overflows on the Internet. And the activities of hate groups are spread not only on the Internet but also in person, with groups conducting hate rallies in the street, organizing into a political parties such as *Nihon Daiichi Tō* ('Japan First'), and nominating candidates for local elections. Yet those people whom these groups target on the basis of imagined 'special privilege' (framed in propaganda as stemmed from their 'special permanent residency') are not eligible to stand similarly for election or even to vote.

In addition, in 2017 bar associations across Japan received a total of 130,000 formal letters demanding that disciplinary measures be taken against member lawyers, including ethnic Korean lawyers and Japanese lawyers, who were engaged in cases seeking parity for Korean schools[49] in Japan in terms of the public subsidy and scholarships programme, among other things.[50] A nationalist blog criticizing the lawyers is believed to

[49] Following the end of World War II, Koreans residing in Japan established Korean schools to restore the ethnic identity that had been violated by Japanese colonialism and to educate their children. It started as Korean language training classes and gradually was organized into a schools system. After the Division of Korea in 1948 and following the Korean War (1950–53), Korean schools started to have relations with North Korea, with which Japan has no diplomatic relations.

Korean schools are now located throughout Japan, ranging from kindergartens to high schools. The nationality of the students attending Korean schools is mainly South Korean (more than 70 per cent), followed by 'Korean', which is a sort of stateless identity (less than 27 per cent), and dual (i.e. South Korean/Korean and Japanese). Classes are taught mostly in the Korean language at Korean schools, and Korean history and society are part of the curriculum, while education on other subjects (such as Japanese, Japanese history, world history, geography, maths, science, social studies, music, physical education, and the arts, etc.), as well as the structure of the curriculum, is similar to that within the Japanese education system.

[50] In Japan, facilities in which foreign nationals provide independent education in their native language, including Korean schools, cannot be authorized schools because 'school' is defined as an educational facility that uses textbooks certified by the government and written in the Japanese language (Fundamental Law of Education, arts 1, 34, 49, 62, 70, and 82). However, as is the case with driving schools, facilities that provide education similar to school education can be authorized as 'miscellaneous schools' by a prefectural governor and many of educational facilities intended for foreign nationals, including Korean schools, fall under that category.

have called on its readers to participate in the letter-writing campaign, which started around June 2016. Such kinds of campaign seem to be the first such incident during the 120-year history of the bar associations in Japan.

It is apparent that this type of campaign is discriminatorily motivated interference with business and hence should be restricted by hate crime law. Because Japan has no law on hate crime, the only recourse open to the lawyers is to file a civil lawsuit. Several lawyers who received similar letters have pursued such cases against the senders, seeking compensation in the Japanese civil courts – but the effect of this situation is that people perceive that supporting the Korean minority and fighting against racism can expose them to a very real risk of being targeted themselves and interference with their own livelihoods. The negative impact of this on anti-racism in Japan is more powerful than the positive impact of the HSEA on hate speech.

The reach of racist groups in Japan is not limited to the domestic sphere but extends into international society. The groups, presenting themselves as legitimate NGOs are submitting counter-reports to UN committees and attending sessions of the UN treaty bodies.[51] Shockingly, they were able to cover the costs of this activity by crowdfunding and through donations from supporters in Japan.

That these activities are spilling beyond cyberspace and the streets of Japan into the international arena even after the enactment of the HSEA demonstrates the impotence of the Act in tackling extremism.

Moreover, in April 2010, Japan introduced a system to exempt tuition fees for public high schools and to supply scholarships to students of national and private high schools, etc. Although foreign schools were also covered by this programme, Korean high schools were excluded because of the diplomatic tension with North Korea.

To date, several Korean schools have filed claims against the government, arguing that the exclusion of Korean schools from the programme is illegal, and court proceedings are still ongoing in each case at time of writing. On 28 July 2017, in a case filed by Osaka Korean High School, Osaka District Court recognized the exclusion of Korean schools as illegal, but the Osaka High Court overturned the judgment on 27 September 2018, ruling the exclusion to be valid. The school appealed to the Supreme Court and this case is pending at time of writing.

In addition, the United Nations has – in the form of recommendations of the UN Committee on Economic, Social and Cultural Rights (E/C.12/JPN/CO/3, 2013), the UN Committee on the Elimination of Racial Discrimination (CERD/C/JPN/10/10-11, 2018) and the UN Committee on the Rights of the Child (CRC/C/JPN/CO/4-5, 2019) – repeatedly advised the Japanese government to apply the programme equally to Korean schools, but the government continues to ignore the recommendations.

[51] For example, Net Far-Right attended a session of the UN Committee on the Elimination of Racial Discrimination (CERD) in 2018 and a session of the UN Committee on the Rights of the Child (CRC) in 2019, held in Geneva.

IV. Conclusion

Korean residents with permanent resident status fall within the scope of the definition of national or ethnic minorities under the International Convention on the Civil and Political Rights (ICCPR) or the Declaration on the Rights of Persons Belonging to National or Ethnic, Religious and Linguistic Minorities (the Declaration on Minority Rights). Yet the Japanese government has never treated Korean residents as such,[52] and it taken no measures to protect and promote the ethnic, cultural or linguistic identity of Korean residents; rather, the government stripped Korean residents of their Japanese nationality against their will and has since excluded them from participation in social society under the nationality requirements set out in various laws. Korean residents in Japan suffer discrimination in myriad forms. Furthermore, the government, the Diet, and courts in Japan share a point of view that derives historically from racism, 'Japanese supremacy', and other such bias. Accordingly, as we saw earlier in this chapter, the police and prosecutors in Japan are tolerant of hatred against Korean minority even in criminal conduct. This allows racist groups to continue to believe that they are delivering 'justice' on behalf of Japanese nationals and it emboldens them towards ever more extreme actions.

To combat such hatred and to establish in Japan a truly democratic society, anti-discrimination legislation is crucial. Once a comprehensive anti-discrimination legal framework has been established, broad governmental action against expressions of hate can have a real impact on the fight against discrimination. Beyond providing legal instruments with which to respond to incitement to hatred, an effective response to hate speech must always include fostering more open and critical conversation that counters such incitement. In limiting the ability of Korean residents and other foreigners to participate in Japanese society, including public office, Japan silences them. In this regard, the UN Special Rapporteur has recommended that:

[52] In the reports it submitted to UN treaty bodies and the Universal Periodic Review (UPR), the Japanese government never treated Korean residents as national or ethnic minorities to be protected under the Article 27 ICCPR or Article 30 of the 1989 UN Convention on the Rights of the Child. For example, the Japanese government reported on policies centred on the Ainu people as an ethnic minority only in its response to previous UPR recommendations: Government of Japan, *Mid-term Report on the Progress Made in the Implementation of the Recommendations Issued during the Second Cycle of the Universal Periodic Review* (January 2017), point 161, available at www.mofa.go.jp/mofaj/files/000225031.pdf [accessed 15 September 2020].

> The promotion and protection of the right to freedom of expression must . . . go hand in hand with efforts to combat intolerance, discrimination and incitement to hatred . . . While laws are certainly necessary and an important component in addressing hate speech, they should be complemented by a broad set of policy measures to bring about genuine changes in mindsets, perception and discourse.[53]

As a third-generation Korean in Japan, I have experienced institutional discrimination at every significant step in my life, including education, employment, housing, marriage, and so on. I continue to experience it explicitly in my daily life, in the form of physical and verbal abuse that was especially common in my schooldays. Since those days, whenever political tensions between the Korean peninsula and Japan have escalated, Korean students in Japan – especially girls – have been targeted by racists and their school uniforms (ethnic dress) have been slashed. Korean students' school uniform have been changed simply because wearing Korean ethnic uniform exposed students to real physical risk. Discriminatory writing and rallies are rampant in Japan. In this situation, many Korean residents in Japan choose to obscure their ethnic names, origin, and identity, and so they have become yet more invisible and yet more marginalized. And yet we have continued to be the most 'perfect' target for extreme racism in Japan. Our ability to participate in Japanese society is limited, our voices are silenced, and we remain subject to deportation even when born in Japan. As a target of hate speech, I am issuing a warning about the situation in Japan today, which is so severe that we might compare it to racism pre-war.

If we are to protect freedom of expression in Japan and open up opportunities to challenge hate speech, we must establish comprehensive anti-discrimination law, including an Act that provides for the prosecution of hate crimes.

[53] See David Kaye, UN Special Rapporteur, *Report on the Promotion and the Protection of the Right to Freedom of Opinion and Expression, Submitted in Accordance with Human Rights Council Resolution 25/2*, 8 September 2015, available at https://undocs.org/A/70/361 [accessed 15 September 2020].

6

The Failure of the Human Rights Vindication Bill

MASAYOSHI KANEKO

I. An Overview of Human Rights Policy in Japan

The concept of human rights emerged on the national policy agenda in Japan after World War II. Although the emperor had granted 'rights of subjects' to his people as an 'act of charity' before the war, those differed from human rights as conceived of today – that is, as inherent and inviolable among all human beings. In addition, no administrative organization was responsible for guaranteeing the rights of subjects nor was the judicial court system independent of the national government.[1]

The August 1945 Potsdam Declaration that ended the war required Japan to accept occupation by the Allied Powers and to establish a system to guarantee human rights; in October, the Supreme Commander of the governing Allied Powers issued a 'Directive for Freedom',[2] ordering Japan's government to abolish all laws, regulations, and organizations constraining its people's rights. The guarantee of human rights then became a national imperative and it was codified in the Constitution of Japan enacted in 1946.[3]

Among the legislative and institutional reforms under the Constitution, the Attorney General's Office was established in 1948 and it encompassed

[1] The constitution before the war (the Constitution of the Empire of Japan established in 1889) adopted the separation of powers, but the Ministry of Justice, which was an administrative body, could manage judges and set the court rules.

[2] The Allied Powers occupied Japan from 1945 to 1952. The Supreme Commander's directives to the Japanese government were called SCAPIN and were numbered sequentially. The Directive for Freedom was SCAPIN-93.

[3] The Constitution of Japan was established as a complete revision of the Constitution of the Empire of Japan. Immediately after the war, the Japanese government refused to revise the Constitution drastically, but the Allied Powers made it clear that the government had no choice but to amend it completely. See Shigenori Matsui, *The Constitution of Japan* (Hart, 2011), 13–16.

the Human Rights Bureau (HRB) as the office overseeing human rights in Japan.[4] The HRB was modelled after the civil rights section of the US Department of Justice and it was Japan's first national administrative organ to feature 'human rights' as its titular charge. While the Attorney General's Office was reorganized as the Ministry of Justice (MoJ) in 1952,[5] the HRB remained intact.[6]

Although the HRB was responsible for investigation, relief, and consultation concerning cases of human rights violation, it alone could not manage cases nationwide. A supporting system of 'human rights volunteers' was therefore established in 1948. Around 100 lawyers and others conversant with human rights were commissioned as human rights volunteers by the Minister of Justice at the time of inception – a number that now stands at some 14,000.[7]

When these volunteers think it necessary to deal with issues as instances of human rights violation after they are consulted on human rights issues in their local communities, they refer the cases to the HRB or its regional branches. However, the HRB lacks the authority to compel investigation or to prosecute human rights violations; it can merely make recommendations, try to persuade perpetrators to change their behaviours, assist victims, and mediate the relationships between parties, all of which actions are voluntary. Although the HRB handles around 20,000 cases annually, about 90 per cent involve only victim assistance. In most instance, the HRB makes no recommendations, no attempt to persuade perpetrators to stop the violations, and no attempt to mediate relationships. Thus the HRB does little to remedy violations or to punish perpetrators even if it accepts petitions seeking its support. Further, the cadre of volunteers is criticized for being inadequately trained and for a lack of diversity in terms of age, gender, and occupation. Japan's nationwide system of civil human rights

[4] See Masumi Takano, 'Nihon no Jinken Yōgo Seido no Genjō to Kadai' ['The current situation and issues with the system upholding human rights in Japan'], in Mainoritī Kenkyūkai [Minority Study Group] (ed.), *Kakkoku no Jinken Yōgo Seido* [National systems upholding human rights] (Kaiho Shuppansha, 1995), 113.

[5] The name of the Ministry of Justice was the same in English both before and after the war, but its name in Japanese differs. The pre-war name in Japanese was *Shihōshō*, whereas it was named *Hōmushō* after the war. The meaning of *Hōmushō* is closer to the 'Ministry of Legal Affairs'.

[6] The HRB has never been accorded high standing in the Ministry of Justice and has been targeted for redundancies, reorganization, or abolition whenever administrative reform has been discussed.

[7] See Masumi Takano, 'Jinken Yōgo Iin Seido no Shikumi to Genkyō' ['The system and current situation of human rights volunteers'] (1998) 523 *Hōgaku Seminā* [Legal seminar] 56.

volunteers may be uncommon in the world, but the effectiveness of its human rights protections is in question.

The MoJ, HRB, and cadre of human rights volunteers are not Japan's only national structures charged with tackling human rights issues, however. Those issues that intersect with concerns about workers, women and children are the focus of separate networks, including the Labour Standards Office, Labour Relations Commission, Child Guidance Centre, and Women's Consulting Office, which have functioned to guarantee human rights and can boast certain achievements. However, these bodies too have limited legislative authority and no comprehensive jurisdiction over human rights. Consequently, what falls outside their specific jurisdictions is beyond the scope of remedy and the pace of intervention is generally slow. Adequate steps have not been taken to protect the rights of LGBTQ+ and foreign people, especially in terms of the education of children.

On the whole, Japan's human rights policy is far from comprehensive and is insufficiently flexible.

II. The Buraku Liberation Policy

Japan's Buraku Liberation Policy[8] (the Dōwa Policy[9]) has been one pillar of its human rights protections. The policy was a concerted effort by national and local governments to address the discrimination against the Buraku community that has persisted in Japanese society since medieval times. The Act on Special Measures Concerning the Dōwa Policy – which was enacted in 1969 and expired in 1982 – provided the Buraku community with medical and educational support, improvements in housing, roads, water, and waste disposal, recruitment efforts, and financial support for businesses. The Dōwa Policy further sought to educate, train, and raise awareness among the public, reaching beyond reforms to social infrastructure in an effort known as the Dōwa education initiative.

Japan's Dōwa Policy lasted until 2002. The ¥14 trillion (US$130 billion) spent nationally and locally under its auspices yielded significant

[8] *Buraku* is a word used to refer to areas that were historically home to communities of people who were ostracized because of their occupations and social status. Buraku discrimination encompasses discrimination against those who have lived among or had relations with *Burakumin* ('Buraku people'). In that sense, it is discrimination against both people and land. See Hitoshi Okuda, *Tochi Sabetsu: Buraku Mondai o Kangaeru* [Discrimination against land: a consideration of Buraku discrimination] (Kaiho Shuppansha, 2006). See also Chapter 4.

[9] *Dōwa* can be translated as 'integration and harmony' or, more aggressively, as 'assimilation'.

environmental and infrastructure improvements, diminishing the physical impact of discrimination. Although its methods and those achievements remain controversial, it became a model of comprehensive action to improve human rights, spanning welfare, medical treatment, education, labour, and social infrastructure. In that sense, the Dōwa Policy is one legacy of human rights policy in Japan.[10]

After the effects of the Dōwa Policy began to become apparent, the government of Japan established the Council for Promotion of Human Rights Vindication in 1997 and consulted with it to scale up the Dōwa Policy into a general human rights policy.[11] The Council's first report recommended extending the Dōwa education initiative towards broader education in human rights. The report prompted legislation: the 2000 Act on the Promotion of Human Rights Education and Human Rights Awareness-Raising.

The Council issued another report in 2001. The 2001 report emphasized the need for simpler, faster, easier, and more flexible mechanisms to resolve human rights violations, and it recommended establishing a human rights commission with a degree of independence from government.[12] According to the 2001 report, the commission would have two pathways through which to resolve violations:

- *simple resolution* would include consultation, mediation, and directive; and
- *active resolution* would involve conciliation, arbitration, recommendations and disclosure of those recommendations to the public, and litigation support.

The 2001 report organized serious human rights violations into four categories that warranted active resolution: discrimination; abuse; violations by governmental agencies; and violations by the media.

In 2002, the MoJ drafted the Human Rights Vindication Bill, which would establish the required commission and grant it authority, and the Cabinet submitted the bill to the Diet. Although the bill was prepared to implement revisions to the Dōwa Policy, it was also a response to

[10] See Kenji Hishiyama, 'Sengo Dōwa Gyōsei no Henyō Katei ni Kansuru Yōin Bunseki' ['Analysis of the factors contributing to the transformation of administrative policy for Buraku liberation after the war'] (2002) 21 *Syakaigaku Jyānaru* [Sociology journal] 69.

[11] The Council was composed of prominent scholars and lawyers, but it included few parties directly involved in human rights issues.

[12] See Toshihiko Nonaka, 'Atarashii Jinken Kyūsai Seido o Motomete' ['Seeking a new system for upholding human rights'] (2002) 1221 *Jurist* 116.

international demands that Japan establish national human rights institutes (NHRIs). Such institutes are domestic mechanisms that implement international human rights standards consisting of international covenants on human rights and other international human rights instruments. The Paris Principles, which provided guidelines for the authority, responsibilities, and composition of NHRIs, were adopted at a workshop of the UN Commission on Human Rights in 1991 and approved by the UN General Assembly in 1993. Since then, the United Nations' human rights treaty bodies have sought to embed NHRIs across UN member governments. In 1998, the UN Human Rights Committee (HRC) and then, in 2001, the UN Committee on Economic, Social, and Cultural Rights (CESCR) urged the Japanese government to establish NHRIs. Other human rights treaty bodies have repeatedly followed suit.

It was against this international backdrop that the 2001 report stated: 'We made deliberations with sufficient consideration of international trends.' In other words, the purpose of the Human Rights Vindication Bill was twofold: it aimed to expand the Dōwa Policy to become a policy of human rights protections in general; and it aimed to establish the NHRIs demanded by international society.

III. The Contents of the Human Rights Vindication Bill

The focus of the Human Rights Vindication Bill was on resolving human rights violations such as discrimination and abuse by establishing a human rights commission as an administrative organ independent of government. The bill defined human rights violations as 'unjust discrimination, abuse and other acts which violate human rights', and it provided that no person shall commit them. It stipulated nine grounds of discrimination: race; ethnic origin; creed; sex; social status; family origin; disability; disease; and sexual orientation. Under the bill, any victim of human rights violations or anyone about to become a victim could petition the commission for resolution and the commission would investigate or take measures to resolve the issue. Those included 'general resolution' and 'special resolution procedures' resembling the 'simple' and 'active' forms of resolution set out in the 2001 report by the Council for Promotion of Human Rights Vindication. The former procedures were voluntary and encompassed all human rights violations; the latter invoked enforceable authority over specific serious violations.

In response to a petition, the commission would first pursue seven *general resolution procedures*:

(1) advice;
(2) introduction to other organizations;
(3) arrangement of legal aid;
(4) other assistance;
(5) persuasion, education or instruction of the perpetrator;
(6) mediation between victims and perpetrators; and
(7) notification of the relevant administrative body.

Under general resolution procedures, the commission could investigate claims ('general investigation'). Neither general resolution procedures nor general investigation would involve enforceable authority over perpetrators to avoid the chilling effects of overly broad scope. The effect, however, risked being that if perpetrators were to dispute petitioners' claims and refuse any procedures, no resolution could be reached.

To address that limitation, the Human Rights Vindication Bill granted the commission enforceable authority to investigate and resolve specific serious human rights violations (the *special resolution procedures*). The 11 violations susceptible to special resolution ('special human rights violations') were:

- discrimination or abuse by public employees;
- discrimination against customers by sellers or companies;
- employer discrimination against an employee;
- unjust and offensive discriminatory behaviour and sexual harassment against a specific person;
- abuse by staff of social welfare or medical institutions;
- abuse by school staffs;
- child abuse;
- domestic violence;
- elder abuse;
- infringement of privacy or excessive media coverage; and
- other serious violations for which victims cannot themselves recover damages.

The commission was to be able to take special resolution procedures in three directions, as follows.

(a) *Conciliation or arbitration* The commission could present contesting parties with a proposal for conciliation or arbitration and reach agreement between them. The commission would have no authority to enforce conciliation or arbitration. However, if perpetrators were to accept either and fail to comply, victims would be able to seek an order to force their performance of the agreement through the judicial process.

(b) *Recommendation and disclosure* The commission could have made public the violations of perpetrators who failed to abide by its recommendation and required them to cease the violations. Although lacking authority to stop human rights violations directly, recommendation and disclosures can invite social sanction.

(c) *Litigation support* When recommendation and its disclosure could not facilitate resolution, the commission was to be able to provide victims with materials and support to help them to pursue civil or administrative litigation. Victims would not always prevail even with commission support, but litigating has significant psychological and financial effects for them.

The commission would also have conducted special investigations in cases qualifying for special resolution. It could compel appearances, submission of materials, and on-site investigations, and it could impose civil fines up to ¥300,000 (US$2,800) on perpetrators who refuse to comply. However, the commission was not to be able to conduct special investigations of the media; only voluntary investigation was to be admitted for the media.

Under the Human Rights Vindication Bill, the commission could file a lawsuit to order an end to discriminatory expression that incites discriminatory behaviour against unspecified people sharing a specific attribute. This concept of the promotion of discrimination covered two actions: the disclosure of information that makes it easy to identify that a group consisting of unspecified people shares a specific attribute; and to publicize the intention of public employees or private corporations to engage in discriminatory treatment of unspecified people. An example of the former is distributing *Buraku-Chimei Sōkan*.[13] An example of the latter is posting notices declaring 'Japanese only'.[14] When it encountered

[13] The *Buraku-Chimei Sōkan* is a book listing the names and addresses of Buraku communities. This sort of book is even now misused for discrimination against Burakumin. See Kenzo Tomonaga, *Ima Aratamete Buraku-Chimei Sōkan Sabetsujiken o Tou* [Rethinking the *Buraku-Chimei Sōkan Dissemination Case*] (Kaiho Shuppansha, 2006).

[14] In 2001, while the Human Rights Vindication Bill was in progress, a discrimination case arose in which three white men who had been refused access to the public bath in Otaru City, Hokkaido, because of their colour and appearance sued an owner of the public bath under the International Convention on the Elimination of All Forms of Racial Discrimination (ICERD). At the entrance to the bath, a signboard declared 'Japanese only'. In 2002, Sapporo District Court accepted the plaintiffs' claim and the upper court affirmed it: Sapporo District Court, 11 November 2002, 1806 Hanji 84 (*Otaru Public Bath*

prohibited acts, the commission was to confront the perpetrator. If the perpetrator were to persist, the commission could take the case to the courts, requesting an injunction. This method of resolution whereby a public institution could sue for an injunction on behalf of victims was new to Japan's judicial system at that time.[15]

IV. Analysis of the Human Rights Vindication Bill

The Human Rights Vindication Bill addressed discrimination, abuse, and human rights violations by the media. Discrimination and abuse included violations perpetrated by public authorities and that perpetrated by people from the private sector. It had, in fact, been possible to pursue some types of perpetrator of abuse under criminal law or tort law even before the bill was proposed. Furthermore, various laws had been enacted regarding abuse, including the Act on the Prevention of Child Abuse and the Act on the Prevention of Domestic Violence.

However, many cases of discrimination were such that it was it difficult to accuse perpetrators under criminal and civil law, and no general legislation then prohibited discrimination. Therefore, matters such as racial discrimination and discrimination against Burakumin remained unresolved. Although the Constitution of Japan prohibits discrimination, it provides for relations between the state and its people, not between people themselves. Consequently, it is difficult to regulate discrimination between private individuals under the Constitution, unless a constitutional provision can interpreted as applying indirectly between private individuals under the civil law.[16]

Although many Western countries have enacted legislation to prohibit discrimination generally, such legislation has not been forthcoming in Japan despite pressure from non-governmental organizations and stakeholders. Only legislation prohibiting discrimination against groups on the basis of characteristics such as gender and disability exists at present (i.e. the Act on Securing Equal Opportunity and Equal Treatment between Men and Women in Employment, and the Act for Eliminating Discrimination against Persons with Disabilities). The present government

Entrance Refusal). Had the Human Rights Vindication Act been in force at the time, the plaintiffs could have sought relief more easily.

15 Thereafter, a similar system was introduced in the form of the Consumer Contract Act of 2007.

16 Compare Supreme Court, Grand Bench, 12 December 1973, 27 Minshū 1536 (*Mitsubishi Plastics*).

is reluctant to enact a general anti-discrimination law even as it will enact specific anti-discrimination laws. Indeed, in recent years, the Hate Speech Elimination Act and the Buraku Discrimination Elimination Act have been brought into force, but these laws are only partial in effect and do not directly regulate discriminatory actions. The Human Rights Vindication Bill, which prohibited a range of discriminatory behaviours, would have been Japan's first comprehensive anti-discrimination law had it passed. Even the attempt to enact it was revolutionary in seeking to secure human rights in Japan.

The bill was problematic in many ways, however, and many criticized it.[17] First, guarantees of the commission's independence of government were insufficient. Although the bill stipulated that 'the chair and commissioners of the Commission [would] exert their authority independently of the government', it placed the commission under the auspices of the MoJ and did not grant it independent staffing authority. It was also supposed that the HRB currently under the control of the MoJ would be transferred into the offices of the commission. While commissioners would be granted authority independent of the government, case workers were incorporated into the employment hierarchy of the MoJ. Thus, there was a risk that true independence could never be secured, and many critics argued that the commission should be established outside of the MoJ and composed of new recruits.

Second, discrimination prohibited under the bill was limited to 'unjust' discrimination; discrimination not perceived as unjust was outside the bill. The bill offered no criteria to define what was just and unjust, and determination would largely be at the discretion of the commission. As precedent shows, many legal actions concerning discrimination in Japan have been dismissed on the basis that they are not 'unjust' discrimination. To avoid perpetuating this absurdity, the criteria informing any such decision should have been clearly specified in the bill.

Third, the bill regarded violations by public authorities and people from the private sector as equal, and tasked the commission with pursuing identical investigations and proposing like resolutions whether they involved public authorities or private actors. Yet public officials or organizations – notably, the police, prosecutors, and officers of detention facilities – exert stronger authority than do private actors. Discrimination

[17] See Kazuyuki Azusawa, Tatsuya Sakuma, and Yasuhiko Tajima, 'Zadankai: Jinken Yōgohōan no Kentō' ['Symposium on the Human Rights Vindication Bill'] (2002) 920 *Hōritsu Jihō* [Legal times] 75.

or abuse by public actors often occurs behind closed doors and evidence is not easily preserved. To set human rights violations by public authorities on a par with those perpetuated in the private sector raised doubts that violations by public authorities would be regulated effectively.

As has already been noted, the bill was based on the 2001 report of the Council for Promotion of Human Rights Vindication. In the report, the Council classifies human rights violations as of four types: discrimination; abuse; human rights violations by (organs of) the state; and human rights violations by media. While the bill was developed in response to the report, it failed to take human rights violations by a public authority – one of the four types of human rights violation highlighted – seriously, instead deliberately incorporating such abuses into discrimination and abuse in general.

Fourth, that the commission's authority over the media might threaten free speech was the most controversial issue arising.[18] The bill allowed those whose reputation or privacy were invaded and to whom excessive media coverage did damage to petition the commission for redress. Given the freedom of the press, the commission was not to be able to exercise special investigation, but it could pursue conciliation, arbitration, recommendation and disclosure, and litigation support. Critics argued that these resolution procedures might have a chilling effect on the media and limit the exercise of free speech as a foundation of democracy. The media themselves particularly criticized this aspect of the bill. In no other nation is invasion of privacy by media an independent human rights violation subject to resolution by the relevant commission. The voices of those who had effectively suffered trial by media were heard in the bill, yet this clause was among the biggest reasons the bill was discarded.

V. Setback and Confusion

The Human Rights Vindication Bill was submitted to the Diet in 2002, tabled three times, and abandoned when the House of Representatives was dissolved in 2003.[19] The main reason why the bill was not approved

[18] See Shigenori Matsui, 'Jinken Yōgohōan to Masu Media no Hyōgen no Jiyū' ['The Human Rights Vindication Bill and freedom of expression in the mass media'] (2002) 924 *Hōritsu Jihō* [Legal times] 52.

[19] In Japan, a bill that has not been passed by the end of the session is abandoned unless it is adjourned to the next session. Furthermore, all bills under deliberation are abandoned simultaneously in the event of the dissolution of the House of Representatives.

and failed to pass was criticism from Diet members, the media, bar associations, and scholars on the grounds noted in the last section. After the bill was first abandoned, some members of the ruling party, the Liberal Democratic Party (LDP), revised it, freezing those clauses that regulated media. Those members were prepared to submit a new bill to the Diet in 2005, but more conservative members of the LDP opposed the new bill and obstructed its submission, primarily because they resisted the enactment of any comprehensive human rights law.[20]

Confrontation based on ideological and political difference has characterized the debate ever since.

While discussions within the LDP stalled, opposition parties, with liberals at their centre, continued to advocate comprehensive human rights legislation. The Democratic Party of Japan (DPJ), leading the opposition, prepared its own bill – the Remedy for Human Rights Violations Bill – and submitted it to the Diet in 2005. But because it had been proposed by the opposition, the government granted it negligible discussion, and this bill too was abandoned when the House of Representatives was dissolved that year.[21]

As human rights legislation stagnated nationally, Tottori Prefecture[22] attempted to implement an original and comprehensive guarantee of human rights in the form of an ordinance.[23] It aimed to establish a 'commission for promotion of relief of human rights violations' to investigate and relieve discrimination complaints. The ordinance covered eight discriminatory acts: unjust discriminatory treatment; unjust discriminatory behaviour; abuse; sexual harassment; calumny, or invasion of privacy; collecting information for discrimination; repeating crude behaviour; and promotion of discrimination. Many provisions of the ordinance overlapped those that had appeared in the Human Rights Vindication Bill. Grounds for discrimination, relief provided by the commission, and the commission's investigative authority and authority

[20] See, e.g., Minoru Kiuchi, 'Jinken Yōgohōan: Nachisu mo Massao no Kikensei' ['The Human Rights Vindication Bill is more dangerous than the Nazis'] (2005) 39 *Gekkan Gendai* [Monthly modern times] 200.

[21] The circumstances within the LDP after the abolition of the Human Right Vindication Bill are detailed in Kōshi Yamazaki, *Kokunai Jinken Kikan no Igi to Kadai* [The significance of and problems with national human rights institutions] (Sanseido, 2012), 147–58.

[22] Tottori Prefecture is in western Japan, facing the Sea of Japan. The area of Tottori is the seventh smallest in 47 prefectures and its population is the smallest.

[23] See Chapter 9 and Masayoshi Kaneko, 'Tottoriken Jinken Kyūsai Jōrei no Igi to Kadai' ['The significance of and issues with the ordinance for promotion of relief of human rights violations'] (2006) 170 *Buraku Kaihō Kenkyū* [Buraku liberation studies] 54.

to punish perpetrators, were almost identical. The ordinance took the bill as its model and sought to establish human rights by means of local political action.

The ordinance was to be implemented in 2006, yet – as they had in the face of the Human Rights Vindication Bill – the media and bar associations expressed reservations that it could restrict freedom of speech. Politicians and scholars also claimed that the commission might abuse its authority. As a result, the ordinance was frozen immediately before being brought into force and it was abandoned in 2009 – and this failure weakened the drive towards legislating for the protection of human rights, as had that of the Human Rights Vindication Bill.

However, a turning point arrived in 2009 when liberals triumphed over conservatives in the general election and the government changed hands. The DPJ took on a main role in government and began to discuss comprehensive human rights legislation – although the DPJ excluded the media from the scope of human rights violations and proposed a commission that would have no enforceable authority to investigate. While the discussion gathered more pace than ever before, it took time to reach agreement within the MoJ. In addition, bar associations and scholars continued to voice their apprehension.[24] At the close of 2010, public approval of the DPJ and its government was in decline, and the government almost collapsed in 2012 – shortly after it had drafted and submitted to the Diet its own bill, the Human Rights Commission Establishment Bill.[25]

That bill sought to establish the long-proposed commission under the auspices of the MoJ. It gave the commission no enforceable powers of investigation and restricted its resolution measures to voluntary methods, such as support and mediation. Even the commission's authority to demand an injunction that halts promotions of discrimination was omitted in this bill, whereas it had been provided for in the Human Rights Vindication Bill. Discriminatory behaviour was excluded from the types of human rights violation that were the subject of resolution by the commission and the substance that would define promotion of discrimination was

[24] See, e.g., Norikazu Kawagishi, 'Jinken Yōgohōan o meguru Shomondai' ['Problems with the Human Rights Vindication Bill'], in Junichi Saitō (ed.), *Jinken no Jitsugen* [Realizing human rights] (Horitsu Bunkasha, 2011), 50.

[25] For more on the path from the abolition of the Human Rights Vindication Bill to the proposal of the Human Rights Commission Establishment Bill, see Miki Ogasawara, 'Aratana Jinkenkyūsaikikan no Secchi o meguru Dōkō' ['The likelihood of establishing a new human rights institution'] (2013) 754 *Reference* 123.

limited to disclosure of information such as the *Buraku-Chimei Sōkan* for the purpose of discrimination. As a whole, the resolution measures available to the commission were significantly weakened.

When the House of Representatives was dissolved after the bill's submission, the bill was abandoned without deliberation. In the 2012 general election campaign, the LDP led by conservative Shinzo Abe, pledged to oppose the establishment of a human rights commission if it won power.

The discussion of comprehensive anti-discrimination law ended when those conservatives did indeed win and again took control of government.

VI. The Human Rights Vindication Bill and Hate Speech

Since 2012, the idea of comprehensive human rights legislation to prohibit discrimination and establish a human rights commission in Japan has lain dormant. No political faction seems interested in serious discussion of this issue. Among developed nations, Japan alone has neither comprehensive human rights legislation nor NHRIs.

In recent years, vicious hate speech targeting Korean residents has engendered controversy in Japan. Had the Human Rights Vindication Act been in place in 2002 and a commission established, could that commission have regulated hate speech? The bill provided for voluntary general procedures and special resolution procedures with enforceable authority. Hate speech would likely have evaded special resolution procedures because, to be subject to special resolution, 'unjust and offensive discriminatory behaviour' must be directed at specific, identifiable persons and hate speech is often directed at a minority group as a whole. Additionally, approaching hate speech as 'promotion of discrimination', which could justify an injunction prohibiting the action, must be defined by either (a) the disclosure of information that makes it easy to identify that a group consisting of unspecified people shares a specific attribute, or (b) a publication of the intention of public employees and private corporations to conduct discriminatory treatment. Hate speech meets neither criterion. Thus, even had the Human Rights Vindication Act been enacted, it would have been difficult for general victims of hate speech to pursue the special resolution procedure or demand an injunction. The Human Rights Vindication Act could not be the anti-discrimination law that the International Convention on the Elimination of All Forms of Racial Discrimination requires Japan to enact.

The Human Rights Vindication Bill did, however, propose to prohibit discrimination on ground of race and ethnic origin, and it made such discrimination subject to general resolution. Such acts as hate speech are eruptions of a discriminatory atmosphere latent in society. As such, eliminating hate speech means urging society to reject it. The general resolution procedures set out in the bill might have had such transformative effects. The bill also allowed the proposed commission to publicize issues and to submit opinions to the prime minister and the Diet. The commission could have broadcast the evils of hate speech, and it could have asked the Diet and the Cabinet to take action. Such efforts could have amplified those transformative effects.

The failure of the Human Rights Vindication Bill has brought all of this to naught. Japan has no NHRIs, despite the United Nations' encouragement, and it resists the global trends towards guaranteeing human rights.[26]

[26] Few Japanese studies examine the National Human Rights Institute. The only systematic literature is Yamazaki, note 21.

PART III

Legal Framework

7

Hate Speech and Criminal Law Frameworks in Japan

OSAMU SAKURABA*

I. Introduction

This chapter focuses on the Japanese criminal law framework as it relates to hate speech, and aims to clarify both practical and theoretical issues and actions.

In section II, an overview of the Japanese Penal Code will be presented, focusing on the provisions regarding defamation and insults. Additionally, with reference to the *Kyoto Korean Elementary School* case, the present situation of and problems with legal practice on hate speech will be examined. Furthermore, those areas in which current criminal law cannot effectively cope with hate speech will be clarified.

Section III outlines a history of theoretical approaches to the criminal regulation of hate speech. In the past, views on criminal regulation largely leaned away from a pro-regulatory approach;[1] however, there have been some signs of change as a result of *Kyoto Korean Elementary School*. In recent years, greater support for regulation has emerged and this has informed development of a new theoretical approach. However, as this chapter demonstrates, there remain issues with arguments advocating regulation.

In section IV, the significance and limitations of criminal law in relation to the regulation of hate speech will be discussed, and the role

* I am deeply grateful to Dr Mariko Hattori, Associate Professor of Administrative Law at Yamaguchi University, for her help in translating this study. This work was supported by JSPS KAKENHI Grant No. JP19K01347.

[1] In this chapter, 'pro-regulatory approach' means an approach that favours the specific criminalization of hate speech per se; 'anti-regulatory approach' means an approach that opposes it. The discussion is limited to the various approaches advocated in theory by criminal law scholars.

of the criminal law in resolving the issue of hate speech itself will be summarized.

II. The Penal Code and Judicial Practice

A. The Japanese Penal Code

The oldest parts of the current Japanese Penal Code date back to 1907. While its 1880 predecessor followed the example of French law, current criminal law in Japan is enacted with reference to the German system. Consequently, in revising and interpreting the Japanese Penal Code, it is commonplace to refer to German criminal law.[2] There are, however, some critical differences between the Japanese and German penal codes as they relate to hate speech.

Following World War II, and in reaction to Nazi persecution of the Jewish people both before and during the Holocaust, Germany established provisions for *Volksverhetzung* ('incitement to hatred') under article 130 of its Penal Code. Acts such as inciting hatred against minority groups are prohibited. It was emphasized in legislative deliberations that public incitement is a serious crime that can lead to the disturbance of public peace. It is regarded not merely as a special form of defamation, but as a crime that requires punishment with heavy statutory penalties.[3]

Under Japanese law, there are no particular provisions supporting the punishment of hate speech per se. This is in reaction to the severe suppression of free speech in Japan during World War II and the dominant theory of prudence in relation to the regulation of free expression. This is illustrative of the impact of their histories on the legislative decisions of Japan and Germany. Additionally, Japanese society, unlike the German people, has been unwilling to admit to the presence of hate speech against minorities and hence the situation has not been raised as a public issue.

In acceding to the United Nation's 1965 International Convention on the Elimination of All Forms of Racial Discrimination (ICERD) in 1995, the Japanese government expressed reservations regarding Article 4(a) and (b), condemning propaganda and the idea of racial supremacy. The article

[2] To be precise, this is a generalization. The Japanese and German penal codes are not the same. There are numerous important differences, including capital punishment.

[3] See BT-Drs. 3/918, S. 3f. For a detailed argument, see Osamu Sakuraba, *Doitsu ni okeru Minshū Sendōzai to Kako no Kokufuku: Jinshu Sabetsu Hyōgen oyobi 'Aushubittsu no Uso' no Keiji Kisei* [The prohibition of incitement to hatred and the struggle to overcome the past in Germany: criminal regulation of racist expression and Holocaust denial] (Fukumura Shuppan, 2012) and Chapter 2 of this volume.

obliges parties to criminalize hate speech, hate crimes, and the financing of racist activities, and to prohibit and criminalize membership of organizations that 'promote and incite' racial discrimination. The UN Committee on the Elimination of Racial Discrimination (CERD) criticized Japan for taking insufficient measures against racist hate speech. The Japanese government responded that clear racial discrimination was not an issue in Japan and legislative measures were not urgent, that it was possible to deal with the issue using existing Penal Code provisions, and that there was a possibility that the punishment required under Article 4 ICERD would conflict with the guarantee of free speech provided for in the Japanese Constitution, on the one hand, and the principle of legality – *nullum crimen, nulla poena sine lege* ('no punishment without law') – on the other.[4]

Japanese public opinion had long held that racial discrimination was not widespread to such an extent that special regulation was required. The subject of debate has therefore been whether punishment under current regulations governing defamation or insult suffices.

B. *Defamation and Insult*

Article 230(1) of the Japanese Penal Code provides as follows:

> **(Defamation)**
> A person who defames another by alleging facts in public shall, regardless of whether such facts are true or false, be punished by imprisonment or imprisonment without work for not more than three years or a fine of not more than 500,000 yen.

In article 231, the Code provides thus for insult:

> **(Insults)**
> A person who insults another in public, even if it does not allege facts, shall be punished by penal detention or a petty fine.

'Penal detention or a petty fine' means imprisonment for less than 30 days or a fine of less than ¥10,000 (about US$90). In other words, insult is regarded as a minor crime.

When interpreting a provision of a criminal code, it is crucial to determine which legal interests (in German, *Rechtsguts*) are protected

4 *Submission of the Opinion of the Japanese Government on the General Findings regarding the Examination of the Japanese Government by the Committee on the Elimination of Racial Discrimination,* available at www.mofa.go.jp/mofaj/gaiko/jinshu/iken.html [accessed 18 December 2018].

by individual provisions. For example, since murder is an act that infringes on one's life, establishing a penalty for murder suppresses such behaviour and protects life. In this example, life is the legal interest protected under the murder provision. Protection of legal interests is one of the most important functions of criminal law.

According to judicial precedent, the legal interest protected under the provisions for defamation and insult is an individual's honour – that is, their reputation.[5] The reason why insult is considered a trivial crime can be explained with an example.

Compared the statement 'Professor X plagiarized Professor Y's material' (defamation) with the statement 'Professor X is incompetent' (insult). The latter exposes Professor X to less risk to reputation, because it is mere abstract judgement unsupported by alleged 'facts' (the plagiarism alleged in the former), as prescribed under article 230 of the Japanese Penal Code.

The most controversial term in the provisions for defamation and insult, however, is 'individuals'. Depending on precedents and the dominant theory, 'individual' – the entity whose honour is at risk – can be interpreted to include both natural persons and organizations such as corporations. Corporations are also subject to the social evaluation that shapes their reputation and they, like natural persons, are involved in social activities. Because social life requires protection of reputation, it is appropriate that corporations are also protected against defamation and insult.[6] Yet, as a consequence of that word, an expression directed at a large group, such as residents of Tokyo or people from Kyushu in general, does *not* constitute either defamation or insult,[7] the idea being that the interests of these groups are too abstract and the individuals affected by such expression are unlikely to suffer detriment to their own reputation.[8]

[5] See Atsushi Yamaguchi, *Keihō Kakuron* [Criminal law: specific offences], 2nd ed. (Yuhikaku, 2010), 134.

[6] *Ibid.*, at 136.

[7] See Supreme Court, 3rd Petty Bench, 24 March 1926, 5 Keishū 117.

[8] For example, unlike an expression targeting X, a specific Tokyo citizen, an expression directed at an abstract entity, such as any Tokyo citizen, is not usually understood to be an expression that reduces the reputation of X. In Germany, insult targeting a large group of people 'diminishes the individual relevance of any single member of the group' such it does not merit punishment. However, a significant difference between the laws of the two countries is that, in Germany, where expression targets a group and the relevance of the individual is recognized, insult is said to have occurred. This interpretation is known as *Kollektivbeleidigung* ('collective insult') in Germany. See Schönke-Schröder, *StGB Kommentar*, 29.aulf. 2014. Vorbem. §§185ff. Rn. 5–8.

C. *Practical Issues*

Groups that share specific characteristics such as race, gender, or nationality are large and so are not considered to have the attributes of a well-defined reputation, as prescribed in articles 230 and 231 of the Penal Code. The hate speech that has arisen in Japan has generally not been directed at specific individuals and organizations, but at groups such as Korean or Chinese people, and hence has not been subject to criminal prosecution.

In the 2009 *Kyoto Korean Elementary School* case, the defendant was convicted of insult and forcible obstruction of business.[9] Because this was an exceptional case of behaviour directed at a school as an organization, legal action was possible. Other instances of hate speech in public spaces have generally not been similarly criminally prosecuted.

Another problem is the extent of the prosecutor's discretion. In *Kyoto Korean Elementary School*, the school had filed a criminal complaint for the crime of defamation. However, the prosecutor charged the alleged offenders with insult, even though what the defendant had said could be categorized as 'alleging facts'.

The defence for defamation, according to article 230–2, is as follows: when defamation 'is found to relate to matters of public interest and to have been conducted solely for the benefit of the public, the truth or falsity of the alleged facts shall be examined, and punishment shall not be imposed if they are proven to be true'. Sangyun Kim, a criminal law scholar, suggests that, in *Kyoto Korean Elementary School*, the utterances were deeply rooted in the history of Japanese colonial rule during World War II and in post-war Japan, and the prosecutor did not want those utterances to be expressed publicly.[10]

Since Japanese prosecutors have wide discretionary power to prosecute,[11] there is a risk that appropriate prosecution will not be brought in cases in which victims belong to persecuted minority groups.

[9] Kyoto District Court, 21 April 2011, unreported. See Chapter 13.

[10] See Sangyun Kim, *Sabetsu Hyōgen no Hōteki Kisei: Haijo Shakai e no Pureryūdo to shite no Heito Supīchi* [Legal regulation of discriminatory expression: hate speech as a prelude to exclusionary society] (Horitsu Bunkasha, 2017), 9. Regarding the specifics of charges, the police asked the lawyer for the Kyoto Korean Elementary School to drop the charge of defamation. See Il-song Nakamura, *Rupo Kyoto Chōsen Gakkō Shūgeki Jiken* [A report on the Kyoto Korean School attack incident] (Iwanami Shoten, 2014), 156. For detailed facts of the case, see Chapter 12.

[11] Article 248 of the Criminal Procedure Code: 'Where prosecution is deemed unnecessary owing to the character, age, environment, gravity of the offence, circumstances or situation after the offence, prosecution need not be instituted.'

In other words, in addition to substantive problems, the regulation of hate speech faces procedural problems.

D. Other Punitive Provisions

Not only are there difficulties in applying defamation or insult provisions to hate speech, but also there is a degree of difficulty in applying other provisions of the Penal Code to the same end.

In the United States, the burning of crosses is an illustrative example of an action equated with hate speech that also manifests *threat or intimidation*. Article 222 of the Penal Code of Japan states that 'a person who intimidates another through a threat to life, body, freedom, reputation or property' has committed the crime of intimidation. The difficulty in applying this provision to hate speech is that threatening hate speech is not normally directed at a specific person. It is not typically a threat such as, 'I am going to set fire to your home'; rather, it is usually directed at a large group, as in 'I will kill all Koreans in Japan'. According to legal precedent, 'the announcement of the intent to harm' is interpreted such that the person must have the ability to directly or indirectly cause the intended harm. This ability is called *shihai kanōsei* ('controllability').[12] Previous judgments suggest that the more widespread the targets of the announced harm, the less controllability the person intended to perpetrate that harm is deemed to have.[13] Thus, when an announcement is directed at a large group identified only generically, it is unlikely to be considered intimidation, because there is little or no controllability.

It has been asserted that hate speech has the potential both to cause post-traumatic stress disorder (PTSD) in victims and to be as harmful as a physical attack. Since the focus is on the emotional trauma caused by hate speech, it is related to *injury* without physical assault. Article 204 of the Penal Code punishes 'a person who causes another to suffer injury'. Judges interpret 'injury' as physiological damage and apply article 204 to disability such as PTSD. In one case, the defendant had continuously and

[12] See Supreme Court, 2nd Petty Bench, 25 July 1952, 13 Keishū 1176.

[13] In one case in which a police officer on patrol was told by the defendant that traitors would be tried and punished through the people's court, the defendant was convicted under the law of intimidation: see Supreme Court, 3rd Petty Bench, 8 June 1954, 6 Keishū 941. However, in another case in which the defendant announced, in front of several hundred police officers, 'At daybreak, a police officer will be executed by guillotine according with the people's court ruling', the judge did not consider it to be intimidation, because the defendant had no ability to effect the announced harm (i.e. no controllability): see Hiroshima High Court, Matsue Branch, 3 July 1950, 3 Kōkeishū 247.

loudly played a radio and sounded an alarm late at night for a period of one-and-a-half years, causing the victim to suffer migraine and sleep disorders, among other things. That impact was considered to be an injury.[14] From the legal point of view, however, it is not easy to establish the effects of hate speech as injury and prosecute it as such.

Incitement constitutes a crime under the Japanese Penal Code. However, under article 61, a person who incites another to commit a crime will be subject to criminal punishment only if the principal offender attempts to put that action into effect. Therefore, even if there has been incitement to act against a minority group, if no one responds to the call to action, the hate speech cannot be punished as incitement. Only a few regulations, such as the Subversive Activities Prevention Act, punish incitement itself as a serious crime. However, this is a rare exception; the typical types of hate speech are not covered by provisions under the Subversive Activities Prevention Act and the classification of incitement as a separate offence has been criticized severely in legal theory.[15]

It is therefore clear that no special punishment measures for hate speech exist within the Japanese Penal Code, and that the application of defamation, insult, and other related clauses to hate speech is extremely limited.

III. The Development of a Theoretical Approach

A. *Previous Theoretical Approaches*

(a) Anti-regulatory Approaches

In contrast to post-war Germany, where provisions banning demagoguery were introduced into the Criminal Code, there was little debate in Japan on the subject of the criminal regulation of hate speech and,

[14] See Supreme Court, 2nd Petty Bench, 29 March 2005, 59 Keishū 54. In this case, the behaviour continued over a long period of time and the court did not regard emotional distress that had not manifested in specific symptoms such as post-traumatic stress disorder (PTSD) to be an injury.

[15] However, this is not necessarily reflected in actual court practice. The Supreme Court relatively often approves the constitutionality of the provocation provisions of the Subversive Activities Prevention Act: see Supreme Court, 2nd Petty Bench, 28 September 1990, 44 Keishū 463. See also Takehiko Sone, 'Hakai Katsudō Bōshihō no Sendōzai Shobatsu Kitei no Gōkensei' ['The constitutionality of the prohibition of incitement in the Subversive Activities Prevention Act'] (1995) 391 *Hanji* 56. For a constitutional law scholar's criticism, see Chapter 2.

when such debate did take place, the dominant argument was anti-regulatory.

When a series of UN human rights covenants came into force in 1976, Tsuneo Kikkawa, a prominent criminal law scholar, examined the relationship between Japanese law and the International Covenant on Civil and Political Rights (ICCPR), which contains numerous criminal human rights provisions. Kikkawa argued that Article 20 ICCPR was the biggest hurdle to Japan ratifying the Covenant. This article requires the prohibition of war propaganda and advocacy of hatred.[16] He maintained that:

> The intent of the Covenant should not be so difficult to comprehend. However, this article originally was a disposition positing a new control regarding free speech, and it was based on a rather undefined concept. Regarding the intention to convert it to a positive law, not only are there many questions of technical feasibility, depending upon the method of regulation, but there are concerns about its potential to qualitatively contradict the Covenant itself, which establishes principle of legality (Article 15) and freedom of speech (Article 19).[17]

Japan has a unique problem in Buraku discrimination – that is, discrimination against *Burakumin* ('Buraku people'), a minority group descended from those who were at the bottom of the pre-modern Japanese caste system.[18] There has been a great deal of debate regarding the regulation of discriminatory expressions[19] targeting this group.

In 1985, *Buraku Kaihō Dōmei* ('Buraku Liberation League') drafted a bill that would regulate discriminatory expression, and under which defamation and insult targeting a Buraku group with discriminatory intention would be prohibited. Criminal law scholar Ikuzo Maeno pointed out that criminalizing discriminatory expression risked infringing on the right to freedom of thought and expression:

> The wording [of the draft bill] is extremely vague, and it does not even make it clear whether punishable behaviour has occurred ... Of course, the question of proportionality with regards to criminal punishment is also

16 Article 20: '1. Any propaganda for war shall be prohibited by law. 2. Any advocacy of national, racial or religious hatred that constitutes incitement to discrimination, hostility or violence shall be prohibited by law.'

17 See Tsuneo Kikkawa, 'Kokusai Jinken Kiyaku to Keijihō' ['International covenants on human rights and criminal law'], in Shigestugu Suzuki (eds.), *Gendai no Keiji Hōgaku Jōkan* [Modern criminal jurisprudence, vol. 1] (Yuhikaku, 1977), 429.

18 *Buraku*, directly translating as 'hamlet', refers to the areas in which these people were required to live. For more on Buraku discrimination, see Chapter 4.

19 At that time, the term *Sabetsuteki Hyōgen* ('discriminatory expression') was generally used rather than 'hate speech' in Japan.

> a problem. There is significant debate in Japanese law regarding the punishment of speech crimes, with arguments that, while legislation regarding public order has many aspects and examples, from the perspective of criminal law, it seems the punishment of speech crimes should not be forgiven as a principle. Rather, speech issues should be resolved with speech.[20]

This anti-regulatory approach was common in the relevant academic circles of the day.

(b) A Pro-regulatory Approach

Although relatively few, there have been some pro-regulatory theories. While the idea of criminalizing incitement per se has been strongly criticized, the proactive approach asserts that it is better not to prohibit incitement of racial discrimination, as stipulated in Article 4(a) ICERD, but to expand the scope of punishment for the crime of insult, which already exists in the Penal Code.[21]

Munenobu Hirakawa, an outstanding criminal law scholar in the field of defamation and insult, has long expressed a unique view on the substance of the legal interest protected under the insult provision[22] and on criminalizing discriminatory expression. Hirakawa maintains that the legal interest protected should be regarded as 'a state in which human dignity is respected and maintained'. He argues that:

> Expressions that harm human dignity are ones that deny the value of a human being and that characterize their targets as having less value than other human beings. This is equivalent to contemptuously comparing people to animals . . . [Human dignity should be equal for all people, yet] the benefit derived from punishing insulting behaviour seems to be greatest for socially vulnerable people. Because these expressions are often directed at those who are mentally and physically disabled or those of a particular minority group, punishing the most malignant cases helps protect the most socially vulnerable individuals.[23]

From this perspective, Hirakawa argues that it is desirable to amend the current definition of insult. First, if the insults to be punished are

[20] See Ikuzo Maeno, 'Shimin Shakai to Hō' ['Civil society and law'] (1986) 86 *Buraku Mondai Kenkyū* [Bulletin of Buraku problems] 14, at 19–20.

[21] See Munenobu Hirakawa, *Keihō Kakuron* [Criminal law: specific offences] (Yuhikaku, 1995), 270.

[22] See Munenobu Hirakawa, *Meiyo Kison to Hyōgen no Jiyū* [Defamation and freedom of expression] (Yuhikaku, 1983), 155–77.

[23] See Munenobu Hirakawa, 'Sabetsu Hyōgen to Kojin no Sonchō' ['Discriminatory expression and respect for individuals'], in Buraku Kaihō Kenkyūjo, *Kenpō to Buraku Mondai [The Constitution and Burakumin]* (Kaiho Shuppansha, 1986), 259, at 281.

malicious expressions that harm human dignity, the current statutory penalty is too light and penalties should be made more severe. Second, criminalizing 'group insults'[24] needs to be considered. Certainly, as it stands, 'defamation and insult cannot be considered as such when directed against large groups . . . [However,] discriminatory defamation and insults against a group have the potential to be the same as denying the dignity of the individuals that make up the collective.'[25] In other words, '[t]hese expressions can be regarded as acts that indirectly infringe on the dignity of individual members of a group'.[26]

Hirakawa's theory has failed to gain support within the academy. His conception of legal interest under the insult provision has been criticized on the basis that 'human dignity is not sullied by insults' and that, 'anyway, it seems too unclear for the legal interest under criminal law'.[27] Others have argued that insults that hurt human dignity are more serious than defamation, which merely harms reputation and that, therefore, 'the legal punishment of both should be reversed'. Despite this, that is not the case under the current law 'and, according to legislative theory, it is unlikely that such an understanding is valid'.[28] However, these criticisms seem to derive from a misunderstanding of Hirakawa's intention. It should be noted that Hirakawa regards the legal interest defended under the insult provision to be a concrete social reality – that is, the 'state in which the dignity of humans is respected and maintained' – distinct from the normative concept of human dignity.[29]

B. Recent Theories

Since 2006, public hate speech – especially that targeting Korean residents voiced by *Zainichitokken o yurusanai shimin no kai* ('Group of

24 In the United States, the terms 'group libel' or 'group defamation' are commonly used. However, Hirakawa uses the concept of 'group insult', which refers only to insult and not to defamation.

25 See Hirakawa, note 21, at 270–71.

26 *Ibid.*, at 271.

27 See Mikito Hayashi, *Keihō Kakuron* [Criminal law: specific offenses], 2nd ed. (University of Tokyo Press, 2007), 113.

28 See Atsushi Yamaguchi, *Mondai Tankyū: Keihō Kakuron* [Search for criminal law problems: specific offences] (Yuhikaku, 1999), 79.

29 In his more recent work, Hirakawa stated that his earlier explanation had been inadequate and that such criticism was inevitable; hence he is reworking his thesis. See Munenobu Hirakawa, *Kenpōteki Keihōgaku no Tenkai: Bukkyō Shisō o Kiban to shite* [Development of constitutional criminal jurisprudence: based on Buddhist thought] (Yuhikaku, 2014), at 270–73.

Citizens Who Do Not Tolerate Privileges for Ethnic Korean Residents in Japan', known as *Zaitokukai*), a well-known xenophobic group[30] – has garnered increasing public attention and attitudes towards hate speech are changing. Scholars are increasingly focused on this new xenophobic movement and some criminal law scholars have begun to study the regulation of hate speech. However, these scholars are still far outnumbered by constitutional law scholars.

(a) First Steps

Akira Maeda, whose research interests include a wide range of legal issues, but focus especially on the rights of minority groups, argues that hate speech should be criminalized in Japan.[31]

In a book spanning more than 800 pages,[32] Maeda argues that hate speech should be criminalized to protect freedom of speech and he has been severely critical of the prevailing view that subordinates the elimination of hate speech to the protection of free speech.

His criticisms are wide-ranging, but certain elements are characteristic. First, Maeda criticizes the idea that hate speech is not a behaviour but an expression that results in mild levels of harm, Drawing on the work of British and US legal scholars and sociologists, he stresses the diverse and multiple damages caused by hate speech and defines it not as an expression but as an action.[33] Second, Maeda argues that hate speech regulation should reflect 'international common sense', based on governmental reports submitted by member states of the CERD on the legislative situation concerning hate speech (98 countries) and the application of hate speech laws (42 countries).[34]

Maeda's research is significant in informing the discussion of hate speech regulation in the Japanese context. It contests the validity of conventional theories by focusing on the actual damage it does. However, this work has yet to be developed into something more than a critique of conventional theories and hence it does not offer a specific interpretive theory of the criminal regulation of hate speech or start to develop legislative theory.

30 See Chapter 5.

31 Akira Maeda, *Heito Kuraimu: Zōo Hanzai ga Nihon o Kowasu* [Hate crime: hate crime destroys Japan], new ed. (San-ichi Shobo, 2013).

32 Akira Maeda, *Heito Supīchihō Kenkyū Josetsu: Sabestu Sendō Hanzai no Keiji Hōgaku* [An introduction to the Hate Speech Act: a criminal law study of incitement to discrimination] (San-ichi Shobo, 2015).

33 See *Ibid.*, at chs 3–5.

34 See *Ibid.*, at chs 6–10.

(b) The Development of Interpretive Theories

Based on German criminal law, Japanese criminal law scholars have begun to promote the idea of criminalizing hate speech. Takashi Kusumoto, whose research has examined article 130 of the German Criminal Code, which relates to *Volksverhetzung* ('incitement to hatred'),[35] asserts the need to create a new regulation to punish defendants in situations such as that involving the Kyoto Korean Elementary School.

He posits two main reasons why hate speech framed as group insult should be specifically punished. First, with reference to the German interpretation of crimes relating to *Kollektivbeleidigung* ('collective insult'),[36] according to the dominant theory in Germany, one criterion characterizing insult at a collective level is the existence of a small and publicly visible group within which the effects of insult are easily spread. Kusumoto argues that when the target of the hate expression is a *persecuted* group, the effect of an insult is extensive:

> [S]uch groups of people are likely to be sensitive to discrimination, and the effects of insults on these groups are more likely to propagate to individual members . . . [B]ecause of the common characteristics of the members of the group, the entire group has, historically, suffered severe discrimination, and when these characteristics become part of the personality of each member, it follows that even large groups can be subject to collective insults.[37]

Second, Kusumoto refers to the German interpretation of incitement to hatred as requiring *Menschenwürde angreifen* ('attack on human dignity'), arguing that a violent insult against a group also constitutes an attack on human dignity. Such characteristics as ethnicity, race, and physical attributes are predetermined factors that individuals cannot change: 'With slander, which is carried out by referring to the core area of a personality that is unavoidable, the effects are not limited to a superficial part of the personality. Rather, it denies the rights to social life that are "the rights to live as individuals with equal values in the community".'[38]

[35] See Takashi Kusumoto, *Keihō Kaishaku no Hōhō to Jissen* [Method and practice on interpretation of criminal law] (Gendai Jinbunsha, 2003), 103–62.

[36] See note 8.

[37] See Takashi Kusumoto, 'Shūdan Bujokuzai to Minshū Sendōzai' ['Group libel and incitement to hate'] (2012) 2 *Ryukoku Daigaku Kyōsei Hogo Sōgō Sentā Kenkyū Nenpō* [Ryukoku Corrections and Rehabilitation Center journal] 38, at 50.

[38] See *Ibid.*, at 51.

Therefore, Kusumoto concludes, '[i]f some of the Kyoto Korean school students victimized by the assault of the Zaitokukai felt they were not being treated as a person with the same value as other people in this country, then, through the actions of the defendants, the dignity of these children was violated.'[39]

Kusumoto's research emphasizes that, based on German criminal law, the essence of hate speech is not an infringement of honour, but rather a violation of human dignity for members of the discriminated group. Furthermore, unlike Hirakawa, Kusumoto has said that attacks on 'human dignity itself' and attacks on the 'condition of human dignity' should be regarded as the same thing. According to Kusumoto, therefore, hate speech is a crime attacking human dignity, which should be considered a crime more severe than defamation.[40]

However, despite their differences, Kusumoto's argument faces similar criticisms[41] as Hirakawa's theory that human dignity itself is a legal interest. Additionally, Kusumoto argues that collective insult should be regulated by new legislation. However, no concrete legislative proposal has been forthcoming.

(c) The Development of Legislative Theories

In recent years, Sangyun Kim has been the most active criminal law scholar in the field of the criminal regulation of hate speech. He advocates a unique theory of the protected legal interests relating to hate speech regulation and also presents specific legislative proposals.

Kim's work on the criminalization of hate speech[42] can be summarized with three main points. First, to counter the anti-regulatory approaches that emphasize freedom of expression, he argues that focus should be directed to the question of why freedom of expression should be guaranteed. Kim extrapolates that if freedom of expression is considered important for maintaining democracy and if hate speech is a threat to democracy, regulating the latter does not conflict with the former. He elaborates on the harm caused by hate speech:

> Hate speech denies 'living in an environment that guarantees the ability to negotiate as a human equal, one in which personal rights and right to life are guaranteed, which is the foundation of a democratic society', implying

[39] *Ibid.*

[40] See *Ibid.*, at 43.

[41] See notes 27 and 28.

[42] See Kim, note 10.

> that people with certain attributes be denied personal rights and right to life while living. As a result, the latter are relegated to an unfair condition in which their personal rights and right to life are violated. This is not temporary, but continues over a period of time.[43]

Second, and leading directly from this first point, Kim argues that the legal interests protected by criminalizing hate speech must be 'socially equal relationships and opportunities for social participation'.[44]

Third, Kim suggests revising article 2 of the Hate Speech Elimination Act to contain a clearer prohibition and, at the same time, establishing the following penalty in the same law:

> **(Punishment for attribution-based insults)**
>
> (1) A person who, contrary to the meaning of the Convention on the Elimination of All Forms of Racial Discrimination, publicly intimidates another through a threat to another's life, body, freedom, reputation or property, or insults another on the grounds of attributes such as ethnicity, descent or family origin, shall be punished by imprisonment for xxxx years.
>
> The same shall apply to a person who, contrary to the meaning of the Convention on the Elimination of All Forms of Racial Discrimination, publicly defames or insults another on the grounds of the above by means of words, documents, images, behaviours, actions or other methods in a widely recognizable way.
>
> (2) 'Another', as described in the preceding paragraph, includes groups that share common attributes such as ethnicity, descent or family origin.[45]

Kim, emphasizing that hate speech is not merely an infringement of honour but also destroys socially equal relationships, has developed a unique view of the legal interest protected by criminalizing hate speech. His work is proving significant in the development of concrete legislative proposals.

C. *The Task Ahead*

A review of the history of criminal law concerning hate speech regulation facilitates identification of the current status of hate speech in criminal law theory. What follows is a summary of these issues, together with an attempt to clarify those that remain unresolved.

[43] See *Ibid.*, at 48.
[44] See *Ibid.*, at 212–28.
[45] See *Ibid.*, at 256.

The biggest obstacle in current criminal law to the regulation of hate speech is that the objects of defamation and insult are limited to specific individuals and organizations. To overcome this barrier, the pro-regulatory approach seeks to establish new standards that punish expressions of hate that target large groups.

However, as a variety of anti-regulatory approaches show, the most important principle of criminal law – namely, the principle of legality (*nullum crimen nulla poena sine lege*) – cannot be overlooked. This means that no one shall be held guilty of any act that does not constitute a criminal offence under law at the time the offence is committed. It also requires that the punishment of criminal conduct must be clearly (the principle of clarity) and appropriately (the principle of appropriateness) prescribed. Inappropriate penalties are defined as those that punish actions that do not infringe or endanger any legal interests, or those that are excessive in light of regulatory objectives.[46]

The scope of punishment in any new hate speech regulations must therefore be limited to clearly defined activities that infringe or endanger a specific legal interest and conform to the original purpose of regulation. However, certain issues remain.

First, the pro-regulatory approach attempts to regulate expression targeting large groups rather than individuals and it attempts to identify legal interests other than honour that might be violated. The legal interests suggested are conceptually too vague to be the grounds for criminal regulation.

As Hirakawa points out, human dignity should be equal for everyone. In theory, this means that group insults directed at minority groups should be as punishable as those directed at majority groups, because both types of insult harm human dignity in the same way. If this is the case, then, to prevent the scope of regulation from becoming excessive, Kusumoto argues that it should be limited to 'those groups of people likely to be sensitive to discrimination'. However, this standard seems too subjective to be used as a criterion to identify whether a group should be protected.[47]

[46] See Atsushi Yamaguchi, *Keihō Sōron* [Criminal law: general], 3rd ed. (Yuhikaku, 2016), 17–21.

[47] Kusumoto's view can also be read thus: in deciding whether or not an infringement of human dignity took place, it matters whether or not the group members *felt* that they were not being treated as humans with equal value. See Kusumoto, note 35, at 51. Japanese criminal law scholars are often critical of this perspective, which positions emotion as a legal interest. See, e.g., Kanako Takayama, 'Kanjō Hōeki no Mondaisei' ['Problems of emotion as a legal interest'], in Kanako Takayama and Soichiro Shimada

Kim's legal interests in 'socially equal relationships and opportunities for social participation' are extremely vague, and recognition of infringement or endangerment may be unfeasible. Thus his ideas too are subject to a great deal of criticism from constitutional law scholars.[48]

The requirement of 'attack on human dignity' for an expression to be considered hate speech is used in relation to incitement to hatred under the German Penal Code.[49] However, this emphasis is placed on specific criteria regarding expression that clearly refers to Nazi propaganda and therefore is associated with the Holocaust.[50] In this context, one important task is to establish how to derive objective and concrete criteria based on known historical facts while clarifying the shape of the legal interest defended under hate speech regulation.

Second, the range of punishment in the proposed legislation is unclear and it is impossible to dispel the concern that it could be excessive. The risks have to be carefully weighed when considering new restrictions on expression. As *Kyoto Korean Elementary School* demonstrates, it is doubtful whether the police and prosecution will make appropriate professional judgments regarding hate speech. There is a danger that hate speech regulations, originally created to protect the minority, might be abused to repress those same minorities (reverse application).[51] In

(eds.), *Yamaguchi Atsushi Sensei Kentei Ronbunshū* [A Festschrift for Atsushi Yamaguchi] (Seibundo, 2014), 1–34.

48 For example, Yuji Nasu, a prominent constitutional law scholar on hate speech regulation, stated at a round table on hate speech regulation, that '[t]here is an argument in Europe and the United States that [the] regulation of hate speech should be carried out with the objective of highly abstract purposes such as correcting structural discrimination and racial equality. However, these are not readily acceptable as a specific legal interest'. See Kensuke Kajiwara *et al.*, 'Riron to Seisaku no Kakyō ni Mukete' ['Bridging theory and policy'] (2016) 736 *Hōgaku Seminā* [Legal seminar] 47, at 50.

49 In Germany, it is common opinion that the legal interest protected under provision of incitement to hatred is not 'human dignity', but 'public peace'. See Schönke-Schröder, note 8, at §130 Rn. 1a. For detailed argument, see Osamu Sakuraba, 'Meiyo ni taisuru Tsumi ni yoru Heito Supīchi Kisei no Kanōsei' ['The possibility of hate speech regulation emerging from defamation'], in Sangyun Kim (ed.), *Heito Supīchi no Hōteki Kenkyū* [A legal study of hate speech] (Horitsu Bunkasha, 2014), at 135–41.

50 See Clivia von Dewitz, *NS-Gedankengut und Strafrecht*, Berlin 2006, S. 182f.; Wilhelm Römer, 'Nochmals: Werden Gastarbeiter und andere Ausländer durch §130 StGB gegen Volksverhetzung wirksam geschützt?', NJW 1971, S. 1736. For a detailed argument, see Osamu Sakuraba, 'Keihō ni okeru Hyōgen no Jiyū no Genkai' ['Limitation of freedom of expression in criminal law'], in Kim, note 49, at 117.

51 Lawyer Yasuko Morooka argues that concerns about such dangers are seen all over the world, but that it is an extreme position to abandon regulating imminent infringement of legal interests because of a danger of abuse. See Yasuko Morooka, *Heito Spīchi to wa Nanika* [What is hate speech?] (Iwanami Shoten, 2013), 164–65.

a country such as Japan, with its extensive prosecutorial discretion,[52] that risk is high.

When creating new criminal regulations, to prevent uses deviating from the original regulatory objectives, Germany's experience must set an example whereby Japan will add provisions that will limit their application. This should be combined with mechanisms to ensure that judgments are appropriate.[53] These are the tasks that must be addressed to establish provisions for punishing hate speech.

IV. The Significance and Limitations of Criminal Regulation

A. *Significance*

In criminal law terms, even if there are problems with the pro-regulatory approach as it is currently shaped, criminal law is not necessarily useless in the regulation of hate speech. The ability to suppress extremely malevolent hate speech is the strongest merit of applying criminal law. However, it should also be remembered that criminal regulation can have strong side effects. It is not realistic to comprehensively regulate all hate speech with the current criminal regulations and the scope of punishment must be refined.

Indeed, so far as it requires the naming of a specific individual or organization, current defamation practice remains inadequate when it comes to victim protection. For legislation that proposes to punish group insult to strengthen victim protection, the issues outlined in this chapter still remain unresolved.[54]

However, it is not necessary to rely on new legislation, because current defamation and insult provisions could be interpreted to extend the punishable range for hate speech. For example, the current defamation clause could be applied to expressions that do not directly reveal the name of a specific person or organization, but which can be regarded as doing so in combination with the location or size of the target group. In fact, such application is the case in German criminal law.[55]

[52] See note 11.

[53] I developed the argument on the mechanism in Osamu Sakuraba, 'Heito Spīchi Kisei ni okeru Unyōjō no Shomondai' ['Procedural problems in hate speech regulation'], in Yasuyuki Tokuda *et al.* (eds.), *Keijihō to Rekishiteki Kachi to Sono Kōsaku* [Criminal law, historical value and its intersection] (Horitsu Bunkasha, 2016), 812–32.

[54] See sections III.B and III.C.

[55] See note 8.

B. Limitations

Attention must also be paid to the fact that criminal regulation cannot remedy the damage caused by hate speech. As Maeda emphasized, the harms caused by hate speech are diverse and multiple. In a criminal trial in which the defendant's specific malignant actions are recognized as a criminal offence, 'remedy' means only the prevention of such acts. Damage such as the deterioration of the relationship between minority groups and the majority community, and their loss of comfort within everyday life, can persist even after the incident is over. Equanimity cannot be recovered by conviction alone.[56]

Measures such as emergency deterrence of problematic behaviour, reflection, and apology by the perpetrators, public education that hate speech is not to be tolerated, correction of a social system that reinforces the discrimination and prejudice that lies behind hate speech, and striving to realize a symbiotic society in which minority groups can live with peace of mind should all be implemented. These are all important; the role of criminal justice in these aims is limited.

Criminal trials criticize the individual actions of perpetrators and their abdication of their social responsibilities, but the social factors leading perpetrators to prejudice and hate are seldom referred to during a trial. It is the political branch, rather than the judicial system, that has the means to address these social issues.

The declarative effect of the law does not necessarily have to be delivered through 'punishment'. For example, in both the Child Abuse Prevention Law and the Act for Eliminating Discrimination against Persons with Disabilities, prohibitive regulations involve no criminal punishment, and yet they are widely applied as ground rules for establishing the execution of administrative measures.

Excessive expectations of the criminal law may obscure such flexible solutions and force damage relief into the narrow arena of criminal justice.[57]

Pro-regulatory approaches do also recognize that criminal law is not a panacea. Given that conventional non-regulatory methods such as anti-discrimination awareness-raising are not sufficiently effective, pro-regulatory

[56] Regarding the various kinds of damage that occurred in the *Kyoto Korean Elementary School* case, see 'Tokushū Heito Supīchi/Heito Kuraimu' ['Feature issue: hate speech/hate crime'] (2015) 726 *Hōgaku Seminā* [Legal seminar] 11.

[57] See Osamu Sakuraba, 'Genzai no Keiji Shihō to Heito Supīchi' ['Current criminal justice and hate speech'] (2016) 735 *Hōgaku Seminā* [Legal seminar] 24, at 27–28.

approaches seek to use criminal law as an antidote.[58] But warning that hate speech is criminally regulated should never be the only reason by a person is dissuaded from uttering it. More resources should urgently be invested in investigating actual situations of hate speech and proposing more effective measures to tackle its root causes.

To appropriately remedy the effects of damage done by hate speech, multidimensional approaches that consider both the strengths and weaknesses of criminal law in Japan, and the legal system as a whole, need to be further explored.[59]

V. Conclusion

This chapter has clarified that:

- current measures controlling defamation are limited to expressions targeting specific individuals or organizations and many forms of hate speech are beyond the scope of criminal provisions;
- there have been remarkable developments in theoretical approaches in recent years, but problems need to be addressed regarding the principles of criminal law; and
- criminal law is not powerless in addressing the damage done by hate speech, but it is capable of addressing the problem only partially.

Until recently, the debate on hate speech regulation focused on criminal regulation. Some scholars have taken a view that the scope of punishment for charges related to hate speech should be greatly expanded under law. Others suggest that action regarding hate speech should be left to civil society – that is, they advocate self-regulation. These arguments have gone to opposite extremes.

[58] See Maeda, note 32, at 120; Sangyun Kim, 'Epilogue', in Kim, note 49, at 183–84.

[59] Hirofumi Uchida, a criminal law scholar engaged in a wide range of human rights issues, maintains the need to distinguish between procedures focused on punishment and procedures focused on promotion of understanding in considering human rights legislation. According to Uchida, in the case of punishment-type procedures, the focus of due process is 'avoidance of misjudgment', whereas in the case of those seeking to promote understanding, the focus is on reaching 'mutual understanding' through dialogue between a perpetrator and a victim regarding the human rights violation. Uchida emphasizes that discussion should begin with the actual damage caused and notes that it is important to design of a system that is appropriate for the relief of each instance only once the specific nature of that damage is properly understood. See Hirofumi Uchida, *Motomerareru Jinken Kyūsai Hōsei no Ronten* [Issues relating to the legal institutions required for remedying human rights] (Kaiho Shuppansha, 2006), 58–60. For the Human Rights Vindication Bill, see Chapter 6.

The Hate Speech Elimination Act has offered unique direction when it comes to the use of non-regulatory methods.[60] Although this chapter does not evaluate that Act, what is certain is that if it is to achieve its nominal goal, a multidimensional approach that spans the legal system as a whole, including policies outside of regulation, must increasingly be debated within Japanese law and society.

[60] See Chapter 11.

8

Tort Liability for Hate Speech in Japan

KENSUKE KAJIWARA*

I. Introduction

This chapter will discuss the extent to which those responsible for hate speech in Japan are liable in tort – that is, to what extent Japanese tort law can offer relief to victims of hate speech.

As has been mentioned in other chapters, there is no law in Japan that penalizes hate speech exclusively.[1] In seeking relief and that a wrongdoer be held legally liable for damage done, the only effective approach available to the victim at the present time is to bring a lawsuit requesting compensation.[2] This is because, in Japan, it is the law of tort that is primarily focused on the recovery of damages and thought to play a role in penalizing or sanctioning the perpetrator. Further, as a secondary effect, if many people are aware of the boundaries between legal acts and illegal ones, as clarified by cases, fewer illegal acts may be expected in the future. However, this approach is not a panacea. This chapter will explore both its advantages and its limitations.

Because a basic knowledge of Japan's tort system is indispensable to what follows, the chapter will first summarize that system. Sections III and IV address what sort of tort liability might be imposed on those responsible for hate speech, while section III considers the effectiveness of the lawsuit strategy, which seeks a judgment against the speakers by categorizing some hate speech as 'defamation'. Section IV examines what tortious elements lie in hate speech other than defamation by looking at judicial precedents, and section V concludes by discussing the merits and

* This work was supported by JSPS KAKENHI Grant No. JP18K12630.

1 See Chapter 11.

2 Injunctive relief is another effective approach to prevent future damage: see Chapter 14.

disadvantages of seeking relief for victims of hate speech in the form of monetary compensation.

II. Japan's Tort Law System

A. Overview

Japanese tort law is basically shaped by statute, especially the Civil Code. However, the Civil Code stipulates only the general concepts and basic rules; the complex and various details of the system of tort in Japan have been informed by case law.[3]

The Civil Code lays down 16 articles (arts 709–24) that provide for tort liability. Article 709, which sets out the basic matter provides as follows:

> **Article 709 (Damages in Tort)**
> A person who has intentionally or negligently infringed any right of others, or legally protected interest of others, shall be liable to compensate any damages resulting in consequence.

As a consequence of this provision, satisfaction of the following four requirements is considered necessary to constitute a tort.

(i) The tortfeasor should be at fault (i.e. have acted either with intent or negligently).
(ii) There should have been infringement of the rights or legally protected interests of others.
(iii) A causal link should exist between the tortious act and the loss.
(iv) Loss should have been incurred.

Articles 710 and 711 offer a clue to what comprises 'any right of others, or legally protected interest of others', as set out in article 709.[4] Article 710 indicates that the actor may be liable at a minimum for infringing the 'property rights of others' or 'the body, liberty or reputation of others'. Moreover, article 711 stipulates that a person who has taken the life of another must compensate the damage done to the victim's family. It

[3] See generally Hiroyuki Kihara, *Tort Law in Japan* (Kluwer Law International, 2015); Hiroshi Oda, *Japanese Law*, 3rd ed. (Oxford University Press, 2009), ch. 9.

[4] Article 710 states that '[p]ersons liable for damages under the provisions of the preceding Article must also compensate for damages other than those to property, regardless of whether the body, liberty or reputation of others have been infringed, or property rights of others have been infringed'. In addition, art. 711 provides that '[a] person who has taken the life of another must compensate for damages to the father, mother, spouse and children of the victim, even in cases where the property rights of the same have not been infringed'.

therefore becomes clear from these two provisions that the 'right of others, or legally protected interest of others', includes 'life', 'body', 'liberty', 'reputation', and 'property rights'.

Although the 'right(s) or interest(s)' referred to in the Civil Code in relation to compensation for damage are 'body, liberty, reputation, life and property' only, it is generally understood that the term is not necessarily limited to these concepts, and the role of interpretation is left to the judiciary. The fact that the 'right or interest relating to person or personality' – that is, *jinkakuken* ('personality right') – is deemed to be included in this 'right(s) or interest(s)' is important to what follows.

As case law developed, the personality right has been growing as a comprehensive concept that includes not only life, body, and reputation, but also the right to privacy and the right to publicity, an interest in sunshine, and a freedom from sexual harassment, among other things. The damage done by hate speech is also understood, in a broad sense, to be a violation of the victim's personality right. Nevertheless, the concept is both broad and ambiguous, and to judge whether or not there has been infringement of the rights or legally protected interests of others, it is necessary to closely analyse what right or interest was actually violated in any given case.

The next point to note about the system of tort in Japan is that compensatory damages are the only monetary relief rendered to the victim and that the tortfeasor will not be required to pay punitive damages.[5] Included in the definition of 'compensatory damages' is, as

[5] There is a case involving a claim by the appellant requesting enforcement of a judgment of the Court of the State of California that ordered the defendants to pay compensatory damages and punitive damages. According to the Code of Civil Procedure and the Civil Execution Act, judgments of a foreign court that are contrary to public order and ethical standards are invalid in Japan. The Supreme Court has said that if an institution that appears in the foreign judgment but does not exist in Japan is contrary to the basic principles or basic ideas of the legal order in Japan, that judgment should be regarded as being against public order. According to the court, it is evident that California's system of punitive damages is designed not only to impose punitive sanctions on the culprit, but also to prevent similar acts in the future, in that the culprit is ordered to pay additional damages on top of the damages for the actual loss. This is similar to criminal sanctions such as fines in Japan. In contrast, the Japanese system of damages in tort is not intended to sanction the tortfeasor or to prevent similar acts in the future. It requires assessment of the actual pecuniary loss and that the tortfeasor compensate the victim for this amount, and thus it enables the victim to recover what they lost. Thus the system of punitive damages was regarded as against the basic principles or basic ideas of the system of compensation in tort in Japan. Consequently, the claim for enforcement of the judgment to pay punitive damages was dismissed. See Supreme Court, 2nd Petty Bench, 11 July 1997, 51 Minshū 2773.

a rule, the loss incurred by the plaintiff individually as a victim by reason of the tortious conduct. Pecuniary losses and non-pecuniary losses are all converted to monetary value to contribute to the total compensatory damages ordered.[6] *Pecuniary* losses include lost profits, in addition to the costs that the victim was forced to cover as a result of the tortious act, such as medical expenses and hospital charges. The typical example of *non-pecuniary* losses is loss as a consequence of mental suffering and emotional harm, which may not be readily and strictly objectively given monetary value. Nevertheless, those victims who suffered non-pecuniary losses are able to obtain compensatory damages and hence the calculation of the appropriate amount is left to the discretion of the judge. (In civil suits in Japan, no jury appears at any stage of the litigation.)

In the next subsection, the current status of case law on a few speech-related torts is introduced. The scope of this introduction is limited, because this chapter seeks more specifically to clarify the extent to which tort law can support relief of the damage done by hate speech.

B. *Tortious Speech*

(a) Defamation

Under defamation law, some judicially created doctrines have been established that are somewhat complex compared to other categories of speech tort. While it is clear from article 710 of the Civil Code that tort law protects reputation, what the 'reputation' referenced therein means cannot be clearly deciphered from the provision itself. The Supreme Court of Japan once defined 'reputation' under the Civil Code as 'an objective evaluation that the person receives in society in terms of [their] personal aspects such as moral character, virtue, fame, and credit etc.',[7] – that is, as 'the person's evaluation in society'. The Supreme Court further stated that it does not include the subjective opinion that the person has of their own personal value – namely, their sense of 'honour'.[8] In that sense, honour can be said to have almost the same meaning as 'pride' or 'self-esteem'.

Moreover, the Supreme Court said that 'whether or not the meanings or contents of an article undermine another person's reputation in

[6] See arts 417 and 722(1) of the Civil Code.

[7] Supreme Court, 3rd Petty Bench, 11 June 1986, 40 Minshū 872; Supreme Court, 3rd Petty Bench, 27 May 1997, 51 Minshū 2024.

[8] Supreme Court, 2nd Petty Bench, 18 December 1970, 24 Minshū 2151.

society should be determined according to the ordinary care and reading manner of ordinary readers of the article'.[9]

The distinguishing characteristics of Japan's defamation law with which readers who are not familiar with Japanese laws should be particularly careful are that:

(a) there is no distinction between libel and slander;[10]
(b) truth is not an absolute defence and falsity is not an indispensable element of defamation; and
(c) an opinion can constitute defamation under tort law.

With respect to this final point, while under criminal law the person who expressed an opinion would not be penalized because stating a fact is a prerequisite for defamation,[11] there is no such restriction under tort law, so that even an opinion could bring about tort liability if it is an expression that tends to diminish someone's reputation in society.

In the event that the tort is established, it becomes possible for the victim to receive compensation for damage from the tortfeasor and, here, the primary damage is a moral one.[12] Furthermore, if there are any calculable special damages unique to the particular case that were caused by the tortfeasor's speech, that sum can naturally be included in the amount of compensation. Under Japanese law, however, special damages are not precondition of tort, regardless of whether or not the target of the speech was a public figure or the contents of the speech were of public concern. The compensation in defamation litigation is, for the most part, a sum aiming 'to value the mental harm inflicted on the victim in monetary terms and to make the tortfeasor pay as a means to recover the damage on the honour – [the] personal value of the victim'.[13] The sum is 'determined by considering the entire circumstances including the

[9] Supreme Court, 3rd Petty Bench, 9 September 1997, 51 Minshū 3804. See also Supreme Court, 2nd Petty Bench, 20 July 1956, 10 Minshū 1059; Supreme Court, 3rd Petty Bench, 27 May 1997, 51 Minshū 2009.

[10] There are no special categories such as 'libel per se' and 'slander per se'. Thus it is not automatically determined whether the speech is defamatory, but is judged separately by the courts.

[11] See art. 230(1) of the Penal Code of Japan.

[12] Article 723 of the Civil Code states that '[t]he court may, at the request of the victim, order a person who defamed others to effect appropriate measures to restore the reputation of the victim in lieu of, or in addition to, damages'. The question of what is included in the 'appropriate measures' mentioned here is again left to case law and previous cases indicate that they may include a court order requiring a publisher to post corrections in a newspaper or magazine, or to publish an apology or the fact that they lost in litigation.

[13] Supreme Court, 1st Petty Bench, 6 October 1983, 37 Minshū 1041.

extent of the moral harm inflicted on the victim, sense or feeling of the victim, [the] attitude of the tortfeasor and other undetermined factors'.[14]

Incidentally, in many defamation litigations, the alleged tortfeasor may be the mass media. Moreover, under Japanese law, truth is not a complete defence to a claim of defamation. In such cases, defamation law may therefore come into conflict with article 21 of the Constitution of Japan, which guarantees freedom of expression. The Supreme Court developed the following rules by gradually confining the scope of the speaker's liability, so as to bring defamation law into line with the Constitution.[15]

In a case of defamation committed by alleging a fact:

> [W]here the act of alleging a fact relates to matters of public interest and was conducted solely for the benefit of the public, the said act is deemed not to be illegal if the alleged fact is proven to be true for its essential part. Even where the truthfulness of the alleged fact is not proven, the person's intent or negligence to infringe the reported person's right or interest shall be denied if the person who conducted the act has a reasonable ground to believe the fact to be true.[16]

It has already been noted that, in tort, even expressions stating an opinion could be judged to be defamation. In the case of defamation committed by manifesting an opinion or criticism based on a fact, the Supreme Court ruled that, 'where the act of manifesting the opinion or criticism relates to matters of public interest and was conducted solely for the benefit of the public, if the alleged fact on which the opinion or criticism were based is proven to be true for its essential part', the defendant shall

[14] *Ibid.*

[15] See Shigenori Matsui, 'Freedom of Expression in Japan' (1991) 38 *Handai Hōgaku* [Osaka University law review] 13, at 26–28; Noriko Kitajima, 'The Protection of Reputation in Japan: A Systematic Analysis of Defamation Cases' (2012) 37 *Law & Social Inquiry* 89, at 91–93.

[16] Supreme Court, 3rd Petty Bench, 9 September 1997, 51 Minshū 3804. See also Supreme Court, 1st Petty Bench, 23 June 1966, 20 Minshū 1118. Relatedly, art. 230–2 of the Penal Code stipulates that even a person who defames another by alleging fact will not be punished if three requirements are satisfied: (a) the alleged fact is found to be a matter of public interest; (b) the act is found to have been conducted solely for the benefit of the public; or (c) the accused succeeds in proving the alleged fact to be true. Furthermore, the Supreme Court said that, 'even if there is no proof of the existence of the facts under Paragraph 1 of Article 230–2 of the Penal Code, no crime of defamation was committed because of the absence of mens rea, when the publisher believed mistakenly in the existence of the facts and there was good reason for his mistaken belief on the basis of reliable information and grounds'. See Supreme Court, Grand Bench, 25 June 1969, 23 Keishū 975. Thus it can be considered that the rule defining the scope of legal liability in the criminal defamation law is the same as the civil rule. See Chapter 7 for more details.

not be liable for damages, 'unless the opinion or criticism does not constitute a personal abuse or otherwise go beyond the bounds of an ordinary opinion or criticism'.[17]

In another case, the Supreme Court affirmed the importance of protecting freedom of expression in defamation trials:

> The requirement for holding a person liable for an unlawful act varies between defamation by alleging a fact and defamation by presenting an opinion or comment, and a person who has defamed another party by presenting an opinion or comment shall not be deemed to have committed an unlawful act unless the contents of such opinion or comment, regardless of whether they are valid or reasonable, go so far as to insult another or go beyond the bounds of opinion or comment, because freedom to present an opinion or comment should be considered to be a core of freedom of expression, which is essential to democratic society, and therefore should be carefully protected.[18]

(b) Other Tortious Speeches

In relation to other speech torts, the Supreme Court has not established rules as detailed as those that govern its treatment of defamation law. For example, with respect to public disclosure of private fact, it has done no more than present the following principle:

> [B]y weighing up the legal interest of not publishing the facts against the reasons for publishing them, and when the former can be regarded as superior to the latter, tort is constituted. . . . Therefore, it is necessary to individually and concretely examine the circumstances concerning the following legal interest of not publishing the facts and reasons for publication, and then make a decision after weighing up.[19]

Neither has the Supreme Court yet set out the criteria defining expression that causes mental suffering by violating emotional interests such as pride and self-esteem. Several of its decisions have, however, suggested that a matter in excess of tolerable limits would constitute a tort.[20]

[17] The Supreme Court modified the rule by referring to the rule of defamation committed by alleging a fact. According to the court, if the person who expresses the defamatory opinion or criticism has a reasonable ground to believe the fact alleged as the basis of the opinion or criticism to be true, that person shall not be liable should it be otherwise. See Supreme Court, 3rd Petty Bench, 9 September 1997, 51 Minshū 3804; Supreme Court, 1st Petty Bench, 21 December 1989, 43 Minshū 2252.

[18] Supreme Court, 1st Petty Bench, 15 July 2004, 58 Minshū 1615.

[19] Supreme Court, 2nd Petty Bench, 14 March 2003, 57 Minshū 229. See also Supreme Court, 3rd Petty Bench, 8 February 1994, 48 Minshū 149.

[20] Supreme Court, 2nd Petty Bench, 15 July 2011, 65 Minshū 2362.

Having outlined Japan's system of tort law, the chapter will now move on to examine how likely it is that someone responsible for hate speech will be held liable in tort – and, to this end, the chapter will introduce some specific cases.

III. Tort Liability for Hate Speech: Defamation

A. *Kyoto Korean Elementary School*

From 2009 to 2010, members of *Zainichitokken o yurusanai shimin no kai* ('Group of Citizens Who Do Not Tolerate Privileges for Ethnic Korean Residents in Japan', known as *Zaitokukai*) and others conducted three demonstrations in front of Kyoto Korean Elementary School.[21] In these demonstrations, the following types of slogan were repeated:

(a) 'The land of this school was illegally occupied!' and 'This school is training North Korean spies!'; and
(b) 'Promises can be made only between humans; no promise can be made between humans and Koreans!', 'Kick out riotous Koreans from Japan!', 'Dispose of Koreans in public health centres!', and 'Cockroaches and maggots must go back to the Korean Peninsula!'

The defendants recorded their demonstrations and published the videos on the Internet.

The corporation that operates the school, Kyoto Chōsen Gakuen, lodged a lawsuit against the demonstrators, claiming that these demonstrations injured its own reputation and credit, disrupted the school's educational operations, and violated its right to provide ethnic education. In 2013, Kyoto District Court acknowledged that a tort was established for defamation and obstruction of business (interruption of the plaintiff's educational activities) and ordered the defendants to pay a compensation for damages in the amount in excess of ¥12 million.[22] Although the defendants subsequently filed appeals, both Osaka High Court and the Supreme Court dismissed them, and confirmed the lower court's decision in favour of the plaintiff.[23]

It is noteworthy that, in the decision, only the (a) type of speech was acknowledged as defamation as alleging facts relating to the plaintiff,

[21] See also Chapters 12 and 13.
[22] Kyoto District Court, 7 October 2013, 2208 Hanji 74.
[23] Osaka High Court, 8 July 2014, 2232 Hanji 34; Supreme Court, 3rd Petty Bench, 9 December 2014, unreported.

Kyoto Chōsen Gakuen. The (b) type of speech that could be assessed as typical hate speech addressed to Korean residents in Japan in general was carefully excluded from the judgment of defamation.[24] Junko Kotani, a leading scholar of hate speech law in Japan, has said that '[i]t must be noted, however, that the hate speech in the Kyoto cases was not the kind of hate speech that commonly takes place in society. In the Kyoto cases, a specific school was the direct target of extremely crude racist remarks made in an aggravated manner.'[25] Indeed, while hate speech that targets and defames a specific person (natural or corporate) as was the case here may constitute the tort of defamation, there is almost no chance that a speaker who spreads hate speech targeting Korean residents in general will be liable for defamation.

How is it that the courts do not recognize hate speech directed towards Korean residents in general as defamation? Kyoto District Court found that:

(a) the defendants disliked Korean residents and thought that they should be expelled from Japan, and they conducted demonstrations to share that thought with society;
(b) various slogans that liken Korean residents to pigs and worms, or which call for their expulsion from Japan, can be judged to be racist speech; and
(c) the acts of the defendant therefore constituted a violation of the International Convention on the Elimination of All Forms of Racial Discrimination (ICERD).

While the court did not opine that such speech itself constitutes another tort other than defamation, it determined that these three points justified increasing the amount of the damages awarded. The court explained its unusual view that it was bound by the ICERD to increase damages for acts of racial discrimination.

Osaka High Court, the court at second instance, evaluated the defendants' hate speech directed at Korean residents as malicious enough to encourage and amplify prejudice and discrimination generally, and it stated that the mental damage suffered by the victims because of irrational racially discriminatory conduct must have been especially serious. However, this court disagreed with the lower court's view that

[24] See Shigenori Matsui, 'The Challenge to Multiculturalism: Hate Speech Ban in Japan' (2016) 49 *UBC L. Rev.* 427, at 451.

[25] Junko Kotani, 'Proceed with Caution: Hate Speech Regulation in Japan' (2018) 45 *Hastings Const. L.Q.* 603, at 613.

the defendants' demonstrations were in violation of the ICERD. Moreover, it also denied the view that acts of racial discrimination should directly increase the amount of damages, since the courts would be bound by the ICERD. It should be noted that, in the High Court, the racially discriminatory nature of the speech was treated only as a factor in assessing the malignancy of the conduct and seriousness of damage under Article 709.

In conclusion, both decisions held that even though the defendants' speech was racist in tone, it did not necessarily establish defamation. Nevertheless, this case is currently understood to be the leading hate speech case in Japan.[26] The reason is the remarkable size of the damages that the courts awarded, emphasizing that some of the defendants' statements in this case were racially discriminatory.

B. *Hoshusokuhō*

In recent years in Japan, there have been occasions on which Korean residents have been labelled 'covert operatives', 'spies', or 'criminals' (or potential criminals), among other things, solely on the basis of their Korean heritage. These slurs censuring Korean residents based on nothing other than their ethnicity are a kind of hate speech. The question is: if such speech were to be directed at a particular Korean resident, would the person responsible for the speech become liable in tort for defamation, having deteriorated their victim's social reputation by publishing a false statement of fact?

One case considered just such a question: whether baselessly characterizing Lee Shinhae, a Korean writer residing in Japan, as a 'Korean operative', a 'North Korean spy', a 'comrade of criminals', and an 'illegal immigrant', among other things, would constitute defamation. The blog that was sued, Hoshusokuhō, is a curation service site that gathers various information available on the Internet[27] and summarizes it for its users. The substance is primarily commentary on politics, the economy, and topics about China and South Korea viewed through the lenses of conservatism, ethnocentrism, and xenophobia, curated from among the large, disorganized mass of information and comments posted on a forum then named 2channel (now 5channel). Since the forum is the

[26] See Matsui, note 24, at 451; Koji Higashikawa, 'Japan's Hate Speech Law: Translation of the Osaka City Ordinance and the National Act to Curb Hate Speech in Japan' (2017) 19 *Asian-Pacific L. & Pol'y J.* 1, at 3.

[27] See Chapter 18.

largest in Japan and a variety of users posting information to it freely and anonymously, it perpetuates inaccurate information and misinformation. Because Hoshusokuhō further selects the posts and skews them to suit its own standards, the contents of the blog are heavily biased and much of it can be characterized as hate speech, the comments on the plaintiff among them.

Osaka District Court nevertheless held that the comments targeting Lee were part of the blog's broader agenda of conservative political thought, which included a lot of content severely and scurrilously criticizing China, South Korea, and North Korea. The court argued that the ordinary reader would not understand these expressions to be true such that they would correspond to defamation.[28] The court held that these were simply bombastic rhetoric aiming to denigrate her and that, while they might be assessed as unacceptable insult, they would not diminish her reputation in society. Neither the High Court nor the Supreme Court overturned this judgment on appeal.[29]

Incidentally, many comments on the defendant's blog criticized, denigrated, and belittled the plaintiff, and the plaintiff argued that the defendant should also be held liable for torts other than defamation. The chapter looks at this argument later.

C. *Group Defamation*

If we look at the few cases establishing hate speech precedent, the subjects are all individual natural persons or legal entity. Utterances that demonstrate contempt for a particular person, stir up hate, and call for that person's expulsion from Japanese society simply because they are a member of a certain group can, of course, be assessed as a type of

[28] Osaka District Court, 16 November 2017, 2372 Hanji 59. The plaintiff in this case claimed that some comments that the defendant placed on an Internet site, other than those expressions mentioned in the text, were also injurious to her reputation. These comments included, in particular, that her remarks in the past constituted intimidations, threats, or defending crimes and that she was intentionally inciting critics for the purpose of getting work as a reporter. The court found that these comments attacked her personality and therefore constituted defamation. The High Court and the Supreme Court upheld this judgment. See note 29.

While these comments certainly constitute defamation, in my view, they cannot be characterized as hate speech. Therefore they are not covered in detail in this chapter dealing with tort liability for hate speech.

[29] Osaka High Court, 19 June 2017, available at www.courts.go.jp/app/files/hanrei_jp/878/086878_hanrei.pdf [accessed 3 June 2019]; Supreme Court, 3rd Petty Bench, 11 December 2018, unreported.

hate speech. However, hate speech is more typically expression that defames and degrades the group itself without specifying a target, advocating the elimination of *all* members of the group, for example abusing Korean residents as a whole using foul language, or claiming that they are not human (and hence are not to be treated as human) by likening them to insects, or to advocating their expulsion from Japan en masse. In this case, is there any hope of relief in tort law?

There have already been some cases that have sought to establish liability for discriminatory speech not directed at any particular individual or entity. One such example is the case in which Shintaro Ishihara, governor of Tokyo at the time and excusing himself by alleging that he was basing his thinking on the ideas of Takafumi Matsui,[30] said that 'the worst, most harmful thing that civilization has brought to us can be said to be a beldam [an old woman]', and that 'for a woman to stay alive after losing reproductive capability is wasteful and a sin'. Women who had seen his comments filed an action for defamation.[31] Tokyo District Court rejected the plaintiffs' claim, finding that Ishihara's speech was an expression of his personal opinion directed to a general and unorganized group

[30] Takafumi Matsui is a Japanese scientist specializing in planetary science and he was a professor at the University of Tokyo at that time. He said later that the purport of his ideas was completely different from Ishihara's statement.

[31] As another example, there occurred a litigation in which plaintiffs sought compensation for damage based on the argument that they had been defamed and that their right not to be discriminated against as the racial minority had been violated by publication of *Ainushi Shiryōshū* ('History of the Ainu, data compilation') in 1980. The Ainu are the indigenous people in Hokkaido and a minority with their own culture. The publication consisted of the writing of a doctor, first published in 1896, gathering medical information on the Ainu and of the records made by police in 1916, compiling the medical history and current health conditions of the Ainu people, which records bore the actual names of the people concerned. The publication included descriptions of the Ainu people as an inferior race destined to die out in the future. The plaintiffs, who are Ainu, brought an action against the publisher in 1998. Sapporo District Court did not approve defamation, stating that the plaintiffs' reputation was not degraded by the publication because their names were not included among the actual names of the Ainu people cited nor was there any reference to the plaintiffs in the publication. It also judged that, even assuming that discriminatory contents were included in the publication, the plaintiffs' 'right not to be discriminated against as a racial minority' was not violated to such an extent as requiring a relief. It therefore reasoned that the direct victims of the discrimination were the persons whose names were cited in the publication, or the Ainu people as a whole, and the right of the plaintiffs was not damaged directly. The court stated that it did not find any justification for special treatment, such as that the plaintiffs' loss as a result of the publication was significant, or that there was the close relationship between the plaintiffs and the direct victims. See Sapporo District Court, 27 June 2002, available at www.courts.go.jp/app/files/hanrei_jp/655/008655_hanrei.pdf [accessed 3 June 2019].

of people, such as 'women who have lost reproductive capability' or 'women', and could not be recognized as directed at each individual member of that group (including the plaintiffs), such that it did nothing to diminish the reputation of each individual plaintiff.[32]

The attitude of the Japanese courts to group defamation is summarized by this case: each member of a defamed group is denied relief because it is said that the act complained of seldom has caused them no individual personal harm. In Japan, as a rule, group defamation has not been recognized as a tort.[33] As a matter of exception, as has been the case in the United States,[34] the only situation in which a group member has successfully brought a cause of action under defamation law for speech that attacks a group is when the defamatory statement can be understood to implicate the plaintiff individually because of the particular nature of the case or because the group is somehow limited.[35]

Consequently, in the case of group defamation where the group is large and the statement cites no specific individuals, it is nearly unthinkable

[32] Tokyo District Court, 24 February 2005, 1186 Hanta 175.

[33] Even under the defamation law in the United States, a plaintiff cannot prevail unless they can prove that 'a reasonable person' could perceive the defendant's statement to be 'of and concerning' the plaintiff. See The Restatement (Second) of Torts §§558 and 564; *New York Times Co.* v. *Sullivan*, 376 U.S. 254, 288 (1964); Joseph H. King, Jr., 'Reference to the Plaintiff Requirement in Defamatory Statement Directed at a Group' (2000) 35 *Wake Forest L. Rev.* 343; Robert D. Sack, *Sack on Defamation: Libel, Slander, and Related Problems*, 3rd ed. (Practicing Law Institute, 2008), §2.9. In particular, it has been thought that it is difficult to meet this requirement in the case of group defamation based on ethnicity or race. See W. Page Keeton (ed.), *Prosser and Keeton on Torts*, 5th ed. (West, 1984), at 784; Michael J. Polelle, 'Racial and Ethnic Group Defamation: A Speech-Friendly Proposal' (2003) 23 *B.C. Third World L.J.* 213, at 243–44; Nat Stern, 'The Certainty Principle as Justification for the Group Defamation Rule' (2008) 40 *Ariz. St. L.J.* 951, at 986–88.

[34] Restatement (Second) of Torts §564A.

[35] As for the latter, Japanese law does not limit the size of the group as strictly as does the US law. In a famous television news programme, information was reported to the effect that the vegetables grown in a certain city (Tokorozawa City, Saitama Prefecture, with a size of about 72 square kilometres) contain toxic dioxin, along with comments that eating the vegetables produced from the region 'is not safe' and that 'there is a risk of causing a health hazard'. Some 376 vegetable farmers in the city sued the broadcasting station for defamation. Saitama District Court held that the broadcast injured the reputation of the plaintiffs. The court explained that it was obvious that the programme damaged public trust in the safety of vegetables grown in Tokorozawa City and diminished the reputation of 'farmers who produce various vegetables within Tokorozawa City'. However, the court rejected the plaintiffs' claim for compensation for damages, because it concluded that the report was in the public interest, broadcast solely for that purpose, and the facts reported were true in large part. See Saitama District Court, 15 May 2001, 1063 Hanta 175.

that the Japanese courts will find the two requirements of causation and loss to be satisfied. In the case of Korean residents in Japan, an investigation by the Ministry of Justice in June 2019 into the number of people with South Korean and North Korean nationality staying in Japan on a mid- to long-term basis found 480,000 (the number exceeds 310,000 even if limited to those with special permanent resident status), and the figure would be even larger if it were to include those who have obtained Japanese citizenship and their descendants.[36]

D. *Solely for the Benefit of the Public*

We now move the focal point of the argument to the relationship between defamation law and hate speech directed to a particular individual or entity. The first challenge is whether the reasonable listener would devalue of the plaintiff as a result of the speech. As we saw earlier in the chapter, the more aggressive the speech is, the more difficult it is to recognize the speech as harming the reputation of plaintiff, because the content of the speech will be perceived to be untrue and/or excessively exaggerated criticism, and not worth taking seriously.[37]

The next challenge, once the hate speech is determined to be defamatory, is whether the speaker is exempted from liability for the reasons already explored. If the speaker is to escape liability, they must persuade the court that:

- the expression relates to matters of public interest;
- it was expressed solely for the benefit of the public; and
- that the content of the expression was true (or there was a reasonable ground to mistakenly believe it to be true).

In many hate speech cases, satisfaction of the second condition – namely, the public benefit requirement – would be denied. Because those who are loudly disseminating hate speech targeting foreigners and Korean residents are generally individuals and groups who have no intention of hiding the hate they seek to amplify, it is easy to determine that the purpose of the speech is indeed to propagate hate against minorities. In other words, it is difficult to understand the conduct as executed solely for the benefit of the public.

[36] Available at www.e-stat.go.jp/stat-search/files?page=1&layout=datalist&toukei=00250012&tstat=000001018034&cycle=1&year=20190&month=12040606&tclass1=000001060399 [accessed 29 January 2020].

[37] See Catherine J. Ross, 'Incredible Lies' (2018) 89 *U. Colo. L. Rev.* 377, at 402.

In *Kyoto Korean Elementary School*, Kyoto District Court found that the defendants hated Korean residents and thought that they should be expelled from Japan, and had conducted demonstrations to amplify that thought among society. Because the purpose of the defendants' demonstrations was not deemed to be 'solely for the benefit of the public', the defendants were not exempted from liability for defamation.

In cases of fierce hate speech expressing an opinion based on hatred, if the courts find the statement to be defamatory, the speaker will not be exempted from liability. Because, such speech would generally not be judged a legitimate criticism. As mentioned above, in the case of defamation committed by manifesting an opinion, the speaker will be held liable if the expression is deemed to be a personal abuse or goes beyond the boundaries of an ordinary criticism.[38]

IV. Tort Liability for Hate Speech: Other Torts

We have seen thus far that there are a few cases in which hate speech constitutes defamation because it is damaging to the reputation of a particular victim and hence the speaker will owe liability in tort. To explore the ways in which victims of hate speech can access relief in tort, it is necessary to analyse the rights and interests other than reputation that are damaged by hate speech, and to explore the possibility of finding the speaker liable in other torts.

A. Insult

There are a handful of precedents that have recognized hate speech directed at an individual as insult – a tort that damages the pride and self-esteem of the victim.

Lee Shinhae instituted a lawsuit for compensation for damages separately from *Hoshusokuhō*, claiming that the speech of Makoto Sakurai (the former chair of Zaitokukai) and his followers constitutes more than one tort. They had questioned Lee's capacity as a journalist, and had made fun of and insulted her figure, both using online streaming services and social media, and during the demonstrations in the bustling streets. Osaka District Court held that defendants' conduct in persistently showing

[38] Thus determination of whether the fierce hate expressed in the opinion can be said to diminish the plaintiff's reputation, i.e. whether the expression is defamatory, would be decisive in the outcome of the case.

contempt for Lee, calling her a 'Korean beldam', or likening her body to Korean foods and vegetables, was insulting conduct beyond socially acceptable limits, which injured Lee's self-esteem and illegally violated her 'personality right'.[39]

However, the court recognized that the defendants had repeated in a series of speeches the same kind of remarks to express their hatred of Koreans, such as 'Koreans must get out of Japan!', that by itself was not recognized in tort. The court nonetheless acknowledged that Zaitokukai's members had been conducting activities aiming to encourage and amplify discrimination against Korean residents, based on their view that these Koreans should be excluded from Japanese society. The court stated that the defendants' insulting remarks in this case could also be assessed as having been made based on an intention that ran counter to the spirit of the ICERD. Further, the court proposed that the viciousness of any such intention will increase the amount of compensation awarded.

Similarly, in *Hoshusokuhō*, the question of whether some expressions in the blog describing plaintiff Lee as 'Ttongsul writer' and 'Hwabyeong writer' corresponded to insult and constituted a tort was at issue. *Ttongsul* is liquor said to be drunk in the Korean Peninsula and said to be made from human excrement. This word is sometimes used to insult Koreans. *Hwabyeong* means psychiatric disorder and frenzy, and is also a word regularly used to insult Koreans. In the blog, in addition to these peculiar words that intentionally diminish Koreans, there were expressions that were wrongfully derogatory to the plaintiff, such as 'cockroach' and 'parasite'. A series of these remarks can be considered a kind of hate speech. Osaka District Court concluded that these expressions considerably damaged Lee's pride and self-esteem, and were insults that exceeded socially acceptable limits, piled one after the other over a long period of time, and hence the speaker could not escape tort liability.

As is evident in these judgments, it is highly likely that hate speech can constitute the tort of insult. However, I might add that, as far as I could investigate, the Japanese courts have recognized liability in insult only with respect to speech that directly targets an individual plaintiff; I could find no case in which compensation was ordered for speech that was directed to a group.

[39] Osaka District Court, 27 September 2016, available at www.courts.go.jp/app/files/hanrei_jp/441/086441_hanrei.pdf [accessed 3 June 2019].

B. Infringement of the Right to Live in Peace and Quiet

Might hate speech not directed at a particular person (natural or corporate) that does not fall under with defamation or insult constitute any other tort?

Jeremy Waldron has argued that, as a harm done by hate speech, members of the victim groups come to be diminished unfairly in society and that the cumulative effect is to deny them equal treatment as members of that society.[40] Even in Japan, there are scholars who agree with this view.[41]

Tokyo District Court has once expressed a view that the interests to be protected in tort include the right to lead a peaceful life.[42] Nevertheless, the court dismissed the plaintiffs' claim in this case that the defendant's speech had violated this interest because it found a lack of causation. Under tort law, no relief will be given to victims unless it is proven that a loss in the interest was in fact caused directly by the speech. Therefore, even if the victim group becomes unable to lead a tranquil life as a consequence of the hate speech, it is very difficult to prove that any particular instance of hate speech violates this interest because the harm tends accumulate gradually over time and with many instances of such speech.[43]

Of course, it is easily imaginable that an individual belonging to a group may become unable to live in peace and quiet as a consequence of mental distress caused by hate speech directed at the group. Inner calm is likely be included in the interests to be protected by tort law. Under tort law of Japan, however, a damage of no more than an offensive, unpleasant, or uneasy feeling would not give rise to a liability in tort. Even though Japanese law would not require the outrageousness of the content of the speech and emotional damage at the level required to prove the tort of intentional infliction of emotional distress in the United States,[44] the plaintiff needs to convince the judge of the intolerable offensiveness of the speech and the causal relationship between that speech and the distress – and neither of those things is easy.

[40] Jeremy Waldron, *The Harm in Hate Speech* (Harvard University Press, 2012), 5.

[41] Kim Sangyun, 'Heito Supīchi Kisei no Igi to Tokushusei' ['The significance and unique characteristics of hate speech regulation'], in Kim Sangyun (ed.), *Heito Supīchi no Hōteki Kenkyū* [A legal study of hate speech] (Horitsu Bunkasha, 2014), 155.

[42] Tokyo District Court, 24 February 2005, 1186 Hanta 175. The court of second instance dismissed the appeal: Tokyo High Court, 28 September 2005, unreported.

[43] See Waldron, note 40, at 4.

[44] The Restatement (Third) of Torts: Liability for Physical and Emotional Harm, §46.

C. *Racial Discrimination*

What, then, of the fact that the content of a speech is racially discriminatory? Does that help to establish any independent tort? Racially discriminatory conduct such as refusing someone the use of facilities or a service on the basis of their race or nationality will constitute a tort, being assessed as infringing on the victim's reputation or personality right.[45] The question here is whether racial discrimination *by itself* might come to be recognized as a new, independent tort.

The judgment of Osaka District Court in *Hoshusokuhō* offered an affirmative answer to this question. It found that, because the blog referred to the plaintiff by using common slurs such as 'Ttongsul' and 'Hwabyeong', and it included aggressive expressions aiming to provoke the target's exclusion from Japan such as 'Kick them out of Japan!', the blog included the type of content that can be characterized as racial discrimination such that it violates several laws, including the Constitution of Japan, the Hate Speech Elimination Act, and the ICERD.[46] The court considered racial discrimination to be a type of infringement of the plaintiff's personality right, like defamation and insult. This positioning of racial discrimination as an independent tort is, however, remarkable and is found in no other judgments.[47] By contrast, Osaka High Court, the court of second instance, while acknowledging that such expression was racial discrimination, rejected the idea that it could be an independent tort. The High Court held that while the fact of racial discrimination will establish the severity of insult and that content corresponding to racial discrimination will heighten the severity of insult or defamation, it refused to add 'racial discrimination' or 'racist speech' to the tort categories already existing.[48]

It is very unlikely that Japanese courts will recognize racist speech or racial discrimination as a separate and independent category of tort in the

[45] See Shizuoka District Court, Hamamatsu Branch, 12 October 1999, 1045 Hanta 216; Sapporo District Court, 11 November 2002, 1150 Hanta 185.

[46] Specifically, the following provisions were mentioned: (a) art. 14 of the Constitution of Japan (guaranteeing equality under the law); (b) arts 1 of the Hate Speech Elimination Act (outlining the purpose of the law) and 2 (defining impermissible 'unfair discriminatory speech and behaviour'); and (c) arts 1(1) ICERD (the definition of racial discrimination), 2(1) (the obligation of State parties to eliminate discrimination and promote understanding), and 6 (the obligation of State parties to provide effective protection and remedies against acts of racial discrimination).

[47] See note 28.

[48] See note 29.

near future and render relief for it. Assuming that some other tort is established, the severity of hate speech as racial discrimination will remain only a factor increasing the amount of compensation awarded.

V. Conclusion

When hate speech targets a particular individual or entity, the victim may win compensation for damages in defamation or insult. Those responsible for more typical hate speech, which has no individually identifiable target, are less likely – if not wholly unlikely – to be found liable in tort.[49]

Incidentally, the remedy of monetary compensation available in tort law may not be exactly what victims are hoping for. It is conceivable that victims may not particularly want money; rather, they may be hoping for public acknowledgement that hate speech is unlawful, for the establishment of new criminal regulations under which those responsible will be penalized and forced to reflect on their conduct, and – above all – the elimination of hate speech in the future.

If we focus on the last point, it should be recalled that one function of tort law is to prevent and reduce wrongdoings. As mentioned at the outset of this chapter, if tortfeasors are ordered to pay compensation for damages, such orders may be expected to have an effect restraining hate speech in the future.[50]

Moreover, there may be unique merit in pursuing relief in tort for damage done by hate speech. Under the Japanese criminal law system, the judgment of whether or not to prosecute a suspect is monopolized by the prosecution, which prosecutes only when it is certain to obtain a conviction. Therefore, even if a law to penalize hate speech were to be enacted, whether a court will be able to pass judgment on the illegality of hate speech will depend on the prosecution first judging the case worthy

[49] See Keizo Yamamoto, 'Sabetsu Hyōgen, Zōo Hyōgen no Kinshi to Minji Kyūsai no Kanōsei' ['The prohibition of hate speech and civil remedies'] (2013) 24 *Kokusai Jinken* [Human rights international] 77, 78–79; Junko Kotani, 'A Comment on the Hate Speech Regulation in Japan after the Enactment of the Hate Speech Elimination Act of 2016' (2017) 21 *Hōsei Kenkyu* [Shizuoka University journal of law and politics] 1, 7; Kotani, note 25, at 613 and 618.

[50] The Supreme Court admitted that sanctions ordering the tortfeasor to pay compensation may have a preventative effect on similar acts in the future. However, the court surmised that this is a merely reflective or secondary effect of imposing on the tortfeasor the duty to compensate their victim for the damage done. See Supreme Court, 2nd Petty Bench, 11 July 1997, 51 Minshū 2773.

of pursuit. In contrast, an individual can exercise the choice to bring a civil lawsuit for compensation, and they can ask a court to assess the hate speech at their own initiative.

This is perhaps the key merit of seeking relief in tort for hate speech in Japan.[51]

[51] See Kensuke Kajiwara, 'Heito Supīchi ni taisuru Minji Kyūsai to Kenpō' ['Civil remedies for victims of hate speech and constitutional law'] (2016) 736 *Hōgaku Semina* [Legal seminar] 30; Masahiro Sogabe, 'Jinken Soshō ni okeru Minji Soshō no Igi' ['The significance of civil suits in human rights litigation'], (2016) 67 *Jiyū to Seigi* [The liberty and justice] 13, at 16–17.

9

The Frameworks of the Hate Speech Local Ordinances

Efforts and Challenges of Local Governments in Japan

HIDEKI NAKAMURA

I. Introduction

In this chapter, I will be focusing on the responses of the Japanese local governments to the issue of hate speech. First, I will briefly discuss the system of local autonomy in Japan and the right to enact local ordinances; then, I will outline the past efforts of the local governments to tackle discrimination and hate speech; finally, I will briefly touch upon what kind of challenges the local governments face when attempting to regulate hate speech. The debate over the pros and cons of regulation itself will be left to other chapters,[1] leaving this chapter free to focus on issues specific to the local governments.

II. The System of Local Autonomy in Japan

A. History

The Constitution of the Empire of Japan enacted in 1889 had no provisions on local autonomy or the local governments. This was because the framers of the Constitution wanted to centralize power and thought that matters of local governance should be determined by the laws of the state. However, as is also evident from the fact that the local autonomy system was established at the same time as the Constitution, the introduction of the local autonomy system was planned right from the beginning of the modernization of Japan, and therefore it is not the case that the policy-makers at the time intended to downplay the role of local autonomy.

[1] See Chapters 1, 7, and 8.

In 1888, the municipal government, together with the town and village system, and in 1890, the prefectural government, together with the county system, were established in law. In this system, however, the governors of the prefectures were officials of the national government and the prefectural assembly members were not directly elected by the residents, but by means of a form of indirect election. Moreover, the municipalities were placed under the robust supervision of the prefectural governors and the Minister of the Interior.[2] Thus, under the Constitution of the Empire of Japan, the local systems were not worthy of the label 'autonomous, being wholly subject to the extensive and watchful supervision of the national government.[3]

After World War II, under the rule of General Headquarters (GHQ), a radical reform of the local autonomy system took place; on 3 May 1947, the Constitution of Japan and the Local Autonomy Act were simultaneously brought into force. The Constitution of Japan, unlike the Constitution of the Empire of Japan, established an independent chapter entitled 'Local self-government' in which the following four articles on basic matters were stipulated:

Article 2. Regulations concerning organization and operations of local public entities shall be fixed by law in accordance with the principle of local autonomy.

Article 93. (1) The local public entities shall establish assemblies as their deliberative organs, in accordance with law.

(2) The chief executive officers of local public entities, the members of their assemblies, and such other local officials as may be determined by law shall be elected by direct popular vote within their several communities.

Article 94. Local public entities shall have the right to manage their property, affairs and administration and to enact their own regulations within law.

[2] See Takeshi Kobayashi and Yoan Tonaki, *Kenpō to Chihō Jichi* [Constitution and local autonomy] (Horitsu Bunkasha, 2007), 15–16.

[3] See Yoriaki Narita, 'Chihō Jichi Sōron' ['General theories of local autonomy'], in Ichiro Osukawa *et al.* (eds.), *Gendai Gyōseihō Taikei 8 Chihō Jichi* [Modern administrative law 8: local autonomy] (Yuhikaku, 1984), 18. In 1925, following the adoption of universal suffrage in the lower house elections, universal suffrage was also implemented in the municipalities and prefectures. In addition, in the 1929 revision of the system, efforts were made to expand and reinforce the authority of the municipalities and prefectures. However, during the time of the Asia–Pacific War, it was the system of central government oversight that came to be strengthened.

Article 95. A special law, applicable only to one local public entities, cannot be enacted by the Diet without the consent of the majority of the voters of the local public entity concerned, obtained in accordance with law.

During GHQ's drafting of the Constitution, local governments were defined as 'communities' and local assemblies were defined as 'legislative assemblies', while the right to frame their own 'charters', which could be termed the 'constitutions of the local governments', was also guaranteed. Yet the principle of federal, decentralized, US-style local autonomy became ambiguous in translation at the hands of Japanese bureaucrats and in the process of negotiations with GHQ.[4] As a result, in the Constitution of Japan, communities are defined as *chihō kōkyō dantai* ('local public entities'), while the legislative assemblies became 'assemblies as their deliberative organs', and 'the right to frame their own charters' became 'the right to enact their own regulations'.

Article 92 of the Constitution of Japan is a general provision confirming that local autonomy is an essential element of an administrative body, while providing that matters concerning local autonomy should be decided by national law and that the basic precept of the principle of local autonomy restricts even the legislative power of the Diet. In response to this, the Local Autonomy Act was enacted as a comprehensive law on local autonomy. Under this law, the democratic and self-rule aspects of the local governments were reinforced by means of strengthening the power of the local assembly, reorganizing and reducing oversight by the national government, changing the status of the prefectural governor, previously an official of the national government, to that of local government official, and introducing a system under which local citizens could directly petition their local government. Meanwhile, many of the national affairs that had formerly been under the jurisdiction of the prefectural governor as an official of the national government were maintained as they were and the *kikan inin jimu* ('delegated functions') entrusted to the chief executive of the local government, as a body of the national government,[5] came to comprise the majority of the administrative affairs of the local governments.

[4] See Miyoko Tsujimura and Hajime Yamamoto (eds.), *Gaisetsu Kenpō Konmentāru* [A summarized commentary on the Constitution] (Shinzansha, 2018), 412–13.

[5] In this system, the chief executive of the local government implemented and managed affairs legally under the jurisdiction of central government ministers and agencies, in effect acting as a local branch of the national government. It has been said that this formed the core of Japan's centralized administrative system. However, it had long been pointed out that not only did this make it unclear exactly who was responsible for dealing with these

The Local Autonomy Act was revised on several occasions. In the 1990s, deregulation and decentralization became the slogan of administrative reform, and in 1999, the Local Autonomy Act underwent fundamental revision. The objective of its amendment was to increase the autonomy and self-rule aspects of the local governments by revising the system of centralized governance. The reform saw delegated functions completely abolished, and administrative affairs were classed into two groups – namely, 'local autonomy functions' and 'statutory entrusted functions'. The local governments were given actual responsibility for both. These functions therefore came to be regulated through the ordinances of the local assemblies and this phase of amendment came to be known as the First Decentralization Reform. Even after this reform, there remained a large number of national laws and regulations that excessively constrained local government. From 2011, the Second Decentralization Reform (more properly, multiple reforms) was implemented under the slogan 'decentralization of legislative authority' to expand the authority to enact ordinances. Yet even this reform did not allow the local governments to 'overwrite' national laws through an ordinance[6] or to enact ordinances contrary to the purpose of the national laws and regulations. Thus the local governments have not yet attained legislative power on a par with the national government.[7]

B. *The Scope and Limits of the Authority to Enact Local Ordinances*

Unlike the United States and other countries, Japan is not a federal state, and there are unique problems concerning the scope of and limits to the local governments' authority to enact ordinances. Needless to say, it is impossible to create local ordinances that violate the Constitution of Japan (see art. 98), while article 94 of the Constitution permits local governments to enact ordinances only 'within law'. In line with this, article 14(1) of the Local Autonomy Act provides for the enactment of

matters, but also it treated local governments as subordinate administrative agencies of the central government. See Council of Local Authorities for International Relations, *Local Government in Japan 2016*, at 14–15, available at www.clair.or.jp/j/forum/pub/docs/jichi-en_1.pdf [accessed 31 March 2019].

6 The 'overwrite' mentioned here is a means of establishing a clause in general laws, such as the Local Autonomy Act, permitting the standards specified by the national government in its laws and regulations to be strengthened, eased, or supplemented by means of a local ordinance.

7 See Tsujimura & Yamamoto, note 4, at 414.

ordinances to the extent that they do not violate national laws and regulations, Cabinet orders, or ministerial ordinances. Consequently, inconsistencies between national laws or regulations and local ordinances can pose a problem. We can assume two things:

- if there are national laws and regulations that govern a certain matter, local ordinances might conflict with them; and
- where the implicit intention of the Diet is for a certain matter not to be governed by laws and regulations, enacting ordinances might conflict with that intention.[8]

The former situation provoked fierce discussion in Japan, reflecting the severity of the pollution problem in the 1960s, when it was unclear whether or not it was possible to set emission standards in an ordinance that were stricter than those set by the national laws (a so-called top-up ordinance). Moreover, local governments setting emission standards for matters that were not regulated at the national level was also the subject of controversy (so-called sidestep ordinances).

The leading criteria on this point emerged from a judgment of the Supreme Court in *Tokushima City Public Safety Ordinance*.[9] According to this ruling, 'whether the ordinance is in violation of national laws does not involve merely looking at their subject matter and prescribed wording, but also necessitates a comparison of the intent, purpose, content and effect of each, and must be decided based on whether a conflict exists'. The court added the following.

(1) Even in the absence of explicit provisions in the national laws and regulations, if the Diet desired that such matters should not be regulated, any ordinance that attempts to regulate them is in violation of those laws and regulations.
(2) Even when national laws and regulations overlap with local ordinances on specific matters:
    (i) where their objectives differ and, moreover, the purpose and effect of the laws and regulations are not hindered in any way

[8] Traditionally, it was considered impossible to enact an ordinance that conflicted with the national laws and regulations. This is called 'pre-emption' under law. The relationship between the laws or regulations and ordinances in Japan differs from the relationship between federal laws and state laws or local government ordinances in the United States, but a similar framework of thinking has also be seen: see *Gade* v. *National Solid Wastes Management Association*, 505 U.S. 88, 98 (1992).

[9] Supreme Court, Grand Bench, 10 September 1975, 29 Keishū 489.

through the application of the ordinance, no conflict exists between the two; and

(ii) even though their objectives are the same, no conflict exists between the two when the national law was not intended to enforce uniform regulations throughout the country.

For the most part, this criteria is the accepted opinion both in theory and in practice, as judicial precedent.

Looking beyond the issue of restrictions on economic freedoms, such as pollution control and land use, to the area in which ordinances impose restrictions on personal freedoms, judicial rulings generally deem ordinances regulating public protests and meetings (demonstrations) and harmful publications to be constitutional.[10] There is, however, strong criticism that insufficient consideration is being given to the nature of the restricted rights. Given that the Supreme Court has taken an impassive attitude towards the protection of personal freedoms and that the ability to formulate ordinances differs among the local governments, it has to be said that there appear to be grounds for such concern. However, when a new problem requiring legal action arises, it may be sufficient for the local governments, which are more familiar with the situation specific to the region, to take precedence over national government in recognizing and analysing the problem. Therefore, even in cases in which it is ultimately preferable for control to be enforced through national laws and regulations, ordinances that roll out advanced and trial strategies should not be ruled out.[11] In particular, examining the legal situation after the decentralization reforms, the trend towards broadening the subject matter of ordinances should be applauded.

In relation to the theme of this chapter, the following two points should also be noted. First, to guarantee the effectiveness of the ordinance or to secure performance of the obligation imposed under the ordinance, the tools that the local government has at its disposal include administrative guidance, public disclosure of a lack of compliance, and punishments restricted to 'imprisonment with or without work for two years or less, a fine of not more than 1 million yen, penal detention, a petty fine or confiscation' and 'a civil fine of not more than 50,000 yen' (art. 14(3) of

[10] See Supreme Court, 3rd Petty Bench, 18 September 2007, 61 Keishū 601; Supreme Court, 3rd Petty Bench, 19 September 1989, 43 Keishū 785.

[11] See Narufumi Kadomatsu, 'Jichi Rippō ni yoru Tochi Riyō Kisei no Sai Kentō' ['A reconsideration of land use regulation pursuant to local legislation'], in Sumitaka Harada (ed.), *Nihon no Toshihō II* [Urban law in Japan II] (University of Tokyo Press, 2001), 326.

the Local Autonomy Act). These measures can be resorted to in instances of hate speech. Moreover, since it is not possible to establish a wholly independent administrative committee by passing an ordinance (art. 138–4 of the Local Autonomy Act), when attempting to set up a committee to examine or recognize hate speech, that committee necessarily becomes an affiliate organization of an executive agency (the chief executive officer), and therefore falls short of independence and neutrality.

III. The Local Government's Approach to Hate Speech

A. *An Overview*

Upholding the values guaranteed by the Constitution is an inherent obligation of all local governments. In addition, Articles 2(1)(a) and (c) and 4(c) of the International Convention on the Elimination of all Forms of Racial Discrimination (ICERD) impose certain responsibilities on the local governments alongside the national government of the Contracting Parties, and local public entities are required to make proactive efforts to eliminate discrimination.[12] In other words, elimination of discrimination in a broad sense is one of the administrative affairs in a local government's region prescribed in article 2(2) of the Local Autonomy Act.[13]

Moreover, article 4(2) of the Hate Speech Elimination Act (HSEA), which aims to eliminate unfair discriminatory speech and behaviour targeting persons originating from outside Japan, imposed an obligation on the local governments 'to take measures in accordance with the actual situation of the region, taking into account the sharing of appropriate roles with the national government', while the Act's Chapter 2 stipulates the content of the basic measures. Specifically, the preparation and maintenance of a consultation system (art. 5), the enhancement of education, etc. (art. 6), and awareness-raising activities, etc. (art. 7) are also required not only of national government, but also of local governments. However, while the national government 'has responsibility' for implementation of these measures, the extent of responsibility of the local governments is left as 'shall endeavour'. The reason for the difference in wording, according to those who drafted the bill, is that the

[12] See Chapters 1 and 3.

[13] Article 2(2) of the Local Autonomy Act provides that 'ordinary local public entities are to process their affairs in the region as well as other affairs, which according to the laws or Cabinet orders based thereon, are to be processed by them'.

percentage of people originating from outside Japan and the frequency of hate speech differs for each local government.[14]

So local governments are required to eliminate discrimination through such means as human rights education and activities aiming to raise awareness of human rights. And since the issue of unfair discriminatory speech and behaviour targeting persons originating from outside Japan causes serious rifts in the local community (as noted in the preamble to the HSEA), it can be supposed that each local government is required to respond to the actual situation specific to its own region.

B. *Previous Efforts*

For a long time, discrimination against *Burakumin* ('Buraku people') was a central issue in Japan.[15] Local governments, led largely by those in western Japan, enacted ordinances named *Jinken Sonchō no Shakai-zukuri Jōrei* ('Ordinances on Community Planning to Respect Human Rights') to provide for their own responsibilities and the formulation of a basic policy, and to establish a council to promote human rights measures.[16] Moreover, to deal with issues such as Buraku discrimination in the areas of marriage and employment, ordinances prohibiting investigation into whether a person lives in or comes from Buraku were enacted by the prefectural governments of Osaka, Kagawa, Tokushima, Fukuoka, and Kumamoto.[17] The reasons thought to have inspired these human rights ordinances include that:

[14] Yuichiro Uozumi *et al.*, *Heito Supīchi Kaishōhō Seiritsu no Keii to Kihonteki na Kangaekata* [The Hate Speech Elimination Act: the background to and basic concept of its establishment] (Daiichi Hoki, 2016), 37–38 (quoting the statement by Katsuo Yakura, a member of the House of Councillors).

[15] Burakumin are a minority group descended from those who were at the bottom of the pre-modern Japanese caste system. *Buraku*, directly translating as 'hamlet', refers to the areas in which these people were required to live. See Chapter 4.

[16] Kenzo Tomonaga, *Buraku Kaihō o Kangaeru: Sabetsu no Genzai to Kaihō no Kenkyu* [Thinking about Buraku emancipation: exploring current discrimination and liberation] (Kaiho Shuppansha, 2015), 157–59. Moreover, arts 1 and 5 of the 2000 Act on the Promotion of Human Rights Education and Human Rights Awareness-Raising established the responsibilities of the national government, local governments, and citizens concerning the promotion of measures related to human rights education and raising awareness of human rights.

[17] The catalyst for these ordinances was the case of the comprehensive list of Buraku that came to light in November 1975. In this case, more than 200 companies purchased the book *Chimei Sōkan* ('list of villages'), which described the locations of Buraku throughout the country, and they then referred to this list when recruiting employees. Since the creators and sellers of these books were investigating agencies, such as credit reference

- because the efforts being made at the national level were apathetic, the marginalized groups asked local governments to promote their own efforts;
- with the progress in the trend towards decentralization, the role of the local governments was growing in all sectors; and
- as the disclosure of information became more prevalent, it became difficult to secure the necessary budgets and to allocate personnel without the legal basis of an ordinance.[18]

One example of a regulatory ordinance cracking down on acts of 'expression' is *Okayama-shi Denshi Keijiban ni Kakaru Yūgai Jōhō no Kiroku Kōi Kinshi ni Kansuru Jōrei* ('Ordinance Prohibiting Acts of Posting Harmful Information on the Okayama City Electronic Bulletin Board'). Okayama City enacted this ordinance in 2002 prompted by a case in which it was discovered that the names of the Buraku had been posted on an electronic bulletin board via the Internet. This ordinance prohibits the writing of harmful information such as 'information recognized as likely to promote unfair discrimination' on the electronic bulletin board managed by Okayama City and imposes a non-penal fine of ¥50,000 or less. Moreover, the 'harmful information' prohibited by the ordinance includes not only expressions that promote discrimination, but also more broadly information constituting an invasion of privacy, information that causes property disadvantage or mental suffering, and sexual information. Furthermore, in addition to harmful information, commercial information and information damaging political or religious neutrality are also subject to deletion. The electronic bulletin board of Okayama City, which was the subject of this ordinance, has since been abolished.[19]

In 2002, the Human Rights Vindication Bill was submitted to the Diet, but the independent nature of the human rights committee that it proposed to establish and the relationship between its provisions and freedom of speech were subject to intense debate.[20] Although the bill was rejected in October 2003, an ordinance on comprehensive human rights relief – the first of its kind throughout the country – which could be said to be a local government version of the originally proposed national bill was passed in 2005. *Tottori-ken Jinken Shingai Kyūsai Suishin oyobi Tetsuzuki ni Kansuru*

agencies and private investigation agencies, the local governments established regulatory ordinances. See *Ibid.*, at 48–55.

18 *Ibid.*, at 153.

19 See www.city.okayama.jp/shimin/jinken/jinken_00026.html [accessed 31 March 2019].

20 See Chapter 6.

Jōrei ('Tottori Prefecture Ordinance on Promotion and Procedures for Relief of Human Rights Violations') prohibits 'unfair discriminatory treatment or discriminatory speech or behaviour carried out on the grounds of race or the like', 'acts of publicly expressing an intention to conduct unfair discriminatory treatment against a large number of unspecified people, who have common attributes such as race, by reason of this attribute', and other similar acts of (broad-ranging) hate speech, defining 'human rights violations' as the repetition of abusive, defamatory, or significantly crude or violent speech or behaviour. When a petition for relief and prevention of a human rights violation is submitted to a committee consisting of five members appointed by the governor and approved by the local assembly, the committee conducts the necessary investigation and requests cooperation of the parties involved, such as participation in a hearing or the provision of information. Any person who refuses to cooperate without just cause will be punished with a fine of not more than ¥50,000. When deemed necessary by the committee, measures are taken such as offering assistance to the victim and issuing guidance to the perpetrators. If it is found that there has been public and repeated discriminatory speech or behaviour, or serious abuse of human rights such as defamation, additional measures may be taken such as issuing a warning to the perpetrator demanding that they cease the violation, or encouraging the perpetrator to participate in human rights training. Moreover, if the perpetrator does not comply with the warning without just cause, this non-compliance may be subject to public disclosure.

The Tottori Prefecture Ordinance was passed in October 2005 by means of assembly-initiated legislation[21] based on the bill proposed by then governor Yoshihiro Katayama. However, immediately after the bill was submitted to the prefectural assembly, criticism poured in from both inside and outside the prefecture, including from the Tottori Prefectural Bar Association. This led Tottori Prefecture to temporarily freeze the ordinance before its enforcement and to establish a review committee of experts to review it. The review committee conducted a survey of the human rights violations committed within the prefecture and concluded that the ordinance could not be expected to be properly implemented since it attempted to deal with human rights issues too extensively and even included quasi-judicial proceedings. The committee also provided some model ordinances,

[21] With regard to Japanese local governments, most of the draft ordinances submitted to the local assembly are prepared by the civil service, and it is rare for assembly members to prepare and submit their own draft ordinances.

such as an ordinance prohibiting discrimination limiting the target to discriminatory conducts, and proposed that the prefectural government design a new system. In response to this, the Tottori Prefecture Ordinance was abolished in April 2009 without coming into force and efforts have since been led by the Advice Network to Create a Society Respecting Human Rights, which bolsters support through advice.[22]

IV. The Osaka City Ordinance Dealing with Hate Speech

Osaka-shi Heito Supīchi e no Taisho ni Kansuru Jōrei ('Osaka City Ordinance Dealing with Hate Speech') – the first ordinance in Japan aiming to deter hate speech – was promulgated on 18 January 2016. The bill had been based on the report of *Osaka-shi Jinken Sesaku Suishin Shingikai* ('Osaka City Human Rights Policy Promotion Council'), published in February 2015 in response to opinions expressed by then Mayor Toru Hashimoto, and it was passed after partial revision by the city assembly.[23]

The immediate catalyst for the enactment of the ordinance came on 3 September 2014, when Mayor Hashimoto asked the Osaka City Human Rights Policy Promotion Council for an expert opinion on 'Measures Required of Osaka City against the Expression of Hate (Hate Speech)'. The report issued by the Council recognized that 'discriminatory behaviour that rejects people of a particular race or nationality, so-called hate speech, is the focus of public attention':

> Amid an environment where there are many foreign nationals, including South Korean and North Korean nationals living in Osaka City, hate speech is indeed being expressed in the city, and therefore, it is necessary for Osaka City, as a core municipality protecting the human rights of its citizens, to show a clear stance that hate speech is not to be permitted through the adoption of its own individual enforceable measures.

22 The Tottori Prefecture Ordinance is available at www.pref.tottori.lg.jp/32501.htm [accessed 31 March 2019]. See also Shunsuke Otawara, 'Tottoriken Jinken Jōrei o Meguru Keii to Kadai' ['Background to and issues affecting the Tottori Prefecture Human Rights Ordinance'] (2008) 36 *Shōgaisha Mondai Kenkyū* [Disability issues research] 48.

23 A provision was added that requires consent by the legislative assembly when appointing a member of the hate speech review board, and the provision concerning financial support for litigation and the victims' other expenses was deleted. For the background to the enactment of the Osaka City Ordinance, see Hiromi Hata, 'Osaka-shi Heito Supīchi e no Taisho ni Kansuru Jōrei' ['Osaka City Ordinance dealing with hate speech, pt 1'] (2018) 667 *Jichi Jitsumu Seminā* [Autonomy practical seminar] 54; Hiromi Hata, 'Osaka-shi Heito Supīchi e no Taisho ni Kansuru Jōrei' ['Osaka City Ordinance dealing with hate speech, pt 2'] (2018) 668 *Jichi Jitsumu Seminā* [Autonomy practical seminar] 56.

The report also advised that '[i]t is appropriate to build a structure based on the viewpoint of defending the human rights of citizens and others rather than the viewpoint of imposing an obligation or other regulations on those engaging in hate speech'. Although the city assembly opposed measures to support litigation for the victim proposed in the same report, most of its other suggestions were reflected in the ordinance.

Article 2 of the Osaka City Ordinance defines hate speech as an act of expression that corresponds to all of the following requirements:

> (1) The act is done with the purpose of any of the following (for the application of subsection (iii), the specified purpose has to be clearly identifiable):
> (i) To exclude any person or group of persons who has or have specific characteristics pertaining to race or ethnic origins (hereinafter referred to as 'specific persons') from society,
> (ii) To limit the rights or freedoms of specific persons;
> (iii) To incite hatred, a sense of discrimination, or violence against specific persons.
> (2) The content of, or the method of, the expression falls within any of the following:
> (i) It is to substantially insult or defame specific persons;
> (ii) It is to make specific persons (or a substantial number of specific persons, if directed to them) feel threatened.
> (3) The act is done in a place where, or in a way that, many unspecified persons would become aware of the content of the act.[24]

Under article 5, the mayor is to take necessary measures to prevent dissemination of the content and is to publish the act that constitutes hate speech, a summary of the content of the expression, the measures taken to prevent dissemination of the expression, and the name of the actor, if the mayor deems that (1) an act of expression conducted within the city corresponds to hate speech, or that (2) an act of expression conducted outside the city corresponds to hate speech, and either (a) the content of the expression is clearly understood as relating to the citizens or (b) the expression, having occurred within the city, is disseminated to an area outside of the city.

In judging whether a particular instance falls within the scope of article 2, the mayor must ask the opinion of the Osaka Hate Speech Review

[24] See Koji Higashikawa, 'Japan's Hate Speech Laws: Translations of the Osaka City Ordinance and the National Act to Curb Hate Speech in Japan' (2017) 19 *Asian-Pac. L .Pol'y J.* 1, at 6–17. The English translation of the provisions is based on the same paper.

Board in advance (art. 6). The board is established as an organ affiliated with the mayor (art. 7), and its five members comprise academic experts or other specialists commissioned by the mayor, with the consent of the city council (art. 8).[25] In addition, the council itself is able to conduct necessary investigations (art. 9), but there are no provisions for measures that guarantee the cooperation of the parties.[26]

A major feature of the Osaka City Ordinance is that it is, in substance, the only law or regulation in Japan that gives a detailed definition of 'hate speech'. Even the HSEA, which is a national law, merely offers an ambiguous definition of 'unfair discriminatory speech and behaviour against persons originating from outside Japan' without using the term 'hate speech'. Since the HSEA is a 'principle law', which provides for no specific means of regulation, it does not strictly define the object of the discrimination. In the case of the Osaka City Ordinance, the requirements corresponding to hate speech have to be stipulated because the mayor adopts measures to prevent the spread of the acts of expression and to disclose the name of the actor. That said, the Osaka City Ordinance, like the HSEA, does not prohibit hate speech. The framework of such an 'imperfect' ordinance derives from its starting point, which was to establish the immediate measures that the local government would be able to take within the current legal system while taking into consideration constitutional rights and freedoms (freedom of expression and personal right).[27] In this sense, the ordinance is experimental in nature.[28]

As of 31 March 2018, the Osaka Hate Speech Review Board had dealt with 34 cases under the Osaka City Ordinance. Four cases were recognized as constituting hate speech, all of which were cases concerning the posting of videos on the Internet. For three of them, the city required the provider to delete the video; in the other, the video had already been deleted when it was recognized under the ordinance.[29] The ordinance has

[25] As of July 2020, the committee is composed of one expert on constitutional law, one expert on international law, one expert on administrative law, and two lawyers.

[26] For the Osaka City Ordinance, see www.city.osaka.lg.jp/shimin/page/0000339043.html [accessed 31 March 2019].

[27] Article 11 of the Osaka City Ordinance provides that '[i]n the application of the Ordinance, due regard must be paid to prevent unjust infringement on the freedom of expression and other freedoms and rights of the Japanese people that are guaranteed by the Constitution of Japan'.

[28] Kazuhiko Matsumoto, 'Osaka-shi Heito Supīchi e no Taisho ni Kansuru Jōrei' ['Osaka City Ordinance Dealing with Hate Speech'] (2017) 1513 *Jurist* 81, at 82.

[29] See www.city.osaka.lg.jp/shimin/cmsfiles/contents/0000339/339043/kennsuuhyou.pdf [accessed 31 March 2019].

been criticized on the grounds that review takes too long, that it is highly difficult to identify the actor because acts of expression on the Internet are mostly carried out using a handle or otherwise anonymously, and that the ordinance does not explicitly specify that hate speech is illegal and prohibited in the first place.[30] Moreover, if hate speech is defined only imperfectly, this may have a chilling effect on expression and hinder the normal workings of the 'marketplace of ideas'. Thus it is necessary to keep the ordinance in constant review, carefully examining its beneficial effects and its potential harms.[31]

If hate speech is posted anonymously on the Internet, to publish the names or other information about the person responsible under article 5(1) of the Osaka City Ordinance, these sorts of information must be obtained from the operator running the site on which the information was posted or otherwise the Internet services provider or another such person. However, it was originally unclear whether this was possible under current law and hence the mayor of Osaka consulted the Osaka Hate Speech Review Board.

In its report submitted in January 2018,[32] the Board concluded as follows.

(1) The establishing of an ordinance on the provision to the city of information held by a provider or other such person for the purpose of publishing the name or other information in accordance with article 5(1), as well as cases in which such provision is made mandatory, violates article 4 of the Telecommunications Business Act, since it impacts the judgment of the provider or other such person and inhibits the act of expression.

(2) It may be possible to ask the provider or other such person to provide information voluntarily for the purpose of supporting those who have suffered an infringement of their rights, rather than for the purpose of publication. However, it is necessary for the city to consider carefully whether or not to implement this measure, since, in its role as the local government, the city is restricted in terms of the measures it may take in response and its effectiveness cannot always be assured.

[30] See Yoshihisa Tajima, 'Osaka-shi Heito Supīchi e no Taisho ni Kansuru Jōrei' ['Osaka City Ordinance Dealing with Hate Speech'] (2018) 757 *Hōgaku Seminā* [Legal seminar] 32.

[31] See Matsumoto, note 28, at 85.

[32] See www.city.osaka.lg.jp/shimin/cmsfiles/contents/0000366/366957/30tousinn5gou.pdf [accessed 31 March 2019].

(3) It is considered necessary under law at a national level to deal with hate speech that is posted on a site and hence, with regard to measures facilitating provision by the provider or other such person of information on the person posting the information, there is similarly a need to seek review at a national level.[33]

In response to this report, the mayor of Osaka submitted a request to the national government in August 2018 for revision of the law to promote the provision by the provider or other such person to the local government of information about the poster.[34]

Incidentally, in October 2018, Tokyo Prefecture – in preparation for its hosting of the Olympic and Paralympic Games 2020 (in 2021) – enacted its Ordinance Aiming to Realize the Principle of Respect for Human Rights as Set out in the Olympic Charter.[35] This ordinance has a framework similar to the Osaka City Ordinance, such as measures intended to prevent the spread of acts of expression and allowing the governor to publish names and other information. However, it does not adopt a rigid definition of the type of hate speech subject to action as does the Osaka City Ordinance and it instead adopts the ambiguous definition found in article 2 of the HSEA.

V. Future Tasks

To close the chapter, let us list the tasks facing local governments in Japan when taking steps to tackle hate speech.

The local governments are required to reliably ascertain the legislative facts constituting the necessity of and reason for legislation. In other words, as a prerequisite to legal regulation, an accurate survey and analysis needs to be conducted in the region to investigate what kind of damage is being suffered by individuals and groups as a consequence of what kinds of content and modes of hate speech. Japan may seem relatively homogeneous, but there appears to be some uneven regional distribution depending on the characteristic subject to discrimination. Thus an ordinance established without appropriate investigation and analysis may not only be deemed by the courts to lack legislative fact, but also renders the purpose of the measures unclear and effective problem-solving impossible.

33 See Chapter 18.

34 See www.city.osaka.lg.jp/hodoshiryo/shimin/0000434133.html [accessed 31 March 2019].

35 See www.soumu.metro.tokyo.jp/10jinken/tobira/pdf/regulations2.pdf [accessed 31 March 2019].

In addition, since there are few judicial rulings on hate speech regulation in Japan, those local governments that are trying to implement regulation will constantly find themselves at risk of litigation on whether or not they are infringing freedom of expression and freedom of assembly. There will always be limitations on the types of regulation that local governments have at their disposal, but considering the risk of litigation and costs of enforcement, it seems that – as is the case with Osaka – there is little option but to adopt less-restrictive means and to revise the regulations in a process of continuous review of whether or not the ordinance is achieving its objective.[36]

Moreover, in a community in which few recognize that 'there is a structure of historically formed discrimination in the background of hate speech, and therein exists an asymmetry between the perpetrator and the target of the discrimination',[37] sanctions against discrimination too readily employed could easily create a public backlash. It is precisely because the local governments are those on the front line that such a backlash risks causing yet further division in the community. The development and dissemination of effective resources and activities raising awareness are undoubtedly more urgent issues for local governments than are sanctions.

Since the enactment of the HSEA, some local governments have formulated guidelines that ban the use of public facilities for hate group meetings.[38] In my own view and in terms of resolving the problem of hate speech, rather than prescribing such measures through guidelines, which are internal regulations, the local government will more effectively prescribe them in ordinance form, raising awareness of the problem among the general public and legitimizing the action through democratic debate.[39]

[36] However, even the Osaka City ordinance, which has adopted only limited means, has been subject to litigation for violating freedom of expression. See www.sankei.com/west/news/180416/wst1804160056-n1.html [accessed 31 March 2019].

[37] In terms of the aspects of historical backgrounds and asymmetry in hate speech, see the discussions in the special issue 'Tokushū Heito Supīchi/Heito Kuraimu – Minzoku Sabetsu Higai no Bōshi to Kyūsai' ['Special issue: hate speech and hate crimes – prevention and remedies regarding damage from ethnic discrimination'] (2015) 726 *Hōgaku Seminā* [Legal seminar] 1.

[38] See Chapter 20.

[39] See Hideki Nakamura, 'Heito Supīchi Shūkai ni taisuru Ōyake no Shisetsu no Riyō Seigen' ['Restrictions on the use of public facilities for hate group meetings'] (2018) 46 *Kitakyūshū Shiritsu Daigaku Hōsei Ronshū* [Kitakyushu Shiritsu Daigaku journal of law and political science] 65.

10

The Legislative Process Leading to the Hate Speech Elimination Act

KATSUO YAKURA

I. Introduction

I am a member of the Komei Party,[1] one of the ruling parties of Japan, and have been a member of the Upper House of the National Diet of Japan since August 2013. In 2016, when I was a director of the Legal Affairs Committee for the Upper House, I proposed and established the Act Concerning the Promotion of Efforts towards the Elimination of Improper Discriminatory Speech and Conduct against People Who Came from Outside Japan,[2] known as the Hate Speech Elimination Act (HSEA), with members of two other ruling parties.

What motivated me to enact a special law against hate speech were stories of reprehensible speech and marches that I heard directly from victims. In 2014, I met some third- and fourth-generation Koreans living in Japan who belonged to the same generation as I. The actual stories of hate speech and demonstration marches I heard from them were truly shocking. The offenders had rushed into a peaceful residential area and shouted abusive remarks such as 'XX people are cockroaches!' and 'Kill them!' I remember some of the victims said, 'I'm really afraid, and scared to go out at night alone', and 'I'm so afraid of getting killed, I can't even get in the elevator.' I committed myself strongly to eradicating hate speech and violent demonstration marches.

[1] *Komeito* ('Komei Party') was founded in 1964 by Mr Daisaku Ikeda, the third president of Soka Gakkai, a Japanese religious organization. Our party's political goals focus on humanism underpinned by Buddhism.

[2] The thinking underlying the legislation was our deep determination to have Komeito's humanitarianism take root not only in Japan, but also all around the world.

It is an honour to be able to describe the legislative process of the Hate Speech Elimination Act and our efforts to eliminate hate speech from our society.

II. The Situation in Japan before the Hate Speech Elimination Act

First, I would like to offer a brief explanation of the situation in Japan before enactment of the Hate Speech Elimination Act. The government had been reluctant to enact any special legislation on hate demonstrations. This was in part because it perceived there to be no legislative basis for creating a law and that it would violate the freedom of expression guaranteed by the Constitution to subject hate speech to criminal punishment, in particular where the expression causes harm to unspecified people.

For example, in response to the report to the United Nations' Human Rights Committee (HRC) under the 1979 International Covenant on Civil and Political Rights (ICCPR), which Japan had ratified, there was a common perception insisting that:

> Article 14 of the Japanese Constitution stipulates the provision of equality under the law, and the government has taken measures to eliminate discrimination, hostility, and violence, a stance which is stated in various fields such as the Penal Code, education laws and labor laws. Japan will take legislative measures 'when a specific adverse effect occurs due to an action that has not been regulated by the current legislation'. However, even in such cases, the freedom of expression guaranteed by the Constitution should be fully considered as long as it will not harm public welfare.[3]

[3] Japan insisted on the following in the Fifth Report of 2006:

> If national, racial or religious hatred, which can incite discrimination, hostility or violence, is advocated and includes content that harms the honour or credibility of a specific individual or organization, the offenders will be punished on the basis of the Penal Code's defamation laws (Article 230), insult laws (Article 231) or laws on damage to the reputation of a business or the obstruction of business (Article 233). If there is threatening content toward specific individuals, the offenders can be punished on the basis of the crimes of intimidation in the Penal Code (Article 222), collective threat charges in the Act Concerning Punishment of Physical Violence and Others (Article 1), and habitual intimidation (Article 1–3); moreover, the offenders can be punished on the basis of inducement (Article 61 of the Penal Code) or accessoryship (Article 62 of the Penal Code).

Furthermore, the government also reported that it was undertaking activities such as raising awareness and drafting guidance with the help of the Ministry of Justice's human rights defence organization, and that it was involved in issuing requests to delete discriminatory expressions published online, the dissemination of such on the Internet having become

Japan also reserved ratification of Article 4(a)[4] and (b)[5] of the International Convention on the Elimination of All Forms of Racial Discrimination (ICERD). Although the UN Committee on the Elimination of Racial Discrimination (CERD) described in Article 8 ICERD recommended on 20 March 2001[6] that Japan consider lifting the reservations, Japan stated in August 2001 that it would not do so, arguing that:

> Article 4(a) and (b) of the said Convention request State Parties to punish dissemination of ideas based on racial superiority or hatred and incitement to racial discrimination. In Japan, it is possible to punish such practices as long as it is compatible with the Constitution; accordingly, Japan fulfills the obligation requested by the said Convention to that extent. However, as stated above, to control all such practices with criminal laws and regulations beyond the current legal system is likely to be contrary to the freedom of expression and other freedoms as guaranteed by the Constitution. This is because the concept referred to in the said Articles may include various practices under diverse conditions. Therefore, Japan has decided to fulfill the obligations stipulated in Article 4 of the said Convention as long as they do not contradict the guarantees of the Constitution of Japan, while paying due regard to the rights proclaimed by the Universal Declaration of Human Rights.[7]

Japan also made the following statement in the same reports:

a major problem at the time. With regard to this problems, the Sixth Report of 2012 stated that the government was supporting activities such as the development of 'guidelines for providing Internet connection services' formulated by the Telecommunications Carriers Association.

4 Article 4(a) ICERD provides:

> (a) To declare that, regardless of whether it be about a race, skin color or group of people of any ethnic origin, the dissemination of ideas based on racial superiority or hatred, the instigation of racial discrimination, acts of violence or the instigation of acts of violence, and assistance (including the provision of funding for activities based on racism) shall fall under crimes which should be punished by law.

5 Article 4(b) ICERD provides:

> (b) To agree to prohibit as illegal any advertising activities or other activities by a group or organization that promotes or instigates racial discrimination, and to acknowledge that participation in such organizations or activities is a crime that should be punished by law.

6 The CERD has the authority to examine the reports submitted to the Committee by the State parties on a regular basis or further to a request from the Committee under Art. 9(1) ICERD, and to make suggestions and general recommendations based on that examination.

7 See Ministry of Foreign Affairs, *International Convention on the Elimination of All Forms of Racial Discrimination (First and Second Reports)*, para. 50, available at www.mofa.go.jp/policy/human/race_rep1/article4.html#1 [accessed 1 June 2020]. See also Chapter 1 in this volume.

> With regard to all dissemination of ideas based on racial superiority or hatred, there are no specific provisions that stipulate what constitutes racially discriminatory expression, that is, dissemination of ideas based on racial superiority or hatred, as a criminal act, taking into consideration the importance of the freedoms of assembly, association and expression as guaranteed by the Constitution. However, if the content damages the honor or credit of a specific individual or group, such dissemination of ideas is punishable as a crime of defamation (Article 230, Penal Code), insult (Article 231), or damage to credit or obstruction of business (Article 233). If such activities include threatening content against a specific individual, they are punishable as a crime of intimidation (Article 222), and collective intimidation and habitual intimidation (Article 1 and Article 1–3 of the Act Concerning Punishment of Physical Violence and Others).
>
> Incitement to racial discrimination is punishable as a crime of instigation (Article 61, Penal Code) or assistance (Article 62) of the crimes if an act constitutes one of the above-mentioned crimes. If an instigation or assistance is a violation of a law prohibiting discriminatory treatment, such as the provision of equal treatment by public officials (Articles 27 and 109 of the National Public Service Act, Articles 13 and 60 of the Local Public Service Act), it shall also be punished.[8]

III. The Rise in Hate Speech in Japan

A. *The Rise in Hate Speech in the 21st Century*

In the 21st century, controversy over the need for specific legislation heightened and there was growing sentiment that the Japanese government should address the issue of hate speech more earnestly, especially after the group *Zainichitokken o yurusanai shimin no kai* ('Group of Citizens Who Do Not Tolerate Privileges for Ethnic Korean Residents in Japan', known as *Zaitokukai*) was established in January 2007. Zaitokukai became widely known for conducting harassing demonstrations against foreign residents in Japan, including Koreans. Its principle claim was that privileges for Koreans in Japan should be abolished, but it did not provide a clear explanation of whether any such privileges actually existed.

B. *Kyoto Korean Elementary School*

One of Zaitokukai's most famous activities was its hate speech demonstrations against Kyoto Korean Elementary School (now the Kyoto

[8] See *Ibid.*, paras 52 and 53. See also Chapter 8.

Chōsen Elementary School).[9] The group marched around the school and used cars to broadcast street propaganda. On three occasions, it directed insulting remarks at the school through loudspeakers. The school corporation that ran the school filed a criminal complaint in December 2009 against Zaitokukai and other groups responsible for the demonstration activities.

On March 2010, Zaitokukai announced a demonstration in advance on the Internet and recruited additional people to participate in it. This prompted the school corporation to petition Kyoto District Court for a provisional injunction to prohibit demonstration activities within a 200-metre radius of the school gates. A provisional injunction was issued, but the demonstration was still held, running from the centre of Kyoto City to a location about 100 metres from the school.

On June 2010, the school corporation filed a civil lawsuit with Kyoto District Court based on its personal rights, seeking compensation for damages, and arguing that the three demonstrations and the release of video footage thereof were illegal. The corporation also requested the prohibition of similar activities.

Kyoto District Court rendered a judgment on 7 October 2013 in response to the civil lawsuit. According to the judgment, in light of Articles 2 and 6 ICERD, 'Japanese courts are obliged to interpret the law in a manner that complies with the provisions of the ICERD, since it has been acceded to'. Furthermore, '[i]n cases where the act of racial discrimination causes specific damage and falls under the illegal actions stated in Article 709 of the Civil Code, the amount of compensation for damages should be determined in compliance with the provisions of the ICERD'. The court concluded that the demonstration activities and release of video footage in this case comprised defamation and obstruction of the plaintiff's business, and accordingly it recognized that illegal acts had been committed. It also stated that, '[o]verall, this is nothing short of racial discrimination as described in Paragraph 1 of Article 1 of the ICERD'. The judgment was not based on so-called hate speech, but on 'racial discrimination' under Article 1 ICERD. The court awarded total damages of approximately ¥11 million as compensation for both tangible and intangible damage.

The defendants filed an appeal with Osaka High Court. However, although the Osaka High Court overruled that part of the lower court's

[9] A kindergarten and elementary school in Kyoto, Japan, attended by Koreans living in Japan. See Chapters 7 and 12.

judgment in which it interpreted the ICERD as governing relationships between private individuals, it upheld the rest of the decision. Osaka High Court adopted the overall purpose of the ICERD, rather than each of its individual provisions, as the criterion for deciding whether the defendants' activities constituted illegal acts under article 709 of the Civil Code of Japan.

The defendants next filed an appeal with the Supreme Court. In December 2014, the Supreme Court dismissed the appeal, and the judgment became final and binding.

The Supreme Court's decision in this case was significant because it would form part of the legislative basis for establishing a specific law against hate speech.

IV. Political Movement towards Eliminating Hate Speech

With the increase in hate speech in Japan, each political party started to take action to address the issue.

A. *The Liberal Democratic Party*

The Liberal Democratic Party (LDP) held its first meeting on the issue on 29 August 2014. This was partly because when the then governor of Tokyo, Yoichi Masuzoe, visited Korea in July 2014, then President Park Geun-hye asked him to take measures against hate speech and Mr Masuzoe conveyed this request to Prime Minister Abe. However, the meeting was based on the premise that the current law would not be changed. Consequently, although meetings were held several times that year, the activities were then discontinued.[10]

B. *Opposition Parties, Including the Democratic Party*

Some members of the opposition parties, including the Democratic Party of Japan (DPJ), the biggest opposition party at that time, were earnest about addressing the issue. They proposed a Bill Concerning the Promotion of Countermeasures for Abolishing Discrimination for Reasons of Race and So On on 22 May 2015.

[10] See Naoto Higuchi, 'Heito ga Ihō ni Naru toki: Heito Supīchi Kaishōhō Seitei o Meguru Seiji Katei' ['When hate becomes illegal: the political process of enacting the Hate Speech Elimination Act'] (2016) 62 *Leviathan* 96.

This bill aimed to abolish not only hate speech, but also all other forms of discrimination against foreigners. It banned anyone from engaging in 'unfair discriminatory speech' and 'unfair discriminatory acts' against unspecified people for reasons of race and so on. However, it did not contain any clear definitions of what constituted 'unfair discriminatory speech' and 'unfair discriminatory acts', and it granted the Cabinet Office the authority to investigate discrimination, including 'unfair discriminatory speech' and 'unfair discriminatory acts', and to recommend to the Japanese government that it take counter-measures. This would be inconsistent with the 'freedom of expression' set forth in article 21 of the Japanese Constitution and therefore it was not the kind of proposal that could gather a consensus.

C. The Komei Party

The Komei Party, to which I belong, had been steadily taking action by means of practical procedures even before the Supreme Court delivered its final decision in *Kyoto Korean Elementary School.*

In September 2014, a Project Team to Deal with Hate Speech Problems (the Komei PT) was established. Mr Kiyohiko Toyama, who also belongs to the Komei Party and is member of the House of Representatives, became the team's chair. The team repeatedly investigated the scenes of hate speech incidents, exchanged opinions with experts, and also looked into counter-measures.

On 2 July 2015, the Komei PT submitted a set of requests to the Japanese Cabinet. Among these were requests to conduct a survey on the actual situation of hate speech in Japan and to take effective counter-measures. Mr Yoshihide Suga, Chief Cabinet Secretary, promised to implement the Komei PT's proposal rapidly and announced that the Cabinet would investigate the issue using a reserve fund in the national budget. After receiving instructions from the Mr Suga, the Ministry of Justice commenced the proposed survey and, in March 2016 of the following year, it released a report based on the results. The report stated that hate speech in demonstration marches and street propaganda activities had not yet abated.

The survey contributed significantly to subsequent legislative activities, because the fact that the Japanese government had admitted that hate speech still existed in Japan would provide the legislative basis supporting the need to create a specific law.

D. *Active Discussions towards Enacting the Hate Speech Elimination Act*

(a) Proposal of the Bill

Following this movement, on 6 August 2015, at a meeting of the Legal Affairs Committee for the Upper House, I made the assertion that a hate speech elimination act was necessary and said that the Komei Party would endeavour to submit such a bill. This was the first formal statement by a lawmaker from one of the governing parties that insisted on the need to enact special legislation regarding hate speech.

The Komei PT, including Mr Toyama and myself, held meetings and had earnest, vigorous discussions with the LDP and other parties. I also had discussions with other members of the Legal Affairs Committee for the Upper House, as one of its directors.

After overcoming many points of contention, on 8 April 2016, the Komei Party and the LDP launched the Governing Parties' Work Team on Hate Speech and examined ways of regulating hate speech. We then framed a bill, the Hate Speech Elimination Bill, and, as the sole proponent in the Komei Party, I submitted the bill to the Upper House and the Legal Affairs Committee for the Upper House on 13 April 2016.

(b) The Content of the Bill

The following is extracted from my explanation of the reasons for this proposal, as a proponent of the Hate Speech Elimination Act:

> In recent years, we have seen unfair discriminatory behaviour promoting the exclusion of people who came from a country or an area outside Japan and legally took up residence here, or the exclusion of the descendants of such people, just because they are considered outsiders. There are a lot of cases in which people who are from foreign countries or their descendants suffer a great deal of pain. Such behaviour is not only a serious threat to the fundamental human rights of individuals: it also spreads a sense of discrimination, hatred, and violence, and undermines the foundations of the community; thus, it is absolutely intolerable.
>
> Of course, freedom of expression is the right that forms the basis of democracy, so regulations concerning the content of expression must be carefully considered; moreover, what should be considered illegal speech and who should judge it, etc., are difficult issues.
>
> However, overlooking this situation and leaving it unaddressed is not an appropriate attitude in light of the position of our country in international society.
>
> Based on this, as an initiative to eliminate discriminatory behaviour against people who are from outside Japan, we aim to establish a basic

> philosophy, clarify the responsibilities of the country, etc., establish basic measures, and then promote them, while taking the freedom of expression guaranteed by the Constitution into consideration. While focusing on so-called hate speech, both inside and outside Japan, we have to show that we uphold the philosophy that unreasonable discriminatory behaviour against people who come from outside of Japan is not permitted, and we the Japanese people should declare ourselves to be for the achievement of a society in which such discriminatory behaviour does not exist.[11]

As well as aiming to set out the basic principles for eliminating hate speech and to clarify the responsibilities of the national government, among other things, the Hate Speech Elimination Bill also aimed to set out and promote the basic measures for addressing the issues (art. 1). It required the Japanese government to implement measures to eliminate 'unfair discriminatory speech and behaviour against persons originating from outside Japan', and it also called for local governments to endeavour to take measures in accordance with the actual situation in their regions, taking into account the appropriate sharing of roles with the national government with respect to the elimination efforts (art. 4[12]). It additionally provided for the 'Preparation and Maintenance of a Consultation System' (art. 5), the 'Enhancement of Education' (art. 6), and 'Activities to Raise Awareness' (art. 7).

Unlike the earlier Bill Concerning the Promotion of Countermeasures for Abolishing Discrimination for Reasons of Race and So On that the opposition parties had submitted, the Hate Speech Elimination Bill offered a definition of 'unfair discriminatory speech and behaviour against persons originating from outside Japan'. Article 2 of the bill defined it as:

> . . . unfair discriminatory speech and behaviour to incite the exclusion of persons originating exclusively from a country or region other than Japan or their descendants who are lawfully residing in Japan from the local community by reason of such persons' originating from a country or region other than Japan, such as openly making proclamations to the effect of harming the life, body, freedom, reputation or property of persons originating from outside Japan with the objective of encouraging or inducing discriminatory feelings against such persons originating from outside Japan.[13]

[11] Taken from the minutes of the meeting of the Legal Affairs Committee for the Upper House of Councillors, 19 April 2016.

[12] See Chapter 9.

[13] This was amended on 12 May 2016 to:

> . . . unfair discriminatory speech and behaviour inciting the exclusion of persons originating exclusively from a country or region other than Japan or their descendants who are lawfully residing in Japan from the local

The bill also called on Japanese citizens to understand the need to eliminate unfair discriminatory speech and behaviour against persons originating from outside Japan, and to endeavour to contribute to the achievement of a society that is free from unfair discriminatory speech and behaviour against such persons (art. 3).

The Hate Speech Elimination Bill did not, however, prohibit discriminatory speech or impose punishments on people who used it; rather, it was a so-called principle law that simply promoted the philosophy, 'Hate speech should not be used.' The provision set out in article 3 was very characteristic of the bill as a principle law.

(c) Discussion of the Bill

The Legal Affairs Committee for the Upper House discussed the bill, and I explained its content and background from the podium over three days, on 19 and 26 April and 12 May 2016.

The main issue raised by members of the Committee was whether a specific law of such a nature, lacking any criminal punishment, would actually be able to eliminate hate speech from society. I repeatedly answered such questions as follows:

> First, we must realize that establishing penalties for hate speech is not easy. If punishments were imposed on the grounds of the content of expression, the government would have the authority to decide which expressions were to be subject to punishment. We are afraid that if that were the case, our society could become a place where any expression by anyone, not just someone who used hate speech, might be monitored by the government. This would result in an obvious violation of the 'freedom of expression' stipulated by the Constitution.[[14]]
>
> More than anything, I think it is important to create a society in which everyone spontaneously raises their own voice and acts 'to eliminate hate speech', rather than being an immature society in which people think, 'Hate speech will not disappear unless it is punished.' I firmly believe that this Hate Speech Elimination Act will help people say 'No' to hate speech and voluntarily create a society where it does not exist.

community by reason of such persons originating from a country or region other than Japan, such as openly making proclamations to the effect of harming the life, body, freedom, reputation or property of, *or to significantly insult*, persons originating from outside Japan with the objective of encouraging or inducing discriminatory feelings against such persons originating from outside Japan. [Emphasis added]

[14] See Chapter 1.

Nevertheless, some opposition party members still attacked us, saying, 'A bill like this is cheating. The Komei Party is taking a cowardly attitude toward hate speech regulation. They are an anti-human rights faction.'

On 27 April 2016, I attended a rally against the proposed Hate Speech Elimination Bill. The reason why these participants were against it was that it was a principle law and neither prohibited discriminatory speech nor imposed punishments on people who used it.

I was the only person from a governing party who participated in the rally, while there were a lot of opposition Diet members on the stage. When they shouted out, one after another, 'It is unthinkable that the LDP and the Komei Party has created such a toothless bill!', I went up on the stage and argued, 'If we do not establish this Hate Speech Elimination Act now, we will never be able to do anything', and 'This legislation is an important step to take now'.

I then shouted, 'I know that many of you will oppose this bill, but I'm definitely going to pass it!'

My remark prompted even more rage.

When I promised, 'I will create a society without hate speech', they retorted, 'You're lying! You can't do anything!'

To this, I instantly replied, 'I vow to create it!'

The rally echoed with a torrent of protests and catcalls, but throughout it all I earnestly spoke my mind to the opposition Diet members and the audience to the extent that I was able.

(d) The Passage and Enactment of the Bill

Looking back at it now, that event could have been the turning point.[15] I felt that the atmosphere in the Legal Affairs Committee for the Upper House had changed. Although there were still differing opinions among the opposition parties, we continued to discuss the bill in earnest, trying to reach a consensus.

One opposition member disagreed with the bill because its definition of 'unfair discriminatory speech and behaviour against persons originating from outside Japan' in article 2 seemed to be limited only to unfair

[15] It was a serious confrontation. After the end of the event, one of the organizers thanked me for attending and apologized for all the rudeness at the venue. He said, 'Your ideas really came across to us well.'

Later, when I met the same person after the Hate Speech Elimination Act had been brought into force, he thanked me again and said, 'Although I was strictly opposed to it then, it is a really good thing that the bill has been passed. The trends have changed a great deal in the wake of it. We are very thankful to you.'

discriminatory speech and behaviour against 'persons' 'who are *lawfully residing* in Japan' (emphasis added). He argued that it would result in the legality of hate speech against persons who are residing in Japan unlawfully and offenders excusing themselves on the basis that, 'Our actions should be legal, because we think they are residing in Japan unlawfully!'

I answered that this was not correct, because the interpretation of the definition in article 2 should be reasonable and objective, and offenders should not have the authority to interpret it arbitrarily. I also said that the goal of the Bill as a principle law was to establish a society in which there was no hate speech against any people, whether they are residing in Japan lawfully or unlawfully, and that it would therefore never result in legality for any form of hate speech.

Another opposition member was concerned that if the bill were enacted, certain kinds of political statement intended to oppose the presence of US forces in Okinawa (such as 'Yankee, go home!') would be deemed to be hate speech.

I answered that such remarks would not be unfair discriminatory speech under article 2 of the bill because they were not prompted simply 'by reason of such persons' originating from a country or region other than Japan', as provided for in article 2, and they would be protected under the 'freedom of expression' stipulated in article 21 of the Japanese Constitution.

Some members expressed the concern that article 2 of the bill seemed to mention 'openly making proclamations to the effect of harming the life, body, freedom, reputation or property of persons' only as a category of 'unfair discriminatory speech and behaviour', and asked us whether it was not hate speech to insult people by making remarks such as 'XX people are cockroaches!'

I answered that 'openly making proclamations to the effect of harming the life, body, freedom, reputation or property of persons' in article 2 of the bill was only one example of 'unfair discriminatory speech and behaviour', and many kinds of remarks could fall under its definition.

In the end, we agreed to amend article 2, and added '*to significantly insult*' to the definition of 'unfair discriminatory speech and behaviour'.

After this partial amendment, a supplementary resolution was added to the bill to the effect that counter-measures against unfair discriminatory speech and behaviour should be considered even after the enactment of the Hate Speech Elimination Act if necessary.

On 12 May, the bill was at last passed unanimously by the Legal Affairs Committee for the Upper House. All members of the Committee applauded when it was passed: it was the first time I had experienced anything like it.

On 13 May, the bill was approved with a large number of affirmative votes in the plenary session of the Upper House and it was sent to the House of Representatives. On 18 May, it was tabled at the Legal Committee of the House of Representatives and we had a question-and-answer session at which I also answered questions on the podium.

Finally, on 24 May, the bill was approved by a majority affirmative vote at the plenary session of the House of Representatives and enacted into law.

The Hate Speech Elimination Act was promulgated as Law No. 68 of 2016 on 3 June and it came into effect on the same day. The establishment of this law was significant and I was extremely proud to have been among its proponents. The reason why our activities bore fruit and this legislation was established in this way is that the efforts of the people who were devoted to this problem, including Diet members of both governing and opposition parties, started to take root in society and I would like to express my respect for all of the parties who conducted these activities.

(e) The Early Effects of the Hate Speech Elimination Act

Just one week after the passage into law of the Hate Speech Elimination Act, Kawasaki City 'declined authorization' for a hate speech demonstration march planned at a park in the city on 31 May 2016.[16] On 2 June, Yokohama District Court's Kawasaki Branch issued a provisional injunction prohibiting demonstration marches within a 500-metre radius of a plaintiff's building in the Sakuramoto district of Kawasaki Ward, which was an area targeted for hate speech activities.

Through the effects of this law, local governments and judiciaries were finally granted the discretion to say 'Hate speech is not acceptable'.[17] Even though the Act is a principle law that has no penalty provisions, it has enabled administrative institutions to significantly change the way in which they deal with these kinds of situations. It has awakened a dormant awareness among people and inspired a mass civil movement aiming to eliminate discrimination. It can be said that the Hate Speech Elimination Act has been effective in initiating efforts towards eliminating hate speech.[18]

[16] See Chapter 14.
[17] See Chapter 9.
[18] See Chapters 9 and 11.

In June 2018, some executives visited my office from the Simon Wiesenthal Center, a human rights organization based in Los Angeles, CA, which confronts the effects of hate and of events such as the Holocaust, perpetrated by the Nazis. One of the visitors said to me, 'If hate speech is left as it is, it can lead to violent confrontation or war. How society deals with hate speech and its potential threats is important. Mr Yakura, you took up the issue, and it lead to a wonderful movement. I'd like to express my respect. Let's create a society without hatred together.'

The issue is far from resolved and the enactment of the new law in Japan is just a first step. I will continue to fight earnestly against all kinds of discrimination, including hate speech, and I am determined to lead this civil movement further.

11

The Hate Speech Elimination Act

A Legal Analysis

SHINJI HIGAKI*

I. Introduction

Hate speech[1] is a serious problem all over the world. It sometimes provokes riots and even genocides. We can recall the incident in August 2017, when white supremacists gathered in Charlottesville, Virginia, waving the Confederate flag.[2] They clashed with their opponents, causing many casualties and forcing the governor of Virginia to declare a state of emergency.

While many European countries, as well as other nations such as Canada and Australia, regulate hate speech to some extent, the United

* This work was supported by JSPS KAKENHI Grant No. 19K13512.

[1] 'Hate speech' is quite a complex term that includes many types of expression. Shigenori Matsui, 'The Challenge to Multiculturalism: Hate Speech Ban in Japan' (2016) 49 *UBC L. Rev.* 427, at 462, pointed towards at least four:

> The first type is the advocacy or incitement of illegal violence, such as homicide or physical attacks, against members of an identifiable group. The second is the defamation, vilification, or insult against members of an identifiable group. The third is the incitement or promotion of discrimination against members of an identifiable group. The fourth is the promotion of hatred against members of an identifiable group.

In this article, however, I use the term in a broader sense to mean speech that attacks a person or group based on their race, religion, sex, sexual orientation, etc. or which incites such discrimination.

[2] During the American Civil War, the Confederate army used the Confederate flag as a battle flag. Afterwards, some organizations such as the Sons of Confederate Veterans adopted the flag as a symbol of Southern states and some states even incorporated it into their flags. The Confederate flag is, however, commonly regarded as a symbol of white supremacy given the role of the Confederacy in perpetuating slavery. See, e.g., James Forman Jr., 'Driving Dixie Down: Removing the Confederate Flag from Southern State Capitols' (1991) 101 *Yale L.J.* 505.

States has no such laws. Freedom of speech is indeed a fundamental right because it is essential to maintain a democratic society. However, the international community in general banned hate speech after World War II,[3] because it was commonly understood that combating racism is essential to protect human dignity,[4] equality,[5] and a multicultural society.[6] It is extremely difficult to strike a balance between freedom of expression and anti-racism in a free and democratic society; we must therefore tackle this aporia head on.

Like the United States, Japan had long had no hate speech laws. However, in 2016, the Japanese Diet enacted the Hate Speech Elimination Act (HSEA), which became the first measure it had passed aiming to tackle hate speech. The law is unusual because while it clearly declares hate speech to be impermissible, it imposes no penalties on offenders. As such, Japanese hate speech law may offer a modest model that strikes an appropriate balance between the freedom of expression and anti-racism.

This chapter describes the past and present status of hate speech regulations in Japan and analyses the HSEA. Section II offers an overview of the process of enacting the HSEA, briefly describing the way in which Japan, which had not enacted any laws relating to hate speech until 2016, ultimately passed the Act.[7] Section III explains the Act's content, analyses some of its many contentious issues, and offers a qualified interpretation of the HSEA.

[3] See Chapter 1.

[4] See, e.g., Jeremy Waldron, *The Harm in Hate Speech* (Harvard University Press, 2012); Steven J. Heyman, *Free Speech and Human Dignity* (Yale University Press, 2008).

[5] See, e.g., Charles Lawrence III, 'If He Hollers Let Him Go: Regulating Hate Speech on Campus' [1990] *Duke L.J.* 431.

[6] Article 27 of the Canadian Charter of Rights and Freedom provides that '[t]his Charter shall be interpreted in a manner consistent with the preservation and enhancement of the multicultural heritage of Canadians'. In *R* v. *Keegstra* [1990] 3 SCR 697, 757–58, the Supreme Court of Canada, which upheld the constitutionality of Canadian Criminal Code s. 319(2), stated that:

> The value expressed in s. 27 cannot be casually dismissed in assessing the validity of s. 319(2) under s. 1, and I am of the belief that s. 27 and the commitment to a multicultural vision of our nation bear notice in emphasizing the acute importance of the objective of eradicating hate propaganda from society … When the prohibition of expressive activity that promotes hatred of groups identifiable on the basis of colour, race, religion, or ethnic origin is considered in light of s. 27, the legitimacy and substantial nature of the government objective is therefore considerably strengthened.

[7] Other chapters explain the same content in detail, but it is related to the content and effect of the HSEA and hence I describe it here in brief.

II. How the Hate Speech Elimination Act Came to Be Enacted

In Japan, hate speech has generally been aimed at *Burakumin* ('Buraku people'), the descendants of that group which once sat at the bottom of Japan's pre-modern caste system. Discriminatory and hateful graffiti was, for example, written about them in public spaces.[8] Burakumin had long called for laws that would regulate hate speech, but the Japanese Diet had been reluctant to respond to those calls. It was not until 2002 that the Diet attempted to legislate hate speech. The first bill proposing to regulate the phenomenon was the Human Rights Vindication Bill,[9] which prohibited undue discriminatory speech.[10] While this bill did not impose penalties on perpetrators and did not regulate hate speech, the media strongly opposed it, asserting that it would impermissibly violate freedom of speech, and the bill ultimately stalled.

Despite sensational coverage in the media, the public seemed largely uninterested in these issues at the time and few were even familiar with the term 'hate speech'.[11] During this period, almost all constitutional law scholars had opposed the regulation of hate speech other than a few, such as Masayuki Uchino and Toshiyuki Munesue.[12] As Shigenori Matsui pointed out, because the Japanese Supreme Court has long been highly deferential to the government and allowed restrictions on freedom of speech too easily, many scholars 'have argued for the introduction of freedom-of-expression jurisprudence from the United States'.[13] Generally speaking, they were interested in the principle of content neutrality that is found in the First Amendment to the US Constitution. These scholars claimed that if the Diet were to enact hate speech regulation, it would be difficult to justify under a doctrine of freedom of expression influenced by the US model. They also criticized the Human Rights Vindication Bill as lacking a concrete definition of discriminatory speech and as discriminating speech based on its

[8] Chapter 4 describes the extent of vicious hate speech against Burakumin.

[9] Chapter 6 overviews the contents of this bill and explains why it could not pass in the Diet.

[10] This bill did not use the term 'hate speech' and it was used in the media only rarely.

[11] According to the newspaper database, Asahisinbun, one of the biggest newspaper companies in Japan, published no articles featuring the term 'hate speech' between 1984 and 2002, whereas it published 1,350 such articles between 2003 and 2018.

[12] See, e.g., Masayuki Uchino, *Sabetsuteki Hyōgen* [Discriminatory expression] (Yuhikaku, 1990); Toshiyuki Munesue, 'Sabetsuteki Hyōgen' ['Discriminatory expression'], in Kazuyuki Takahashi and Makoto Oishi (eds.), *Kenpō no Sōten* [Issues of constitutional law], 3rd ed. (Yuhikaku, 1999), 104.

[13] See Chapter 2.

content.[14] In addition, many scholars were not as familiar with the problem of hate speech as were many citizens because hate speech aimed at Burakumin had not yet been explicit in form.[15]

In recent years, however, the issue of whether the government should regulate hate speech has become a pressing problem in Japan. The number of xenophobic groups has risen rapidly since the early 2000s, as has the number of anti-Korean and anti-Chinese rallies and demonstrations.[16] Moreover, a growing number of Japanese people now appear to harbour hostility towards the Korean Peninsula and China; according to research conducted by the Cabinet Office, the percentage of those who feel close to South Korea has decreasing swiftly since 2011.[17]

Zainichitokken o yurusanai shimin no kai ('Group of Citizens Who Do Not Tolerate Privileges for Ethnic Korean Residents in Japan', known as *Zaitokukai*), one of the most well-known xenophobic groups in Japan, was established in 2006. Zaitokukai and other xenophobic groups believe that Korean residents in Japan[18] are granted special privileges, misinterpreting the meaning of special permanent residency and alleging special welfare and preferential tax treatment. These groups insist that granting such special privileges to Korean residents in Japan amounts to reverse discrimination against Japanese people. As such, members have marched in the Korean communities, such as Shin-Okubo in Tokyo and Tsuruhashi in Osaka, using loudspeakers to shout highly discriminatory insults. Additionally, members have recorded their rallies and released them on online sites such as YouTube to disseminate their assertions.

Zaitokukai had also marched in front of Korean schools, established by Korean residents after the Pacific War to teach their children the Korean language, culture, and history. These schools are not officially acknowledged

[14] See, e.g., Shigenori Matsui, *Masu Media no Hyōgen no Jiyū* [Freedom of expression of the mass media] (Nihon Hyoronsha, 2005), 187–91.

[15] According to Magazineplus, one of the most famous databases on academic papers in Japan, only 22 papers on hate speech were prepared before December 2012. In contrast, there were 565 papers prepared between January 2013 and April 2019.

[16] Chapter 5 illustrates current trends in hate speech targeting Korean and Chinese residents in Japan.

[17] Cabinet Office, *Public Opinion Survey on Diplomacy* (2015), available at http://survey.gov-online.go.jp/h27/h27-gaiko/zh/z14.html [accessed 17 January 2018].

[18] Today, some 450,000 Koreans who do not have Japanese citizenship live in Japan. The Ministry of Justice releases the statistics on foreign residents in Japan every year. See www.moj.go.jp/nyuukokukanri/kouhou/nyuukokukanri04_00068.html [accessed 17 January 2018].

as schools under the School Education Act, because they do not meet the requirements of the Japanese Ministry of Education, Culture, Sports, Science and Technology. Some Korean schools are said to use textbooks that glorify Kim Il Sung and Kim Jong Il, and to hang their pictures on the classroom wall, and so xenophobic groups have criticized the Korean schools for their educational content.

One of the most memorable recent instances in which Zaitokukai and other groups protested in front of such a school is that which gave rise to the *Kyoto Korean Elementary School* case.[19] In this incident, the Kyoto police arrested some members of Zaitokukai, who were prosecuted for forcible obstruction of business,[20] insult,[21] and damage or destruction of structure.[22] Kyoto District Court found them guilty on 21 April 2011.[23] One of the defendants appealed to Osaka High Court, but the lower court's judgment was affirmed.[24] The same defendant then appealed to the Supreme Court, where the appeal was dismissed.[25] The school then filed a suit against some participants of the protest and Kyoto District Court ordered these groups to pay damages amounting to approximately US$120,000 on 7 October 2013,[26] which is an exceptionally large sum for a Japanese civil lawsuit. The defendants appealed to Osaka High Court, but again the judgment was affirmed.[27] They then appealed to the Supreme Court, but it too dismissed the appeal.[28] This case demonstrated that some aspects of hate speech can be regulated by existing laws for defamation, threat, or insult. At the same time, however, it also revealed the limitations of existing laws, Kyoto District Court clearly stating that there is no remedy in law for hate speech that is not directed at a specific target.

Major newspapers devoted space to this incident. According to an official survey conducted by the Centre for Human Rights Education and Training at the behest of the Ministry of Justice, while there had only been one newspaper article that had mentioned 'hate speech' in 2012, the

[19] Chapter 12 offers a detailed history of this case, while Chapter 13 analyses it from a legal perspective.
[20] Penal Code, art. 234.
[21] Penal Code, art. 231.
[22] Penal Code, art. 261.
[23] Kyoto District Court, 21 April 2011, unreported.
[24] Osaka High Court, 28 October 2011, unreported.
[25] Supreme Court, 23 February 2012, unreported.
[26] Kyoto District Court 7 October 2013, 2208 Hanji 74.
[27] Osaka High Court, 8 July 2014, 2232 Hanji 34.
[28] Supreme Court, 3rd Petty Bench, 9 December, 2014, unreported.

number has been rapidly rising since 2013,[29] especially in the aftermath of the civil judgment in *Kyoto Korean Elementary School*. In fact, an opinion poll conducted in 2017 shows that almost all respondents were familiar with the phrase 'hate speech' as used in the news media.[30] In other words, the case is the one of the major reasons why many Japanese citizens came to understand the harsh reality of hate speech in Japan and became interested in the issue. The case triggered a nationwide debate about whether and how the Japanese government should regulate hate speech, ultimately leading to public demands to enact hate speech laws.

In response to public opinion, the opposition parties – that is, the Democratic Party and the Social Democratic Party – presented a bill in 2015, which provided that no one shall commit unfair discriminatory behaviour and speech.[31] In 2016, a ruling coalition of the Liberal Democratic Party (LDP) and Komeito Party formed a working group on this issue and presented another bill. Ultimately, the Diet enacted the HSEA on 24 May 2016, which clearly declares that hate speech is 'not permissible'. The law assigns various duties to national and local governments to tackle hate speech, but it does not impose penalties because of concerns that sanctions might deprive individuals of their freedom of expression.

Around this time, some constitutional scholars began to assert that hate speech regulation could be justified under article 21 of the Constitution of Japan.[32] They realized that the facts of the case were such as to justify the introduction of hate speech regulation, even though

29 Ministry of Justice, *Heito Supīchi ni Kansuru Jittaichōsa Hōkokusho* [Report on the survey on the actual situation concerning hate speech] (March 2016), available at www.moj.go.jp/content/001201158.pdf#search=%27%E6%94%BF%E5%BA%9C+%E7%B5%B1%E8%A8%88+%E3%83%98%E3%82%A4%E3%83%88%E3%82%B9%E3%83%94%E3%83%BC%E3%83%81%27 [accessed 17 January 2018]. According to this survey, 235 newspaper articles mentioned 'hate speech' in 2013; in 2014, the figure rose to 324.

30 *Jinken Yōgo ni Kansuru Seronchōsa* [An opinion poll on the protection of human rights] (December 2017), available at https://survey.gov-online.go.jp/h29/h29-jinken/zh/z18.html [accessed 17 January 2018].

31 *Jinshutō o Riyū to suru Sabetsu no Teppai no Tame no Seisaku no Suishin ni Kansuru Hōritsuan* [The Bill on the Promotion of Measures to Eliminate Discrimination Based on Race and Other Reasons], House of Representatives, 189th Session (Regular Session), 2015, available at www.shugiin.go.jp/internet/itdb_gian.nsf/html/gian/honbun/houan/g18902007.htm [accessed 17 January 2018].

32 I claimed that, because it was a refusal to recognize minority people as equal citizens and thus would violate human dignity, hate speech could be regulated under article 21 of the Constitution: Shinji Higaki, *Heito Supīchi Kisei no Kenpōgakuteki Kōsatsu* [A constitutional analysis of hate speech regulation] (Horitsubunkasha, 2017).

most scholars remains reluctant.[33] The prevalent thinking was that although the hate speech that had been aimed at Koreans, including children, had been severe, it was dangerous to regulate it because the terms 'hate speech' was highly ambiguous and its regulation could easily be extended to legitimate political speech[34] – one of the reasons why the Diet did not criminalize it.[35]

III. The Hate Speech Elimination Act

A. An Overview

As already noted, the Japanese Diet enacted the HSEA in 2016. This Act consists of only seven provisions, a preamble, and supplementary provisions, which makes it short and to the point compared to many other laws.

The preamble explains the legislative facts, and declares that unfair discriminatory speech and behaviour inciting 'the exclusion[36] of persons and their descendants, who are residing lawfully in Japan, from local communities in our country by reason of such persons originating from a country or region other than Japan' will not be tolerated.

33 See Yuji Nasu, *Heito Supīchihō no Hikaku Kenkyū* [A comparative study of hate speech laws] (Shinzansha, 2019), 448–81.

34 On 28 August 2014, the LDP held a meeting for the project team considering countermeasures for hate speech. Sanae Takaichi, chair of the LDP Policy Research Council at that time, said that regulation for public demonstration around the Parliament building should have been considered together with hate speech regulation in this meeting. As her utterance suggests, the LDP sometimes attempts to restrict freedom of speech, assembly, and public demonstration in the name of public welfare. See Chapter 2. In addition, because the Supreme Court is highly deferential to the government, most Japanese constitutional law scholars, strongly affected by the US doctrine, are sceptical about the court and reluctant to introduce regulations in general. They have claimed that the harm in hate speech should be resolved by means of education and more dialogue among the parties affected.

35 It can be easily recognized that the drafters of the HSEA were influenced by the mainstream doctrine of constitutional law scholars and the US doctrine behind them. See Nasu, note 33, at 390–91. They sometimes referred to the principle of content neutrality during deliberations in the Committee on Judicial Affairs. For example, Katsuo Yakura pointed out that 'freedom of expression is the right that forms the basis of democracy, so regulations concerning the content of expression must be carefully considered'. See Chapter 10.

36 The word 'exclusion' in this Act refers to the social exclusion of minorities, rather than the legal exclusion of such persons. As the legislative fact of this Act showed, minority residents have repeatedly suffered as the targets of demonstrations by hate speakers such as Zaitokukai. These demonstrators have repeatedly shouted that Koreans should get out of the neighbourhood. This may have had some influence upon the drafters of the HSEA.

Article 1 sets out the purpose of the Act. It declares that Japan will tackle unfair discriminatory speech and behaviour, as pressing issues. Article 2 defines 'unfair discriminatory speech and behaviour against persons originating from outside Japan' as 'unfair discriminatory speech and behaviour to incite the exclusion of persons originating exclusively from a country or region other than Japan or their descendants and who are lawfully residing in Japan . . . from the local community by reason of such persons originating from a country or region other than Japan'. As such, it covers in part that hate speech which is directed towards a general group, which does not fall within the scope of any previously existing law. As we will see, however, this definition is problematic.

Article 3 asserts the moral duty of the general public. It declares that the 'general public shall further their understanding of the need to eliminate unfair discriminatory speech and behaviour', as defined in article 2, and 'shall endeavour to contribute to the realization of a society free from' unfair discriminatory speech and behaviour. Article 4 establishes that the law assigns various duties to both national and local governments in tackling hate speech. Article 5, 6, and 7 provide basic measures regarding these obligations.

B. The Act as Government Speech

The HSEA requests that national and local governments implement educational activities to eliminate unfair discriminatory speech and behaviour, as well as to raise awareness among the general public about this issue. In response to this Act, the human rights organizations of the Ministry of Justice are actively working to increase public awareness of hate speech, to make it clearly understood that such hate speech is unacceptable. These awareness campaigns utilize media such as newspaper advertisements, posters and leaflets, public transport advertisements, and Internet ads, as well as spot video on YouTube. In addition, the Ministry intends to expand opportunities to raise awareness through human rights training and other classes, and to enhance public information and public relations through the Counselling Service.[37] Such government's activities can be interpreted as a type of 'government speech'.

[37] *Hōmushō: Heito Supīchi ni Shōten o Ateta Keihatsukatsudō* [The Ministry of Justice: promotion activities focusing on hate speech], available at www.moj.go.jp/ENGLISH/m_jinken04_00001.html [accessed 17 January 2018].

Although article 21 of the Japanese Constitution limits the government's ability to regulate freedom of expression, it does not constrain the government from speaking. A law prohibiting certain types of speech based on its content would be fundamentally unconstitutional unless it passed strict scrutiny. In other words, such a law is justified only when it is narrowly tailored to serve a compelling governmental interest. However, when the government is acting as a speaker and not as a regulator, it is unfettered by constitutional prohibitions on content and viewpoint discrimination.[38] This can be referred to as the 'government speech doctrine', developed in the US Supreme Court.[39] That court pointed out that, '[w]hen government speaks, it is not barred by the Free Speech Clause [of the First Amendment to the US Constitution] from determining the content of what it says'.[40] It also stated that 'it is not easy to imagine how government could function if it lacked th[e] freedom' to select the messages it wishes to convey.[41] In other words, in democratic countries, governments are required to explain their position[42] and they do not have to be content- or viewpoint-neutral when they speak or subsidize private institutions.[43]

According to Charlotte H. Taylor, 'government speech offers a third path', which 'can be used deliberately to discourage and deter' hate

[38] Charlotte H. Taylor, 'Hate Speech and Government Speech' (2010) 12 *U. Pa. J. Const. L.* 1115, at 1120.

[39] See, e.g., Mark G. Yudof, 'When Governments Speak: Toward a Theory of Government Expression and the First Amendment' (1979) 57 *Tex. L. Rev.* 863; Steven Shiffrin, 'Government Speech' (1980) 27 *UCLA L. Rev.* 565; Andy G. Olree, 'Identifying Government Speech' (2009) 42 *Conn. L. Rev.* 365.

[40] *Walker* v. *Texas Division, Sons of Confederate Veterans*, 135 S.Ct. 2239, 2245 (2015) (citing *Pleasant Grove City* v. *Summum*, 555 U.S. 460, 467–68 (2009)).

[41] *Summum*, 555 U.S. at 468.

[42] Randall P. Bezanson, *Too Much Free Speech?* (University of Illinois Press, 2012), 106, pointed out that 'speech by the government is essential to our democracy' and asserted that:

> We live in a country [the United States] premised on the individual's control, through the vote or the power of our own speech to others about government, through challenges to administrative action in the federal, state, and local bureaucracies, and through our right to petition government and to take to the streets, sidewalks, and parks in protest to its actions. To do these things we need information from the government. What policies is it supporting, what reasons justify government actions, what consequences will befall us? To hold government and its agencies and its employees accountable we need to hear from them.

[43] See, e.g., *Walker*, 135 S.Ct. 2239; Joseph Blocher, 'View Point Neutrality and Government Speech' (2011) 52 *B.C. L. Rev.* 695.

speech.[44] She claims that 'because government expression is not binding on citizens as laws and court decision are, it does not amount to impermissible content or viewpoint discrimination'.[45] She emphasizes that since government speech is softer than legal regulation, it 'might be expected to produce less resentment and ensuing resistance',[46] and that it 'would have the benefit of giving potentially empowering information to targets of hate speech'.[47] Because government speech has such advantages compared to regulation, it therefore has the potential to strike an appropriate balance between freedom of speech and anti-racism. The HSEA can be interpreted as a motion whereby the Diet asks the national and local governments to declare their position – namely, to oppose and criticize hate speech. In addition, it asks the governments to enhance educational activities, which is a very typical example of government speech.[48] In this case, because the government does not have to be content- or viewpoint-neutral, it can avoid the constitutional problems in the definition of hate speech provided in article 2 of the HSEA. For example, the government can use this Act as a guideline to select which private institution to subsidize.

Of course, some fear that government speech may be too powerful and can distort the 'marketplace of ideas'. John Owen Haley suggested that, compared to Western law, Japanese law is effective even absent the power to enforce it.[49] In Japan, there are many principle laws or basic laws that impose *the obligation to make an effort* to achieve legislative ends, but impose *no sanctions*. Despite this absence of formal enforcement mechanisms, the Japanese people have generally obeyed such laws and fulfilled

[44] Taylor, note 38, at 1120.

[45] *Ibid.*, at 1122.

[46] *Ibid.*, at 1181.

[47] *Ibid.*, at 1179.

[48] It should be noted that there are many kinds of government speech and some of them are verging on regulation. Thus we must explore which types of government speech are appropriate to our goals. See *ibid.*

[49] See John Owen Haley, *Authority without Power: Law and the Japanese Paradox* (Oxford University Press, 1991), emphasizing the separation of authority and power in Japan, and the relative weakness of most forms of law enforcement.

Craig Martin summarizes Haley's observation. He points out that Japanese law 'often operates effectively to govern and modify behavior without the application of sanctions to enforce compliance', and has 'relied to a much greater extent upon informal social mechanisms for mobilizing compliance with criminal law'. See Craig Martin, 'Laws without Sanction: Hate Speech Laws and Balancing of Rights in Japan', in Keiichi Ageishi *et al.* (eds.) *Gendai Nihon no Hōkatei: Miyazawa Setsuo Sensei Koki Kinen* [The legal process in contemporary Japan: a Festschrift in honor of Professor Setsuo Miyazawa's 70th birthday] (Shinzansha, 2017), at 169–70.

such obligations. In other words, Japanese law has depended on an 'extralegal, informal mechanism of social control as a means of maintaining societal order with a concomitant transfer of effective control over the rules and norms that govern society to those who are able to manipulate these informal instruments of enforcement'.[50] In light of this perspective, government speech may be problematic and therefore the government should be careful to declare specific messages to be impermissible. As Mark G. Yudof pointed out, the government 'is forbidden from using a particular technique for indoctrination'.[51] At the very least, the government should not use its own speech to coerce people into having, or not having, specific ideas. In the case of the HSEA, however, since the message that the government declares 'impermissible' is a discriminatory insult that can be prohibited if it is aimed at a specific target, such government speech correlates with the idea set out in the Constitution.[52]

C. *Is the Act Problematic? Some Issues with the HSEA*

As government speech, the HSEA can be assessed as striking an appropriate balance between freedom of speech and anti-racism, but there are some critiques of this Act. One is that it does not encompass hate speech targeted towards ethnic minorities originating within Japan and illegal immigrants. The ethnic composition of Japan is not as diverse as that of other counties, but some ethnic minorities are indeed indigenous to Japan, such as the Ainu people in Hokkaido and the Ryukyu people of Okinawa. It should be noticed that both Houses of the Diet adopted the Supplementary Resolution to the HSEA, which states that 'it is not correct to believe that certain form[s] of discriminatory speech and behaviour may be allowed as long as [they are] not the "unfair discriminatory speech and behaviour against persons originating from outside Japan" provided for in Article 2', and that 'all discriminatory speech and behaviour shall be dealt with appropriately'.[53] However, the definition of

[50] Haley, note 49, at 13–14.

[51] Yudof, note 39, at 891.

[52] Toru Mori, 'Kenpō Soshō no Jissen to Riron (1): Heito Demo Kinshi Karishobun Meirei Jiken' ['The practice and the theory of constitutional litigation (1): The case of the order of provisional disposition prohibiting hateful demonstration'] (2017) 2321 *Hanji* 3, at 6.

[53] *Honpōgai Shusshinsha ni Taisuru Futō na Sabetsuteki Gendō no Kaishō ni Muketa Torikumi no Suishin ni Kansuru Hōritsuan ni Taisuru Futaiketsugi* [Supplementary Resolution for the Act on the Promotion of Efforts to Eliminate Unfair Discriminatory

hate speech provided in article 2 is apparently the type of viewpoint discrimination that the US Supreme Court held to be unconstitutional in *R.A.V.* v. *City of St. Paul*.[54]

Another issue has been raised regarding article 2 of the HSEA. It encompasses incitement of the exclusion of persons originating exclusively from a country or region other than Japan and/or their descendants, which is not a crime in itself unless it is directed at a specific target. The HSEA acknowledges incitement of hate speech to be impermissible even if it does not have clear and present danger. This is problematic because even incitement for crime cannot be prohibited unless such risks are evident. In other words, the HSEA is overly broad because it declares specific expressions, including lawful speech, to be impermissible. It is therefore in question whether the definition of hate speech provided in article 2 is sufficiently limited.[55]

The most important and controversial issue pertaining to this Act is that it does not criminalize hate speech, but rather assigns various duties to national and local governments to tackle hate speech. In this sense, the Act is nothing more than a 'principle law', which simply declares a basic principle. On the one hand, one might argue that the Act properly balances equality and freedom of speech. Since Japanese courts have been highly deferential to the Diet and have not rigorously undertaken any judicial review of free speech,[56] scholars claim that the problem of free speech must be discussed with more care, and therefore the evaluate this Act favourably. On the other hand, one might question the effect of this law in combating hate speech. For example, Craig Martin indicates that the HSEA 'leave[s] the vulnerable group exposed and unprotected, notwithstanding that the very enactment of the law acknowledges their plight', and that it is 'helping [to] mask the continued violation'.[57] He points out that although this Act is directed at the national and local governments, as well as the general public, it 'is not directed at, nor does it even refer to, the individuals or entities engaging in the communication of hate speech'.[58]

Speech and Behaviour against Persons Originating from Outside Japan], available at www.moj.go.jp/content/001199555.pdf [accessed 17 January 2018].

[54] *R.A.V.* v. *City of St. Paul*, 505 U.S. 377 (1992); see also Matsui, note 1, at 473–75.

[55] Matsui pointed out that 'the ban should be limited to extreme hate speech and willful promotion of hatred toward minority groups': Matsui, note 1, at 475–76.

[56] See, e.g., Shigenori Matsui, 'Freedom of Expression in Japan' (1991) 38 *Osaka University L. Rev.* 13, at 14–18.

[57] Martin, note 49, at 171.

[58] *Ibid.*, at 175.

This Act does not criminalize hate speech, but we can see that 'it can function as a guideline for the courts and the government' and that it has 'changed the attitude of national and local governments'.[59] In fact, during deliberations on the bill before the House of Councillors Committee on Judicial Affairs, one of the members stated that it could be a guideline for the interpretation of various laws.[60] Moreover, one scholar pointed out that the HSEA is intended to be an interpretational guideline for the courts,[61] as evidenced in the *Sakuramoto* case that was held a few days before the enforcement of the Act. In 2016, a xenophobic group announced that it would march in the district of Sakuramoto in Kawasaki City, Kanagawa Prefecture, where many Koreans live.[62] To prevent this protest, a social welfare corporation, whose president and the majority of whose staff are Korean-Japanese or Koreans who are permanent residents in Japan, filed a suit for an injunction prohibiting the demonstration. Yokohama District Court Kawasaki Branch accepted the claim, citing the HSEA, and it prohibited the xenophobic group from demonstrating within 500 metres of the social welfare corporation.[63] The court found that the speech intended by the xenophobic group fell within the definition of 'hate speech' in article 2 of the HSEA and that such speech would violate the personality rights of the victims. It was in this way that the court clearly used the HSEA as a guideline for the authority to control the demonstration.

Subsequently, the xenophobic group applied to use a public park for its demonstration. Freedom of assembly and freedom of speech are protected by article 2 of the Japanese Constitution,[64] and article 244(2) of the Local Autonomy Act provides that local government shall not deny the use of public facilities without 'legitimate reason'.[65] In other words,

[59] Junko Kotani, 'A Comment on Hate Speech Regulation in Japan after the Enactment of the Hate Speech Elimination Act of 2016' (2017) 21 *Hōsei Kenkyū* [Shizuoka University journal of law & policy] 1, at 9.

[60] *Dai 190 kai Kokkai Sangiin Hōmuiinkai Kaigiroku dai 8 gō* [The Minutes of the House of Councillors Committee on Judicial Affairs], 190th Diet, 19 April 2016, available at http://kokkai.ndl.go.jp/SENTAKU/sangiin/190/0003/19004190003008a.html [accessed 17 January 2018].

[61] Kensuke Ueda, 'Case Comment' (2016) 433 *Hōgaku Kyōshitsu* [Law classroom] 153.

[62] A xenophobic group had held a demonstration twice before this instance, chanting extremely abusively, and the group declared on its website that it would demonstrate again. Chapter 14 explains this case in detail.

[63] Yokohama District Court, Kawasaki Branch, 2 June 2016, 2296 Hanji 14.

[64] Constitution of Japan, art. 21(1): 'Freedom of assembly and association as well as speech, press and all other forms of expression is guaranteed.'

[65] Local Autonomy Act, art. 244(2): 'Ordinary local public entities shall not deny the use of public facilities by local residents without legitimate reasons.'

the government shall not reject an application unless there is 'clear and present danger' to human life, safety, property, or public safety.[66] Although it is difficult to meet this standard, as defined by the Japanese Supreme Court, Kawasaki City cited the HSEA and rejected the xenophobic group's application to use the public park. The city emphasized that the group had protested twice before in this area, shouting highly discriminatory insults each time. The city asserted that if the group were to march in the same way, there was substantial possibility that their protest would violate residents' rights to live in peace.

It should be reiterated here that the HSEA makes no provision for its enforcement and it merely declares basic principles. It is nothing more and nothing less. In other words, it does *not* regulate hate speech. This is why one of the drafting members of the HSEA, during deliberations before the House of Councillors Committee on Judicial Affairs, asserted that the definition of 'unfair discriminatory speech and behaviour' should have been interpreted loosely because it was principle law.[67] In other words, the Diet did not find it necessary to define hate speech narrowly for the Act to pass the strict scrutiny of judicial review precisely because the HSEA is a principle law and therefore does not regulate freedom of speech. In *Sakuramoto*, however, the HSEA had a legally binding power as a guideline for interpretation of other laws and hence it was used to regulate hate speech in practice.

To this extent, the HSEA is apparently content discrimination, according to *R.A.V.*, in which the US Supreme Court struck down the city of St. Paul's Bias-Motivated Crime Ordinance.[68] In *R.A.V.*, the Supreme Court stated that content discrimination could be justified only in the following situations:

[66] Supreme Court, 3rd Petty Bench, 7 March, 1995, 49 Minshū 687.

[67] *Dai 190 kai Kokkai Sangiin Hōmuiinkai Kaigiroku dai 10 gō* [The minutes of the House of Councillors Committee on Judicial Affairs], 190th Diet, 26 April 2016, available at http://kokkai.ndl.go.jp/SENTAKU/sangiin/190/0003/19004260003010.pdf [accessed 17 January 2018].

[68] In this case, the St. Paul's ordinance provided that:

> Whoever places on public or private property a symbol, object, appellation, characterization or graffiti, including, but not limited to, a burning cross or Nazi swastika, which one knows or has reasonable grounds to know arouses anger, alarm or resentment in others on the basis of race, color, creed, religion or gender commits disorderly conduct and shall be guilty of a misdemeanor.

St. Paul, Minn., Legis. Code, § 292.02 (1990); *R.A.V.*, 505 U.S. 377 (1992).

(1) if 'the basis for the content discrimination consists entirely of the very reason the entire class of speech at issue is proscribable, no significant danger of idea or viewpoint discrimination exists';[69]
(2) a 'content-defined subclass of proscribable speech is that the subclass happens to be associated with particular "secondary effects" of the speech';[70] and
(3) 'the nature of the content discrimination is such that there is no realistic possibility that official suppression of ideas is afoot'.[71]

The HSEA, however, does not fall within these exceptions.[72] Hate speech directed against Koreans is specifically harsh, but the kind of hate speech that the HSEA intends to prevent is aimed against persons originating exclusively from a country or region other than Japan, and/or their descendants, who are lawfully residing in Japan. It does not encompass hate speech against illegal immigrants and ethnic minorities indigenous to Japan.[73] Thus the HSEA is impermissibly content discrimination and

[69] *R.A.V.*, 505 U.S. at 388.

[70] *Ibid.*, at 389.

[71] *Ibid.*, at 390.

[72] In light of the past disposition of the Japanese Supreme Court, it appears incredible to me that it will never adopt the *R.A.V.* standard. However, the viewpoint neutrality principle is a fundamental element of the free speech principle and, accordingly, it naturally has universal appeal. The Japanese Supreme Court does not clearly endorse the principle, but it adopts the distinction between content-based and content-neutral regulation developed by the US Supreme Court. It can therefore be said that the Supreme Court of Japan implicitly accepts the viewpoint neutrality principle. In addition, most Japanese scholars support the US doctrine on freedom of speech and hence the Japanese government should enact laws accordingly.

[73] In *Virginia* v. *Black*, 538 U.S. 343, 362–63 (2003), the U.S. Supreme Court implied that the Virginia statute prohibiting cross-burning was constitutional because it met *R.A. V.* exception (1). Virginia statute §18.2–423 provided: 'It shall be unlawful for any person or persons, with the intent of intimidating any person or group of persons, to burn, or cause to be burned, a cross on the property of another, a highway or other public place. Any person who shall violate any provision of this section shall be guilty of a Class 6 felony.'

The US Supreme Court stated that 'the Virginia statute does not single out for opprobrium only that speech directed toward "one of the specified disfavored topics" ', and that it prohibited true threat, which is a particularly virulent form of intimidation:

> Instead of prohibiting all intimidating messages, Virginia may choose to regulate this subset of intimidating messages in light of cross burning's long and pernicious history as a signal of impending violence. . . . A ban on cross burning carried out with the intent to intimidate is fully consistent with our holding in *R. A. V.* and is proscribable under the First Amendment.

Unlike the Virginia Statute, the HSEA apparently discriminates based on viewpoint.

its scope is not narrowly tailored. If the HSEA were to have legally binding power, it could be facially unconstitutional. As such, the Act should not be interpreted as a guideline for other laws.

IV. Conclusion

The majority of Japanese constitutional law scholars have been strongly influenced by the doctrine of US constitutional law, especially in the area of freedom of speech.[74] In regard to hate speech, many scholars are highly supportive of *R.A.V.* In other words, most Japanese constitutional law scholars have considered hate speech regulations to be fundamentally unconstitutional. However, as noted earlier, the Japanese Supreme Court has been highly deferential to the Diet. In fact, many scholars criticize the Supreme Court for failing to take seriously the value of the freedom of expression. Other scholars foresee that if the Diet were to enact laws regulating hate speech, the Supreme Court would likely uphold their constitutionality[75] and therefore endanger that freedom. Regardless of such risk, however, more than a few are seeking further regulation, such as criminal punishment, in light of the recent escalating situation.

The Japanese government appears to remain reluctant to further regulate hate speech. In 2017, the United Nations' Human Rights Committee revealed that the Japanese government had submitted a report to the Committee in which it stated that Japan does not need to strength its hate speech regulation, because incitement of racial discrimination rarely occurs in the country. Such a position, however, does not indicate that the Japanese government is supportive of the freedom of speech.[76]

Under current circumstances, hate speech regulation must be implemented deliberately in Japan. The HSEA may be a second-best way of preventing hate speech, at the very least,[77] but it may be the most suitable

[74] See Chapter 1, section I.

[75] See, e.g., Kotani, note 59, at 223.

[76] For example, Japan ranked 72nd in the World Press Freedom Index. Reporters without Borders stated that '[m]edia freedom in Japan has been declining ever since Shinzo Abe became Prime Minister again in 2012' and pointed towards various problems, such as Kisha clubs ('reporters' clubs'), which eliminate freelancers and foreign reporters. See https://rsf.org/en/japan [accessed 17 January 2018].

[77] I believe that there are better measures with which to combat hate speech, but it is always difficult to find the most appropriate policy in the real world. The HSEA and the whole framework of the Japanese model are suitable for the time being, but it is still far from the optimal solution.

model of hate speech law in the world. There are several points that we might highlight as its strengths of the HSEA. First, it respects the 'marketplace of ideas', which is based on the fundamental principles of modern law, such as freedom, autonomy, and self-realization. Second, numerous works on hate speech have argued that the criminal regulation of public discourse will cause undesirable backlash, produce martyrs, or drive dangerous speech underground, but the Japanese non-regulatory model is immune to these problems.[78] Finally, by condemning hate speech by means of the HSEA, the Japanese government sends a clear message of its condemnation of hate speech to its own people, as well as to other countries.

Hate speech is a serious problem not only in Japan, but also all around the globe, yet freedom of speech is one of the most fundamental rights with which we maintain democracy. Many liberal and democratic countries struggle to balance the freedom of speech with anti-racism.[79] As government speech, the HSEA can be used to discourage and deter hate speech, while avoiding constitutional problems. It is one of the most rational ways of striking a balance between the freedom of speech and anti-racism, and it may also be the most appropriate alternative path to discourage and deter hate speech without regulating the freedom of expression.

[78] As Chapter 7 points out, we already have some provision to regulate hate speech targeting particular persons, corporations, or associations. It is in this sense that Japan regulates hate speech. In addition, the HSEA does not provide any regulations and therefore we used the term 'non-regulatory approach' when referring to the methodology adopted under the Act.

[79] See, e.g., Michael Herz and Peter Molnar (eds.), *The Content and Context of Hate Speech: Rethinking Regulation and Responses* (Cambridge University Press, 2012); Erik Bleich, *The Freedom to Be Racist? How the United States and Europe Struggle to Preserve Freedom and Combat Racism* (Oxford University Press, 2011); Ivan Hare and James Weinstein (eds.), *Extreme Speech and Democracy* (Oxford University Press, 2009).

PART IV

Cases

12

Kyoto Korean Elementary School Case

The Facts

IL-SONG NAKAMURA, TRANSLATED BY MANA SATO

I. Introduction

On 4 December 2009, *Kyōto Chōsen Daiichi Shokyū Gakkō* ('Kyoto Korean No. 1 Elementary School'), which was located in Minami Ward, Kyoto City, came under attack by xenophobes. Most of the 11 attackers belonged to racist group *Zainichi Tokken o Yurusanai Shimin no Kai* ('Association of Citizens against Special Privileges of the Zainichi'[1]), commonly known as *Zaitokukai*.[2] This was the first in a series of attacks on the school. After this first attack, the perpetrators posted online to incite others to participate in two more discriminatory demonstrations planned for the vicinity of the school, at which the demonstrators were protected by several hundred police officers. At this time, Zaitokukai was only beginning to expand its sphere of influence, its members in east and west Japan escalating the extremity of their words and deeds in competition with each other. Happening during the first wave of xenophobic movements that are unprecedented in Japan, this incident is one of the pivotal moments informing discussion of hate speech in Japan. More than ten years have passed since then, yet the racists continue to spew hate however they please.

1 A short form of *Zainichi Chōsenjin* ('Koreans living in Japan') or *Zainichi Kankokujin* ('nationals of the Republic of Korea living in Japan'). *Zainichi* is a term used to refer generally to those ethnic Koreans who migrated to the mainland Japan during Japan's colonial rule over Korea and to their descendants.

2 Zaitokukai is a racist group formed in 2007 under the leadership of Makoto Takata, more widely known as Makoto Sakurai, a blogger whose primary interest lies in insulting the Republic of Korea (ROK). Zaitokukai accuses those from ex-Japanese colonies of having 'privileged' legal status in Japan (which is not the case) and also makes demands such as the abolition of the livelihood protection scheme (the Japanese welfare system). Sakurai later formed and became leader of political party *Nippon Daiichitō* (Japan First Party), which promotes xenophobic agendas.

The racist attacks shattered the daily lives of all those targeted. The school and parents came together to discuss how to cope with the situation. After nights of heated arguments, they reached a decision: they would launch a legal battle against the racists. They were fully aware of the possible drawbacks such as retaliation or drawing out the period during which they had to deal with the aftermath of the incidents. Nevertheless, they were determined to take the risk and endure the pain that would accompany the battle. Eventually, four of the attackers were convicted in a criminal trial, and a civil suit resulted in the courts ordering Zaitokukai and the attackers to pay ¥12.26 million in compensation and banning them from demonstrating within a 200-metre radius of the school's main gate.

The civil suit ruling was only the third ever case in Japan to cite the International Convention on the Elimination of All Forms of Racial Discrimination (ICERD). It was also the very first case in Japan's judicial history in which 'a social environment in which the Zainichi provide ethnic education' was regarded as a legal interest. By the last stages of the hearings, hate speech had become a social issue in Japan. Citizens began to protest *against* the racists – activists commonly referred to as *kauntā* ('counter-demonstrators') – and several members of the Diet made statements expressing concern about these xenophobic demonstrations. The mass media thus described the Kyoto incident as 'the starting point of the hate speech issue', and the liberal papers and television stations largely celebrated the school's legal victory.

However, an array of problems still awaits resolution. The plaintiff (the school) and the parents fought their legal battle under slogans such as 'Create a hate crime-free society!' and 'Secure the right to ethnic education [*minzoku kyōikuken*]!' As regards the first of these goals, the Japanese criminal justice system still lacks clear standards for aggravated crimes motivated by discrimination. Japan has no effective legal system regulating incitement to discrimination (i.e. hate speech) that induces hate crimes. These are factors that allow perplexing spectacles to survive in Japan, where dozens and sometimes hundreds of police officers will guard a handful of chauvinists as they march in the streets. In other words, in practice nothing has changed in the ten years since Kyoto Korean No. 1 Elementary School was attacked.

Likewise, the second goal, 'securing the right to ethnic education', is yet to be fulfilled. The incident and the court battle were concurrent with a process whereby the Japanese government excluded Korean schools[3] – and only Korean schools – from its programme waiving high-school tuition fees. What we see here is a discrimination double standard: a state that established the Hate Speech Elimination Act as an effort to eliminate discrimination by citizens[4] is taking the lead in discriminating against Korean schools. Acting substantially in concert with the state, prefectures such as Tokyo, Saitama, and Osaka withheld or abolished existing subsidies for Korean schools. While such action is spreading across the country, it does not attract as much attention as xenophobic demonstrations do. The schools filed lawsuits against the state, but all lost their cases. The authorities – both executive and judicial – are, in effect, sending a message that, 'We can do whatever we want to Korean schools'. This is nothing other than state-level incitement to hate crime.

In this chapter, centring on the results of interviews with parties involved, I build a picture of the actual harms perpetuated by the Kyoto incident, the pain and hopes of the parents and teachers who went on to fight back in court, and the problems that remain even after they achieved legal victory.

II. An Overview of the Incident

On the afternoon of 4 December 2009, 11 individuals gathered at the south gate of the Kyoto Korean No. 1 Elementary School. Most of these individuals were members of racist associations, including Zaitokukai.[5] The school did not own its playground; rather, under a tripartite agreement with the neighbourhood community and Kyoto City, the school used a neighbouring City-owned park as its playground. The attackers alleged that this constituted Koreans 'unlawfully occupying' Japanese national territory. Gathering at the school with the agenda of 'taking back the park', they established themselves in front of the main school

[3] The term 'Korean school(s)' technically includes not only those run by Chongryon, but also the Korean Residents Union in Japan, which is an ROK-related organization. However, the Korean schools excluded from the tuition waiver programme are specifically those run by Chongryon; hence the 'Korean school(s)' discussed in this chapter refer to these Chongryon-affiliated schools.

[4] While the Act did not include any provision to prohibit hate speech or to prescribe penalties, it stated that the national government would take responsibility for working towards the elimination of hate speech.

[5] Some of the attackers belonged to another racist group, *Shuken Kaifuku o Mezasu Kai* ('Association Aiming for Recovery of Sovereignty'), commonly known as *Shukenkai*. The 11 attackers acted in concert at the time, calling themselves *Chīmu Kansai* ('Team Kansai').

gate, demanded that teachers 'open the gate', and shouted through loudspeakers for nearly an hour, all while children were in the school.

The rally started when lunch break was almost over. The attackers approached several third-graders (i.e. children aged 8 or 9) when they went out to the faucet area in the courtyard to brush their teeth. A video of the attack, uploaded to a video-sharing website by the attackers themselves as evidence of their 'spoils of war', shows children, visibly scared, scurrying past behind two teachers facing the attackers. The echoing roars and the hostile atmosphere pinned one of the girls to the spot as though she were struck by lightning. The pupils rushed back into their classroom on the second floor and reported to their homeroom teacher. Soon after, the attackers started showering the School with abuse and insults:

> This piece of land was taken [by Koreans] during the War, raping and massacring women to seize this land while the men were away!
> This land belonged to the Japanese to begin with. You took it from us after the War, isn't that right!?!
> This is an act of invasion, you know, by North Korea . . .
> They are taking advantage of the Japanese people who had to start over from the ruins after the War, seizing land everywhere in Japan under the façade of these ethnic schools, fights for ethnic education and stuff . . .
> This place is an academy for North Korean spies!
> These are descendants of illegals!
> You criminal Koreans!
> Kids educated by criminals!
> I don't see any kids; they're kids of spies!
> You should've stayed on the side of the road from the beginning!
> Promises are made between human beings. Promises don't work between human beings and Koreans!
> You Korean mobsters! You're in trouble big time . . .

The third-grade pupils were old enough to understand the slogans to some extent. The first to burst into tears was a girl who was celebrating her birthday that day. Her sobs were contagious and, in no time, more than half of the class were crying. Their sobs and cries were so frantic that their teacher feared 'they might just shatter into pieces'. With first-, second- and third-grade classrooms all on the same floor, two female teachers were hard pressed to attend to all of the shocked children. In the auditorium located on the north side of the third floor, some 120 pupils were in a joint class, gathering fifth- and sixth-graders from the four Korean primary schools that then existed in Kyoto and Shiga Prefectures. Doing their best to muffle the shouts and roars of the attackers, the teachers closed all of the curtains and turned up the music they were using for recreational activities. It was impossible to shut them out entirely. Male teachers went down to the ground floor to prevent the attackers from entering the school's premises. They, along with some 50 parents and former students who had heard the news and came rushing to the school, one after another, faced the attackers from inside the gates.

In fact, the attackers had issued notice beforehand that they planned to launch this attack. During a discriminatory rally that took place in front of the Kyoto Prefectural Committee of *Zai-Nihon Chōsenjin Sōrengōkai* ('General Association of Korean Residents in Japan'), commonly known as *Chongryon*, the previous month, they had bellowed, 'We can't say when, but we'll go to your schools!' They then posted an 'announcement video' recorded in the school's neighbourhood to a video-sharing website. Thus put on notice, the school had been on alert and had even consulted the police. The school had agreed upon two points in advance: they would not resort to force to confront the racists, and they would not let the attackers onto the school's premises. Chongryon, an organization that functions as DPRK's de facto embassy and controls Korean schools, is policed and monitored by the Japanese Public Security Bureau. Should a scuffle have broken out between the school and the attackers, it was likely that blame would be placed solely upon the school, resulting in large-scale raids.[6] The biggest reason why they agreed on a policy of non-resistance, however, was that the school and parents did not want to resort to violence in a space meant for children and their education.

Police officers arrived at the scene of the attack some 10 minutes after the school's emergency call – and they gave the situation their tacit approval. Emboldened by the school's non-resistance and police silence, the attackers' actions became more aggressive. They knocked down the soccer goal post that the school had placed in the park (which was also used by local Japanese boys). They dragged out the platform used for morning assemblies that had been placed in the corner of the park and

[6] There have been countless cases in which the police launched large-scale raids of Chongryon and schools to confiscate items, including lists of names. The spurious grounds for such raids were petty offences including parking violations and technical offences pertaining to administrative procedures; even worse, other charges were wholly false. To give an example from Kyoto, in June 1994, the Kyoto police mobilized 350 officers to raid targets including Chongryon's headquarters, claiming that Chongryon had failed to stamp a seal necessary in the process of a land transaction (the procedures had, in fact, been completed appropriately). Two years previously, 100 officers had raided Shiga Korean Primary School on ground that it was keeping a car at a place not registered in its parking space certificate.

smashed it against the school gate. They destroyed the speakers installed on the park's backstop, took them to the gate, and demanded that the school collect the broken equipment.

The fifth- and sixth-graders soon noticed that something was wrong. One girl I interviewed, who had been a fifth-grader at the time, recalled what happened:

> One of my classmates came upstairs and told me that things are going crazy downstairs. I hurried downstairs and found the kids sobbing and crying frantically in the classroom. At that point, I had no idea what was going on outside. So, I asked them, 'What's wrong?' But they just cried and cried. I rushed back upstairs to get my friends, and then just hugged the younger kids, rubbed their backs, and told them, 'It's okay', 'Everything's fine', 'No need to be scared'.

The rally lasted for nearly an hour, during which the school staff stationed in the courtyard bore the full brunt of the hate speech. They stood dazed even as the attackers left, shouting 'We'll be back!' over their shoulders.

Park Chong-im, head of the *omonikai* ('mothers' association') at the time, described what it was like immediately everything was over: 'Nobody said anything. The atmosphere was chilling.' Had they retaliated, they would have been met with further hateful blows. The children were right behind them. The long hours during which the school, parents, and children had waited for the incident to pass had stripped them of words. This is an example of the so-called silencing effect of hate speech.

The police tolerated the attackers on that day, allowing them to do whatever they wanted – and this was far from the only time the police gave their support to the racists. Soon after the school submitted its criminal complaint, the attackers planned a second demonstration, for 14 January of the following year. Again, that demonstration started in the park next to the school and, again, it was scheduled in the daytime on a weekday, when children would be at the school. The police nonetheless approved the demonstration and it went ahead as planned. On 28 March, immediately after Kyoto District Court had granted the 'provisional disposition forbidding demonstrations' that the school had requested of it, another discriminatory demonstration was planned in Higashi-Kujo, an area with the largest Zainichi Korean population in Kyoto. As they had for the second demonstration, the police approved the plans and dispatched 100 riot police personnel to protect the racists as they marched. In June 2016, expressions that incite discrimination were declared to be unacceptable under the Hate Speech Elimination Act[7] (although it prescribes no penalties). Despite this, we in Japan still continue to witness police officers – frequently outnumbering demonstrators more than tenfold – being sent out to protect the racists from counter-protestors.[8] Thus the issue of hate demonstrations is simultaneously an issue of institutional discrimination within the police and, in this sense too, the Kyoto incident can be seen as the prototype of the many similar demonstrations that took place thereafter in Japan.

III. Korean Schools: The Target of the Attacks

The Korean school that was the target of the attacks is one of the self-initiated schools for Zainichi Koreans living in Japan. Aiming to nurture the children's ethnic identity as Koreans as well as their bonds with *dongpo* ('fellow countrymen'), these are operated as full-time schools adopting the 6–3–3 system like Japanese schools.[9] At time of writing, 65 Korean schools are operating in Japan, with a total of more than 6,000 students. However, these schools are legally defined as *kakushu gakkō* ('miscellaneous schools'), which are not 'schools' as defined in article 1 of the School Education Act of Japan. Korean schools therefore do not qualify for Japanese governmental subsidies; instead, the schools have sought subsidies from municipalities as a result of the long-standing rights movement led by Zainichi Koreans and their Japanese supporters. However, the amount of the subsidies is meagre and, in many cases, the administration prescribes how the money should be used, forbidding the schools from using it to pay teachers or cover other labour costs.[10] Worse

[7] The Hate Speech Elimination Act is the first anti-racism Act in Japan. However, as a symbolic law that prescribes no penalties, the Act bears little legal validity. The Act is limited in its scope as well, covering only people 'originating from outside Japan' who 'live [in Japan] legally', such as Zainichi Koreans and South Koreans. This has a limited impact on Zaitokukai, since the group raised its profile by framing its attacks as against 'foreigners without residential status'. Moreover, Zainichi are not the only targets of hate speech in Japan; various groups, such as *Burakumin* ('Buraku people', i.e. descendants of feudal-era outcast groups), the Ainu people, the Ryukyuan people, and LGBTQ+ people are targeted.

[8] On 9 March 2019, while I was writing this chapter, a racist demonstration 'commemorated' this incident, with 150 police officers 'guarding' a mere four participants.

[9] With the establishment of *Chōsen Daigakkō* (Korea University) in 1956, an integrated ethnic education system for Korean children came into existence, reaching from primary school to university.

[10] The subsidies are to be used only for certain predetermined purposes, such as expenses for learning materials and 'expenses for international exchange' (i.e. for exchange projects with Japanese schools).

yet, in synchronization with the recent exclusion of Korean schools from the high-school tuition waiver programme[11] (started in April 2010), prefectures such as Tokyo, Saitama, and Osaka have declared that they will suspend these subsidies. Similar moves are being made by municipalities across the country.

The origin of Korean schools lies in Japanese colonial rule of Korea. In August 1945, Emperor Hirohito accepted the Potsdam Declaration (unconditional surrender) and the Korean Peninsula, which had been annexed (colonized) by the Japanese Empire, was liberated. At this time, there were as many as 2 million Koreans in Japan (i.e. mainland Japan), according to some sources; some 1.4 million had returned to Korea by the following year. The policy that imperial Japan adopted towards Koreans was one of assimilation, whereby the Koreans were forced to worship at Shintō shrines, adopt Japanese names (*sōshi-kaimei*), and use the Japanese language. Immediately after the liberation of the Korean Peninsula, Koreans living in Japan initiated their children into Korean-language education, seeking to regain the ethnic identity that had been stripped from them under colonial rule. *Kokugo kōshūjo* ('Korean national language schools'), each of them small-scale, and voluntarily and autonomously managed with private funding, mushroomed across the country. These kōshūjo were the prototypes of present-day Korean schools. As their history clearly shows, Korean schools started as an exercise in the anti-racism and decolonialization long led by Korean people themselves. In October 1945, *Zainihon Chōsenjin Renmei* ('League of Koreans in Japan'), commonly known as *Chōren*, a nationwide organization for rallying left-wing Zainichi Koreans, was formed. Chōren was the first to consolidate the kōshūjo around Japan, elevating them as Korean ethnic schools. As of April 1948, there were 566 such institutions at primary school level (48,930 pupils) and seven at secondary school (2,416 students). There were also institutions at high school level at that time, although their specific substance remains unclear. The total number of students in these schools surpassed 50,000.[12]

Yet this progress was partnered with persistent attacks by an institutionally biased Japanese government on Korean schools as the product of colonial rule and a mechanism through which the memory of a criminal

[11] A scholarship programme for high-school children introduced by the Democratic Party in government.

[12] *Minju Choson*, May 1950.

past that the Japanese government seeks to erase is passed from generation to generation. These attacks were in line with the so-called reverse course: a qualitative change in the nature of the US occupation of Japan stemming from the intensification of East–West confrontation. First came the forced closure of Korean schools. Starting with the notification 'On the Treatment of Schools Established by Koreans',[13] issued in January 1948, the closure was bulled through over that year and the next. With Koreans resisting fiercely across Japan, the closures triggered significant repercussions. On 24 April 1948, after negotiating with Korean protesters, the governor of Hyogo declared that he would revoke his order for the closure of Korean schools. Further, the turmoil led General Headquarters (GHQ) to declare 'a state of emergency' for the first and only time during the occupation. In Osaka, a police officer shot point blank and killed a 16-year-old Korean boy. According to some sources, 1 million people joined the protests, 2,900 of whom were arrested. It is said that the prison terms of all those who were convicted in military court added up to 116 years.

In September 1949, Chōren was forced to dissolve and most of the schools that had lost their backing were closed. Education for the inheritance of Korean ethnic identity nonetheless continued in various forms and, eventually, it was again consolidated by Chongryon, which was formed in 1955 as the overseas citizens' organization of the Democratic People's Republic of Korea (DPRK). This marked the birth of present-day Korean schools.

The next wave of attacks on Korean schools came in the 1960s. On 23 April 1965, the 26th meeting of the Committee on Legal Status of Koreans in Japan took place as a part of talks between the Republic of Korea (ROK) and Japan. During this meeting, Jirō Ishikawa, a councillor within the Japanese Education Minister's Secretariat, was faced with a question from Representative Lee Kyung-Ho of ROK: 'Oughtn't the Japanese government to close down Chongryon-affiliated schools which provide communist education aiming at communizing ROK, Japan, and eventually the entire world?'

Despite noting that 'this is an internal affair that the Japanese government should take responsibility in solving', Ishikawa answered, 'When it comes to school issues, we are also deeply troubled by Chongryon-affiliated ones.'

[13] Stating that those who reached school age must enter Japanese public/private schools even if they are Korean, this notification was in practice a rejection of ethnic education.

He then asked, in return, 'Assuming the Japanese government *does* regulate Chongryon-affiliated schools: could there be objections from the viewpoint of protecting [Korean] nationals abroad?'

Representative Lee answered, 'There would never be such objections... Should anyone ever object to closing down communist training schools, they would be ***, ***, *** out of their minds.'[14]

Given ROK's word that it would 'tolerate' such interventions, the Japanese government began to crack down on Korean schools. In December that year, a notification from the Administrative Vice-Minister of Education, titled 'On the Treatment of Educational Facilities Housing Koreans Only', was issued to prefectural governors and boards of education. The notification stated three principles on how Korean schools are to be treated:

(1) Korean schools were not recognized as 'schools', as defined in the School Education Act;
(2) since 'granting the status of miscellaneous schools to Korean schools whose aims are to cultivate Korean ethnicity or nationality cannot be recognized as having positive significance for our nation's society', approvals of new miscellaneous schools and school incorporations were to be withheld; and
(3) the policing of and orders imposed on existing *ichijōkō* ('article 1 schools') and miscellaneous schools should be intensified.

At the end of the notification, it was noted that a unified treatment of schools for foreign nationals would soon be discussed.

The following year, the Foreigners' School Bill was drafted. The aim of the bill was to transfer administrative authority over schools for foreign nationals (from approving through to closing such schools) from the hands of the prefectural governors to the Minister of Education. This was an attempt to silence resistance at the municipal level to the state's policies of oppression, stripping local governments of the power to approve new miscellaneous schools or to provide subsidies to these schools – of the power to resist in action. The 12-article bill consisted only of provisions pertaining to policing and monitoring, such as 'correction orders', 'closure orders', 'reporting and investigating', or 'suspension orders', and included no provisions on rights such as university entrance qualifications or subsidies proportionate to those available to private schools. The bill was approved by the Cabinet in 1966 and was

[14] *** indicates words not appropriate for print.

laid before the Diet multiple times until 1972, before it was finally discarded because of widespread objection.

Alongside the government's oppression of Korean schools, compulsory police investigations targeting Korean schools and their teachers frequently took place during this period. A common pretext for such investigations was that teachers had failed to carry their certificates of alien registration. Hate crimes against Korean schools and their students also occurred frequently, committed by Japanese right-wing high school students, mobsters, and right-wingers who engaged in propaganda activities using sound trucks.[15] Media coverage of these incidents spread the impression that Korean schools were 'dangerous places'. That impression was further amplified by the images of DPRK and Korean schools that were disseminated by official entities including the Liberal Democratic Party's Research Commission on National Security. The DPRK was depicted as 'a threat to security' and Korean schools, as organizations affiliated with Chongryon, which is connected to DPRK, were imagined to be 'bodies subject to security controls'. Documented cases of hate crime surged: 37 cases in 1963, 3 in 1964, another 3 in 1965, 7 in 1966, 14 in 1968, 20 in 1969, and 45 in 1970. A discriminatory and chauvinistic mentality was circulating between the government sphere and the civil sphere, continuously amplifying itself.[16]

Thereafter, every time diplomatic or political issues were trumpeted in the mass media, hate was directed towards Korean schools and their students. Especially targeted were female students in *chima jeogori*, a traditional Korean ensemble for women consisting of *chima* (skirt) and *jeogori* (top). Such students were insulted, beaten, or had their chima jeogori uniforms slashed with knives as they made their way to school. These so-called chima jeogori incidents occurred frequently after the Rangoon bombing of October 1983 and the Korean Air Flight 858 bombing of November 1987, as well as when the Pachinko Scandal[17]

[15] Examples include the Kanagawa incident of November 1962, in which a student of Kanagawa Korean Middle School who visited Hōsei Daini Senior High School's festival was beaten to death by a Hōsei Daini student, and the Jūjō incident of April 1963, in which nearly 20 mobsters with baseball bats and clubs attempted to burst through the main gate of Tokyo Korean Middle School, throwing beer bottles, rocks, and square timber into the school, while screaming, 'Do the Korean school in!', before running away.

[16] Yusaku Ozawa, *Zainichi Chōsenjin Kyōikuron: Rekishihen* [On Zainichi Korean education: a history] (Aki Shobo, 1973), 456–66.

[17] The 'Pachinko Scandal' refers to a series of reports in weekly magazine *Shūkan Bunshun*, published by Bungei Shunju, which problematized big-name members of the Social Democratic Party of Japan who were receiving donations from the *pachinko* (a pinball-

surfaced in August 1989, when the DPRK withdrew from the Treaty on the Non-proliferation of Nuclear Weapons in April 1994, and after the missile test[18] of August 1998. To ensure the safety of female students in these circumstances, Korean schools across Japan introduced secondary sets of uniforms (blazers and ordinary skirts) to be worn when commuting to and from school.

Meanwhile, the impact of the Zainichi Korean rights movement, invigorated by victory in the 1974 *Hitachi Employment Discrimination* case,[19] had started to extend to Korean schools. In the 1990s, Korean school students were finally allowed to compete in sports and cultural competitions from which they had been excluded, and Japan Railways decided that the season tickets of Korean school students were now to be treated 'like those of Article 1 school [students]'. These were all results of sustained campaigning by Koreans themselves. Another achievement came in the area of university entrance qualifications. In 1998, Kyoto University made a ground-breaking move, allowing a Korea University graduate to take the entrance examination for one of its graduate schools. A year later, the Ministry of Education, Culture, Sports, Science and Technology (MEXT) reversed its policy, allowing those who graduated from schools for foreign nationals to enter Japanese graduate schools.

All of these trends, however, were immediately subject to pushback. On 17 September 2002, the DPRK admitted to abducting Japanese citizens.[20] A survey conducted by *Zainichi Korian no Kodomotachi ni Taisuru Iyagarase o Yurusanai Wakate-Bengoshitachi no Kai* ('Association of Young Lawyers Who Do Not Tolerate Harassment against Zainichi Korean Children') outlines what happened next.

type gambling game) industry, known for having many Zainichi business owners. In reality, however, Liberal Democratic Party (LDP) legislators received larger amounts in donations from the industry. Kazuyoshi Hanada, then editor-in-chief of *Bunshun*, later took post as editor-in-chief with the publisher for another magazine in which he oversaw an article perpetuating Holocaust denial. Since leaving Bungei Shunju, Hanada has successively worked as editor-in-chief for several far-right publications.

18 Chōsen Jihō Shuzaihan, *Nerawareru Chima Chogori: Gyaku-Kokusaika ni Yamu Nihon* [Targeting chima jeogori: Japan suffering reverse globalization] (Takushoku Shobo, 1990).

19 In 1970, a second-generation Zainichi Korean man who passed the entrance exam for Hitachi Ltd using his common name (Japanese-style names used by Zainichi Koreans) was fired upon revealing to the company as South Korean. The Kawasaki Branch of Yokohama District Court recognized the discrimination and ordered compensation.

20 In the Japan–North Korea summit meeting between Prime Minister Junichiro Koizumi and General Secretary Kim Jong-il, Kim admitted to abducting Japanese citizens – an act that the DPRK had been denying thus far – and apologized.

According to their survey, between October 2002 and March 2003, more than 1,000 hate incidents (321 of which occurred in the Kantō region) were documented across Japan. Many of these incidents involved abusive language.[21] The next year, the new flexible admissions scheme qualified graduates from schools-for-foreign-nationals to apply for Japanese universities;[22] yet, following the missile test of July 2006 and the nuclear testing that followed in October, cases of discrimination targeting Korean schools continued to rise.

On 16 September 2009, the Democratic Party government was newly elected, having included the high school tuition waiver programme as one of its main campaign policies. The policy aimed to realize Article 13(2) of the International Covenant on Economic, Social and Cultural Rights (ICESCR) – namely, the right to free education – and, for the first time in the history of Japanese educational policies, it was to include schools for foreign nationals (although limited to those recognized as miscellaneous schools). However, the policy made slow progress, held up by objections from right-wing party members who fought against the inclusion of Korean schools. Bringing up the abduction issue as their ground for objections, many problematized Korean schools in official spaces, including the Diet. Eventually, the Democratic Party launched the programme in April 2010 while putting only Korean schools on hold.[23]

Unlike the 1960s, municipal leaders chose to act in concert with right-wing Diet members. As if to respond to the discussions at the national level, then Mayor of Osaka Toru Hashimoto commented on 3 March: 'That country, North Korea, is basically like a crime syndicate. Is giving subsidies to schools that associate with crime syndicates the right thing to do?' He then proposed principles for re-examining the subsidy

[21] Zainichi Korian no Kodomotachi ni Taisuru Iyagarase o Yurusanai Wakate-Bengoshitachi no Kai (eds.), *Zainichi Korian no Kodomotachi ni Taisuru Iyagarase Jittai: Chōsahōkoku* [The reality of harassment targeting Zainichi Korean children: an investigative report] (Zainichi Korian no Kodomotachi ni Taisuru Iyagarase o Yurusanai Wakate-Bengoshitachi no Kai, 2003).

[22] Still, it should be noted that Korean high-school students must gain permission from the respective universities to which they apply, while those from non-Korean foreign national schools automatically qualify for application upon graduation.

[23] Korean schools were kept on hold for an excruciatingly long time, including the period during which the screening process was suspended as a result of the bombardment of Yeonpyeong in 2010. In December 2012, when the screening was still pending, the LDF government was re-elected to replace the Democratic Party government. In February 2013, the Second Abe Cabinet forced, as the first task after its formation, a complete exclusion of Korean schools from the tuition waiver programme, which led to the current situation.

programme, laying out four requirements that Korean schools must satisfy should they wish to participate in it – namely, that they must:

(1) distance themselves from Chongryon;
(2) 'remove the portraits [of father and son Kim Il-sung and Kim Jong-il that were hung in the classrooms]';
(3) provide education that conforms to Japan's curriculum guidelines;[24] and
(4) disclose the schools' financial information to the public.[25]

The attack by civil racists on Kyoto Korean No. 1 Elementary School was congruent with these discriminatory moves by the governments.

IV. Myriad Psychological Harms

The children who were exposed to the hate demonstrations suffered serious damages. Since the day of the first attack, habits such as bed-wetting or crying during the night returned to some of them, in a form of acute shock. One child became very upset whenever they saw seeing people in working overalls, worrying that 'Zaitokukai is here', because the attackers had worn similar clothes on the day of the demonstration. The children became especially sensitive to sounds. Even some of the teachers said that loud voices, such as the wailing of a child or the shouts of a drunkard waiting for a train, triggered memories of the scene of the attack. Even if the children did not completely understand what the attackers screamed at them, the experience of being shouted at through loudspeakers had scarred them. There were those who would be frightened by voices booming through the loudspeakers of refuse collection vehicles or campaigning cars. One parent told me that things get tough during election season, with her child becoming mentally unstable.

In some cases, the shock fuelled aggression. One second-grade boy is a case in point. This boy always brought four sharpened pencils to school, so that he could use one for each of the four classes he had in a day. However, after the incident, he refused to use two of them, sometimes even walking around clutching them in his hands. On being asked why, the little boy announced that he would 'fight against Zaitokukai with these [pencils]'. This boy was not the only child who may have been trying to act tough, displaying bravado perhaps in a vain attempt to hide

[24] *Gakushū shidō yōryō* ('curriculum guidelines') are education guidelines for cultivating the Japanese nation. 'Conforming' to such guidelines erases the identity of Korean schools.

[25] Another requirement – 'to remove the portraits from the staff room as well' – was added later, making the final total of the requirements five.

their fear. When Zaitokukai disclosed its plan for their second demonstration, this child pleaded with his mother, tears in his eyes, 'No way, I can't do this'.

I interviewed the victims over the course of about a year, starting in 2013 – three years after the incident. Even then, deep psychological scars remained. One child refused to enter a local chain restaurant, insisting that 'Zaitokukai is there'. Others, accidentally encountering footage of hate demonstrations on news programs, directed their anger towards their parents, berating them for having the television on. Some even told their parents, 'I guess I should just become Japanese now'. Three-and -a-half years after the attack, there was one boy who had not managed to overcome his fear of staying home alone. Many children visibly feared distorted noise or angry shouts, as if having an 'allergic' reaction to loudspeakers.

Symptoms of post-traumatic stress disorder (PTSD) can surface long after the event that caused it and even though the causal relationship between the symptoms and the event is unclear. In the case of the attack on the Kyoto Korean No. 1 Elementary School, there was one child who, three years after the incident, suddenly became incapable of going to the bathroom alone at night. What scared the child was the sound of the toilet flushing. According to a study conducted by Hyogo Prefectural Board of Education,[26] tracking psychological trauma in secondary and high school students after *Hanshin Awaji Daishinsai* ('Great Hanshin Earthquake'),[27] the number of 'children in need of psychological care' peaked (4,106) not in the direct aftermath, but three years after the event. The Board of Education dealt with this by, for example, sending additional counsellors and 'teachers in charge of psychological care' to schools. However, in this case, because the Korean school was a miscellaneous school, Kyoto City dispatched no such personnel. That the children were not offered the professional treatment that they evidently needed is another major source of concern.

One female interviewee had been a pupil in the school at the time of the attack, but was in Kyoto Korean Middle School by the time of the

[26] See Hyogoken Kyōiku Iinkai [Hyogo Prefectural Board of Education], 'Saigai o Uketa Kodomotachi no Kokoro no Rikai to Kea' ['Understanding and caring for the hearts of children who have experienced natural disasters'] (March 2011), available at www.hyogo-c.ed.jp/~somu-bo/bosai/kokorokea.pdf [accessed 16 September 2020].

[27] The Great Hanshin Earthquake occurred early in the morning of 17 January 1995, the focus of the quake being Hyogo Prefecture. Some 6,434 people were killed in the earthquake.

interview.[28] She told me: 'There are a lot of tourists walking up and down Ginkakuji-michi [the path that leads to her school], but they make me nervous even when they're just asking me how to get to places. When I go to school, I use the back gate and avoid Ginkakuji-michi, because there are too many tourists out there.' In other words, she was trying to avoid situations in which her memories might be triggered.

Needless to say, it is not only memories that haunt her; she has no choice but to stay vigilant every day to protect herself from very real threats: 'When I have to go places wearing a jeogori for club activities, I worry about people watching me. Also, our textbooks are written in Hangul [the Korean alphabet], so I get nervous when I must open them in the bus or the train.'

She also described to me her experience of attending the civil trial:

> I knew that the Zaitokukai people and the lawyers would be Japanese, but come to think of it, the chief judge is Japanese too, and the people sitting in the gallery are also Japanese, right? I learned later that most of them were supporting us and was relieved. But, at first, I feared that they're all on 'their' side and became very nervous.

There also was a moment when she realized she had become aggressive in spite of herself. She spoke of clashing with a *netouyo* – that is, one of the *Netto Uyoku* ('Net Far-Right'), Japanese neo-nationalists who are active on the Internet – of more or less the same age as her on a social networking service. She had hurled insults at him, using words that surprised even her. This story is hardly unique, of course. According to one parent, 'Ever since what happened, when my child hears the word "Japanese", he sometimes seems to fly off the handle'.[29] Many parents spoke of the difficulties they face at home, stating that they now have to 'emphasize that Zaitokukai represents only a part of the Japanese people, and that most of the Japanese people are basically nice'.

Those who could not so easily share their own vulnerability, such as parents and teachers, were also scarred deeply. Phrases such as 'an away game', 'sense of loss', 'powerlessness', and 'being dragged back' came out of their mouths. What lies at the roots of these words is a collapsed sense of trust at not being recognized as human – as equal. Such a feeling

[28] *Kyoto Chōsen Chū-Kōkyū Gakkō*, or *Kyoto Joseong Jung-go-geub Haggyo*, is a Korean school located in the north-east of Kyoto City. Also translated as 'Kyoto Korean Junior High School', it is a combined school providing both secondary and high school education.

[29] This then-student's recollection of the past ten years was published in the 4 March 2019 edition of *Choson Sinbo*.

connects them not only to their own childhoods, but also to the situation in the past about which their parents and grandparents had told them.

Kim Sang-gyun, a parent, rushed to the school on receiving news of the attack and was exposed to the abuse for several tens of minutes. (He also witnessed the two demonstrations that followed.) He began to realize the 'harms' that had been done to him only that night, hours after the event. This was characteristic among my interviewees, who commonly finally began to recognize the damage they had suffered a few hours or even a few days after the attack, having found themselves unable to think at all in the very moment of the attack.

In Kim's case, the attack recalled the discrimination he had experienced while in a Japanese primary school:

> I guess it was when I went up to second grade. Back then, I went by my common name, 'Kaneshiro'. When I stepped out from the ground-floor corridor, I got surrounded by five or something kids. They went, 'Kaneshiro, you're chonko [a racial slur], right? Chonko eat bamboo, right? Dude!' So, even second graders knew this. Even if we call ourselves 'Kaneshiro', just having the Chinese character *kin* [derived from the Korean surname 'Kim'] in our surname made it obvious that we were Koreans. I guess it's that these kids had been listening to what their parents had been saying back home.

Kim was 'dragged back' into such childhood memories. What the children meant by 'bamboo' was probably kimchi (Korean pickles). The children presumably meant that kimchi is not something human beings eat. Those who eat kimchi are not humans like them – not equal to them. It was a 'formal notice' that Koreans are inferior to them by a notch or two. Kim and the children began to scuffle on the spot – although, said Kim, 'I don't think that was because I wanted to defend my roots or my name or anything'.

Kim himself is second-generation Zainichi Korean, with parents from Jeju Island in present-day ROK. His parents spoke Korean at home and he grew up surrounded by Korean culture. He says, 'In that sense, there was no way that I could hide the fact that I was Korean, and my parents thought the same'. However, they would not intentionally make it public; that was the golden rule. Kim explained:

> That was when I thought that my name was something very bad. That my background was something very embarrassing. Like, I got possessed of the idea that those were nothing I could be proud of. Even after that, I never had any first-hand experience that could give me a sense of positivity. Even when we learned about Korea in social studies class at school, I feared, 'Isn't somebody going to find out about me?'

Kim himself did not go to a Korean school, and while he participated in local Korean language classes for Korean schoolchildren, his daily life did little to instil in him a sense of self-esteem. He says that, while in high school, he flew into numerous fist fights when his background was insulted.

He decided to change his life and stopped using his common name upon entering university:

> On my first day in university, I see my own name as 'Kim', but you know, I'm not familiar with it. It was kind of strange, but still, refreshing. I'm using my real name, which means that, from now on, I don't have to worry about people discovering my secrets. I thought that, should something happen because of this, the future would take care of itself.

Kim joined a dongpo society in university. There, he learned about his own roots and strengthened his bond with dongpo of the same generation. However, even now, he struggles with the personal impact of discrimination: 'Suppose someone asks me if I have a sense of self-esteem, I can't just say, "Yes, I do". The negative ideas I cultivated in the past still pop up in unexpected moments. I can't have a complete sense of self-esteem. Or, perhaps I should say, "I can *never* have"?

Kim says that he sent his three children to Korean school because he wanted them to grow up without the sort of skewed sense of self or inferiority complex that he had. Kim's wife went to Japanese schools as well. 'For us, it's an "experiment" ', he says, while acknowledging that this is not the whole picture. Providing a space in which the children 'don't have to deal with things they shouldn't have to worry about' was also about motivating Kim himself to live as Zainichi: 'In my case, half [of the reason for sending the children to Korean school] was for myself. It's that I wanted to elevate my awareness and motivate myself constantly.' For this reason, he became a member of the parents' association board, and worked on school management and events. Yet his hopes - the motivation he had strived to sustain since university – were dashed by the hate speech:

> As members of Japanese society, I believe that we've been working hard in various ways. From the 1990s, the Japanese society started discussing stuff like 'multicultural coexistence', and discriminatory measures against Korean schools were mended, although little by little. Despite all this, that rally completely destroyed the sense of and the perception I had towards, or rather accumulated in the face of, the Japanese society. I was dragged back into what I experienced in primary school. What we worked so hard to elevate, that rally just knocked it down to the ground, *wham*.

> They told us stuff like, 'Stay on the side of the road', and 'Promises are made between human beings. Promises don't work between human beings and Koreans.' They basically told us that we're not equal humans. My mind went completely blank. It was indeed a 'sense of loss' that I felt.

During the interviews, many told me that 'the moment' still comes back to them as they speak and that they continue to suffer from stomach pains or palpitations, especially when they watch the videos of the attack. Several interviewees even started to cry as they talked, overcome with emotion. And this was three-and-a-half years after the attack.

Park is a parent who also rushed to the school immediately after the first attack and went on to play a central role in taking counter-measures. She told me that she 'feels a contracting pain in her womb' when she watches the videos of the attack. As was the case for Kim, what haunted Park after the attack was the discrimination she faced as a fifth- or sixth-grader in a Korean primary school.[30] What she felt was a sense of loss, having the 'sense of trust' – something she managed to accumulate after her primary school days – knocked out of her:

> I used to play with [Japanese] kids in the neighbourhood, but whenever we had an argument, they'd tease me, '*Chōsen* [Korea], chōsen', and that was it. There was a time I got so angry that I scuffled with them and we never played together ever again. Then, one day, when I was walking down the street with my little sister, wearing our Korean school uniform and carrying our *randoseru* [a leather backpack for primary school children], the boys came up from behind us. One of the boys shouted, 'Chōsen!' and grabbed the top of my sister's randoseru, pulled her down to the ground, and spat all over her face. I ran after him and knocked him over, along with the bicycle he was riding. Then I basically beat the hell out of him.

She always gave tit for tat. The bullies, however, were persistent:

> They always told me, 'Go away, chōsen'. There was even a day when they pulled out my abacus from my randoseru and whacked my head with it from behind, shouting, 'Chōsen!' Having these memories, I always had . . . how can I describe it, a sense of estrangement, maybe? All because, you know, I was bullied like this. . . . There are people who hate Koreans, that's what I felt.

For Park who was persecuted 'because' she was Korean, chōsen was also a derogatory term. And yet her daily experience of Korean school itself managed to slowly melt away the negative impression she had of 'Korea':

[30] This was a school that used to exist in the north of Kyoto City.

'My teacher wrote "Korea" on the blackboard in *hiragana* [the Japanese alphabet], Hangul and *kanji* [the Chinese alphabet], and explained to us, "It means that the morning (*chō*/*cho*) is bright (*sen*/*son*)". Then she played the organ and sang a song for us. The characters were shining bright in front of my eyes.'

After graduating high school, Park was employed in a Chongryon-affiliated workplace surrounded by dongpo. However, after she gave birth to her two children, she had them looked after in a Japanese daycare centre for a short period of time:

> For me, that was like making a debut in Japanese society. Seeing a Japanese nurse feeding baby food to my children, I entertained the idea of 'living together' for the first time. You know, I grew up in an area with a large concentration [of Koreans] and went to Korean school. With my experiences in the past, I sort of had my guard up against Japanese people. But then I started to think, 'Wait, many of them are actually good people'. I guess that was when I first became a 'Zainichi' parent.

Park still keeps in touch with the nurses from that daycare centre. The rally, however, unsettled the foundations of the trust she had developed in Japanese society. Park says, 'I have been telling my children over and over again that they should treat Japanese people just "as people" and not "as Japanese", even after the incident'. This presumably reflects a hope that her daughter, who will reside permanently in this society, can build 'a sense of trust'.

After the incident, Park, then head of the omonikai, suffered a 'sense of powerlessness' at having been unable to prevent it despite being given notice. She had agreed that she would not come to the school in the actual event of an attack – yet she could not help but rush to the school when it happened. On the way to the school and after she got there, she kept blaming herself, repeating the same words in her mind: 'I let this happen, I let this happen.' She continued to blame herself for some time after the incident: 'Later, our lawyer told me that the mothers of the Morinaga Milk arsenic poisoning incident[31] victims were in a similar state to mine, blaming themselves for feeding poisoned milk to their children.'

I interviewed several *omoni* ('mothers') in a roundtable-style session. The omoni of the girl who had her birthday on 'that day' found out about

[31] A large-scale arsenic poisoning incident in 1955 caused by Morinaga Dry Milk, a Morinaga Milk product. More than 100 infants died as a consequence, and the health of more than 10,000 was adversely affected nationwide.

the incident only when her daughter came home: 'I hadn't received any news whatsoever from the School. Hearing the story from my daughter, I called the school up and found out that a classmate of hers came across [the attackers] and things went crazy.'

Her daughter could not stop crying, even at home, and repeated that she was 'scared to go to the park'. The mother told me:

> I guess it was pretty terrifying for her. Back when we were little, other kids would sometimes tell us, 'go back to Korea', or throw stones at us. But those were kids of the same age, plus we fought back. Back then, we had lots of Koreans in the neighbourhood. But now, we live separated from each other here and there, and our kids are facing grown-ups. These people are acting so cruel and mean towards little kids.

Another omoni is still very vocal in her anger about how the school dealt with the situation at the time:

> My child came back home as usual, but when I asked, I was told that there were weird people at school who told the kids that being 'Korean' is a bad thing. I made an inquiry to the school and found out about the incident. It didn't make sense to me at all. Why would you let the kids go back home on their own, then? You could have at least made them leave school in groups or asked us parents to come pick them up. I watched the video later and found out that the route my child takes to come home was the same as the one Zaitokukai took when they left. Just why!

Even though Zaitokukai had made an announcement beforehand, the approaching peril of the rally was made known only to the school staff and a fraction of the parents. This added to the confusion right after the incident, as well as the distrust and anger of the parents towards the school. Moreover, many of the parents had studied and played in Korean schools in the 1970s and the 1980s. Whether at first or second hand, they had formative experiences that allowed them to imagine the actual fear that their children tasted. In other words, they had painful experience into which they could be 'dragged back'. For instance, there was one omoni who recalled the experience of having her jeogori slashed with a knife on her way to school:

> It was when I was in secondary school, and after some kind of incident happened, I guess. When I got off the train I took to school, I felt that it was kind of chilly around here [the back of her waist]. I looked and found out that the fabric was slashed wide open. I was horrified. But that day, my parents went the other way around and scolded me, 'This was so expensive, why on earth did you let someone ruin it!'

Another omoni narrated her own experience:

> When I was on my way to school by bus, a guy who probably was drunk suddenly whacked my classmate with an umbrella. The bus driver and the adults around us just turned a blind eye, like they would today. The fact that we were so suddenly attacked was shocking, but we were all quite feisty back then. The *jung-go* [a Korean abbreviation for Kyoto Korean Middle School] students on the same bus all got together to catch the guy, dragged him out of the bus at the next stop, and turned him over to the police station.

While both episodes come with 'punchlines', they are more than enough to share what it means to be Korean in Japan. It might be that, if they were not to sugar-coat them with humour, these stories would stick in the women's throats as they tried to tell them. Most of the chima jeogori incidents remain unsolved. The women who went through such experiences had nevertheless believed that things had improved since their own school days, only to have that illusion shattered by the attack. This was another example of an uprooted 'sense of trust'.

There was an omoni who began her talk by telling me jokingly, 'Our kids were the receptionists that greeted Zaitokukai'. This was her way of humorously describing the fact that her child was beckoned by the perpetrators to 'come over here'. Again, this mother presumably attempted to narrate by sugar-coating with humour her anxiety that her child and others are still exposed to hostility from a wide and random range of people. She also told me that, when she first saw the video of the Incident, tears were streaming down her cheeks before she knew it: 'My husband had been telling me not to watch it. For a moment, I thought that I didn't want to send [my children] to [Korean] school. At that moment, I thought, "So, we're really playing an away game here". That was probably the first time I ever felt that way.'

Despite the interviews taking place three years after the incident, it was not uncommon for my interviewees to have already forgotten the details of what happened. However, the emotions were still fresh. Even though the detail had dissipated, the anxiety and fear engendered in that moment lingered, still raw. What especially pained these omoni were the questions their children asked: 'Is being Korean wrong?' 'Is Korean school a bad place?' '*Omma* ['mommy' in Korean], are we doing something wrong?' 'Is "Korean" a bad word?' 'Why are we living in Japan?'

Park Chong-im, who tended to the mothers as the head of the omonikai, told me:

> The children in Korean school, especially the little fourth- or fifth-generation kids, are completely unaware that the word *chōsen* is sometimes used with

> discriminatory malice. The omoni were troubled because they had no idea how to explain this to the kids. Should they tell the kids that there are people who use the word *chōsenjin* ['Koreans'] in a derogatory way? Honestly, that's not something we want to teach our children, and that's why the parents send their children to Korean school in the first place. They want the children to grow up carefree, away from things they shouldn't have to worry about.

These were questions Park herself was repeatedly asked. She told me about a moment in her local supermarket right after the incident, when her daughter called out 'Omma!' in a loud voice. Chills immediately ran down her spine. She was about to cover her daughter's mouth with her hand on impulse:

> I want my children to use the language of their nation naturally in Japanese society. This was one of the things I hoped for when I sent them to Korean school, but [at that moment] I felt fear before joy. That describes how much stress I was under. But I can't tell them to call me *okāsan* or *mama* outside, right? I thought that, if I wavered in my beliefs, my children would too. So, I was having emotional conflicts all the time. . . . Ever since the incident, I had been worn out. I felt rejected from and negated by Japanese society, and that maybe it can't be helped because I'm Korean. But I would never want to tell my children '[we are being rejected] because we're Korean'. And there was nowhere to direct my anger. . .

Roughly two weeks after the first attack, the school and parents lodged a criminal complaint against the perpetrators for charges including defamation. Nevertheless, the attackers continued their demonstrations. What should never have happened to begin with took place two further times with the police's approval and indifference among the societal majority. Each time, it was Korean youth who kept watch on the discriminatory demonstrations and protected the school from attacks, all while bearing the full brunt of abuse and putting themselves at risk. One of the parents said, 'The first time, we were shocked. But the second and third times, we were terrified.' Other parents said, 'Nobody ever came to protect us', and 'I realized that we had to protect ourselves'. The school staff agreed that 'they would never resort to force'. Should there be a clash and should arrests happen of school staff or parents, right-wing media outlets such as *Sankei Shimbun* would have trumpeted that fact, claiming that 'Chongryon assaulted civil activists'. The ensuing battle in court was like 'walking on thin ice'.

V. Classifying the Harms

I would now like to classify the psychological harms that surfaced in my interviews. US social psychologist Craig-Henderson recognizes a pattern of psychological harms that are almost always inflicted upon hate crime victims:

(1) extended emotional distress;
(2) a shattering of assumptions;
(3) feelings of deviancy;
(4) errors in attribution; and
(5) effects on the victim's in-group.[32]

'Extended emotional distress' applies directly to the rage and pain of the victims. They ruminated on the abuse that was hurled at them, remembered their own childhoods, and felt unending anxiety about the next attack. In this specific case, videos uploaded online contributed to the perpetuation of that emotional distress. There were parents who suffered flashbacks when accidentally encountering the videos of the attack. Similarly, when hate speech became a social issue in 2013, there were students who panicked when they saw other hate demonstrations on the television.

'A shattering of assumptions' means that the minimum assumptions the victims had about Japanese society in the 21st century were disrupted. Most of the parents are third- and second-generation Zainichi. Their grandparents and parents had lived through eras during which discrimination had been far more public and explicit. Despite sharing that collective memory, these parents had been feeling that today's Japanese society was becoming a society worth living in – that their lived experiences tomorrow would be better than those of today. The xenophobes shattered all such beliefs.

'Feelings of deviancy' means that the victims feel as though they must be bad beings who deserve to be attacked. Children asking questions such as 'Is being Korean a bad thing?' is the epitome of such feelings. At its most basic, a major reason why parents send their children to Korean school is to nurture their sense of self-esteem. 'I wanted to give them a school environment where they could bring kimchi for lunch without worrying that somebody would make a big deal out of it': these are the

[32] K. Craig-Henderson, 'The Psychological Harms of Hate: Implications and Interventions', in B. Perry *et al.* (eds.), *Hate Crime: The Consequences of Hate Crime* (Preager Perspectives, 2009), 15–30.

words of the head of the omonikai. 'I wanted my children to use the word "Korea" in a carefree way', said another omoni. The parents and teachers wished to protect the children from this very 'deviancy' – from seeing their Korean-ness as something bad. The school was the space dedicated to the children for this purpose. It was attacked, however, for the very reason that it was a Korean school raising Koreans.

'Errors in attribution' means that those subjected to attacks for absurd reason try to attribute those attacks to something that might be explained rationally. In this case, this included that they ought not to have placed school equipment in the park or that the school's stance towards the attackers was not tough enough. Some among the dongpo who had no children in the school (or in any Korean school, for that matter) criticized the school's policy of non-resistance, saying that teachers and parents 'should have done something'. According to those who were at the scene on the day, 'what really hurt to be honest' was that their own dongpo criticized them when they had swallowed their anger simply because they did not want to subject their children to the sight of violence. There were also those dongpo who would more casually ask those involved, 'That was the school's fault, right?' While this could demonstrate insensitivity, it could also represent 'error in attribution' stemming from anger.

I did not interview students that went to other schools in my 2013–14 interviews; in 2015, however, after the Supreme Court decision granted the plaintiffs victory, I conducted a joint survey on hate speech involving 1,453 high school students of Korean origin around Japan.[33] Looking at the results, 87 per cent of the respondents confirmed that they knew about the Kyoto incident. When asked what they felt at the time (multiple answers were allowed), 74.7 per cent answered 'anger' and 51.2 per cent answered 'fear'. Likewise, when asked how they felt now about 'demonstrations taking place around Japan', 76 per cent felt 'anger' and 46.1 per cent felt 'fear'. Moreover, in response to the open-ended question, five students who belonged to Korean schools outside Kyoto confessed that they feared for their lives. They said, 'I'll be killed someday' and 'I'm going to die'. One respondent even wrote, 'We have to physically

[33] Of the respondents, 93 per cent were Korean school students; the rest belonged to South Korean schools, South Korean international schools, or Japanese public/private schools. See the report for the research project *Heito Supīchi ni yoru Higai Jittai Chōsa to Ningen no Songen no Hoshō* ('A study of the actual damage caused by hate speech and the securing of human dignity') (2016), funded in 2015 by *Ryūkoku Daigaku Jinken Mondai Kenkyū Iinkai* ('Ryukoku University Human Rights Issues Research Committee'). The principal investigator was Kim Sang-gyun.

annihilate [the racists]', which can be understood as an extreme reaction to the threat to their own life. These answers to the survey offer us examples of the 'effects on the victim's in-group'.

As such, the psychological harms that became evident from sources such as my interviews with the parents and the children fit exactly into the pattern that Craig-Henderson describes.

VI. Economic and Social Harms

The harms caused by the attack were not only psychological; economic and social harms were grave as well. Park, head of the omonikai at the time of the attacks, was swamped with the task of taking countermeasures and had to quit two of her three jobs. The teachers especially grew increasingly worn out day by day, having to care for the traumatized children while preparing to defend them against new attacks. Later in the civil lawsuit, it was found that 765.5 hours had been spent on countermeasures in response to the incident between 25 November 2009 and 24 March 2011 – that is, over a period of approximately 16 months. Most of this time was spent patrolling and guarding the school, as well as the paths the children took to travel to and from the school. This vigilance was not only against 'activists' such as Zaitokukai members, but also against those who came to harass them after watching the videos on the Internet.

Kim Ji-sung, the curriculum coordinator at the time, played a central role in these vigilance efforts. It was during the 1980s and the 1990s that Kim had spent his days as a student, decided on his career, and started his life as a teacher. This was a time when Japan was being 'forced' to accede international human rights treaties such as the International Covenants on Human Rights in 1979 and the Convention Relating to the Status of Refugees in 1981 as a result of pressure from Europe and the United States. Domestically, the fingerprinting refusal movement[34] was spreading, spanning different nationalities and ethnicities, despite the Japanese government's bare-knuckled measures of oppression including arrests, prosecutions, and refusal of re-entry into Japan.

Under such circumstances, Kim, as a young teacher, witnessed incremental improvements in the treatment of Korean schools:

[34] The fingerprinting resistance movement was a battle against the mandatory fingerprinting of foreign nationals in Japan, which was stipulated under the Alien Registration Act. Nicknamed the 'civil rights movement of Japan', it was a symbol of anti-discrimination struggles in the 1980s.

> When I was in middle school, we weren't allowed to participate in Japanese sports competitions. Since we couldn't compete on an equal footing with Japanese kids of the same age, we told ourselves, 'We should never lose in a fist fight, then'. Otherwise, we would deal with practice matches as if our lives depended on it. But now that we can compete with them under the same rules without presenting a bold front, we found goals to strive for. Ever since the doors started to open, more and more kids are putting sincere efforts into soccer practice.

Emboldened by the fact that Korean schools were getting more and more recognition and prospects for 'coexistence' were opening up, Kim Ji-sung, in cooperation with Kim Sang-gyun of the parents' association, embarked on a new challenge: educating a disabled child. When Kim Ji-sung was appointed to Kyoto Korean No. 1 Elementary School, there was a third-grader with Down syndrome in his homeroom class. For Korean schools with minimal equipment and staffing, taking in children with disabilities is a difficult task. There have been many cases in which parents, despite hoping their children would receive ethnic education, have had to give up on that dream. To help the pupil learn, Kim set about scheduling pull-out tutorials. He recruited student volunteers to help. Making the most of his networking with Japanese teachers, he acquired know-how through workshops.

When the incident happened, the child was in the sixth grade. However, swamped with the task of responding to the series of discriminatory demonstrations, it became increasingly difficult for Kim Ji-sung to hold the pull-out tutorials. Looking back, he says:

> What we wish to do as teachers not only for this student but also for everyone is to offer substantial teaching by building on what they did not get to learn, so that the second year would be better than the first and the third better than the second. But ever since the incident, that became impossible for us to manage. Ultimately, they [Zaitokukai] became the central issue in school management, and all the teachers had to devote their energy there. We teachers work with children all throughout our career, but for the individual children, naturally, being in primary school is a once-in-a-lifetime experience. I feel terribly sorry that we couldn't help them make the most of this period.

As a teacher, he worries about the future of these children:

> We've been telling the children daily, 'Being Korean is not a bad thing', 'Let's live our lives with pride in our hearts'. But then, we found ourselves in a situation where we had to take every word that contradicted what we taught. These are words and that's why they stay. I'm concerned that this

> is going to impact them over the course of the future. Not only one but three demonstrations took place right in front of the eyes of the children. What I want to ask is, is the Japanese society okay with this? Was what we thought we had built up nothing but a house of cards?

The discrimination that Korean schools suffer may be described as a normalized state of exception. When an emergency happens, this state becomes all the more evident in the form of an absolute lack of tangible and intangible resources. Korean schools are already forced into a situation in which they are barely continuing to operate. If teachers must additionally act as police officers and guards, it is inevitable that the pupils will be left to study on their own for a longer period of time. Declines in the pupils' academic abilities were grave back then. Declines in physical strength were obvious as well, since they could not hold proper physical education classes in the park that had been the trigger of the whole ordeal. And the pupils enrolled at the time of the attack were not the only ones affected. The period from December to March, during which the school was swamped with all of the consequences of the attacks, was also a crucial time of the year for the recruitment of new pupils and students. Nobody turned up for the first information session of the year, which was scheduled for the day after the first attack. Only ten children ended up entering the kindergarten and the primary school, respectively, which was half the usual number.

The school became a 'place of pilgrimage' for Zaitokukai members after the incident and suspicious persons with cameras repeatedly appeared in the neighbourhood. The police were called out frequently and, every time they were, Kim Ji-sung was summoned to the police station to answer questions. The school was flooded with complaints and nuisance calls. When nobody was available, Kim himself patrolled the area in between making handouts and chairing staff meetings. He offered explanations to parents and dealt with outside entities such as the police and the authorities. As such, the daily life of Kim Ji-sung, who was becoming a veteran teacher, was overwhelmed by counter-measures for the incident. In late December, just as the second semester was over, Kim Ji-sung fell ill from overwork. More than half of the teachers who worked at the school during this period resigned within three-and-a-half years of the incident, a major cause cited being overwork as a consequence of the incident.

Further, the repeated discriminatory demonstrations brought about a typical harm caused by hate – one that is also very common in the case of sexual violence: victim blaming. After the incident, the Korean school gradually came to be seen as a nuisance in the area. The three discriminatory demonstrations, accompanied by a squad of police officers, destabilized the relationship between the half-century-old school and its local community. They could no longer use the park as they had done, based on the tripartite agreement. The park was redesigned, to include highway girders. With benches and artificial hills blocking the space, the new park could no longer be used as a school playground. The redesign had been approved by the neighbourhood association without consulting the school. The school's educational environment was destroyed completely. It consequently had to accelerate its pre-existing plan to relocate and the school closed without ceremony or celebration, two-and-a-half years after the incident.

VII. The Difficulties of the Legal Battle

So how should the school deal with all of this? Since it could not retaliate with force, the only counter-measure available was legal action. However, it took a long time to reach the decision to fight back in the courts. One reason for this is that being treated as inferior within a society leads a group to develop, with reasonable justification, a distrust of the judicature. In Japan, lawsuits regarding post-war compensation or the legal status of Zainichi Koreans had never before ended in victory. To make matters worse, Chongryon and Korean schools are subject to security controls by the Japanese authorities. 'The Japanese judicature isn't going to protect us Koreans nor Korean schools after all', said several of those who were involved in the incident. Forced into a state of exception, which is exemplified in the numerous cases of institutional oppression, the group will commonly resign itself to likely failure when it tries to consider how to resolve an issue within the existing societal system. This can be characterized as another example of damage caused by discrimination. When discussing the option of lodging a complaint, one of the parents who was against the idea said through his tears, 'We don't have human rights in the first place'. With these words, he reveals the depth of despair that sees some simply hold their tongues in the face of discrimination. Indeed, he and others are living in a society in which police officers, who were present at the time of the attack but did nothing to defend the school, are said to have performed their duties 'faultlessly'.

The school, with bold determination, filed a criminal complaint two weeks after the incident. Yet the progress of the investigation was extremely slow and the second attack was launched against the school with complete disregard for the legal action. To push the investigation forward – that is, to demonstrate its determination that it would use all means available to it – the school also filed a civil lawsuit in July 2010. One-and-a-half months after that filing and a staggering eight months after the filing of the criminal complaint, the Kyoto police at last arrested four of the attackers. But while the parents and school had insisted on filing a claim in defamation, the prosecutor in charge required that it be downgraded to the lesser charge of insult. One omoni said, 'After insisting so much on "defamation", I couldn't help but think, "What were our efforts all about?" ' In light of the need to value freedom of expression, which is the basis of a democratic society, it is natural that defamation is difficult to prove in court, but the effect of this difficulty is that prosecutors steer away from that tort when laying charges. If they try to pursue it, not only do prosecutors risk the sentence pronounced being much lighter than requested, but also – in the worst-case scenario – they risk defendants being acquitted (which taints a prosecutor's career).

The civil lawsuit also faced an array of problems. One of them surfaced very early on during formation of the complaint: who should the plaintiff be? Most straightforwardly, the rights of the pupils and students to receive ethnic education were violated by the attack. Making them the plaintiffs would be a clear step – but the effect of that would have been to hand over to the defendants the personal information of the children as the litigators. This was out of the question. When I asked some of the parents whether they had contemplated making the children the plaintiffs, almost all of them immediately answered, 'No way'. They made the school corporation the plaintiff, stating that its right to deliver ethnic education had been violated. This was only one of the issues that had to be ironed out before the case even reached the court.

What is worse is that a court battle meant that the victims were necessarily exposed to the risk of being dragged back into 'that moment' – reliving the painful experience – at any given time. The civil suit was not simply a healing process through which the victims could legally call the attackers to account and be exonerated of blame in public; it also offered opportunities for the defendants, who mischaracterized their actions as 'justified' and 'rightful', to speak. For victims sitting in the gallery, this equated to yet another hate demonstration.

In cross-examination, the principal offender who had planned the series of attacks expressed his opinion that 'education in Korean schools deserves no consideration whatsoever' and that 'it is an adult's responsibility to teach the children [that they are unlawfully occupying the land]'.

It became evident that statements such as 'This piece of land was taken [by Koreans] during the War, raping and massacring women' were unfounded and that claims the group had sent out questionnaires to the neighbourhood thorough which they confirmed that the neighbours were troubled by the Korean school were fabricated. In a private handbook used for the first rally, the offender wrote that they would begin their rally with microphones, 'crazed like a man with split personalities'. When the plaintiff attorney asked about it, he replied casually, 'Well, it's for laughs, so'.

Those in the gallery were aware that if they were to shout at the defendants in anger, they would be ordered to leave the court. Thus, instead of shouts of anger, sneering laughter echoed in the court again and again, resulting in the judge repeatedly warning the public, albeit softly, 'Allow me to remind you, you are in court now'. Some of the parents sat with their eyes fixed ahead, their lips tightly closed: the attackers took aim at their children's hearts so casually.

Some said that they 'decided to think of [the defendants] as nonsensical beings' or that they were able to 'rather detach [themselves from the defendants], since it was so ridiculous that they believed in such things'. However, not everyone can necessarily dissociate in that way. There was a moment when an omoni in the gallery broke down in tears. The last straw for her was what the defence attorney said. Drawing fully upon rumours of unknown source and tell-all books about Korean schools published when there was stronger emphasis on political and ideological education, the defendants' counsel argued, 'It cannot be helped that [ethnic education itself] is regarded as "hate speech education" '.

Those victims who acted as witnesses, striving to appeal to the judges, were necessarily dragged back into the moment of the attack. Several parents spoke to me of the pain they felt when a video of the attack was shown in the eighth oral proceedings. Before the showing, it was announced that those in the gallery 'may leave' and that 'a waiting room was available'. A Zaitokukai executive who was in court said, 'Yeah, get out of here'. One of the parents said that his voice was still ringing in their ears. It was not only the attackers' words that pained them; one of the parents said, '[The plaintiffs' statements] reminded me of being teased, "chōsen, chōsen", when I was small. I wondered why this discrimination has lasted for 30 years, 40 years'. There also were omoni who recalled their student days in the 1980s when classmates in jeogori were beaten and insulted in public.

Teachers and parents who gave their statements in court had to bear a massive psychological burden. Park was continuously dragged back into 'the moment' while she was preparing for the lawsuit. She kept having dreams in which she was desperately explaining her thoughts and feelings to the chief judge seated in front of her. She woke up crying every time. 'Until just before the trial began, I was seriously wishing that I'd be injured in a traffic accident or suddenly become sick', she says.

Kim Ji-sung, the teacher, was asked by the judges if he had any final remarks to make. He said:

> [The racists] justify their actions saying that 'this is not a school', but it's just a school where Koreans learn about Korean culture. They're not just words, they stay precisely because they're words. We teachers are also deeply hurt because what we had been learning thus far was completely denied. We want to solve this as soon as possible and send out a strong message that things like this will never happen again to the children as well as the parents who send their children to us from far away.

The court battles concluded with the attackers being convicted of criminal offences (although they were given suspended sentences).[35] The civil lawsuit also ended in victory – although it took about six years to be finalized before the Supreme Court, only partly because the attackers appealed twice.

Among those who had been against lodging the claims, the keenest concern had been that 'if we provoke them [the racists], the children will be in danger'. This risk lingered throughout the whole of the six-year period as an actual threat to children's safety. On the day of the Supreme Court decision, the school made the children come to and leave school in groups to prepare for the worst.[36]

Further, the biggest difficulties when minorities themselves launch a legal battle is that it sometimes forces them to face the discrimination they have internalized as a discriminated people. In other words, they

[35] Three of the four who were convicted in this case repeated hate demonstrations thereafter. Two of them burst in upon a pharmaceutical company that had featured a South Korean actress in its commercials. They were sued on suspicion of extortion, had their suspension of sentence revoked, and were eventually imprisoned. The very fact that suspended sentences were given to those who would clearly repeat hate crimes demonstrates the court's lack of understanding. In fact, the three are repeating discriminatory demonstrations even today.

[36] What the school feared was the racists attacking them yet again in 'retaliation'. They expected such retaliations to happen regardless of the outcome of the decision, but they anticipated more extreme actions should the school lose.

have to face their own anger and hurt – the authentic self they have swallowed down when swallowing the injustices.

After the Supreme Court decision, Kim Sang-gyun, who led the battle, recalled: 'I guess I was a nuisance in a sense. Think of our situation as having an unduly curved spine. People were saying, "I don't mind because I won't die from this", and I was basically telling them, "No, no, let's have it straightened". Facing these things head-on involves pain.'

VIII. 'Dissonance' within the Mass Media

In 2013, just as the court battle entered its final stages, many more reporters started to attend the trial – but there was a desperate dissonance between the Koreans themselves and those reporters.

The plaintiffs sought to 'create a hate crime-free society' and to 'secure the right to ethnic education', but the interest of the media (which tends to reflect the position of the majority group) lay only in the former. To them, the Kyoto incident was nothing but 'the starting point of the hate speech issue'.

This is reflected, for one thing, in the number of newspaper articles relating to Kyoto Korean No. 1 Elementary School. For example, in *Mainichi Shimbun* in 2010, when the criminal and civil complaints were filed, 16 articles included reference to the school, whereas there were only three in 2011 and none in 2012. In 2013, however, the total number of such articles suddenly surged to 28, staying high, at 26, in the year that followed. The media did not report on Zaitokukai between 2009 and spring 2010, when the attacks were in full swing, other than in a few exceptional instances,[37] fearing protests from 'opinionated people'. However, things took a sharp turn in February 2013, when kauntā came to the fore in Tokyo and Osaka, and some lawmakers problematized the situation in the Diet. All of a sudden, hate demonstrations became valuable media content.

The number of articles skyrocketed from zero in 2012 to 127 in 2013 and 267 in 2014. If we add the keyword 'hate speech' to 'Kyoto Korean No.1 Elementary School', 24 articles emerge for 2013 and 2014, respectively. However, if we add the keyword 'ethnic education', the number of articles drops to six and four. *Asahi Shimbun* also displayed a similar

[37] The papers that reported the incident before the criminal complaint was filed were *Tokyo Shimbun*, *Kyoto Shimbun*, and *Asahi Shimbun*, all of which were exposed to violent protests from the racists. The attackers also swarmed to the Kyoto Bar Association, which issued a statement criticizing Zaitokukai.

tendency. Despite the fact that what came under attack was a space for 'ethnic education' through which 'witnesses to history' are constantly reproduced and 'the others' within society are guaranteed their own authentic existence, the words that pinpoint this core issue were discarded.

As will be detailed in the next chapter by Shiki Tomimasu, which offers legal analysis of the case, Osaka High Court recognized 'a social environment in which the Zainichi provide ethnic education' as an interest protected by law (i.e. a legal interest), which was ground-breaking in the judicial history of Japan. However, local paper *Kyoto Shimbun* was the only one to use the term 'ethnic education' in its headlines and it did so only for a city news page article supplementing the front-page article reporting the legal victory.[38] In other words, few would come to understand the wish to 'secure the right to ethnic education' that was crucial to the parents and the school's staff. 'We felt somewhat left behind', said some, including Park, baffled by the sudden increase of media attention.

Each media outlet can pick and choose on which aspects of a story they report and how. However, the choices made in this case, which tend to reflect the received wisdom of the societal majority, reflected the shallowness of their understanding of racism. The fact that they translated the term 'hate speech' mechanically as *zōo hyōgen* is one instance of the ways in which media, including conservative media such as *Yomiuri Shimbun* that continue to use this translation at time of writing, missed the essential truth: that hate speech is discrimination and incitement.

I sensed this 'dissonance' acutely during a workshop held just after the victory in Osaka High Court, in which supporters, parents, and school staff made the contents of the judgment into drawings. This project was aimed at translating the very technical and complicated judgment into plain words and creating an illustrated booklet aiming to communicate the outcome of the trial not only to the direct victims, but also to Korean school children across Japan. The idea behind it was that the Osaka High Court decision, which concluded that the actions of Zaitokukai were 'racial discrimination' and declared that the core of the moral interest of Korean schools was 'ethnic education', would empower children and teachers of other Korean schools, as well as the parents. The project further had in mind the students of Japanese schools with whom the Korean schools had exchange programmes.

[38] Takanobu Honda and Tomoya Tsuji, 'Minzoku Kyōiku Kachi Mitomeru' ['Osaka High Court acknowledges the value of the ethnic education'], *Kyoto Shimbun*, 9 July 2014, 27.

Several students who went to Kyoto Korean No. 1 Elementary School back then participated in the workshop. The judgment contains specific details of the incident as found facts. For a moment, I feared that these students would suffer flashbacks. However, that was a needless fear. The participants were divided into several groups, and the judgment was segmented and a segment assigned to each group. The rough sketches that the participants drafted were perfected by professional illustrators, who volunteered their work for free. Some of the participants completed high-level sketches that would not really require polishing, while others' drawings looked like an infant's doodle or a poor attempt at Cubism. Showing their drawings to each other, participants burst into laughter. The workshop progressed in an atmosphere so cheerful and harmonious that one of the parents said, 'I have never laughed this much talking about the incident'.

To conclude the workshop, each group displayed their 'works', and the participants explained the thoughts and feelings that had gone into their own drawings. Looking at several of the drawings by high school students who were in the primary school at the time of the attack, I stood aghast. The drawings depicted scenes of parting in which their classmates, with whom they had studied since they were little, left the Korean school. Although there were various reasons why they had changed schools, one was 'the lack of future prospects' they had to suffer in a Korean school. The State of Japan and its municipalities continue to butcher such prospects with policies that discriminate against the children. When the emotional damage inflicted upon these children by hate crimes finally begins to heal, they will be faced with a social structure – the very cause of the crimes – that has not changed and they will be scarred even more deeply. This is a secondary damage stemming from hate-driven violence.

In fact, concurrent with the trials, official discrimination against Korean schools crossed a line. Symbolic of this was the re-examination of local government subsidy provision in response to the exclusion of Korean schools from the national tuition fee waiver programme. Toru Hashimoto, then governor of Osaka, took the initiative in this re-examination. After throwing Korean schools into confusion by laying down jug-handled conditions, such as taking down portraits, ending the schools' relationship with 'North Korea' or Chongryon, and aligning their education with Japanese curriculum guidelines (i.e. abandoning ethnic education), Hashimoto, on the basis of his feelings towards a specific country, ended up abolishing the subsidies that Osaka had granted. Those subsidies had been much-needed security for the students' right to study, something born of the relationship between the municipality and local residents. In one fell swoop, Hashimoto destroyed the very conception of 'local residents' that had been the foothold for foreign nationals' rights movements since the 1970s. While in the courts, civil hate speech was illegalized, discrimination in the official sphere has gone unchallenged. The trend of suspending subsidies spread across Japan as if in approval of what Hashimoto declared. Their drawings of the scenes in which they bid their friends farewell clearly show that the students had a firm grasp on this very real threat.

The readily apparent chauvinism and exclusionism are not the only forms of discrimination; forced assimilation – that is, not allowing 'the other' to exist as authentically themselves – is no less discrimination. Yet few acknowledge the absurdity that Hashimoto speaks of countering hate in the same breath as he sets about destroying Korean schools at the municipal level – the epitome of an illness that plagues Japanese society.

IX. Remaining Problems

The legal victory accelerated national discussion of hate speech regulation and brought about the Hate Speech Elimination Act (HSEA), the first ever 'anti-racism Act' in Japan. However, problems are still piling up, the first on the list being the weakness of the HSEA itself as nothing more than a symbolic law providing no sanction capable of stopping hate demonstrations in practice. Every year, around 4 December – the day on which the first attack happened – chauvinists who celebrate the incident as 'the day we recaptured our national territory from *futei senjin* [outlaw Koreans]' plan a commemorative demonstration. In 2019, which was the tenth anniversary of the event, a demonstration had already taken place on 9 March.[39]

On 13 December 2019, the city government of Kawasaki City, Kanagawa, unanimously passed an ordinance that makes vicious, persistent hate speech directed towards those with non-Japanese ethnic roots criminally punishable.[40] This was the first ever law in Japan in

[39] Despite there being only four racists participating in the demonstration, the Kyoto police deployed 150 riot police personnel and guarded the demonstrators from the counter-demonstrators throughout. See www.youtube.com/watch?v=I6bVgrJj7eg [accessed 16 September 2020].

[40] The Kawasaki City Ordinance for Discrimination-Free, Human-Rights-Respecting City Buildings, tackles: (a) inciting expulsion of, or declaring the expulsion of, minorities from where they live; (b) inciting or declaring attacks against minorities, aiming to kill them or

which racism was explicitly declared a crime and playing a key role in the process was the local anti-hate speech movement, which grew powerful enough to sway the city government. However, even this ultimately testifies to the impotence of state-level laws in dealing with hate speech. The reality is that the Japanese state government has taken no practical measures to tackle discrimination, leaving people no choice but to turn to their local governments. Above all, even after hate speech (the incitement of discrimination) was illegalized, the State of Japan and its municipalities have continued to cross the line, discriminating against Korean schools explicitly even as they enact the HSEA. We see here a double standard: is discrimination to be a privilege of government, just like killing (i.e. the death penalty)?

As a response to the exclusion of Korean high schools from the tuition fee waiver programme, five of the ten Korean high schools in Japan lodged lawsuits against the state. However, only the Osaka District Court decision of July 2017 was in favour of the school and even this 'ground-breaking victory' was nullified by the September 2018 judgment of Osaka High Court. In August 2019, the Supreme Court rejected appeals regarding two lawsuits filed in Osaka and Tokyo. From a legal and factual viewpoint, these lawsuits are far from unreasonable. The high school tuition fee waiver was a school-expenses support programme that heralded 'equality of educational opportunity' for all children regardless of nationality or origin, of which the children were the beneficiaries. Nevertheless, the state raised political and diplomatic reasons such as the 'abduction incident' for excluding Korean schools in the programme, and summarily deleted the provisions on which they had based their applications – pulling the rug out from under even those schools who applications were already in progress. The judicature 'authorizes' such visible malfeasance because 'Korea bashing' is the basis of the Japanese government. In Japan, where the Cabinet appoints Supreme Court judges and the Supreme Court then nominates judges of the lower courts, such judges rarely make decisions that stand in opposition to the state.

In October 2019, state-wide policies were enacted for the free preschool education programme through which education and childcare for

physically harm them, restricting their freedom, defaming them, or damaging their property; and (c) making egregious insults such as likening minorities to vermin. The city mayor, with input from an advisory board consisting of experts, can issue recommendations or orders to offenders and may also publish their names, if necessary. If the offenders do not adhere to the orders, the city will press charges against them. Offenders could be fined up to ¥500,000. The ordinance does not cover online action.

preschoolers was to be made free, under the auspices of the Liberal Democratic Party–Komeito coalition led by Prime Minister Shinzo Abe. Korean kindergartens, however, were excluded from the scope of the programme. When politicians use children as tools to maintain their power and the judicature sanctions that oppression, both fail the children. The administration, the legislators, and the judicature are officially inciting hate crimes, sending out an implicit message that, 'We can do whatever we want to Korean schools because they are connected to North Korea and Chongryon'. In this light, the next Kyoto Korean No. 1 Elementary School attack is surely only a matter of time.

Japan has become the 'isolated island' of East Asia, where what little 'decency' and 'intellect' that had existed are being cast away, the light disappearing as the tunnel closes in. Nevertheless, every week and every month, students, graduates, and supporters of Korean schools continue to stand in front of the MEXT, in front of the Osaka prefectural government office, in station squares, and on downtown streets, voicing their anger towards discrimination, speaking up for equality, and calling for solidarity. Writing this chapter, I have renewed my determination to follow them their lead – their anger and courage – and to fight for the society we deserve: a society in which everybody is granted equality, freedom, and dignity.

13

Kyoto Korean Elementary School Case

A Legal Analysis

SHIKI TOMIMASU

I. Introduction

A. The School's Simple Desire to Restore a Peaceful Study Environment

When the Kyoto Korean School Corporation, the educational institution that administered the Kyoto Korean First Elementary School, chose to file a criminal complaint against the xenophobic perpetrators of an attack on the school in December 2009, it did not aim to rectify the widespread hate speech problems in Japanese society. What the school corporation, along with school parents and teachers, desired desperately was simple: to restore a safe school environment for the children. It seemed that securing legal protection, which at the early stages meant immediate arrest of the offenders and subsequent police protection, would be straightforward, once the case was brought formally to the police in the form of a criminal complaint. The allegation of a clear violation of the Penal Code was supported by solid evidence, including video clips uploaded to YouTube. Direct observations by multiple police officers who had rushed to the scene of the crime reinforced the evidence solidly proving the need for criminal sanctions.

The later development of civil proceedings into a wide variety of legal procedures became necessary only because the police were frustratingly slow to respond. The proceedings expanded to include a request for a civil injunction, the indirect execution of a restraining order, and a civil claim in tort. It was a great surprise to parents, teachers, and supporters of the school's ethnic education effort that the Japanese court consistently ignored the racial nature of the case to such an extent that it might be labelled intentional 'bleaching', as explained later in this chapter, and that they had to wait several years until Osaka High Court finally held ethnic education to be worthy of protection in the ratio of the ruling.

B. *Two Viewpoints for Analysis of the Different Judgments*

Over time, parents and teachers have come to realize the importance of actively seeking recovery of ethnic dignity, in addition to prevention of the recurrence of physical damages.

One of the factors contributing to this shift was that the school was repeatedly targeted for subsequent street demonstrations. People could no longer claim that the first demonstration in December 2009 had been an isolated incident. It had long been pointed out that discrimination against Koreans living in Japan is deeply embedded in Japanese society, and that the Internet has been a powerful tool with which it has been echoed and amplified.

It was around this time in 2009 that such discrimination began to emerge from the underground of the Japanese society. School teachers and parents in Kyoto, who had been wishfully thinking that their own children's safety would not be affected, could no longer deny the seriousness of the situation when sentiment became physical attack conducted in front of a school gate.

A turning point in the school's response came in February 2010, when police pressed the school to drop the charges of defamation. The police advised the school to seek a lesser charge, to simplify the criminal investigation and ensure the timely arrests of the perpetrators. However, the school, after a series of serious discussions, concluded that if it were to place too much emphasis on its physical security, they may leave the attacks on ethnicity unquestioned. The attacks on their ethnic identity aimed to fundamentally undermine the educational message the school and the parents had worked hard to convey to children at the school.

By the time the third demonstration was conducted in March 2010, the school had decided to seek official court judgment on two main points:

(1) condemnation of the perpetrators for their discriminatory behaviour; and
(2) recognition that Korean ethnic education has significant social value.

This incident occurred in the context of ethnic education, which is a symbolic locus of the passing of ethnic identity from one generation to the next. This was the true reason why the school was attacked by the racists. And because it was such a symbolic place, the Zainichi Korean people in Kyoto were deeply shocked by the attack.

It was recognized that there was a need to examine the likely stance of the Japanese judiciary in an actual instance in which the development and maintenance of ethnic self-esteem among Zainichi Koreans was threatened. It was considered important to seek recognition in court of these two aspects and that such judgment would contribute to shaping Japanese public opinion.

Even though it has not been discussed sufficiently in the literature, there was a stark difference among the three major court decisions on the incident in relation to the points pursued. The first of these was the criminal judgment of Kyoto District Court (21 April 2011); the second, the civil judgment of Kyoto District Court (7 October 2013); the third, the appellate judgment rendered by Osaka High Court (8 July 2014), later affirmed by the Supreme Court (9 December 2014).

The failure to address either of the two essential elements in the criminal case should be understood as intentionally 'bleaching' the racial or ethnic components out of the incident. Even in the well-received Kyoto District Court civil decision, a similar treatment is evident in evaluation of the damages. Only in the appellate decision was a judgment rendered in which both essential elements were afforded fair attention and clearly expressed as part of the ratio.[1]

C. *Who Sued Whom and for What Actions? Selecting the Plaintiff, Defendants, and Subject Matter*

Analysis of these court cases should start with an observation of how those persons (natural and corporate) who were to be positioned as plaintiffs and defendants were selected differently for each procedure, and why.

[1] This analytic framework can be usefully applied to the *Tokushima Teachers' Association* case, in which different judges and prosecutors came to different conclusions about a similar offence. In *Tokushima*, members of Zaitokukai and their sympathizers – 16 in total – raided a small office of the Association in April 2010, shouting racist slogans through megaphones. Despite general public support, and clear condemnation of the group by Kyoto District Court and Osaka High Court in the case described in this chapter, Tokushima District Court took a step backwards on 27 March 2015, denying that the act was motivated by racism (point (1))). The plaintiff in *Tokushima* consequently regarded the decision as a complete loss, despite being awarded a high monetary amount in damages. On appeal, Takamatsu High Court rendered its judgment on 25 April 2016, LEX/DB25543016. See Tamitomo Saito, 'Heito Supīchi to Jinshu Sabetsu Teppai Jōyaku ['Hate speech and the ICERD'] (2018) 1518 *Jurist* 296 for detailed analysis. It recognized the malicious racism at play (point (1)) and it has been applauded for that. At the same time, however, the appellate court failed to address important elements of point (2). It failed to evaluate fully the damage done to the precious relationships and goodwill accumulated through decades of dedicated support activities for Korean schools. See Shiki Tomimasu, 'Re-evaluation on the Function of Torts Law's Compensatory Principle in Cases of Hate Speech' (2018) 61 *Kanazawa Law Review* 199, at 208.

First, there were three different demonstrations that could form the subject matter of each procedure – namely, those of 4 December 2009, 14 January 2010, and 28 March 2010. The choice made by the prosecutor in the criminal trial to prosecute only the first of these reflects his assumption that a series of hate-fuelled demonstrations could be reduced to nothing more than their physical aspects. Such selective prosecution contributed to the erasure of the racial and ethnic aspects from the final criminal judgment.

In the civil case, the school corporation (the plaintiff) included all three demonstrations as subject matter to capture their cumulative damage and the peculiar defiance the perpetrators exhibited in the face of a legal order.

These choices offer us some insights into how each of these actors, in addition to different courts, in criminal or civil procedures contributed to the final outcome for each case. These differences in attitude are indicative of the prospects and limitations of tackling these issues through conventional civil and criminal means.

(a) How the Plaintiff Was Selected in the Civil Case

In a criminal procedure, it is the prosecutor – representing the Japanese government – who has the exclusive authority to initiate and maintain a case, seeking a guilty verdict with adequate sentencing.

In the civil procedure, directors, teachers, and parents concluded that the educational institution (Kyoto Korean School Corporation) should act as plaintiff – although there had been serious discussion of whether the school children, teachers, and parents themselves should become plaintiffs jointly. Either way, it had already been decided that the plaintiff would be represented by more than 100 attorneys volunteering their time pro bono and hence the discussion of who should be the plaintiff was shaped by the advice of this group of professionals.

Clearly, the children were the victims most directly affected by the incident. There were, however, strong concerns about potential harassment in the future if their names and addresses were to be made public, as procedurally required. The same concerns applied in the case of the teachers and the parents, as necessarily named individuals.

Unfortunately, those concerns were not unfounded in the context of widespread discriminatory sentiment against Korean minorities and consequently we had to give up on the idea of fulfilling the right to court procedures of children, school parents, and teachers. We hoped that the courts should understand and acknowledge the special function that the school corporation would assume as their representative, given the practical difficulties of positioning these vulnerable individuals as plaintiffs.

(b) The Accused in Criminal Procedure and the Defendants in Civil Procedure

In the criminal case, the prosecutor selected four people who played a major role in the first December demonstration as those who deserved formal indictment. These four accused were later found guilty.

When filing the civil cases in tort, the plaintiff added the person who played a major role in creating and proliferating the YouTube video clips. Several others were added such that the eventual defendants were one organization and nine individuals, including the four convicted in the criminal case.

While adding these defendants was important for the purpose of deterrence, the victim (plaintiff) in this case, as in any other civil actions, had to be able to identify the defendant and their place of residence to make them party to a lawsuit. In perpetrating hate crimes, people often pay special attention to preserving anonymity, so that they cannot be held accountable. It takes victims great effort to identify perpetrators, generating yet further barriers to seeking remedy in the courts. This is a consistent characteristic among those who perpetrate hate speech: on the one hand, they emphasize the importance of their own freedom of expression and yet, on the other hand, they seek to suppress constructive discussion, evading counter-arguments in open forums. They rarely shy away from threatening physical violence in combination with their incitement of discrimination all under cover of anonymity.

(c) Selecting the Subject Matter

Of the three demonstrations held in the vicinity of the school, on 4 December 2009, 14 January 2010, and 28 March 2010, the prosecutor limited the subject matter of the criminal case to the first.[2] The plaintiff in the civil case made sure to include all three demonstrations as the subject matter of the civil case.

A comparison of the different choices made by the prosecutor in the criminal case and the plaintiff's attorneys in the civil case in framing the subject matter for trial foreshadows the decisive roles they played in

[2] The criminal charge in *Tokushima Teachers' Association* (see note 1) was later incorporated (joinder).

directing the course of legal procedure to be followed. To ensure that a final judgment properly addresses the harm caused, it is of crucial importance that the charges or claims accurately capture the essence and gravity of damages particular to those caused by racist aggression. These roles are supposed to be fulfilled when a prosecutor properly exercises their discretion and indicts in the criminal case. Similarly, a plaintiff's appropriate description of the damages and facts supporting the claims in a civil case is crucial. In both situations, the legal profession's depth of understanding about the characteristics of hate-motivated incidents is important in advancing the anti-discrimination cause cumulatively through judicial remedies and judgments.

II. The Criminal Case (Kyoto District Court)

A. *An Overview*

In the criminal case, four members of the Zaitokukai were indicted and convicted of various offences: 'Breaking into a Residence' (Art. 130 of the Penal Code), 'Damage to Property' (Art. 261), 'Forceful Obstruction of Business' (Art. 234) and 'Insults' (Art. 231). The prosecution could have resorted to the provision of defamation (Art. 230(1)) instead of insults. However, in the case of defamation, unlawfulness of an act could be precluded by the motif of public interest and the proof of truthfulness of facts, making the task of the prosecution more cumbersome. The accused were sentenced to suspended penal servitude of 18 to 24 months, as their acts also involved other offenses including forceful obstruction of business and breaking into a residence.

The court plainly dismissed the defendants' various claims based on constitutional freedom of expression (art. 21), which was an obvious conclusion in light of precedents in Japanese courthouses.[3] There is little worthy of note in this analysis from a legal perspective in the context of constitutional freedom of expression. Presenting this case as a juxtaposition of minority rights and freedom of expression gives too much credit to those peddling hate.

[3] Shin Hae Bon, 'Legal Responses to Racial Hate Speech in Japan' (2018) *Droits fondamentaux*, no. 16, January–December. As Shin points out, '(c)oncerning the vociferation, the Kyoto District Court rejected the argument of the defense that it was an act of legitimate political expressions, holding that the act of yelling insulting speech at a high volume by means of megaphones for over 46 minutes in front of the school, added to the fact that the defendants caused a tumult by using material force such as displacing the property of the victims, left no room for being admitted'. *Ibid.*, at 11–12.

B. The Prosecutor's Choice of Insult (Art. 231) as the Charged Offence

Many criticize Kyoto District Court for rendering a criminal judgment that applied the law on insult,[4] rather than defamation,[5] under the Penal Code. The ruling has been criticized as not capturing the essence and gravity of victimization as a hate crime. However, the focus of criticism should be the prosecutor, who was responsible for choosing insult as the offence charged. It is important to recognize the decisive influence exerted by the prosecutor in the choice of the charge. Japanese criminal procedural law gives prosecutors full discretion in deciding whether to indict or to drop the case, in defining the counts for indictment, and in determining the choice of the charges to be prosecuted under the Penal Code. And once a prosecutor submits an indictment with a particular count described with citation to a specific article of that Code, judges, in principle, are required to respect that submission and to proceed within that framework.

The institutional racism is deeply rooted in every aspect of the hierarchical organizational structure of state prosecution. A lack of motivation to pursue a heavier penalty was by no means peculiar to the prosecutor in this case.

The responsibility of the prosecutor becomes even clearer in light of the previous opinion recommending defamation, which was passed on to the prosecutor by the Kyoto Prefectural Police.

Generally speaking, additional preparation for the rebuttal of any possible defence based on what is called 'Special Provision for Matters Concerning Public Interest'[6] becomes necessary if the prosecutor chooses to indict for defamation. The police, which were in charge of the investigation before handing it over to the prosecutor, understood the special importance of securing a defamation judgment in the minds of the minority – namely, Zainichi Korean teachers, parents, and children. The damaged dignity of these individuals and communities could not be

[4] Penal Code, art. 231 ('Insults'): 'A person who insults another in public, even if it does not allege facts, shall be punished by misdemeanour imprisonment without work or a petty fine.'

[5] Penal Code, art. 230(1) ('Defamation'): 'A person who defames another by alleging facts in public shall, regardless of whether such facts are true or false, be punished by imprisonment with or without work for not more than three years or a fine of not more than 500,000 yen.'

[6] Penal Code, art. 230–2(1): 'When an act prescribed under paragraph (1) of the preceding Article is found to relate to matters of public interest and to have been conducted solely for the benefit of the public, the truth or falsity of the alleged facts shall be examined, and punishment shall not be imposed if they are proven to be true.'

remedied merely by condemning these actions as insult. This would indicate to Zainichi Koreans that the Japanese judiciary considered the racist attacks to be minor and that the likely light sentencing for the minor charge would effectively tell the perpetrators that they were forgiven.[7]

C. *Complete 'Bleaching' in the Criminal Decision*

The omission in the criminal decision of the racist and ethnic elements of the incident are its most prominent characteristics.

The essence of the Kyoto incident is the clear racist motives of perpetrators who targeted a school that practises ethnic education. The perpetrators acted on their intent to discriminate based upon ethnicity. And it is clear that the ethnicity of Koreans in Japan was targeted. This point was immediately obvious to anyone who watched the YouTube video of the demonstration. Nevertheless, the ruling completely avoided any mention of ethnicity and there is no reference in the verdict to any assessment of the malevolent discriminatory motive.

Moreover, schools exist to protect, nurture, and educate children. Appropriate effort should have been made to grasp the actual damage caused to these children by the wrongdoers. The prosecutor and the court should have centred the impact of this harmful behaviour as a formative experience in the development of the Zainichi Korean children.

Similarly, the parents and other parties related to the school have a strong sense of belonging to the school community. Such sentiment is rooted in the fact that the school acted as sanctuary and place for sustaining and passing on their cultural heritage to the next generation.

Although it should have been natural and proper that ethnicity should be centred as a basis for examinations in court, the prosecutor ignored these circumstances entirely. As a result, the judge did not assess the problem and the issue was wholly absent in the ratio of the judgement.

[7] The prosecutor's justification for dropping a defamation charge was that the perpetrators' intention must be judged from the overall course of their actions and it was alleged that it was 'clearly' that of insult. From the victims' perspective, nothing justified that assessment. No matter the perpetrators' intention, members of the public viewing the YouTube videos were likely to mistake the perpetrators' allegations for facts rather than as unsubstantiated emotional insults. And it was clear that substantial damage was done to the social reputation of the victims, aggravated by discriminatory sentiment, fuelled by unjust biases and prejudices, which were widely shared among Japanese people. With regards to how the civil courts can address a perpetrators' unjust intention to make use of widespread bias to amplify the impact of their racist attack, see Tomimasu, note 1, at 222.

D. *The Aftermath of Sentencing: Recurrent Criminal Engagement*

It was no surprise that the overly lenient sentencing of the criminal judgment rendered on 28 April 2011 was less than effective in deterring subsequent racist 'speech' activities. However, its failure to prevent recurrent 'physical' assaults was surprising. The extremist group Zaitokukai led similar demonstrations that featured increasingly violent and physical obstruction. Two of the accused did not stop until they were again arrested for (and later convicted of) extortion against Rohto Pharmaceutical in March 2012. The four-year probationary period that had been handed down in the *Kyoto Korean Elementary School* criminal case had barely elapsed when the accused committed extortion.

In other words, Kyoto District Court failed to properly assess the risk of repeat offences when attaching suspension to the sentencing. The lesson may be that, for a hate crime offender who maintains racist opinions even in open court hearings, it is not enough to warn them that if they commit another offence, that suspension will be cancelled and they will be sent straight to prison.

In addition, to recognize that 'the fear and humiliation felt by the victim is significant, and it is natural to show strong feelings of victimization', the judgment itself pointed out that 'the defendants exhibited no attitude of remorse'. Their lack of remorse is evident in their statements at the court hearing. Here, the court refers to the repeated discriminatory comments made by those accused at the court hearing, attempting to link the school with criminal activities conducted by the North Korean government. At the end of the trial, one accused stated that the damage done to the school by their 'protests' were too soft and lukewarm (as a response to what he alleged the school was engaged in), and he argued that therefore these protests were acceptable in Japanese society. The accused had stated that the school should be thankful that the demonstrators had limited themselves to only this degree of damage.

School officials received the court's sentencing decision with surprise. The ruling stated the ratio for the suspension, despite the offenders' evident lack of remorse, as follows: '[T]he accused have stated that if their past conduct is deemed illegal, they will change the method of their activities.' When the accused made this pledge in court, it comprised nothing more than that they would 'not do the same thing' and would 'not get arrested'. There was no hint of remorse for the hateful motivation with which they incited ethnic discrimination and contempt.

The court therefore appears to have evaluated the risk of reoffending only to the extent of whether or not the offenders would repeat physical acts disrupting the school's business. In this sense, the nature of the damage in this case was reduced to nothing more than the type of physical disruption that any loud street demonstration or other activity would cause, should it take place without consideration of time, place, or occasion.

Later, on 18 December 2012, Osaka District Court ruled in the Rohto extortion criminal case that the actions of the defendant were 'malicious offence whereby the perpetrators burst in on the victims' office completely uninvited and threatened them. If left unaddressed, [the defendants] shall soon pose a serious social threat.' We must remind ourselves that such a ruling was quite possible eight months earlier, at the time of the Kyoto District Court decision. Kyoto District Court's criminal sentencing should be regarded as a judicial failure. Similar mistakes occurred when the Kinki Regional Parole Board evaluated two convicted offenders for early release (parole), based upon 'signs of substantial reformation' (under art. 28 of the Penal Code). After their release, the two yet again committed hate-related crimes in 2017 and 2018.[8]

The insufficient criminal response to the school's case, with its meagre effect on prevention, warrants a comprehensive revision of the Japanese criminal justice system. It is as if, once thrown into the context of hate-motivated crime, the legal system suddenly malfunctions. In the *Kyoto Korean Elementary School* case, as well as in the *Tokushima* case, the main factors that prolonged the distress of the victims were administrative – namely, failings in the practice of criminal investigation and indictment. In other words, the root problem lies in unfair implementation of procedural law. The issues in these cases were not so much about the lack of a substantive law, as loudly claimed by those advocating for a new hate speech regulation.[9] This point is widely misunderstood by the

[8] One of the accused, Hitoshi Nishimura, was indicted on 20 April 2018 for defamation conducted on 23 April 2017. Another, Yasuhiko Aramaki, was reportedly arrested and charged with two different assaults: on 14 August 2018, in Kawasaki (*Sankei News Webnews*, 29 January 2019); and on 18 November 2018, in Osaka (*Sankei West Webnews*, 19 November 2018). For more detailed analysis, see Shiki Tomimasu, 'The *Kyoto Korean School* case' (2019) 258 *Bessatsu Hōgaku Seminā* [Bessatsu legal seminar] 100.

[9] Discussions of hate speech have centred on the issue of substantive laws, such as the constitutionality of new proposed regulations, along with appropriate delineation, both in terms of extent and clarity, of the regulations and punishments. However, more relevant discussion may have focused in practice on the operation of existing criminal procedural

Japanese public. Some possible options for effective revision of the system might therefore include publishing prosecution guidelines,[10] or sentencing guidelines to which courts can refer in these cases, developing and implementing a correctional programme focusing on hate crime offenders. Instituting appropriate standards for parole examinations may also be beneficial, accompanied by proper assessment of the degree of remorse inspired by correctional measures and a reduced risk of reoffending.

III. The First Civil Judgment (Kyoto District Court)

A. *Introduction*

In June 2010, the plaintiff filed a civil lawsuit with Kyoto District Court, in parallel with the criminal prosecution. Along with an injunction prohibiting similar intimidating demonstrations in the future, the plaintiff sought damages of ¥10 million per intimidating demonstration (¥30 million in total).

In the civil trial, the plaintiff made an extra effort to present the importance of the right to ethnic education. The Korean schools project is essential if individual Zainichi Korean children are to exercise and fulfil that right.

By the time the first hearing of the civil trial had been filed, the plaintiff's lawyers group had summarized the elements of ethnic education, as conducted at Kyoto Korean Elementary School, as follows in its first brief submitted to the court.

(1) If new generations are to inherit language and culture, it is necessary to secure a place in which teachers and students who share the language and culture can gather as a group.

laws to ensure the effective investigation and prosecution of hate crimes. Even if some hate speech regulations are enacted as substantive law in the near future, there is no guarantee that they will be applied as the legislature envisions absent the systemic improvements that will facilitate prompt arrests and detentions, and reliable prosecutions. Standards of sentencing, including discussion of suspended sentences, would be beneficial to prevent overly lenient decisions influenced by general discriminatory sentiment against minority victims. Sufficient protection, both in terms of formal legal protection and civil society's support, should be instituted to decrease minority victims' fear of retaliation should they institute legal action.

[10] International comparison is warranted. See James Morsch, 'The Problem of Motive in Hate Crimes: The Argument against Presumptions of Racial Motivation' (1991) 82 *Journal of Criminal Law and Criminology* 687 for the discussion of the situation some 30 years ago in the United States.

(2) To foster sound ethnic self-esteem in those children, a safe and secure learning environment shielded from ethnic insults and discriminatory remarks is essential.

While the main effort of the Korean schools project is placed on the succession of ethnic language and traditional culture, significant emphasis is placed on interaction and mutual understanding with Japanese residents in surrounding communities.

(3) Experiencing, from an early age, friendly exchanges that transcend nationality and ethnicity is considered to have significant impact on fostering healthy ethnic self-esteem.

The Korean schools project is based in the idea that the children will develop a sense of security that they will be respected as a person in Japan even if they reveal their Korean heritage. All of these experiences aim to shape young people who feel able to behave confidently with ethnic dignity in later life.

It was later revealed that the first brief played an extremely important role in establishing a relationship of trust between the Zainichi Korean community surrounding the school and the plaintiff's lawyers' group. Because these lawyers were mainly Japanese, there had been some scepticism about whether they could really understand the importance of a Korean ethnic education for Zainichi Koreans in Japan. The first brief gave the Koreans hope that if they were to explain their position sincerely, the lawyers would understand it and it would eventually be possible to persuade even the Japanese judges.

B. *An Overview of the Judgment*

(a) Common Scholarly Assessment in Jurisprudence

The civil trial at Kyoto District Court was concluded on 7 October 2013, some three years after the first oral argument was delivered on 16 September 2010. As many as 18 oral hearings had been held at the court house, including the testimonial hearing.

Professor Shin Hae Bon has correctly summarized the civil judgment rendered by Kyoto District Court as follows:

> In a civil lawsuit filed by the educational institution, the Kyoto District Court ordered [payment of] a total of over 12 million yen for a series of acts as compensation in damages for tort, recognizing that the acts amount to racial discrimination in the sense of the International Convention on the Elimination of All Forms of Racial Discrimination (ICERD). . . . The Court

held: '[. . .] [T]he obstruction of business and slander, into which discriminatory remarks against Koreans residing in Japan were interwoven, were both conducted with the intention of appealing discriminatory ideas against the Koreans to the public, thus amount to exclusion based on ethnic origin as Koreans residing in Japan which has the purpose of impairing the enjoyment for Koreans residing in Japan, on an equal footing, of human rights and fundamental freedoms. Therefore, as a whole, they are nothing short of racial discrimination as provided in the ICERD. [. . .] In making monetary evaluation of immaterial damages, the seriousness of the damage and the gravity of unlawfulness of the act of infringement are considered.'[11]

(b) Dismissing the Freedom of Expression Defence

The District Court ruling dismissed the defendants' allegation that their conduct was justified on the basis of constitutional freedom of expression.[12]

Many of the defendants' statements in court proceedings had been provocative and highly discriminatory. They had been effective in creating 'topical' content for the media and attracting attention, acting in defiant character even in an open court, with consistently immature, reckless, and even playful attitudes, complete with insincere grins and smirks, and not a hint of remorse. Such extremism in a criminal courthouse was completely

[11] See Shin, note 3.

[12] It stated:

> The above case law exempts defamatory expressions only when they are expressed solely for the benefit of the public, whether they are factual or commentary.
>
> It is extremely difficult to find that the defamatory comments mentioned in (2) to (4) above in the Activities were expressed solely for the benefit of the public. This is because of the following characteristics: the Demonstration Activities were conducted loudly in the vicinity of the School with amplification by loudspeaker; Demonstration Activities 1 involved the use of physical force near to the School to knock down the soccer goal placed in the Park, cut off the speaker wiring, and remove the morning assembly platform; Demonstration Activities 2 and 3 involved the use of a propaganda demonstration truck (equipped with loudspeakers and intimidating confrontational appearance). Expressions intended to serve the public interest generally are not coercive with the use of physical force.
>
> In addition, as mentioned above, the Activities as a whole are acts of racial discrimination that are interwoven with discriminatory remarks appealing the legitimacy of discrimination against Koreans in Japan to the public, and asserting, in a public place, their view that Koreans in Japan should be excluded from Japanese society, denying [their right to live] on an equal footing with Japanese people and other foreigners in Japanese society. Such acts can no way be deemed to have been conducted for the purpose of 'solely for the benefit of the public'.

unconventional in terms of prioritizing their impact on and appeal to the public over the possibility of lesser sentencing should they appear to sincerely exhibit remorse and promise accountability, pledging never again to perform similar unlawful conduct.

It is important to understand these efforts as quite different from the search for truth through a series of fair discussions, which is the basic premise for evoking constitutional protection of expression. A court procedure should be an ideal stage on which any accused can play out a discussion of the 'reason' for their actions, had there been any. However, these defendants dared instead to repeat provocative and defiant utterance.[13] Looking back, a similar trend was obvious in the actual criminal scene of 2009 and 2010, and it is consequently reasonable to conclude that this was the defendants' true aim: they simply wanted to attract media and public attention by acting out outrageously.

Their goal, it appeared, had never been persuasion of those who might be receptive to discussion of their 'reasons'; rather, the purpose of their campaign, which were continued even in the courthouse trial, was to appeal mostly to those who want to share extremism and discriminatory propaganda. They showed little interest in engaging in the type of constructive discussion that might eventually build public support, based on some sort of inherent truth.[14]

Osaka High Court confirmed and developed further the District Court's assessment of the case.[15]

[13] We might also be alarmed that those advocating a pro-regulatory approach are starting to belittle the idea of constructive discussion. In recent years, it has become common for those advocating regulation to use personal attacks to silence those who advocate against it and emphasize the importance of 'freedom of expression'. As a result, there also have been a number of situations in which the healthy, constructive exchange of opinions is no longer possible about the subject of hate speech regulation.

The termination of such discussions by silencing opposition has gained public support in general. However, we should not overlook that such effects have something in common with hate demonstrations themselves as attempts to suppress unpleasant speech by force.

[14] See Chapter 12 for more on why peaceful educational efforts inspire a vehement emotional response among some majority Japanese.

[15] Osaka High Court stated:

> The appellees voluntarily approached the School and engaged in an illegal act of interfering with the appellee's business and dishonouring the appellee's reputation. It cannot be denied that the persons concerned at the School who objected to the unlawful acts of the appellant and others made hostile attitudes and statements toward the appellants, but the appellant and others merely caused such objections by their illegal acts, and the manner in which they provoked the appellant and further escalated discriminatory words and deeds by taking advantage of the expected friction.

The accused intentionally chose to continue offending and attacking their victims even at the court where they were indicted, as though it meant nothing to them other than a bigger stage from which to promote their hate message. Such an attitude is diametrically opposite of an apology hoping to calm anger and reduce victims' pain. The accused's persistent defiance was certainly a shock to the Zainichi Korean people – but the subsequent lenient sentencing of the court in the face of such clear defiance was a far bigger shock, entrenching the feeling of hopelessness shared among those within the Zainichi community.

C. *'Bleaching' of the Victim's Ethnicity*

Nevertheless, even Kyoto District Court's decision, which clearly took a firm stance against the perpetrators' racism, carefully 'bleached' the ethnic nature of the victim's business. In other words, the judgment consistently avoided analysing the case through the lens of the right to and social value of Korean ethnic education.

Certainly, Kyoto District Court can be applauded for its approach to carefully observed facts relating to the damages done to the school and for its courage to order high compensation in proper appreciation of those damages – but it overlooked their qualitative essence. The judgment presents these damages merely as a hindrance to education of the same type as it would be had the attack affected any school corporation; it carefully avoided recognition of the ethnic aspect of the education conducted at the school. The court's attention was limited to physical damage – namely, the 'adverse effect' such as 'organizational confusion, retention of regular work, generation of time and effort to keep the organization calm or to calm the confusion'.

In this case, the hate-motivated conduct and the damage done to the school hinged on the concept of ethnic self-esteem. The two were flip sides of the same coin: a vicious act of hate speech is wrongful behaviour that harms ethnic self-esteem and increases discrimination in society. For this reason, the plaintiff hoped that if the courts were to understand the core of the (psychological) damage a hate crime does, then they would naturally engender appreciation of the importance of ethnic education for minority Koreans in Japan. And, as a result, the plaintiff fully expected to see the social importance of ethnic education underlined in the ratio of the verdict.

In its statements, the plaintiff repeatedly emphasized that school's programme focuses on fostering ethnicity among students and that this had special significance to the case. Indeed, in the course of trial, this is not something that the defendants contested, so it was reasonable to expect the court to recognize it – the court's meticulous omission was both surprising and deeply disappointing to both parents and teachers.

It can be argued that this careful erasure, or 'bleaching', of the ethnic aspects of the case from its decision was deliberate on the part of the court. That the omission of the infringed interest was both unnatural and inappropriate is indicative that it was intentional – and it was certainly consistent with the criminal decision in which issues of ethnicity and racism had been stubbornly ignored.[16]

D. *In the Name of 'Immaterial Damages': Awarding Punitive Damages Contrary to Supreme Court Precedent?*

Many regarded the Kyoto District Court decision as awarding punitive damages against Supreme Court precedent. The idea that the court took such action was a major point of dispute when the defendants immediately sought to appeal. As Professor Shin Hae Bon states:

> Significantly, [Kyoto District] Court held that, in awarding compensation in damages for racial discrimination, the amount has to be decided so that it would provide effective protection and remedy for the act of racial discrimination, citing the statement of the Japanese government that had been made public before the treaty body, on an occasion of periodic examination of State reports, to the effect that, in criminal proceedings concerning the cases of racism, judges often take the element of maliciousness into their consideration of sentences.[17]

The Court held that:

[16] As a related issue, 'bleaching' in media coverage is worth noting. Even though the verdict attracted strong media attention, there was a peculiar absence of media coverage linking the Kyoto incident to violence and harassment motivated by bias in the past. For more on the criminal assault and injury of Korean schoolgirls wearing traditional chima jeogori uniforms, and the obvious link between those attacks and the more recent racist attacks, see Chapter 12.

Looking further back, one should note the commonalities between the violent acts committed by Zaitokukai and those perpetrated by the Japanese government itself in 1948. The government exercised police force in the compulsory shutdown of Korean schools, resulting in the death of 16-year-old Kim Tae-il. It is not a coincidence that the fiercest forms of violence have been directed at Korean ethnic schools, whether by government or by private individuals motivated by hate, despite that the schools are home to many young and innocent children in need of protection.

[17] See Shin, note 3.

> [T]he government of Japan, [...] in the Committee on the Racial Discrimination established under the ICERD, in response to a question whether the courts in criminal cases consider 'racial motivation' of crimes, replied that 'in cases of racism, judges often refer to the element of malice, which is then reflected on the sentence'; in response, the Committee called on the Japanese government 'to take additional measures to address expressions of hate and racism and, in particular, to ensure the effective implementation of the provisions of the Constitution, the Civil Code and the Penal Code'. That is, in deciding the sentences in criminal case, racial discrimination as the motivation of the crime being an element aggravating the sentence, it is plainly admitted that the ICERD directly influences interpretation and application of law. Similarly, in cases where a tort such as slander equally amounts to racial discrimination, or where a tort is motivated by racial discrimination, it cannot be denied that the ICERD directly influences the interpretation and application of civil law, becoming an element aggravating the amount of compensation for immaterial damages. Also, as stated above, in this case in which the obstruction of business and slander against the plaintiff were conducted as racial discrimination, the Court is under obligation, under Art. 2(1) [and] Art. 6, to interpret and apply law in compliance with the provisions of the Convention. As a result, monetary evaluation of the immaterial damages by the Court cannot be but expensive in amount.[18]

The District Court was careful to confine and bracket the punitive character within the terminology of 'immaterial damages', which are widely precedented. However, as the analogy with sentencing in a criminal judgment clearly shows, the court's intention to impose a penalty on the perpetrator rooted in the maliciousness of their behaviour is evident. The legal reasoning behind its increase of the amount of damages seems to be exactly the kind of punitive damages that the Supreme Court of Japan nullified in *Mansei Kōgyō*.[19] In that decision, Supreme Court presented the Civil Code of California as a contrasting example,[20] to illustrate the compensatory philosophy behind tort law in Japan:

[18] Translation cited *ibid.*

[19] Supreme Court, 2nd Petty Bench, 11 July 1997, 51 Minshū 2573.

[20] The Supreme Court state:

> The Civil Code of the State of California, USA, has a provision which allows the plaintiff to receive punitive damages for the purpose of deterrence and sanction on the defendant in addition to damages for the actual loss in litigation on the ground of breach of non-contractual duties, if there was an fraudulent act or similar acts on the part of the defendant (Article 3294) . . . It is evident that the system of punitive damages as provided by the Civil Code of the State of California (hereinafter, 'punitive damages') is designed to impose sanctions on the culprit and prevent similar acts in the future by

> [T]he system of damages based upon tort in Japan assesses the actual loss in a pecuniary manner, forces the culprit to compensate this amount, and thus enables the recovery of the disadvantage suffered by the victim and restores the status quo ante (Judgment of the Supreme Court, 1988 (O) Case No. 1749, Judgment of the Grand Bench, 24 March 1993, Minshū 47-4-3039), and is not intended for sanctions on the culprit or prevention of similar acts in the future, i.e. general prevention. Admittedly, there may be an effect of sanctions on the culprit or prevention of similar acts in the future by imposing a duty of compensation on the culprit, but this is a reflective and secondary effect of imposing the duty of compensation on the culprit, and the system is fundamentally different from the system of punitive damages whose goals are the sanctioning of the culprit and general deterrence. In Japan, sanctioning of the culprit and general deterrence is left to criminal or administrative sanctions. Thus, the system in which in tort cases, the victim is paid damages for the purpose of imposing sanction on the culprit and general deterrence in addition to damages for the actual loss should be regarded as against the basic principles or basic ideas of the system of compensation based upon tort in Japan.

This section illustrates that the court was committed to condemning the perpetrators for their discriminatory behaviour even as it ignored the significant social value of Korean ethnic education.

IV. The Second Civil Judgment (Osaka High Court)

A. A Common Assessment of the Judgment

The defendants appealed the lower court ruling ordering them to pay about ¥12 million. However, Osaka High Court dismissed the appeal on 8 July, closing the case with only one hearing. The defendants had continued to make various arguments based on freedom of expression, but Osaka High Court gave them short shrift.

In contrast with the decision at Kyoto District Court, the ruling of Osaka High Court clearly recognizes the social importance of Korean ethnic education in Japanese communities.

In its own judgment, the appellate court deleted the descriptions in the characteristic part of the first-instance judgment, including most of those that have already been cited in this chapter. However, it upheld that court's evaluation of the malicious nature of the perpetrators' racism and its recognition of the many ways in which they obstructed the school's

ordering the culprit who had effected malicious acts to pay additional damages on top of the damages for the actual loss, and judging from the purposes, is similar to criminal sanctions such as fines in Japan.

business, condemning their discriminatory behaviour. In addition, the judgment added that 'the degree of mental damage inflicted by the unreasonable act of racism was enormous'.

It can therefore be said that this judgment takes the view of the first-instance court one step further, delving more deeply into the specific effect of racism on the wrong done to the victim. The High Court reiterated that '[t]he degree of mental damage caused by the unreasonableness and absurdity of racial discrimination was enormous'. In this way, it merged its condemnation of the perpetrators for their discriminatory behaviour with its recognition of the significant social value of Korean ethnic education, rather than treating each as an independent factor constituting damage in tort.

The heart of this ruling lies in its 'victim first' approach to fact-finding, as well as its discussion of technical legal questions and application of international treaties. It is this approach that enabled judges to proceed so far as to recognize the importance of ethnic education.[21] The High Court held:

> When racially discriminatory remarks against those who belong to certain groups are made between private individuals, and the remarks lack reasonable grounds and infringe legal interest of others beyond the limit tolerable in society in light of Arts. 13 and 14 of the Constitution and the object of ICERD, we should interpret that the requirement that it 'infringed any right of others or legally protected interest of others' in Art. 709 of the Civil Code is fulfilled, and realize the object of the Convention to eliminate racial discrimination even between private individuals by making the perpetrator compensate for the damages caused. . . . [T]he object of the Convention to eliminate racial discrimination becomes the basis in evaluating the maliciousness of tort. Evidently, it should be

[21] Shin Hae Bon (note 3) correctly summarizes the judgment thus:

> In the appeal, the Osaka High Court modified the method of interpretation by the first instance that had relied solely on the ICERD, invoking both the Constitution and the ICERD as standards of interpretation of the Civil Code. On the other hand, the High Court clearly admitted that the object of the Convention becomes the basis in evaluating the maliciousness of tort, maintaining the amount of compensation in damages awarded by the first instance. The Court also rightly evaluated the seriousness of the acts of the defendants aggravated by uploading the films on the internet. In evaluating the immaterial damages incurred by the school, the Court noted the seriousness of the moral damages caused by racial discrimination. The Court also recognized that the school has legal interest to conduct ethnic education to Koreans in Japan, whereas the activities by the appellants abusing the freedom of expression do not enjoy legal protection.

> considered in terms of the gravity of immaterial damages such as the sense of victimization by unreasonable tort and moral damages.[22]

This premise conforms better to Supreme Court precedents,[23] in comparison with the Kyoto District Court judgment.

The High Court also stated that:

> According to the facts, it is clear that the appellants negated the personality of Koreans in Japan and the appellee, appealed the legitimacy of discrimination against Koreans in Japan to the public, and claimed, in public places, their view that Koreans in Japan should be excluded from Japanese society. Moreover, in addition to the facts that their acts were persistently repeated for three times, the third demonstration was especially of highly unlawful nature in that it was conducted in violation of the decision of temporary injunction in this case. Furthermore, publicizing the films shooting the scenes of demonstrations in this case by uploading them on movie site on the internet, with titles put from the position of the groups of the appellants [. . .], making them viewable by unidentified numbers of people, not only aggravated damages by widely disseminating the films but also makes it possible that the damages be reproduced in the future by being conserved in destinations where the films are disseminated. Considering the circumstances as above in total, it is clear that the activities in this case, as a whole, are malicious acts that promote and

[22] Translation cited in Shin, note 3.

[23] *Mitsubishi Plastic, Inc.* (Supreme Court, Grand Bench, 12 December 1973, 27 Minshū 1536) ruled:

> [E]ach of the above provisions of the Constitution, like other provisions of Chap. 3 of it guaranteeing other basic rights of freedom, aiming at the vindication of the fundamental freedom and equality of individuals from governmental actions of the state or public entities and is not expected directly to regulate the mutual relations between private parties . . . [I]t is not a proper interpretation that the provisions which guarantee fundamental and constitutional rights should apply directly or by analogy to the mutual relations between private parties . . . [However,] concrete and socially inadmissible infringement in private control relationships, or the risk thereof, can be recovered through remedial measures taken by legislature. And also in some cases we may be able to make a proper adjustment between the principle of private autonomy on one hand and the benefits of fundamental freedom and equality on the other against socially inadmissible infringement thereon by properly applying Arts. 1 and 90 of Civil Code (which provide general limitation on private autonomy) and other various provisions relating to unlawful acts. It is a matter of course there that we should think much of fundamental freedom and equality of the individual as a very important legal benefit, but at the same time it is not proper to regard this as an absolute one and it goes without saying that one cannot regulate this relation according to the same concepts and standards as those in case of governmental actions.

> aggravate social prejudices and the idea of discrimination against the appellee educating Koreans in Japan and their children.
>
> The appellee not only incurred serious impediment to its operation of ethnic education by the above acts of the appellants but also was exposed to unreasonable expressions of hate. As a result, their business has been obstructed, social reputation degraded, and their personal interest greatly damaged [. . .]. Also, the 134 students enrolled in the school at the time of the incident were, in spite of the fact that they had evidently nothing [for which] to be blamed, exposed to scornful and degrading attacks by the appellants only for the reason of their ethnic origin (even if the children had not been present, it is easily presumable that they would have recognized the situation of the incident). It is admitted that the degree of moral damages incurred by them due to unreasonable acts of racial discrimination was significant, and the appellant will have to pay considerable efforts to alleviate the sufferings of those students.
>
> The appellee, as the contents of its personal interest, has the interest to retain the honour, which is an objective evaluation by the society on the personal values such as the raison-d'être as an educational institution and its qualification, and to conduct ethnic education of Koreans in Japan as an educational business in the school in this case. On the other hand, the activities in this case obstruct the educational business of the appellee in the school in this case, significantly impairing the honour of the appellee as an educational institution. There is no choice but to say that they are contrary to 'public welfare' in Art. 13 of the Constitution, as abuse of the freedom of expression, and do not merit legal protection.

These sections indicate Osaka High Court's commitment to amplifying the social value of ethnic education.

B. Including the Victim's Ethnicity in the Legal Analysis

Despite this, no scholarly reviews, including Professor Shin's analysis, have yet pointed out the import of the court in citing 'Plaintiff Exhibit (kō) 152, 153, 191'. The court consciously did so to specify the meaning of the notion 'ethnic education' in the judgment. This citation appears in the following section of the judgment, pointing out the 'social value' of the Korean school programme in Japan, of which Kyoto Korean Elementary School is a part:

> [T]he appellee was a school corporation approved in 1953 and was engaged in ethnic education of Korean residents in Japan by establishing and operating the school, for the purpose of carrying out education for Korean people and general cultural education projects. The Korean schools, including the Kyoto Elementary School at issue, numbered about 120 schools and about 12,000 students nationwide, and have

> formed a social reputation as a place for implementing ethnic education (Plaintiff Exhibit (kō) 152, 153, 191).
>
> The appellant's act in this case damaged the Korean school's social significance and reputation as a manifestation of the interests in personality rights of the school corporation ... [T]he act in this case not only hindered the educational activities of the school and undermined the educational environmental of Korean residents in Japan, but also undermined the social environment of the school.

The ruling proclaimed that these elements – 'ethnic education', 'the purpose of carrying out education for Korean people', 'general education projects (for Korean children)', and 'a social reputation as a place for implementing ethnic education' – would be subject to legal protection under tort law in Japan. These protections were not mere formal recognition; such protection would allow victims to seek concrete reparations from perpetrators if infringements were to occur. Considering that the school system has historically been targeted as a subject of persecution by the Japanese government,[24] Osaka High Court's clear declaration that Korean ethnic education is to be protected is epoch-making, however obvious this should be.

Moreover, the fact that the ruling went out of its way to deliberately cite three works submitted as Exhibit (kō) 152, 153, and 191 – namely, Kicahng Song, *Katararenai Mono to shite no Chōsen Gakkō* [The Korean schools as untold entity] (Iwanami Shoten, 2012), *Chousengakkou No Shakaigakuteki Kenkyu* [A sociological study of a Korean school] (Doshisha University Sociology Department, 2008), and Il-song Nakamura, *Rupo: Kyoto Chōsen Gakkō Shūgeki Jiken* [Reportage: Kyoto Korean School raid case] (Iwanami Shoten, 2014) – to define the substance of the school's 'social significance and reputation' gave special hope to the Korean community. These books depict in detail the specific practices of ethnic education and became the basis of recognition of the value of the educational endeavour. This allows Korean people to feel optimistic about the prospect of wide acceptance within the Japanese community of the same.[25]

[24] See details of the death of Kim Tae-il and other racist harassment outlined at note 16.

[25] One of the most important contributions of this decision has to be the empowerment of the young children who were victimized – some 12,000 students from 120 Korean schools across Japan. They were worried about the future of their own schools. The court support organization Korumu prepared and distributed illustrated leaflets for the children. While students at these Korean schools have no difficulty reading and writing Japanese, in accordance with the spirit of respect for ethnic education in the ruling, Korumu prepared Korean versions of all five issues: see https://blog.goo.ne.jp/kopponori/e/c48d6715e96284029b01c10bb2211a8e [accessed 30 January 2020].

V. Conclusion

A. *How Many Zainichi Koreans May Perceive the Japanese Justice System*

Since the beginning of Japanese colonial rule, many in the Zainichi Korean community have viewed the Japanese criminal justice system as a powerful organ of government oppression. Criminal prosecutions have unfairly targeted the Korean minority, and the Japanese courts have often coldly dismissed grievances and requests for judicial relief submitted by Korean or other minority victims of discrimination. It is regretful that one cannot deny that such unfair use of law has cast a shadow among the Japanese public more generally.

Deprived of the legal system as a viable means to address injustices, it is understandable that the Korean community has had to resort to self-help measures to a certain extent. However, this practice can further distance a group from legitimate judicial processes and make it increasingly difficult for community members to foster a sense of belonging in Japanese society.

The Osaka High Court judgment in the civil torts case will be remembered by the Korean community as the first favourable ruling to properly address the Korean victims' emotional injuries. In this highly publicized case, the court listened carefully to the Korean victims' stories and exhibited in its ruling sympathy to their plight and the plight of the Korean minority as a whole, giving the case special significance in Japanese legal history. The judgment offered hope that we might raise the Japanese judicial system to a level such that Japanese communities and Zainichi Korean communities are judged fairly under the same universal legal standards – although careful attention must be paid to make sure the majority Japanese do not again end up forcing the Zainichi Korean minority to assimilate in the course of such efforts. A fair universal standard must incorporate the core constitutional value of respect for individual dignity and the dignity of minority groups, and must be designed in such a way that fosters multiculturalism and ethnic education.

B. *Proposing a Restorative Model in Addressing the Phenomenon of Hate Speech*

With respect to the opportunities and limitations of the Japanese legal system when it comes to tackling hate-motivated crimes, *Kyoto Korean Elementary School* provides us with some unique insights.

As this chapter has shown, in its earlier phases, the criminal verdicts and even the highly acclaimed civil Kyoto District Court decision actually exhibited resistance to the promotion of Korean ethnic education. This may well be reflective of Japanese society's overall attitude about minority issues in general. The Japanese public may share general abhorrence when confronted by a peculiar form of racist demonstration – especially those accompanied by physical criminal offences – but their abhorrence of the perpetrators may not be coupled with sympathy for the minority victims. It is no surprise that many majority Japanese find it difficult to truly understand at a gut level the need among Zainichi Korean to foster an ethnic dignity and to differentiate themselves from majority Japanese culture to maintain their own sense of dignity and integrity. For that reason, we should always be cautious that the driving social force behind the institution of the Hate Speech Elimination Act (HSEA) pivot in the near future, demanding suppression of minority opinions, including those coming from Zainichi Koreans.

This case was, first and foremost, about recovering the safety of school children, in face of a discriminatory criminal justice system. After minimal physical safety was secured, the emphasis gradually shifted to recovery of the Zainichi Korean's ethnic dignity. Among several different procedures within the current Japanese legal system, what has proven to be most effective in advancing the special needs of a damaged minority was the compensatory framework of civil tort. The criminal court decision, as well as the civil Kyoto District Court decision based on the punitive framework of tort law, suggests in hindsight that adversarial procedures may not have been optimal venues in which to seek recovery of ethnic dignity. What enabled true recovery, as the judgment of Osaka High Court suggested, was a 'victim first' approach exploring thoroughly the positive social value of ethnic education rather than a perpetrator-centred condemnation of unacceptable behaviours.

In this case, monetary compensation was not at all the first priority of the Zainichi minority and the school corporation, although the relatively high amount of damages awarded by the court contributed to increasing its news appeal and attracting social attention. Such high awards, however, can make it less likely that the perpetrators will come to accept their fault and express sincere apology. Rather than strengthening a punitive approach in the Japanese legal system, it may be more constructive to build a restorative procedure. Such a procedure may focus on positive outcomes and be optimized to raise awareness and public understanding of the nature of hate speech, hate crimes, and victimization. It could be achieved with similar hearings as those performed de facto in compensatory tort trials, as shown in the Osaka High Court judgment described in this chapter. Such a system may better foster mutual understanding between divided groups.

Ultimately, we may need to aim to rehabilitate and return perpetrators into society rather than to exclude them. Perhaps only then will we encourage their recognition of ethnic dignity of the ones they damaged and eventual sincere apology.

C. *Paradoxical Japanese Public Opinion and Its Implications for Anti-hate Efforts*

To conclude this chapter, I would like to pose the following two questions.

(1) Why does the inward, harmless practice of ethnic education in Korean schools create such vehement emotional resentment within these racist groups? Does the average majority Japanese person also share, at least partially, similar negative sentiment against the refusal of minorities, including Zainichi Koreans, to assimilate?

(2) If we suppose the driving force behind the institution of the HSEA was increased understanding of and sympathy with minority Zainichi Koreans among average Japanese voters, then how could those voters support seemingly contradictory discriminatory policies? How do we explain the sentiment of a majority public who vehemently condemn Zaitokukai's racist demonstration at the same times as they support the government's highly discriminatory policy of excluding Korean schools from the high school tuition fees exemption programme?

With regard to the first question, the daily activities of Korean schools are conducted peacefully and involve young, powerless children. It is a very modest effort, the impact of which on Japanese people and the community is minimal or nil.[26] Nevertheless, such peaceful school education has, for some reason, repeatedly inspire an urge to 'smash and destroy'. Such urge is sometimes sufficiently strong to fuel the effort involved in organizing large-scale racist rallies. And a similar urge – whether bias or

[26] Its amicable impact should be noted. Korean schools in Japan open every school event to their neighbouring communities so that local residents gain insight into, understanding of, and sympathy for their efforts. It is consequently obvious that the accusation that they are 'spy schools' is unfounded.

something more – among Japanese government officials, commonly shared by the Japanese public at the time, may have been the main driving force for the violent forced closure of Korean schools during the Hanshin educational struggle in the 1940s. After decades, we can suspect that the same urge informs the discriminatory economic policy that has seen Korean schools excluded from the high school tuition fees exemption programme since 2010. This assumption would provide a possible explanation of why the government regards it as such an important political issue, given that the size of the budget at issue is so small.

Building on these observations, we might develop a hypothesis. Is there a common obsession behind all of this that tries to force resident Koreans to assimilate into the Japanese society? Is there a common angst about the development of diverse society in Japan? Among the Japanese majority – even within any minority communities – there are people who have urged assimilation for various reasons.[27] There are also those who believe that the coexistence of different values will destabilize Japanese society. For these people, would it not be natural to see Korean schools as a threat to the realization of Japan as a racially homogeneous nation?

Legislation regulating hate speech can never effectively soothe that type of anxiety, however groundless it may be. Even if such regulation against hate speech becomes strict, some other legitimate and 'lawful' oppression of Korean schools will certainly continue, reflecting persistent

[27] Japanese society is characterized by a patriotism that can be discriminatory. One of the discourses is that Japan should be a 'beautiful country', based on a 'single-ethnic' state view.

Suppose that an individual internalizes this goal and, with it, develops a sense of discrimination against their own self. Suppose that the individual has desperately kept their minority identity secret in an effort to 'assimilate' into Japanese people and society. One day, that individual may visit a Korean school. At that school, they may see children confidently speaking their own language and practising their own culture cheerfully and enthusiastically. That individual may be unsettled – distressed, even. This is because the scene clearly reflects symbolically another future for Japan. It shows that some kind of 'foreign culture' can be inherited intact and passed on from generation to generation, which would appear in this individual's eyes to be persistent defiance and antagonism against Japan. Remember, the individual has mistakenly understood that the concept of 'Japanese society' is a rigid one and hoped that assimilation into it will bring inner peace. But this school offers an alternative: it disrupts the illusion – the fundamental (mis) conception of a homogeneous, rigidly defined 'Japanese society' as an ultimate goal. The Korean school may appear in the eyes of individual as threat to and denial everything with which he has struggled over the years. If this is the case, then it is no wonder that nothing more than peaceful school activities can cause intense anxiety and emotional reactions within such an individual.

negative sentiment against multiculturalism among Japanese public. Eventually, Zaitokukai will achieve its racist goals.

Indeed, the idea of 'assimilation' may offer insight into the second question. Several politicians, including Prime Minister Abe, have justified the need to institute new hate speech regulations with comments like this: 'because these acts are shameful conduct in light of the nobility and politeness of traditional Japanese nationals'.[28]

These comments, which in many ways reflect general public sentiment, represent an aversion to difference. The first observation we can make is that this discourse falsely draws boundaries around what is and is not 'Japanese', setting the stage for divisions. Those who make such comments commonly pay little attention to their assumptions and the underpinning social psychology of 'assimilation', both of which take effect in the exclusion to those who are struggling with ethnic (and other marginalized) identities and with their sense of belonging or otherwise to this fictitious singular 'Japanese' community.

A second important observation is that these comments are obsessed with the social graces or otherwise of the perpetrators, independent of the actual lived experience of minority victims. It is as though these politicians are focused only on how 'Japanese' is viewed outside of Japan, so they desperately condemn the perpetrators, seeking to distinguish them from the rest of the 'humble and virtuous' Japanese people. Because these comments are not motivated by sympathy with the victimized minority, they express nothing of the essence of Zainichi Koreans' deep emotional pain in a historical context of colonial oppression. The driving principle is to restore the comfort of the Japanese majority, and the effect is to perpetuate the same division and exclusion that characterizes the hate speech itself. And it may well be the case that those who identify with this fictitious 'Japanese' persona, who is ruled by deep-rooted sentiment and

[28] Prime Minister Abe commented, 'Hate speech is, in my understanding, . . . racist, or sexist slander that incites hatred. We, the Japanese, have always believed that we should be polite, tolerant of people, and humble at all times . . . It is extremely regrettable that there are now words and actions to exclude some countries and peoples': Upper House of the Diet, Budget Committee, 7 May 2013.

Councillor Shoji Nishida (Upper House) responded, 'There is a common understanding that so-called hate speech is something that Japanese people should be ashamed of . . . I'd like to ask you to share the purpose of this, and I'd like you to make sure that people who engage in hate speech are aware that it's a shameful act, and that they take it upon themselves [to change their behaviours].'

Representative Sanae Takaichi (Lower House) went so far as to propose regulating ordinary demonstrations under the newly stipulated law against hate speech.

cannot free themselves from their own obsession with self-image, already condemn Korean schools as 'foreign elements' and thus as objects to be excluded.

If such conditions do exist, one effective approach would be to educate the Japanese majority, learning from the rich, trial-and-error experiences of Zainichi Koreans, who have long embraced community-building and building relationships with their surrounding Japanese neighbourhoods. There are as many and as diverse stories as the number of Korean schools scattered across and rooted in local neighbourhoods all over Japan, including the Higashi-Kujou neighbourhood of Kyoto, once home to the Korean First Elementary School.

A multicultural society should not be envisaged as a space in which 'Everybody is smiling happily'. The practice of multicultural symbiosis often implies a clash of different values. It means a way of life in which we embrace the reality that mutual understanding may not be achieved and accept that different, mutually exclusive, opinions may necessarily coexist. Multicultural symbiosis is not a project aiming to create a society in which each member feels comfortable; rather, it is a society in which each side agrees to coexist with a number of discomforting opinions. At the same time, though, it is a society that does not allow identities and individual dignity to be crushed, whether deliberately or neglectfully, by the majority. Individuals belonging to the ethnic majority will naturally encounter Zainichi Koreans in their daily lives. This may grant them opportunities to learn the history and way of life of this valuable minority culture. In these natural, casual interactions, any individual may gradually come to recognize that they too have some characteristics that differ from those of that fictitious 'Japanese' avatar. As the individual comes to understand themselves more fully and recognize the value that difference can add, feeling comfortable with that difference and gradually freeing themselves of the obsession with 'assimilation', it will become apparent that continuous interaction with a minority community has significantly enriched that individual's worldview and life.[29]

[29] The hypothetical individual (see note 27) may have imagined that, one day, their quest for assimilation would be at an end – that they would have fully sublimated his minority characteristics. And that individual might have imagined that this would bring about inner peace and eventually social stability, as every other Korean resident in Japan consummates their own like missions. These are illusions and the paranoia at their root – that multicultural symbiosis poses a threat to social stability – is what fuels hate crimes. Needless to say, this is not a minority issue, but a majority issue.

Encouraging more individuals to practise multicultural symbiosis will *never* be a 'threat to society'. The first step in our anti-hate efforts should be to convince individuals, one by one, of its value by reflecting back at them their own personal experiences. We can remind them of the thrill of authenticity – and we will achieve concrete change of the sort that can never be effected by ad hoc regulations on hate-motivated expressions and dependency on the whim of national government.

In our jurisprudence, we should seek to strengthen of the compensation doctrine in civil tort, rather than to amplify punitive sanction. In addition to the existing civil and criminal procedures in Japan, we might propose and institute various restorative judicial mechanisms. In either case, we should be reminding ourselves to focus on efforts to deepen understanding of the lives of minority victims and to generate empathy.[30] We must distinguish clearly between the points set out at the start of this chapter and make a conscious effort to steer away from condemnation (a focus on the perpetrators) towards understanding of the social value harmed (sympathy with the victims).

The Osaka High Court judgment contained some encouraging signs of movement in such a restorative direction. However, looking at the shape of the debate since then, it seems that the implications of this ruling have been neither fully recognized nor implemented. It is never too late to affirm the social significance of the Osaka High Court judgment. By focusing on restoration rather than condemnation, the High Court judgment warrants further analytical, scholarly attention and, in such analysis, careful comparison with the precedent criminal and civil Kyoto District Court judgments will be useful.

[30] It would also be effective to conduct various surveys on lived experiences of – actual damage done by –various aspects of discrimination in various regions. This would require proper allocation of public funds or support by private donation. It will be important not only to amplify those voices, but also to clearly and repeatedly highlight the benefit to Japanese society of learning from those minority experiences. For this purpose, such surveys must be conducted and designed carefully not with curiosity, but with sincere objectives. Such efforts are likely to contribute to creating a relationship of trust between the Japanese majority and Zainichi Korean and other minority groups, as well as ensure that anti-hate messages permeate every corner of Japanese society.

14

An Injunction Banning a Xenophobic Group from Demonstrating

Kawasaki Case

TORU MORI

I. Introduction

Groups voicing hate speech against Korean residents often hold demonstrations in the areas in which these people have gathered to live – and they do so specifically so that they can convey their hostility most effectively. The residents there are frightened when they hear insulting and offensive words during the demonstrations. Some have tried to stop the demonstrations by seeking a civil injunction against them.

An injunction is an effective remedy for residents genuinely at risk of attack. Because it means the prior restraint of speech, however, it should not be ordered generously. Before a demonstration begins, no one knows exactly how extreme it will be. An order forbidding the demonstration in advance might restrict the constitutional freedom of expression too broadly and hence each case should be decided carefully.

In the case on which this chapter focuses, a court issued an injunction prohibiting a demonstration planned by a xenophobic group in an area of Kawasaki City in which many Korean residents live. It has drawn considerable attention because the court condemned hate speech with clear reference to the Hate Speech Elimination Act (HSEA), which had just been enacted. Although it is the decision of a district court, the case is seen as an important precedent in the struggle against hate speech. We should therefore analyse it carefully to assess whether the court supported its order persuasively.

II. An Outline of the Case

In recent years, Kawasaki City has seen many demonstrations organized by a body calling for the exclusion of Korean residents. Since 2015, two demonstrations have been planned in district A, where many Korean residents reside. However, because counter-protesting residents and their supporters barred the demonstrators' passage, they did not advance up to the area in which the homes of Korean residents are concentrated. In those demonstrations, participants held placards saying, for example, 'Korean residents are bloody liars!' or 'Go back to the [Korean] Peninsula!' During the demonstration, harsh sentiment was loudly proclaimed through speakers and megaphones, such as 'We will kick all of you out on your ear!', 'We are demonstrating to expel maggots and ticks from Kawasaki!', and 'Cockroach Koreans, go back to your own country!'

The members of this group planned to hold a third demonstration on 5 June 2016 in district A and they invited others to participate. Seeking to foil the plan, a social welfare corporation with an office in the same district (X), which operates various facilities used by many Korean residents, sought an order for a provisional injunction prohibiting the demonstrators (Y and others) from holding, within a 500-metre radius of the office entrance, demonstrations that announced their intention to inflict harm on Korean residents or defamed them, or engaging in other similar activities.

III. The Gist of the Decision

Yokohama District Court, Kawasaki Branch, ordered as follows and admitted X's petition:

> Everyone will earn from society an evaluation of his or her personality, including character, deeds, reputation, and credibility, while building his or her personality by living in his or her house in peace as the basis of livelihood and engaging in activities freely; the rights to live in his or her house in peace, freely engage in activities, and maintain his or her honour and credibility are strongly protected as personal rights derived from Article 13 of the Constitution and are guaranteed equally for those who reside in the country lawfully.
>
> For the people coming from countries or regions outside Japan and their descendants who reside lawfully in Japan (hereinafter 'Persons of Foreign Origin'[1]), such as the Korean residents who relate to the present case, the right not to be discriminated against or excluded from local

[1] This phrase is used in the HSEA to define the persons who should be protected against the hate speech.

communities in Japan solely on the grounds of the countries or regions of origin outside Japan should form the foundation necessary for them to (i) live in peace in their houses as the basis of their livelihood in local communities in Japan, (ii) build their personality, (iii) freely engage in activities, and (iv) earn and maintain honour and credibility, and these rights must be strongly protected as a premise ensuring that they will have and enjoy those personal rights.

It must be said that such protection is crucially important, especially in the light of the fact that (i) the respective provisions of the International Convention on the Elimination of All Forms of Racial Discrimination ratified by our country and Article 14 of the Constitution prohibit discrimination on the basis of race or others, and (ii) Hate Speech Elimination Act was enacted and will come into force as needed due to the social situation in recent years. The court believes that feelings, emotions, and beliefs harboured by persons of foreign origin towards their ethnicity or the countries or regions of origin are the foundation of their character building and are most deeply rooted in individual dignity, and they must not be illegally infringed by any persons in Japan but respected mutually.

Accordingly, it can be appreciated that discriminatory speech and behaviour, which falls under Article 2 of the Hate Speech Elimination Act, of publicly announcing the intention to inflict harm on the life, bodies, freedom, honour, or properties of persons of foreign origin, injuring the honour of or seriously insulting those persons, and thereby instigating the exclusion of those persons from local society on the grounds of countries or regions of origin outside Japan, solely with the aim of promoting or inducing a discriminatory attitude against those persons, constitutes a tort as an illegal act of infringement of the above personal right to live in his or her house in peace.

Furthermore, when so significant is the extent of infringement of personal rights of those living in their houses in peace where the infringers, making discriminatory speech and behaviour, hold a demonstration, roam about, use campaign vehicles or speakers, or raise a loud voice in the neighbourhood, though those rightful persons live in their houses in peace and the infringers are in fact or easily aware of such fact, then it is reasonable to appreciate that those rightful persons have the right to seek an injunction against such discriminatory speech and behaviour as a right to demand elimination of the disturbance under the personal right to live in their houses in peace.

However, when an act of infringement of personal rights takes the form of a rally or collective demonstrative action by the infringers, it is necessary to make an adjustment to the freedom of assembly and expression under Article 21 of the Constitution; to prohibit in advance the act of infringement, it is reasonable to examine the degree of illegality in correlation between the kind/nature of the infringed rights and the mode/graveness of the infringing act.[2]

[2] Yokohama District Court, Kawasaki Branch, 2 June 2016, 2296 Hanji 14.

In the present case, in light of the significance of the personal rights (the infringed rights) and the mode of discriminatory speech and behaviour (the act of infringement), the act of infringement was held to be 'remarkably illegal'. It was said that it:

> . . . obviously exceeds the scope of the freedom of assembly and expression guaranteed under the Constitution and may also be appreciated under private law as abuse of rights. In addition to the foregoing, when taking into consideration the fact that it is extremely difficult to recover personal rights once infringed, it is reasonable to deem that prohibiting the act in advance is acceptable, and the right to demand prevention of disturbance under the personal rights should be affirmed.[3]

In the present case, while X was a juridical person, it also had personal rights, including the right to conduct business in peace free from hindrance and the right to protect its good name, and it was entitled to demand an injunction against acts of infringement.

IV. Examination

A. *The General Difficulty with a Civil Remedy for Hate Speech*

In recent years, Japan has often seen hate speech aimed at Korean residents and it has become a major social problem. When the control of hate speech is discussed in the context of constitutional law, what has been mainly considered is whether a penalty against it is acceptable under the Constitution. It is natural to assume a criminal penalty as a typical example of national control. In the context of comparative law, the discussion seems to have centred on the theme of what stance Japan should take in comparison with European countries that have laws that punish certain hate speech and approve their constitutionality, and the United States, which does not have such laws and where people have strong doubts about the constitutionality of such laws. Moreover, much attention has been given to discussion of Japan's reservation of Article 4(a) and (b) of the International Convention on the Elimination of All Forms of Racial Discrimination (ICERD), which require the signatory countries to make it a crime to incite racial discrimination. When Japan joined the Convention, it declared that it would fulfil these paragraphs only insofar as they are compatible with constitutional rights such as freedom of assembly, association, and expression.[4]

[3] *Ibid.*
[4] See Chapter 3.

However, I believe that one more reason why no civil settlement but a criminal penalty was assumed is that, generally speaking, in the case of hate speech slandering a specific group and asserting their exclusion from society, it is doubtful whether there are any persons whose individual rights are thereby infringed. Defamation and intimidation against specific persons are subject not only to a criminal penalty, but also to compensation for damage done to victims as a civil tort. However, it is unreasonable to think that any right is infringed should someone simply hear an insult of the ethnic group to which they belong. As long as there is no identifiable person whose rights are infringed, it is not possible to argue successfully in a civil suit the illegality of such an act of infringement.[5]

In a civil suit filed by Kyoto Korean Elementary School against Zaitokukai (one of the most active groups responsible for hate speech against Korean residents), in response to an incident in which members of Zaitokukai visited the school and held a demonstration, shouting (among many other things) 'Kick them out!', much attention was drawn to the fact that Kyoto District Court held that the attack could be characterized as 'racial discrimination' under the ICERD and that this was taken into consideration as a 'factor increasing intangible damages to be acknowledged'. However, the ruling also stated that 'it will be deviated from the due construction of the Civil Code' if 'a court construes, when racist speech is aimed at the people in whole belonging to a given group, that the act falls under a tort under Article 709 of the Civil Code just because an act of racial discrimination was committed, despite no concrete damage caused to any individual'.[6] In that case, it was obvious that the act perpetrated by Zaitokukai corresponded to defamation and obstruction of business targeting a specific school. The court therefore did not need to consider the difficult question of under what circumstances one may file a civil suit against hate speech aimed at no specific individual or body, or under what circumstances such an act does damage to a specific individual or body that should be remedied by law.

If the hate speech does not target a specific person or institution, however, it comes into question whether there is any person whose rights can be said to have been concretely infringed by the act. It is extremely

[5] See Chapter 8. See also Keizo Yamamoto, 'Sabetsu Hyōgen/Zōo Hyōgen no Kinshi to Minji Kyūsai no Kanōsei' ['Comment: prohibition of hate speech and civil remedies'] (2013) 24 *Kokusai Jinken* [Human rights international] 77, at 78–80.

[6] Kyoto District Court, 7 October 2013, 2208 Hanji 74. See Chapters 12 and 13.

difficult to assert in the courts that any Korean resident may claim damages against utterances such as 'Get out of Japan, Korean residents!'

B. The Substance of the Rights to Be Protected that the Decision Acknowledges

The present case seeking a provisional injunction against hate demonstrations was a more complex affair than that of *Kyoto Korean Elementary School* in terms of whether the rights of any specific individual were being infringed. According to the court's fact-finding, while hate speech against Korean residents in general was fully recognized in the past two demonstrations in the district, no attack had been delivered against any specific individual or body, including the social welfare corporation that sought the provisional injunction. Who, then, can demand an injunction against such demonstrations and what rights can they claim that are to be protected under law?

In such a case, it will be difficult for residents in the district to base a suit on the grounds of defamation because the honour of no individual was specifically injured. In a modern society that no longer has a caste system, the reputation of a group is not directly linked to the reputation of individual members of that group. Each person can establish themselves independently of the group to which they belong. A modern legal system should maintain this individualism in principle. Even if there is, in fact, a person who is strongly discomforted by words insulting a group to which they belong, such a feeling does not itself deserve legal protection. The purpose of an expression is to psychologically affect its recipients and what the freedom of expression implies is exactly this: anyone can freely engage in activities that have such effects on others. Since a negative emotional reaction is among such effects, it is not reasonable to control an expression just because it arouses a negative emotional reaction in others. Additionally, if a verbal attack on a group were easily seen to be an injury to its individual members, a person engaging in such an act would be held accountable for defamation in an unexpected manner and there may be a chilling effect on free speech about the activities of various legal or political groups, which are often the subject of controversy.[7]

[7] Toru Mori, 'Heito Supīchi no Hōteki Kisei ni tsuite' ['On the legal restraint of hate speech'] (2014) 176 *Hōgaku Ronsō* [Kyoto law review] 210, at 218–21. It is true that, in exceptional cases, an expression that diminishes the reputation of a group can be said to have injured the honour of any individual belonging to that group. The German Federal Constitutional Court admitted that Holocaust denial might be understood as an insult to individual Jews

The decision recognized that not the honour itself but the 'right to live in his or her house in peace' should be a right to be protected here as a personal right derived from article 13 of the Constitution. The right to live in peace not disturbed by noise or vibration issued by factories, cars, and planes has become sufficiently accepted in court precedent relating to torts. However, an act limiting that personal right would not immediately be held illegal. When leading a life in society, no individual can escape entirely from the unpleasant intrusion of their environment and the issue is whether that intrusion is within tolerable limits or not.[8] In particular, obtaining not only damages against past acts but also a prospective injunction will require proving the seriousness of the infringement and the difficulty in recovering the rights once injured.[9] Demonstrations, unlike a pollution incident that gives rise to constant noise or vibration, cause only temporary noise damage. It is questionable whether any instance exceeds the tolerable limit. It is even more so when taking into consideration the fact that the act of infringement was an action of expression.

The difficulty in this case comes from the fact that this personal right was employed to acknowledge that even hate speech specifying no specific person would infringe the specific rights of the Korean residents in the district. The primary question in the present case was not whether the noise was within tolerable limits but how to evaluate the harmful effect caused by the specific contents of the demonstration (hate speech). The decision attempted to consider this question within the framework of an established right: the right to live in one's house in peace. For that reason, the decision associated, somewhat artificially, the right to live in one's house in peace with the 'right to maintain his or her honour and credibility', and attributed it to article 13 of the Constitution by emphasizing the value of personality. It clarified that

living in Germany. See BVerfGE 90, 241 (1994). This decision is readily understood only as a consequence of the exceptionally tragic experience of the Jews, however.

[8] See, e.g., Supreme Court, 1st Petty Bench, 24 March 1994, 1501 Hanji 96 (in which the noise and dust caused by a factory injured the interests of its neighbours illegally only when the harm exceeded the tolerable limit).

[9] See Supreme Court, 2nd Petty Bench, 7 July 1995, 49 Minshū 2599 (a case of noise and dust pollution caused by a major road in which the court suggested that, to get injunctive relief, more severe illegality needs to be proven than that required to justify the award of damages); Supreme Court, Grand Bench, 11 June 1986, 40 Minshū 872 (when seeking a provisional injunction against publication of a magazine that includes an article seriously insulting an election candidate, the candidate must clearly prove the illegality of the insult and the likely difficulty of rebuilding their injured reputation).

the term 'peace' in this right implies not only physical quietness but also a state of mind. Furthermore, the decision states that, as a premise for this personal right, the 'right not to be discriminated against or excluded from local communities in Japan solely on the ground of the countries or regions of their origins outside Japan' will be protected for those who lawfully reside in Japan. However, the 'right not be excluded' is an abstract expression and the two rights seem to be associated quite unnaturally.

Moreover, a major characteristic of the decision is that it holds the feelings and beliefs harboured by persons of foreign origin towards their ethnicity or the countries (or regions) of their origin to be 'the foundation of their character building and (be) most deeply rooted in individual dignity'. This idea makes it possible to evaluate a statement injuring those feelings or beliefs as grossly prejudicial to a peaceful life. The judgment treats this as grounds for deciding that a hate demonstration's infringement of the right to live in one's house in peace is serious, such that it emphasizes the seriousness of the infringement of rights in the present case.

It is undeniable, however, that this finding is not free of questions. If, for members of a given group, the specific shared identity can be identified as the foundation of character-building among the individuals, then slander against the group or incitement to exclude it from society can be appreciated as acts prejudicial to each individual belonging to the group. However, according to the individualism at the heart of the modern legal system, each person should be able to freely decide what to centre within their identity and any public authority should be extremely cautious of labelling the characteristics of each member of a given group. It is this very factor that makes it difficult to restrict hate speech and any ruling of the court that gives little attention to this factor must be criticized for carelessness. I do not deny that the identity of Korean residents is firmly connected to their ethnicity; however, the court should not be satisfied with such a generalized observation, but must take into consideration expressly the special circumstances in which Korean residents have been placed in Japanese society.

Either way, the decision does not hold such feelings and beliefs harboured by persons of foreign origin towards their ethnicity or the countries/regions of their origin to be legal interests in and of themselves. The court might have thought that it should ground its decision on an established right. It recognized, after all, the personal right to live in one's house in peace as the right to be protected and it used those feelings as a reason to explain why a hate demonstration would grossly infringe this right. Unlike the noise or vibration of factories, cars, or planes, hate demonstrations do not continuously disturb a peaceful life. If the court wanted to claim, despite such fact, that infringement of personal rights in the present case was serious and even that an injunction against expressive activities was acceptable, it had to emphasize the qualitative significance of the damage. Not only was loud speech harmful to physical peace, but also its content grossly damaged the peace of mind of residents. Substantially, therefore, the decision relied on the injuriousness of the hate speech to its targets.

I continue next to examine how persuasive the court is in this.

C. *Employment of the Hate Speech Elimination Act*

The Act on the Promotion of Activities towards Elimination of Unjust Discriminatory Speech and Behaviour against Persons of Foreign Origin passed in 2016 – that is, the Hate Speech Elimination Act (HSEA) – declares in its preamble that 'unjust discriminatory speech and behaviour [that incites the exclusion of persons of foreign origin from local communities on the ground of their origin] is unacceptable', and it provides for basic measures towards the elimination thereof. However, it does not contain any provision that prohibits such speech or behaviour, because the Diet considered there to be a risk that prohibition of expressive activities would infringe the freedom of expression guaranteed constitutionally (art. 21(1) of the Constitution).

An official state ideology does not in and of itself restrict the freedom of expression. However, if the state declares that a given ideology is true or false, it will have significant effects on the citizens as government speech. This is even more so when it is provided for by law. Accordingly, in general terms, such acknowledgment requires prudence. If the government endorses an ideology affirming the discriminatory treatment of social minorities, social pressure targeting them would increase and it would have a considerable chilling effect on the minorities' own expressive activities. If an inevitable relationship were to be perceived between an official ideology of the government and concrete social pressure against minorities, it would be possible to detect infringement of the freedom of expression by the public authority.

However, this may be an unnecessary concern in the context of the HSEA. The word 'unacceptable' therein is aimed at intimidating or intensely insulting speech and behaviour against social minorities that constitutes the kind of expressive activities that are obviously illegal when aimed at specific individuals. A nation enacting a passive value judgement on such speech and behaviour conforms to the idea of the protection of human rights. It is also unthinkable that social pressure against persons engaging in such activities would be increased to such an extent that it can be treated as equivalent to a legal restriction.

Nevertheless, it is undeniable that this law's official value judgment on discriminatory speech and behaviour may affect judicial judgments in various instances involving hate speech. The *Kawasaki* decision cites this law exactly to point out the importance of protecting the 'right [of Korean residents] not to be excluded from local communities'. Furthermore, it defines the acts deserving of an injunction in complete reliance on the law's language of 'unjust discriminatory speech and behaviour', and it acknowledges 'discriminatory speech and behaviour that falls under Article 2 of Hate Speech Elimination Act' as a tort infringing personal rights. Although this law does not contain any direct prohibitive provisions, this civil decision employs it as a supplement to the substance of another established right and one basis on which it sanctions an injunction.[10]

As noted already, that part of the decision acknowledging that feelings and beliefs harboured by persons of foreign origin towards their ethnicity or the countries/regions of their origin form the foundation of character-building for individuals is insufficiently grounded. It might be conceived that the decision supplements this point with the fact of enactment of the HSEA. After acknowledging that 'in recent years in Japan', persons of foreign origin have been 'tremendously anguished' by unjust discriminatory speech and behaviour, the preamble to the HSEA urges efforts towards the elimination of such unjust discriminatory speech and behaviour. If the state authority clarifies, in the form of law, a judgment that, in present-day Japan, Korean residents in fact suffer serious damage from hate speech and it is an issue that cannot be left unattended as nothing more than the subjective reaction of individuals, no one would be surprised if it were to affect a court's assessment of social reality.

However, since the HSEA in and of itself does not contain any provision to restrict such expressions, one cannot think that an act that can be defined as unjust discriminatory speech and behaviour of any sort may

[10] Kensuke Ueda said that it corresponds to the intent of the legislature to use the HSEA as 'a guideline for the interpretation of other laws by the courts': Kensuke Ueda, 'Case Comment' (2016) 433 *Hōgaku Kyōsitsu* [Law classroom] 153.

always be prohibited.[11] It should be appreciated as only one factor to be considered in assessing the seriousness of the infringement of the rights directly concerned. In this regard, I believe that it is excessively generalized thinking to claim that, under the HSEA, a hate demonstration may be always held illegal as an act infringing the rights of individuals belonging to the targeted group to live in peace in their houses.

D. *The Meaning of the Fact that It Was Planned for an Area in which Homes of Korean Residents Are Concentrated*

In assessing the illegality of the hate demonstrations banned in the present case in relation to the rights to be protected, it would be no less important that they were scheduled to be held in an area in which the homes of Korean residents are concentrated. Y and others fully intended to incite the exclusion of Korean residents in that area and that their intimidating and insulting language should be directly heard by those residents. X, the social welfare corporation that requested the injunction, can be said to have acted on behalf of the Korean residents in the area. It may be for that reason that the decision emphasizes the personal rights of individuals and acknowledges the adjacent right of corporation X, the actual petitioner, 'to conduct business in its office in peace'.

The fact that Korean residents make up a relatively high proportion of its staff members and facility users is mentioned in context to illustrate that the demonstrations would considerably affect the business of X. The 'peculiarity' of district A where the 'houses of Korean residents are concentrated' is mentioned as the reason to believe that Y knew or should have suspected that the demonstration would infringe the personal rights of X to conduct its business in peace. However, in determining the illegality of the demonstration, the decision does not attach importance to the fact that the demonstration was planned for an area in which the homes of Korean residents are concentrated. Because X operates facilities for local residents, that fact can be raised as part of the evaluation of X's infringed rights.

According to the logic of the decision, even outside a district where the homes of Korean residents are concentrated, hate demonstrations against them would injure the personal rights of individual Korean residents. If so, individual Korean residents living outside such

[11] See Chapter 11.

a concentrated residential area could be said to be entitled to demand prohibition of a demonstration in their residential neighbourhood when the hate demonstration is planned in their district. The decision certainly opened such possibility when it found that discriminatory speech and behaviour will harm the foundation of the personalities of individuals belonging to a group at which the demonstrations were aimed. However, in real terms, such a judgment may have an effect that makes it extremely difficult to hold any demonstration when hate speech is expected during it. That does not seem to conform to the spirit of the HSEA, which aims for elimination not through direct legal prohibition but through various other efforts. If it were to have an effect that makes it extremely difficult to hold any outdoor demonstration or rally, it would give rise to serious problems in connection with the freedom of expression and assembly.

In practice, it is expected that provisional injunctions will mostly continue to be sought for those hate demonstrations that are planned for an area in which many Korean residents live. Since such hate demonstrations aim to arouse a real sense of fear in Korean residents in the area, acknowledgment that individuals suffer infringement of their concrete rights is easier to obtain. While the present case benefited from a corporation that could represent local residents, such a body does not necessarily always exist. Even in such cases, however, on the grounds of the characteristics of an area in which many Korean residents live, slander in a hate demonstration not aimed at any specific person can be acknowledged to be targeted directly at the local residents and it should be possible to prove that the personal rights of individual Korean residents in the area are concretely infringed. I believe that if such a claim were to be filed by multiple residents, it would be reasonable to expect them to be successful.

There would, however, be considerable difficulty in legally prohibiting demonstrations in ordinary business quarters that do not have similar distinctive characteristics. The decisive factor should be the seriousness of the infringement of rights that would be caused if a hate demonstration were to be held in the area. Depending on where the hate speech is uttered – that is, whether in a district where the homes of Korean residents are concentrated or in an ordinary business district – the harmful effect caused to Korean residents seems to be qualitatively different. In the former case, discriminatory speech and behaviour can be seen to demand the exclusion from society of local residents; in the latter, it is difficult to prove that hate speech targeting a group is directly aimed at individual local residents belonging to that group.[12] Even if, in present-day Japan, hate speech against Korean residents can be proven to be prejudicial to the core identity of the individual persons attacked en masse, the latter case is materially different from the former in terms of the degree of threat to a peaceful life.

E. *The Need to Protect Hate Speech as Expressive Activity*

To demand prohibition of hate demonstrations broadly, it would be necessary to assess the value of hate demonstration as expressive activities as very low. In that respect, too, the decision of the court in this case is informative. It held that engaging in an act of 'unjust discriminatory speech and behaviour' as defined in the HSEA by issuing loud sound from campaign vehicles is 'remarkably illegal' and 'obviously exceeds the scope of the guaranteed freedom of assembly and expression'. For such an act not deserving of protection, it would be possible to appreciate quite loosely the requirements for an injunction against it.

However, the HSEA does not directly prohibit unjust discriminatory speech and behaviour. Neither is there legal judgment demonstrating that, by becoming subject to the Act, speech and behaviour will lose its value as an expressive activity. Such a judgment would be hasty from the perspective of the guaranteed freedom of expression. Discriminatory speech denying the right to live in a community together to a given group or denying that the people within it are human and equal to the speaker is indeed contrary to the spirit of the Constitution – but, even then, the Constitution does not deny that expressive activities contrary to its spirit have some value. The Constitution of Japan recognizes the freedom to express any kind of ideology. If the state prohibits any specific ideology based on its contents, it will unsettle the core of the freedom of

[12] Referring to Larry Alexander, *Is There a Right of Freedom of Expression?* (Cambridge University Press, 2005), at 56–81, Yuji Nasu distinguishes the one-step harms caused by speech from the two-step harms. The former means those harms that are conveyed directly from the speaker to the audience; the latter are the harms that are inflicted on victims via others' reactions. Nasu said that the two-step harms are not recognized as reasonable cause to restrict hate speech, although the one-step harms could justify the restriction if they were vicious enough. See Yuji Nasu, 'Heito Supīchi Kiseihō no Iken Shinsa no Kōzō' ['Hate speech and the judicial review structure'] (2009) 59 *Kansai Daigaku Hōgaku Ronshū* [Kansai University law review] 391, at 400. In this context, I can add to this distinction that the seriousness of the one-step harms done by the hate speech varies according to the areas in which it is made.

expression and the free democracy it realizes. In abstract terms, even speech asserting that specific people are not actors entitled to enjoy human rights has to be protected under the freedom of expression as a political assertion. Prohibition is not possible unless an expressive activity gives rise to a concrete danger.

More specifically, if an injunction is demanded, there is a risk of chilling speech and behaviour that might earnestly be considered to be political assertion. Legal treatment of a group is often the subject of political controversy and, in connection with Korean residents, their status under the current domestic law may be naturally discussed. An assertion that Korean residents enjoy undue privilege, regardless of whether or not it is true, should be permitted as political assertion and its prohibition should be granted only exceptionally. Even when the organizers of a demonstration are making a sincere political demand, there is always the possibility that participants may exhibit excessive speech or behaviours to attract attention. If an organizer were held strictly responsible for such participants, it would be very difficult for them to hold the demonstration at all. The potential chilling effect on expressive activities deserving of protection therefore cannot be ignored.

That part of the decision concerned with unjust discriminatory speech and behaviour should be considered to relate only to the specific hate demonstrations in question. From the perspective of the freedom of expression, one should refrain from careless generalizations. After all, the decision has only limited meaning regarding the acceptability of hate demonstrations held in an ordinary business quarter and the balance of interests should be assessed on a case-by-case basis by taking into consideration the characteristics of the district.

Supplementary comment

In 2019, Kawasaki City enacted an ordinance that forbids hate demonstrations in public places. If persons do not follow the advice of the city not to hold such a demonstration and try to repeat it, the ordinance permits the mayor to order them not to do so. If they breach this order, they will be punished by a fine of not more than ¥500,000. Unlike the HSEA, this ordinance prohibits hate speech clearly and makes perpetuating it a crime.

Groups attacking Korean residents in Japan often plan to demonstrate in areas in which the homes of those residents are concentrated. Such zones in Kawasaki are especially targeted, as the court decision discussed in this chapter shows. Kawasaki City has therefore decided to take a further step to rescue its Korean residents from hate demonstrations. This ordinance is the only law in Japan to date that imposes a punishment on hate speech against certain groups. If someone is accused of committing this crime, the constitutionality of the ordinance will be surely fought over in the courts.

PART V

Multidisciplinary Debates

15

Free Speech Jurisprudence in Japan

The Influence of Comparative Constitutional Law*

KEIGO OBAYASHI

I. Introduction

How many decisions might we guess the Japanese Supreme Court has handed down declaring a statute to be unconstitutional regarding freedom of expression? Given that there have been ten cases declared unconstitutional by the Supreme Court,[1] is would be reasonable to assume that there would be at least two or three – but the truth is surprising: there have been no decisions at Supreme Court level finding a statute to be unconstitutional in terms of freedom of expression.[2] Despite the fact that it has struck down laws as unconstitutional violations of economic rights, which are generally regarded as inferior to other personal rights, the Supreme Court has never held any law or governmental action to violate the right to freedom of expression.

* For useful edits and specific suggestions, thanks to Craig Martin.

1 When it comes to cases that have held statute to be unconstitutional, there have been ten (1947–2019): Supreme Court, Grand Bench, 4 April 1973, 27 Keishū 265 (*Parricide*); Supreme Court, Grand Bench, 30 April 1975, 29 Minshū 572 (*Regulation of Geographical Location under Pharmaceutical Affairs Law*); Supreme Court, Grand Bench, 14 April 1976, 30 Minshū 223 (*Malapportionment (1)*), Supreme Court, Grand Bench, 17 July 1985, 39 Minshū 1100 (*Malapportionment (2)*); Supreme Court, Grand Bench, 22 April 1987, 41 Minshū 408 (*Limit of Spirit about Community Forest under the Forest Law*); Supreme Court, Grand Bench, 11 September 2002, 56 Minshū 1439 (*Exemption under the Postal Law*); Supreme Court, Grand Bench, 14 September 2005, 59 Minshū 2087 (*Right to Vote of Japanese Residing Abroad*); Supreme Court, Grand Bench, 4 June 2008, 62 Minshū 1367 (*Nationality of Illegitimate Child*); Supreme Court, Grand Bench, 4 September 2013, 67 Minshū 1320 (*Heritage of Illegitimate Child*); Supreme Court, Grand Bench, 16 December 2015, 69 Minshū 2427 (*Period of Prohibition of Remarriage*).

2 Although the Supreme Court has never struck down a free speech case, some lower-court decisions have been held to be unconstitutional. See, e.g., Tokyo District Court, 8 August 1954, 286 Saiji 6 (*Tokyo Metropolitan Ordinance*).

Why might this be? Is it because there are few laws or regulations that might impinge upon freedom of speech? This cannot be true because there are many cases regarding free speech. So if not that, is it because the Court underestimates the value of freedom of expression? The Court has sometimes stated that freedom of expression is important to democracy in Japan. For example, *Zeikankensa*,[3] the Court said that 'freedom of expression should be regarded as occupying an extremely important place among [the] fundamental human rights guaranteed by the Constitution'. It nevertheless appears that the Court has readily approved constraints on that freedom. Indeed, when a case alleges violation of that right to freedom of expression, the Court has typically applied a mere 'reasonableness' test to justify limitations of the right. As such, it is possible to argue that the Court has failed to exercise the proper rule of constitutional judicial review.

Japanese constitutional scholars have tried to change this situation through the study of comparative law.[4] First of all, cases and theories regarding freedom of expression from the United States were studied and introduced to Japan.[5] It was argued that the Japanese Supreme Court should take into account the same constitutional rule of review as had been developed by the US Supreme Court.[6]

Other scholars have examined the German approach. The former Meiji Constitution of 1889 was strongly influenced by the Prussian Constitution.[7] The comparative study of Germany constitutional law continued even after the promulgation of the current Constitution of Japan. A central feature of the German approach to constitutional review is the proportionality principle.[8] This method is different from the US-

[3] Supreme Court, Grand Bench, 12 December 1984, 38 Minshū 1308, at 1320.

[4] See Chapter 2, which deals with the judicial framework of freedom-of-expression cases and overviews academic criticism of the case law.

[5] See, e.g., Yasuhiro Okudaira, *Naze Hyōgen no Jiyū ka* [The basic theory of 'freedom of expression'] (University of Tokyo Press, 1988); Yasuhiro Okudaira, *Hyōgen no Jiyū o Motomete: Amerika ni okeru Kenrikakutoku no Kiseki* [Exploring 'freedom of expression': the path to acquiring the right] (Iwanami Shoten, 1999).

[6] See, e.g., Masami Ito, 'Hanzai no Sendō to Kenpō 21 Jō' ['Sedition and article 21'], in Sakae Wagatsuma and Toshiyoshi Miyazawa (eds.), *Zoku Hanrei Hyakusen* [A sequel to 100 cases] (Yuhikaku, 1960), 78–79. Professor Masami Ito suggested that the Japanese Supreme Court should consider adopting the 'clear and present danger' test that prevails in the United States.

[7] Miyoko Tsujimura, 'Joron' ['Introduction'], in *Gaisetsu Kenpō Konmentāru* [The constitutional commentary] (Shinzansha, 2018), 1.

[8] Kazuhiko Matsumoto, 'Doitsu no Hirei Gensoku no Fuhensei to Tokushusei' ['The universality and the peculiarity of the proportionality principle in Germany'] (2013) 75 *Hikakuhō Kenkyū* [Comparative law journal] 228.

style constitutional rules because it weighs the balance between governmental interest and individual right without using a test such as a rule. This approach has drawn a lot of attention within the new Japanese law school system that was established in 2004. Those teaching law have needed to adopt a more practical approach to constitutional cases and some think that the US approach is useless in practice in more cases than might be expected. They argue that the German approach is both more logical and more suited to practical application.

Despite introduction of these approaches to Japan by legal scholars, the judgments of the Japanese Supreme Court have tended to go in a different direction. It seems that the Court takes an approach that both balances interests *and* applies a kind of rule. While the Court seems to use a US-style categorical approach, the Court has not actually developed or adopted categories of exclusion based on the substance of expression, but rather has created a dichotomy between expression and conduct.

This chapter deals with how these legal doctrines or methods developed outside of Japan have affected the constitutional judicial review within Japan of cases involving freedom of expression and the debates in Japan relating to hate speech. Section II explores the approach of the Japanese Supreme Court in the early years of the 1947 Constitution. The problems with its original approach are what fuelled a search for other approaches and led Japan towards comparative law research. Section III examines that comparative research on freedom of expression, with a focus on the debate over adoption of the US constitutional tests or the German principle of proportionality. In general, the US approach in constitutional review involves establishing a rule or a test limiting the likelihood of arbitrary judgments, while the German approach grants the judge discretion to review the constitutionality of any given law.[9] There is clear difference in effect between the impact of the categorical approach of the United States and the balancing approach of Germany on freedom of speech. And while it has been said that the Supreme Court of Japan has begun to adopt a categorical approach, detailed examination of the case law suggests that this is not true. In section IV, based on consideration of

9 Larry Alexander, 'Constitutional Rules, Constitutional Standards, and Constitutional Settlement: *Marbury* v. *Madison* and the Case for Judicial Supremacy' (2003) 20 *Const. Comment.* 369, at 374. Professor Alexander distinguishes between constitutional rules and constitutional standards, saying that 'the latter [standards] are essentially delegations to future decisionmakers to determine what really is just, fair, and reasonable. The former [rules] are preemptive of future decisionmakers' own normative judgments.'

the relationship between these constitutional theories and the constitutional jurisprudence of the Japanese Supreme Court, I will clarify the true nature of the doctrine employed in the constitutional cases. Finally, I will explore the issue of hate speech from the perspective of this controversy over the doctrine employed in free speech cases.

II. From Public Interest to Constitutional Test

A. *Prevailing Public Interest*

The current Constitution[10] gives the Supreme Court the power of judicial review. Article 81 provides that 'the supreme court is the court of last resort with power to determine the constitutionality of any law, order, regulation or official act'.[11] Under this provision, the Court has the duty to protect the individual rights, including freedom of expression, and – for the first time – it is granted the power of constitutional judicial review. The Meiji Constitution had not provided the judiciary with that power and hence the Court had no test of constitutionality to apply at the outset.

Immediately after the current Constitution became effective, the Supreme Court focused on those constitutional provisions that refer to the 'public interest' as the basis for justifying limits on rights, including individual rights that do not include that language.[12] In early constitutional rights cases, the Court would simply examine whether the law sought to further the public interest, referring to the relationship between the law and public interest, but not sufficiently taking into account the value and nature of the rights at issue. This came to be called the public interest approach.[13]

[10] The first Japanese Constitution was enacted 1889 and it was called *Dainihon Teikoku Kenpō*, or the Meiji Constitution. In 1946, the current Constitution, *Nihonkoku Kenpō*, was made as a revision of the Meiji Constitution. Although it was formally revision, the current Constitution dynamically changed the Meiji Constitution: it shifted the subject of sovereignty, protected constitutional rights substantively, and declared pacifism.

[11] Although the text seems to grant the power of judicial review only to the Supreme Court, it is thought that the lower courts also have that power.

[12] The articles referring to public interest are arts 12, 13, 22, and 29. Although the text of these articles speak of 'public welfare', that is equivalent to public interest. For example, art. 12 provides: 'The freedoms and rights guaranteed to the people by this Constitution shall be maintained by the constant endeavour of the people, who shall refrain from any abuse of these freedoms and rights and shall always be responsible for utilizing them for the public welfare.'

[13] Yoichi Higuchi, 'Kōkyō no Fukushiron no Genjō to Yukue' ['The current situation and the prospect of the theory of public interest'] (1972) 5 *Jurist* 37.

The public interest approach sees the Court reviewing the constitutionality of the law based on a syllogism:

(1) the public interest may limit individual rights;
(2) the law in question is based on furthering the public interest; and
(3) therefore this law is constitutional.[14]

It seems that this approach is one of the tests or standards of judicial review whereby the courts can examine whether a law is constitutional or not. However, the Supreme Court has not explained in any case why the public interest takes precedence over the rights of the individual. Although the Court is expected to explain the reason why the law's limitation of a right is justifiable, the Court really mentions nothing more than the construction of the law as 'reasonable' regulation. Constitutional scholars therefore concluded that the Court judged the constitutionality of law without using any constitutional test against which to measure the 'reasonableness' of the law.[15]

B. *The Advent of a Constitutional Test*

The public interest approach was widely criticized.[16] The most challenging critique was that it was too abstract. Professor Nobuyoshi Ashibe, one of its major critics, charged the public interest approach with being too formalistic and conceptual.[17] He argued that the public interest approach provided no satisfactory explanation that how the courts examines the constitutionality of the laws. He thought that it was necessary for a court to propose the method on which that court relied in judging the constitutionality of legislation.

Furthermore, another problem was apparent in terms of how the Supreme Court appeared to understand the concept of public interest itself. The Court was criticized because it had used the existence of a public interest as a conclusive factor.[18] Although public interest itself is a ground for restricting individual rights, it ought not always to precede

[14] Nobuyoshi Ashibe, *Kenpōgaku II* [Constitutional jurisprudence II] (Yuhikaku, 1994), 202.

[15] Hidenori Tomatsu, *Kenpō Soshō* [Constitutional litigation], 2nd ed. (Yuhikaku, 2008), 274–82.

[16] Hidenori Tomatsu, 'Kenpōhandan no Hōhō (5): Kōkyō no Fukushiron' ['The method of constitutional judgement: public interest theory'] (1996) 186 *Hōgaku Kyōshitsu* [Law classroom] 16, at 17.

[17] See Ashibe, note 14, at 200.

[18] Kenji Takahara, 'Shihōkatei ni okeru "Kōkyō no Fukushi" ' [Public interest in the "judicial process" '] (1962) 5 *Hōgaku Kyōshitsu* [Law classroom] 126, at 127.

those rights; whether the public interest prevails should be weighed on a case-by-case basis. Yet public interest has been used as a trump card.

These criticisms led to shifts in the conception of public interest. According to Ashibe, the Supreme Court began to compare each interest in line with the theory that regards the 'public welfare' (public interest) in some provisions of constitutional law as colliding with individual rights.[19] In short, the Court began to take a balancing approach.

However, if this is based on nothing more than an ad hoc exercise, it will be unpredictable and wholly at judges' discretion.[20] An ad hoc balancing exercise cannot inform decisions in future cases because each case is merely decided on its particular facts. Without more developed rules or tests, then, there is no restraint on a judge's discretion.

Considering these problems, Ashibe proposed a constitutional test.[21] He introduced a so-called double standard theory, based on the constitutional theories and constitutional jurisprudence of the United States.[22] The double standard theory distinguishes between spiritual freedoms[23] (which concern civil, political, and personal rights), and economic freedoms. On the one hand, based on this distinction, this theory requires that US-style strict scrutiny should be applied to spiritual freedoms, because it is necessary to maintain proper political process in a constitutional democracy. On the other hand, less rigorous review, such as US-style rational basis review, might be applied to economic freedoms because it is more appropriate for the court to defer to the judgment of the political branches on issues of socio-economic policy that are the product of the political process.

This two-tiered approach owes much to the famous 'footnote 4' in *United States* v. *Carolene Products Co.*[24] The Supreme Court of the United States held that the law regarding the economic sphere was presumptively constitutional because it was within legislative discretion. Footnote 4, which Justice Stone went on to write, instructed the Court that it should apply strict scrutiny. According to him, when the law

[19] See Ashibe, note 14, at 200.

[20] Kazuyuki Takahashi, 'Shinsa Kijunron no Rironteki Kiso (Jō)' ['Theoretical Foundation of Constitutional Test I'] (2008) 1363 *Jurist* 64, at 67–68.

[21] Nobuyoshi Ashibe, *Kenpō* [Constitutional law], 7th ed. (Iwanami Shoten, 2019), 103–07.

[22] See *ibid.* at 104.

[23] Naoki Kanaboshi, 'Competent Persons' Constitutional Right to Refuse Medical Treatment in the US and Japan: Application to Japanese Law' (2006) 25 *Penn St. Int'l L. Rev.* 5, at 59–65. In Japanese constitutional theory, freedom of conscience, religious freedom, freedom of expression, and academic freedom are collectively called *seishinteki jiyūken* ('spiritual freedoms' or 'spiritual rights').

[24] *United States* v. *Carolene Products Co.*, 304 U.S. 144 (1938).

reflected prejudice against discrete and insular minorities and seriously curtailed the operation of political processes, strict scrutiny should be applied. Many Japanese constitutional scholars,[25] including Ashibe, regarded this doctrine as a two-tiered approach because it distinguishes levels of scrutiny that the court should apply in its review of legislation, based on the category of rights that are implicated by the law. The double standard consequently developed into doctrine in Japan based in large part on footnote 4 of the US case *Carolene Products.*[26]

The double standard became the general basis for constitutional doctrine in Japan. Following this underlying principle, individualized constitutional tests were introduced in relation to each right, again influenced by US jurisprudence. Yet, notwithstanding these developments, the standard developed to apply to freedom of expression cases was remarkable in that it did not incorporate the US doctrine, nor did the Court apply a stricter level of scrutiny even though freedom of expression is considered a fundamental individual right and one that is essential to the operation of liberal democracy.[27]

III. Constitutional Test vs Proportionality Principle

A. *The Constitutional Test in Freedom of Expression*

Many constitutional rules or tests concerning freedom of expression in the United States have been introduced to Japan. The most referred to is strict scrutiny.[28] Although the Supreme Court of the United States has set forth several different specific formulations of the strict scrutiny test in the context of freedom of speech, the basic framework is a determination of whether the law is narrowly tailored to serve a compelling state interest. Many other tests have also been developed for freedom of speech cases, including actual malice, the *O'Brien* test, and the *Central Hudson* test.[29] Particularly, it is said that the compelling state interest and the

[25] Shigenori Matsui, *Nijū no Kijunron* [Double standard theory] (Yuhikaku, 1994).

[26] See Ashibe, note 14, at 214–15. Ashibe explicitly mentioned that the double standard originated in *United States* v. *Carolene Products Co.*

[27] Masato Ichikawa, 'Hyōgen no Jiyū to "Kōkyō no Fukushiron" ' ['Freedom of speech and public interest theory'] (1997) 202 *Hōgaku Kyōshitsu* [Law classroom] 70. Professor Ichikawa points out that the Japanese Supreme Court pays little attention to that point despite the fact that freedom of expression was regarded as core to democratic process.

[28] See Ashibe, note 21, at 204.

[29] Actual malice means that, in defamation, the plaintiff must prove that the defendant had knowledge that their statement was false or spoke with reckless disregard of whether or not it was false.

'clear and present danger' definitional approach should be adapted in Japan.[30]

Apart from these individual tests, one of the general principles in freedom of expression is a 'content dichotomy' between content-based regulation and content-neutral regulation, again deriving from the United States.[31] According to this dichotomy, strict scrutiny should be applied to content-based regulation because it restricts the substance of the expression (i.e. the message), while intermediate scrutiny should be applied to content-neutral regulation because it restricts only the means, such as the time, the place, and the method of delivery, without regard to the substance of the message.

At the same time, the level of scrutiny required will depend on the content of speech. On the one hand, political expression is valuable because it concerns the democratic process. As a result, political expression triggers strict scrutiny. On the other hand, some expression such as sedition, obscenity, and defamation is excluded from or receives a lower level of constitutional protection. In that case, the level of scrutiny is weakened drastically. This is what is known as a value-based approach.

The *O'Brien* test was introduced in *United States* v. *O'Brien*, 391 U.S. 367, 377 (1968): '[I]f it is within the constitutional power of the Government; if it furthers an important or substantial governmental interest; if the governmental interest is unrelated to the suppression of free expression; and if the incidental restriction on alleged First Amendment freedoms is no greater than is essential to the furtherance of that interest.'

The *Central Hudson* test was introduced in *Central Hudson Gas & Electric Corp.* v. *Public Service Commission*, 447 U.S. 557, 566 (1980):

> At the outset, we must determine whether the expression is protected by the First Amendment. For commercial speech to come within that provision, it at least must concern lawful activity and not be misleading. Next, we ask whether the asserted governmental interest is substantial. If both inquiries yield positive answers, we must determine whether the regulation directly advances the governmental interest asserted, and whether it is not more extensive than is necessary to serve that interest.

See also Ashibe, note 21, at 200 (actual malice), 201–02 (*Central Hudson* test), and 205–07 (*O'Brien* test).

[30] Koji Sato, *Nihonkoku Kenpōron* [Japanese constitutional law theory] (Seibundo, 2011), 262. 'Compelling interest' means that the regulation has to have inevitable governmental interest. 'Clear and present danger' means that the regulation is needed to avert obvious and imminent danger. 'Definitional approach' means that it is necessary to define the range of expression excluded from constitutional protection.

[31] See Ashibe, note 21, at 203–07.

These tests are parts of a categorical approach, in that they require the court to decide, depending on the type of the regulation limiting speech and based on the nature of the expression, which category of speech the particular expression falls into.[32] In short, one form of constitutional standard is based on this kind of categorical approach whereby different levels of scrutiny, or tests, are applied depending on the category of the regulation and the particular speech implied in the case.

The categorical approach functions to limit judicial discretion. Within a categorical framework, judges have to make decisions in accordance with a predetermined rules. Judges must:

(1) decide which categories the regulation and speech in question fall into;
(2) choose the constitutional tests that apply to these categories; and then
(3) apply the test to the case.

Although some US Supreme Court justices, such as Stephen Breyer, favour the balancing approach rather than the categorical approach,[33] most cases have taken the categorical approach.

B. *The Proportionality Principle*

Another approach has been introduced to Japan as a result of studies in comparative law. Because the Meiji Constitution was strongly influenced by German constitutional law, Japanese constitutional scholars have traditionally looked to Germany; since the promulgation of the current Constitution, they have continued to study German approaches.

According to the German approach to constitutional judicial review, the court judges the constitutionality of the laws based on a three-step process.[34]

(1) The court decides whether the conduct of the claimant is protected as a constitutional right.
(2) The court judges whether the law, policy, or governmental action or inaction violates the constitutional right.

[32] Rodney A. Smolla, 'Categories, Tiers of Review, and the Roiling Sea of Free Speech Doctrine and Principle: A Methodological Critique of *United States* v. *Alvarez*' (2013) 76 *Ala. L. Rev.* 499, 509–19.

[33] Jerome A. Barron, 'Electronic Media and the Flight from First Amendment Doctrine: Justice Breyer's New Balancing Approach' (1998) 1 *U. Mich. J. L. Reform* 817.

[34] Go Koyama, 'Daisanshō Sōsetsu' ['Chapter 3 overview'] [2011] *Shinkihonhō Konmentāru* [New basic law commentary] 69, 75–77.

(3) If the court finds that claimant's conduct is protected by a right and that the governmental action does limit or infringe the right, then the court examines whether the violation can, in any event, be justified.

It might therefore be said that the three-step standard is a logical stepwise framework for examining constitutionality.[35]

In the third step of the standard, the court reviews the law or governmental action based on the proportionality principle.[36] Under this principle, after first determining its purpose and importance, the court investigates three factors, aiming to establish the importance or legitimacy of the constrained rights. If the purpose of the law or governmental action is upheld, the three factors at which the court will look are:

(1) the congruency, or rational connection, between the purpose of the law and the means with which it aims to achieve that purposes;
(2) the necessity of those means; and
(3) the proportionality of the harm done by the rights violation in comparison with the benefit should the law achieve its purpose.

The congruency element requires that the means set out in the law actually facilitates achieving its purpose. The second element requires that even if the means are congruent with the purpose, they must also be the least restrictive means possible (known as the least restrictive alternative), carefully tailored to suit the purpose and to violate constitutional rights only if unavoidable. Finally, the relationship between the harm caused by the violation and the benefit should the purpose of the law be achieved must be proportional.

The proportionality principle is equivalent to an end–means review because it checks whether the purpose and the means are both reasonable and necessary. An end–means review is similar to a constitutional test. But, compared to the constitutional test in the US categorical approach, the proportionality principle provides the judge with more discretion, particularly in the balancing exercise that comprises the third factor.

The difference between the constitutional tests approach and the proportionality principle becomes apparent in the context of freedom of expression. Strict scrutiny should be applied when it comes to content-

[35] Kazuhiko Matsumoto, 'Sandankai Shinsaron no Yukue' ['The prospect of a three-step test'] (2011) 83 *Hōritsu Jihō* [Legal times] 34, at 35.

[36] Go Koyama, *'Kenpōjō no Kenri' no Sahō* [The way of 'constitutional rights'], 3rd ed. (Shogakusha, 2016), 70–71.

based cases infringing on freedom of expression, because freedom of expression takes precedence over other rights such as economic right under the double standard. Furthermore, judicial discretion is controlled by the categorical approach. Generally speaking, however, the proportionality principle does not establish in advance a certain rule or test in a case of freedom of expression. The balancing element in the proportionality principle allows judges to consider the case flexibly on its facts. Thus the constitutional test limits the scope of judges' discretion when taking a categorical approach, while granting them broad discretion under the proportionality principle.

C. *Controversy*

In terms of the approach of the Japanese Supreme Court to constitutional judicial review, the constitutional test had been employed more commonly that the proportionality principle until, in 2004, the law school system was established in Japan as a result of legal reforms.[37] With system established, the bar examination system was also changed. The new bar exam questions on constitutional law now require students to refer to constitutional case law more than they did before and to apply the framework developed in practical constitutional judgments.

This was a turning point, because it was increasingly argued that the proportionality principle was more suitable as an analytical framework for responding to questions in the new examination corresponding to practical constitutional judgment. There are several reasons why we might favour the proportionality principle.[38] First, there is commonly a gap between the constitutional test and the facts of the case in practice. Although comments a have been made in few cases that seem to refer to the double standard theory,[39] the Supreme Court has never struck down any law or governmental action as a violation of freedom of expression.

[37] Keigo Komamura, *Kenpō Soshō no Gendaiteki Tenkai* [The contemporary turn of constitutional law litigation] (Nihon Hyoronsha, 2013), 1–2.

[38] Kenji Shibata, 'Kenpōjo no Hirei Gensoku ni tsuite (1): Doitsu ni okeru sono Hōteki Konkyo Kisozuke o meguru Giron o Chūshin ni' ['The constitutional proportionality principle (1): focusing on the German theory of legal ground and foundation'] (2010) 116 *Hōgaku Shinpō* [Chuo law review] 183, at 184–90.

[39] At least, three cases have mentioned that strict scrutiny applies to spiritual freedoms or freedom of expression, unlike economic rights. See Supreme Court, Grand Bench, 22 November 1972, 26 Keishū 586 (*Public Market Place Act*); Supreme Court, Grand Bench, 30 April 1975, 29 Minshū 572 (*Regulation of Geographical Location under*

The German three-step standard including the proportionality principle therefore provides a more viable alternative formula for examining constitutionality.[40] Proponents of the proportionality principle in Japan argue that cases such as *Yakujihō Kyoriseigen* can be explained well from the three-step perspective because the judgment was itself structured as three steps.[41]

Second, the proportionality principle includes the use of a case-specific balancing approach rather than a rigid rule. Justice Katsumi Chiba, concurring in *Horikoshi*,[42] explicitly mentioned that the Court had used a balancing approach rather than a test. If so, then the proportionality principle should be familiar to judges, because it has already been used in Japanese case law. A categorical approach based on constitutional tests might provide simpler answers, because it applies a simple formula to the facts, but it lacks more nuanced consideration of the issues and it can be inflexible.

Some scholars have tried to respond to this criticism of the categorical approach and favouring of the proportionality principle. Professor Kazuyuki Takahashi, for example, has pointed out some flaws in the proportionality principle.[43] He has argued that the balancing test under the proportionality principle informs only vague decision-making, resulting in a sliding scale of ad hoc judgments. He condemned the principle as a 'bare balancing test'.[44] He concludes that the proportionality principle gives judges far too broad a discretion, and results in a loss of predictability and legal stability.[45]

Furthermore, Takahashi has insisted that the significant difference between the constitutional tests approach and the proportionality principle is that the former provides for different tests responding to each different category, while the latter responses by applying a balancing test

Pharmaceutical Affairs Law); Supreme Court, 3rd Petty Bench, 7 March 1995, 49 Minshū 687 (*Izumisano City Civic Center*).

[40] See Komamura, note 37, at 1–12. Komamura does not propose that the three-step test be adopted, but analyses the background to the test.

[41] See Koyama, note 36, at 18–21.

[42] Supreme Court, 2nd Petty Bench, 7 December 2012, 66 Keishū 1337 (Chiba J., concurring).

[43] Kazuyuki Takahashi, 'Tsūjōshinsa' no Imi to Kōzō' ['The meaning and the construction of regular review'] (2011) 83 *Hōritsu Jihō* [Legal times] 12.

[44] Kazuyuki Takahashi, 'Ikenshinsa Hōhō ni Kansuru Gakusestu Hanrei no Dōkō' ['The development of theory and the case regarding the method of judicial review'] (2009) 61 *Hōsō Jihō* [Lawyer times] 3609.

[45] See Takahashi, note 43, at 19.

in all cases.[46] This causes different results in the area of freedom of expression.

A constitutional test generally requires strict scrutiny of spiritual freedoms such as that in content-based cases involving freedom of expression.[47] On the one hand, strict scrutiny is required because freedom of expression is an important right informing individual self-fulfilment and it is also crucial to the democratic process. On the other, the proportionality principle supports a regularized balancing test even in cases involving freedom of expression.

Even if the proportionality principle is flawed, the fact that the Court does not use strict scrutiny in relation to freedom of expression seems to suggest that the proportionality principle might be better suited to constitutional case law.

IV. The Real Approach of the Supreme Court

A. *Not Categorical Speech Exclusions, but Dichotomy of Expression and Conduct*

It has been said that the Japanese Supreme Court should take a categorical approach to the review of freedom of expression cases, based on the value of certain kinds of expression, similar to the approach taken in the United States.[48] Low-value expression, such as sedition, obscenity, and defamation, are not protected or are less protected as freedom of speech, while high-value forms of expression such as political speech are strongly protected.

However, the Supreme Court of Japan has never held a law that limits political speech to be unconstitutional nor has it ever held that low-value speech is entirely excluded from constitutional protection. As an example of cases involving political speech, *Sarufutsu*[49] upheld the constitutionality of article 102(1) of the National Public Service Act, which bars public servants from engaging in certain forms of political activity.[50] In this case, the defendant, who was a public servant at the post office, was prosecuted for

[46] See *ibid.*, at 18.

[47] Masami Ito, 'Kenpō Kaishaku to Rieki Kōryōron' ['Constitutional interpretation and balancing approach'] (1977) 638 *Jurist* 198, at 204.

[48] See Ashibe, note 21, at 204.

[49] Supreme Court, Grand Bench, 6 November 1974, 28 Keishū 393.

[50] Article 102(1) provides: 'Officials shall not solicit, or receive, or be in any manner concerned in soliciting or receiving any subscription or other benefit for any political party or political purpose, or engage in any political acts as provided for by rules of the National Personnel Authority other than to exercise his/her right to vote.'

engaging in political campaigning for an upcoming election. Following a labour union resolution, he had put up posters supporting an election candidate on the public bulletin board when off-duty. The District Court[51] held that the provision was unconstitutional, at least as applied to the particular facts of this case, because while the objective of ensuring political neutrality among public officials was important, the provision failed the LRA test.[52] The High Court[53] affirmed the decision, but the Supreme Court reversed it. The Supreme Court held that the provision was constitutional because it was reasonable regulation. Some scholars regarded the judgment as using the rational basis test/the reasonable relevance test, while others thought it had simply adopted a balancing approach.[54] The Court held that:

(1) the purpose of the challenged law was legitimate;
(2) there was a rational connection between the purpose of the challenged law and the means adopted in the law to achieve that objective; and
(3) the public interest protected in the law and the loss or harm caused by the law's limitation of the right infringed was proportionately balanced.[55]

The Court held that the provision passed its test.

The dissenting opinion held that the criminal regulation of political activity should be subject to stricter scrutiny such as requiring proof that the law served a compelling state interest and that the means adopted was the least restrictive.[56] In any event, the point is that the majority opinion applied a low-level constitutional test even in a case involving the limitation of political expression.[57]

[51] Asahikawa District Court, 25 March 25, 1968, 28 Keishū 676.

[52] Itsuo Sonobe, 'Iwayuru Sarufutsu Daiisshinhanketsu' ['The *Sarufutsu* case in the District Court'] (1968) 224 *Hanta* 77, at 80. Professor Itsuo Sonobe pointed out that this case applied the test that was used in the United States.

[53] Sapporo High Court, 24 June 1969, 28 Keishū 688.

[54] There has been discussion of whether this method instructed the constitutional test or not. For example, Ashibe regarded this test as the reasonable relevance test, while Takahashi thought it to be ad hoc balancing. See Ashibe, note 21, at 219–20, 292–93; Takahashi, note 20, at 70–71.

[55] *Sarufutsu*, 28 Keishū at 399–400 (note 49).

[56] *Ibid.* at 410–24 (Kenichiro Osumi, Kosato Sekine, Nobuo Ogawa, and Yoshikatsu Sakamoto JJ., dissenting).

[57] George Shishido, ' "Sarufutsu Kijun" no Saikentō' ['Reconsideration of the "*Sarufutsu* test" '] (2011) 83 *Hōritsu Jihō* [Legal times] 20, at 21. Although it seemed to adopt a constitutional test like that of the United States, the academy criticized *Sarufutsu* at the outset as cherry-picking from the constitutional litigation theory of the United States.

While the Court has not adopted a categorical approach based on the differentiated value of speech, it has made distinctions between expression and conduct. In *Shibuya Riot*, the Court agreed that seditious activity that was prohibited under the Subversive Activities Prevention Act[58] was expressive action. The defendants, who had disagreed with the Okinawa Reversion Agreement, had exercised their right to assembly, inciting the crowd to riot. The Court held that such expressive action was not worthy of constitutional protection, and hence it excluded sedition from constitutional protection based on the dichotomy between expression and conduct, not on a value-based categorical approach.

Even though the case concerned political expression, the Court regarded it as a matter of expressive *action* rather than the content of the expression itself. *Sarufutsu*, in which it was held that the law restricting the political activities of public servants applied to the defendant, who had put campaign posters on a public bulletin board, was constitutional, was also considered as a matter of expressive action rather than expression itself. In the application of the balancing element of the test, the Court estimated that the harm to freedom of speech was light, because the limitation merely involved the indirect and incidental restriction of expression rather than directly limited the expression of the complainant's thoughts. *Tachikawa Handbill Distribution*[59] also reflected this approach. This case similarly concerned political speech, and yet the Court easily upheld the constitutionality of the application of criminal prohibitions on trespassing[60] to prosecute someone for distributing handbills within a Self-Defence Force family residential complex. In the judgment, the Court characterized the case as the mere regulation of expressive acts. The Court said that, 'in this case, the point at issue is not the constitutionality of punishing the expression itself but the

[58] Article 40 stipulates: 'A person who, with the intent to promote, support or oppose any political doctrine or policy, has prepared, plotted or induced any of the following crimes, or Incited others to commit the crime with the intent to cause it to be committed, is punished by imprisonment with or without work for a term not exceeding three years.' Article 4(2) provides: 'In this Act, the term "Incite" means, with the intent to cause a particular act to be committed, allowing a person, by means of any document, picture, speech or action, to decide to commit the act, or to be provided with a stimulus of sufficient power to promote a decision already in the process of being made.'

[59] Supreme Court, 2nd Petty Bench, 11 April 2008, 62 Keishū 1217.

[60] Article 130 of the Penal Code stipulates: '[A] person who, without justifiable grounds, breaks into a residence of another person or into the premises, building or vessel guarded by another person, or who refuses to leave such a place upon demand shall be punished by imprisonment with work for not more than three years or a fine of not more than 100,000 yen.'

constitutionality of punishing the act of entering the "premises guarded by another person" without permission of the manager in order to distribute the leaflets, a means of expression'.[61]

Regarding low-value speech, it might seem that the Court does take a categorical approach. In spite of the fact that the regulation of low-value expression such as sedition, obscenity, and defamation does constitute a content-based limitation of expression, the Court has readily approved the constitutionality of such regulation. However, the Court did not mention that any low-value expression was excluded from constitutional protection. That it always upholds the constitutionality of such regulation does not mean that the Court has held that such forms of speech are outside of the scope of the right; it means only that the Court applies a very low-level constitutional test.

Looking at the case law about obscenity, the Court has separated obscenity from other forms of sexual expression by means of definition.[62] When an expression has been judged to be obscene under that definition, any restriction on expression has been upheld because the expression was deemed to be harmful to public interest. But the Court did not state that obscenity was excluded from constitutional protection. Similarly, in defamation cases, when the expression harms reputation of someone else, the Court reviews whether the expression is true or not. When the defendant shows that they had probable cause to believe the expression to be truthful, the defendant will not be charged;[63] otherwise, the defendant incurs liability. However, just because the defendant is liable for defamation does not mean that the untruthful expression is excluded from constitutional protection.

Sedition cases, however, took another approach. From the beginning of the current constitutional era, the Supreme Court has held that sedition is outside of the scope of freedom of expression, while the valid criticism of governmental policy is within the scope of the right.[64] Some 40 years later, the Court held that the punishment of sedition was constitutional because the law regulated expressive activity, not

[61] *Tachikawa Handbill Distribution*, 62 Keishū at 1225 (note 59).

[62] Supreme Court, Grand Bench, 13 March 1957, 11 Keishū 997 (*Lady Chatterley's Lover*). According to the definition, when material is appealing to the prurient interest, harming the sense of shame and contradicting sexual morality, it will be obscenity.

[63] Supreme Court, Grand Bench, 25 June 1969, 23 Keishū 975 (*Yūkan Wakayama Jiji*).

[64] Supreme Court, Grand Bench, 18 May 1949, 3 Keishū 839 (*Emergency Food Supply Order*).

expression itself.[65] In other words, it held the regulation to be constitutional simply because it regulates expressive activity, not because sedition is excluded from constitutional protection.

In sum, therefore, the Court has not adopted a categorical approach in freedom of expression cases – but we cannot say that the Court completely disregards the categorical approach, because some cases have mentioned the importance of political speech and referred to the necessity of stricter scrutiny.

B. *Emphasizing the Importance of Freedom of Expression*

Hoppō Journal,[66] which involved claims of defamation, held that 'the freedom of expression, especially the freedom of expression relating to public matters, must be respected as a particularly important constitutional right in a democratic nation'. In light of this, the Court imposed a strict rule of proof that had to be satisfied by plaintiffs who sought to obtain a court-ordered prior restraint of publication to protect their honour.[67]

Sarufutsu also mentioned that freedom of expression formed the foundation of democratic society and was especially important for the protection of other constitutional rights.[68] Following this case, *Horikoshi* stated that:

> [C]onsidering that this freedom of mind is a fundamental human right that is indispensable in the political process based on constitutional democracy and it is a material right that underpins democratic society, the scope of legal prohibition of public officials' engagement in political acts for the above-mentioned purpose should be limited to the level of a necessary and inevitable restriction on freedom of political activities that they should be guaranteed to enjoy as Japanese citizens.[69]

In this judgment, the right to freedom of speech for purposes of engaging in political expression was recognized as an especially important constitutional right. As a consequence, the scope of regulation should impose only necessary and inevitable restriction on freedom of

[65] Supreme Court, 2nd Petty Bench, 28 September 1990, 44 Keishū 463 (*Shibuya Riot*).

[66] Supreme Court, Grand Bench, 11 June 1986, 40 Minshū 872, at 877.

[67] *Ibid.*, at 879. It is approved only 'when it is obviously found by materials presented by the petitioner that the contents of the expression is not true, that the objective of the expression is not to promote solely the public interest, and, moreover, when fear exists that the petitioner may suffer serious and irreparable damage'.

[68] *Sarufutsu*, 28 Keishū at 398 (note 49).

[69] *Horikoshi*, 66 Keishū at 1342 (note 42).

political activities. Although this case does not refer to constitutional tests, because the Court decided the case on the basis of whether the statute covered the defendant's conduct rather than on the basis of the constitutional issue, the reference to requiring the restriction to be 'necessary and inevitable' implies that a stricter scrutiny applies to the regulation of political expression.

We therefore cannot conclude that the Court never considers or applies constitutional tests or a categorical approach. It is unclear whether the Court applies a constitutional test or adopts the proportionality principle. But the Court has been careful in more recent cases to avoid upholding laws merely by invoking public interest. The Court has tried to explain some factors in its judgments on the constitutionality of challenged laws, such as whether the speech in question comprised expressive activity or was expression itself, and whether the law constituted a direct regulation or an indirect regulation of speech, and whether it was balancing the public interest with the harm caused by the limitation of the right.

For example, in *Sarufutsu*, the Court used three factors to review the constitutionality of the law:

(1) its objective;
(2) the rational connection between the objective and the means employed; and
(3) the relationship between the benefit of achieving the law's objective and the harm caused by limiting freedom of speech.

This method seems to be a kind of constitutional test. But it also seems to have a kind of proportionality test because the third factor involves balancing. In any case, the judgment includes some factors that display both a constitutional tests approach and a proportionality principle approach.

As we have seen, the Court tends to examine whether the case involves expressive activity or pure forms of expression and whether the regulation of speech is direct regulation or indirect regulation. We can therefore assume that the Court examines some factors such as the expressive act or expression itself, the nature of the regulation as direct or indirect, the relationship between the purpose and the means, and a balancing of benefits and harms. Although it must do better, it seems that the Court's approach seems to have been evolving incrementally to inform construction of the judgment.

C. The Implications for Hate Speech

There are, then, three approaches that we might take when examining the constitutionality of the regulation of hate speech from the perspective of constitutional judicial review: constitutional tests, the proportional principle, and case law. I will here attempt to apply each of these approaches to hate speech.

If we were to adopt a *constitutional test* approach, there is a possibility that some aspects of hate speech may be excluded from the scope of the right to freedom of speech, or be less-protected forms of speech, in the same way as are obscenity and defamation. Professor Masato Ichikawa points out that a law prohibiting hate speech would be constitutional only if the law were to regulate an extremely narrow range of speech, such as seditious hate speech and particularly terrible expressions of contempt.[70] The constitutionality of hate speech regulation will focus on the definition of the hate speech that is to be regulated. The Court will determine whether the law strictly defines the range of speech that is prohibited. In any particular case, the Court would be required to assess whether the speech in question, which is said to have violated the law, falls within the scope of the definition of hate speech.

If the Court thinks that hate speech falls within the scope of the freedom of expression protected by the Constitution, hate speech may be regulated only to the extent that the restrictions are necessary and reasonable. Professor Shigenori Matsui mentions that 'the protection of freedom of expression theoretically covers even hate speech. But, of course, freedom of expression is not absolute and can be made subject to necessary and reasonable restrictions to secure important or compelling public interests.'[71] Here, it is necessary to examine which constitutional test should be applied. According to Matsui, if the law regulates hate speech simply because it harms other people emotionally, it will burden freedom of speech. He therefore thinks that hate speech should be regulated only if the *Brandenburg* test or the 'clear and present danger' test are satisfied.[72]

Furthermore, it is necessary to focus on the nature of the hate speech regulation. Professor Yasuo Hasebe points out that the necessity and

70 Masato Ichikawa, *Hyōgen no Jiyū no Hōri* [The doctrine of freedom of expression] (Nihon Hyoronsha, 2003), 63.

71 Shigenori Matsui, 'The Challenge to Multiculturalism: Hate Speech Ban in Japan' (2016) 49 *U.B.C. L. Rev.* 427, at 463.

72 Shigenori Matsui, *Masu Mediahō Nyūmon* [An introduction to mass media law] (Nihon Hyoronsha, 2013), 167–68.

reasonableness of hate speech regulation should be carefully considered because it is content-based.[73] In other words, strict scrutiny would be applied in the case of hate speech regulation.

In light of this analysis, the scope of the definition of hate speech should be limited. Although the level of scrutiny is changeable depending on the method of regulation, the Court should at least apply strict scrutiny such as the *Brandenburg* test or the 'clear and present danger' test.

If we were instead to apply the *proportionality principle*, the courts would check:

(1) whether the purpose is congruent with the means;
(2) the necessity of the means; and
(3) the proportionality of the means.

The primary issue is whether the regulation can be weighed against the value of freedom of expression. The current hate speech law[74] in Japan has no mandatory provisions – that is, it prohibits no speech or conduct whatsoever and provides for no sanction. It simply stipulates that the public and government must make efforts to reduce 'unfair discriminatory speech' against persons who originate from outside of Japan. Its impact on freedom of expression is therefore light.

Even if a law that criminalized hate speech were to be enacted,[75] however, it is possible that it may be upheld. Professor Masayuki Uchino attempts to examine the constitutionality of any criminalization of hate speech.[76] According to him, the regulation of hate speech is necessary to protect an individual's honour. Although it is said that equal protection under law requires that hate speech be regulated, he points out that equal protection is not a reason to regulate hate speech because it prohibits only the discrimination not the expression of that discrimination.[77] He thinks that any such criminal regulation needs to restore the dignity of victims damaged by hate speech.[78] Analysing the constitutionality of the criminal regulation of hate speech, he suggests that it can be expected that the law

[73] Yasuo Hasebe, 'Zōo no Hyōgen to Hō Kisei' ['Expression of hate and its legal regulation'], *Asahi Shimbun*, 21 July 2015, at 9.

[74] The Act of Promotion for Elimination of Unduly Discriminatory Words against People from Outside Japan, known as the Hate Speech Elimination Act (HSEA).

[75] See Chapter 7, which analyses the criminal regulation of hate speech and recent debates about its criminalization.

[76] Masayuki Uchino, *Sabetsuteki Hyōgen* [Discriminatory expression] (Yuhikaku, 1990), 135–75.

[77] See *ibid.*, at 161–62.

[78] See *ibid.*, at 163.

will prevent hate speech in the future and remedy its damages effectively.[79] Although he does not mention the proportionality principle explicitly, he argues that the regulation hate speech is constitutional based on a balancing of the costs of free speech and the benefits of regulation.

Finally, we might judge the constitutionality of hate speech based on case law. When plaintiffs argue that hate speech constitutes a tort or when the prosecution argues that the hate speech is illegal because it is defamation, there is chance that the regulation of hate speech is restricting freedom of speech.

If the Supreme Court reviews the constitutionality of the law on hate speech, we might assume that it will first examine whether the case concerns freedom of expression after referring to the importance of freedom of speech as general theory. Next, the Court will review the legitimacy of the purpose of the law – that is, whether prohibiting speech that unduly discriminates against persons who originate from outside of Japan is in the public interest. In its judgment, the Court will not be likely to refer to the value of such speech. If regulation is held to be in the public interest, the Court will next review whether the law regulates the content of expression directly or indirectly. Finally, the Court will balance the benefit to be obtained by regulating hate speech with the harm caused by limiting freedom of expression.

Furthermore, there remain facial challenges to the law on hate speech in cases of defamation. Although there are few cases that have been so reviewed, it may be that the Court will check the breadth of the law. If the defendant argues that the law is overly broad because it regulates not only unprotected speech, but also protected speech, the Court will review whether the law is only as broad as it needs to be.[80]

V. Conclusion

The Japanese Supreme Court has decided free speech cases in its own unique way. The Court's approach in the judgments in freedom of expression cases has been different from those suggested by the constitutional academy. However, the continuous efforts scholars have made to suggest different methods and the academic criticism

[79] See *ibid.*, at 164–67.

[80] Supreme Court, 3rd Petty Bench, 18 September 2007, 61 Keishū 601 (*Motorcycle Gang Ordinance*). In this case, the court reviewed whether the ordinance was excessively broad or not.

of judgments based purely on public interest have been worthwhile. Given the suggestions of ways in which the Court might adopt a more logical and predictable approach, based on either the US or German models, the Court has begun to examine some common factors in assessing constitutionality. The academic project aiming to improve constitutional judicial review is still a work in progress.[81] The Court needs to refer to both the constitutional tests, to maintain the predictability and the legal stability that results when judges' discretion is bounded, and the proportionality principle as a basis for more logical judgments of the constitutionality of laws limiting freedom of expression.[82]

[81] See, e.g., Tatsuhiko Yamamoto and Keigo Obayashi, *Ikenshinsa Kijun: Amerika Kenpō Hanrei no Ima* [Constitutional test: the current of constitutional cases in the United States] (Kobundo, 2018).

[82] Craig Martin, 'Striking the Right Balance: Hate Speech Laws in Japan, the United States, and Canada' (2018) 45 *Hastings Const. L.Q.* 455, at 511–30. There might be a third approach. Professor Craig Martin compares hate speech laws in Japan with those in United States and Canada, and argues that Japan should refer to the Canadian approach, because it considers equal protection as well as free speech.

16

Japan's Postcolonial Hate Speech

NAOTO HIGUCHI*

I. Introduction

As other chapters have mentioned, the Japanese Diet passed the Hate Speech Elimination Act (HSEA) in May 2016. Because it was enacted under the hostile political environment of the rightist Abe Cabinet, the law neither prohibits hate speech nor punishes it.[1] Nevertheless, it is significant that the Diet passed the Act nearly unanimously just three years after it was introduced to the phrase 'hate speech'. The major battleground to regulate hate speech then shifted from the Diet to municipalities such as Osaka and Kawasaki, in which civic groups have strongly lobbied to pass local ordinances under which hate speech can be penalized.[2] This steady progress has been accomplished as a result of civic groups' struggles to combat nativism.[3]

From a sociological perspective, legal measures against hate speech cannot solve the root cause of the problem, because hate speech is not a cause (independent variable) but a result (dependent variable) of nativism. Different approaches, which clarify the causal relations that produce hate speech, are also needed to tackle this issue. One of the most promising ways of doing so would be to focus on the

* This work was supported by JSPS KAKENHI Grant No. 17H01005.

[1] Craig Martin, 'Striking the Right Balance: Hate Speech Laws in Japan, the United States, and Canada' (2018) 45 *Hastings Const. L.Q.* 455, at 464. See also Chapter 11.

[2] See Chapter 9.

[3] Naoto Higuchi, 'When Hate Becomes Illegal: Legislation Processes of the Anti-hate Speech Law in Japan', in Myongkoo Kang *et al.* (eds.), *Beyond Hate and Fear: Hate Speech in Asia and Europe* (Routledge, 2020). In this chapter, nativism is defined as 'an ideology, which holds that states should be inhabited exclusively by members of the native group ("the nation") and that non-native elements (persons and ideas) are fundamentally threatening to the homogeneous nation-states': Cas Mudde, *Populist Radical Right Parties in Europe* (Cambridge University Press, 2007), 19.

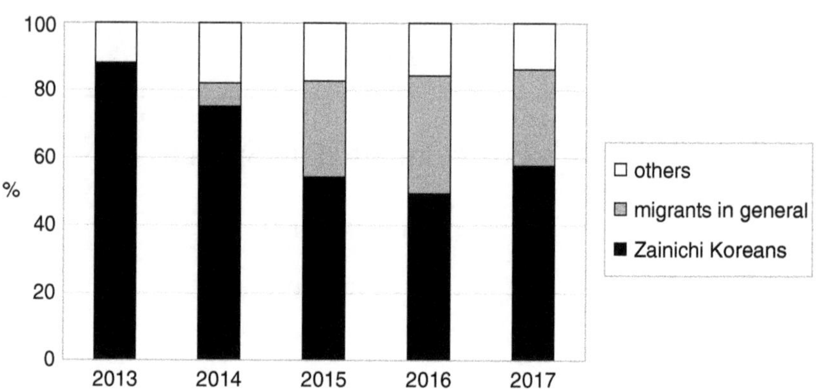

Fig. 16.1 Possible victims of hate speech in newspapers
Source: *Asahi Shimbun*

targets of hate speech, which embody the historical and structural conditions of the rise of nativism. Figure 16.1 illustrates press representation of the actual and potential victims of hate speech since the term first appeared in Japanese newspapers in 2013.[4] The most striking feature of this data is the predominance of Zainichi Koreans.[5] They accounted for the overwhelming majority of victims in 2013 and 2014, in coverage of court decisions on hate crimes such as *Kyoto Korean Elementary School*.[6] Although the proportion of Zainichi Koreans reported as victimized has significantly decreased since 2015, this is not because Japan witnessed new victims of hate speech; rather, submission of the anti-racism bill to the Upper House in 2015 by opposition parties[7] led to the argument on hate speech being abstracted to include migrants in general as assumed victims. In fact, newly arrived migrants have seldom been attacked by hate groups. Other minorities, such as women, disabled people, indigenous Ainu and Okinawan people, and LGBTQ+ persons, appeared in only a few articles.[8] In addition, a recent survey shows

[4] I first collected articles using the phrase 'hate speech' in the *Asahi Shimbun* from 2013 to 2017, and then counted how many of those referred to actual and potential victims.

[5] *Zainichi* (literally, 'resident in Japan') is used largely to refer to ethnic Koreans who came to Japan as colonial citizens and their descendants. See also Chapter 3.

[6] See Chapter 13.

[7] See Chapter 10.

[8] This is why Japan's hate groups are motivated by nativism, so I use 'nativists' and 'hate groups' interchangeably in this chapter.

that the general public are much more tolerant of hate speech against Zainichi Koreans than of that against other minorities.[9]

We can therefore safely say that Zainichi Koreans are at the core of debates around hate speech in Japan. In this chapter, I will examine what is behind Japan's hate speech by answering the following research question: why are Zainichi Koreans targeted by hate groups? At first glance, it seems natural that they attack Zainichi Koreans because they have long been a disadvantaged minority.[10] However, discrimination against them was weakened, and socioeconomic disparity between Japanese and Zainichi Koreans had almost disappeared by the turn of this century.[11] It should be noted that hate groups were established only after Zainichi Koreans were socioeconomically integrated. My research question is thus important because it can clarify the characteristics of hate speech in Japan.

II. Analytical Viewpoint

I have elsewhere examined conventional theories on xenophobia, such as the losers of modernization or competition theories, and shown that they cannot explain the rise of hate groups in Japan. Instead, I concluded that Japan's nativism should be understood as a variant of the historical revisionism that justified pre-war Japanese imperialism and colonialism.[12] While revisionist views have taken root among conservatives throughout the post-war era, Japan has seen a rise in historical revisionism since the late 1990s. Its impact has been significant, ranging from the publishing of revisionist history textbooks to the worsening of relations with South Korea and China. Turning our attention to historical revisionism enables us to elucidate what distinguishes Zainichi Koreans from other victims of hate and discrimination. When they migrated to Japan under the colonial rule from 1910 to 1945, these people were considered Japanese nationals.[13] The rights and status of Zainichi Koreans as a group have been associated

[9] Masaru Kono and Yoshitaka Nishizawa, 'Hate Speech Kisei eno Sanpi wa Dō Kimaru noka' ['What determines attitudes toward legal regulation of hate speech'] (2019) 133 *Chūo Kōron* 166, at 177–78.

[10] George Hicks, *Japan's Hidden Apartheid: The Korean Minority and the Japanese* (Avebury, 1997).

[11] See generally Naoto Higuchi, 'Dynamics of Occupational Status among Koreans in Japan: Analysing Census Data between 1980–2010' (2016) 2 *Seoul Journal of Japanese Studies* 1.

[12] Naoto Higuchi, *Japan's Ultra-Right* (Trans Pacific Press, 2016).

[13] Eiji Oguma, *The Boundaries of the Japanese, Vol. 2: Korea, Taiwan and Ainu 1868–1945* (Trans Pacific Press, 2017).

with their history as nationals deprived of citizenship in post-war Japan, which reminds the Japanese of things they would rather forget.

This historical context has brought about ambivalence towards Zainichi Koreans. On the one hand, the Japanese government had to respect their presence as former nationals different from other foreigners, because their status was dealt with through bilateral negotiations between Japan and South Korea in the decolonization process.[14] On the other hand, since Zainichi Koreans have been dependent on Japan–Korea relations, worsening bilateral relations can jeopardize this status. We must consequently suppose there are two factors that are crucial to our analytical viewpoint: decolonization; and the effect of bilateral relations on Zainichi Koreans.

A. *Postcolonial Melancholia in Post-war Japan*

In terms of the relationship between decolonization and hate speech against Zainichi Koreans, British cultural studies have extensively explored a connection between the postcolonial predicament and racism. Especially important for our purpose is the work of Paul Gilroy, who used the term 'postcolonial melancholia' to analyse British racism.[15] It refers to 'an inability even to face, never mind actually mourn, the profound change in circumstances and moods that followed the end of the empire and consequent loss of imperial prestige'.[16] The historical roots of racism are important, but he goes beyond this to focus on collapse of the empire, which is more closely related to British attitudes that regard post-war migrants as alien intruders. It is associated with the neo-traditional pathology of what has been identified as the morbidity of heritage.[17]

Gilroy borrowed the idea of melancholia from the work of Alexander and Margarete Mitscherlich, who analysed post-war German attitudes towards Nazism and World War II.[18] They pointed out two behavioural patterns typical of Germans: denial of defeat; and resultant sluggishness of reaction.[19] Although the only possible response to German guilt would

[14] Because of the lack of diplomatic relations with North Korea, the legal status of those affiliated to North Korea was not determined by bilateral negotiations.

[15] Paul Gilroy, *Postcolonial Melancholia* (Columbia University Press, 2005).

[16] *Ibid.*, at 90.

[17] *Ibid.*, at 99–100.

[18] Alexander Mitscherlich and Margarete Mitscherlich, *The Inability to Mourn: Principles of Collective Behaviour* (Grove Press, 1975).

[19] *Ibid.*, at 7.

have been mass melancholia,[20] there was cognitive disparity between perpetrators and victims. Germans could forget the dark side of history without mourning for Hitler, their own dead, and innocent victims,[21] which inhibited any capacity for responsible reconstructive practice.[22]

Likewise, because the British people have failed to appreciate the brutalities of colonial rule and to understand the damage it did to their political culture, they cannot adjust to the horrors of their own modern history and build a new national identity.[23] As Gilroy emphasizes, such melancholia is not unique to Britain; other countries that were involved in colonial expansion, including Japan, have also experienced similar problems.[24]

What characterizes Japan is the influence of its defeat in World War II and the subsequent Cold War on the decolonization process. First, because Japan's surrender brought about the end of the colonial rule, decolonization was forced from above – instead of being the product of anti-colonial struggle from below. In Japan, 15 August is designated as the date marking the anniversary of the end of the war in 1945, but the Chinese Civil War was still raging and, within a few years, the Korean Peninsula was plunged into a state of full-scale war.[25] The result was the division of both China and the Korean Peninsula, but it was actually this very situation that proved useful in ensuring that the issues of Japan's colonial rule would remain vague. Japan escaped from its responsibility of invasion and colonization by taking advantage of divisions in Korea and China.

American control in the context of the occupation also prevented a true decolonization process being realized.[26] Under the Cold War, the United States preferred securing military bases to investigating Japan's war responsibility, and it was acquiescent in the construction of relations with Japan's nearest neighbours that left the issue of responsibility in an ambiguous state. The Cold War structure has permitted the vague

20 *Ibid.*, at 55.
21 *Ibid.*, at 103.
22 Gilroy, note 15, at 96.
23 *Ibid.*, at 99.
24 *Ibid.*, at 100.
25 Takeshi Komagome, *Shokuminchi Teikoku Nihon no Bunka Tōgo* [Cultural integration in the Japanese colonial empire] (Iwanami Shoten, 1996).
26 See generally Xavier Robillard-Martel and Christopher Laurent, 'From Colonization to Zaitokukai: The Legacy of Racial Oppression in the Lives of Koreans in Japan' [2019] *Asian Ethnicity* 1, at 5.

treatment of the colonial settlement, which exempted Japanese from suffering postcolonial melancholia until the end of the Cold War.[27]

B. *Brubaker's Triad Model*

Roger Brubaker's studies of Eastern European nationalism provide a valuable guide when considering the situation in which Zainichi Koreans find themselves.[28] With the existence of multiple ethnic groups that could potentially constitute nation-states in the countries of Eastern Europe, the reconstruction of nations that accompanied the end of the Cold War has given rise to a complex situation. Specifically, the succession states to the previous multi-ethnic socialist states have been redefining themselves as nation-states since the end of the Cold War. Examples such as the former Soviet Union and the former Yugoslav Republics, formed in the division of Yugoslavia, are easily understood, but other new problems erupted everywhere, such as that of the treatment of people of Belarusian descent within Poland. Brubaker sees the ethnic conflicts arising as part of these processes of national reconstruction as resulting from the existence of a triad that includes a 'national minority', a 'nationalizing state', and a 'national homeland' (see Figure 16.2).

Nationalizing states are defined as 'ethnically heterogeneous yet conceived as nation-states, whose dominant elites promote (to varying degrees) the language, culture, demographic position, economic flourishing, or political hegemony of the nominally state-bearing

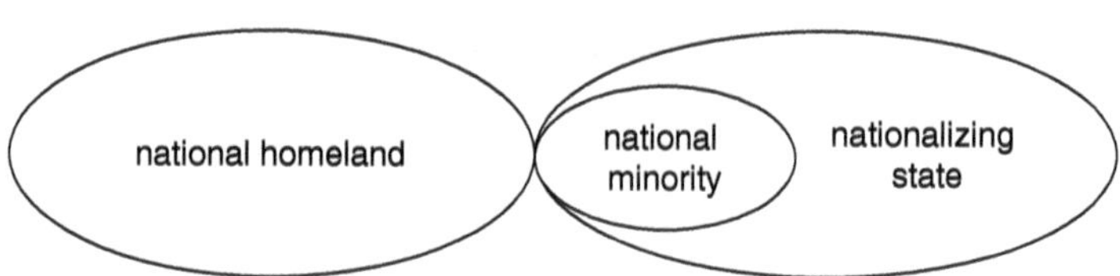

Fig. 16.2 Triad model of ethnic conflict

[27] Some other factors also characterized Japan's decolonization process. For example, Ching points out factors such as the sudden disappearance of the Japanese empire after Japan's defeat, the subsequent US hegemony in the region, authoritarian rule in Taiwan and South Korea, and Japan's postwar economic ascendancy: Leo T. S. Ching, *Anti-Japan: The Politics of Sentiment in Postcolonial East Asia* (Duke University Press, 2019), at 30).

[28] Rogers Brubaker, *Nationalism Reframed: Nationhood and the National Question in the New Europe* (Cambridge University Press, 1996).

nation'.[29] For example, the socialist state of Czechoslovakia split into two independent states for the two main ethnic groups, the Czechs and the Slovaks, following the end of the Cold War. In Brubaker's terminology, these are examples of the 'ethnically homogenous nation state',[30] several of which emerged in Eastern Europe. These are not, in reality, ethnically homogeneous nations; Slovakia is a multi-ethnic nation, which is home to Hungarians from Hungary with which it shares a border, but is an attempt to create a state predominantly comprising Slovakians.

National homeland refers to a situation in which 'political or cultural elites define ethnonational kin in other states as members of one and the same nation, claim that they "belong," in some sense, to the state, and assert that their condition must be monitored and their interests protected and promoted by the state'.[31] To return to the above example, because of historical circumstances, whereby Hungary had controlled Slovakia, the two countries did not enjoy amicable relations. However, in 1995, a treaty of friendship was concluded as a sign of historical rapprochement, which led to the recognition of language and cultural rights for the Hungarians living in Slovakia.[32] As their national homeland, Hungary exerted considerable influence on the rights of Hungarians in Slovakia.

Finally, *national minority* is a 'political stance' that displays the following characteristics: '(1) the public claim to membership of an ethno-cultural nation different from the numerically or politically dominant ethno-cultural nation; (2) the demand for state recognition of this distinct ethno-cultural nationality; and (3) the assertion, on the basis of this ethno-cultural nationality, of certain collective cultural or political rights'.[33] Instead of the dyad model, which regards relations between the national minority and the nationalizing state as being concluded domestically inside one nation, Brubaker explicitly established that this is affected by relations between the two nations. The destiny of national minorities is at the mercy of conflicts between the 'nationalizing state' and the 'national homeland'.[34]

[29] *Ibid.*, at 57.

[30] See generally Rogers Brubaker, 'Migrations of Ethnic Unmixing in the "New Europe" ' (1998) 32 *International Migration Review* 1047.

[31] Brubaker, note 28, at 58.

[32] Hanna Vasilevich, 'Majority as Minority: A Comparative Case of Autochthonous Slavs in Lithuania and Hungarians in Slovakia after the Second World War', in Julien Danero Iglesias, Nenad Stojanović, and Sharon Weinblum (eds.), *New Nation–States and National Minorities* (ECPR Press, 2013).

[33] Brubaker, note 28, at 60.

[34] *Ibid.*, at 5.

III. Structural and Historical Contexts

A. *The SCAP and Japanese Government Policy towards Zainichi Koreans*

In this section,[35] I show how the combination of incomplete decolonization and the triad relationship determined governmental policies towards Zainichi Koreans. The expansion and collapse of the Japanese empire brought about the ethnic mixing and unmixing of Japanese and Koreans: in the territories of the Japanese empire, ethnic mixing proceeded as emigrants from Japan and migrants from the colonies mixed with each other. At that time, the assimilation of Koreans was seen as possible because the Japanese were argued to be ethnically diverse to win over and control different ethnic groups.[36] After Japan's annexation of Korea, Koreans who crossed over to Japan were treated as Japanese under the law and Korean men had voting rights. The process of the dissolution of the Japanese empire following defeat led to the liberation of the Korean Peninsula, but a significant number of Koreans continued to live in Japan.

The Japanese government encouraged Zainichi Koreans to return to their own country; it insisted on limiting the rights of Korean residents in Japan. Post-war Japan, as a 'nationalizing state', was to be promoted by forcing Koreans, as the 'national minority', to return to their 'national homeland' and by treating those who stayed behind inhospitably. In December 1945, the franchise was suspended for people from Japan's former colonies (mostly Koreans and Taiwanese) and they were thus divested of their voting rights. This political decision was taken out of fear of the political influence of Zainichi Koreans.[37]

The occupation period was also the time when the immigration control regime that was established in 1952 was formulated. The basic policy towards Zainichi Koreans was decided by the lopsided dyad of the Japanese government, which was aiming for the creation of an 'ethnically homogeneous nation-state', and Zainichi Koreans who had no one to

[35] This section is based on my argument in Higuchi, note 12, ch. 8.

[36] Eiji Oguma, *A Genealogy of 'Japanese' Self-Images* (Trans Pacific Press, 2002).

[37] See generally Naoki Mizuno, 'Zainichi Chōsenjin Taiwanjin Sanseiken "Teishi" Jōko no Seiritsu: Zainichi Chōsenjin Sanseiken Mondai no Rekishiteki Kentō (1)' ['The bringing into effect of the stipulations "suspending" the voting rights of Zainichi Koreans and Taiwanese: a historical examination of the Zainichi Korean voting rights issue (1)'] (1996) 1 *Sekai Jinken Mondai Kenkyū Sentā Kenkyū Kiyō* [Bulletin of the Kyoto Human Rights Research Institute] 43.

back them. Although the Republic of Korea (ROK) and the Democratic People's Republic of Korea (DPRK) were founded in 1948, Japan did not have diplomatic relations with them. The Japanese government took advantage of the lack of the ethnic homelands as negotiating partners. In addition, the Japanese government made use of the US anti-communism doctrine to gain approval for a policy of 'unmixing'. The Japanese government, with the acquiescence of the Supreme Commander for the Allied Powers (SCAP), oriented itself towards ethnically homogeneous nation-state-building, and this is the reason why they promoted the repatriation of Zainichi Koreans and the removal of their rights.[38] Once the San Francisco Peace Treaty came into effect in 1952, people from Japan's former colonies officially lost their Japanese citizenship. Following this development, Zainichi Koreans, as foreign nationals, came under the control of the Immigration Control Act and the Alien Registration Act, in which they were granted tentative legal status as '126-2-6 aliens' under Law No. 126.[39]

B. *From the 1952 Immigration Control System to Special Permanent Residency*

Under the Cold War regime, the Korean Peninsula was divided into two successor states, South Korea and North Korea, which greatly influenced the legal status of Zainichi Koreans. Their status was one of the topics prioritized at the negotiations between Japan and South Korea seeking to normalize their diplomatic relations. However, because the goal of the Japanese government at this time was unmixing, its initial proposals at the Japan–South Korea negotiations were restrictive: fresh applications would have to be required for Zainichi Koreans to qualify for permanent residence; and welfare recipients were to be forcibly repatriated.[40] In

[38] Tessa Morris-Suzuki, *Borderline Japan: Foreigners and Frontier Controls in the Postwar Era* (Cambridge University Press, 2010); Taeki Kim, *Sengo Nihon Seiji to Zainichi Chōsenjin Mondai: SCAP no Taizainichi Chōsenjin Seisaku 1945–1952 nen* [Postwar Japanese politics and the Zainichi Korean issue: SCAP policy towards Zainichi Koreans 1945–1952] (Keiso Shobo, 1997).

[39] Bumsoo Kim, 'From Exclusion to Inclusion? The Legal Treatment of "Foreigners" in Contemporary Japan' (2006) 24 *Immigrants & Minorities* 51, at 57–58.

[40] Yongho Choe, 'Shūsenchokugo no Zainichi Chōsenjin/kankokujin Shakai ni okeru "Hongoku" Shikōsei to Daiichiji Nikkan Kaidan' ['Homeland orientation of Zainichi North and South Korean communities in postwar Japan and the inaugural Japan–Korea Conference'], in Jongwon Yi, Masafumi Kimiya, and Toyomi Asano (eds.), *Rekishi to shite no Nikkan Kokkōseijōka II: Datsushokuminchika hen* [The normalization of Japan–

reality, the Japanese government regarded Zainichi Koreans as a burden and thus gave substantial assistance to efforts to return people to North Korea.[41]

After the start of Park Chung-hee's administration in South Korea, however, *Mindan* ('Association of Koreans in Japan') came under its control and support,[42] which enabled joint negotiations to resist Japan's efforts at unmixing. As a result of the negotiations, treaty permanent resident status was created for Zainichi Koreans with South Korean nationality in 1965 and their status thus became relatively stable.[43]

However, those without South Korean citizenship – mostly affiliated to *Soren* (the pro-North-Korea 'General Association of Koreans in Japan') – remained tentative '126-2-6 aliens', which produced a division in legal status among Zainichi Koreans themselves. Moreover, the Japanese government tried to revise the Immigration Control Act in the late 1960s, which included restrictions on the political activities of foreigners. Now that the triad included a nationalizing state (Japan), a national minority (Koreans without South Korean nationality) and a national homeland (North Korea) that was also an 'enemy state', the Japanese government would never change its unmixing policy.

It was the ratification of the International Covenant on Economic, Social and Cultural Rights in 1979 and the Convention Relating to the Status of Refugees in 1981 – factors beyond the level of the triad – that promoted partial change to these conditions. This led to legal amendments in the form of the Immigration Control and Refugee Recognition Act, which resulted in Zainichi Koreans without South Korean nationality[44] gaining permanent resident status. In addition, all Zainichi Koreans were given access to the social security system in areas such as government pensions, childcare allowances, and access to public housing.

South Korea diplomatic relations as history, vol. II: decolonization] (Hosei University Press, 2011).

41 Tessa Morris-Suzuki, *Exodus to North Korea: Shadows from Japan's Cold War* (Rowman & Littlefield, 2007).

42 Kiyong Roh, 'Zainichi Mindan no Hongoku Shikō Rosen to Nikkan Kōshō' ['The homeland-oriented alignment of Mindan and Japan–South Korean negotiations'], in Yi *et al.*, note 40.

43 It should also be noted that favourable policy towards South Koreans was limited to legal status. Despite the establishment of this more stable residential status, all Zainichi Koreans continued to be excluded from many of the social rights.

44 Yasuaki Onuma, *Shinpan Tanitsu Minzoku Shakai no Shinwa o Koete* [Beyond the myth of a racially homogeneous society], new ed. (Toshindo, 1993).

The final change came about as a result of negotiations on the legal status of third-generation Zainichi Koreans with South Korean nationality, designed to review the Treaty on Basic Relations between Japan and the Republic of Korea 25 years after it first came into being. At this time, the South Korean government released nine demands taken from the ideas of Mindan and, following discussions with the Japanese government, the Agreement between Japan and the Republic of Korea Concerning the Legal Status and Treatment of the People of the Republic of Korea Residing in Japan was released. This was a case of the triad that had excluded North Koreans effecting a revision of legal status.[45] However, the Special Act on Immigration Control, enacted in 1991, saw the application of permanent resident status to both South and North Korean nationals for the first time.

C. *Prolonged Processes of Decolonization*

It is the influence of the logic of the colonial settlement that brought about the biggest difference between Zainichi Koreans and other foreigners. Nevertheless, at the time of the enactment of the 1952 Immigration Control Law and the Alien Registration Act, neither the colonial settlement nor the history of settlement in Japan were taken into account. When Japan and South Korea ratified the Treaty on Basic Relations, Japan did acknowledge the status of this national minority as treaty permanent residents. However, the logic of the triad under the Cold War resulted in differential status being granted to South Koreans and North Koreans. In terms of the legal status, this division was not dissolved until the Diet passed the Special Act on Immigration Control in 1991. It took 46 years from the end of World War II to settle the legal status of Zainichi Koreans.

The decolonization process was prolonged by the reluctance of Japan as a nationalizing state. There were three major points of progress in the legal status of Zainichi Koreans, but none of them was initiated by the

[45] As used here, 'North Korean' does not imply that all such people possess North Korean nationality. There are some North Koreans who identify with North Korea, but others who do not. In the immediate post-war period, Koreans living in Japan were recorded as Koreans (a geographical name because no state existed there before 1948) under the alien registration system. Since then, some have taken South Korean nationality and some have continued on as Korean, but the Japanese government has regarded the latter as North Koreans. Since Japan does not recognize North Korea as a state, North Koreans have been placed in a situation close to statelessness.

Japanese government: bilateral negotiations between South Korea and Japan resulted in permanent resident status in 1965 and 1991, and ratification of UN conventions led to permanent resident status for North Koreans in 1982. However, South Korea had already demanded the sort of treatment that now applies to special permanent residents before 1965, during negations surrounding the Treaty on Basic Relations between Japan and the Republic of Korea.[46] The issue of legal status ought to have been decided back then, but the Japanese government had been unwilling to grant stable legal status to Zainichi Koreans. The Japanese government had failed to see this as its own issue to resolve.

IV. Fertile Ground for Hate Speech against Zainichi Koreans

A. *Changing Enemies for Japan's Radical Right*

While South Koreans were better treated in the decolonization process during the Cold War, they have become the primary target of hate speech in the last decade. This is closely related to the radical right changing their targets in post-Cold War Japan.[47] Consider the result of a web poll conducted in May 2013 by Zaitokukai, which became defunct in 2016 but was by far the largest of hate groups in Japan at the time of the poll.[48] Of the 5,272 people who voted, 78 per cent (4,123 people) said 'the country that I hate the most' is South Korea. The score for China was 12 per cent (652 people), and North Korea, 4 per cent (246 people). This conspicuous 'hatred of South Korea' is in a way surprising, because Japan's hypothetical enemies are North Korea and China. In addition, abductions of Japanese nationals by North Korea in the 1970s and 1980s triggered extreme antipathy nationwide.[49] In this section, I will illustrate

[46] See generally Taeki Kim, 'Zainichi Kankokujin Sansei no Hōteki Chii to "1965 nen Kannichi Kyōtei" (1)' ['The legal status of third-generation Zainichi Koreans and the "1965 South Korea–Japan Agreement" (1)'] (1991) 105 *Ikkyō Ronsō* [Hitotsubashi review] 43; Taeki Kim, 'Zainichi Kankokujin Sansei no Hōteki Chii to "1965 nen Kannichi Kyōtei" (2)' ['The legal status of third-generation Zainichi Koreans and the "1965 South Korea–Japan Agreement" (2)'] (1991) 106 *Ikkyō Ronsō* [Hitotsubashi review] 82.

[47] In my classification, hate groups belong to the third and newest wave of the radical right. For details, see Naoto Higuchi, 'The Radical Right in Japan', in Jens Rydgren (ed.), *The Oxford Handbook of the Radical Right* (Oxford University Press, 2018).

[48] Higuchi, note 12. See also Chapter 5.

[49] See generally Brad Williams and Erik Mobrand, 'Explaining Divergent Responses to the North Korean Abductions Issue in Japan and South Korea' (2010) 69 *Journal of Asian Studies* 507.

how the triad and postcolonial melancholia nonetheless positioned South Korea as a bitter enemy and generated hate against Zainichi Koreans.

To begin with, Figures 16.3 and 16.4 show how the end of the Cold War shifted the concerns and targets of the radical right. The data examine the interests of the radical right with the aim of elucidating its designation of enemies, and are based on the titles of issues of the major right-wing monthly journals *Shokun!* and *Seiron* between 1982 and 2015.[50]

The end of the Cold War was accompanied by the rise of identity politics among Japan's radical right. Figure 16.3 shows the direction of right-wing interests. Until the mid-1980s, the number of articles related to military affairs and defence sometimes exceeded 10 per cent of the total. After that, they ceased to be central concerns for the radical right, replaced by history-related articles that exceeded 10 per cent for the first time in 1997. The peak in the proportion of history-related articles at over 20 per cent in 2005 overlapped with anti-Japanese demonstrations in China, Prime Minister Koizumi's visit to the Yasukuni Shrine, and the selection of revisionist textbooks in the Japanese curriculum. The increasing number of history-related articles was triggered by a backlash against statements by non-LDP[51] Prime Ministers Morihiro Hosokawa (in 1993) and Tomiichi Murayama (in

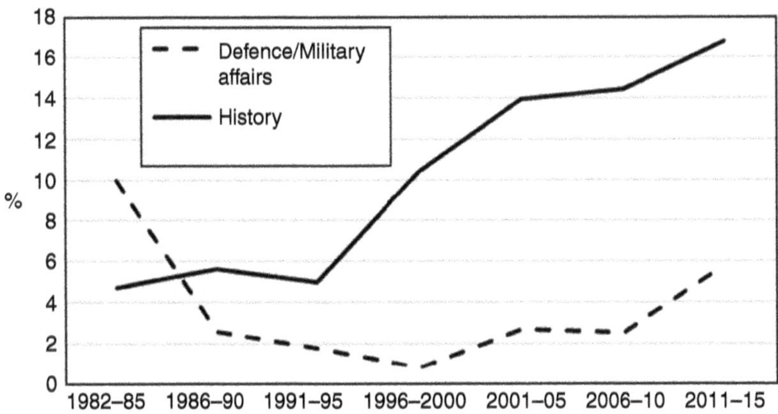

Fig 16.3 Shifting interests of right-wingers

[50] Because *Shokun!* ceased publication in 2009, I replaced it with *WiLL* from that point onwards. For details, see Higuchi, note 12, appendix.

[51] The conservative Liberal Democratic Party (LDP) has been ruling since the war, except for two short periods from 1993 to 1994 and from 2009 to 2012. These statements were made by non-LDP prime ministers.

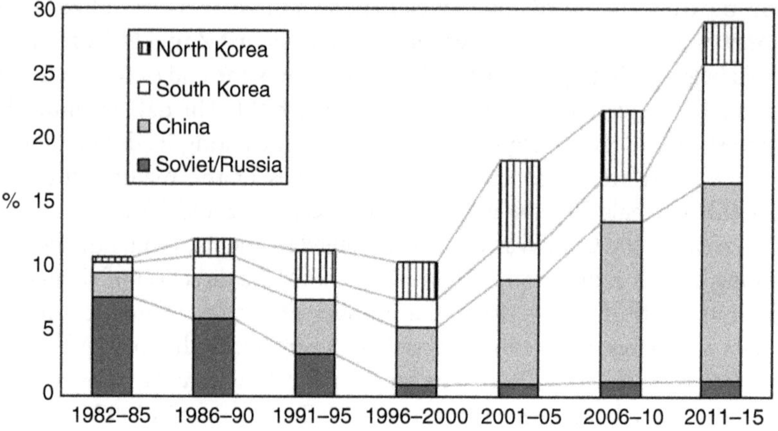

Fig 16.4 Respective frequencies of appearance of countries

1995) acknowledging Japan's war responsibility. The rising awareness of Japan's aggression in South Korea and China also contributed to intensification of conflict over war memories.

Since the post-Cold War world widely witnessed politicization of cultural trauma such as the Katyn massacre in Poland,[52] the way in which Japan faced historical issues such as the 'comfort women' is rather a familiar story. What characterizes Japan is that a rising interest in history was accompanied by a change of target for the radical right. Figure 16.4 plots the frequency with which the Soviet Union (Russia), China, South Korea, and North Korea appeared in articles between 1982 and 2015. It reflects which countries Japan's radical right has viewed as enemies, and it shows three broad changes in the 1990s and the 2000s.

First, throughout the 1980s, the frequency with which the Soviet Union appeared remained high. Conversely, the proportion of mention of China, South Korea, and North Korea remained low. The Soviet Union was by far the most important hypothetical enemy, in terms of both anti-communism and nationalism (territorial disputes). This changed in the 1990s, although the Soviet Union continued to be of interest until its dissolution, after which its frequency of mention dropped dramatically and failed to return to its former levels.

[52] Jeffrey Alexander *et al.*, *Cultural Trauma and Collective Identity* (University of California Press, 2004).

Second, East Asian countries took the Soviet Union's place in the late 1990s and even surpassed it with the advent of this century. While articles related to East Asian countries made up only 4.7 per cent of articles in the 1980s (lower than the 6.5 per cent earlier devoted to the Soviet Union), they skyrocketed to 9.6 per cent in the 1990s and then to 22.2 per cent between 2001 and 2015. Although Japan's radical right had looked favourably on South Korea as an anti-communist ally, after the Cold War ended, it began to regard all other East Asian countries (China, North Korea, and South Korea) as 'anti-Japanese' enemies.

Third, these tendencies are the most salient for South Korea. Figure 16.5 shows that historical disputes with China have been constant since the 1980s, such as those surrounding the Nanjing Massacre and history textbooks issues. Historical problems concerning South Korea, however, did not begin to influence bilateral relations until 1991, when former 'comfort women' came forward after the democratization of the country. While history has been only one of the important issues between China and Japan, it has become the biggest unresolved diplomatic problem between South Korea and Japan in the post-Cold War era. This shows that while the biggest 'enemy' for Japan's radical right is China, with whom there is all-out confrontation, South Korea is its enemy primarily with regard to the understanding of history.[53]

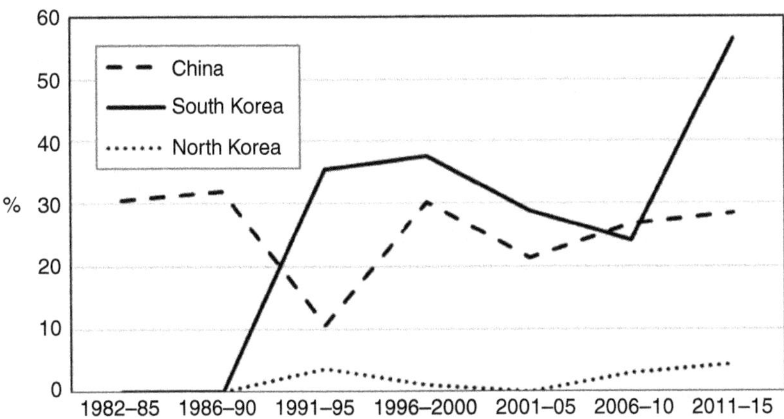

Fig 16.5 Proportion of history-related articles

[53] Alexix Dudden, *Troubled Apologies: Among Japan, Korea and the United States* (Columbia University Press, 2008).

B. *Hate Speech as a Spinoff of Historical Revisionism*

Although Japan's right-wing establishment has criticized hate groups as extremely shameful, both share revisionist ideologies of history. They are not directly associated with each other, but their views on history are surprisingly similar.[54] In fact, most activists within hate groups were not originally interested in Zainichi Koreans; they were first attracted to historical revisionism or indignant about the 'anti-Japanese behaviours' of neighbouring countries.[55] Their hatred of Zainichi Koreans is no more than a variant of such feelings.[56] So why did they set their sights on Zainichi Koreans?

This is the key to answering our research question. While hate groups also harbour hatred towards China and North Korea,[57] this is not enough to explain why they feel stronger animosity towards South Korea.[58] What is unique to South Korea is the importance of historical issues, which threatens Japan's sense of moral superiority. Unlike the communist and authoritarian Chinese and North Korean regimes, it is difficult to criticize the legitimacy of democratized South Korea's protest of historical issues. Hatred of South Korea can be regarded as backlash against challenges to Japan's moral position on historical issues.[59]

Likewise, Zaitokukai alleges four 'special privileges' granted to Zainichi Koreans: special permanent residency; the issuing of subsidies to Korean schools; the system of aliases (the use of Japanese names); and favourable welfare provisions. All of them are no more than demagogic, but we should examine the historical nature of these claims: all but welfare provisions are rooted in the colonization of the Korean Peninsula. Special permanent residency is a kind of compensation for

[54] Analysis by Fabian Schäfer and his colleagues also suggests that online hate speakers served as de facto subcontractors of the right-wing establishment: Fabian Schäfer, Stefan Evert, and Philipp Heinrich, 'Japan's 2014 General Election: Political Bots, Right-Wing Internet Activism, and Prime Minister Shinzo Abe's Hidden Nationalist Agenda' (2017) 5 *Big Data* 294.

[55] Higuchi, note 12, ch. 4.

[56] Enemies are directed by group leaders in accordance with the movement's strategy. See generally Yuki Asahina, 'Becoming Right-Wing Citizens in Contemporary Japan' (2019) 31 *Contemporary Japan* 1.

[57] In fact, Zaitokukai repeatedly attacked pro-North Korea schools, as Chapters 12 and 13 show.

[58] It is also insufficient to explain stronger antipathy towards South Korea as the result of enduring discrimination against Koreans.

[59] See generally Shogo Suzuki, 'Japanese Revisionists and the "Korea Threat": Insights from Ontological Security' (2019) 32 *Cambridge Review of International Affairs* 303.

Zainichi Koreans deprived of their Japanese citizenship; Korean schools have long been subject to oppression since the colonial era;[60] and the Japanese colonial authority imposed the system of aliases on Koreans, who were denied the right to use their authentic names. All of these shed light on the dark side of Japan's modern history. Thus when Zainichi Koreans share their stories of postwar marginalization, members of Zaitokukai and others experience cognitive dissonance,[61] which has triggered a revisionist backlash against these supposed 'special privileges'.

These 'special privileges' are nothing new. Other than those that are part of the Special Act of Immigration Control enacted in 1991, they have been part of life in Japan since the 1950s. Nevertheless, it was not until the late 2000s that Japan first saw the rise of the organized nativist movement. How can we understand this time lag? It is because of the triadic sequence of Japan's nativism: the radical right hates South Korea because its harshest criticisms expose the reality that Japan can no longer consider itself free of blame for incomplete decolonization. The result is the rise of historical revisionism since the late 1990s. At first, the main target of historical revisionism was non-LDP politicians who made 'masochistic' statements regarding Japan's invasion during World War II, but these sights soon shifted to neighbouring countries. Hate groups applying the logic of historical revisionism decided that Zainichi Koreans were their most proximate enemies.

V. Conclusion

Every variant of hate speech has its own historical context. In this chapter, I have attempted to clarify the nature of hate speech in Japan by answering the question of why Zainichi Koreans have become the primary target of hate groups. In so doing, I first focused on the effect of colonial rule on Zainichi Koreans and found two things: Japan enjoyed prolonged postcolonial settlement; and the legal status of this group was determined by triadic relations. I then examined the timing of the rise of hate groups – that is, after open discrimination against Zainichi Koreans had diminished and their socioeconomic disadvantage had all but disappeared.

[60] See generally Ryuta Itagaki, 'The Anatomy of Korea-phobia in Japan' (2015) 35 *Japanese Studies* 49. See also Chapter 12.

[61] Carol Gluck, 'The Past in the Present', in Andrew Gordon (ed.), *Postwar Japan as History* (University of California Press, 1993), at 89.

Hate speech accompanied the proliferation of historical revisionism and worsening relations between Japan and neighbouring countries in the 2000s. Zainichi Koreans became targets of hate speech because they were seen as belonging to another government and a different regime, and not because of their socioeconomic conditions.[62] Under normal conditions, for example, Mindan's campaign for local voting right should be understood as a willingness to integrate politically in Japan. However, Japan's right-wingers mobilized against this, claiming that it would serve as a Trojan horse for invasion of political actors from Korean homelands.[63]

It is the unfinished processes of decolonization that has brought about the triadic logic of Japan's nativism. Japan's postcolonial melancholia is rooted in its 'inability even to face the profound change that followed the end of'[64] the exceptional period that exempted Japan from taking responsibility for its past misdeeds under the Cold War regime. If we recognize that historical revisionism is an attempt to erase the history of colonialism and to deny incomplete decolonization, embodied in the 'comfort women' issue, we can see how these discourses coalesce to fuel nativism.[65] In fact, Prime Minister Shinzo Abe himself has been strongly committed to historical revisionism since his early political career.[66] I conclude, therefore, that the present Cabinet is responsible for creating such hate speech (through its promotion of historical revisionism), even while reluctantly tackling its results (by enacting the Hate Speech Elimination Act).[67]

[62] Didier Bigo, 'From Foreigners to "Abnormal Aliens": How the Faces of the Enemy Have Changed Following 9/11', in Elspeth Guild and Joanne van Selm (eds.), *International Migration and Security: Opportunities and Challenges* (Routledge, 2005), at 69.

[63] Higuchi, note 12, ch. 7.

[64] Gilroy, note 15, at 90.

[65] Remi Joseph-Salisbury, 'Does Anybody Really Care What a Racist Says? Anti-racism in "Post-racial" Times' (2019) 67 *Sociological Review* 63, at 65–66.

[66] James Babb, 'The New Generation of Conservative Politicians in Japan' (2013) 14 *Japanese Journal of Political Science* 355, at 362–63.

[67] Higuchi, note 3.

17

A Quantitative and Theoretical Investigation of Racism in Japan

A Social Psychological Approach

FUMIAKI TAKA*

The aim of this chapter is to discuss hate speech in current Japan from a social psychological perspective. Social psychologists have long explored intergroup phenomena and have contributed greatly to the understanding of stereotypes, prejudice, and discrimination. Social psychology does not stand apart from other disciplines such as sociology, political science, and information science, but shares common goals of understanding social phenomena. In this chapter, I will introduce the findings and implications of social psychological research, and that of adjacent fields, to illuminate their contributions to the studies of hate speech in contemporary Japan.

I. Basic Concepts

In social psychology, intergroup phenomena such as hate speech can be understood through classification into three concepts: stereotypes, prejudice, and discrimination. Although these concepts are related to one another, it is important to recognize that these concepts also have distinctive characteristics in the following ways.

A. Stereotypes

A widely accepted definition of *stereotype* today is 'a set of beliefs about the personal attributes of a group of people'.[1] The term was first coined in

* This work was supported by JSPS KAKENHI Grant Nos JP26870662, JP16K21443, and JP18K03019. The author is also grateful to Makiko Deguchi, Sophia University, Japan, for help in the editing of this chapter.

[1] Richard Ashmore and Francis Del Boca, 'Conceptual Approaches to Stereotypes and Stereotyping', in David Hamilton (ed.), *Cognitive Processes in Stereotyping and Intergroup Behaviour* (Psychology Press, 1981), at 16.

1922 by Walter Lippmann, a prominent journalist, to represent fixed internalized images; it was then adopted as scientific terminology to represent fixed images of social group characteristics. Although early theorists incorporated descriptors, such as 'wrong', 'exaggerated', 'fixed', 'shared', or 'negative', in the definition of stereotypes, these were eventually dropped.

This 'simplification' of the definition of stereotypes aimed to capture the optimal concept for conducting scientific analyses. For example, the descriptor 'wrong', which was included in an earlier definition, was problematic because scientists would have had to first resolve the issue of whether the belief was indeed incorrect before they could use the word. This posed a dilemma because the objective realities of psychological traits and behavioural characteristics, in which social psychologists are interested, is a question of scientific investigation itself. Previous research that investigated the accuracy of 'stereotypes' has shown that many of them in fact tended to be accurate.[2]

Even if a 'stereotype' or a general description of average group members may in fact be fairly accurate, applying this stereotype to an individual is often unjust or unfair. For example, in Japan, it is true that not a small percentage of female workers discontinue their work after marriage or having a child.[3] However, it is still unfair and unjustifiable to treat individual female workers or jobseekers as though they are bound to leave their jobs. Although it is worth knowing whether or not a stereotype is accurate, psychologists today tend not to use this or other criteria to define them.

B. *Prejudice*

Prejudice refers to the attitudes held towards members of social groups. In psychology, prejudice is defined as 'the set of affective reactions we have towards people as a function of their category memberships'[4]. The difference between attitudes and beliefs (i.e. stereotypes) is the presence or absence of a reference to affective or evaluative components. In a study

[2] For a review, see Lee Jussim *et al.*, 'The Unbearable Accuracy of Stereotypes', in Todd D. Nelson (ed.), *Handbook of Prejudice, Stereotyping, and Discrimination* (Psychology Press, 2009), ch. 10.

[3] Gender Equality Bureau Cabinet Office, *Toward Active Participation of Women as the Core of Growth Strategies* (2013), at 8, available at www.gender.go.jp/english_contents/about_danjo/whitepaper/pdf/2013-01.pdf [accessed 29 January 2019].

[4] David J. Schneider, *The Psychology of Stereotyping* (Guilford Press, 2004), 27.

that was conducted in the 1950s with Japanese students ranging in age from junior high school to college, it was found that students associated attributes such as 'slovenly', 'physically dirty', and 'foul-smelling' with Koreans.[5] Here, statements used in the questionnaire such as 'Koreans are slovenly' refer to cognitive rather than affective meanings and are therefore are considered beliefs. However, because all of these attributes have negative evaluative connotations, those who are associated with these attributes might be evaluated negatively (i.e. disliked or evaluated unfavourably). In fact, the respondents ranked the Koreans as the most unfavourable people among 12 racial or ethnic groups listed in the questionnaire (followed by Jewish and Black people).[6] These affective evaluations, often based on specific beliefs, are called 'attitudes'. In this sense, stereotypes and prejudice are interrelated, but distinguishable for social psychologists. It is especially important to distinguish cognitive and affective components of intergroup psychological phenomena when discussing racism and the issues around hate speech in the digital age.

The definition of prejudice has similarly evolved. Gordon Allport, a pioneering figure in the study of prejudice in psychology, defined ethnic prejudice as 'an antipathy based upon a faulty and inflexible generalization'.[7] Allport focused on prejudice as negative attitudes, although he fully recognized that both negative and positive biases exist towards members of any group. Indeed, positive biases towards members of dominant groups are as problematic as biases against members of subordinate groups because these biases might contribute to maintaining an unjust and unequal system. In addition, social psychologists today would emphasize that attitudes towards social group members often consist of both positive and negative attributes. Susan T. Fiske and colleagues demonstrated that just because a social group was evaluated positively on one dimension did not result in their attributes being regarded positively. Jews and Asians, for example, were ranked higher in competence, but lower in warmth, by American students and non-student samples. In other words, Jews and Asians are perceived as having positive attributes in one dimension, but negative attributes in another.

[5] Tatsuo Haratani, Yasuo Matsuyama, and Yutaka Minami, 'Minzokuteki Sutereotaipu to Kōo Kanjō ni tsuiteno Ichikōsatsu' ['Study of stereotypes and preferences among Japanese students toward themselves and other national and ethnic groups'] (1960) 8 *Kyōiku Shinrigaku Kenkyū* [Japanese journal of educational psychology] 1.

[6] *Ibid.*

[7] Gordon W. Allport, *The Nature of Prejudice*, 25th anniversary ed. (Perseus Books, 1954/1979), 9.

Correspondent to this ambivalence, the affective reaction (i.e. prejudiced emotion) of American college students towards members of these groups was a mixture of admiration and envy.[8] It therefore seems reasonable to include both positive and negative attitudes in the concept of prejudice, although the former often need explicit marks. Similarly, modifiers such as 'faulty' and 'inflexible' are not required in current definitions.

C. *Discrimination*

Discrimination refers to behaviour and is considered distinct from cognitive or affective biases. For example, a Japanese man who dislikes Koreans might avoid becoming friends with them or prevent Koreans from being promoted in an organizational context. In these cases, negative attitudes (i.e. prejudice) result in negative behaviours (i.e. discrimination). However, not all behaviours that are advantageous or disadvantageous to members of certain groups can be called discrimination. John F. Dovidio and colleagues noted that '[discrimination] implies more than simply distinguishing among social objects, but refers also to inappropriate and potentially unfair treatment of individuals due to group membership'.[9] In other words, discrimination connotes inappropriate or potentially unfair behaviour based on certain criteria.

It is worth noting that there is no single criterion of appropriateness or fairness that all people can agree to use in all occasions. One type of criterion is legal regulation (e.g. laws, ordinances, international treaties, and agreements), For example, the International Convention on the Elimination of All Forms of Racial Discrimination (ICERD) defined *racial discrimination* as 'any distinction, exclusion, restriction or preference based on race, colour, descent, or national or ethnic origin' in its Article 1 and declared all states' duty to promote elimination of racial discrimination in Article 2. In other words, some biological or cultural characteristics are explicitly stated as being an inappropriate basis for unequal treatment. Meanwhile, many countries have domestic laws that ban or restrict unequal treatments based on certain biological or cultural

[8] Susan T. Fiske *et al.*, 'A Model of (Often Mixed) Stereotype Content: Competence and Warmth Respectively Follow from Perceived Status and Competition' (2002) 82 *Journal of Personality and Social Psychology* 878.

[9] John F. Dovidio *et al.*, 'Prejudice, Stereotyping and Discrimination: Theoretical and Empirical Overview', in John F. Dovidio *et al.* (eds.), *The Sage Handbook of Prejudice, Stereotyping, and Discrimination* (Sage, 2010), at 8.

characteristics, and legislative status. For example, Japan has the 2016 Hate Speech Elimination Act (HSEA) (with respect to residents' origin), 1985 Equal Employment Opportunity Act (with respect to jobseekers' gender), and so on. However, having a legal system does not necessarily mean that all relevant characteristics are taken into account. Moreover, the legal system itself can often be regarded as having laws that are unfair based on certain criteria – laws that ban same-sex marriage, for example. Discrimination can be endorsed by formal institutional systems.

When the legal system is insufficient or inadequate, the average person's 'good sense' can provide an alternative measure of appropriateness or fairness. The average person's objections (including those of targeted minorities, of course) sometimes mobilize policymakers and contribute to the enactment of new legal standards. However, good sense is not necessarily objective and not everyone can agree on what is appropriate or fair. More important is the fact that, in many cases, discrimination is deeply embedded in societal cultures. For example, the avoidance of *Burakumin* ('Buraku people') in marriage widely exists in Japan even today,[10] even though there are no legal restrictions for cross-class marriage and the hereditary caste system has been long repealed in Japan. When societies approve discrimination, in turn, the legal system can confront such behaviours by restricting unequal treatments or promoting counter-measures. For example, laws based on article 14 of the Japanese Constitution, which declares equality of all people under the law, provide a good basis to counteract discriminatory public mindsets. Philosophical discussion by the experts and voices of people in disadvantaged status might provide other basis of appropriateness and fairness – but they also have difficulties to reach an agreement.

Some behaviours are inappropriate or unfair based on one set of criteria, but are not when based on another set. Likewise, behaviours that one person regards as appropriate can be regarded as inappropriate by others. I am not arguing that all behaviours labelled by some as discrimination are justifiable or that discrimination is based on subjective judgments; my point is that although I use the term 'discrimination' to describe inappropriate or potentially unfair treatments, I also acknowledge the potential difficulties in reaching agreement on which behaviours count as such.

[10] *Buraku* ('hamlet') refers to the areas which those at the bottom of Japan's pre-modern caste system once lived. Naoko Saito, *Kekkonsabetsu no Shakaigaku* [The sociology of marriage discrimination] (Keiso Shobo, 2017).

D. The Relationship between the Three Concepts

I have discussed three important concepts: stereotypes, prejudice, and discrimination. In considering the main theme of this book – hate speech – the most relevant among them is the concept of discrimination, because expressions of hate constitute overt behaviour. This is not to say that the other two concepts are unimportant, of course. In psychology, we think in the following terms: 'People who believe that members of group A have unfavourable attributes will dislike them and as a result place them in disadvantaged positions (stereotype cause prejudice and, in turn, prejudice causes discrimination).'

However, there are other causal relationships that can be surmised from cognitive dissonance theory, which suggests that how people feel tends to be aligned with how they act.[11] In other words, the act of discrimination can give rise to prejudice. This is especially problematic when existing legal systems or cultures justify discrimination. Socially sanctioned discrimination enforces or maintains prejudicial attitudes and, in turn, prejudicial attitudes can drive discriminatory behaviour at the individual level and/or contribute to enforcing or maintaining unfair systems and social norms. Once discriminatory laws are repealed, however, it is possible for prejudice to be reduced, sometimes quickly. For example, Gallup polls show that, in May 2004, slightly before Massachusetts became the first state to allow same-sex couples to register their marriage in the United States, only 42 per cent of US respondents supported same-sex marriage, while the majority, 55 per cent, opposed it. Since 2008, many other US states have legislated same-sex marriage laws and, in 2015, the US Supreme Court ruled that same-sex couples must be guaranteed the same rights as other couples in all states. Consequently, these legal changes increased the number of same-sex marriages in the United States, resulting in a steady increase in support for same-sex marriages since the late 2000s, reaching 67 per cent (vs 31 per cent remaining opposed) in May 2018.[12]

Another important point to understand about discrimination is that discrimination does not always correlate strongly with prejudice or stereotypes. Although the psychological concept of attitude was introduced to capture behavioural predispositions, there are many cases in

[11] Leon Festinger and James M. Carlsmith, 'Cognitive Consequences of Forced Compliance' (1959) 58 *Journal of Abnormal Psychology* 203.

[12] Justine McCarthy, 'Two in Three Americans Support Same-Sex Marriage', *Gallup* (23 May 2018), available at https://news.gallup.com/poll/234866/two-three-americans-support-sex-marriage.aspx [accessed 1 February 2019].

which people behave in incongruent manners compared to their attitudes. For example, even if an individual in Japan is extremely interested in using cocaine, that individual may never act on it because of strict laws prohibiting drug use, as well as intense public denouncements of drug users within Japanese society. In other words, people act not only according to their own attitudes, but also those of others – that is, in adherence to formal or informal social norms.[13] In addition, whether or not there exist opportunities or resources that allow an individual to act on something easily is another important factor.[14] For example, in Japan, smoking is prohibited under the age of 20. Japanese adolescents are unable to purchase cigarettes from stores or vending machines, thus have limited opportunities to engage in the act of smoking. Under such circumstances, adolescents who have a desire to smoke and are unconcerned by social norms may nonetheless end up not smoking because of the lack of opportunities. Meanwhile, those who have just a little interest in smoking but have peers around them who provide them with cigarettes may easily end up taking up smoking to satisfy their curiosity. Thus it is not always the case that stronger attitudes predict stronger or more frequent behaviours.

In the contexts of hate speech, it is important to understand the effects of social norms on the relationship between attitudes and behaviour. On the one hand, those who hold certain prejudices may express them freely if social norms do not prevent them from doing so. Moreover, if it is regarded as desirable to discriminate members of a certain group in a society – that is, if social norms promote discrimination – then those people who previously held no such prejudicial attitudes may behave in a discriminatory manner. On the other hand, if there are strong social norms against discrimination, people may choose not to outwardly express their inner prejudices.

The omnipresence of opportunities for delivering hate speech is another important problem, especially in the Internet age. People can post hate speech online anonymously (i.e. without risking social sanctions for breaching social norms), for little or no cost (e.g. monetary costs of publishing, time required searching for potential targets), at any hour of the day they wish to. Under such circumstances, it is easy to imagine the ease with which Internet users who may not have strong prejudicial

[13] Icek Ajzen, 'The Theory of Planned Behavior' (1991) 50 *Organizational Behavior and Human Decision Processes* 179.

[14] *Ibid.*

attitudes against a certain minority group might post hate speech online. People now have the tools to spread false rumours about certain minority groups without any scrutiny and can come to harass minority groups just for fun or to kill time, without any strong sense of mission. A study that looked at hate crimes found that only a strikingly small percentage of hate crimes – less than 1 per cent – were in fact driven by a strong sense of mission to exclude minorities; rather, the majority of hate crimes (66 per cent) were driven by a desire for excitement or thrill. Offenders in these cases had simply been 'bored' when committing these crimes, and found convenient targets with reference to their own biases and social norms.[15] Likewise, a strong desire to damage and exclude minorities is not needed to prompt someone to post hate speech on the Internet.

E. A Short Summary

I have discussed the basic social psychological concepts relevant to hate speech. Understanding how these concepts are interrelated – especially regarding when and how discrimination and the other components are congruent or incongruent – is useful and informative when discussing laws regulating hate speech.

I will now introduce relevant applied research in the field of hate speech in Japan using these concepts.

II. Applied Research

In this section, I will discuss contributions by social psychological research regarding the racial and ethnic discrimination in Japan. Japanese social psychologists, compared to their counterparts in other parts of the world, have been rather hesitant to study 'delicate' or 'controversial' social issues. One exception is my study on anti-Korean racism that resulted in publication of the book *Reishizumu o Kaibōsuru: Zainichi Korian eno Henken to Intānetto* ('The anatomy of racism: prejudice against Zainichi Koreans in the age of the Internet') in 2015.[16] This book was considered ground-breaking in light of how few

[15] Jack McDevitt, Jack Levin, and Susan Bennett, 'Hate Crime Offenders: An Expanded Typology' (2002) 58 *Journal of Social Issues* 303.

[16] Fumiaki Taka, *Reishizumu o Kaibōsuru: Zainichi Korian eno Henken to Intānetto* [The anatomy of racism: prejudice against Zainichi Koreans in the age of the Internet] (Keiso Shobo, 2015).

psychologists enter this area of research. It has yet to be translated into English and has not been available to the foreign community of prejudice and discrimination scholars. Thus I will start this section by introducing my contribution; then, I will review the literature from within and outside of Japan in the field of social psychology and other disciplines.

A. *Analyses of Racism against Koreans among Japanese Social Media*

(a) An Overview of the Study

Reishizumu o Kaibōsuru contains eight studies, among which the first three (Studies 1–3) quantitatively analysed Japanese tweets (i.e. posts on Twitter, one of the most popular social networking services in Japan) to understand discriminatory climates on the Internet.[17] I will briefly explain Study 1 and its supplemental section, which analysed remarks on Koreans.

Data collection took place between November 2012 and February 2013, and was conducted by using rich site summary (RSS), a technology for accessing regularly changing web content such as Twitter. Searches were conducted on individual tweets using keywords in Japanese such as *Kankoku-jin* ('South Koreans'), *Chōsen-jin* ('Koreans'), '*Zainichi*',[18] and *Chon.*[19] After tweets that included those words but were not relevant to Koreans were deleted, 109,589 tweets were available for analysis.[20] In short, Japanese tweets that explicitly referred to the Koreans were sampled regardless of their residential status (i.e. whether they lived in or outside of Japan). Tweets that referred to specific Korean names or replies for Korean accounts were not collected, although these tweets were obviously relevant to Koreans. During approximately the same period, 114,932 Japanese tweets were collected by using a wildcard search, which means that a certain amount of Japanese tweets were sampled regardless of their relevance to Koreans.

[17] *Ibid.*, ch. 2.

[18] *Zainichi* ('resident in Japan') is commonly used as a single word to mean Zainichi Koreans (Korean residents in Japan). It is also used in other compound nouns that refer to individuals, groups, and organizations, such as *Zainichi Beigun* (US military stationed in Japan).

[19] *Chon*, an abbreviation of *Chōsen-jin*, is a slur used against Koreans.

[20] This was not the whole sample, but a small sample of relevant tweets posted within the data collection period.

(b) Findings about Basic Attributes

First, the rate of retweets was calculated for each sample. 'Retweet' is a unique form of tweet, whereby users share other users' tweets with their own followers. Among Korean-relevant tweets, retweets comprised 44.7 per cent of sampled tweets and 9.4 per cent among wildcard tweets. Thus it was shown that Korean-relevant tweets were more likely to be retweets compared to general Japanese tweets.

The number of accounts included in the Korean-relevant sample was 43,619. Among these accounts, 77.6 per cent were captured only once in the sample, while 0.11 per cent (47 accounts) were captured more than 100 times. The latter accounts posted obviously discriminatory tweets multiple times and the maximum number of captured tweets posted by a single user was 1,644. Judging from their posting frequency and the clients they used to post on Twitter, they seemed to be bots (computer programs designed to automatically post tweets according to certain rules). Meanwhile, the number of followers of these bot accounts ranged from 182 to 15,499, with a median of 2,135. Compared to ordinal Japanese Twitter users, the bots had obtained impressively large numbers of followers.

The share of top accounts that had been captured many times was calculated for Korean-relevant tweets. The top 25 and 50 accounts (0.05 per cent and 0.11 per cent of captured accounts) had posted 10.1 per cent and 12.8 per cent of sampled tweets, respectively. Thus it was evident that a small proportion of users tended to post a large number of tweets.

To evaluate the collected tweets' valence towards Koreans, 150 tweets were randomly sampled from the Korean-relevant sample and evaluated independently by two trained coders. The two evaluations were highly congruent; where evaluations of the tweets differed, the averages of the two were calculated. Of these, 70 per cent was of negative valence, 17.3 per cent positive, and 12.7 per cent neutral or 'cannot be determined'. Composition rates for the entire sample are not exactly the same as these figures and have certain ranges of error because these figures were drawn from a small subsample. However, it is quite obvious that the valence of Korean-relevant tweets were predominantly negative against Koreans.

(c) Findings from Frequently Appearing Codes

Quantitative text analyses of collected tweets were conducted by using KHCoder.[21] After morphological analysis and quantitative tabulations,

[21] Koichi Higuchi, 'A Two-Step Approach to Quantitative Content Analysis: KH Coder Tutorial using Anne of Green Gables' (2016) 52 *Ritsumeikan Social Science Review* 77;

the content of tweets were qualitatively analysed. Table 17.1 is a list of codes applied to a set of Korean-relevant tweets that correspond to certain themes. Some of these themes were drawn from the findings of previous research (i.e. through a top-down approach) and others were

Table 17.1 *Codes applied to various Korean-relevant tweets*

Label	Theme of tweets (Examples of words needed for applying codes)	% among Korean-relevant tweets	% among wildcard tweets
Modern racism	Rights of Koreans frequently noted as 'privilege' (*tokken* ['privilege'], *seikatsu-hogo* ['welfare'], *nenkin* ['pension'])	12.2	0.1
Old-fashioned racism	Inferiority of Koreans in morality and/or ability (*hanzai* ['crime'], *kyōaku* ['vicious'], *gōkan* ['rape'])	10.8	0.3
Historical issues	Historical issues between Japan and Korea (*syokuminchi* ['colony'], *shinryaku* ['invasion'], *ianfu* ['comfort women'])	11.3	0.2
Diplomatic issues	Diplomatic issues between Japan and Korea other than historical issues (*Takeshima, Dokdo, misailu* ['missiles'])	4.5	0.1

Koichi Higuchi, 'A Two-Step Approach to Quantitative Content Analysis: KH Coder Tutorial Using *Anne of Green Gables* (Part II)' (2017) 53 *Ritsumeikan Social Science Review* 137.

Table 17.1 (*cont.*)

Politics	Government, politicians, political parties (*seifu* ['government'], *Jimintō* ['LDP'], *Minsyutō* ['DPJ'])	20.7	0.7
China	China or the Chinese (*Chūgoku* ['China'], *Shina, Shina-jin*[22])	9.0	0.1
Mass-media	Mass-media (not specific media companies) (*masukomi* ['mass communication'], *nyūsu* ['news'], *terebi* ['television'])	9.1	0.7
Enemy of Japan	Anti-Japan agents or organizations (*Han-nichi* ['anti-Japan'], *Baikoku* ['betrayal of Japan'], *Baikoku-do* ['betrayer of Japan'][23])	7.6	<0.1
Hidden truth	Hidden truth that the Japanese should know (*shinjitsu* ['truth'], *giwaku* ['doubt'], *uso* ['lie'])	8.2	0.3

[22] *Shina* is a derogatory noun meaning China. *Shina-jin* means people in or from *Shina*.

[23] *Baikoku-do* has a strong flavour of militarism and fascism, because this word is known to have been used to oppress people who were not devoted subjects of imperial Japan. A couple of decades ago, this word was used mainly in the context of criticism and satire on past Japan. However, today, there are many people who use it to attack those whom they regard as not beneficial to Japan.

Table 17.1 (*cont.*)

Derogatory words	Blatant usage of derogatory words (*baka* ['fool'], *kiseichū* ['parasites'], *gokiburi* ['cockroaches'])	5.0	1.0
2channel	2channel or curator sites of 2channel [*2channel-matome-sites*] (2ch, *sokuhō* ['news flash'],[24] *Nyūsoku*)[25]	5.2	0.3
Call for dissemination	Call for dissemination (*kakusan* ['dissemination'], RT*kibō* [asking for retweet][26])	5.8	0.4
Hashtags	Use of hashtags #, ＃	17.3	6.3

Source: Retrieved and modified from Taka (2015), pp. 38 and 40

drawn from observations of tweets in the sample (i.e. through a bottom-up approach). A necessary condition in applying a code to a tweet was to include at least one conditional word and hence two or more codes may be applied to a single tweet.

Among these codes, 'old-fashioned racism' and 'modern racism' were based on theoretical and empirical analyses by David O. Sears, John B. McConahay, and their colleagues.[27] The distinction between the two types of racism had been proposed and developed to capture the more

[24] In this context, *sokuhō* was used mainly in the names of 2channel-matome blogs.

[25] *Nyūsoku* is the abbreviation of a phrase meaning 'news flash', which refers to *Ita* (a category of bulletin board system) in *2 channel.*

[26] *Kakusan* and RT*kibō* were often used with angle brackets as a call to action for retweeting.

[27] John B. McConahay, 'Modern Racism, Ambivalence, and the Modern Racism Scale', in John F. Dovidio and S. L. Gaertner (eds.), *Prejudice, Discrimination, and Racism* (Academic Press, 1986), ch. 4; David O. Sears, 'Symbolic Racism', in P. A. Katz and D. A. Taylor (eds.), *Eliminating Racism: Profiles in Controversy* (Plenum Press, 1988), ch. 4.

contemporary prejudice against Black people in the United States. They proposed that compared to old-fashioned, blatant racism, which is based on beliefs on inferiority of Black people, racial prejudice in recent years has taken more subtle forms. Specifically, modern or symbolic racism is based on four distinctive but interrelated beliefs:

(1) discrimination has already been resolved;
(2) thus the disadvantaged conditions of Black communities are a direct result of their lack of effort;
(3) meanwhile, Black people have continued protesting against non-existent discriminations; and
(4) as a consequence, Black people have more privileges in society than they deserve.

This type of prejudice can be endorsed and expressed even under the current social norms that restrict racial discrimination because it seems to be based not on antipathy towards the Black communities, but on their breach of individualistic social norms. In other words, modern racism at first glance appears not to be about race or racism. However, it has been shown that this type of racism nevertheless *is* racism.[28]

Although the concept of modern racism originated from research on racism against Black communities in the United States, the same principles were found to apply to prejudice against other types of target (e.g. modern sexism[29] and modern heterosexism[30]). Thus the belief that Black people are afforded privileges seems to reflect not the reality of Black lived experience, but the dominant group's psychological responses to improvements made in guaranteeing rights for people in subordinate or marginalized groups.

Hate speech against Zainichi Koreans today seems to be a combination of modern racism and old-fashioned racism. The 'accusation' that Zainichi Koreans benefit from *Zainichi-Tokken* ('Zainichi Korean privilege') and utterances opposing such imagined privilege are the most prevalent form of hate speech against Zainichi Koreans. This type of hate speech saw a rise in Japanese Internet communities beginning in the

[28] For a review, see David O. Sears and P. J. Henry, 'Over Thirty Years Later: A Contemporary Look at Symbolic Racism' (2005) 37 *Advances in Experimental Social Psychology* 95.

[29] Janet K. Swim *et al.*, 'Sexism and Racism: Old-Fashioned and Modern Prejudices' (1995) 68 *Journal of Personality and Social Psychology* 199.

[30] N. Eugene Walls, 'Toward a Multidimensional Understanding of Heterosexism: The Changing Nature of Prejudice' (2008) 55 *Journal of Homosexuality* 20.

early 2000s, but soon seeped into offline lives. Meanwhile, the more blatant type of racism, which alleges that Zainichi Koreans have lower moral dispositions or inferior abilities, is a more traditional form of prejudice against them, as shown in section I.B. Expression of this blatant type of racism are common within Internet spaces and among messages delivered by xenophobia groups.[31] Thus the codes of both types of racial prejudice were included in analyses.

All codes described in Table 17.1 appeared much more frequently in Korean-relevant tweets than in wildcard tweets and they represent a broad summary of tweets related to Koreans. Tweets that applied 'modern racism' and 'old-fashioned racism' comprised 12.2 per cent and 10.8 per cent, respectively, of the Korean-relevant sample. However, because these codes were applied automatically as the basis of inclusion of some words, not all tweets necessarily contained expressions of prejudice. Importantly, there are users who are critical of racism yet use the same terms as the racists. Thus the valence of these tweets towards Koreans was evaluated with the same method noted above. For tweets that were given a 'modern racism' code, 95.3 per cent, 1.3 per cent, and 3.3 per cent were negative, positive, and neutral or 'cannot be determined', respectively. For 'old-fashioned racism' tweets, they were 91.3 per cent, 2.0 per cent, and 6.7 per cent, in the same order. Thus tweets that were given racism codes were overwhelmingly constituted by negative tweets. In other words, most of them were expression of racial prejudice, rather than mere mentions of racism-relevant words. In addition, many tweets that contained obviously derogatory words such as 'fool', 'parasites', 'cockroaches', and so on, are clearly considered discriminatory as well.

Frequent mentions of historical issues and other diplomatic issues may be important to note. Japanese sociologist Naoto Higuchi pointed out, through findings mainly from qualitative studies, that the xenophobic climate in Japan was closely linked to East Asian geopolitics.[32] Interest in these issues may give rise to antipathy towards Koreans, especially during periods when international conflicts intensify.

A striking finding is the frequent appearance of 'enemy of Japan' and 'hidden-truth' codes. The former includes offensive words that were used during Japan's imperial rule and show intolerance towards those who are seen as not beneficial to Japan. The tweets that were given the latter codes

[31] See Chapters 5 and 18.

[32] Naoto Higuchi, *Nihongata Haigaishugi: Zaitokukai, Gaikokujinsanseiken, Higashi Ajia Chiseigaku* [Japan's ultra-right: Zaitkukai, foreigner's suffrage and East Asian geopolitics] (Nagoya University Press, 2014).

of 'hidden truth', which represents beliefs whereby the Japanese had the truth hidden from them and have now uncovered it. In other words, the code implies a strong suspicion of socially accepted truth and strong trust of an alternative interpretation (what the alleged truths were will be discussed later). These two findings illustrate the rising political polarization and a 'Post-Truth Era' in Japan.

There are two codes that relate to different types of media in Table 17.1. The first type is 'mass media'; the other is '2channel' – the most popular and well-known anonymous bulletin board system site in Japan during the data collection period,[33] which resembles 4chan in the English Internet sphere. Because of the anonymity of users and a passive administrative stance in relation to cyber-bullying and harassment, 2channel has been a major centre of online discrimination since around 2000. *2channel matome-sites*, or curator sites, are names for another type of social media, many of which are in the form of blogs that extract posts from 2channel and edit them (e.g. rearrange, add colour, or increase text size) to make their meaning clearer and more appealing. Many 2channel matome-sites run articles that seek to belittle, insult, or intimidate of groups or individuals of minority status.[34]

Other noteworthy codes were 'call for dissemination' and 'hashtags'. The former literally means posts asking other users to retweet them; the hashtag is another function of Twitter, which makes it easier to find and share tweets on certain themes with other users. In conjunction with the finding that Korean-relevant tweets are more likely to be retweets than wildcard tweets, tweets that refer to Koreans tended to be posted with an obvious intention to disseminate or share them among other users – an intention that was fulfilled.

'China' was the only code that referred to states or regions other than Korea and Japan. Frequent appearance of this code among a Korean-relevant sample implies that the Japanese feel antipathy towards East Asian countries, and associate them in similar ways.

Findings from the Co-occurrence of Codes I also analysed the co-occurrence of these codes. The codes in Table 17.1 applied most frequently were 'politics' and 'hashtags'. These codes co-occurred with each other, and both codes co-occurred frequently with codes 'modern racism' and 'enemy of Japan'. These associations imply that a lot of tweets claiming that some

[33] 2channel was renamed 5channel in 2017 and a clone site is now called 2channel instead.
[34] See Chapter 18.

political agent (e.g. the government,[35] political parties, or politicians) was acting to enhance Zainichi Koreans' privilege instead of the interests of the Japanese and that any such agent was anti-Japan or betraying Japan, were posted with the intention that other users would share them.

The code 'call for dissemination', which is relevant to interaction among users besides 'hashtags', also co-occurred with 'modern racism'. Thus the expression of modern racism was especially likely to be accompanied by intention to disseminate among other users.

Another code that frequently co-occurred with 'call for dissemination' was 'hidden truth'. 'Hidden truth', in turn, co-occurred also with the 'historical issues' and 'old-fashioned racism' codes. The former association implies that alleged 'truths' hidden were likely to be about historical issues. It appeared in tweets that demonstrated leanings towards historical revisionism. For example, users were claiming that Japan's 'wartime crimes' were not actually crimes but were appropriate behaviours, or that Japan's colonial rule was in fact merciful and beneficial to Korea. When it came to the association with 'old-fashioned racism', the 'hidden truths' code appeared in tweets that claimed to uncover Koreans' 'criminal nature'. Many of these tweets accused Koreans of being criminals, regardless of whether or not the crimes to which they referred had actually been committed by a Korean.

This 'hidden truth' code co-occurred also with two media codes (i.e. 'mass media' and '2channel'). However, when qualitatively interpreted, these two types of media were associated with 'hidden truth' in different ways. On the one hand, the mass media was frequently referred to as an agency that hides the truth. According to associations with other codes, the truths that mass media were alleged to hide were especially about issues relevant to old-fashioned racism and historical issues. For example, users would claim that the mass media had hid the 'true' ethnic nature of Koreans as vicious criminals or that they unfairly blamed Japan for 'fake' wartime crimes. On the other hand, 2channel and 2channel-matome-sites were frequently referred to as information sources (in many cases, reference to these websites included names of the sites, hashtags relevant to them, and web addresses). In other words, many Twitter users claimed that they had learned the truth from these media. It seems rather ludicrous to distrust the mass media, which is run by well-trained experts, and to trust instead non-trained, unauthorized

[35] Until late-December, 2012, the government was led by Prime Minister Noda, who belonged to the Democratic Part of Japan (DPJ).

incognitos. However, this may be one of the most significant aspects of the Post-Truth Era in and outside Japan.

Finally, the 'modern racism' code co-occurred also with 'historical issues' and 'old-fashioned racism'. The former association appeared in tweets that had claimed the protection of Zainichi Koreans' rights in Japan to be fundamentally unjustifiable because the Japanese do not have any responsibility for the past. The latter association was evident in tweets claiming that Zainichi Koreans have the privilege of being able to hide their true names and identities when they commit crimes.

(d) Other Studies and Implications

Study 3 collected Japanese tweets posted between March 2012 and February 2013 which included the word *Nihon-jin* ('the Japanese').[36] Among this sample, the rate of tweets that also referred to Korea and the Koreans was 11.9 per cent. This exceeded those mentioning China and Chinese (6.2 per cent), the United States and Americans (4.1 per cent), and other states and regions (each of which was less than 1.3 per cent). This implies that the most salient outgroup for the Japanese when they think about their own group was the Koreans and not the Americans, at least during the data collection period. Japan has maintained by far the closest relationship with the United States in the economic, diplomatic, and military fields, and it is beyond question that Americans had been the most salient 'other' for the Japanese for many decades. However, it seems that the situation is different in today's Japanese Internet age.

With regards to studies conducted by other scientists, Kyongho Cho, a sociologist in Japan, analysed tweets about foreigners posted in Japanese language immediately after the 2016 Kumamoto Earthquake.[37] In short, he found that a small proportion of captured accounts (3.8 per cent) had posted a large proportion of captured tweets (25.0 per cent), which was quite similar to my own finding.

In another study, Cho analysed users' comments on *Yahoo! News*, the most famous news portal site in the Japanese Internet sphere.[38] Users are

[36] Taka, note 16, section 4 in ch. 2.

[37] Kyongho Cho, 'Intānettojō no Saigaiji "Gaikokujin Hanzai" no Ryūgen ni Kansuru Kenkyū: Kumamoto Jishin Hassei Chokugo no Tsuittā no Keiryōtekisutobunseki' ['A study of groundless rumours of "crimes by foreigners" on the Internet during disasters: quantitative text analysis of Twitter after the Kumamoto Earthquake'] (2018) 60 *Ōyō Shakaigaku Kenkyū* [Journal of applied sociology] 79.

[38] Kyongho Cho, 'Intānettojō ni Okeru Korian ni Taisuru Reishizumu to Taisaku no Kōka: "Yahoo! Nyūsu" no Komento Dēta no Keiryōtekisutobunseki' ['Quantitative text analysis

able to post their own comments if news providers allow them to and these comments are shown below the original news articles. Cho was given comments posted in July 2016 and sampled Korean-relevant ones from among them. Again, he found that a small proportion of sampled accounts (1.0 per cent) had posted a large proportion of Korean-relevant comments (25 per cent). In addition, he found that approximately 90 per cent of the sampled comments had negative valence against Koreans and that almost all of the codes shown in Table 17.1 could be applied to large numbers of Korean-relevant comments on *Yahoo! News*. The few exceptions were either absent or comprised only a small proportion of 'hashtags', 'dissemination', and '2channel' codes. The results regarding the former two codes may simply be because *Yahoo! News* does not provide hashtags or retweet-like functions. This study implies that the frequent themes that appeared in Korean-relevant tweets were rather similar to those appearing in other social media outlets in Japan.

Although Cho made no any clear suggestions about whether or not the 'heavy users' among his samples were bots, some studies on tweets about different issues in different states agreed on the significance of bot accounts in political discourse (e.g. the 2014 general election in Japan,[39] the 2016 Brexit referendum in the United Kingdom,[40] the 2016 presidential election in the United States).[41] Bot accounts had created a large proportion of traffic relevant to these issues, and they were often responsible for spreading misinformation and extreme political attitudes.

It is worth noting that the notion of the 'marketplace of ideas' does not always work as expected. If people were to select ideas based on informational validity, it would work – but information often undergoes

of "Yafū! Nyūsu": focusing on comments on Koreans'] (2017) 59 *Ōyō Shakaigaku Kenkyū* [Journal of applied sociology] 113.

39 Fabian Schäfer, Stefan Evert, and Philipp Heinrich, 'Japan's 2014 General Election: Political Bots, Right-Wing Internet Activism, and Prime Minister Shinzo Abe's Hidden Nationalist Agenda' (2017) 5 *Big Data* 294.

40 Philip N. Howard and Bence Kollanyi, 'Bots, #StrongerIn, and #Brexit: Computational Propaganda during the UK–EU Referendum', Working Paper No. 2016.1, *Oxford Project on Computational Propaganda* (21 June 2016), available at https://comprop.oii.ox.ac.uk/research/bots-strongerin-and-brexit-computational-propaganda-during-the-uk-eu-referendum/ [accessed 15 February 2019].

41 Bence Kollanyi, Philip N. Howard, and Samuel C. Woolley, 'Bots and Automation over Twitter during the U.S. Election', Data Memo 2016.4, *Oxford Project on Computational Propaganda* (17 November 2016), available at https://comprop.oii.ox.ac.uk/research/working-papers/bots-and-automation-over-twitter-during-the-u-s-election/ [accessed 15 February 2019].

emotional selection, rather than informational selection, and memes that inspire strong emotion win out regardless of their validity.[42] In such a situation, what is advantageous are extremeness, shamelessness, and persistence, and not integrity, thoughtfulness, or cautiousness.

These and my findings imply that bots and bot-like people can distort political discourse and harm democracy. With regards to racism, it was revealed that exposure to hate speech increases prejudice against targeted groups.[43] However, not all users are exposed directly to hate speech created by bots or bots-like human users. The maximum number of followers of presumed bot accounts in my sample, one of which had posted Korean-relevant tweets most frequently, exceeded 15,000. Although this figure is large enough to be made by those who automatically spread hate, this was only a small part of Twitter users in Japan (estimated to be approximately 18 million in 2013).[44]

There might nonetheless be a large problem. According to Nicholas Christakis and James Fowler's review, beliefs, attitudes, and behaviours can be transmitted indirectly, person to person via other people even with three or more order effects.[45] Misinformation and negative attitudes can be transmitted from bots and bot-like users to vast amounts of other users through indirect means. Showers of hate speech can weaken perceived social norms that otherwise suppress discrimination, regardless of whether or not the perceiver is exposed directly to the speech. Thus it is possible that a relatively small number of accounts, including bots, bias the entire Internet community using the same language towards creating a discriminatory climate.

In short, quantitative analyses of my studies and those of other researchers have revealed the prevalence of discrimination on the Internet in Japan, and thus raise our awareness of this alarming situation, pointing towards a gloomy future.

[42] Chip Heath, Chris Bell, and Emily Sternberg, 'Emotional Selection in Memes: The Case of Urban Legends' (2001) 81 *Journal of Personality and Social Psychology* 1028.

[43] Wiktor Soral, Michal Bilewicz, and Mikołaj Winiewski, 'Exposure to Hate Speech Increases Prejudice through Desensitization' (2018) 44 *Aggressive Behavior* 136.

[44] Statista Research Department, 'Number of Twitter Users in Japan from 2013 to 2021', *Statista* (24 September 2019), available at www.statista.com/statistics/381839/twitter-users-japan/ [accessed 16 February 2019].

[45] Nicholas Christakis and James Fowler, *Connected: The Amazing Power of Social Networks and How They Shape Our Lives*, Epub ed. (HarperCollins, 2009).

B. *Analyses of the Effects of Internet Usage on Prejudice*

(a) The Internet and Racial Prejudice

If there are large amounts of hateful content on the Internet, then, does Internet usage come to be associated with prejudice in the users' minds?

An early investigation regarding this issue looked at prejudice against Black communities in the United States. Debra B. Melican and Travis L. Dixon assessed respondents' prejudice, using the Modern Racism Scale, comparing the credibility of different news sources on the Internet: online traditional news associated with mass communication (CNN, NY Times, etc.), and non-traditional news outlets.[46] They found that those who trust non-traditional news outlets more than traditional media scored higher on the Modern Racism Scale.

In terms of racism in Japan, in 2010 my Study 6 investigated the relationship between Japanese university students' racial prejudice against Zainichi Koreans and media usage by means of a self-reporting questionnaire.[47] Measures of racial prejudice were threefold: the Modern Racism Scale; the Old-Fashioned Racism Scale; and a Feeling Thermometer. The former two were developed by McConahay,[48] and then modified and adapted to the context of racism against Zainichi Koreans by Taka and Amemiya.[49] Compared to the two scales, which measure racial prejudice based on specific beliefs, as described in section II.A(c), the 'Feeling Thermometer' can be regarded as a measure of relatively pure emotional response (e.g. like–dislike, warm–cold). Among these measures, the Modern Racism Scale is that which especially relates to the cognitive, rather than affective, aspects of prejudice.[50] Variables of media usage were time spent on the Internet and television per day, and reading or not reading newspaper(s) more than once a week.

Correlation analysis and structural equation modelling (SEM) analysis revealed that Internet usage was especially associated with the strength of

46 Debra B. Melican and Travis L. Dixon, 'News on the Net: Credibility, Selective Exposure, and Racial Prejudice' (2008) 35 *Communication Research* 151.

47 Taka, note 16, section 1 in ch. 4.

48 McConahay, note 22.

49 Fumiaki Taka and Yuri Amemiya, 'Zainichi Korian ni Taisuru Kotenteki/Gendaiteki Reishizumu ni Tsuite no Kisoteki Kentō' ['A basic investigation of old-fashioned and modern racisms against Zainichi Koreans'] (2013) 28 *Research in Social Psychology* 67; Fumiaki Taka, 'Zainichi Korian ni Taisuru Kotenteki/Gendaiteki Reishizumu Shakudo no Kakuninteki Inshibunseki to Kisoteki na Kentō' ['Confirmatory factor analysis and basic investigations of old-fashioned and modern racism scales against Zainichi Koreans'] (2013) 180 *Studies in Humanities* 69.

50 McConahay, note 22; Taka, note 48.

modern racism. The association between old-fashioned racism and Internet usage was statistically significant in the correlational analysis, but marginal in the SEM analysis. The feeling thermometer showed no significant association with Internet usage in either analysis. This implies that the effects of Internet usage are primarily cognitive. In other words, the Internet might alter users' belief structures by transmitting information or stereotypes, and effects on emotional aspects are secondary if any.

Another interesting finding from this study was that Internet usage was associated with social dominance orientation (SDO), but not right-wing authoritarianism (RWA). The former is the tendency to justify inequalities among groups;[51] the latter is the tendency to submit to authority, to aggressively challenge those who do not submit to authorities, and to observe conventions.[52] These two were originally proposed as personality traits, but recent social psychologists have come to regard them as ideologies, which are based on both personalities and beliefs in the nature of the social world.[53] Although both form the basis of attitudes such as prejudice against various kinds of minorities and support for conservative policies, they are distinctive concepts: SDO corresponds to economic conservatism; RWA, to cultural conservatism. With regard to prejudice, SDO predicts prejudice against 'derogated' people and RWA predicts prejudice against 'dangerous' people.[54]

The discriminatory climate on the Internet in Japan in recent years seems to be well understood from this association between Internet usage and SDO. Today, many minorities other than Zainichi Koreans, such as women, immigrants, LGBTQ+ people, people on welfare, and disabled people, are typical targets of hate speech on the Internet in Japan (and in other countries). The common characteristics of these targeted groups are perceived low-quality or competence. In other words, these are people whom one can easily derogate. Thus hate speech on the Internet seems to be related to SDO rather than RWA, although the causal relationships (i.e. high SDO among Internet users inducing hate speech against these groups on the Internet, the rampancy of hate speech on the

[51] Felicia Pratto *et al.*, 'Social Dominance Orientation: A Personality Variable Predicting Social and Political Attitudes' (1994) 67 *Journal of Personality and Social Psychology* 741.

[52] Bob Altemeyer, *The Authoritarian Specter* (Harvard University Press, 1996).

[53] John Duckitt, 'A Dual-Process Cognitive-Motivational Theory of Ideology and Prejudice' (2001) 33 *Advances in Experimental Social Psychology* 41.

[54] John Duckitt and Chris G. Sibley, 'Right-Wing Authoritarianism, Social Dominance Orientation and the Dimensions of Generalized Prejudice' (2007) 21 *European Journal of Personality* 113.

Internet strengthening Internet users' SDO, or other mechanisms) have not yet been clarified.

The amount of time spent watching television was not significantly associated with prejudice or ideology measures and reading newspapers was positively associated only with RWA.

In Study 7, I investigated which kinds of websites and web services especially predicted prejudice against Zainichi Koreans among university students in 2013.[55] The study revealed that stronger prejudice in one or more measures among three (i.e. the Modern Racism Scale, the Old-fashioned Racism Scale, the Feeling Thermometer) are predicted by use of 2channel-matome-blogs and shorter use of social networking services.[56] Again, the importance of 2channel-matome-blogs had been likewise indicated by findings from analyses of tweets. Some of my follow-up studies (not yet published) have used online questionnaire methods to focus on determining the causal relationships and identifying mediating or moderating effects of suspicion on mass media.

(b) The Internet and *Netto-Uyoku*

Before I published my 2015 book, Daisuke Tsuji, a Japanese sociologist, had investigated the nature of *Netto-Uyoku* ('Net Far-Right') by administering an online survey among adult Japanese.[57] He found that 1.3 per cent of his sample matched his operational definition of Netto-Uyoku and 3.1 per cent matched when a broader definition was used. Respondents who had similar attitudes as Netto-Uyoku (e.g. unfavourable attitudes towards Korea and China, support for a public visit to the Yasukuni Shrine by government officials), but did not meet the operational definition for the behavioural dimension (e.g. having voiced their opinions or thoughts on other people's blogs in the past year), and whom he thus called latent supporters of Netto-Uyoku, counted 2.8 per cent or 8.3 per cent of his sample, depending on narrower and broader definitions, respectively. He also found that users characterized as Netto-Uyoku evidence stronger distrust of the mass media and tend to be users of 2channel, while frequently using the Internet in other ways (e.g. to send emails).

[55] Taka, note 16, section 2 in ch. 4.

[56] In this survey, Twitter usage was measured independently from other social networking services, such as Facebook.

[57] Daisuke Tsuji, 'Kenkyūshitsu kara no Media Ripōto: Chōsa Dēta kara Saguru "Netto Uyoku" no Jittai' ['Characteristics of the Japanese alt-right: a survey report'] (2009) 226 *Journalism* 62.

Tsuji conducted an online survey again in 2014 and published the results in 2017.[58] He found that the ratio of Netto-Uyoku had not significantly increased between 2007 and 2014, and he inferred that such users comprised less than 1 per cent of Japanese Internet users in general. However, he also found that latent support of Netto-Uyoku had dramatically increased (a 174 per cent gain) during the same period. In other words, although the ratio of Japanese Internet users who were actively voicing their opinions had not increased, Internet users' attitudes had leaned in that direction. Among attitude measures, unfavourable attitudes towards Korea and China had especially gained in popularity. Another important finding is that although Netto-Uyoku tend to use various kinds of website, frequency of usage of 2channel and 2channel-matome-sites predicted a xenophobic attitude and the effect of time spent using the Internet in general ceased when this factor was put into analysis.

In an even more recent study, Tsuji investigated the causal relationships between Internet usage and xenophobic attitudes among the Japanese by using an instrumental variable method.[59] He found that Internet usage increased not only negative attitudes towards immigrants, but also positive attitudes.

In short, Japanese Internet communities can be associated with xenophobic attitudes in Japan and at least one study indicated that this association was causal rather than merely correlative. However, not all Internet use increases xenophobic attitudes and the strengthening effects of Internet usage are not limited to negative attitudes. Discourse on hate speech on the Internet will be more effective when we discover when, how, and for whom exposure to information on the Internet has unfavourable effects.

III. Conclusion

In this chapter, I have described various scientific studies on intergroup phenomena relevant to hate speech issues, especially those that occur in

[58] Daisuke Tsuji, 'Keiryō Chōsa kara Miru "Netto Uyoku" no Purofairu: 2007nen/2014nen Webu Chōsa no Bunseki Kekka o Moto ni' ['A profile of "Net Far-Right": quantitative data analysis of online questionnaire surveys in 2007 and 2014'] (2017) 38 *Nenpō Ningen Kagaku* [Annals of human sciences] 211.

[59] Daisuke Tsuji, 'Intānetto Riyō wa Hitobito no Haigaiishiki o Takameru ka: Sōsahensūhō o Mochiita Ingakōka no Suitei' ['Does use of the Internet make people more racist? A causal analysis based on a synchronous effects model using the instrumental variable method'] (2018) 63 *Soshioroji* [Sociology] 3.

Japan. Discussion of the basic concepts of prejudice and discrimination showed the importance of social norms and opportunities. Not every individual who holds prejudices or negative stereotypes delivers hate speech, but those who have only a little prejudice or negative stereotypes may do so under some conditions. How norms and opportunities are provided is a practical question. Adequate legislative regulations can provide social norms that restrain discrimination and reduce the opportunities to easily deliver hate speech, although there might be some problems that should be resolved before Japan enacts such.

Applied research successfully demonstrated the xenophobic climate of Japanese Internet communities. Most of the Korean-relevant tweets and comments on a news portal have negative valence towards Koreans. Among Korean-relevant tweets, frequent expressions of old-fashioned racism and modern racism were evident. Other themes frequently appeared in Korean-relevant tweets composed by hate-oriented complexes of beliefs and attitudes. Service providers have failed or been unmotivated to address this rampant spread of hate speech.

In addition, exposure to some information sources on the Internet above others have detrimental effects: 2channel and 2channel-matome-blogs. There are analogues of 2channel that use languages other than Japanese, such as 4chan and 8chan (the latter have been expelled from the global web community after the El Paso mass shooting in August 2019). Anonymous online communities can easily turn hateful if administrators do not take a sufficiently active role. Curator sites[60] are run by drives different from anonymous bulletin board system sites. Contents creators of curator sites extract and arrange information from other sources, and most of them earn advertising fees per hit. They are therefore incentivized to disseminate evocative (mis)information. One cannot doubt there are some sites that are paid to do so for some political purposes.

Although freedom of speech is essential to democracy, the notion of the 'marketplace of ideas' often fails because of its very nature. Ideas win out when they induce strong emotion and not because they are valid or reasonable. Relatively small numbers of social networking service users who post persistently, including bots, can overwhelm others. Thus the marketplace of ideas is susceptible to propaganda. When such propaganda is directed towards minorities and wielded for other anti-

[60] Although *matome-sites* ('curator sites') approximately corresponded to *2channel-matome-blog* ('curator sites of 2channel') when I conducted the surveys described in this chapter, many of them take other forms today; some extract information from websites other than 2channel (e.g. Twitter, blogs) and are not blogs.

democratic purposes, Information Age societies can be easily exploited. We need to put in place defence measures that are not limited to enacting more law regulations.

Thus far, I have discussed the phenomena of hate speech on the Internet. This is simply because the previous social psychological research relevant to hate speech in Japan has focused on these phenomena, because the content and effects of hate speech on the Internet can be easily analysed quantitatively. However, it is important to note that hate speech is not limited to online phenomena. Furthermore, some components of hate speech on the Internet are supported or promoted by Japanese authoritative figures. Historical revisionism, oversimplified perception which categorizes people into pro- and anti-Japan, slander against the mass media, and allegations that minorities have 'too many' rights characterize not only online discourse, but also political discourse in the real world in Japan today. Rampant hate speech delivered incognito on the Internet has evolved alongside a political discourse delivered by right-wing authorities and media. To date, social psychologists studying Japanese society have not sufficiently investigated these offline phenomena; future research should seek to do so – and to reveal the interrelationship of online and offline hate speech.

PART VI

Current Issues

18

Hate Speech on the Internet

KAZUSHI OGURA

I. Introduction

In recent years, the number of Internet users has increased in Japan, partly owing to the provision of services by Internet Initiative Japan, which was the first to promote its Internet connection service in 1993. In 1997, the number of users was 11.55 million and the population penetration rate was 9.2 per cent. By 2003, that number had grown to 77.3 million users and a population penetration rate of 64.3 per cent. The number of users climbed to 100.84 million people by the end of 2016, corresponding to a population penetration rate of 83.5 per cent.[1] As is the case of many Western countries, Japan is designated an 'Internet developed country'. According to data from the World Economic Forum last updated (at time of writing) in December 2019, Japan ranked 12th in the world in terms of its IT industry's international competitiveness. Among the G7 countries, it ranked fourth, after the United States, Germany, and the United Kingdom.[2]

This study focuses on the struggle to deal with hate speech (particularly that targeting Koreans living in Japan) and discriminatory expressions on the Internet, including concrete examples and an examination of the basic measures that Japan needs to put in place to address this problem. It should be noted that discriminatory expressions related to the *Burakumin* ('Buraku people'[3]) have been a problem in Japan since feudal times and discussion of discriminatory expressions against them forms the basis of the current debate on hate speech. While this chapter uses both 'hate speech' and 'discriminatory expression' to highlight these

[1] Ministry of Internal Affairs and Communications, *Heisei 29nendoban Jōhō Tsūshin Hakusyo* [Information communication White Paper] (Nikkei Insatsu, 2017), 282.

[2] 'IT Competitiveness International Ranking', *Global Note* (25 December 2019), available at www.globalnote.jp/post-1523.html [accessed 15 September 2020].

[3] *Buraku* ('hamlet') refers to those areas in which, historically, groups at the bottom of the pre-modern Japanese caste system lived. See Chapter 4.

problems, we would like to emphasize that we do not consider the two terms to be equivalent in meaning and impact.[4]

II. Specific Examples Related to the Internet

A. *The Situation to the Present Day*

Discriminatory expressions in Japan have often targeted the Burakumin. What follows are examples of problematic online communications involving such discrimination. In 1994, there was a case involving an attempt to identify the locations of Buraku in Ishikawa Prefecture on the bulletin board system NIFTY-serve; this occurred again in 1995. In a 1997 case, a person impersonating a Fukuoka City staff member sent an email that included discriminatory expressions, which was later posted on NIFTY-serve. Moreover, in 1989, there were cases in which lists of Buraku were circulated, along with discriminatory expressions in Osaka and Wakayama Prefectures, using amateur radio.[5]

In a case dating from 1996, in the early days of the Internet, discriminatory expressions targeting the Burakumin were posted on an electronic bulletin board operated by the Osaka University Buraku Liberation Research Association. A year later, discriminatory expressions targeting Burakumin, Koreans living in Japan, and people with disabilities were posted on the website of the Yamato Race Protection Group.[6] In addition, there are many examples involving:

- the exposure and identification of Burakumin individuals, aiming to cause them shame;
- references to Burakumin as 'not human', or the targeting of Burakumin and Koreans living in Japan with expressions such as 'Die!' and 'Exterminate them!'; and
- the circulation of information identifying specific Burakumin and Koreans living in Japan, putting those individuals at risk of harassment and violence.[7]

[4] In Japan, defamation and insult towards the Burakumin were called 'discriminatory expression' until recently, but the phrase 'hate speech' is now widely used.

[5] Kenzo Tomonaga, 'Intānetto to Buraku Sabetsu' ['Internet discrimination against the Burakumin'] (1997) 117 *Gekkan Hyūman Raitsu* [Human rights monthly] 16, at 17.

[6] *Yamato* is the ethnicity of the Japanese majority.

[7] Kazushi Ogura, *Saibāsupēsu to Hyōgen no Jiyū* [Cyberspace and freedom of expression] (Shogakusha, 2007), 191–92.

These types of hate speech and discriminatory expressions continue on the Internet. Notably, quantitative and qualitative changes can be seen increasingly on large Internet bulletin boards. Discriminatory websites are using a wider range of media, and video-upload sites are increasingly being used to spread hate speech and other discriminatory activities. For example, the 2channel[8] forum became the focus of attention in May 2000 in the wake of a criminal declaration posted on the site in discussion of the hijacking of a bus in Fukuoka, commonly known as the Nishitetsu busjacking incident.[9] This incident triggered criticism that discriminatory expressions formerly seen only on individual websites and bulletin boards had inappropriately migrated to the public 2channel site, and that, because 2channel was lax about its administrative responsibilities for discriminatory posts, there was also a shift towards relaxing anti-discrimination policies on other Internet bulletin boards, such as megaBBS and Yahoo![10]

It has been indicated that technology has allowed discriminatory expression to appeal increasingly visually, such as with images, video data, and Google Maps street view. An example is the 2006 case in which detailed maps of Buraku in Aichi Prefecture, photographs of residences and factories in the districts, and videos filmed from bicycles were posted on a website along with discriminatory text. Subsequently, the creator was convicted and imprisoned for a year, with an additional four-year suspended sentence for the crime of defamation. Another case occurred in Sumida Ward, Tokyo, where photographs of Buraku houses and factories were posted along with discriminatory text on a website launched in March 2007. There were also cases in Tottori Prefecture, where the locations were displayed using the 'My Maps' function of Google Maps, with discriminatory text added in the explanations.[11]

Furthermore, there was recently a case in which the Cabinet Office removed the discriminatory and defamatory posts on the website of

[8] 2channel (now 5channel) is Japan's most popular Internet bulletin board service.

[9] A 17-year-old boy hijacked the Nishitetsu bus, and three passengers were killed and injured.

[10] Shigeshi Tabata, 'Zōkasuru Sabetsujirei to Tōmen no Kadai' ['Increasing discrimination-related incidents and immediate tasks'] (2008) 599 *Buraku Kaihō* [Buraku liberation] 92.

[11] Calls for the Establishment of Buraku Liberation and Human Rights Policy, *Zenkoku no Aitsugu Sabetsujiken* [Discrimination cases nationwide] (Kaiho Shuppansha, 2008), 83–85 and 90; Calls for the Establishment of Buraku Liberation and Human Rights Policy, *Zenkoku no Aitsugu Sabetsujiken* [Discrimination cases nationwide] (Kaiho Shuppansha, 2011), 14–15 and 97. More recently, there have been cases of discriminatory posts regarding Ainu on blog sites and Twitter.

monitors on national policy that was established to solicit opinions from the public.[12] On the website Roundup, the administrator quoted posts from 2channel and Twitter that were defamatory and discriminatory on the basis of ethnicity, targeting a freelance writer who is Korean living in Japan, and the court held the administrator liable for damages, ordering the site to pay ¥2 million in compensation.[13] There is also a case in which the crime of defamation was applied to find an individual liable for damages of ¥100,000 for posting defamatory remarks based on ethnicity at 2channel targeting Koreans resident in Okinawa.[14]

B. *Recent Court Rulings*

In recent times, problems related to hate speech and discriminatory expressions on the Internet have made their way into the courts. The cases that follow are not cases of discriminatory expressions simply being posted on the Internet, but are examples of public demonstrations or rallies that have taken place in offline contexts and have subsequently been filmed, photographed, and uploaded to video-sharing sites.

(a) *Suiheisha Museum*

In January 2011, executives of an ultranationalist group calling itself *Zainichi Tokken wo Yurusanai Shimin no Kai* ('the Association of Citizens against the Special Privileges of Koreans Living in Japan') (*Zaitokukai* for short), issued a declaration of their views while they were gathered in front of Suiheisha Museum in Gosho City, Nara Prefecture, which was hosting a special exhibit called 'Korea and Japan: 100 Years since Korean Unification'. Zaitokukai's statement was to the effect that the exhibition included erroneous information, particularly in relation to the 'comfort women'.[15] In addition, the group's statements included slander against Koreans living in Japan and North Korea, as well

12 'Naikakufu Saito ni "Zainichikankokujin Tatakidase" ' [' "Kick out Koreans living in Japan" on the Cabinet Office's website'], *Hokkaido Shimbun*, 2 May 2018 (Evening edition).

13 Osaka District Court, 16 November 2017, 2372 Hanji 59; Osaka High Court, 28 June 2018, unreported; Supreme Court, 3rd Petty Bench, 11 December 2018, unreported.

14 'Netto no Heito Tōkō ni Hatsu no Shobatsu' ['First punishment for posting hate speech on the Internet'], *Abema Times* (8 February 2019), available at https://abematimes.com/posts/5687925?categoryIds=537591 [accessed 4 March 2019].

15 'Comfort women' were women who were forced to provide sexual services to soldiers during World War II.

as discriminatory expressions against Suiheisha Museum[16] and Burakumin. The group also made a video of its discriminatory protest and uploaded it to YouTube, where hundreds of thousands of people viewed it. Later, the Museum filed a lawsuit seeking damages from the group.

Nara District Court indicated that words such as *eta* ('people working with carcasses') and *hinin* ('non-humans'), which are used to defame or insult the Burakumin, constitute unfair discriminatory terms. It held that, '[c]onsidering the purpose and activity of the plaintiffs and the timing and location of the defendants' behaviour, it is reasonable to assume that the defendants' behaviour was equivalent to defamation of the plaintiff', and that 'tangible and intangible damage to the plaintiff was caused by the illegal acts of the defendants'. The court awarded ¥1.5 million to the plaintiff.[17] Thus the court affirmed that discriminatory expressions are illegal under the Japanese Civil Code and that the amount of compensation in such instances should be high compared with that in other cases involving intangible damage. This court ruling has acted as a precedent in subsequent cases.[18]

(b) *Kyoto Korean Elementary School*

In December 2009, and again in January and March 2010, members of Zaitokukai staged an aggressive demonstration near Kyoto Korean First Elementary School in Fushimi Ward, Kyoto City, which included the use of discriminatory expressions and a notable display of force. A video was uploaded on YouTube and Niconico, a Japanese video-sharing service. Kyoto Korean Gakuen, the corporation that operates the school, sued for the restitution of damages and to curtail future demonstrative activities.

Kyoto District Court found that this demonstration and the released videos that showed illegal acts were highly detrimental to the dignity of the subjects and disturbed the educational work of the school. Further, the videos were held to contribute to the exclusion of Koreans living in Japan based on their ethnic origin. Because these factors imply an

[16] This museum has kept and exhibited the materials of Zenkokusuiheisha, which was established in March 1922 and which has taken the lead in the Buraku Liberation Movement.

[17] Nara District Court, 25 June 2012, unreported.

[18] Masaaki Furukawa, 'Suiheisha Hakubutsukan Sabetsu Gaisen Jiken' [Discrimination incident that occurred in the street protests in front of the Suiheisha Museum'], in Akira Maeda (ed.), *Naze Ima Heito Supīchi Nanoka* [Hate speech: why now?] (Sanichi Shobo, 2013), 66–78.

intention to hinder the enjoyment of human rights, fundamental freedoms, and equality for Koreans living in Japan, the court ruled that there were grounds for claiming illegal racial discrimination, as described in Article 1(1) of the International Convention on the Elimination of All Forms of Racial Discrimination (ICERD).

Based on Article 2(1) of the Convention, which requires member countries to implement measures to prohibit and terminate racial discrimination, and Article 6, which seeks to ensure that effective relief of racial discrimination can be accessed through the courts, Kyoto District Court considered itself obliged to interpret the Japanese legislation in line with international law. More significantly, if a crime is found to be racially motivated, it qualifies as having an extra degree of seriousness and a correspondingly heavier sentence. In civil cases involving illegal activities motivated by racial discrimination, the Convention directly influences the application of civil law and its interpretation, and becomes a factor in calculating the total intangible damages to be awarded. The court granted the school ¥12,263,140 in compensation and prohibited future demonstrations within a 200-metre radius of its gates.[19]

Osaka High Court later approved Kyoto District Court's ruling and recognized the 'interests of ethnic education', which the lower court had not mentioned.[20] In addition, the Supreme Court dismissed Zaitokukai's further appeal and affirmed the lower courts' findings.[21] In the criminal case that had preceded the civil case, the accused had been convicted, with imprisonment for up to two years and a four-year suspended sentence for the interruption of business and insulting action.[22]

Kyoto District Court's 2013 decision in *Kyoto Korean Elementary School* can be seen not only as consistent with Nara District Court's previous ruling, but as an expansion and clarification of that decision. In other words, discriminatory expressions applied to an entire group of people correspond to racial discrimination, as described in Article 1(1) ICERD. However, when there is no specific damage to individuals, it is held to be impossible (unless new legislation is created) to consider it a tort and therefore it does not qualify for compensation.

This provision acknowledges only cases in which illegal acts are committed using discriminatory expressions and the court ruling defines the

19 Kyoto District Court, 7 October 2013, 2208 Hanji 74.

20 Osaka High Court, 8 July 2014, 2232 Hanji 34.

21 Supreme Court, 3rd Petty Bench, 9 December 2014, unreported.

22 Kyoto District Court, 21 April 2011, unreported; Osaka High Court, 28 October 2011, unreported; Supreme Court, 1st Petty Bench, 23 February 2012, unreported.

limits of the definition of illegal acts. The racial discrimination described in Article 1(1) ICERD has been identified in civil cases as adding weight to intangible damages and as a factor to be taken into account when sentencing in criminal cases. This court ruling clarifies the reason for the high amount of compensation.[23]

III. The Response in Japan

This section discusses the regulation of discriminatory expressions and hate speech according to (the drafts of) acts and ordinances tested by national and local public bodies in Japan, and in the context of Japanese constitutional theory on discriminatory expressions and hate speech.

A. *Constitutional Theory*

Constitutional theory in Japan is strongly influenced by that which dominates in the United States and by the doctrine of judicial precedent. Regarding the regulation of discriminatory expressions and hate speech directed towards a group with certain attributes (as opposed to a specific individual or organization), a negative or cautious stance is often taken.

Professor Shigenori Matsui, who is generally critical of hate speech regulation, characterizes discriminatory expression as:

(1) expression that incites harm to racial minorities and others;
(2) expression that promotes discrimination of racial minorities and others;
(3) expression that causes injury to the dignity of racial minorities; and
(4) insults targeting minority groups and others.

The first two can be regulated under the Constitution if they qualify as illegal incitement per the *Brandenburg* test – that is, as constituting expressions that encourage or induce imminent illegal behaviour – or when there is a 'clear and present danger' that the harm or discrimination might occur.[24] However, in cases (3) and (4), regulation cannot be

[23] Shiki Tomimasu, 'Kyōto Chōsen Gakkō Syūgeki Jiken' ['Kyoto Korean School attack incident'], in Maeda, note 18, 32–50; Junko Kotani, 'Nihon Kokunai ni okeru Zōo Hyōgen no Kisei ni tsuite no Ichikōsatsu' ['An analysis of hate speech regulation in Japan'] (2014) 87 *Hōgaku Kenkyū* [Legal studies] 385; Yuji Nasu, 'Ōkina Igi o Motsu Kyōto Chisai Hanketsu' ['Kyoto District Court's highly significant decision'] (2013) 282 *Jyānarizumu* [Journalism] 110. See also Chapters 12 and 13.

[24] *Brandenburg* v. *Ohio*, 395 US 444 (1969).

constitutionally justified.[25] This approach places emphasis on the 'marketplace of ideas' theory, which states that the best way of arriving at the truth is to start from a place where people can freely express what they think and believe, and where people can challenge each other's differing perspectives. In other words, when direct harm is caused, as in fighting words or expressions that violate privacy (other than in exceptional cases that cannot be considered 'more speech'), state intervention is acceptable.

According to some scholars who support the idea of some limited regulation, discriminatory expressions can be classified into three groups:

(i) expressions that insult a minority group;
(ii) expressions inciting discriminatory treatment; and
(iii) expressions that encourage or promote discriminatory treatment.[26]

Regarding the characteristic feature of this theory in relation to (i), the reason for the regulation of discriminatory expressions targeting minority groups is to protect the dignity and emotions of said individuals, and the regulation becomes constitutional only in the case of a particularly malicious act done with the purpose of perpetrating insult. Otherwise, (ii) is judged according to the *Brandenburg* test and (iii) is judged based on the perspective of privacy protection, allowing partial regulation. This theory supports freedom of expression based on its individual value as an attempt at self-realization and its social value whereby it contributes to better political decision-making or self-governance. The expressions presented in these cases are regarded as 'low-value expressions', and thus it is not necessary to exercise strong guarantees against such expressions.

The point on which these two theories differ is whether to regulate 'extremely malignant expressions performed with the particular intention of insulting a minority group'. However, such expressions are exceptional and there are relatively few expressions that can be subject to regulation. In respect to a limited pro-regulatory approach, therefore it

[25] Shigenori Matsui, 'Intānettojō no Hyōgenkōi to Hyōgen no Jiyū' ['Freedom of expression on the Internet'], in Kazuyuki Takahashi *et al.* (eds.), *Intānetto to Hō* [Internet and Law], 4th ed. (Yuhikaku, 2010), 39. See also Shigenori Matsui, 'The Challenge to Multiculturalism: Hate Speech Ban in Japan' (2016) 49 *U.B.C. L. Rev.* 427.

[26] Masayuki Uchino, *Jinken no Omote to Ura* [The two sides of human rights] (Akashi Shoten, 1992), 199–203; Junichi Hamada, 'Intānetto ni yoru Sabetsu no Sendō' ['Incitement of discrimination on the Internet'] (1999) 126 *Burakukaihō Kenkyū* [Buraku liberation research] 44, at 56–57.

is not reasonable to accept restrictions that would pose a threat to the broader freedom of expression to regulate only a few discriminatory expressions. In addition, there is criticism that relaxing the guarantees of protection of freedom of expression may lead to confusion between constitutional interpretation and policy theory.[27]

Regardless of theory, the general understanding is that discriminatory expressions should be handled without distinction between whether they were carried out offline or on the Internet. However, those scholars supporting limited regulation state that discriminatory expressions on the Internet are often more aggressive than those expressed through traditional media, owing to features such as ease of expression, anonymity, depth and breadth of distribution, and ease of obtaining information. It is worth noting that when, there is a high probability of causing damage, there are claims that broader regulations should be implemented, especially for discrimination involving people trying to identify Burakumin individuals or disseminating lists of Buraku.[28]

B. *(Drafts of) Acts and Ordinances*

Regarding the regulation of discriminatory expressions, many of the constitutional theories within Japan take a negative or cautious stance; the position of the government is similar. On joining the ICERD, the Japanese government identified a possible conflict of Articles 21(1) ICERD (on 'Freedom of Expression, Freedom of Assembly/Association') and 31 ('Due Process and Fair Procedure') with the Constitution of Japan, and it reserved Article 4(a) and (b). Article 20(2) of the International Covenant on Civil and Political Rights (relating to the prohibition of hate advocacy) corresponds with a measure under article 14 of the Constitution concerning equalities appealing for elimination of discrimination, hatred, violence, and exclusion in criminal law, educational law, employment law, and other areas. In the event that concrete adverse effects arise owing to acts that cannot be regulated even under such current legislation, the government will discuss legislation with due consideration of the freedom of expression.

[27] Tatsuya Fujii, 'Heito Supīchi no Kisei to Hyōgen no Jiyū' ['Hate speech regulation and freedom of expression'] (2005) 9 *Kokusai Kōkyō Seisaku Kenkyū* [International public policy study] 14; Junko Kotani, 'Amerika ni okeru Heito Supīchi Kisei' ['Hate speech regulation in the United States'], in Keigo Komamura and Hidemi Suzuki (eds.), *Hyōgen no Jiyū I* [Freedom of Expression I] (Shogakusha, 2011), 472–73.

[28] Hamada, note 26, at 57–58.

This approach obviously renders immediate response unnecessary. However, even in Japan, there have been movements to establish legislation to deal with discriminatory expression.

(a) The Human Rights Advocacy Bill and the Tottori Prefecture Ordinance

The Human Rights Advocacy Bill is an early example of an attempt to regulate discriminatory expressions. In March 2002, the bill was submitted to the Diet to establish a human rights committee in the external bureau of the Ministry of Justice. This legislation meant that, in the event of a human rights violation, when (1) further unfair discriminatory treatment, (2) unfair discriminatory behaviour, (3) acts promoting discrimination, or (4) abuse, among other things, take place, a summons, requests for submission of documents, or on-the-spot investigations would take place and human rights relief would be sought through special relief procedures, such as mediation, arbitration, recommendation, and litigation aid, in accordance with the response procedures in place, such as appointed investigations, advice, guidance, and coordination. For (3), it was also possible to bring a lawsuit seeking an injunction or to announce counsel details. However, the bill was discarded by the House of Representatives in October 2003 because:

(i) it was deemed ambiguous, and the object it aimed to provide relief for was unclear and overly extensive;
(ii) it was questionable whether human rights violations of public authority can be effectively dealt with by the external bureau of the Ministry of Justice; and
(iii) correctional fines were to be imposed on the investigation conducted by the proposed human rights committee, as well as various other problems, such as a warrant being unnecessary.

In Tottori Prefecture, which aimed to introduce a similar system at the local level, a Tottori Prefecture Ordinance on the Promotion of Relief and Procedure of Human Rights referring to the failed bill was approved in October 2005; however, the ordinance was abolished in April 2009without being brought into force.

(b) The Bill for Elimination of Racial Discrimination and the Hate Speech Elimination Act

Subsequently, although there was no movement towards legislation other than submission of the Bill on the Establishment of the Human Rights

Commission under the Democratic Party administration in November 2012 (discarded owing to the dissolution of the House of Representatives in the same month), the situation on the streets escalated and anti-foreigner demonstrations took place in the Korean towns in Shin Okubo (Shinjuku Ward, Tokyo) and Tsuruhashi (Ikuno Ward, Osaka). To cope with this and the increase of discriminatory expression on the Internet, the Bill for the Elimination of Racial Discrimination was submitted to the Diet and a Osaka City Hate Speech Prohibition Ordinance (draft) was submitted to the Osaka City Council in May 2015.

The Bill for the Elimination of Racial Discrimination was submitted by the opposition parties, including the Democratic Party of Japan and Social Democratic Party. The bill aimed to prohibit discriminatory acts targeting a specific person (natural or corporate) on the grounds of race or the like, or discriminatory behaviour against unspecified persons sharing common attributes such as race, although it did not contain penalty provisions in the event of violation. Alongside this bill, national and local governments requested provisions with which to formulate and implement policies concerning the prevention of discrimination, to include collaboration with private organizations. Concerning discriminatory expressions on the Internet in particular, the bill was supposed to contain a mechanism to support voluntary efforts among businesses. However, in the House of Councillors Legal Committee and Plenary Session of May 2016, the ruling parties opposed and rejected the bill.

Meanwhile, although the ruling parties had taken a negative stance to legislative development thus far, they quickly switched track and submitted a Bill Concerning the Promotion of Efforts to Resolve Unreasonable Discriminatory Behaviour against Foreign Nationals from Outside Japan (the Hate Speech Elimination Bill) to the Diet (House of Councillors) in April 2016. After amendment in the House of Councillors, the bill was passed in May 2016 with the agreement of opposition parties (including the Democratic Party and Japan Communist Party) in the House of Representatives Legal Committee and Plenary Session.[29]

According to article 2 of the Hate Speech Elimination Act (HSEA), which was brought into force in June of the same year, discriminatory expressions included those aimed at promoting or inducing discriminatory attitudes towards 'those who are originally from countries or

[29] In addition, the Act on the Promotion of Elimination of Discrimination against Burakumin was established in December 2016 and took effect in the same month. There is no penalty provision in this law either.

regions outside the territory of Japan or their descendants living in Japan lawfully', as well as 'announcements that harm the life, body, freedom, dignity, or property of the public; unfair expression that constitutes significant insult to those from outside the country; and promoting or inciting exclusion of the latter from the community based on their being from outside of the country or region'. In addition, the law established, as a basic point of policy, the obligation of national and local public bodies to implement measures to resolve these matters (art. 4), and to implement systems for counselling, enhancing education, and raising awareness (arts 5–7).

Regarding discriminatory expressions on the Internet, the clause 'implement countermeasures to deal with individuals or groups promoting unjustifiable discriminatory expression against persons from overseas or from outside Japan and to eliminate acts that promote unfair discriminatory behaviour on the Internet' is included in the supplementary resolutions of both the House of Representatives and House of Councillors as an issue for special consideration.

However, the law imposes no penalty provisions on those who have carried out unfair discriminatory behaviour against foreign nationals from outside Japan. There is consequently debate over the effectiveness of the law and the likelihood that it will be subject to interpretation in the civil law courts (similar to the role of Kyoto District Court in *Kyoto Korean Elementary School*), and that it may exert certain influence on local government permission or rejection of meetings using public facilities, such as demonstrations and rallies.[30]

(c) The Osaka City Ordinance

The Osaka City Hate Speech Prohibition Ordinance deals with instances in which Osaka citizens or organizations suffer damage as a result of the diffusion of hate speech, including Internet expression, in or around Osaka City and citizens – or the mayor of the city of Osaka – may request that steps be taken to curb hate speech. In addition to publicizing the names of those individuals and organizations responsible for the hate speech, the ordinance as drafted proposed, among other things, to support plaintiffs with litigation expenses so that they could pursue civil claims. In addition, the draft ordinance was supposed to establish an Osaka City Hate Speech Investigation Committee as an organization that would assess whether or not an expression constitutes hate speech, as

[30] See Chapters 10 and 11.

well as measures enacted by the mayor, the content of disclosures, and the merit of requests for litigation expenses loan applications.

The ordinance passed only after the provision concerning the financial support system for the costs of litigation was omitted. The ordinance was revised to require the consent of the city council for the commission of members of the Hate Speech Investigation Committee. The ordinance was enacted in January 2016 and came into effect in July of the same year, at which point complaints alleging damages arising from videos of hate speech demonstrations on blogs and Twitter were filed.[31] Based on the report of the Committee, if the mayor of Osaka judges that the expression reported can be defined as hate speech, as prescribed in the ordinance, the name of individuals and organizations responsible for the expression and an outline of its content will be announced on the city website, and measures necessary to prevent hate speech from spreading will be taken, such as requesting the provider or site administrator to delete the expression (art. 5). Efforts to use the same ordinance to deter hate speech on the Internet were also seen.[32]

Furthermore, the Osaka City Hate Speech Investigation Committee had discussed the possibility of requiring Internet services providers to disclose the real names of individuals and organizations post anonymously on the internet, but it concluded that it would be difficult to enforce this obligation and that it should instead ask the government to amend the Telecommunications Business Act and Provider Liability Limitation Act.[33]

IV. Review

Finally, we will consider a few more cases. In cases in which discriminatory expression is directed at a specific individual or organization, it may be considered a crime as defamation under article 230 of the Criminal

[31] 'Osakashi Heitojōrei Sekō' ['Osaka City Hate Ordinance enforcement'], *Hokkaido Shimbun* (1 July 2016) (Evening edition).

[32] See Chapter 9.

[33] 'Heito Supīchi ni kakaru Hōkaisei no Yōbō ni tsuite' ['About the request for amendment to existing laws on hate speech'], available at www.city.osaka.lg.jp/shimin/cmsfiles/contents/0000366/366957/30tousinn5gou.pdf [accessed 15 December 2018]. However, a person whose account name was disclosed has filed a lawsuit alleging the same unconstitutionality of publishing a real name and infringement of his freedom of expression and right of privacy: 'Osakashi no Heito Nintei: Jitsumei Yamete' ['Osaka City recognized hate speech: please do not disclose real name'], *Asahi Shimbun* (16 April 2018) (Morning edition).

Code, insult (art. 231), intimidation (art. 222), or obstructing someone's business (art. 234). Finding the activity illegal as defamation, interfering with someone's business, or racial discrimination may affirm the liability for tort under article 709 of the Civil Code. However, when it comes to a group with certain attributes, regulation under the current law is not feasible, even from the perspective of allowing new legislation. Similarly, in terms of freedom of expression, a general understanding of constitutional law will support the view that the scope of regulation is limited. This point applies whether the expression is offline or on the Internet.

Meanwhile, the response among providers that mediate information on the Internet has been based on the terms of their user contracts. Indeed, measures such as deletion of accounts or blocking access have been implemented for some of the concrete examples introduced in this chapter. Contract terms are prepared by individual providers, but in November 2006 'Model Contract Clause Items concerning Illegal or Harmful Information and Counter-measures' were formulated by the Telecommunications Carriers Association, Telecom Service Association, Japan Internet Provider Association, and Japan Cable Television Federation (at time of writing, most recently revised in April 2016). Among the items prohibited are: obscene expressions and the transmission of child abuse images; the act of infringing on privacy, the rights to use one's likeness, or intellectual property rights, and so on; engaging in unfair discrimination against another by means of defamation and insults or promoting such behaviour; damaging others' dignity or harming people's trust in them; and disrupting public order and morals, or other behaviour that infringes on other people's rights. If a complaint is made that can be characterized as any one or more of these prohibited actions and the provider adjudges the claim to be appropriate, the actor responsible is asked to stop the behaviours corresponding to the prohibited matter, or to discuss the matter to resolve the complaint. The provider is to delete the expression, suspend the user's access, and cancel their contract. These items function as a literal 'model' contract for providers.[34]

In addition, the Human Rights Organs of the Ministry of Justice (Legal Affairs Bureau, or District Legal Affairs Bureau) have previously requested deletion of providers, and the methods and response

[34] Shuji Matsui, 'Intānettojō no Sabetsuteki Hyōgen o meguru Kadai o Kangaeru' ['Reconsidering issues surrounding discriminatory expressions on the Internet'] (2013) 302 *Gekkan Hyūman Raitsu* [Human rights monthly] 2, at 8–9.

procedures have been clarified by its revision of the Provider Liability Limitation Act Guidelines Relating to Defamation and Privacy (October 2004). In cases in which a request for deletion is made to the provider in accordance with these guidelines, there is no particular reason to deny the request as long as there are reasonable grounds on which to believe that the rights of others have been unjustly infringed upon. Provided that the provider has assured minimum measures to prevent transmission of discriminatory expression and the like, it is understood that providers can escape liability for damages from those people whose activity they curtail.

However, with regard to contract terms, if the prohibited items and their provisions are unclear, if it is difficult to assess the expression as prohibited matter, if the complaint procedure is unclear, or if there is not enough incentive to support deletion (e.g. in cases in which the content is not illegal and does need not to be deleted, where no damage liability arises), it may be the case that many discriminatory expressions will remain on the Internet without a provider taking action. Regarding a request for deletion by the human rights organs, however, it may be that any delay to the action requested will lead to greater damage.

There is a significant difference between discriminatory expressions attacking socially vulnerable minorities and expressions attacking the government and a socially strong majority, which have become the focus for debate on regulation. However, while discriminatory expressions are unpleasant, because they are based on thoughts or ideas that many people strongly dislike, they remain mere expressions and should be treated as such because, according to the principle of the 'marketplace of ideas', it is inevitable that we must cope with 'more speech'. It should not be overlooked that discriminatory expressions often take on a political character because they are focused on emphasizing equality. Regulation under the law should be rooted in freedom of expression and the goal of eliminating discrimination itself, and the latter calls for a blend of education and awareness-raising activities. Any focus on discriminatory expressions on the Internet should be on minimizing resolution by law and aiming to encourage voluntary initiatives (self-regulation) among providers.

Although the recently implemented Act and ordinance offer some consideration of freedom of expression, a closer examination is required. The idea that speech should be fundamentally free and that, as a matter of principle, public authorities – particularly the government – must intervene carefully is not uncommon. Many identify a range of doubt regarding the government's control of the flow of information, but in particular they challenge the perception that there are stop signs controlling that flow. We must keep an eye on the trends that the Osaka City Hate Speech Investigation Committee and Osaka City represent. Where the Committee defines hate speech broadly, a heavy-handed content-based regulation of expression may emerge. Conversely, should it be narrowly defined, more kinds of expression will be tacitly accepted. It can be assumed that any sort of expressions spread widely on the Internet. Any entity that regulates the flow of this information will have to deal with this ambivalence in its own response to the issues of the day.

19

Hate Groups and the Use of Public Facilities

Striking a Balance between the Right to Assembly and the Interests of Minority Residents

YUJI NASU*

I. Introduction

In this chapter, I will address issues regarding the use of local public facilities by hate groups in Japan. I will examine them mainly through the lens of a guideline issued by Kawasaki City in Kanagawa in November 2017, and the guidelines subsequently issued by Kyoto Prefecture and Kyoto City in 2018. After the surge of hate speech by extreme far-right groups in the late 2000s, several such groups attempted to use local public facilities to promulgate hate speech chiefly against Koreans. This gave rise to the difficult question of how to strike the balance between freedom of assembly (and expression),[1] on the one hand, and the interests of minority residents, on the other.

In this chapter, I will argue that local governments[2] can sometimes refuse hate groups use of their facilities, to protect local minority residents, and that the guidelines issued by three local governments (Kawasaki City, Kyoto Prefecture, and Kyoto City) are constitutional despite some notable defects. Many constitutional law scholars in Japan will certainly oppose this conclusion, but I will contend that their

* This work was supported by JSPS KAKENHI Grant No. 20K01305.

[1] Article 21(1) of the Constitution of Japan protects freedom of assembly and speech in the same clause ('Freedom of assembly and association as well as speech, press and all other forms of expression are guaranteed'). Although freedom of assembly is different in nature from that of speech and these differences might affect this chapter's analysis to some extent, both largely overlap in their protections. I therefore presume that those two freedoms do not require different levels or forms of judicial scrutiny in this context.

[2] Japan has 47 prefectures and approximately 1,700 municipalities (cities, villages, and towns), to which I refer as 'local governments'. Chapter 9 overviews various local government measures against hate speech.

position cannot be supported, because it overcategorizes conflicting interests and abstracts highly complex factors. It must be recognized that there are exceptions to free speech protections in certain categories of hate speech. Some cases on the use of public facilities by hate groups constitute an example of such exceptions, because certain uses will clearly harm minority residents and contravene the purpose of the establishment and operation of those facilities. Certainly, guidance must be clear if it is to minimize potentially chilling effects and not comprise an abuse of power. The three guidelines issued to date (at time of writing) successfully avoid unconstitutionality, but more work needs to be done to refine them in this respect.

Section II will clarify some legal terms and concepts in advance and introduce relevant legal provisions. I will then describe cases of the Supreme Court of Japan pertinent to this context and summarize its doctrine in section III. In section IV, I will offer an overview of the Kawasaki guideline, including a short history of its path to enactment. I will also consider the guidelines enacted by Kyoto Prefecture and Kyoto City. Section V will introduce academic debates on this subject and illuminate how the two opposing camps support their positions. I will seek to accommodate both camps and find a reasonable solution to this novel legal question in section VI, before concluding the chapter in section VII.

II. Terms and Concepts

It is useful to expound on some preliminary matters beforehand. I will first present the definition of *ōyake no shisetsu* ('public facilities') of local governments. This term appears in article 244 of the Local Autonomy Act, defined as 'facilities for use of local residents to promote their welfare'.[3] This is an extremely vague and broad definition, and, in fact,

[3] Article 244 provides that: '(1) Ordinary local public entities shall establish facilities for use of local residents to promote their welfare (hereinafter "public facilities"). (2) Ordinary local public entities shall not deny the use of public facilities by local residents without legitimate reasons. (3) Ordinary local public entities shall not discriminate local residents when they use public facilities.' This provision was introduced in 1963 by the 17th amendment of the Act. Before that amendment, the term *eizōbutsu* ('construction') had been used. It was a broad concept, which basically referred to public facilities, but it even included personnel working there. It was an old and vague concept that smacks of the so-called *tokubetsu kenryoku kankeiron* ('special power relationship theory') that legitimatized strong governmental powers, originating from German public law jurisprudence. In the 1963 amendment, it was replaced by the term 'public facilities', and more emphasis was

it has been interpreted to include a wide variety of facilities, such as parks, civic centres, water and sewage plants, roads, and even baseball stadiums.[4] In this chapter, I will confine my object of discussion to facilities that are suitable for assembly, such as parks, civic centres, and public halls.

It would also be beneficial to introduce the wider concept of *gyōsei zaisan* ('administrative properties'), as developed in Japanese public law scholarship. This includes two types of government property: those for *kōkyōyō* ('public use') and those for *kōyō* ('non-public use').[5] The idea of public facilities explained above is almost identical to the former.[6] However, the latter is often used to refer to sites of assembly as well. This is referred to as *mokutekigai riyō* ('unintended use') of public properties. An example of such an unintended use is when a citizen's group rents a conference room in a city hall for its activities by obtaining permission from the city.[7] Much wider administrative discretion is allowed in such cases. However, it is sometimes difficult to distinguish between uses of public properties for non-public and public purposes. For instance, the Supreme Court held, in one typical case of unintended use, that a local government had abused its discretionary power by denying permission for the use of a public school facility for an assembly planned by a teachers' union.[8] In this incident, the local government had taken such measures in fear that hostile groups would break the peace. This precedent suggests that a government's discretion is not unlimited, even in cases of unintended use. However, I will not discuss this topic in

placed upon welfare and the rights of local residents. See Yasushi Mino, 'Article 244', in Jun Murakami, Hiroyuki Shirafuji, and Takeshi Hitomi (eds.), *Shin Kihonhō Konmentāru, Chihō Jichihō* [New commentary on the Local Autonomy Act] (Nihon Hyoronsha, 2011), 357. Ōyake no shisetsu is distinguished from *kōkyō shisetsu*, although both are translated into 'public facilities' in general. Kōkyō shisetsu is sometimes used as a statutory term. See, e.g., art. 4(14) of the City Planning Act. Since ōyake no shisetsu is a term in the Local Autonomy Act, it is used to mean public facilities of local governments. On the other hand, kōkyō shisetsu include not only local facilities, but also those of the national government. Ōyake no shisetsu and kōkyō shisetsu are difficult to translate into different terms, and so I use the blanket term 'public facilities' here, despite the potential for confusion.

4 See Katsuya Uga, *Chihō Jichihō Gaisetsu* [General survey of the Local Autonomy Act], 8th ed. (Yuhikaku, 2019), 383–85.

5 See art. 238(4) of the Local Autonomy Act.

6 Those two concepts are the same thing defined from different perspectives. The public facility is a concept defined from the perspective of administrative management, while the property for public use is a concept defined from the perspective of properties.

7 See art. 238.4(7) of the Local Autonomy Act.

8 See Supreme Court, 3rd Petty Bench, 7 February 2006, 60 Minshū 401.

this chapter, because there cannot be many cases in which hate groups use administrative properties for unintended purposes.[9]

The Local Autonomy Act addresses only local matters, but some national facilities are also suitable for assembly. For example, national parks or streets are often used for such purposes. In fact, a well-known Supreme Court case originated in denial of permission for a planned assembly in the outer garden of the Imperial Palace in Tokyo, which has been a national park.[10] Discussions in this chapter will also be applied to national facilities, *mutatis mutandis*.

The relevant legal provisions should also be explained.[11] Laws at the national level regulating the use of parks include the Urban Park Act and the Regulations on National Parks, the Chidorigafuchi National Cemetery, and the Memorial for the Dead Who Were Detained and Used as Forced Labourers in Siberia after the Second World War (hereinafter 'Regulations on National Parks'). Article 18 of the Urban Park Act delegates detailed provisions to Cabinet order and local ordinance. With respect to civic centres, public halls, or other similar facilities on the local level, article 244 of the Local Autonomy Act is a basic norm, and many local ordinances (and subordinate rules) are enacted under its authority. I should also note that article 94 of the Constitution is relevant, because it provides that local ordinances shall be enacted within the confinement set out by national laws.[12] If local ordinances violate article 21 of the Constitution, they will certainly have no 'legitimate reasons' in the words of article 244(2) of the Local Autonomy Act and will infringe on article 94 of the Constitution.

Because the Urban Park Act and the Local Autonomy Act are laws that regulate the administration of public facilities, regulations or ordinances enacted by these delegations should not control matters unrelated to this

[9] *National Socialist White People's Party* v. *Ringers*, 473 F.2d 1010 (4th Cir. 1973) and *Knights of Ku Klux Klan, Realm of Louisiana* v. *East Baton Rouge Parish School Board*, 578 F.2d 1122 (5th Cir. 1978) are rare cases of unintended use of public facilities in the United States. Both cases were concerned with the applications to use school facilities by extreme right-wing organizations. In both cases, courts accepted claims by those organs. See also note 104.

[10] See Supreme Court, Grand Bench, 23 December 1953, 7 Minshū 1561.

[11] On a detailed overview of relevant provisions, see Yoshihiro Saito, 'Shūkai no Jiyū to Kōkyō Shisetsu no Riyō (1)' ['The right of assembly and the use of public property (1)'] (2000) 9 *Fukuoka Kenritsu Daigaku Kiyō* [Fukuoka Prefectural University bulletin] 17, at 19–22.

[12] It provides that '[l]ocal public entities shall have the right to manage their property, affairs and administration and to enact their own regulations within law'.

purpose. These laws therefore should not be applied to maintain public order around the public facilities unless such order is directly connected to the administration or operation of said facilities; otherwise, it would become an exercise of 'police power', as some minority opinions of the Supreme Court have pointed out.[13]

Although these laws set various requirements for permission for public assembly, most of them set only extremely vague standards. For example, the Urban Park Act prohibits conduct that *is likely to seriously prevent the public use of urban parks.*[14] Park administrators can take various measures, including revoking permission once given, when such conduct is recognized.[15] In local ordinances on parks, civic centres, or civic halls, the requirements are *not to break the public order,*[16] *annoy others,*[17] or *harm public interests.*[18] In some ordinances, general discretionary powers are given to administrators by adding phrasing such as 'or other conducts that prevent administration' after enumerating particular prohibited conducts.[19] Surprisingly, the Regulations on National Parks do not provide any standards on which administrators rely and only enumerate some prohibitory conducts.[20] It can be argued that these regulations are clearly violating article 21 of the Constitution, and that they are facially unconstitutional on the grounds of vagueness and overbreadth. However, as will be explained, it is rarely argued that these vague provisions should be held unconstitutional on their face, because the Supreme Court held the ordinance's provision having such characteristics to be constitutional by reading it down.

There are multiple remedies for those who claim violation of the right of assembly. The most widely used provision is article 1(1) of the State

[13] See, e.g., Supreme Court, 3rd Petty Bench, 7 March 1995, 49 Minshū 687, at 702–03 (Sonobe, J., concurring).

[14] See Urban Park Act, art. 11(1)(4). Similar words appear at local ordinances enacted by the delegation of this Act. See, e.g., Fukuoka City Park Ordinance, art. 4(4); Akita City Urban Park Ordinance, art. 3(3); Naha City Park Ordinance, art. 3(4).

[15] See Urban Park Act, art. 27(2)(2).

[16] See, e.g., Akita City Urban Park Ordinance, art. 3(3); Hamamatsu City Park Ordinance, art. 3(4)(1); Takatsuki City Cultural Hall Ordinance, art. 7(1)(1); Sapporo City Education and Culture Hall Ordinance, art. 9(1).

[17] See, e.g., Fukuoka City Park Ordinance, art. 4(4)(1); Akita City Urban Park Ordinance, art. 4(1)(8); Naha City Park Ordinance, art. 3(4)(2).

[18] See, e.g., Fukuoka City Park Ordinance, art. 4(4)(2); Naha City Park Ordinance, art. 3(4)(5).

[19] See, e.g., Naha City Park Ordinance, art. 3(4)(6); Kawagoe City Urban Park Ordinance, art. 2(4)(3); Takatsuki City Cultural Hall Ordinance, art. 7(1)(3).

[20] See reg. 4(1).

Redress Act.[21] Citizens may also start actions for the revocation of dispositions under the Administrative Case Litigation Act.[22] This procedure can be used only after the application is denied or when the permission, once given, is retracted. Plaintiffs have also been able to claim provisional orders of *mandamus* since the 2004 amendment of this Act.[23]

It is assumed that there are two levels of right, *statutory* and *constitutional*, when referring to the 'right' to use public facilities. Although the Japanese Supreme Court does not clearly recognize the statutory right to use public facilities, it narrowly limits administrative discretion and seems to recognize it implicitly. Moreover, most scholars clearly endorse that right. In fact, article 244(2) and (3) of the Local Autonomy Act could be rightly interpreted to include statutory rights. Thus it is almost useless to discuss the existence of the statutory right to use public facilities.

What is more controversial, however, is whether citizens have the *constitutional* right to use them. In the United States, this right is plainly approved by its Supreme Court, which developed the doctrine of public forum that classifies public properties into traditional, designated, and non-public fora.[24] Citizens are allowed to engage in a wide variety of speech activities as part of their constitutional rights, especially in traditional and designated fora.[25] The Supreme Court of Japan does not adopt the same doctrine, but some minority opinions openly refer to it.[26] Furthermore, commentaries by law clerks of the Supreme Court frequently mention the US public forum doctrine,[27] which could indicate

[21] It provides that, '[w]hen a public officer who exercises the public authority of the State or of a public entity has, in the course of his/her duties, unlawfully inflicted damage on another person intentionally or negligently, the State or public entity shall assume the responsibility to compensate therefor'.

[22] See art. 3(2) of the Administrative Case Litigation Act.

[23] See art. 37-5 of the Administrative Case Litigation Act. See also Okayama District Court, 15 October 2007, 1259 Hanta 182.

[24] As a classic statement to protect the right to use public places for assembly, see *Hague* v. *CIO*, 307 U.S. 496, 515–16 (1939). On concise explanation of the three categories of public fora, see *Perry Education Association* v. *Perry Local Educators' Association*, 460 U.S. 37, 44–46 (1983). For an introduction to the US public forum doctrine in Japan, see, e.g., Masako Kamiya, 'Paburikku Fōramu' ['Public forum'] (1988) 50 *Kōhō Kenkyū* [Public law review] 103.

[25] See *Perry Education Association*, 460 U.S. at 45–46.

[26] See, e.g., Supreme Court, 3rd Petty Bench, 18 December 1984, 38 Keishū 3026, at 3030–33 (Ito, J., concurring); Supreme Court, 3rd Petty Bench, 3 March 1987, 41 Keishū 15, at 17–25 (Ito, J., concurring).

[27] See, e.g., 'Commentary on *Ageo City Welfare Hall*' (1996) 1 *Saikō Saibansho Hanrei Kaisetsu Minjihen* [Commentary on Supreme Court precedent: civil cases] 208.

that the Court has been conscious of it in cases on the right to assembly. In addition, it can be safely said that most Japanese legal scholars would recognize the constitutional right to use public facilities for assembly.[28]

What are termed 'public facilities' in article 244 of the Local Autonomy Act includes parks and streets, which are classified as traditional fora under the terminology of the US Supreme Court. Most facilities, however, are designated ones. At first glance, designated fora sound inferior to traditional fora in the context of the constitutional protection of assembly rights, but this is a misunderstanding; rather, many designated fora, such as civic centres or public halls, are uniquely designed for assembly and are better suited in terms of architecture than are traditional ones.

Finally, I would like to add some comments on terminology within this chapter. I refer to scholars that oppose hate speech regulations as 'oppositionists' and those who support limited regulations as 'regulationists'. When I mention 'Koreans', this term includes both Korean Japanese who have Japanese nationality and Koreans who hold permanent residential status, but do not have Japanese nationality.

III. Precedents

The Supreme Court of Japan has heard several cases on the right to assembly in public facilities and has established some important rules. While these cases are highly significant, they do not provide a direct answer to the subject matter of this chapter.

A. Izumisano Civic Hall[29]

During construction of Kansai International Airport in Izumisano City, Osaka, some extreme left-wing organizations fiercely protested against the project.[30] One such group applied for use of the Izumisano Civic Hall to hold a rally to oppose the construction.[31] The city turned down the

[28] See, e.g., Saito, note 11, at 31; Masato Ichikawa, 'Shūkai no Jiyū' ['The right to assembly'] (1997) 207 *Hōgaku Kyōshitsu* [Law classroom] 42, at 47.

[29] Supreme Court, 3rd Petty Bench, 7 March 1995, 49 Minshū 687.

[30] On the facts of this case, see *ibid.*, at 690–95.

[31] This group called itself by a neutral name, the *Zen Kansai Jikkō Iinkai* ('All Kansai Action Committee'), but it was in fact the *Kakumeiteki Kyōsan Shugisha Dōmei Zenkoku Iinkai* ('Japan Revolutionary Communist League'), often referred to as the *Chūkakuha* ('Core Faction'). For this group's official website, see www.zenshin.org/english/index.htm [accessed 17 September 2020].

application because it would violate article 7(1) and (3) of the Izumisano Civic Hall Ordinance that was in operation at that time, which provided that the city reserved the right to reject an application if the use was likely to cause a breach of the public order (art. 7(1)) or to interfere with the administration of the hall (art. 7(3)). It was feared that hostile groups would intervene in the assembly, disrupting the peace at the hall and in its surrounding area. The city was even concerned about the physical safety of the hall's officials and local residents.

Consequently, the group sued the city, arguing that article 7(1) and (3) of the ordinance infringed article 21 of the Constitution, and that the ordinance was therefore unconstitutional on its face. It also asserted that the city's disposition was unconstitutional, violating both article 21(1) of the Constitution, which provides for the right to assembly, and article 21(2), which prohibits censorship,[32] as well as article 244 of the Local Autonomy Act. Moreover, the group claimed compensatory damages based on article 1 of the State Redress Act.

The Supreme Court rejected all of the plaintiff's claims, but it significantly read down the ambit of article 7 of the ordinance. It first recognized the need to balance the right to assembly with conflicting interests. It also emphasized the importance of assembly rights and adopted the double standard doctrine developed in the United States, which weights spiritual freedom more heavily than economic freedom.[33]

The Court then narrowly interpreted the possibility of causing a breach of the public order in article 7(1) and permitted the denial of applications only in cases in which *obvious and imminent dangers can be concretely predicted to occur*. It also demanded evidence that the *occurrence of such dangers could be predicted concretely and obviously, in light of objective facts.*[34]

The Court added that local governments should not deny the use of their facilities *solely because of the character of the group*. Moreover, it introduced the hostile audience doctrine, which was developed particularly in the United Kingdom[35] and the United States,[36] stating that

[32] Article 21(2) of the Constitution provides that '[n]o censorship shall be maintained, nor shall the secrecy of any means of communication be violated'.

[33] See note 29, at 696–97.

[34] See *ibid.*, at 697–98.

[35] See, e.g., *Beatty* v. *Gillbanks* [1882] 9 QBD 308, (1882) 15 Cox CC 138; *Redmond-Bate* v. *DPP* (1999) 7 BHRC 375, [1999] Crim LR 998.

[36] See, e.g., *Terminiello* v. *City of Chicago*, 337 U.S. 1 (1949); *Edwards* v. *South Carolina*, 372 U.S. 229 (1963); *Gregory* v. *City of Chicago*, 394 U.S. 111 (1969). The doctrine was

governments cannot deny the use of their facilities by one group only because other groups hostile to it will try to prevent and disrupt its assembly.[37]

The Court, however, accepted the city's claim in this case, because the plaintiff had repeated illegal conduct and had long-term conflicts with opposing groups. The Court's judgment was that the plaintiff's assembly would cause serious disruption within and outside of the hall, and that this danger could be concretely predicted based on objective facts.[38]

B. Ageo City Welfare Hall[39]

The Japan Confederation of Railway Workers' Union (JRU) planned to hold a mass funeral in February 1990 for a member who had been murdered on his way home.[40] Some media outlets suspected that he had been murdered in an intragroup conflict. The union applied for the use of the Welfare Hall of Ageo City, Saitama, for this purpose. However, the head of the hall knew about the intragroup conflict and declined JRU's application, in fear that the peace would be breached by those who were hostile to the JRU. The applicant sued the city and claimed compensatory damage, based on article 1 of the State Redress Act.

Although the Tokyo High Court denied the plaintiff's claim, the Supreme Court overturned the decision. The Supreme Court remanded the case, and it ordered the High Court to determine the existence and degree of damage. It basically concurred with *Izumisano Civic Hall*, but developed its hostile audience doctrine to further protect the freedoms of expression and assembly. It held that local governments could deny applications for peaceful assemblies on the grounds that hostile audiences are likely to interrupt and disturb such gatherings, but *only when regular police or security forces are not available to prevent a breach of the peace.*[41]

affirmed in the context of hate speech regulations. See *Village of Skokie* v. *National Socialist Party of America*, 69 Ill.2d 605, 616–19 (1978).

37 See note 29, at 699–700.

38 See *ibid.*, at 700–01.

39 Supreme Court, 2nd Petty Bench, 15 March 1996, 50 Minshū 549.

40 On the facts of this case, see *ibid.*, at 551–54.

41 See *ibid.*, at 554–56.

C. *The Doctrine of the Court*

The Court's doctrine can be summarized as follows.

- The right to assembly is balanced against conflicting interests, but more weight should be placed on this spiritual right than on economic rights.
- Governments can deny the use of facilities in cases in which assemblies are feared likely to cause public disorder, but only when 'clear and present danger' can be concretely predicted to occur. In such cases, governments are required to submit evidence of the danger, in light of objective facts.
- Governments are prohibited from denying the use of facilities based only on the characters of the applicant groups.
- Governments can deny the use of facilities to certain groups on the basis that hostile groups are likely to try to disrupt its assembly, but only when regular police or security forces are not available to prevent any breach of the peace.

This established doctrine should be praised for emphasizing the importance of the right to assembly, but it does not provide a perfect answer to the question of how to balance the rights and interests in conflict. The main concern here is that assemblies by hate groups will cause harm to minority residents. In light of the Court's doctrine, we can confidently state that it is unconstitutional for a local government to restrict a hate group's assembly on the grounds that the government opposes that group's policy or that the assembly might cause a breach of the peace when such danger is not objectively certain. However, if the local government's reason for restriction is to prevent harm to minority residents at and around the facility, the constitutionality of this restriction remains unclear.

IV. The Guidelines

A. *A History of the Problem*

In Japan, the use of public facilities by hate groups first emerged as an issue in Yamagata Prefecture in June 2013. The *Zainichi Tokken o Yurusanai Shimin no Kai* ('Association of Citizens against the Special Privileges of Korean Residents in Japan'), commonly known as *Zaitokukai*, applied for the use of the prefecture's Lifelong Study Centre. The centre rejected the group's application, relying on a provision that authorizes it to deny an application when the use will benefit groups that are likely to continually or collectively conduct violence or tort.[42] It was not clear whether this provision could be applied to this case and there was some controversy over the proper standard in such cases.[43]

The same problem surfaced in 2014 in Kadoma City, Osaka. After rejecting an application from a far-right group for use of the municipal Cultural Centre, the city began to develop a policy with which it could deny hate groups' use of its facilities. Eventually, the city published its view that it would accept all applications in principle, but deny some applications if they violated existing provisions.[44] Although the city also emphasized that it would combat discriminatory speech and stand up for human rights protection, it was not clear exactly when these existing provisions would be applied.

Many local governments have similarly been troubled with this problem, and scholars and attorneys have been divided in their views. On 7 September 2015, *Tokyo Bengoshi Kai* ('Tokyo Bar Association', or TBA) published an expert opinion,[45] arguing that local governments should not endorse racial discrimination by renting their facilities to hate groups given Japan's ratification of international treaties including the International Convention on the Elimination of All Forms of Racial Discrimination (ICERD). The TBA therefore asserted that local governments could deny the use of public facilities in appropriate circumstances.[46]

However, the TBA emphasized the significance of free speech and attempted to clarify certain points to consider when limiting the use of

42 See 'Anti-Korean Group's Plea to Use Public Facility Nixed', *Japan Times* (online), 29 June 2013, available at www.japantimes.co.jp/news/2013/06/29/national/social-issues/anti-korean-groups-plea-to-use-public-facility-nixed/ [accessed 17 September 2020]; 'Genron, Sukumu Jichitai' ['Speech, cringing local government'], *Asahi Shimbun*, 2 May 2014, at 30.

43 For opposing views of Japanese scholars, see *Japan Times*, note 42.

44 See 'Kadoma-shi, Shisetsu Shiyō no Kenkai Kōhyō, ['Kadoma City published its view on the use of its facilities'], *Mainichi Shimbun* (Osaka ed.), 19 April 2014, at 20.

45 See Tokyo Bengoshi Kai [Tokyo Bar Association], 'Chihō Kōkyō Dantai ni taishite Jinshu Sabetsu o Mokuteki to suru Kōkyō Shisetsu no Riyō Kyoka Shinsei ni taisuru Tekisetsu na Sochi o Kōzuru Koto o Motomeru Ikensho' ['Opinion paper calling for local public entities to take proper measures against application for the use of public facilities for the purpose of racial discrimination'], 8 September 2015, available at www.toben.or.jp/message/pdf/20150907.pdf [accessed 17 September 2020].

46 See *ibid.*, at 6. Article 2(1)(b) ICERD provides that '[e]ach State Party undertakes not to sponsor, defend or support racial discrimination by any persons or organizations'.

public facilities. First, it called on local governments to set concrete and clear requirements by making new ordinances or interpretive guidelines, because of the vagueness found in the Local Autonomy Act, most local ordinances, and rules made for each facility.[47]

Second, it insisted that local governments should establish rigid requirements, since limitations will have the nature of prior restraints to free speech and assembly. The TBA therefore argued that local governments could reject the use of facilities only in cases in which danger of racial discrimination is demonstrated in light of objective facts.[48]

Third, it claimed that local governments should provide procedures to guarantee opportunities to applicants and it suggested the establishment of expert committees to assess the merits of proposed denials.[49]

Finally, it proposed some alternative responses from among which local governments might choose when receiving applications from hate groups, including 'warning', 'permission with conditions', or 'denial of permission'.[50]

The TBA made pamphlets based on this paper and distributed them to local governments.[51] However, the controversy did not end there and some local governments seemed sceptical of the TBA's view. For example, an expert committee established by Osaka City published a report on the possible measures that the city could take.[52] Simply put, this report asserted that it was difficult for local governments to deny applications made by hate groups, in light of the *Izumisano* and *Ageo*.[53]

[47] See Tokyo Bar Association, note 45, at 7–8.

[48] See *ibid.*, at 8–9.

[49] See *ibid.*, at 9.

[50] See *ibid.*

[51] See Masakatsu Yamamoto, 'Heito Supīchi, Shūkai Kyohi Dekiru, Tokyo Bengoshi Kai ga Panfu' ['Assemblies for hate speech can be denied, the Tokyo Bar Association made a pamphlet for local governments'], *Mainichi Shimbun*, 10 January 2016, at 27.

[52] See Osaka-shi Jinken Sesaku Suishin Shingikai [Council on Human Rights Policy of Osaka City], 'Heito Supīchi ni taisuru Osaka-shi to shite Toru beki Hōsaku ni tsuite (Tōshin)' ['About possible measures taken by Osaka City against hate speech (Reply Paper)'], February 2015, available at www.city.osaka.lg.jp/shimin/cmsfiles/contents/0000007/7141/tousinkagamituki.pdf [accessed 17 September 2020]. This paper became the basis of the city's hate speech ordinance (see Chapter 12). For a full English translation of the ordinance, see Koji Higashikawa, 'Japan's Hate Speech Laws: Translations of the Osaka City Ordinance and the National Act to Curb Hate Speech in Japan' (2017) 19 *Asian Pac. L. Pol'y J.* 1, at 6–17.

[53] See Council on Human Rights Policy of Osaka City, note 52, at 9–10. As a result, the ordinance did not provide measures authorizing city officials to deny applications for facility use by hate groups.

B. *Enactment of the Kawasaki City Guideline*

Kawasaki City has been vexed by many right-wing extremists who persistently advocate the exclusion of Koreans from its communities.[54] On 31 May 2016, the city rejected an application from some extremists to use a park to conduct a demonstration.[55] On 2 June 2016, Yokohama District Court's Kawasaki Branch issued an injunction against the same extremists who planned to demonstrate on public streets in the Sakuramoto district, which has been traditionally populated by many Korean residents.[56] The extremists changed their plans after their application was rejected and instead conducted a demonstration on a public street in another area. However, their progress down the road was blocked by numerous counter-demonstrators. They cancelled their march within minutes, after some persuasion by the police.[57]

The city received complaints that it had arbitrarily turned down an application to use the park. It therefore started to work on drafting a guideline that it could consult in the event of future applications. On 9 November 2017, Kawasaki City's Guideline for Judgments on Applications to Use Public Facilities was published.[58] This was the first

[54] See Appendix A.

[55] See 'Jidai no Shōtai' Shuzaihan ['Hidden Truth of the Age' Coverage Team at *Kanagawa Shimbun*], *Heito Demo o Tometa Machi: Kawasaki Sakuramoto no Hitobito* [The city that stopped hate demonstrations: people of Sakuramoto, Kawasaki City] (Gendai Shicho Shinsha, 2016), 161–63.

[56] Yokohama District Court Kawasaki Branch, 2 June 2016, 2296 Hanji 14. Chapter 14 provides detailed analysis of this case. See also 'Court Bars Anti-Korean Group from Holding Kawasaki Hate-speech Rally Sunday', *Japan Times* (online), 3 June 2016, available at www.japantimes.co.jp/news/2016/06/03/national/crime-legal/court-bars-anti-korean-group-holding-kawasaki-hate-speech-rally-sunday/ [accessed 17 September 2020]; Tomohiro Osaki, 'Japanese Court Issues First-ever Injunction against Hate-speech Rally', *Japan Times* (online), 3 June 2016, available at www.japantimes.co.jp/news/2016/06/03/national/crime-legal/japanese-court-issues-first-ever-injunction-hate-speech-rally/ [accessed 17 September 2020].

[57] See 'Anti-Korean Hate Speech Rally Called off in Kawasaki amid Protests', *Japan Times* (online), 5 June 2016, available at www.japantimes.co.jp/news/2016/06/05/national/anti-korean-hate-speech-rally-called-off-kawasaki-amid-protests/ [accessed 17 September 2020].

[58] A full document is published at the city's website, available at www.city.kawasaki.jp/250/cmsfiles/contents/0000088/88788/gaidorainn.pdf [accessed 17 September 2020]. See also 'Kawasaki Draws up Japan's First Local Guidelines to Prevent Hate Speech', *Japan Times* (online), 11 November 2017, available at www.japantimes.co.jp/news/2017/11/11/national/social-issues/kawasaki-draws-japans-first-local-guidelines-prevent-hate-speech/ [accessed 17 September 2020].

guideline of its kind in Japan[59] and, thereafter, some local governments published their own.[60]

The guideline is based on article 244(2) of the Local Autonomy Act,[61] which prohibits local governments from denying the use of public facilities by local residents 'without legitimate reasons'. The city has some ordinances that state concrete requirements under the delegation granted by that clause and the guideline has a role in further clarifying those requirements in the context of hate assembly. It authorizes the city to restrict the use of public facilities when it recognizes a concrete likelihood that 'unfair discriminatory speech and behaviour' will be conducted. The definition of 'unfair discriminatory speech and behaviour' basically follows article 2 of the Hate Speech Elimination Act (HSEA).[62] The guideline consequently mainly covers utterances that target people who are (or originates) from other countries, and incite the public to exclude them, and aim to promote and encourage discriminatory attitudes.[63] Types of restriction that can be imposed in such circumstances include 'warning', 'permission with conditions', 'denial of permission', and 'revocation of permission'.[64]

'Denial of permission' and 'revocation of permission' are harsh restrictions that can be issued only when both of the following requirements are met.[65]

[59] See 'Kawasaki Issues Japan's First Guidelines on Public Facility Use Based on Risk of Hate Speech', *Mainichi* (online, English ed.), 10 November 2011, available at https://mainichi.jp/english/articles/20171110/p2a/00m/0na/001000c [accessed 17 September 2020]; 'Kawasaki Draws up Nation's First Guidelines for Eliminating Hate Speech', *Japan Times* (online), 16 June 2017, available at www.japantimes.co.jp/news/2017/06/16/national/social-issues/kawasaki-draws-nations-first-guidelines-eliminating-hate-speech/ [accessed 17 September 2020].

[60] See notes 73–74 and accompanying text.

[61] See note 3.

[62] See Guideline, note 58, at 2. An English translation of the HSEA is available at www.moj.go.jp/content/001199550.pdf [accessed 17 September 2020]. See also Higashikawa, note 52, at 17–22. See Chapters 10 and 11 on the details of the HSEA.

[63] However, the Guideline does not exclude discriminatory speech directed to other groups from its ambit, considering the ICERD and the supplementary resolutions attached to the HSEA by the Judiciary Committees of each House of the Diet. See Guideline, note 58, at 3. English translations of those resolutions are available at www.moj.go.jp/content/001199551.pdf [accessed 17 September 2020] (Supplementary Resolution by the House of Councillors Committee on Judicial Affairs); www.moj.go.jp/content/001199555.pdf [accessed 17 September 2020] (Supplementary Resolution by the House of Representatives Committee on Judicial Affairs).

[64] See Guideline, note 58, at 5–6.

[65] See *ibid.*, at 3–6.

(1) The *speech requirement* obliges the city to establish that it is genuinely likely that unfair discriminatory speech and behaviour will be conducted.
(2) The *annoyance requirement* obliges the city to establish that it is highly likely, in light of objective facts, that the use of facilities by applicants will annoy other users.

Moreover, in the event that these two restrictions are established, the city is required to consult the special expert committee set up as a branch of the Kawasaki City Council on Human Rights Policy, which is an advisory organization to the mayor. Opinions submitted by the committee will be published on the city's website.[66]

It is evident that this guideline is strongly influenced by the TBA's opinion paper and is roughly modelled on its framework. While some maintain that this guideline is constitutional, oppositionists view it as unconstitutional. The next chapter overviews these academic debates.

Kawasaki still remains at the forefront of the battle between rights and lefts. For example, after implementation of the guideline, conservative activists who had repeated hate demonstrations in Kawasaki planned to host a speech by a famous conservative blogger and applied for use of Kawasaki Education and Culture Hall. The city issued permission, but the speech was cancelled, because of a fierce counter-demonstration. The mayor then emphasized freedom of assembly and criticized counter-demonstrators.[67]

On a few occasions, the city issued 'permission with warning' to applicants.[68] If the city ascertained that applicants have conducted hate demonstrations before, it will opt for this measure. To date (at time of writing), 'denial of permission' and 'revocation of permission' have not yet been exercised.[69]

[66] See *ibid.*, at 6–7.

[67] See Shigehiro Saito, 'Kawasaki Shichō "Shishin no Unyō, Tekisetsu": Haigai Demo Dansei Keikaku no Kōenkai Kyoka' ['The Kawasaki mayor said, "it was an appropriate application of the guideline", concerning the permission to use a facility for a lecture by a man who had participated hate demonstrations'], *Asahi Shimbun* (Kanagawa ed.), 6 June 2018, at 23.

[68] See, e.g., 'Shisetsu Riyō de Keikoku, Kawasaki-shi, Heito Jizen Kisei de Hatsu no Shidō' ['"Warning" issued for the use of a facility in Kawasaki City for the first time after the implementation of hate regulation'], *Nikkei Shimbun* (online), 2 December 2018, available at www.nikkei.com/article/DGXMZO38445920S8A201C1CC1000/ [accessed 17 September 2020].

[69] Kawasaki is still a frontrunner on the field of hate speech. It recently enacted a new ordinance called *Kawasaki-shi Sabetsu no nai Jinken Sonchō no Machidukuri Jōrei*

C. *Enactment of the Kyoto Prefecture Guideline*

Following the lead of Kawasaki City, other local public entities also enacted guidelines. For example, Kyoto Prefecture published its guideline in March 2018.[70] This guideline is similar to that of Kawasaki, but different in one important respect: the Kyoto Prefecture guideline allows the prefecture to reject application if either of the following two conditions is met.

(1) There is concrete and high likelihood, in light of objective facts, that 'unfair discriminatory speech and behaviour' will be conducted.
(2) There is an exceptional situation in which the following two requirements are satisfied:
   (i) there is concrete and high likelihood, in light of objective facts, that a disturbance will ensue, because it is highly likely that 'unfair discriminatory speech and behaviour' will be conducted, and that it will become difficult to operate facilities; *and*
   (ii) it is expected that the police will be unable to prevent the disturbance.

Requirement (1) corresponds to the 'speech requirement' of the Kawasaki guideline, while (2) is comparable to its 'annoyance requirement'.[71] However, in the Kyoto Prefecture guideline, the prefecture needs only to prove *either* (1) or (2), while the Kawasaki guideline requires the city to satisfy *both* of the two requirements.

('Kawasaki City Ordinance on Establishing a City with No Discrimination and Respecting Human Rights'). See the City's website, available at www.city.kawasaki.jp/250/cmsfiles/contents/0000113/113041/jyoureil.pdf [accessed 17 September 2020] for the full text. It was a first attempt to criminalize hate speech in Japan. It includes one chapter exclusively focusing on hate speech. This ordinance contains a provision relating to this chapter's topic (art. 16), according to which the mayor is supposed to provide necessary standards to tackle with hate speech in public facilities. Because the existing Kawasaki City guideline is thought to be exactly one of this 'standards' (see the Interpretive Guideline of the ordinance, at 51, available at www.city.kawasaki.jp/250/cmsfiles/contents/0000113/113041/sisinn2.pdf [accessed 17 September 2020]), it is unclear whether the new ordinance will bring some change for actual operation of the Guideline.

[70] 'Kyoto-fu Ōyake no Shisetsutō ni okeru Heito Supīchi Bōshi no tame no Shiyō Tetsuduki ni Kansuru Gaidorain' ['The Guideline for the application procedure to prevent hate speech in Kyoto Prefecture's public facilities'], March 2018, available at www.pref.kyoto.jp/jinken/documents/kyotogl.pdf [accessed 17 September 2020].

[71] Requirement (2) tracks the doctrine developed in the *Ageo* and *Izumisano* cases more accurately than the Kawasaki Guideline.

According to Kyoto Prefecture, in the case of (1), it is appropriate to reject or revoke permission, *because public order or morality will be impaired.*[72] This can be interpreted as demanding a minimum level of civility at public facilities for users. Although the guideline explains that it drew this requirement from *Izumisano*, that case involved breach of the peace in a physical sense. The Kyoto Prefecture illustrated its own interpretation of *Izumisano* to position 'morality' as a ground of rejection or revocation of an application.

D. *Enactment of the Kyoto City Guideline*

Kyoto City followed Kyoto Prefecture, publishing its own guideline in June 2018.[73] This guideline looks quite similar to the Kyoto Prefecture guideline and it features a twofold requirement, the parts of which are connected by the conjunction 'or', as in the Kyoto Prefecture Guideline.

Although requirement (2) is exactly the same as that found in the Kyoto Prefecture guideline, requirement (1) is different. This difference looks small, but it is actually important. It allows the city to turn down an application if there is concrete and high likelihood, in light of objective facts, that 'unfair discriminatory speech and behaviour' will be conducted and that *fundamental human rights, including the right to personality, will be infringed*. The latter part is added to requirement (1) under the Kyoto Prefecture guideline. Drafters may have been concerned about the vague concept of 'unfair discriminatory speech and behaviour' borrowed from the HSEA and attached an additional phrase for clarity.

This trend towards establishment of guidelines at the local level is followed by many local public entities.[74]

[72] See note 70, at 5.

[73] 'Heito Supīchi Kaishōhō o Fumaeta Kyoto-shi no Ōyake no Shisetsutō no Shiyō Tetsuduki ni Kansuru Gaidorain' ['The Guideline for the procedure of using Kyoto City's public facilities in the light of the Hate Speech Elimination Act'] June 2018, available at www.city.kyoto.lg.jp/sogo/cmsfiles/contents/0000239/239850/GL2.pdf [accessed 17 September 2020].

[74] Those local public entities include Kameoka City, Kyoto, Ide Town, Kyoto, and Edogawa City, Tokyo. Recently, Tokyo Metropolitan Government enacted a human rights ordinance containing a provision that restricts the use of public facilities for events that will include discriminatory speech and conduct. See 'Ordinance Aiming to Realize the Idea of Respect for Human Rights in the Olympic Charter', available at www.soumu.metro.tokyo.jp/10jin ken/tobira/pdf/regulations2.pdf [accessed 17 September 2020]. See also Magdalena Osumi, 'Tokyo Adopts Ordinance Banning Discrimination against LGBT Community', *Japan Times* (online), 5 October 2018, available at www.japantimes.co.jp/news/2018/10/05/

V. Scholarly Debates

Some scholars have already published their general opinions on the Kawasaki guideline. Some oppose the denial of applications to use public facilities on the grounds that hate speech will be uttered. Toru Enoki, a professor of constitutional law at Senshu University, makes just such an argument –that local governments should not deny the use of public facilities by hate groups. According to him, this sort of measure is not effective in eliminating hate speech or hate crime; instead, he suggests that national and local governments should work on background social problems such as discriminatory consciousness, prejudice, or economic divides. He claims that although hate speech regulation is a global standard, Japan should adhere to article 21 of its national Constitution in this context.[75]

Yasuo Hasebe, a professor at Waseda University and an eminent constitutional scholar, also belongs to this camp. He argues that, according to *Izumisano Civic Hall*, governments have no power to regulate hate speech without the concrete likelihood that a 'clear and present danger' will manifest. He claims this to be the standard for judging lawfulness when local governments deny the use of public facilities.[76]

In contrast, some commentators argue for denial of the use of public facilities by hate groups in some contexts and they endorse the Kawasaki guideline. In particular, Yasuko Morooka, an attorney and a leading advocate for hate speech regulations, is one such enthusiastic supporter.[77] She is known to be an architect of the TBA's opinion paper, in which her own theoretical position is reflected. She particularly emphasizes Article 2 ICERD.[78] She argues that if a local government were to rent a facility to a hate group, it would 'sponsor, defend or support racial discrimination', in the words of said provision, and that a hate

national/tokyo-adopts-ordinance-banning-discrimination-lgbt-community/ [accessed 17 September 2020].

[75] See Toru Enoki, 'Heito Supīchi, Heito Kuraimu Kisei' ['Regulation of hate speech and hate crime'] (2017) 89 *Hōritsu Jihō* [Legal times] 26, at 31.

[76] See 'Zōo no Hyōgen to Hōkisei' ['Expression of hate and its legal regulation'] *Asahi Shimbun*, 21 July 2015, at 9 (citing comments by Hasebe). This article is a record of the forum in which Hasebe participated and includes some participants' comments.

[77] See Yasuko Morooka, 'Kawasaki-shi ni yoru Heito Supīchi e no Torikumi ni tsuite – Kōkyō Shisetsu Riyō Gaidorain o Chūshin ni' ['On some measures of Kawasaki City to combat hate speech: with special reference to the Guideline for public facilities'] (2018) 757 *Hōgaku Seminā* [Legal seminar] 34.

[78] See note 46. Chapter 3 describes the ICERD and other international human rights treaties in detail.

assembly would contradict some provisions of the rules of each public facility.[79] Naturally, she also points out the relevancy of the HSEA in this context.[80]

Morooka insists that *Izumisano* cannot be applied to cases in which hate speech would harm minority citizens and inflict unbearable pain upon them.[81] Furthermore, she claims that hate assemblies held in not only *open* facilities (e.g. parks or streets) but also *closed* ones (e.g. civic centres or halls) should not be permitted, because hate speech uttered in the latter would still be promulgated via the Internet and the harm will not be confined to the limited spheres of the facility.[82] In light of these reasons, she praises the Kawasaki guideline as a first attempt to combat hate assembly.[83] She argues, however, that the annoyance requirement should be eliminated as redundant, stating that the speech requirement is enough to satisfy the purpose of the HSEA.[84]

Masayuki Uchino, a professor at Chuo University and a renowned regulationist, also argues that some hate assemblies can be excluded from public facilities. He makes the same arguments as Morooka and asserts that hate assemblies might contravene local governments' principles, such as the promotion of multiculturalism. Moreover, governments would effectively be endorsing hate assemblies if they were to rent facilities to such groups.[85] Notably, Uchino had argued that, when freedom of speech is restricted by the provider of the forum, the violated right should be referred to as *han jinken* (a 'semi-human right'), not *kanzen jinken* (a 'perfect human right').[86] This logic might well explain Uchino's position on the subject at hand.

79 See Yasuko Morooka, *Heito Supīchi to wa Nanika* [What is hate speech?] (Iwanami Shoten, 2013), 183–84.

80 See Morooka, note 77, at 35.

81 On the same argument, see Akira Maeda, 'Kōkyō Kūkan ni okeru Heito no Kisei' ['Regulation of hate in public spaces'] (2017) 737 *Buraku Kaihō* [Buraku liberation] 62, at 65.

82 See Morooka, note 77, at 36.

83 See *ibid.*, at 35.

84 See *ibid.*, at 36.

85 See Masayuki Uchino, 'Heito Supīchi' ['Hate speech'] (2014) 403 *Hōgaku Kyōshitsu* [Law classroom] 62, fn. 12. Hiromichi Endo, who is an attorney and a former professor of constitutional law at Tohoku University, supports Uchino's argument: Hiromichi Endo, 'Heito Supīchi Kaishōhō to Ikiru [Living with the Hate Speech Elimination Act'] (2017) 436 *Hōgaku Kyōshitsu* [Law classroom] 48, at 53.

86 See Masayuki Uchino, *Hyōgen, Kyōiku, Shūkyō to Jinken* [Expression, education, religion, and human rights] (Kobundo, 2010), 40.

Some commentators endorse only limited restrictions. Toru Mori asserts that rejecting applications from xenophobes is not permissible under the Constitution in terms of the idea of public forum.[87] However, he admits that such rejection is constitutional, to some extent. The gist of his argument is distinguishing between indoor and outdoor facilities. By *indoor* facilities, he probably means the facilities that are surrounded by walls and which contain sound within them. Community centres or civic halls operated by local governments are among these. *Outdoor* facilities are probably those that have no walls or roof and from which sound escapes into surrounding area. Public parks or civic plazas are typical instances.

According to Mori, it is possible for a local government to deny the use of *outdoor* facilities in limited circumstances. For example, hate speech in an area in which there is a substantial minority population is likely to impair the personality right of targeted residents. It is argued that this is sufficient reason to reject applications.[88] However, hate assembly in *indoor* facilities will not threaten residents in usual circumstances and so it is difficult to deny the use of those facilities even by hate speakers. Mori does, however, offer a highly limited possibility of exceptions even in this case. If the assembly were mostly filled with abusive words targeting a specific group, local government could deny permission to use the facility on the basis that, in this case, speakers would be violating a 'minimum level of civility' required for the use of public facilities.[89]

Hideki Nakamura similarly argues that local governments can reject applications by hate groups only in the case of open facilities in areas with large minority populations, but not closed ones. He asserts that it is only in the former case that other users' rights would likely be infringed.[90] But he attempts to limit the possibility of denial more narrowly than does Mori: he allows no limited exception for denial of use in the case of closed indoor facilities. Nakamura is strongly against the idea of governments denying applications so as to send a message against hate speech, arguing that this would be a dangerous idea if it were to extend to other kinds of

[87] Mori's argument on hate speech is developed in this volume. See Chapter 14.

[88] See Toru Mori, 'Kenpō Soshō no Jissen to Riron, Dai Ikkai: Heito Demo Kinshi Karishobun Meirei Jiken' ['Theory and Practice of constitutional litigation, no. 1: the case of injunction against a hate demonstration'] (2017) 2321 *Hanji* 3, at 8.

[89] See *ibid.*, at 8–9.

[90] See Hideki Nakamura, 'Heito Supīch Kaishōhō o Uketa Chihō Kōkyō Dantai no Torikumi to Kadai' ['Efforts and challenges of local public entities after the Hate Speech Elimination Act'] (2018) 757 *Hōgaku Seminā* [Legal seminar] 37, at 41. On his view about local governments' policies against hate speech, see Chapter 9.

assemblies.[91] He refuses to endorse the idea of 'civility' and, in this way, he departs from Mori.

VI. Possible Accommodations

A. *The Rule-Oriented Nature of the Oppositionists' Theory*

How can we accommodate these conflicting opinions? In my view, the oppositionists' argument cannot be supported, for their argument over-categorizes conflicting interests and abstracts highly complex factors.

The nature of the oppositionists' position can be illuminated through the lens of the 'rule vs standard' debate in the United States, where this dichotomy has been an important theme of discussion for some decades among legal scholars.[92] 'Rule' values the rigid application of laws, while 'standard' allows their flexible application. Alternatively, we can use the concept of 'categorization' in this field of debate. Rule-oriented methods favour categorization, while standard-oriented ones tend to prefer 'particularization', or case-specific methodologies. It is a well-known fact that the Supreme Court of the United States has preferred the method of 'rule' or 'categorization' in the area of free speech in general and hate speech in particular.[93]

Here, I will examine Hasebe's theory proposing a deeper analysis. The main points of his arguments on hate speech are as follows.[94]

- Content (and viewpoint) regulations should be suspect in principle, because it is likely that they reflect improper motivations among legislators. Because hate speech regulations typically bear this character, we should hesitate to implement them.
- It is doubtful that there are legitimate governmental interests in regulating hate speech. Some forms of hate speech may cause hate crimes in some cases, but Japan has not faced such dangers – at least to date.
- Hate speech regulations are not consistent with the Supreme Court's precedents. According to the *Izumisano* and *Ageo* cases, governments

[91] See *ibid.*

[92] See, e.g., Kathleen M. Sullivan, 'Foreword: The Justices of Rules and Standards' (1992) 106 *Harv. L. Rev.* 22; Pierre J. Schlag, 'Rules and Standards' (1985) 33 *UCLA L. Rev.* 379; Frederick Schauer, *Playing by the Rules: A Philosophical Examination of Rule-Based Decision-Making in Law and in Life* (Clarendon Press, 1993).

[93] See generally Frederick Schauer, 'The Exceptional First Amendment', in Michael Ignatieff (ed.), *American Exceptionalism and Human Rights* (Princeton University Press, 2009), 29.

[94] See note 76, at 9 (comments by Hasebe).

have no powers to regulate hate speech without a concrete likelihood that a clear and present danger will manifest.

- Hate speech is distinguished from hate crime and the latter can be regulated constitutionally. Abuse of governmental powers is not so grave in the case of hate crime regulations and the harms of hate crime are much more damaging than those of hate speech.

As is clear from the above, Hasebe's argument is quintessentially rule-oriented. However, he is not alone in this and in his hesitation to embrace hate speech regulation. Other oppositionists, such as Shigenori Matsui, Koichi Yokota, and Toru Enoki, take similar approaches.[95] For example, Matsui and Yokota are strong opponents of hate speech regulations. They support regulation only in severely limited contexts, such as when governments are able to demonstrate a high likelihood of imminent dangers, or when hate speech is directed against individual victims.[96] Not coincidentally, all of these scholars specialize in US constitutional law. In this context, it can be safely said that rule orientation is the exact reflection of US free speech jurisprudence. Hasebe's argument on the use of public facilities by hate groups is an example of his rule-oriented theory on hate speech in general, as is that of Enoki.

B. The Need for Particularization

How can we evaluate the oppositionists' theory? In this context, we should first note that there are numerous categories of hate speech. Indeed, hate speech regulations can be classified in terms of various elements such as targets, harms, actions, media, manner, consequences, and regulatory modes. These constitute one portion of the varied forms of hate speech regulation, and it is impossible to designate them under a single category of content regulation and subject them all to strict scrutiny.

In this light, Hasebe's arguments appear to be overly rule-oriented. First, his application of the content-neutrality principle is too categorical. While

[95] See, e.g., Shigenori Matsui, 'The Challenge to Multiculturalism: Hate Speech Ban in Japan' (2016) 49 *U.B.C. L. Rev.* 427; Koichi Yokota, 'Jinshu Sabetsu Teppai Jōyaku to Nihonkoku Kenpō: Hyōgen Kisei ni tsuite' ['International Convention on the Elimination of All Forms of Racial Discrimination and the Constitution of Japan: on the regulation of free expression'], in *Gendai Rikken Shugi no Tenkai* [Development of modern constitutionalism], vol. 1 (Yuhikaku, 1993), 715; Enoki, note 75. Matsui explains about his position on this volume: see Chapter 2.

[96] See Matsui, note 95, at 475; Shigenori Matsui, *Masu Mediahō Nyūmon* [Introduction to mass media law], 5th ed. (Yuhikaku, 2013), 167–68; Yokota, note 95, at 736–37.

it is quite possible for some extreme varieties of hate speech to be extracted as exceptions to that principle, he does not acknowledge this by any means.

Second, it seems natural for a government to find legislative interests in restricting hate speech in this increasingly charged climate of hate in Japan, but Hasebe affirms that he still sees no legislative facts supporting hate speech regulation.

Third, the *Izumisano* and *Ageo* cases should be distinguished from those involving hate groups. As Morooka correctly argues, they do not apply to hate assemblies. In both cases, a hostile audience was involved. It is wholly inconsistent with free speech values if a government denies hate groups its permission to use public facilities for the reason that it would cause a breach of the peace by a hostile audience, because this grants that audience a 'heckler's veto'. However, the true problem of hate groups' assemblies is that they harm local residents' interests in pursuing peaceful lives. It was a mistake for the Kawasaki guideline to use the word 'annoyance' in this respect, as Morooka duly notes. Indeed, we cannot describe harms to minority residents only as 'annoyance'; it should be people around facilities other than those being targeted who will be annoyed by hate speech. The guideline appears to have chosen this particular term because it refers to *Izumisano* as a relevant precedent.[97]

Fourth, Hasebe's distinction between hate speech and hate crime is also too categorical. Sometimes, hate speech can be more harmful than hate crime and distrust of the government can be minimized even in the case of hate speech regulation when the types of unprotected speech can be successfully categorized.

This rule orientation of Hasebe is conspicuously shared by other oppositionists. Noted oppositionists such as Shigenori Matsui, Koichi Yokota, or Toru Enoki, who are influenced by US First Amendment jurisprudence to a great extent, openly endorse rule-oriented interpretation of article 21 of the Constitution of Japan.[98]

C. *Proper Levels of Categorization*

As has just been seen, forming some categories of exceptions for the content-neutrality principle is unavoidable.[99] Some content regulations

[97] See note 58, at 20–26 (appendix 9 cites the full text of *Izumisano*).

[98] See Yuji Nasu, *Heito Supīchihō no Hikaku Kenkyū* [A comparative study of hate speech laws] (Shinzansha, 2019), 484.

[99] The following argument is developed in detail in Yuji Nasu, 'Jiko Tōchi: Genron no Jiyū no Kachi to Hōri no Kakyō ni tsuite no Ichishiron' ['Self-governance: the relationship

may be permitted if violation of the core principle of viewpoint neutrality can be avoided. It is impossible to establish the content-neutrality principle as an absolute category in a mature society in modern democracies in which a limitless variety of social interests conflict with each other.[100] Speech against private persons involves especially numerous elements, making it highly difficult to balance interests. Hate speech is exactly such a case[101] and some exceptions must be made to the content-neutrality principle.

I contend that the following four elements, in particular, should be considered in classifying harmful speech: values of speech, civility, harms, and line-drawing.[102] Some forms of speech that have extremely low value, lack civility, and cause severe harms should be permitted to be regulated constitutionally if we are also to be sensitive to line-drawing concerns. In addition, hate speech can sometimes be more easily regulated in limited contexts, such as schools, prisons, or the workplace.

From this point of view, some sorts of hate speech restrictions do not violate the content-neutrality principle, including, among others, criminal prohibitions of extreme hate speech directed face-to-face at minority people, injunctions against demonstrations that are likely to see desperate epithets flung at minority populated residential areas,[103] or imposing sanctions on employees who utter hate speech in a highly uncivil way in and outside of their workplace.

D. *The Constitutionality of the Three Guidelines*

I firmly believe that denying the use of governmental properties to hate groups in some contexts is also a permissible exception to the content-neutrality principle. As Uchino argues, this is not a case of content *regulation* such as criminal punishment but of *discrimination* based on content in a limited context. Content neutrality should therefore not be applied too rigorously. Certainly, parks and civic halls are traditional or designated (sometimes limited) public fora, in words of the US Supreme

between values and doctrines of free speech'], in Keigo Komamura and Hidemi Suzuki (eds.) *Hyōgen no Jiyū I: Jōkyō e* [Freedom of expression: to the current situations] (Shogakusha, 2011), 41.

100 See Jamal Greene, 'Forward: Rights as Trumps?' (2018) 132 *Harv. L. Rev.* 28, at 32–33.

101 See Jeremy Waldron, *The Harm in Hate Speech* (Harvard University Press, 2014), 201–03.

102 I developed detailed arguments in Nasu, note 98, at 501–19.

103 See the case referred to on note 56.

Court, and the discretion of local governments should be minimized. However, hate groups are still allowed to use other public places for demonstrations and they can also utilize various alternative media, such as books, magazines, and the Internet.

In the event that a hate group is denied the use of public facilities, the prior restraint doctrine should not be applied too rigorously either. This is not a complete ban of particular expressions or a total exclusion of them from the marketplace of ideas; rather, it is simply keeping some extreme expressions out of certain public facilities. These conclusions are reinforced by relevant provisions of the ICERD and the HSEA, as Morooka asserts.

Although the US courts apply the public forum and prior restraint doctrines rigidly to the problem of hate assembly in public facilities,[104] Japanese courts can be more flexible, considering their traditional, standard-oriented methodology, which allows them to take multifaceted elements into account in judicial review.[105]

This analysis clarifies that the guidelines of Kawasaki City, Kyoto City, and Kyoto Prefecture do not violate general doctrines of content neutrality, public forum, or prior restraint. However, it is crucial to explore whether those guidelines are constitutional in the light of some theories described in the previous section.

Here, I tentatively provide a formula for judging the constitutionality: *when a hate assembly is predicted to involve extreme and uncivil speech with a high likelihood of severe harms, a local government can deny the use of facilities so long as it adheres to a published guideline with clear and articulate phrasing.*

I do not mean that this is an absolute requirement for local governments to satisfy, but they can safely avoid the problem of unconstitutionality by crossing this threshold in drafting ordinances or guidelines.

I will elaborate on this formula for further refinement of the guidelines.

(1) Local governments cannot deny applications merely on the grounds that hate groups' use of public facilities will contradict the government's visions or ideals, such as equality, justice, multiculturalism, or

[104] See, e.g., *Ringers* and *Knights of Ku Klux Klan*, note 9. See also *Matter of Rockwell* v. *Morris*, 12 A.D.2d 272 (N.Y. App. Div. 1961). In the United States, it is considered unconstitutional to require applicants to buy extraordinary amounts of insurance in application for the use of public facilities. See *Collin* v. *Smith* 447 F.Supp. 676, 684–86 (N. D. Ill. 1978); *Collin* v. *Smith* 578 F.2d 1197, 1207–10 (7th Cir. 1978); *Collin* v. *O'Malley*, Docket. No. 76C2024 (unpublished).

[105] See Chapter 15 on this point.

coexistence. Instead, governments should be required to demonstrate certain harms that are caused by hate groups' assemblies.

(2) A hate group's assembly should not be prohibited based only on the character of the group. This is the rule established by *Izumisano Civic Hall*. Local governments are permitted to deny the use of public facilities to the *yakuza* (organized crime syndicates in Japan) because of its character as a gangster organization, but this is an exception. Furthermore, it should be pointed out that because the Japanese government has reserved Article 4(b) ICERD,[106] hate groups are not deemed illegal as such in Japan.

(3) The harms that local governments establish must be severe and significant, not only immediate.

(4) Before local governments may deny applications to use public facilities, they may think it necessary to investigate the past speech and conduct of the relevant persons and groups. This raises serious privacy concerns and is in danger of becoming an unjust prior restraint.

(5) In deciding to issue permission for the use of facilities, local governments may consider *forms* of facilities, especially whether they are open or closed.

Principles (1) and (2) can be a logical extension of the viewpoint-neutrality principle. Viewpoint neutrality is a firmly established principle of free speech and so viewpoint-based regulations are prohibited as a rule.[107] When such a regulation is tolerated, there is a danger that regulations will be motivated solely by the government's own interests.[108] Moreover, it would surely undermine individual autonomy by inviting paternalism.[109] To preclude impermissible viewpoint regulations from sneaking into laws, courts should require governments to establish at least some existence of harm. Indirect and long-term harms in speech restrictions will also be suspect, for those harms are vague and difficult to

[106] It provides that state parties '[s]hall declare illegal and prohibit organizations, and also organized and all other propaganda activities, which promote and incite racial discrimination, and shall recognize participation in such organizations or activities as an offence punishable by law'.

[107] See, e.g., Erwin Chemerinsky, 'Content Neutrality as a Central Problem of Freedom of Speech: Problems in the Supreme Court's Application' (2000) 74 *S. Cal. Rev.* 49, at 56–59.

[108] See Elena Kagan, 'Private Speech, Public Purpose: The Role of Governmental Motive in First Amendment Doctrine' (1996) 63 *U. Chi. L. Rev.* 413, at 451–53.

[109] See David A. Strauss, 'Persuasion, Autonomy, and Freedom of Expression' (1991) 91 *Colum. L. Rev.* 334, at 339–40.

establish, which can lead to governments abusing their power or invading the sphere of individual autonomy.

Certainly, the guidelines are not to be blamed with respect to (1) and (2), because they clearly make harms by hate assembly grounds of restraint. Morooka argues that if a local government were to rent a facility to a hate group, it would 'sponsor, defend or support racial discrimination' in the words of Article 2 ICERD – but this logic cannot be used as a freestanding ground for denial of permission.[110] We should require demonstration of some harms as a threshold requirement for the denial, considering the value of the right to assembly and expression. However, I should add that, as explained shortly, where a minimum level of civility were violated, local governments could issue denials without demonstration of harms.

The guidelines appear to be seriously problematic in terms of (3). They reduce situations in which applications are denied, based on concepts such as 'concrete' and 'high likelihood' established by the Supreme Court precedents explained above, but they do not mention any gravity of possible harms. They should have targeted only harmful expressions beyond a certain level of gravity.

Where Kyoto Prefecture and Kyoto City guidelines are lacking a requirement of annoyance, they depart from the Kawasaki guideline. The Kyoto Prefecture guideline permits the denial of using facilities if it is concretely and highly likely, in light of objective facts, that unfair discriminatory speech and behaviour will be conducted. The Kyoto City guideline added the phrase '*fundamental human rights, including the right to personality, will be infringed*'. Although they might be unconstitutionally applied to hate demonstration causing little harm, these conditions are thought to be constitutional, so long as they are rigorously

[110] In the United States, this issue can be discussed within the framework of state action doctrine. In *Ringers*, note 9, a school board rejected an application from an extreme right-wing party to use a school facility. The Court of Appeals for the Fourth Circuit examined whether the state action doctrine required denial of an organization that practises a racially discriminatory membership policy. The court held that the state is not to be considered as espousing, encouraging, or supporting discriminatory membership policies when it permits an assembly of such an organization to meet in a public facility. The court simply denied that the state action doctrine is not applicable in that context. See *Ringers*, 473 F.2d at 1016–17. In *Knights of Ku Klux Klan*, note 9, the KKK was once permitted to use a school facility by the school board, but the board later withdrew that permission. In this case, the applicability of state action doctrine was also discussed by the Court of Appeals for the Fifth Circuit. The court rejected the existence of state action in this situation. See *Knights of Ku Klux Klan*, 578 F.2d at 1128.

applied. The courts should carefully read down the phrase 'unfair discriminatory speech and behaviour'. Kyoto City can be praised for adding the words 'fundamental human rights' or 'the right to personality', so as to heighten a threshold of harm.

The guidelines are not sensitive to the problem described in (4), because they clearly allow officials to consider the nature of applicants and the history of their activities without any limitations on the judgment of applications.[111] In my opinion, local governments should restrict the scope of denial more narrowly than do the guidelines. Other local governments may alternatively exclude a 'denial' option completely and set up only a 'revocation of permission'. This means that almost all applications will be received automatically, but revoked afterwards when they violate the rules.

Scholarly opinions are divided regarding (5). As mentioned, Mori and Nakamura argue that local governments, in principle, can deny only the use of open facilities, such as parks and streets, where minority residents are more vulnerable to extreme hate speech.[112] However, as Morooka asserts, local governments can also deny applications for the use of closed facilities, such as civic centres and public halls, when hate groups apply for assembly using extremely derogatory language.

In May 2014, Zaitokukai applied to use the civic hall in Kadoma City for an event with the title *Chōsen no Shokufun Bunka o Sonchō Shiyō* ('Respect the Korean Culture of Eating Faeces').[113] The group's application was initially accepted, but later revoked by the city. This assembly utterly contradicted the purpose of the establishment and operation of public facilities. Furthermore, it can be said to be a typical abuse of rights, because the group clearly made the application for the purpose of attacking minority residents. The concept of civility is particularly relevant here. As Mori asserts, assembly in public facilities needs to demonstrate a minimum level of civility. Mori rightly argued that local authorities could deny the use even of indoor facilities in the event of an extreme situation violating minimum civility standards. The applicant in Kadoma clearly violated such standards.

The Kyoto Prefecture guideline might be condemned in that it allows the authority to reject applications only when public order or morality

[111] See Kawasaki Guideline, note 58, at 4; Kyoto Prefecture Guideline, note 70, at 4; Kyoto City Guideline, note 73, at 6.

[112] See text accompanying notes 88–91.

[113] See Morooka, note 77, at 36. On the Kadoma incident, see text accompanying note 44.

will be impaired. Indeed, this might undermine freedom of speech and assembly, depending on the actual practice of applications. Moreover, 'morality' is an old-fashioned legal concept, which is vague and malleable. The Kyoto Prefecture guideline could, however, be read as introducing the concept of civility described above. It should be constitutional, so long as it will be moderately applied in extreme cases like that of Kadoma. Although the Kyoto City guideline added the concepts of fundamental human rights and the personality right to the requirement of the Kyoto Prefecture guideline, the basic idea of civility is thought to be endorsed there as well.

In sum, it is fair to state that, in the case of open facilities, it is easier to justify denial of use of facilities, but that, even in cases of closed facilities, local governments could issue denials in highly exceptional cases of incivility.

Despite some defects, the guidelines are within the ambit of constitutionality, since they narrow the concept of likelihood and require objective and clear evidence. It is also commendable that the Kawasaki guideline makes it essential to consult a special committee in cases of 'denial of permission' and 'revocation of permission'. However, the three guidelines can be ameliorated in some aspects, as I have argued, and other local governments should be more deliberate in drafting similar guidelines.

Other concerns may be raised. First, the guidelines may be criticized as overstepping the scope set out by national law and violating article 94 of the Constitution. However, after the 1999 local governance reform, each local government has been given wide discretion on interpretation of article 244(2) of the Local Autonomy Act.[114]

Second, some oppositionists may argue that the guidelines go beyond the delegation of article 244 and allow the local government to exercise police power. However, harms to minority residents by a hate assembly originate from hate speakers and the assembly itself, not from a hostile audience or another third party disturbing the peace. Administrators of public facilities who have the responsibility of promoting the welfare of local residents[115] are engaging in the day-to-day operations of facilities when they protect residents from egregious hate.

[114] See Hideki Nakamura, 'Chihō Kōkyō Dantai ni yoru Heito Supīchi e no Torikumi to Kadai [Efforts and challenges of local public entities against hate speech'] (2016) 736 *Hōgaku Seminā* [Legal seminar] 41, at 43.

[115] See art. 244(1) of the Local Autonomy Act.

VII. Conclusion

An overly rule-oriented methodology may interfere with constructive debate and productive solutions to current hate speech problems. The case of local public facilities in Japan aptly illustrates this point. It is highly misleading to equalize the *Izumisano* and *Ageo* cases with those involving typical hate assemblies. Harms done by hate assemblies must be taken seriously, but denials of permission must be narrowly limited to extreme situations.

The problem of hate assembly in local public facilities is relatively novel in academic discussions, even outside of Japan. Countries that regulate hate speech do not permit hate groups to assemble in public facilities and countries that do not regulate it accept their assembly.[116] Japan is attempting to find a middle ground. Its solution is far from perfect and leaves much yet to be considered, but it certainly provides valuable lessons for other countries that are experiencing similar issues.

Update

Tokyo Metropolitan Government enacted its own guideline under the Ordinance Aiming to Realize the Idea of Respect for Human Rights in the Olympic Charter in March 2019.[117] The requirements under this guideline for limiting the use of public facilities are relatively strict, in that facilities managers must demonstrate both that hate speech will be uttered and that hate speech is likely to cause security problems within the facilities.

On 17 August 2020, Tokyo Metropolitan Government accepted an application from a right-wing organization for the use of a public park. This organization had tried to protest the memorial ceremony for Korean victims of the Kantō Massacre. Although Tokyo Metropolitan Government had officially recognized some of the organization's utterances as 'hate speech' the previous year, the government accepted the 2020 application on the basis of respect for freedoms of speech and assembly.

[116] See Orange County Human Relations Commission, 'Free Speech vs Hate Speech: Practical Guidelines for Managing Public Forums', January 2014, available at www.ca-ilg.org/sites/main/files/file-attachments/free-speech-vs-hate-commission-guidelines-12.12.2013.pdf [accessed 17 September 2020]. (In this guideline, a local government in the United States clearly permits hate speech in public facilities.)

[117] See www.metro.tokyo.lg.jp/tosei/hodohappyo/press/2019/03/29/documents/29.pdf [accessed 17 September 2020].

Nagoya City, Aichi, is also in the midst of the debate over the use public facilities by hate groups. The Aichi chapter of far-right *Nippon Daiichitō* ('Japan First Party') attempted to hold an event in a facility managed by Nagoya City. This organization's discriminatory speech at a past event had provoked controversy. The city accepted the application in September 2020, although Aichi Prefecture had withdrawn its permission for that same organization's use of a public facility the previous year.

20

Hate Speech in the Mass Media

A Dispute over Broadcasting in Japan

SHINJI UOZUMI

I. Introduction: Hate Speech in the Print Media

In March 2016, Japan's Centre for Human Rights Education and Training released the results of a hate speech survey sponsored by the Ministry of Justice.[1] One of its statistics shows the number of hate speech demonstrations per season (three months) from 2012 through 2015. Hate speech demonstrations (or 'demos' for short) in Japan often try to inflame animus against Korea and China. The general public realized that it had become a social issue when an underage demo participant yelled *Tsuruhashi Daigyakusatsu* ('Massacre Koreans in the Tsuruhashi area!') in February 2013.[2]

The number of demos peaked during the early spring of 2013 (102), the early summer of 2014 (104), and the summer of 2014 (105). Altogether, 311 of 1,152 demos (14 seasons[3]) took place in these three seasons. The same survey also found that major newspapers in the country and public broadcaster NHK ran 235 stories about hate speech in 2013 (four seasons) and 324 in 2014 (four seasons) out of 740 stories between 2012 and 2015 (the full 16 seasons). That figure decreased to 180 in 2015. Only one story appeared in 2012.[4]

[1] Centre for Human Rights Education and Training, *Heito Supīchi ni Kansuru Jittai Chōsa Hōkokusho* [Report of a fact-finding survey concerning hate speech], Ministry of Justice, March 2016, available at www.moj.go.jp/content/001201158.pdf [accessed 17 January 2019].

[2] The neighbourhood in Osaka is well known for its concentration of Korean residents.

[3] The survey could not trace the number of demonstrations for the full 16 seasons (2012–15), but it was able to count all of the news stories.

[4] Il Song Nakamura provides more detailed analysis of newspapers in Chapter 12 of this volume.

If it can be inferred from the survey that newspaper readers and television viewers were exposed to hate speech more often during 2013 and 2014, the same can be said of readers of books and magazines. Because of the difficulty of defining the term *Heitobon* ('hate speech books'), the exact number is not known.[5] However, Motohiko Kimura, a journalist who follows the hate movement, points out that 2014 was a 'bubble' of anti-Korea and anti-China publishing.[6] In 2013–14, some publishers found that 'hate' contents sold well, so they increased the pages describing Korea and China as enemies of Japan in their monthly magazines. Other publishers brought out books filled with negative descriptions about Korean society, culture, and people. Some went further to label newspapers such as *Asahi Shinbun* as *han nichi* ('anti-Japan') or *baikoku* ('traitor to Japan'), since it reported on the issue of Korean 'comfort women' actively and critically.[7] Books and magazines from the other publishers opined that the Japanese military and the government had nothing to do with recruiting 'comfort women' in Korea during the Pacific War. Moreover, they attacked *Asahi Shinbun* for spreading 'fake news' worldwide and damaging Japan's reputation.[8]

Bookstores in Japan stocked several hate books on their shelves during 2013 and 2014. One editor of such books recalls with regret that publishers demanded editors set out their purpose as *ryūin o sageru* ('to give relief') to right-wingers and people critical of Korea.[9] While acknowledging freedom of the press, Motohiko Kimura warns that books and magazines of this sort are purposely selecting negatively skewed information and misleading the public. The effect may have been somewhat

5 Hate books contain extreme language directed against Koreans and Chinese. Those books often use conspiracy theories to inflame discriminatory and suspicious sentiments.

6 Mitsunari Oizumi, Naoki Kato, and Motohiko Kimura (eds.), *Saraba Heitobon!* [Farewell, hate speech books!] (Korokara, 2015), 15, according to which some 200 hate books were published in 2013–14.

7 In general, *Asahi Shinbun*, *Mainichi Shinbun*, and *Tokyo Shinbun* are considered 'liberal'. *Yomiuri Shinbun*, *Sankei Shinbun*, and *Nikkei Shinbun* are thought of as 'conservative'. All six are critical of hate speech.

8 *Asahi Shinbun* admitted that one part of its series of reports about Korean comfort women was not based on fact. See Reiji Yoshida, '*Asahi Shinbun* Admits Errors in Past "Comfort Women" Stories', *Japan Times*, 5 August 2014, available at www.japantimes.co.jp/news/2014/08/05/national/politics-diplomacy/asahi-shimbun-admits-errors-in-past-comfort-women-stories/#.XFJmWXnxpzk [accessed 30 January 2019]. The error probably made it easier for conservatives to bash not only the newspaper, but also others who sympathized with the Korean comfort women.

9 Oizumi *et al.*, note 6, at 26–27.

ameliorated by Japan's enactment of the Hate Speech Elimination Act in 2016.[10]

II. The Problem: Hate Speech on the Television

People worldwide are decreasing the time devoted to legacy media such as newspapers and television and radio as they pay more attention to digital media such as social networking services and YouTube. Japan is no exception.[11] According to the Ministry of Internal Affairs and Communications (MIC), people read newspapers for 10.2 minutes on average per day (Monday–Friday) in 2017, compared to 11.8 minutes in 2013.[12] They watched broadcast television an average of 159.4 minutes per day in 2017, compared to 168.3 minutes in 2013. However, daily time spent on the Internet rose from 77.9 minutes in 2013 to 100.4 minutes in 2017. Thus, although the trend is clear, the Japanese were still spending more time with their televisions than the Internet in 2017.

Several factors explain why broadcast television remains Japan's major medium. Senior citizens account for a large percentage of the population and they prefer television. An Internet search requires typing on a keyboard – a skill that many older people never acquired. The Japanese educational system has long been based on writing by hand. This demographic also tends to be less devoted to smartphones than younger generations, in part because the small screens may tax their aging eyes.

Other factors, even more salient, may be governmental policy and law. Both have been supportive of maintaining the status quo of legacy industries. A legal border remains in place between broadcast media and common carriers even though technological convergence continues

[10] For the text of the Act in English, see www.moj.go.jp/content/001199550.pdf [accessed 18 January 2019]. In this Act, hate speech is 'unfair discriminatory speech and behaviour'. Kotani explains that these are expressive activities that 'incite the exclusion of persons' who originate from outside Japan yet lawfully reside in Japan by making statements that have the effect of harming their life, body, freedom, reputation, or property, or by severely insulting them in public with the intent of inducing discriminatory feelings against them. Kotani questions the Act's restraining power since it does not penalize or criminalize those activities. See Junko Kotani, 'Proceed with Caution: Hate Speech Regulation in Japan' (2018) 45 *Hastings Const. L.Q.* 603, at 605. For more detail and discussions of the Act, see Chapter 11. See also Chapter 3.

[11] For hate speech on the Internet, see Chapter 18.

[12] Information and Communications Statistics Database, Ministry of Internal Affairs and Communications, available at www.soumu.go.jp/johotsusintokei/whitepaper/ja/h30/html/nd252510.html [accessed 17 January 2019].

apace. Various barriers constructed by policy and the law have resulted in newcomers facing difficulty in expanding beyond the market. The team of Rupert Murdoch and Masayoshi Son, the founder of the common carrier SoftBank, failed to buy out TV Asahi in 1995. Young IT ventures such as Rakuten failed to take over Tokyo Broadcasting System (TBS) between 2005 and 2009. Public sentiment was on the side of the broadcasters in both cases. It should also be noted that Japanese television networks have close ties with major newspapers.[13] Japanese newspapers will not allow outsiders to break into the broadcast market, especially terrestrial broadcasting in Japan.

As sacred as the broadcasting market is, broadcast content is regulated under the Broadcasting Act of Japan, enacted in 1950. Under the law, broadcast programmes should not contain messages that harm morals or public safety. Also, politically biased messages and distorted facts should not be broadcast in news reporting. A station that fails to screen out such problematic content from its programmes might jeopardize its broadcast licence.[14]

While some indecent programmes have snuck in, not many viewers would have expected to watch a programme that contained 'hate' until the broadcast of a particular show called *News Joshi* ('News Girls'). *News Joshi* is a series of *mochikomi bangumi* ('brought-in programmes'),[15] the number of which is increasing on local terrestrial television stations – mainly a result of the shrinking market in rural areas. Independent television stations are losing the financial and human resources with which to produce their own original content. Even some network affiliates in rural areas have started to depend on opening up part of their schedule to channel-shopping shows that are brought in.

[13] Consider Nippon TV and TV Asahi, for example. The former has capital ties with *Yomiuri Shinbun* (*Yomiuri Shinbun* holds more than 14 per cent of shares of Nippon TV); the latter, with *Asahi Shinbun* (*Asahi Shinbun* holds more than 24 per cent of shares of TV Asahi).

[14] The Ministry for Internal Affairs and Communications, the broadcast licensing authority in Japan, warned in 2016 that the government can suspend broadcasting for a violation of the law: see 'Sanae Takaichi Warns That Government Can Shut Down Broadcasters It Feels Are Biased', *Japan Times*, 9 February 2016, available at www.japantimes.co.jp/news/2016/02/09/national/politics-diplomacy/minister-warns-that-government-can-shut-down-broadcasters-it-feels-are-biased/#.XJzjIXnxpzk [accessed 20 March 2019]. It is true that art. 79 of the Radio Act gives power to the Minister to revoke the licence of a radio station; however, the Radio Act is intended to oversee *technical* standards and it is questionable whether art. 79 can be applied to regulate the *content* broadcast.

[15] The station is paid to broadcast the programme.

III. *News Joshi* and Its Episodes #91 and #92

News Joshi is a weekly, 60-minute programme that local terrestrial broadcaster Tokyo Metropolitan TV (MXTV) has aired since 2015. The show is sponsored and produced by a business entity called DHC and its subsidiary.[16] MXTV was simply selling the time slot to DHC and airing the content that *News Joshi* delivered. Nevertheless, MXTV was still responsible for the show under the Broadcasting Act, because it was MXTV that had the licence to broadcast. As the licensee, MXTV had a responsibility to screen the content of *News Joshi* before putting it on air.

The show's title suggests that it is a newscast, but it is actually an infotainment/variety show. Panellists, such as journalists and professors, discuss current topics based on video clips, with only young women as studio guests. *News Joshi* advertised on its website that the show would reveal deep truths hidden from existing news stories with which people are familiar. In other words, it declared that it would challenge the typical news coverage that the major media had been presenting. Although MXTV stopped running the programme at the end of March 2018, *News Joshi* is still produced for Internet distribution, satellite television, and other local stations.[17]

Episode #91, aired on 2 January 2017, was subtitled 'Okinawa Kinkyū Chōsa: Masukomi ga Hōdō shinai Shinjitsu' ('Urgent research on Okinawa: the truth the mass media do not report'). It featured protests in Okinawa against US military bases, including the construction of helipads in the Takae area.[18] The episode devoted approximately its first 19 minutes to the story, taking a negative tone towards protesters. The mainstream media, by contrast, often described protestors rather positively as 'peace activists'.

A journalist calling himself a specialist in military affairs visited Okinawa for the show. In the video, he said that the protesters were too

[16] DHC Corporation, a cosmetics manufacturer based in Tokyo, had a subsidiary company called DHC Theater (now DHC Television). DHC Theater co-produced *News Joshi* with an outside production firm called Boy's TV Direction Company.

[17] It is now known that other stations dropped some shows after screening them. Miyagi TV dropped episode #91 after its screening: see 'Naiyō Ippōteki to Handan, Nyūsu Joshi Hōsō Sezu, Miyagi Terebi' ['Miyagi TV did not air *News Girls* because it was biased'], *Okinawa Times*, 28 January 2017, available at www.okinawatimes.co.jp/articles/-/81706 [accessed 17 January 2019].

[18] Episode #91 can be found online at https://dhctv.jp/movie/100690/ [accessed 31 January 2019].

dangerous to ask for an interview. Instead, he talked to a few people who were critical of the protests. One of the interviewees told the journalist that the protesters were brutal enough to stop an ambulance from rescuing a riot police officer who had been injured during protests. The journalist and an interviewee went so far as to suggest that the protesters were akin to 'terrorists'.

After the video footage from Okinawa was shown, the studio panel discussion began. The journalist suggested that some of the protesters might be from Korea and China. A studio guest asked: why would Koreans protest the US helipads, while China could be concerned with the construction of an additional US military facility in Okinawa? Another panellist answered, 'Because some Koreans were pro-North Korea'.

The journalist and panel also alleged that the protesters and citizen reporters had come from mainland cities such as Tokyo. With some evidence in hand, the journalist suggested that some people from the mainland were not volunteers, but paid participants in the protest. At that point, the studio conversation and some captions on the television screen implied that a particular *Zainichi* ('resident in Japan')[19] Korean woman, one of the co-leaders of a citizens group,[20] was hiring the people. Another panellist responded that the woman had been active in several protests, spanning anti-nuclear power plants, anti-discrimination, and anti-hate speech.

The next week, the first 9 minutes of episode #92 justified the journalist's view that China had something to do with the Okinawa protest. It was suggested that the ultimate goal might be the independence of Okinawa from Japan. An official pamphlet issued by the Public Security Intelligence Agency of Japan was shown.[21] The journalist and panel seemed to be confident of their critical perspective towards news coverage presented by the major networks.

News Joshi could be regarded as a unique programme showing a very different perspective. But there were problems: did *News Joshi* really try to seek the truth based on facts, or did it slander the protesters and citizen reporters? The leader of a citizens' group, described in the show as

19 Zainichi Koreans mainly came from colonized Korea. They and their descendants formed Korean communities in certain parts of cities and towns in Japan.

20 This citizens' group is known for protesting hate speech, racism, and discrimination against minorities. Its website can be found at https://norikoenet.jp/ [accessed 31 January 2019].

21 Episode #92 can be found online at https://dhctv.jp/movie/100691/ [accessed 31 January 2019].

a behind-the-scenes fixer of protests, demanded a remedy. These problems were discussed for months, and the resolution was eventually announced by the Broadcasting Ethics and Program Improvement Organization (BPO).

IV. The Broadcasting Ethics and Program Improvement Organization and Its History

The BPO does not have legal powers to bind broadcasters, but broadcasters generally respect its opinions and decisions. They promised that they would follow its suggestions when the BPO was created. In the absence of such an institution, broadcasters might face direct governmental pressure. The ultimate goal of the BPO is that broadcasters will follow the Broadcasting Act[22] and adhere to ethical standards established by the broadcasters themselves.[23]

As already mentioned, a legal boundary exists between broadcast media and telecommunications in Japan. One regulation that is applicable only to broadcast programmes[24] and not to Internet TV, such as AbemaTV,[25] is the 'fairness doctrine'. Although the principle is similar to the US Fairness Doctrine (repealed in 1987), the details of the Japanese version are somewhat different.[26] The Japanese fairness doctrine is set out in article 4 of the Broadcasting Act of Japan. It says that broadcasters should take care:

(i) not to negatively influence public safety or good morals;
(ii) to be politically fair;

[22] English texts of the Broadcasting Act are available at www.soumu.go.jp/main_sosiki/joho_tsusin/eng/Resources/laws/pdf/090204_5.pdf [accessed 30 January 2019].

[23] English texts of the Fundamental Code of Broadcasting Ethics that was established by the Japan Commercial Broadcasters Association (JBA) and NHK in 1996 are available at www.j-ba.or.jp/files/jba101019/Fundamental%20Code%20of%20Broadcasting%20Ethics.pdf [accessed 30 January 2019].

[24] It should be noted that the Japanese fairness doctrine covers cable television programmes too. That makes running public access channels extremely difficult on cable television. The purpose of those channels is to host a wide range of views, beliefs, and values.

[25] AbemaTV is one of Japan's live-streaming video services. It depends on sponsors just like a regular broadcast commercial television station. It was started in 2016 as a joint venture by TV Asahi and CyberAgent, Inc.

[26] The US Fairness Doctrine had two basic elements: it required broadcasters to devote some of their airtime to discussing controversial matters of public interest, and to air contrasting views regarding those matters. See Steve Rendall, 'Broadcasters Should Be Required to Air a Variety of Opposing Views', in Roman Espejo (ed.), *Mass Media* (Farmington Hills, 2010), 63.

(iii) not to distort the facts; and
(iv) to clarify the points at issue from as many angles as possible where conflicting opinions are present.[27]

These four subsections may seem to be fair as 'guidelines'. The problem, however, is who should make the judgments concerning them, especially of political fairness. If it is the government, can broadcast journalism criticize the government? If journalism cannot condemn a questionable policy taken by the government, how can people evaluate their representatives?

The US Fairness Doctrine originated in 1949 because of channel scarcity. It was always controversial, though, because of the potential for infringement of freedom of speech and press. One of the main reasons that the US Federal Communications Commission (FCC) repealed the Fairness Doctrine in 1987 was to escape from this controversy. It thought that more channels provided by the cable television boom of the 1980s would solve the channel scarcity issue.

There seemed to be less concern about fairness when Japan enacted its Broadcasting Act in 1950. The law was designed to be run by an independent regulatory organ called *Denpa Kanri Iinkai* ('Radio Regulatory Commission'). When the independent commission was abolished in 1952, the government – namely, the Ministry of Post and Telecommunications (MPT)[28] – took over the authority to enforce the Broadcasting Act. But the Ministry was wise enough at the outset not to act with a heavy hand.

The mid-1980s brought a number of controversies and the government started to claim that it had the authority to judge the content of broadcast programmes. There were many incidents of violence, indecency, fake documentaries, news hoaxes, defamatory reporting, and harmful cartoons for kids broadcast in a quest for high ratings. Following an infamous remark in 1993 by Sadayoshi Tsubaki, then news division chief of TV Asahi,[29] an official from the MPT declared that the government would stop particular broadcasting stations from operating based on the MPT's judgment of programme content. Pressed

[27] See www.japaneselawtranslation.go.jp/law/detail/?id=2954&vm=04&re=01 [accessed 20 March 2019].

[28] The MPT was reorganized in 2001 into the Ministry of Internal Affairs and Communications (MIC).

[29] In October 1993, *Sankei Shinbun* reported that Tsubaki had revealed his policy, as head of a news department, at the closed JBA meeting held in September of that year. In his remarks, Tsubaki disclosed that he ordered his news staff to broadcast anti-Liberal Democratic Party material during the election period of 1993.

by public criticism of television, NHK and the members of the Japan Commercial Broadcasters Association (JBA) reached an agreement to create an entity to improve broadcasting in Japan:

> NHK and JBA established the Broadcast and Human Rights Committee in 1997 to advocate for basic human rights from an independent, third-party standpoint with the power to enforce corrective measures promptly and effectively. In 2000, the Youth Committee was established to deal with problems in broadcasting concerning youth. This was followed by the Programming Committee. In 2003, these Committees were integrated into the Broadcasting Ethics & Program Improvement Organization (BPO). In 2007, when falsified/fabricated programs became a major issue, the Programming Committee was dissolved and then replaced by the Committee for the Investigation of Broadcasting Ethics to deal with both falsified/fabricated programs and broadcasting ethics.[30]

The BPO set out its mission as being 'to improve the quality of broadcasting and promote higher ethical standards, while ensuring freedom of speech and expression. The BPO deals with complaints and ethical issues by conducting investigations into problematic programs and giving recommendations and/or opinions to either all broadcasters, or to the particular broadcaster concerned.'[31]

Currently, the BPO has three committees:

- the Broadcast and Human Rights/Other Related Rights Committee (BRC), originally formed in 1997 for human rights issues;
- the Committee for the Investigation of Broadcasting Ethics (CIBE), reformed in 2007 for ethical issues; and
- the Broadcast Committee for Youth Programming (BCYP), originally formed in 2000 for youth programming issues.[32]

Each committee comprises 6–10 commissioners, coming from the fields such as law, education, and journalism. Since their opinions and recommendations are based on laws, codes, and standards, their documents are often written in a legal style.

The formation process of the BPO was so distinctive that its role can be described as 'the Japan model' of ethical broadcasting. In the United States, a member of the public is able to file complaints about programme

[30] English texts of the BPO's official web pages are available at www.bpo.gr.jp/?page_id=1092 [accessed 30 January 2019].

[31] *Ibid.*

[32] 'Neither CIBE nor BYCP are official abbreviations used by the BPO. The two are abbreviated as such only for the purpose of this chapter.

content with the FCC. If the complaint is gravely serious, a broadcaster's licence might not be renewed, although this rarely happens.[33]

V. The BPO's Discussion about *News Joshi*

On 27 January 2017, a representative of a citizen's group filed a complaint with the BRC, claiming defamation by *News Joshi*. After the failure of conciliation talks with MXTV, the BRC officially decided in May to begin *shinri* ('examinations'). However, in February of that same year, the CIBE had already decided to start *shingi* ('deliberations') in relation to complaints against the shows.[34] After several exchanges of communications between MXTV and the BPO (BRC and CIBE), as shown in Table 20.1, the CIBE issued its *ikensho* ('opinion report') (CIBE Decision #27)[35] in December, stating that *News Joshi* had severely violated ethical standards for broadcasters. In addition, the BRC announced its *kankoku* ('recommendations') (BRC Decision #67)[36] in March 2018, saying that it found human rights violations in *News Joshi* and strongly recommending MXTV take measures to prevent any future problems of that sort.[37]

According to CIBE Decision #27, the CIBE interviewed staff members of MXTV for eight hours, including two members in charge of screening the show's content, two in charge of programming, and one in sales and

[33] A famous case that demonstrates 'the US model' is the WLBT dispute in the late 1960s. See Ernest Holsendolph, 'Blacks May Soon Direct Big Mississippi TV Station', *New York Times*, 20 November 1978, available at www.nytimes.com/1978/11/20/archives/blacks-may-soon-direct-big-mississippi-tv-station-division-of.html [accessed 30 January 2019].

[34] The CIBE distinguishes *shingi* ('deliberations') from *shinri* ('examinations'). Since the CIBE does not provide English translations for either term, I am providing my own here. They could be superseded if the CIBE were eventually to provide official translations. The CIBE uses shingi when the programme in question may have been unethically produced. It uses shinri when the programme may have both been unethically produced and contained falsehoods. The BRC does not have a shingi process.

[35] An abstract and the full text of CIBE Decision #27 (in Japanese) is available at www.bpo.gr.jp/?p=9335&meta_key=2017 [accessed 31 January 2019].

[36] An abstract and the full text of BRC Decision #67 (in Japanese) is available at www.bpo.gr.jp/?p=9428&meta_key=2017 [accessed 31 January 2019].

[37] These *ikensho* ('opinion reports') and *kankoku* ('recommendations') issued by the BPO have no binding power on the broadcasters in question. Nevertheless, the broadcaster supporting members of the BPO have promised to respect its decisions. A rare case of counter-argument occurred when NHK resisted BRC Decision #62, issued on 10 February 2017. NHK made a statement on 9 May 2017 that it took the decision seriously, but it expressed a difference of opinion on the BRC's findings of human rights violations.

Table 20.1 *A timeline of the* News Joshi *dispute*

Year	Date	Event
2015	7 October	MXTV started airing *News Joshi.*
2017	2 January	MXTV aired *News Joshi* episode #91, labelling protesters in Takae, Okinawa, as 'terrorists' in its first 19 minutes.
	9 January	MXTV aired *News Joshi* episode #92, justifying the reporter's view in episode #91 in the first 9 minutes.
	20 January	A representative of the citizens' group sent a letter of complaint to MXTV, alleging that she had been defamed by *News Joshi.*
	27 January	A petitioner, the representative of the citizens' group, filed a complaint with the BRC, claiming that *News Joshi* had defamed her, and demanding an apology and correction broadcast of MXTV.
	10 February	The CIBE decided to start *shingi* ('deliberations') for the complaints against *News Joshi.*
	27 February	MXTV announced its view that the episodes in question were compliant with the Broadcasting Act and its programme guidelines.
	27 April	MXTV submitted a document to the BRC that claimed there was no defamation because the term 'terrorists' was not used for the petitioner; rather, it was used as a metaphor to describe *kyōkō* ('hard-line') aspects of the protest.
	16 May	The BRC decided to start *shinri* ('examinations') for the *News Joshi* dispute.
	1 July	MXTV overhauled its *kōsa* ('audit') office to strengthen its screening ability towards brought-in programmes (and the office has increased its number of staff since April 2018).
	30 September	MXTV aired its own original programme concerning Okinawa that contained both pro and con voices towards the US military base.
	14 December	The CIBE issued its opinion report (CIBE Decision #27), finding that *News Joshi* had significantly violated ethical standards for broadcasters. MXTV announced that it would take CIBE Decision #27 seriously.
2018	16 February	MXTV invited some members of the CIBE to hold a workshop on broadcast ethics.

Table 20.1 (*cont.*)

Year	Date	Event
	19 February	MXTV held a workshop on broadcast ethics to more deeply understand CIBE Decision #27.
	8 March	The BRC announced its finding (BRC Decision #67) that *News Joshi* had abused human rights and issued *kankoku* ('recommendations') to MXTV to take preventive measures for future broadcasts. MXTV announced that it would take BRC Decision #67 seriously.
	9 March	MXTV recanted the view it had expressed on 27 February 2017.
	14 March	MXTV issued a progress report to the CIBE that explained MXTV's efforts to respond to CIBE Decision #27.
	31 March	MXTV and some ten other television stations cancelled *News Joshi.*
	27 April	The CIBE sent a letter of additional inquiries to MXTV, asking for more detailed explanations concerning the 14 March report.
		MXTV invited some members of the BRC to hold a workshop studying human rights.
	31 May	MXTV submitted a supplementary report responding to the CIBE's additional inquiries on 27 April. The CIBE accepted the report.
	1 June	MXTV invited an official from the Tokyo Legal Affairs Bureau to hold a workshop on human rights.
	8 June	MXTV submitted a progress report to the BRC that explained MXTV's efforts in responding to BRC Decision #67. The BRC accepted the report.
	20 July	MXTV officially apologized to a representative of the citizens' group.

Source: www.bpo.gr.jp/ [accessed 30 January 2019].

marketing. The purpose was to determine whether they had screened episode #91 properly. In addition to interviews with the MXTV staff, the CIBE itself conducted its own original research to verify certain 'facts' by means of hearings with six people in Okinawa and staff members of the citizens' group. After these efforts, it concluded that MXTV had seriously violated broadcast ethics because of six failures in its screening process.

(1) MXTV did not question the lack of interviews with protesters in the journalist's video footage. The show's aim was to critically inform the audience about the true identity of the protesters. To pursue that truth, should the protesters in question now have been interviewed? Although *News Joshi* was thought of as an infotainment/variety show, it still should have been subjected to careful screening to ensure that it dealt ethically with facts.

(2) MXTV did not fact check whether protesters had forced an ambulance to stop its official duties. Stopping an ambulance is a serious crime. If the show had shed light on this act, MXTV should have confirmed it with the police or the fire department. The single witness who appeared in the video footage and the Internet search was not enough.

(3) MXTV did not check whether the term *nittō* ('daily pay') was appropriate to describe the money that a citizens' group provided for its people. One of the journalist's pieces of evidence to prove protesters were hired was a flyer made by the citizens' group. The flyer called for citizen reporters to come to Okinawa from the mainland. The flyer said it would pay *kōtsū hi* ('transportation expenses'), not nittō. Another piece of evidence shown in the video was an envelope on which a particular name was written. The journalist for *News Joshi* suggested that someone with this name had received nittō. However, this was not enough to prove that participants in the protest were hired in return for daily payments.

(4) MXTV allowed emphasized captions to be aired that could imply that the protesters were 'crazy'. The captions *kichi no soto* ('outside the base') in Chinese characters could be wrongly and easily read as *kichigai* ('crazy'). MXTV had to be aware of the possible misreading of these particular emphasized characters.[38]

(5) MXTV neglected to check for insult. In the video footage, the journalist called protesters *hantai ha no renchū* ('bunch of protesters'), 'having two days off, Saturdays and Sundays', and *kageki ha demo no butō ha shūdan* ('a militant group for radical demos').

[38] This technique, applying different Chinese characters to camouflage negative Japanese words, can often be seen on the Internet. MXTV had overlooked this camouflage done by the *News Joshi*.

MXTV should have respected JBA's Broadcasting Standards,[39] which require broadcasters to avoid indecent expressions that can offend and hurt people's feelings.

(6) MXTV did not screen the show when it was in its final format. Brought-in programmes should be assessed only when they are in a complete format because broadcasters are not often involved in actual production. However, MXTV screened only a part of the episode that was in development. Final editing, such as adding captions to the recorded show, was not completed when MXTV screened the show's content.

According to the BRC Decision #67, the Committee examined both episodes #91 and #92 to find whether there was a case for 'defamation'[40] and whether there were issues of broadcast ethics. The BRC reached a conclusion that *News Joshi* had defamed the petitioner and found two ethical problems in MXTV's screening process: it had ignored the lack of interviews with the petitioner, and it had been careless in dealing with racial and ethnic matters.[41]

The BRC discussed three detailed issues concerning 'defamation':

(1) whether there were actual presentations in the episodes that caused harm to the social reputation of the person;
(2) whether the episodes served the public interest or benefited the public; and
(3) whether the episodes presented the truth.[42]

For issue (1), the BRC found two matters to be in question. One was the suggestion that the petitioner was a 'black curtain', or fixer, behind the movement to oppose the bases, and had repeatedly committed illegal and violent acts (matter A). The other representation was that the petitioner mobilized participants by paying them a daily allowance (matter B).[43]

[39] English texts of the JBA's Broadcasting Standards are available at www.j-ba.or.jp/files/jba101019/jbastd2014.pdf [accessed 30 January 2019].

[40] Note that the BPO does not have binding authority over broadcasters, even though committee members use legal terms and standards in their decisions. For legal standards of defamation in Japan, see Chapters 2 and 8.

[41] According to Chapter II, article 10 of the JBA's Broadcasting Standards, due consideration must be given to the feelings and sentiments of the people concerned in handling matters relating to races and nations. Accordingly, there should be no chance of hate speech being used in broadcast programmes.

[42] These three issues are the bases for defamation under Penal Code of Japan, art. 230.

[43] See Shin Sugok, 'The Recent Merging of Anti-Okinawa and Anti-Korean Hate in the Japanese Mass Media' (2019) 17 *Asia-Pacific J.* 1.

The BRC concluded that both matters caused harm to the social reputation of the petitioner.

For issue (2), the BRC concluded that there was public interest and benefit in the broadcast because of the nature of the topic: Okinawa protests against military bases. Thus it said that there would be no case for defamation if MXTV were to prove both matters A and B to be true – that is, MXTV could escape liability if issue 3 were satisfied.

To prove matter A to be true, MXTV submitted video that contained remarks by the petitioner at a past gathering somewhere in Tokyo. The petitioner had made a contentious remark in the video; however, the BRC thought it insufficient to prove she was a 'black curtain'. To prove matter B, MXTV pointed to another remark made by the petitioner in the video. However, the BRC found that MXTV could not prove the payment to have been an allowance. Decision #67 thus concluded that neither of matters A nor B were proven to be true. As a result, a case of defamation had been presented.

On 20 July 2018, MXTV officially apologized to a representative of the citizens' group. Some parties, however, were not convinced by the BPO's conclusions. They included a media watchdog group and a sponsor company of *News Joshi*. On 31 December 2017, *Sankei Shinbun* reported that the director of watchdog group *Hōsōhō junshu o motomeru shichōsha no kai* ('Audience Group Demanding Compliance with the Broadcasting Act')[44] had commented that 'the BPO has double standards; it's too soft on liberals. We need a new system to *kanshi* ["watch"] broadcasting if the BPO cannot secure impartiality.'[45] In the same article, *Sankei* questioned the propriety of the BPO's system for selecting committee members.[46] A few months later, the president of DHC, a sponsor company of *News Joshi*, contributed his opinion to one of the news sites run by *Sankei*, criticizing the BPO.[47] The president claimed that most of

44 Its web page can be found at http://housouhou.com/ [accessed 17 January 2019].

45 'BPO no Chūritsusei ni Gigi' ['Questions arise concerning BPO's neutrality'], *Sankei Shinbun*, 31 December 2017, available at www.sankei.com/entertainments/news/171231/ent1712310019-n1.html [accessed 17 January 2019].

46 Fuji TV, a part of the Fuji-Sankei media group, is also a supporting member of the BPO. If there really is a problem in the selection of BPO committee members, *Sankei Shinbun* should explain that problem in detail; otherwise, it will not obtain a social consensus to reform the BPO.

47 ' "BPO wa Shōki ka", Nyūsu Joshi Sōdō, DHC Kaichō ga Shōgeki no Hanron Shuki' ['"BPO insane?" *News Girls* dispute; DHC president contributing a counterargument with impact'], *Sankei Shinbun*, 1 May 2018, available at www.sankei.com/entertainments/news/180501/ent1805010002-n1.html [accessed 17 January 2019].

the BPO members were *han nichi* ('anti-Japan') and *sayoku* ('leftish').[48] *Sankei* and its supporters seem to have a very different perspective towards human rights.

VI. Conclusion

On 15 March 2018, *Kyodo News* revealed internal documents drafted by the government to repeal article 4 of the Broadcasting Act, the Japanese fairness doctrine, so that the legal border between broadcasting and the Internet would be diminished.[49] It is highly likely that those documents reflect the intention of Prime Minister Shinzo Abe.[50] These internal documents also suggested that, in the future, there would be no need for broadcasters other than the public broadcaster NHK. The implication was that the government was considering making commercial broadcasters give up frequencies[51] and move to the Internet.

A coalition of commercial broadcasters and newspapers, including the *Yomiuri*, which often supports the prime minister, strongly opposed the plan. Probably for that reason, the prime minister's intention was omitted from an official proposal, issued on 4 June 2018, by the Cabinet Office's Regulatory Reform Promotion Council. However, it is still too early to say that he is giving up on the plan; the demand for frequencies for the mobile phone market is surely destined to increase.

Jiro Mizushima, a well-known scholar of politics, has offered some ideas about broadcasters surviving in their current form.[52] He says that existing political parties are losing their powers while the radical voice of the anti-establishment is attracting people's support. The world

[48] His opinion (in Japanese) is available at https://ironna.jp/article/9559?p=1 [accessed 20 March 2019].

[49] 'Japan Gov't Mulls Abolishing Political Fairness Clause in Broadcasting Law', *Kyōdō News*, 15 March 2018, available at https://english.kyodonews.net/news/2018/03/6a6269da7b20-govt-mulls-abolishing-political-fairness-clause-in-broadcasting-law.html [accessed 17 January 2019].

[50] One of Abe's Cabinet members, the then Minister of Internal Affairs and Communications, was criticized by the US Human Rights Report of 2016 for remarks that she could shut down broadcast stations based on art. 4 violations. See US Department of State, *2016 Country Reports on Human Rights Practices: Japan*, available at www.state.gov/reports/2016-country-reports-on-human-rights-practices/japan/ [accessed 16 September 2020].

[51] It has been said that the government is planning to use those frequencies for a future auctioning of the spectrum.

[52] Jiro Mizushima, 'Musoshikisō, "Nakanuki Seiji" Michibiku' [People who do not belong to associations lead to politics without intermediate organ'], *Nihon Keizai Shinbun*, 31 January 2019.

witnessed businessman Donald Trump winning the US presidency by means of a social media campaign attacking the political establishment. Mizushima sees this type of populism as resulting from the decline of intermediate organs, such as farmers' groups and trade unions. In the past, people were attached to the existing political parties through these intermediate organs, whereby people took time to discuss the policies that were presented to them. Nowadays, though, every individual directly follows instant outcries through social media.

Under such circumstances, when political leaders start to label particular news reporting as 'fake news', that should be seen as a warning sign. In November 2018, the White House revoked a press pass for a CNN reporter after his contentious questions and actions in a news conference. Is it appropriate for democratic leaders to avoid particular reporters because they ask tough questions? Should the democratic leaders tell people which news outlets to hate? Newspapers and broadcast television provide information to their communities as a form of journalism. They may be the last intermediate organ for people who pursue deliberative democracy.

Back in Japan, individuals incited by a right-wing blog post titled 'Yomei Sannen' ('Three years left to live')[53] sent letters to the Tokyo Bar Association in June 2017, demanding that certain lawyers be reprimanded. More than 1,000 of those letters bore the same reason: the Association allegedly committed a crime when it supported ethnic Korean schools in Japan. It is true that the Association made a statement in 2016 that Korean schools in Japan should be included in a national policy subsidizing high school tuition fees, but that policy suggestion would seem to fall far short of criminal behaviour.

Broadcast news programmes reported the story and warned that lawyers were starting to sue individuals who recklessly submitted disciplinary requests. NHK revealed that some individuals had accepted mediation to settle the cases before they went to the court.[54] Osaka broadcaster MBS received so much attention for its coverage of the cases that it won an award.[55]

[53] It is said that an Internet service provider removed the blog post. However, some blog posts with a similar title remain.

[54] Public broadcaster NHK described the story in detail: 'Naze Okita? Bengoshi eno Tairyō Chōkai Seikyū' ['Why so many disciplinary requests against lawyers?'], *Close Up 'Gendai [Today]' Plus*, aired 29 October 2018.

[55] *Mainichi Hōsō* ('Mainichi Broadcasting System') (MBS) aired 'Bashhingu: Sono Hasshingen no Haigo ni Nani ga' ['Bashing: what lies behind the source'], *Eizō '18* [Image of 2018], on 16 December 2018. It received a Galaxy Award, selected by members of the Japan Council for Better Radio and Television, for its high production values.

Lawyer Yoshiharu Kawabata, a former chair of the BPO's CIBE, suggests that the BPO can help to improve the image of broadcast television. He says that, by acting ethically, broadcasters can differentiate themselves from other media: 'We only broadcast the facts that are bound close to the truth.'[56] And, he says, 'broadcasting is hate-speech free media'.

[56] Yoshiharu Kawabata, 'Terebi, Jiyū ni Kizen to' ['TV, be free and be firm'], *Asahi Shinbun*, 26 May 2019.

APPENDIX A

A Chronology of Events and Legislation Related to Hate Speech in Japan

This chronology was written by Toshihide Yamamura, lecturer, Tokai Gakuin University.

13 Aug. 1960	*Dōwa Taisaku Shingikai Setchihō* ('Anti-discrimination Measures Council Act') was enacted.
11 Aug. 1965	*Dōwa Taisaku Shingikai Tōshin* ('Report from the Anti-discrimination Measures Council') was submitted.
10 July 1969	*Dōwa Taisaku Jigyō Tokubetsu Sochihō* ('Act on Special Measures Concerning Projects for Anti-discrimination Measures') was enacted.
Nov. 1975	The press revealed that *Buraku Chimei Sōkan* ('Geographical Dictionary on Buraku Communities') had been secretly sold to personnel officers of companies throughout Japan. (*Buraku* is a term used to refer to a group of people historically discriminated against and ostracized in Japan.)
31 Mar. 1982	*Chiiki Kaizen Taisaku Tokubetsu Sochihō* ('Act on Special Measures Concerning Remedies to Improve Living Standards of Communities') was enacted.
27 Mar. 1985	*Osaka-fu Buraku Sabetsu Jishō ni Kakawaru Chōsatō ni Kansuru Jōrei* ('Osaka Prefecture Ordinance on Investigations into Discrimination of People Born in Buraku Communities') was enacted.
31 Mar. 1987	*Chiiki Kaizen Taisaku Tokutei Jigyō ni Kakawaru Kuni no Zaiseijō no Tokubetsu Sochi ni Kansuru Hōritsu* ('Act Concerning Special Government Financial Measures for Designated Projects to Improve Living Standards of Communities') was enacted. (This was temporary legislation for five years and it was then extended for five more years. It was revised and retained for another five years until the end of March 2002, when it expired.)

(*cont.*)

16 Mar. 1995	*Kumamoto-ken Buraku Sabetsu Jishō no Hassei no Bōshi oyobi Chōsa no Kisei ni Kansuru Jōrei* ('Kumamoto Prefecture Ordinance to Prevent and Investigate into Discrimination of People Born in Buraku Communities') was enacted.
20 Oct. 1995	*Fukuoka-ken Buraku Sabetsu Jishō no Hassei no Bōshi ni Kansuru Jōrei* ('Fukuoka Prefecture Ordinance to Prevent Discrimination of People Born in Buraku Communities') was enacted.
15 Dec. 1995	Japan acceded to the International Convention on the Elimination of All Forms of Racial Discrimination (ICERD) as the 146th signatory nation. However, Japan registered a reservation with respect to Article 4(a) and (b).
14 Jan. 1996	The ICERD came into force in Japan.
26 Mar. 1996	*Kagawa-ken Buraku Sabetsu Jishō no Hassei no Bōshi ni Kansuru Jōrei* ('Kagawa Prefecture Ordinance to Prevent Discrimination of People Born in Buraku Communities') was enacted.
25 Dec. 1996	*Tokushima-ken Buraku Sabetsu Jishō no Hassei no Boushi ni Kansuru Jōrei* ('Tokushima Prefecture Ordinance to Prevent Discrimination of People Born in Buraku Communities') was enacted.
26 Dec. 1996	*Jinken Yōgo Sesaku Suishinhō* ('Act on the Promotion of Measures for Human Rights Protection') was enacted.
25 Mar. 1997	Based on the Act on the Promotion of Measures for Human Rights Protection, *Jinken Yōgo Sesaku Suishin Shingikai* ('Promotion of Human Rights Protection Council') was formed.
6 Dec. 2000	*Jinken Kyouōiku oyobi Jinken Keihatsu no Suishin ni Kansuru Hōritsu* ('Act on the Promotion of Human Rights Education and Human Rights Awareness-Raising') was enacted.
25 May 2001	*Jinken Kyūsai Seido no Arikata ni Tsuite (Tōshin)* ('On the Ideal Method of the Human Rights Relief System (Report)') was submitted.
8 Mar. 2002	*Jinken Yōgo Hōan* ('Human Rights Vindication Bill') was introduced to the Diet. However, this bill was discarded on the dissolution of the House of Representatives on 10 October 2003.

(*cont.*)

1 Aug. 2005	The Democratic Party of Japan, an opposition party, introduced a bill to the Diet called *Jinken Shingai ni yoru Higai no Kyūsai oyobi Yobōtō ni Kansuru Hōritsu-an* ('Bill on Restitution for and Prevention of Damage Based on the Violation of Human Rights', or the Human Rights Violations Relief Bill).
12 Oct. 2005	*Tottori-ken Jinken Shingai Kyūsai Suishin oyobi Tetsuzuki ni Kansuru Jōrei* ('Tottori Prefecture Ordinance Regarding the Promotion of and Procedure for the Restitution for Human Rights Violations') was passed in the Tottori Prefectural Assembly.
24 Mar. 2006	*Tottori-ken Jinken Shingai Kyūsai Suishin oyobi Tetsuduki ni Kansuru Jōreitō no Teishi ni Kansuru Jōrei* ('Tottori Prefecture Ordinance to Suspend the Ordinance Regarding the Promotion of and Procedure for the Restitution for Human Rights Violations') was approved, and the Tottori Prefecture Ordinance Regarding the Promotion of and Procedure for the Restitution for Human Rights Violations was therefore suspended indefinitely to undergo reconsideration.
Dec. 2006	*Zainichi Tokken o Yurusanai Shimin no Kai* ('Association of Citizens against the Special Privileges of Korean Residents in Japan'), commonly known as *Zaitokukai*, was founded.
25 Mar. 2009	*Tottori-ken Jinken Sonchō no Shakai Dukuri Jōrei no Ichibu o Kaiseitō Suru Jōrei* ('Tottori Prefecture Ordinance to Revise a Portion of the Ordinance for the Social Formation of Respect for Human Rights') was approved. Consequently, the Human Rights Violations Restitution Ordinance was repealed without being enforced.
Dec. 2009	*Kyoto Korean Elementary School*: The first demonstration against the school was carried out.
Jan. 2010	*Kyoto Korean Elementary School*: The second demonstration against the school was carried out.
Mar. 2010	*Kyoto Korean Elementary School*: The third demonstration against the school was carried out.
1 Dec. 2010	Tokushima District Court ruled on *Tokushima Prefecture Teachers' Union* (criminal case); the accused did not appeal and guilt was established. Three out of the accused six were determined guilty and the remaining three were merged into the proceedings of *Kyoto Korean Elementary School.*

(*cont.*)

21 Apr. 2011	Kyoto District Court ruled on *Kyoto Korean Elementary School* (criminal case).
28 Oct. 2011	Osaka High Court ruled on *Kyoto Korean Elementary School* (criminal case).
23 Feb. 2012	The Supreme Court dismissed the appeal in *Kyoto Korean Elementary School* (criminal case).
25 June 2012	Nara District Court decided in the *Suiheisha* ('National Levellers' Association') *Museum* case.
9 Nov. 2012	*Jinken Iinkai Setchi Hōan* ('Human Rights Commission Bill') was submitted to the Diet. However, this bill was discarded on the dissolution of the House of Representatives on 16 November 2012.
9 Feb. 2013	Yasumichi Noma and persons concerned founded *Reishisuto o Shibakitai* ('Party to Attack Racists').
14 Mar. 2013	Led by Yoshifu Arita, a House of Councillors member belonging to the then Democratic Party of Japan, a number of like-minded Diet lawmakers held an in-house session to criticize hate demonstrations.
12 May 2013	*Hannichi Kyokusa to Futei Gaikokujin kara Kawasaki o Mamoru Demo* ('Demonstration to Protect Kawasaki from Anti-Japan Extreme Left and Lawless Foreigners') was carried out around Kawasaki Station. Since then, many hate demonstrations have been repeatedly held in the same area.
12 June 2013	When Zaitokukai applied for the use of the *Yamagata-ken Shōgai Gakushū Sentā* ('Yamagata Prefecture Lifelong Study Centre') to host a lecture, the Centre did not issue a permit because it determined that the event fell under a requirement to exclude 'circumstances considered to be beneficial to an organization that is likely to collectively or habitually carry out acts of violence or tort'.
7 Oct. 2013	Kyoto District Court ruled on *Kyoto Korean Elementary School* (civil case).
2 Dec. 2013	The term 'hate speech' was placed among the top 10 of 'U-CAN New Language Buzzword Awards 2013'.
Apr. 2014	Diet members who held the in-house session played a key role in founding the non-partisan *Jinshu Sabetsu Teppai Kihon-hō o Motomeru Giin Renmei* ('League of Representatives Demanding the Fundamental Law of Elimination of Racial Discrimination') that aims to listen to the voices of victims

(*cont.*)

	and non-governmental organizations and to study hate speech issues (chaired by Toshio Ogawa, a House of Councillors member belonging to the then Democratic Party of Japan).
27 Feb. 2014	The US Department of State issued *Country Reports on Human Rights Practices for 2013: Japan*. This report expressed concern that blatant hate speech against Korean residents in Japan was being perpetrated.
19 Apr. 2014	Kadoma City in Osaka Prefecture announced its position on the use of its public facilities, such as community centres and parks. The city stated that while it indiscriminately accepts and permits use in principle, irrespective of the activity content of applicant individuals and groups, it will resolutely respond to any act that incites discrimination.
May 2014	When the Prime Minister, the Minister of Justice, and others were questioned about hate speech in the parliamentary proceedings, they mentioned words such as *yūryo* ('anxiety') and *zannen* ('regret').
8 July 2014	Osaka High Court ruled on *Kyoto Korean Elementary School* (civil case).
23 July 2014	The United Nations Human Rights Committee held its 3091st (CCPR/C/SR.3091) and 3092nd (CCPR/C/SR.3092) meetings, and announced in its Concluding Observations on the Sixth Periodic Report of Japan. On this occasion, the Committee recommended that the government legally regulate hate speech.
Aug. 2014	The Project Team on Measures for Hate Speech of the Liberal Democratic Party was founded (chaired by Katsuei Hirasawa, House of Representatives). In the first meeting in August, Sanae Takaichi, the then Policy Research Council chair, stirred controversy by stating that regulation of demonstrations around the Diet building would be considered as well, because they were noisy and disturbed their work.
28 Aug. 2014	In its 2320th and 2321st meetings, the United Nations Committee on the Elimination of Racial Discrimination announced its Concluding Observations on the Combined Seventh to Ninth Periodic Reports of Japan. On this occasion, the Committee strongly advised the country to

(*cont.*)

	provide comprehensive policies on the elimination of discrimination, such as enacting a racial discrimination prohibition law in addition to legal regulation of hate speech and hate crime. In light of this United Nations recommendation, multiple opinion briefs calling for the state to take measures were submitted one after another, beginning with Kunitachi City Council of metropolitan Tokyo, from September onwards.
Sep. 2014	The Project Team on Measures for Hate Speech of the Komeito was founded (chaired by Kiyohiko Toyama, House of Representatives).
3 Sep. 2014	Toru Hashimoto, then mayor of Osaka, referred 'With respect to measures that Osaka City should take about *zōo hyōgen* ["hate speech"]' to Osaka City Council for Promotion of Human Rights Measures.
19 Sep. 2014	Kunitachi City in metropolitan Tokyo submitted a 'Suggestion to Introduce Legislation that Prohibits Discrimination, Including Hate Speech, against Racial and Social Minorities' to the state. This later expanded to other local governments throughout Japan, and similar suggestions and resolutions were adopted in many local councils.
23 Jan. 2015	The inaugural meeting of *Heito Supīchi o Yurusanai Kawasaki Shimin Nettowāku* ('Kawasaki Citizens' Network that Does Not Tolerate Hate Speech') was held.
Feb. 2015	*Gaikokujin Jinkenhō Renrakukai* ('Foreigners' Human Rights Law Liaison Committee') published a model bill for a fundamental law on the elimination of racial discrimination.
2 Feb. 2015	*Hannichi Kyūdan in Kawasaki Kōki 2673 Nen* ('Denouncement of Anti-Japan People in Kawasaki, Imperial Year 2673 [a system of counting the years from the beginning of Emperor Jinmu's reign in 660 BC]') was held. In Kawasaki Station, a hate demonstration participant with an imitation sword provoked an incident that resulted in injury.
25 Feb. 2015	Osaka City Council for Promotion of Human Rights Measures submitted a report titled *With Respect to Measures that Osaka City Should Take about Hate Speech* to the mayor of Osaka.
14 Mar. 2015	The *Hannichi o Yurusuna!* ('Don't Tolerate Anti-Japan People!') Kawasaki demonstration from Inage Park to Kawasaki Station was carried out.

(*cont.*)

19 Mar. 2015	The Association that Calls for the Promotion of Effective Hate Speech Measures to Kyoto Prefecture and Kyoto City was founded.
27 Mar. 2015	Tokushima District Court ruled on *Tokushima Prefecture Teachers' Union* (civil case).
7 May 2015	The Japan Federation of Bar Associations announced *Jinshutō o Riyū to suru Sabetsu no Teppai ni Muketa Sumiyaka na Sesaku o Motomeru Ikensho* ('Suggestion that calls for prompt measures aimed at elimination of discrimination based on racial and other characteristics').
22 May 2015	Seven members of the opposition belonging to the League of Representatives Demanding for the Fundamental Law of Elimination of Racial Discrimination submitted *Jinshutō o Riyū to Suru Sabetsu no Teppai no tame no Sesaku ni Kansuru Hōritsuan* ('Bill Regarding the Promotion of Measures for the Elimination of Discrimination Based on Race and Other Characteristics', or the Bill on Promotion of Elimination of Racial Discrimination) to the House of Councillors. Osaka City submitted *Osaka-shi Heito Supīchi e no Taishō ni Kansuru Jōreian* ('Osaka City Ordinance Bill to Deal with Hate Speech') to the city council.
2 July 2015	Komeito's Project Team on Measures for Hate Speech submitted a paper to the Cabinet Office and the Ministry of Justice, demanding a fact-finding investigation into racial discrimination and settling on policies for its elimination. In response, the government announced that it would carry out a fact-finding investigation into hate speech within the year.
6 Aug. 2015	The Committee on Judicial Affairs of the House of Councillors began its deliberation on the Bill on Promotion of Elimination of Racial Discrimination. The Committee did not reach a consensus after seven meetings and therefore the bill was carried over for further discussion.
7 Sep. 2015	The Tokyo Bar Association announced *Chihō Kōkyō Dantai ni taishite Jinshu Sabetsu o Mokuteki to Suru Kōkyō Shisetsu no Riyō Kyoka Shinsei ni taisuru Tekisetsu na Sochi o Kōzuru Koto o Motomeru Ikensho* ('Suggestion to local governments to take appropriate measures against permit applications to use public facilities with the purpose of racial discrimination').

(*cont.*)

8 Nov. 2015	*Kawasakihatsu! Nihon Jōka Demo [Hannichi o Yurusuna]* ('From Kawasaki! Cleanse Japan Demonstration [Don't Tolerate Anti-Japan People]') was held.
9 Nov. 2015	The Supreme Court dismissed the appeal in *Kyoto Korean Elementary School* (civil case).
22 Dec. 2015	The Human Rights Bureau of the Ministry of Justice acknowledged that then Zaitokukai president Makoto Sakurai's words and deeds in front of Korea University constituted human rights violations and advised him not to repeat similar acts in the future.
15 Jan. 2016	The Osaka City Ordinance to Deal with Hate Speech was enacted in Osaka City (promulgated on 18 January).
31 Jan. 2016	*Kawasakihatsu! Nihon Jōka Demo 'Dai Nidan!' [Hannich o Yurusuna]* ('From Kawasaki! Cleanse Japan Demonstration Part 2! [Don't Tolerate Anti-Japan People]') was performed.
5 Feb. 2016	Under the alias Tottori Loop, Tatsuhiko Miyabe began accepting advance orders for *Zenkoku Buraku Chōsa – Fukkokuban* ('Nationwide Investigation of Buraku Communities – reprinted edition').
10 Mar. 2016	The Liberal Democratic Party's Project Team on Measures for Hate Speech was reorganized into *Sabetsu Mondai ni kansuru Tokumei Iinkai* ('Special Mission Committee on the Issues of All Forms of Discrimination') of the Liberal Democratic Party Policy Research Council.
20 Mar. 2016	Propaganda activities in front of Kawasaki Station by *Ishin Seitō Shimpū* ('Restoration Political Party: New Wind') were held. A demonstration participant was arrested for beating a counter-protestor.
22 Mar. 2016	In the Committee on Judicial Affairs of the House of Councillors, four persons were questioned regarding the Bill on the Promotion of the Elimination of Racial Discrimination.
28 Mar. 2016	Yokohama District Court issued an order suspending the sale of *Zenkoku Buraku Chōsa – Fukkokuban*. Both claims of an individual creditor and *Buraku Kaihō Dōmei* ('Buraku Liberation League') were approved.
30 Mar. 2016	The Ministry of Justice announced the results of its fact-finding investigation into the damage of hate speech: *Kōeki Zaidan Hōjin Jinken Kyōiku Keihatsu Sentā* ('Public Interest

(*cont.*)

	Incorporated Foundation – Centre for Human Rights Education and Training), *Heito Supīchi ni Kansuru Jittai Chōsa Hōkokusho* ('Report on the Fact-Finding Investigation into Hate Speech').
31 Mar. 2016	Ten members of the Committee on Judicial Affairs of the House of Councillors inspected the neighbourhood of Sakuramoto in Kawasaki City, which is an area that is particularly populated by Korean residents in Japan.
8 Apr. 2016	Both members of the Liberal Democratic Party and Komeito submitted a bill called *Honpōgai Shusshinsha ni taisuru Futō na Sabetsuteki Gendō no Kaishō ni Muketa Torikumi no Suishin ni Kansuru Hōritsu* ('Act on the Promotion of Efforts to Eliminate Unfair Discriminatory Speech and Behaviour against Persons Originating from Outside Japan', or the Hate Speech Elimination Act') to the House of Councillors.
18 Apr. 2016	The Sagamihara branch of Yokohama District Court issued an order to suspend posting on the *Zenkoku Buraku Chōsa – Fukkokuban* website.
13 May 2016	The Bill on the Promotion of the Elimination of Racial Discrimination was rejected in the plenary session of the House of Councillors.
24 May 2016	The Hate Speech Elimination Act was approved in the plenary session of the House of Representatives and then enacted.
31 May 2016	Norihiko Fukuda, mayor of Kawasaki, determined to reject an application for the use of a park on 5 June.
2 June 2016	The Kawasaki branch of Yokohama District Court, admitting the claim of social welfare corporation Seikyūsha based in Sakuramoto, issued an order prohibiting hate speech and hate demonstrations within a radius of 500 metres from its office.
3 June 2016	The Hate Speech Elimination Act was promulgated and came into effect. The National Police Agency provided each prefectural police an official notice that promotes activities for the elimination of hate speech.
5 June 2016	*Kawasakihatsu Nihon Jōka Demo 'Dai Sandan!'* ('From Kawasaki Cleanse Japan Demonstration – Part 3!') was held. The meeting venue had been changed from the original location to a park in Nakahara Ward, but the demonstrators failed to depart because of resistance by counter-protestors.

(*cont.*)

	Ultimately, the demonstration was cancelled in response to a request by the police. The Ministry of Justice dispatched vehicles advertising 'Stop Hate Speech' at this location.
July 2016	Former Zaitokukai president Makoto Sakurai ran in the Tokyo gubernatorial elections that were held on 31 July, received 114,171 votes, and came in fifth place.
1 July 2016	In Osaka City, the Osaka City Ordinance to Deal with Hate Speech came into effect in its entirety.
2 Aug. 2016	The Human Rights Bureau of the Ministry of Justice, as of 1 August, acknowledged that the hate speech demonstrations and propaganda activities around Sakuramoto and other areas on 31 January in the same year fall under human rights violations and advised the organizer of this demonstration not to repeat similar acts in the future.
29 Aug. 2016	*Nippon Daiichitō* ('Japan First Party') was founded, with Makoto Sakurai as the party leader.
1 Nov. 2016	The Supreme Court dismissed the appeal in *Tokushima Prefecture Teachers' Union* (civil case).
9 Dec. 2016	*Buraku Sabetsu Kaishō Suishinhō* ('Act on the Promotion of the Elimination of Buraku Discrimination') was enacted.
16 Dec. 2016	Buraku Sabetsu Kaishō Suishinhō came into effect.
28 Dec. 2016	Osaka District Court issued an order prohibiting hate demonstrations in an area of Tsuruhashi in Osaka City that is particularly populated by Korean residents in Japan.
27 Dec. 2016	The Kawasaki City Human Rights Measures Promotion Conference reported on matters for reference to the mayor. This conference reported the following needs: (1) to establish a guideline regarding use of public facilities; (2) to enact measures on the Internet; and (3) to legislate an ordinance. *Heito Supīchi o Yurusanai Kawasaki Shimin Nettowāku* ('Kawasaki Citizens' Network that Does Not Tolerate Hate Speech') submitted a written request to the mayor, aiming to enact the Racial Discrimination Elimination Ordinance (tentative name).
From the end of 2016	The Human Rights Bureau of the Ministry of Justice began to provide local governments with a document that specifies criteria to authorize permission for use of public facilities and typical forms of hate speech.

(*cont.*)

16 Mar. 2017	Yokohama District Court reached a decision regarding the objections to temporary restraining order against the Yokohama District Court decision of 28 March 2016 and against Yokohama District Court Sagamihara Branch's decision of 18 April 2016. With respect to the former, the objection by a debtor to an individual creditor was rejected and the objection to creditor Kaihō Dōmei was approved.
16 June 2017	In relation to the Yokohama District Court decision of 16 March, Tokyo High Court determined to reject the appeals of both the debtor and the creditor Kaihō Dōmei.
19 June 2017	In a case in which Makoto Sakurai, former head of Zaitokukai, was alleged to have defamed a female journalist, Osaka High Court accepted the journalist's argument that Sakurai's speech had fallen into intersectional forms of discrimination (discrimination based on sex and ethnicity).
28 Sep. 2017	Tokyo High Court approved, with some modifications, the Yokohama District Court decision that refused a conservation appeal against Yokohama District Court Sagamihara Branch's decision of 18 April 2016.
9 Nov. 2017	Kawasaki City announced *Honpōgai Shusshinsha ni Taisuru Futō na Sabetsuteki Gendō no Kaishō ni Muketa Torikumi no Suishin ni Kansuru Houritsu ni Motoduuku 'ōyake no Shisetsu' Riyō Kyoka ni Kansuru Gaidorain* ('Guideline Regarding the Use Permit for "Public Facilities" Based on the Act on the Promotion of Efforts to Eliminate Unfair Discriminatory Speech and Behaviour against Persons Originating from Outside Japan').
10 Nov. 2017	The Supreme Court dismissed a special appeal against the aforementioned Tokyo High Court decision of 16 June.
17 Jan. 2018	The Osaka City Hate Speech Committee submitted *Intānettojō no Tōkō Saito o Riyō Shite Okonawareru Heito Supīchi o Okonatta Mono no Shimei Matawa Meishō o Tōgai Tōkō Saito no Un'eisha kara Shutoku Suru tame ni Osaka-shi to Shite Toriuru Hōsaku ni tsuite (Tōshin)* ('With respect to measures that Osaka City can undertake to obtain the names or screen names of users who conduct hate speech via posting sites on the Internet from the administrators of concerned sites (Report)') to the mayor of Osaka. Osaka City cannot demand disclosure of sender information of users who

(*cont.*)

	conduct hate speech on the Internet, because the city ordinance does not prove hate speech to be illegal, and the name publication system is limited to purposes of awareness-building, not punishment, according to the Report.
22 Jan. 2018	The Supreme Court dismissed an appeal against the Tokyo High Court decision of 28 September 2017.
Mar. 2018	Kyoto Prefecture announced *Kyoto-fu Ōyake no Shisetsu ni Okeru Heito Supīchi Bōshi no tame no Shiyō Tetsuzuki ni Kansuru Gaidorain* ('Guideline on the Use Procedure for Prevention against Hate Speech in Public Facilities in Kyoto Prefecture'), which came into force the same month.
19 Mar. 2018	Daini Tokyo Bar Association announced *Intānettojō no Jinshu Sabetsuteki Heito Supīchi Bokumetsu no tame ni Tekisetsu na Taiō o Motomeru Ikensho* ('Suggestion that calls for appropriate measures to be taken for the eradication of racial hate speech on the Internet').
Apr. 2018	Hitoshi Nishimura, a former executive of Zaitokukai, was prosecuted without physical restraint for defamation, because he harmed Kyoto Korean Elementary School's reputation with a loudspeaker at a Kyoto City South Ward park, which adjoins the vacant lot where the school used to be located, and transmitted a video of the event via the Internet.
1 Apr. 2018	*Setagaya-ku Tayōsei o Mitomeai Danjo Kyōdō Sankaku to Tabunka Kyōsei o Suishinsuru Jōrei* ('Setagaya City Ordinance for the Promotion of Gender Equality and Multicultural Symbiosis') came into effect.
May 2018	Controversial comments that discriminated against Korean residents in Japan on the Cabinet Office's online forum on national policy, called the Government Monitor System, aroused concern.
3 June 2018	Conservative blogger Hiroyuki Seto planned a lecture at *Kawasaki-shi Kyōiku Bunka Kaikan* ('Kawasaki Civic Auditorium of Culture and Education') and obtained permission for use. However, this lecture was cancelled because of fierce objection by counter-protesters on that day.
7 June 2018	Tokyo Bar Association announced a model ordinance bill on the elimination of racial discrimination.

(*cont.*)

8 June 2018	Tokyo Bar Association announced *Chihō Kōkyō Dantai ni Jinshu Sabetsu Teppai Jōrei no Seitei o Motome, Jinshu Sabetsu Teppai Moderu Jōreian o Teian Suru Koto ni Kansuru Ikensho* ('Suggestion for local governments to enact ordinances for the elimination of racial discrimination and proposing a model ordinance bill on the elimination of racial discrimination').
28 June 2018	The journalist who had sued Makoto Sakurai, former head of Zaitokukai (*see* 19 June 2017), had also sued 2channel-matome site *Hoshu Sokuhō* for defaming her by aggregating hate comments. Osaka High Court recognized that such aggregation amounts to intersectional forms of discrimination and that the aggregated comments would have unique meaning, not only the repetition of each comment.
29 June 2018	Kyoto City announced *Heito Supīchi Kaishōhō o Humaeta Kyoto-shi no Oyake no Shisetsutō no Shiyō Tetsuzuki ni Kansuru Gaidorain* ('Guideline Regarding Use Procedure for Public Facilities, etc. in Kyoto City based on the Hate Speech Elimination Act'), which came into effect on 1 July.
28 Aug. 2018	Osaka City demanded that the Ministry of Justice and the Ministry of Internal Affairs and Communications deal with hate speech on the Internet.
5 Oct. 2018	Tokyo Metropolitan Government enacted *Tokyo-to Orinpikku Kenshō ni Utawareru Jinken Sonchō no Rinen no Jitsugen o Mezasu Jōrei* ('Ordinance Aiming to Realize the Idea of Respect for Human Rights in the Olympic Charter'), which included provisions relating to discriminatory speech and conduct in public facilities, as well as necessary measures against discriminatory speech and conduct, such as disclosing the content of a particular hate activity.
2 Dec. 2018	Kawasaki City, based on a guideline regarding use for public facilities, permitted the use of its own facility to a group that applied to use the venue, with a warning to avoid discriminatory words and deeds. This case was the first application of prior restraint based on a guideline.
3 Aug. 2019	In a press release, Tokyo Metropolitan Government announced that some utterances by members of a conservative organization at the memorial ceremony for Korean victims

(*cont.*)

	of the Kantō Massacre could be defined as discriminatory speech and conduct under the Ordinance Aiming to Realize the Idea of Respect for Human Rights in the Olympic Charter.
16 Oct. 2019	In a press release, Tokyo Metropolitan Government announced that some utterances by extremists on the streets in Tokyo could be defined as discriminatory speech and conduct under the Ordinance Aiming to Realize the Idea of Respect for Human Rights in the Olympic Charter.
27 Oct. 2019	After the controversial Aichi Triennale 2019, which provoked conservatives' rage with political exhibitions including a statue of the 'comfort women', the Aichi chapter of Japan First held an event called 'Aichi Torikaenahāre 2019' mocking the Triennale, which was criticized as containing explicitly discriminatory expressions.
29 Nov. 2019	Hitoshi Nishimura, who had been prosecuted for defamation in August 2018, was found guilty at Kyoto District Court. The court recognized that some of his utterances were for public purposes and imposed only a fine (¥500,000), instead of imprisonment. This result provoked criticism by the victim and its attorneys.
12 Dec. 2019	Kawasaki enacted *Kawasaki-shi Sabetsu no nai Jinken Sonchō no Machidukuri Jōrei* ('Kawasaki City Ordinance on Establishing a City with No Discrimination and Respecting Human Rights'). This became the first ordinance imposing a criminal penalty upon hate speech in Japan.
27 Dec. 2019	Under the Osaka City Ordinance for Dealing with Hate Speech, Osaka City disclosed the names of two persons who uttered hate speech. This was the first disclosure of the names of hate speakers by a local government.
17 Jan. 2020	In a case in which a plaintiff challenged the constitutionality of the Osaka City Ordinance for Dealing with Hate Speech, Osaka District Court upheld its constitutionality.
1 July 2020	Kawasaki City's Ordinance on Establishing a City with No Discrimination and Respecting Human Rights was fully brought into force.
2 July 2020	An employee of Fuji Corporation Ltd (a real estate company in Osaka) had sued the corporation and its president for damages caused by harassment (the dissemination of discriminatory

(*cont.*)

	documents within the workplace). Those documents were alleged to be discriminatory against Koreans. Osaka District Court's Sakai Branch accepted the claim and ordered the corporation and its president to pay damages amounting in total to ¥1.1 million.
5 July 2020	At the Tokyo gubernatorial election, Makoto Sakurai, leader of Japan First Party, earned about 170,000 votes, ranking fifth.
Aug. 2020	The organization, members of whom were recognized to have uttered hate speech in August 2019, again applied to use a public place near the site of memorial ceremony for Korean victims of the Kantō Massacre. Tokyo Metropolitan Government approved its use despite the previous year's utterances.
26 Aug. 2020	Fukuoka Regional Legal Affairs Bureau officially recognized Makoto Sakurai's election speech around Kyushu Korean Junior and Senior High School in 2019 as hate speech.
Sep. 2020	Japan First Party again planned to hold its event *Aichi Torikaenahāre*. Aichi Prefecture withdrew its permission for the use of its facility once given, but some press reports indicate that Nagoya City accepted its application.
14 Sep. 2020	Osaka High Court dismissed the appeal of Hitoshi Nishimura against Kyoto District Court's decision of 29 November 2019. The court maintained the controversial lower court's reasoning on the 'public purpose' of Nishimura utterances.

APPENDIX B

Lists of Japanese Acts, Bills, Ordinances, and Other Materials

Acts

English	Japanese	Chapter(s)
Act for Eliminating Discrimination against Buraku (Buraku Discrimination Elimination Act)	Buraku sabetsu kaishō suishinhō, Act No. 109 of 2016	4, 6, 18
Act for Eliminating Discrimination against Persons with Disabilities	Shōgaisha sabetsu kaishō suishinhō, Act No. 65 of 2013	6, 7
Act for Promotion of Human Rights Protection Measures	Jinken yōgo shisaku suishinhō, Act No. 120 of 1996	4
Act for Securing the Proper Operation of Worker Dispatching Undertakings and Improved Working Conditions for Dispatched Workers (Act for Worker Dispatching)	Rōdōsha haken Jigyō no tekisetu na unei no kakuho oyobi haken rōdōsha no shūgyō jōken no seibitō ni kansuru hōritsu, Act No. 88 of 1985	1
Act on Social Welfare	Shakai hukushihō, Act No. 45 of 1951	4
Act on Special Measures concerning Community Improvement	Chiiki kaizen taisaku tokubetsu sochihō, Act No. 16 of 1982 (repealed)	4

(*cont.*)

English	Japanese	Chapter(s)
Act on Special Measures concerning Projects of Dōwa Policy (Dōwa Project Special Measures Act)	Dōwa taisaku jigyō tokubetsu sochihō, Act No. 60 of 1969 (repealed)	4, 6
Act on Special Measures of National Finance concerning Specific Project of Community Improvement	Chiiki kaizen taisaku tokutei jigyō ni kakawaru kuni no zaiseijō no tokubetsu sochi ni kansuru hōritsu, Act No. 22 of 1987 (repealed)	4
Act on the Prevention of Child Abuse (Child Abuse Prevention Law)	Jidō gyakutai bōshihō, Act No. 82 of 2000	6, 7
Act on the Prevention of Domestic Violence	DV bōshihō, Act No. 31 of 2001	6
Act on the Promotion of Efforts to Eliminate Unfair Discriminatory Speech and Behaviour against Persons Originating from Outside Japan (→Hate Speech Elimination Act)	Honpōgai shusshinsha ni taisuru futō na sabetsuteki gendō no kaishō ni muketa torikumi no suishin ni kansuru hōritsu, Act No. 68 of June 3, 2016	→Hate Speech Elimination Act
Act on the Promotion of Human Rights Education and Human Rights Awareness-Raising (Act on Promotion of Human Rights Education and Enlightenment)	Jinken kyōiku oyobi jinken keihatsu no suishin ni kansuru hōritsu, Act No. 147 of 2000	4, 6, 9
Act on the Punishment of Physical Violence and Others	Bōryokukōitō shobatsu ni kansuru hōritsu, Act No. 60 of 1926	10
Act on the Securing of Equal Opportunity and Treatment between Men and Women in Employment (Equal	Koyō no bunya ni okeru danjo no kintō na kikai oyobi taigū no kakuhotō ni kansuru hōritsu (Danjo	6, 17

(*cont.*)

English	Japanese	Chapter(s)
Employment Opportunity Act)	koyō kikai kintōhō), Act No. 113 of 1972	
Administrative Case Litigation Act	Gyōsei jiken soshōhō, Act No. 139 of 1962	19
Alien Registration Act	Gaikokujin tōrokuhō, Act No. 125 of 1952	12, 16
Broadcasting Act	Hōsōhō, Act No. 132 of 1950	20
Civil Code	Minpō, Act No. 89 of 1896	1–6, 8, 10, 11, 13, 14, 18
Civil Execution Act	Minji shikkōhō, Act No. 4 of 1979	8
Civil Rights Commissioner Act	Jinken yōgo iinkaihō, Act No. 139 of 1949	5
Code of Civil Procedure	Minji soshōhō, Act No. 109 of 1996	8
Constitution of Empire of Japan	Dainihon teikoku kenpō	2, 9
Constitution of Japan	Nihonkoku kenpō	1–11, 13–15, 17–19
Consumer Contract Act	Shōhisha keiyakuhō, Act No. 61 of 2000	6
Employment Security Act	Shokugyō anteihō, Act No. 141 of 1947	1
Food Management Act (Food Supply Control Act)	Shokuryō kanrihō, Act No. 40 of 1942	2
Fundamental Law of Education	Kyōiku kihonhō, Act No. 25 of 1947 (as amended 2006)	5
Hate Speech Elimination Act	Heito supīchi kaishōhō	1, 3–12, 14–20
Immigration Control and Refugee Recognition Act (Immigration Control Act)	Shutsunyūkoku kanri oyobi nanmin ninteihō, Cabinet Order No. 319 of 1951	16
Labour Standards Act	Rōdō kijunhō, Act No. 49 of 1947	1
Labour Union Act	Rōdō kumiaihō, Act No. 174 of 1949	1

(*cont.*)

English	Japanese	Chapter(s)
Local Autonomy Act	Chihō jichihō, Act No. 67 of 1947	2, 9, 11
Local Public Service Act	Chihō Kōmuinhō, Act No. 261 of 1950	10
Metropolitan Park Act (Urban Park Act)	Toshi kōenhō, Act No. 79 of 1956	2, 19
National Park Act	Kokuritsu kōenhō, Act No. 36 of 1931 (repealed)	2
National Public Workers Act (National Public Service Act)	Kokka kōmuinhō, Act No. 120 of 1947	2, 10, 15
Natural Park Act	Shizen kōenhō, Act No. 161 of1957	2
Newspaper Act	Shinbunshihō, Act No. 41 of 1909 (repealed)	2
Penal Code (Criminal Code)	Keihō, Act No. 45 of 1907	1–8, 10, 11, 13, 15, 18, 20
Provider Liability Limitation Act	Purobaida sekinin seigenhō, Act No. 137 of 2001	18
Publication Act	Shuppanhō, Act No. 15 of 1893 (abolished)	2
Public Office Election Act	Kōshoku senkyohō, Act No. 100 of 1950	1, 2
Public Safety Preservation Act	Chian-ijihō, Act No. 46 of 1925, Act No. 54 of 1941 (repealed)	2
Radio Act	Dempahō, Act No. 131 of 1950	20
Road Traffic Act	Dōro kōtsūhō, Act No. 105 of 1960	2
School Education Act	Gakkō kyōikuhō, Act No. 26 of 1947	11, 12
Special Act on the Immigration Control of, Among Others, Those Who Have Lost Japanese Nationality Pursuant to the Treaty of Peace with Japan (Special	Nihonkoku tono heiwa jōyaku ni motozuki nihon no kokuseki o ridatsusita monotō no shutsunyūkokukanri ni	16

(*cont.*)

English	Japanese	Chapter(s)
Act on Immigration Control)	kansuru tokureihō, Act No. 71 of 1991	
State Redress Act	Kokka baishōhō, Act No. 125 of 1947	19
Subversive Conducts Prevention Act	Hakaikatsudō bōshihō, Act No. 240 of 1952	2, 7, 15
Telecommunications Business Act	Denki tsūshin jigyōhō, Act No. 86 of 1984	9, 18
Worker Dispatching Act (Act for Worker Dispatching)	Rōdōsha hakenhō, Act No. 88 of 1985	1

Bills

English	Japanese	Chapter(s)
Bill concerning the Promotion of Counter-measures for Abolishing Discrimination for Reasons of Race and so on (Bill on the Promotion of Measures to Eliminate Discrimination Based on Race and Other Reasons)	Jinshutō o riyū to suru sabetsu no teppai no tameno shisaku no suishin ni kansuru hōritsuan	10, 11, 18
Bill concerning the Promotion of Counter-measures toward the Elimination of Improper Discriminatory Speech and Conduct against People Who Came from Outside Japan	Honpōgai shusshinsha ni taisuru hutōna sabetsuteki gendō no kaishō ni muketa torikumi no suishin ni kansuru hōritsuan	10, 18
Bill on the Establishment of a Committee of Human Rights (Human Rights Commission Establishment Bill)	Jinken iinkai secchi hōan	4, 6, 18
Bill on the Remedy and Prevention of Damages from Human Rights	Jinken shingai niyoru higai no kyūsai oyobi yobō tou ni kansuru hōritsu an	4, 6

(*cont.*)

English	Japanese	Chapter(s)
Violations (Remedy for the Human Rights Violation Bill)		
Foreigners' School Bill	Gaikokujin gakkō hōan	12
Human Rights Vindication Bill	Jinken yōgo hōan	4, 6, 7, 9, 11, 18

Ordinances

English	Japanese	Chapter(s)
Akita City Urban Park Ordinance	Akita-shi toshi kōen jōrei, Akita City Ordinance No. 35 of 1964	19
Fukuoka City Park Ordinance	Fukuoka-shi kōen jōrei, Fukuoka City Ordinance No. 18 of 1958	19
Hamamatsu City Park Ordinance	Hamamatsu-shi kōen jōrei, Hamamatsu City Ordinance No. 243 of 2005	
Kannonji City Park Ordinance	Kannonji-shi kōen jōrei, Kannonji City Ordinance No. 155 of 2005	2
Kawagoe City Urban Park Ordinance	Kawagoe-shi toshi kōen jōrei, Kawagoe City Ordinance No. 25 of 2005	19
Kawasaki City Ordinance on Establishing a City with No Discrimination and Respecting Human Rights	Kawasaki-shi Sabetsu no Nai Jinken Sonchō no Machidukuri Jōrei, No. 35 of 2019	
Naha City Park Ordinance	Naha-shi kōen jōrei, Naha City Ordinance No. 6 of 1970	19
Ordinance Aiming to Realize the Principle of Respect for Human Rights as Set out in the Olympic Charter (Ordinance for Realization of the Olympic Charter Goal of Respect for Human Rights)	Tokyo-to orinpikku kenshō ni utawareru jinken sonchō no rinen no jitsugen o mezasu jōrei, Tokyo Metropolitan Ordinance No. 93 of 2018	1

(*cont.*)

English	Japanese	Chapter(s)
Ordinance for the Promotion of Gender Equality and Intercultural Co-Living	Tayōsei o mitomeai danjo kyōdo sankaku to tabunka kyōsei o suishin suru jōrei, Setagaya Ward Ordinance, No. 15 of 2018	1
Ordinance for the Protection of Human Rights Aiming to Eliminate All Forms of Discrimination	Arayuru sabetsu no teppai o mezasu jinken yōgo jōrei, Oizumi Town Ordinance No. 2 of 2017	3
Ordinance on Community Planning to Respect Human Rights	Jinken sonchō no shakai-zukuri jōrei, Osaka Prefecture Ordinance No. 42 of 1998	9
Ordinance on Regulations of Investigation on the Buraku Discrimination in Osaka Prefecture	Osaka-hu buraku sabetsu jishō ni kakaru tyōsatō no kisei tō ni kansuru jōrei, Osaka Prefecture Ordinance No. 2 of 1985	4
Ordinance on the Elimination of Discrimination against Buraku and Protection of Human Rights in Anan City	Anan-shi buraku sabetsu teppai jinken yōgo ni kasuru jōrei, Anan City Ordinance No. 27 of 1993	4
Ordinance Prohibiting Acts of Posting Harmful Information on the Okayama City Electronic Bulletin Board	Okayama-shi denshi keijiban ni kakaru yūgai jōhō no kiroku kōi kinshi ni kansuru jōrei, Okayama City Ordinance No. 6 of 2002	9
Osaka City Ordinance for Dealing with Hate Speech	Osaka-shi heito supīchi eno taisho ni kansuru jōrei, Osaka City Ordinance, No. 1 of 2016	1, 3, 9, 18
Sapporo City Education and Culture Hall Ordinance	Sapporo-shi kyōiku bunka kaikan jōrei, Sapporo City Ordinance No. 14 of 1977	19
Takatsuki City Cultural Hall Ordinance	Takatsuki-shi bunka kaikan jōrei, Takatsuki City Ordinance No. 18 of 1991	19
Tottori Prefecture Ordinance on Promotion and Procedures for Relief of Human Rights Violations	Tottori-ken Jinken Shingai Kyūsai Suishin Oyobi Tetsuzuki ni Kansuru Jōrei, Tottori City Ordinance No. 94 of 2005	4, 6, 9, 18

Other Materials

English	Japanese	Chapter(s)
Emergency Food Supply Order	Shokuryō kinkyū sochirei, Imperial Ordinance No. 86 of 1946 (repealed)	2
Order for Closure of Korean Schools	Chōsen gakkō heisarei (October 1949, notified by the Ministry of Education)	12
Regulation on National Parks, the Chidorigafuchi National Cemetery, and the Memorial for the Dead Who Were Detained and Used as Forced Labourers in Siberia after the Second World War	Kokumin kōen, chidorigafuchi senbotsusha boen narabini sengo kyōsei yokuryū oyobi hikiage sibotsusha ireihi enchi kanri kisoku, Ordinance of the Ministry of Health, No. 13 of 1959	19

This comparative table relies primarily on the Japanese Law Translation Database System, available at www.japaneselawtranslation.go.jp/law/?re=02 [accessed 19 September 2020]. It should be noted that these translations are not official text.

INDEX

Ingram Content Group UK Ltd.
Milton Keynes UK
UKHW021814040723
424316UK00035B/583